Mastering
InDesign® CS5
for Print Design and Production

Pariah S. Burke

WILEY

Wiley Publishing, Inc.

Acquisitions Editor: Mariann Barsolo

Development Editor: Tom Cirtin

Technical Editor: Samuel Klein

Production Editor: Dassi Zeidel

Copy Editor: Linda Recktenwald

Editorial Manager: Pete Gaughan

Production Manager: Tim Tate

Vice President and Executive Group Publisher: Richard Swadley

Vice President and Publisher: Neil Edde

Book Designers: Maureen Forys, Happenstance Type-O-Rama; Judy Fung

Compositor: JoAnn Kolonick, Happenstance Type-O-Rama

Proofreader: Publication Services, Inc.

Indexer: Robert Swanson

Project Coordinator, Cover: Katie Crocker

Cover Designer: Ryan Sneed

Cover Image: © Pete Gardner/Digital Vision/Getty Images

Copyright © 2011 by Pariah S. Burke

Published by Wiley Publishing, Inc., Indianapolis, Indiana
Published simultaneously in Canada

ISBN: 978-0-470-65098-1
ISBN: 978-1-118-01656-5 (ebk)
ISBN: 978-1-118-01658-9 (ebk)
ISBN: 978-1-118-01657-2 (ebk)

For general information on our other products and services or to obtain technical support, please contact our Customer Care Department within the U.S. at (877) 762-2974, outside the U.S. at (317) 572-3993 or fax (317) 572-4002.

Wiley also publishes its books in a variety of electronic formats. Some content that appears in print may not be available in electronic books.

Library of Congress Cataloging-in-Publication Data is available from the publisher.

Dear Reader,

Thank you for choosing *Mastering InDesign CS5 for Print Design and Production*. This book is part of a family of premium-quality Sybex books, all of which are written by outstanding authors who combine practical experience with a gift for teaching.

Sybex was founded in 1976. More than 30 years later, we're still committed to producing consistently exceptional books. With each of our titles, we're working hard to set a new standard for the industry. From the paper we print on, to the authors we work with, our goal is to bring you the best books available.

I hope you see all that reflected in these pages. I'd be very interested to hear your comments and get your feedback on how we're doing. Feel free to let me know what you think about this or any other Sybex book by sending me an email at nedde@wiley.com. If you think you've found a technical error in this book, please visit http://sybex.custhelp.com. Customer feedback is critical to our efforts at Sybex.

Best regards,

Neil Edde
Vice President and Publisher
Sybex, an Imprint of Wiley

For Mom, Ma, Dad, Schentel, Mikayla, Joanna, Stevie, and Ann(a). This book exists because of your unflappable faith, love, and support.

Acknowledgments

One name goes on the cover, but a book is always a team effort—this one more than most. I'd like to acknowledge those whose names also belong on the cover.

First and foremost, I want to offer a sincere thank you to each and every person who read and liked the previous edition of this book, who helped make it a success. This CS5 edition is for you. In Appendix B I'll list the names of everyone who bought a copy of the last edition. The 3-column list shouldn't take more than 200–300 pages. (Hopefully I'll have enough page count left to write about InDesign.)

My wife Schentel, who, shortly after our wedding, was widowed to the book. Thank you for putting up with my long hours at work, darling, and for being everything I ever wanted in a wife, a friend, and a partner.

Mikayla, aka Doodle Butt, I know you didn't understand why a book takes so much concentration and time, but you respected my need for both. Thank you, honey. But, just so you know, you're grounded until the next edition of this book is published.

Sarah Taylor, Mom. Thank you for teaching me to crawl, run, and pick myself up when I stumble.

Chloe. Thank you for not biting me *every* time I said, "Daddy's busy."

Chris Bellido. All these years and you never ran short of faith in, and friendship for, me. You honor me, my friend.

Mariann Barsolo, acquisitions editor at Wiley, who somehow managed to find several nice ways of saying, "Hurry up and write!" Mariann has to be the nicest person in publishing.

Thomas Cirtin, developmental editor. Man, you rock! The book is much better for your ideas and feedback, and it was a joy to work with you.

Samuel John Klein, technical editor and friend. Thank you for making sure my Ctrl+Ts were crossed and Cmd+Is were dotted—even without functioning software half the time.

Dassi Zeidel, production editor, and Linda Recktenwald, copy editor. The devil really is in the details. A tweak here, a pluck there. Thank you for finding and fixing all the little things that slipped by the rest of us. Without you, well, we'd all look pretty foolish. The book looks great!

David Fugate, for the Pariah-to-English translations, encouragement, and advocacy.

Thank you to the InDesign community, programmers and experts, friends and colleagues, cohorts and collaborators (in alphabetic order): Barry Anderson, David Blatner, Diane Burns, Scott Citron, Sandee Cohen, Tim Cole, Anne-Marie Concepcion, Sally Cox, Rufus Deuchler, Steve Dolan, Mordy Golding, Lynn Grillo, Dov Isaacs, Bob Levine, Ted LoCascio, Whitney McCleary, Claudia McCue, Branislav Milic, Mark Niemann-Ross, Michael Ninness, Pam Pfiffner, Dee Sadler, Dave Saunders, Chad Siegel, Steve Werner, Zak Williamson, and AJ Wood.

Thank you Johannes Gutenberg, Aldus Manutius, Claude Garamond, John Warnock, Chuck Geschke, Paul Brainard, Tim Gill, Steve Jobs, Bill Gates, and everyone else who got us to InDesign CS5.

About the Author

~~Call me Ishmael...~~
~~It was the best of times, it was the worst of times...~~
~~It was a dark and stormy night...~~
~~The name's Burke. Pariah Burke.~~

The author is just like you: He has square eyeballs and paper-cut-scarred fingers, and his mother doesn't quite understand what he does for a living. He loves designing and the process of designing, and his greatest honor in life is helping others express their creativity efficiently.

Pariah S. Burke began freelance illustration work at the age of 14, apprenticed in a screen print shop at 16, and was designing brochures and Yellow Pages ads with hand-cut Zip-A-Tone, Rubylithe, and rub-on lettering by age 17. When the Desktop Publishing Revolution began, he was loitering around a typesetting shop ignoring the proclamations that "PostScript is a fad" and "Computers will never take the place of wax paste-up." He fell in love with PageMaker, QuarkXPress, and Adobe Illustrator the minute he got his marker-stained hands on them—and he never regretted it.

Lacking the funds to attend college despite eager invitations from the professors at the Savannah College of Art and Design, Pariah embarked on a learn-by-doing educational path, taking any job that would teach him something about graphic design, illustration, prepress, printing, and publishing. His education included stints as production artist (numerous times), bindery operator, color corrector, scanner operator, photo retoucher, lead designer on membership directories, (paste-up) stripper, RIP operator, photographer's assistant, photographer, waiter, forklift driver, jewelry salesman, and a host of other things—many concurrent with one another. He has co-owned a prepress service bureau; been a creative director for a small magazine; made over the look of several magazines, newsletters, and newspapers; and been principal of a design studio whose client list included Time-Warner, Spike Lee, and *Playboy*.

At the turn of the century, Pariah went to work for Adobe, training the Adobe technical and expert support teams to use Adobe software and related technologies and to understand and speak the language of design and prepress. While with Adobe, Pariah was the support teams' technical lead for InDesign, InCopy, PageMaker, Illustrator, Acrobat, and Photoshop. He was the unofficial QuarkXPress guru in residence.

After leaving Adobe in 2004, Pariah became a man of many hats, returning to freelance graphic design; hitting the road as a traveling design, production, and publishing workflow consultant and speaker; and teaching the tools of the trade in classrooms, conference rooms, and back alleys throughout North America. He also began writing. Pariah has published articles on everything from copyright and intellectual property for creative professionals to contract negotiation best practices, from in-depth software reviews to lauded tutorials describing advanced techniques in InDesign, InCopy, QuarkXPress, Photoshop, Illustrator, and Acrobat. His articles have appeared in *Macworld*, *Publish*, *PDFZone*, *Creativepro.com*, *CreativeLatitude.com*, and, most frequently, *InDesign Magazine*. He has written books on Adobe Illustrator, InDesign, and QuarkXPress. He has been a speaker at the InDesign Conference and the InDesign Seminar Tour, among others, has produced e-seminar videos for Adobe, and has been interviewed by numerous media in the United States and the United Kingdom regarding his opinions of Adobe, Quark, the creative pro software market, and the business of design and publishing.

When magazines and magazine-style websites couldn't find spaces for his articles fast enough, Pariah established his own publications. He created the *Design Weblog*, the *Magazine Design Weblog*,

and the *(Unofficial) Photoshop Weblog* for AOL's Weblogs, Inc. He also created the preeminent international authority on the war between desktop publishing giants InDesign and QuarkXPress, *Quark VS InDesign.com*, and founded *Designorati*, an organization and publication with the broad focus of covering any subject that falls under the umbrella of professional creativity.

Born in Boston and having grown up in the hustle and bustle of the East Coast, Pariah now lives among the idyllic beauty and friendly people of Portland, Oregon. He shares his life with his wife, Schentel, their daughter, Mikayla, a dog, and four cats. In his spare time (ha!), Pariah enjoys driving his convertible very, very fast through the Columbia River Gorge, playing chess and MMORGs with his family and friends, and reading Dean Koontz, Robert Ludlum, and Star Wars novels. Once in a while he sleeps.

Pariah's Projects

Pariah is principal of *Workflow: Creative* (www.WorkflowCreative.com), a consultancy and training group providing creative pro software training, migration, and workflow optimization to design, advertising, and publishing teams throughout the world.

The Workflow Network (www.WorkflowNetwork.com) is the hub for all of Pariah's creative professional-focused websites, online services, and online communities, including:

◆ WorkflowPrePress.com

◆ WorkflowFreelance.com

◆ WorkflowFlash.com

◆ WorkflowWordPress.com

◆ Designorati.com

◆ QuarkVSInDesign.com

◆ And many more

Pariah's other projects include: *Design Jobs Live* (www.DesignJobsLive.com), the world's single most extensive index to full-time, part-time, and freelance job and contract openings in the creative professional and production professional industries.

Gurus Unleashed (www.GurusUnleashed.com), scouring the Web 24/7 for the best Photoshop, InDesign, Illustrator, InCopy, Fireworks, QuarkXPress, Dreamweaver, and Acrobat tutorials, tips, tricks, articles, news, and reviews so you don't have to.

eSeminars/Webinars with Pariah Burke: Pariah presents at seminars and conferences frequently, but he also does a lot of e-seminars and webinars—many free to attend. The subjects range from just about everything to do with InDesign (naturally), InCopy, Adobe Illustrator, Photoshop, PDFs, e-publishing, the business of design, freelancing, typography, WordPress, design and production workflows, and anything else he knows or can learn that could help his fellow creative professionals. If you think you might be interested in attending any of his in-person or online seminars, or in catching the recordings of past seminars, visit http://iampariah.com/projects/appearances.

Personal website, blog, and portfolio (www.iamPariah.com).

Watch iamPariah.com for even more new seminars, videos, web, e-publication, and print publication projects from Pariah S. Burke to *Empower, Inform, Connect Creative Professionals*™.

Contents at a Glance

Contents

Introduction

Creativity. It's one of my favorite words of all time, a word I utter with reverence. *Efficiency,* another of my favorite words. Combining the two—*creative efficiency*—describes what I consider the single most venerated concept in the whole of professional creative industries. Creative efficiency. It means freedom—freedom to be imaginative and experimental in your design as well as freedom from as many of the time-consuming, distracting, unproductive mechanical steps you need to take to achieve a design as possible. It's a doctrine of sorts, one that I hold sacred, one that I preach from pulpits of wood, metal, plastic, pixels, and, like this one, pulp. As an ideal, creative efficiency is about making every task, every flick of the mouse or stroke of the keyboard, forward movement in the progression toward a finished design. Its ultimate goal is directing every movement and every thought toward the design, not toward the tools or processes we must employ to construct a design.

We graphic designers and press and prepress operators enjoyed creative efficiency once, not too long ago, in a way our cousins on the sidewalks of public markets and beach boardwalks enjoy still. A painter, working in oil, acrylic, gauche, pastel, or watercolor, has creative efficiency. Every stroke of the brush, whether on the canvas or mixing a color on the palette, is active, forward motion toward the completion of the art on the canvas. When illustrators' hands bore more calluses induced by the smooth plastic pipes of Rapidographs and lacquered wood of Prismacolor pencils than by mice and styluses, when prepressmen's shoulders bent over X-Acto, Rubylith, and Zip-A-Tone instead of over QWERTY, Logitech, and Wacom, we enjoyed creative efficiency. With a page before us, few of our motions and thoughts did not directly contribute to the final design. Now, however, in the age of InDesign, Photoshop, and Illustrator, with creative horizons wider than any even we of limitless imaginations had ever conceived possible, we have lost creative efficiency. Too much of our time is now spent thinking about the tools of our trade, about how to use them to achieve a design. We still have our creativity, but we have been foiled in our pursuit of creating productively and efficiently. Indeed, too often the creativity itself is handicapped by the increasing amount of time and thought devoted to divining the mysteries of the tool, and often failing to find the means by which the tool wants us to do something, we compromise the design.

This book is about helping you achieve creative efficiency within InDesign. It is not for the beginning InDesign user, although professional users proficient with previous versions of InDesign will find in this book exactly what they need to translate their prowess in InDesign CS3 and CS4 into the new CS5. Ultimately, this book is for those who can already produce projects in InDesign but who want to know how to increase their productivity, to produce those projects faster, better, more easily, and, most of all, more creatively. This book is about helping you achieve—or regain—creative efficiency.

Hallelujah, brothers and sisters in the Fellowship of Ink on Paper. Hallelujah!

What You Need

Naturally, you need *your* copy of InDesign CS5, but it would also be helpful to call on a colleague who also has InDesign CS5 to look over the results of the self-test Master It exercises in this book. Moreover, several of the exercises are built around collaboration techniques and teamwork, so if you can work with someone else using InDesign, it will be a big help.

If you work with editorial personnel at all, get a hold of InCopy CS5—even if it's just the free 30-day trial version from Adobe.com. In Chapter 14, "Collaboration," we'll talk quite a bit about InCopy and how integrating it into your workflow takes the responsibility of copyediting and those endless changes completely out of your hands and puts it back in the editorial department where it belongs. With InCopy on your computer, you'll be able to gain a better understanding of just how easy and important it is to return control of editorial content to the editorial department.

Once in a while over the following pages, we'll slip out of InDesign and into other tools of the trade. Although not required, for some portions of the book it would be helpful if you had access to recent versions of Acrobat, Photoshop, and Illustrator. Adobe offers fully functional 30-day trial versions of those, too, if you need to download them.

You'll probably want to don your sense of humor, too. Some of my jokes will admittedly strike you as lame. That's okay because I believe in the philosophy that if you just keep shooting spitballs toward the front of the class, you'll eventually hit the intended target (the teacher). There are enough jokes, quips, and innuendos in this book that at least *some* of them will be funny—as long as you start out with a sense of humor. If you just don't have one, well, interspersed between the humor are a few tidbits of good information, case studies, and advice, too.

The Mastering Series

The Mastering series from Sybex provides outstanding instruction for readers with intermediate and advanced skills in the form of top-notch training and development for those already working in their field and clear, serious education for those aspiring to become pros. Every Mastering book features:

- The Sybex "by professionals for professionals" commitment. *Mastering* authors are themselves practitioners, with plenty of credentials in their areas of specialty.

- A practical perspective for a reader who already knows the basics—someone who needs solutions, not a primer.

- Real-World Scenarios, ranging from case studies to interviews, that show how the tool, technique, or knowledge presented is applied in actual practice.

- Skill-based instruction, with chapters organized around real tasks rather than abstract concepts or subjects.

- Self-review test Master It problems and questions, so you can be certain you're equipped to do the job right.

What Is Covered in This Book

Mastering InDesign CS5 for Print Design and Production is organized a little differently than most computer books. First, you'll notice that each chapter title is a single word, and the chapter is all about that word. Chapter 13, "Efficiency," for example, is about working with the tools, styles, and procedures of InDesign in the way that enables you to get the most work done with a minimum of headaches and problems. And, topics are covered entirely in their individual chapters. You won't have to stick your pinky in the index and jump all around the book reading a paragraph *here*, a page and a half *there*, another paragraph *over here* just to piece together complete information about one topic. Go on. Compare this book's index to that of any other InDesign CS5 book on the bookstore shelf. How many page numbers are listed for a given topic in each index? The more page numbers, the more you'll be flipping hither and yon to get what is, in large part, the same information as this book puts in one place, in one contiguous discussion. Of course, *this* book goes deeper into the topics and level experienced pros need. In *this* book, you won't have to weed through the beginner-level, intro-to-InDesign stuff either—this is the first InDesign book written *by* a print design and press professional *for* print design and press professionals.

Here's a brief synopsis of what you'll find in each chapter:

Chapter 1: Customizing In order to have creative efficiency, you must minimize the impact of your tools on the process of creating. That requires modification of tools: making InDesign work like you do as much as possible. How you customize InDesign directly affects how efficiently you use this page-layout application to learn and use anything else you might read in this volume. Customizing InDesign shifts that dividing line between the software working for you and you working for the software further toward the former.

Chapter 2: Text InDesign operates on a content-to-container premise. Everything within InDesign is either content—text and imagery—or a container to hold text, imagery, or another container. At the lowest level, the pasteboard is a container that holds everything you might place in InDesign. Then there are pages and layers—more containers—and *then* the real content enters the picture—text and imagery. In this chapter, you will learn to create and fill text frames, format text frames, format paragraphs, compose paragraphs, span and split columns, and use paragraph rules for organization and special effects.

Chapter 3: Characters InDesign is the world's most advanced typesetting platform. In fact, type set in InDesign is almost as good as type set on a letterpress. The few sacrifices you make by setting type in InDesign instead of in lead tend to be balanced by the time savings—you can set much faster than one page every four hours—and by the lack of ink perpetually embedded under your fingernails. This chapter is a deep dive into working with characters. In this chapter, you will learn to format characters, transform characters, insert special characters, work with OpenType font features, and use the Glyphs panel.

Chapter 4: Drawing InDesign is *not* Illustrator, and it never will be. Fortunately, however, the Illustrator team happily shares its code with the InDesign team. Consequently, many of the most common drawing tasks can be done directly within InDesign, without the need to load up Illustrator and then move artwork from it into InDesign. It's a matter of efficient creativity—those two words again! In this chapter, you will learn to draw precise paths with

the Pen tool, freehand draw paths with the Pencil tool, combine and subtract shapes and convert from one shape to another, modify any vector artwork, and turn type into a container to hold images or text.

Chapter 5: Images InDesign's greatest strength is its type-handling and type-rendering features. Fortunately, it's just as good with imagery—especially in CS5—as you'll learn when we place image assets, import images without place, manage placed assets, work with the new Live Captions feature, and go native in your workflow.

Chapter 6: Objects If there's a "coolest subject" in this book, this chapter contains most subjects that would fit the description—at least, from a standpoint of creativity and creative productivity. As with drawing in InDesign, the name of the game when applying transparency and effects to objects is efficiency through doing as much as possible *within* InDesign; it's about resorting as infrequently as possible to creating objects in Photoshop or Illustrator. This chapter will teach you to use attribute-level transparency and object effects, design custom stroke styles, create mixed ink swatches, manage and share swatches, work with anchored objects, set type on a path, step and repeat, transform again, and use InDesign CS5's new Gridify tool behaviors and the Gap tool.

Chapter 7: Pages Pages are the foundation of every document in InDesign. How they're created, modified, and managed directly affects their ability to print, their fitness to purpose. InDesign has always offered tremendous ease in working with pages, and the options and control over pages have improved with each successive release. In InDesign CS5, a large portion of the new features and refinements of existing features is centered on the Pages panel and controlling pages—including the Holy Grail of page layout, multiple page sizes and orientations in a single document! In this chapter, you will learn to create pages with bleed, slug, and live areas; manage pages in and between InDesign documents; and master master pages.

Chapter 8: Stories Once you've mastered setting and styling type on a page, it's time to think about writing, editing, and flowing text across multiple pages. It's time to think about stories. In this chapter, you will learn to thread and unthread text frames and flow text; create bulleted and numbered lists; write and word process in InDesign; and fix, find, and change text.

Chapter 9: Documents Working with documents involves knowing how to move around in them, change viewing options, and compare views. Working with longer documents efficiently means mastering InDesign's unique long-document features such as indexing, creating tables of contents, and working within the timesaving and collaboration-ready atmosphere of book files. In this chapter, you will learn to interact with documents visually to change zoom level, view modes, and display performance; build and manage grids and guides; create and manage book files; index terms and create an index; and create a table of contents.

Chapter 10: Preflight At the end of the day, it's all about printing—more precisely, it's about printing well and accurately. It's about getting what you see on screen onto paper or another substrate and getting the two to match as closely as possible. Everything we do in InDesign leads up to that ultimate, defining moment when we watch with bated breath as the job rolls off the press. In this chapter we get into what happens after design, into the ramp-up to outputting a job. Preparing a job for print, ensuring the document doesn't contain errors that could alter or halt the process of printing, checking for broken links and bad fonts, and managing color for accurate translation from screen to substrate.

Chapter 11: Print The ultimate purpose of any InDesign document is to be consumed. The most common final form an InDesign document will take is ink on paper. Ink must be managed and defined, trapping and overprinting defined, and paper characteristics accounted for. Your document may be one sheet or many, bound booklets or loose pages; it can be printed out on an ink-jet or laser printer or sent to a commercial printing press. However your InDesign document will be rendered to hard copy, it's essential that you understand the processes and controls to produce the output you envision. You'll learn in this chapter how to manage the inks used in a document, set an object's colors to overprint, print documents with various options, produce booklets and output in printer's spreads, and package documents, images, and fonts for delivery or archival.

Chapter 12: Export Printing is not the only way in which documents leave InDesign. As often as not, they're exported to PDF to stay in that format or be RIPped and printed from, to ePUB for consumption in an e-book reader, to IDML for use by earlier versions of InDesign, to XML for content repurposing, or to Flash, HTML, or JPEG for use onscreen. In this chapter, you will learn to export documents to IDML, XML, HTML/XHTML, and ePUB formats, generate PDFs for both print and onscreen use, and export pages as images and Flash content.

Chapter 13: Efficiency Professional creatives have deadlines, budgets, and (sometimes) even personal lives to get to. In this chapter, the focus is on getting the job done expeditiously, productively, and without sacrificing quality or creativity. You will learn to work efficiently with text, tables, and objects.

Chapter 14: Collaboration Few InDesign users operate in a vacuum, creating documents start to finish all on their own. The majority of modern workflows, even among freelancers, entails some form of collaborative content creation. This chapter starts with the collaboration features offered by InDesign CS5 and then moves into the when, why, and how of saving, reusing, and sharing project consistency presets; collaborating with editorial personnel through the InDesign-InCopy LiveEdit Workflow; and breaking the one document: one designer and one page: one designer limitations to effect genuine production team collaboration with the Book File Collaboration Workflow and the author's original Placed Page Collaboration Workflow.

Appendix: The Bottom Line Test yourself and evaluate your results with this Appendix, which gathers together all the Master It exercises from all 14 chapters. Each Master It exercise provides the solution and description for the expected results.

Downloading Companion Files

The book's download page is home to samples and resource files mentioned in the book. That page is http://www.sybex.com/go/MasteringInDesignCS5.

How to Contact the Author

This book came about largely because people like you *asked* me for it. Most of my articles, e-seminars, conference sessions, and other projects get started the same way—someone tells me about a need or asks me a question. So, if *you* have a question or would like to see me cover another topic—in a printed book, e-book, article, or somehow—please drop me a line. I can't guarantee I'll write, record, or speak about the topic you suggest, but I promise to consider doing so. At the very least I'll reply to your email.

Even if you don't have a question or book topic in mind, I'd sincerely love to hear about how well my book worked (or didn't) for you, about your experiences trying the techniques and advice it contains, or any other feedback you may have about this book, whether unadulterated adulation or scathing but constructive criticism. No threats of bodily harm or marriage proposals, though, please.

Please feel free to drop me a line any time at MasteringInD@iampariah.com.

You'll always find me ready to help out on Twitter on the ID @iampariah (http://Twitter.com/iampariah).

If you like this book, please leave a testimonial to that fact on its Amazon.com page: http://www.amazon.com/Mastering-InDesign-Print-Design-Production/dp/0470650982/ref=sr_1_1?s=gateway&ie=UTF8&qid=1285001221&sr=8-1.

Want to go beyond this book and have me analyze and optimize *your* unique workflow and train your team in person at your offices or remotely via videocast and screensharing? Please visit www.WorkflowCreative.com.

Sybex strives to keep you supplied with the latest tools and information you need for your work. Please check its website at www.sybex.com, where we'll post additional content and updates that supplement this book if the need arises. Enter the search terms "InDesign," "Burke," or the book's ISBN, 978-0-470-65098-1, and click Go to get to the book's update page.

Chapter 1

Customizing

"Creative efficiency." If you read the refreshingly short introduction a few pages previous, you know that I believe the phrase "creative efficiency" to be among the most important ideals of our profession of designing for, or placing, ink on paper. To realize your creative potential, to enable the creatives working under you to realize their creative potential, you must minimize the impact of your tools on the process of creating. Accomplishing that requires modifying tools like InDesign, making *them* emulate how *you* work as much as possible. Software—computers in general—is far from the point where it will truly work the way humans work, the way humans think. We are still forced to conform our methodologies and thinking processes to fit within the narrow boxes sitting under our desks—to a point. Whenever possible—and, with InDesign CS5, much is possible—customize the software to fit your work and the Preferences as closely as you can.

While the idea of rearranging panels or modifying menus may seem superfluous compared with other topics in this book, I've placed this chapter first because, ultimately, how you customize InDesign directly affects how efficiently you use the page layout application to learn and use anything else you might read in this volume.

Customizing InDesign shifts that dividing line between the software working for you and you working for the software further toward the former.

In this chapter, you will learn to

+ Organize panels and use the panel docks

+ Customize keyboard shortcuts

+ Remove parts of InDesign to create lean, workflow-specific installations

+ Change the default font, colors, and more

+ Carry your personalized InDesign work environment in your pocket or on your iPod

Panels

Since April 2005, when Adobe and Macromedia announced their intent to merge, users of InDesign or any of either company's products have speculated about the user interface that would result from combining two of the most acclaimed user interface design teams in the business. Creative Suite 3 was that result—the Adobe UI—which Creative Suite 5 continues to improve upon and refine.

The Adobe UI is growing ever more efficient in its use of screen real estate and ever more user customizable to facilitate your personal productivity within InDesign and the other Creative Suite applications. *Panels* can be free-floating, tabbed, stacked, grouped together into vertical panel bars à la the old Macromedia applications, and condensed into narrow icon and title tiles. Given the fact that InDesign CS5 has an unprecedented 56 panels, you'll likely employ several panel arrangement forms concurrently.

Hands down, the most efficient way to organize the InDesign workspace is across dual (or triple) monitors—preferably monitors of the same size and resolution. Although the vast majority of users don't need all 56 panels opened at once, many panels—such as Layers, Pages, Swatches, Index, Hyperlinks, Scripts, Links, and the five styles panels—tend to grow in utility and convenience according to their heights. The more space you give such panels, the less scrolling you'll have to do, which means the faster you can access the layer, page, swatch, style, or whatever it is you need.

 **Real World Scenario**

USING MULTIPLE MONITORS

On my primary production computer, I use six monitors, with the first containing the InDesign application itself and the Control and Tools panels, the second completely filled with my most-often-used 28 panels, and several other panels, those I use once in a while, taking up about half of the third monitor in their collapsed button states. The remaining two and a half monitors I use for whatever other application I need open concurrently with a particular InDesign project. Often that's InCopy, but just as often it's a digital asset manager like Bridge or ThumbsPlus, and sometimes Illustrator, Photoshop, or multiple windows of Microsoft Word or Acrobat.

Another interesting multiple-monitor InDesign scenario I've seen is two 32-inch Apple Cinema displays stacked vertically, rather than the more common setup of side-by-side monitors. The stacked monitors are used by a newspaper workflow for which I consulted in InCopy and InDesign. With the monitors stacked, the layout editor can proof two complete spreads (four pages) of the paper—one spread per monitor—simultaneously while keeping them large enough on screen to actually read most text.

Ultimately, like RAM, designers can never have too much screen real estate when dealing with panel-based creative pro applications.

The point is, Adobe knows that InDesign is a forest of panels. The vast majority of the application's functions are contained on panels, which is a far more efficient way of doing it than in dialog boxes. Dialog boxes, while open, prohibit accessing the document; to do something to two objects individually via a dialog box requires more steps than doing it through panels, which are always onscreen. The downside to panels is, of course, that they're always onscreen, always taking up space.

Next, we'll go through the various methods Adobe has built into InDesign to enable you to organize panels. I'll also offer some advice on which ones you can safely keep off your screen.

The Panel Dock

The dock is InDesign's attempt to organize panels on single-monitor systems—or anywhere—where space is at a premium.

Dragging panels to the side of the application window causes them to become labeled icons in the panel dock, a top-to-bottom reserved area of the application window (see Figure 1.1). In some programs, such as Photoshop and Illustrator, the icons initially appear unlabeled, resulting in a much slimmer dock (and consequently a wider document working area).

FIGURE 1.1
The InDesign
panel dock

InDesign can have icon-only docks too; they just don't appear that way in the default workspace. To slim down an InDesign dock to icon-only mode and reclaim most of the horizontal space for the working area, drag one edge of any collapsed panel in the dock toward the opposite screen edge (refer back to Figure 1.1). When you get to within 18 or so pixels of the edge, the dock will snap into icon-only mode. Conversely, dragging outward from the screen edge will widen the dock, first making labels appear, perhaps truncated, and then increasing the space for them.

Adobe branded nearly all its applications and technologies with color-coded, two-letter signifiers strongly reminiscent of elements on the periodic table. The kaleidoscope of icons makes for a brighter desktop, Start Menu, or OS X Dock, while, as a counterpoint, the workspaces of Adobe applications themselves become a cool cornucopia of grayscale icons—every panel now has its own associated icon displayed within the application dock. For easy reference, Table 1.1 pairs all the panels with their associated icons. Astute observers will note that the table includes only 53 icons. The Tool and Control panels cannot be collapsed fully, so they have no icons. Nor does the Cross-References panel, which is permanently fused to the bottom of the Hyperlinks panel despite having a separate Show/Hide command under Window ➤ Type & Tables.

To use a panel in the dock, click its collapsed icon or icon and title. It will expand out to the side, revealing the entire panel. Collapse it back into the panel either by clicking the double arrows pointed toward the dock, by clicking on the title tab of the panel, or by clicking its icon (or icon and title) again.

Only one panel per dock may be extended at once, and by default, the last-used panel will remain extended until you collapse it. If you'd prefer that panels immediately collapse back to their icon or tile state as soon as you finish with them, right-click the dark gray dock title or an empty area of the dock itself and choose Auto-Collapse Icon Panels (you'll also find the same choice in the Preferences on the Interface pane).

TABLE 1.1:   InDesign panels and their icons

ICON	PANEL	ICON	PANEL	ICON	PANEL
	Access CS Live		Flattener Preview		Preflight
	Align		Glyphs		Preview
	Animation		Hyperlinks		Script Label
	Assignments		Index		Scripts
	Attributes		Info		Separations Preview
	Background Tasks		Kuler		Story
	Bookmarks		Layers		Stroke
	Buttons		Links		Swatches
	Cell Styles		Media		Table
	Character		Mini Bridge		Table Styles
	Character Styles		Notes		Tags
	Color		Object States		Text Wrap
	Conditional Text		Object Styles		Timing
	CS News and Resources		Pages		Tool Hints
	CS Review		Page Transitions		Track Changes
	Data Merge		Paragraph		Transform
	Gradient		Paragraph Styles		Trap Presets
	Effects		Pathfinder		

Expand or contract the *entire* dock, inclusive of all the panels it contains, by clicking the double-arrow symbol at the very top of the panel. When the panel is in icon-only or collapsed tile mode, arrows will point inward, toward the application workspace and away from the edge; when the panel is expanded, arrows will point outward toward the edge of the screen. You can also double-click the empty, dark title bar of the dock or Cmd+click/Ctrl+click it to toggle between expanded and collapsed states.

Arranging Panels

To add a panel to the default dock, drag the panel's title tab over the empty area of the dock beneath the lowest panel. When your cursor is in position, a colored horizontal line will appear across the dock. Release the mouse button to drop the panel into the dock at that point.

Remove panels from the dock by dragging the title or icon (not the gray bar above them) out from the dock into the empty application area. When you release the mouse, the panel will become free floating.

Some panels, you'll notice, are grouped—when you click the title of one to extend it, other panels are tabbed behind it (see Figure 1.2). These are grouped panels. Collapsed, their grouped arrangement is indicated by their icons or tiles contained within a light gray rectangle, with a common gray bar atop them. If you *do* drag the gray bar away from the dock, you'll detach the entire group of panels. Once detached, they will be a free-floating group of tabbed panels. Grouped panels, both on the dock and free floating, are one-at-a-time views. In other words, if the Stroke and Color panels are grouped (as they are in the default Essentials workspace), you can view only one or the other, not both simultaneously.

FIGURE 1.2
Grouped panels extended with other groups collapsed

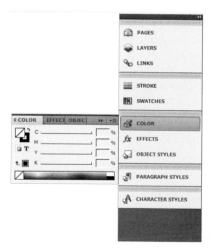

Rearrange panels in the dock by dragging their icons or tiles vertically. A horizontal line will indicate the new location of the panel should you drop it. A rule between the panel groups, in the dark area of the dock background, will reposition the panel or group to that point outside other groups. Dropping it within the area of a group of icons or tiles, however, will add the panel to the group. Dragging the gray bar of a grouped set of panels will reposition the entire group or merge it into an existing group.

InDesign can actually contain docks on *both* sides of the application window and can have multiple columns of panels arranged side by side in the dock. Just as with adding panels to the default right-side dock, creating and managing side-by-side docks is done by dragging. Begin by creating the first dock, and then drag another panel (or panel group) to the screen edge. Bypass the *horizontal* line indicating that the new panel will appear below the one already there, and keep going to the screen edge, whereupon a *vertical* line will appear. When you let go, the previous dock area will be pushed inward, with the new panel forming a column on the outside. Similarly, you'll see a vertical line at the *inner* edge of an existing dock as well, enabling you to add a dock inward rather than outward of existing docks.

You can keep going, adding columns as you like, but only within the application window. If the dock expands so far that it reaches the other side of the window, panels will begin to automatically collapse into their labeled icon tiles. The width of each dock can be set independently, enabling you to have a wide, labeled tile panel dock beside a narrow, icon-only dock.

Stacked Panels

Detached or free-floating panels have similar arrangement options. Drag the tab of one panel atop another free-floating panel or group of panels to group them into tabs. When your cursor is in position, a bold outline will appear all the way around the target panel. If you drag too close to the bottom of another panel, you'll see a horizontal line appear only there, indicating that the panels will stack rather than group (see Figure 1.3).

Stacked panels work similarly to docked panels but with several distinct advantages. You can see and work with multiple panels at once just as you would free-floating panels, and they aren't limited to positioning at the screen edge. Like docked panels, stacked panels can be expanded or contracted into just their icons or icon and title tiles selectively, or an entire stack can be expanded or contracted with a single click of the mouse.

At the top of a stack is a double-arrow collapse/expand button. Clicking it—or double-clicking an empty area of the bar containing the collapse/expand double arrow—collapses all panels in the stack into their low-profile, docked form or expands them all. A single close button also hides the entire stack of panels. When you move a stack by dragging the top bar, all the panels move with it.

FIGURE 1.3
Stacked panels

Many panels—the Pages and Swatches panels, for instance—are resizable. Within a stack, they can be resized by hovering the cursor along their bottom edge, at the point where they join the next panel down, and dragging up or down. The cursor will become a double-headed arrow as a visual cue.

Multistate Panels

Many panels have expanded views with additional options, controls, or fields hidden by default. Switch between the compact and expanded views by choosing Show Options or Hide Options from the panel flyout menus. As we deal with each panel's expanded controls throughout the rest of the book, I'll usually remind you to show the expanded view. However, since this book is written as a focused manual for using InDesign in professional print design and production workflows rather than as a soup-to-nuts InDesign CS5 reference book, some panels won't even be mentioned in later chapters. Always check for the Show Options command on a panel's flyout menu.

Another way to discern if a given panel has multiple states is the presence of double (stacked) arrows in the title tab (see Figure 1.4). Clicking the arrows cycles through the states of any palette—condensed, expanded, and minimized. Double-clicking the title tab of the panel itself accomplishes the same state cycling as clicking the arrows.

FIGURE 1.4

A multistate panel, the Gradient panel, shows a double arrow in its title tab. (Left) The condensed state. (Right) The expanded or options state.

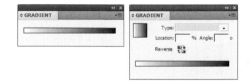

The Tools Panel

You'll use the Tools panel more than any other. All your tools are there, as are basic fill and stroke color controls and preview modes. In Figure 1.5, I've identified each of the tool icons and different parts in an exploded view of the Tools panel.

Customization options for the Tools panel are limited to two choices:

◆ Whether it's docked or free floating

◆ How its tools are arranged—in the now-standard single-column array, as a single row, or in the nostalgic two-column format (see Figure 1.6)

The first option, docked or floating, is set in the same manner as any other panel—drag it toward or away from the screen edge. When docked, it uses the entire screen's worth of vertical space because other panels cannot be docked beneath or above the Tools panel. That's the con. The pro, of course, is that, when the Tools panel is docked, document windows automatically resize around it, never over- or underlapping it as they would do in versions of InDesign prior to the introduction of docking in InDesign CS3.

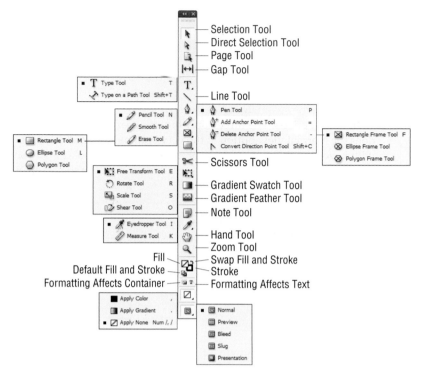

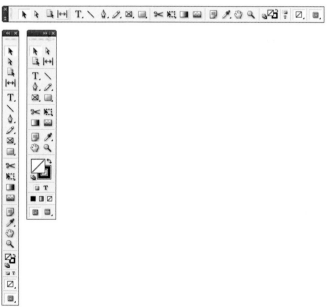

The second option, whether to display the Tools panel in single-column, double-column, or single-row mode, is set in the Interface pane of InDesign's Preferences (InDesign ➤ Preferences on the Mac and Edit ➤ Preferences on Windows). Easier than going that route, however, is to click the double arrows at the top of the Tools panel. When the Tools panel is floating, the double arrows will cycle it through the three states. If docked, however, the double-arrow button will toggle only between vertical single- and double-column modes. Although the single-column and single-row modes have the advantage of consuming less screen real estate, they have a seeming drawback as well; fewer options. The three apply buttons near the bottom don't fit in the slimmer modes, nor does the Normal view button at the very bottom. Fortunately, Adobe made up for their absence with keyboard shortcuts. If you opt to use one of the Tools panel's slimmer arrangements (or just like the efficiency of keyboard shortcuts), memorize the shortcuts in Table 1.2.

TABLE 1.2: Keyboard shortcuts for Tools panel features hidden by single-column and single-row modes

SHORTCUT	FUNCTION
, (comma)	Apply solid color to fill or stroke.
. (period)	Apply gradient to fill or stroke.
/ (slash)	Remove color from fill or stroke.
W	Toggle between normal mode and the selected preview mode.

The Control Panel

The Control panel, a favorite among users since its introduction in InDesign CS (1) PageMaker Edition, is context sensitive to the tool and task at hand, offering a compact quick access point for the most common features and options. While you're editing text, for instance, the Control panel goes into Character or Paragraph mode, two transposable sets of fields and controls that offer, among many other things, the ability to change the font family, style, and size as well as paragraph alignments, spacing, and indents. When you're working with tables, though, the Control panel transforms to offer table-specific controls such as the number of rows and columns, cell alignments, and insets. In all, there are four modes dependent upon what you're actually doing in the document—working with objects, characters, paragraphs, or tables. Figure 1.7 shows all four modes.

FIGURE 1.7
The four modes of the Control panel: (top to bottom) Object, Character, Paragraph, and Table

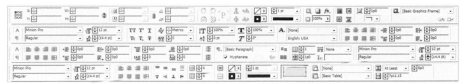

The very last object on the Control panel's right end, a button that looks like three horizontal lines, is the Control panel's flyout menu. Like the face of the Control panel, the commands on the flyout menu are context variable. At the bottom of the list, the Customize command is constant and opens the Customize Control Panel dialog box (see Figure 1.8). Here, by unchecking the show box in the expanding lists, you can selectively disable groups of controls or an entire mode. Maybe, while working with general objects, you'd rather not see the new Corner Shape controls section on the Control panel. To hide the Corner Shape controls, expand the Other section of the Customize Control Panel dialog box and uncheck Corner Shape. The same goes for anything else you'd rather not see on the Control panel.

Also on the Control panel flyout menu are commands to dock the panel to the top of the application window, its default location, dock it to the bottom, or float it free à la PageMaker's Control palette and QuarkXPress's Measurements palette. Once free floating, the Control panel can be positioned anywhere you like onscreen but always horizontal. In addition to using the menu commands, dragging the vertical double bar of dotted lines on the left edge of the panel moves the panel around as well, attaching it to, or detaching it from, the top or bottom edge of the application. When you drag a floating Control panel close enough to either the top or bottom edge, a thick horizontal line, similar to the one you see when docking other panels, will appear above or below the panel; release the mouse button and the panel will snap into its docked position.

If you're running a monitor with a horizontal resolution greater than 1024 pixels, you should take advantage of dynamic controls in the Control panel. All the primary controls of each mode are contained within the first 1024 pixels. After the primary controls have been rendered, several modes of the Control panel will present additional controls for your convenience. In Character mode, for example, more paragraph-centric fields and options will fill the extra space after all character-centric fields. In Paragraph mode, more of the character-centric controls slip in there. The idea, of course, is that if you have the space to use, InDesign will use it to save you a few times toggling between Character and Paragraph modes.

FIGURE 1.8
Customizing the
Control panel

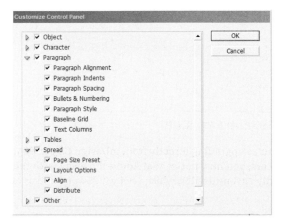

Panels You Don't Need

So upgraded is the Control panel, in fact, that it negates the need to use some other panels almost entirely. Conversely, you can elect to hide the Control panel, saving yourself some vertical screen real estate. The main advantage to using the Control panel is its context-sensitive nature;

depending on the task at hand, it contains the majority of controls, options, fields, and buttons from the Transform, Align, Character, Paragraph, and Table panels, as well as some from the Stroke, Text Wrap, Effects, Character Styles, Paragraph Styles, Object Styles, and other panels. All these controls share the same space onscreen, which is far less real estate than the respective panels consume individually—even with panel docking and other space-saving options.

Although the options on the Control panel are not comprehensive replicas of all the dedicated panels mentioned in the previous paragraph, you may need more only on rare occasions. Consider your unique workflow and examine what is and isn't available on the Control panel to be sure, but you can probably safely hide the following stand-alone panels and reclaim the space they would occupy for other panels not duplicated on the Control panel:

- Character

- Paragraph

- Table

- Transform

- Align

On the other hand, if you prefer using the individual panels (personally, I prefer using the Character, Paragraph, and Table panels rather than the Control panel most of the time), drop the Control panel and reclaim *that* space. With such a panel-laden application, where docking, grouping, and stacking panels and multiple monitors merely mitigate screen overcrowding and a claustrophobic document workspace rather than *solve* it, repossess any pixels you can.

Bars

With 56 default panels, Adobe could market InDesign under the tagline "There's a panel for that!" Of course, that would infringe on Apple's "There's an app for that!" trademark, but in the ongoing feud between Apple and Adobe, one more tiff would hardly be noticed.

By the same token, InDesign could also infringe on the trademark of Apple partner AT&T with "Fewer bars in more places." That's right, folks; InDesign has toolbars, though it has fewer bars than your average cell phone.

COMMAND BAR, R.I.P.

If you're upgrading directly from InDesign CS3 to CS5, as are many of your peers and this book's readers, you may notice that Adobe did away with the Command Bar. Or, you might not notice; hardly anyone used it, which is why it disappeared as of version CS4.

Activated from Window ➤ Object & Layout ➤ Command Bar in CS3, this horizontal toolbar included buttons for common functions like Save, Open, Print, and Check Spelling; buttons to toggle bullets, numbering, and left and right indents on or off; and quick-launch buttons for Photoshop, Illustrator, and Acrobat. If you're among the proud few who used the Command Bar, I have the sad duty to inform you that it is no longer a part of InDesign. With the exception of the quick launch buttons, all its functions are now exclusively part of the Control panel or menus…

…Or a new toolbar, called the Application bar, that has a half-finished look and an in-some-future-release-I'll-be-a-better-Command-bar vibe.

Application Bar

In an ongoing effort to get people to use the entry-level digital asset manager Adobe Bridge (and through it buy stock photography and subscribe to Adobe RSS newsfeeds), Adobe has, since the initial release of Bridge in Creative Suite (1), been integrating (some say infiltrating) all the major applications like InDesign with commands and buttons to launch Bridge. InDesign CS3 brought us a Control panel button named Go to Bridge, which also doubled as a menu to access the short-lived Adobe Stock Photos. As a part of the Control panel, that Go to Bridge button/menu could be easily hidden via the Customize Control Panel dialog box, which may be part of the reason Adobe Stock Photos never succeeded and was killed by the time CS4 debuted.

Adobe Stock Photos- and Adobe RSS newsfeeds-free Bridge CS4 found its way into InDesign CS4 not as a Control panel section that a user could hide but instead as a Browse in Bridge command on the File menu (which is obliterable via menu customizations) and as a nonremovable Go to Bridge button on the new Application bar. It remains in both places in InDesign CS5; CS5 also includes the Mini Bridge panel, but that's a topic for a different chapter.

On the Mac, the Application bar can be toggled on or off with a command at the bottom of the Windows menu. Within the Application bar you'll find the application icon (the stylized ID for InDesign); a Go to Bridge button; and alternate, menu-driven means of accessing document zoom level, common show/hide commands from the View menu, preview modes, and workspaces. In addition, exclusive to the Application bar and available nowhere else in InDesign, the Arrange Documents menu enables you to arrange multiple open documents' windows in a dizzying variety of stacks, tiles, and flotillas (see Figure 1.9). You'll also find a search field to help you find topics in the InDesign help as well as a button to access the new CS Live online features of Creative Suite 5.

FIGURE 1.9

The Application bar on the Mac (top) and Windows (bottom)

Showing the Application bar on the Mac will cause the document zoom percentage display to disappear from the status bar; hiding the Application bar puts the zoom percentage display back in the status bar.

The Application bar is very different on Windows. It contains all the same features as the Mac version. A bigger difference, though, is that the Application bar can't be hidden on Windows. Whether you want them or not, Go to Bridge and the other menus and buttons are a permanent fixture in your copy of InDesign CS4 or CS5. There is a silver lining, though: Unlike on a Mac, the Windows version of the Application bar is (usually) low profile. It's unified with the application menus and minimize, maximize, and exit buttons to form a concatenated single Application bar that takes up very little extra vertical space than that required by the menus. Even the screen-wasting title bar is omitted!

Note that in some default workspaces on Windows, the Application bar appears as its own toolbar independent of the menu bar and thus takes more vertical screen space. Despite the obvious ability of the InDesign engineers to reposition the Application bar, there remains no user interface for you and me to move or hide it.

Application Frame

Exclusive to the Mac version of InDesign, owing to the differences in the way Mac and Windows handle application and document windows, is the option to attach all the panels and toolbars to a document window.

Normally on a Mac, the Application bar and Control panel are docked directly beneath the menu bar; the Tools panel is docked to one side of the screen; and other panels are docked to the other side of the screen. Document windows are their own constructs that can be moved and resized without affecting the positioning on these other elements. To facilitate multiple-application workflows, however, you can invert the behavior that treats toolbars and panels as application—or screen—affixed objects and make them part of the document window (see Figure 1.10).

Choosing the Application Frame command at the bottom of the Window menu sticks panels and toolbars to the document window, enabling you to resize and reposition your work area, which makes switching back and forth between InDesign and another application easier. Note that Illustrator and Photoshop CS4 and CS5 have similar commands to ease all sides of a back-and-forth with InDesign.

FIGURE 1.10
Panels and toolbars affixed to the document window via the Application Frame command

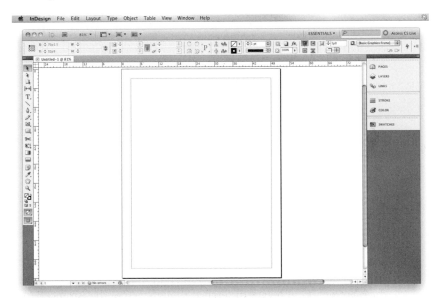

Keyboard Shortcuts

Somebody far back in time invented computer keyboard shortcuts, the ability to press a few keys simultaneously to produce the same effect as, and in lieu of, reaching for the mouse and navigating a menu. I don't know who came up with the idea of keyboard shortcuts —I think it was Cro-Magnon man, but there's a strong case being built that it might have been the newly discovered Ardipithecus Ramidus ("Ardi"). Whomever it was should have a statue erected in his honor. Maybe there already is; I haven't visited the Smithsonian in a few years.

Keyboard shortcuts save tremendous time and effort and are, in my opinion, the greatest productivity-enhancing invention since instant coffee (created by Saint Juan Valdez circa 35,000 BCE). InDesign is loaded with keyboard shortcuts to speed your work. And, at this point in the narrative, many software book authors would launch into several pages of keyboard shortcuts or direct you to the back of the book, to an index of the same. Me? Well, I have precious few pages in which to cram all the advanced InDesign info I can. I'm not going to waste 3 to 10 or so of those with something I can give you in a different medium (see the sidebar "InDesign CS5 Keyboard Shortcuts"). More important, I can give you something even better than a list of keyboard shortcuts: I can show you how to set your own keyboard shortcuts for just about everything.

INDESIGN CS5 KEYBOARD SHORTCUTS

Even with the ability to customize every keyboard shortcut in InDesign, sometimes it's nice to have a list in front of you. So, I made one.

Visit `http://iampariah.com/projects/other-projects` to download a free and printable PDF containing every keyboard shortcut for InDesign CS5 and InCopy CS5 on both Windows and Mac.

If you choose Edit ➤ Keyboard Shortcuts to launch the Keyboard Shortcuts dialog box (see Figure 1.11), you can assign a keyboard shortcut to any command in InDesign, change the shortcuts already assigned, and create portable sets of shortcuts (more on portability later).

FIGURE 1.11
Editing keyboard shortcuts

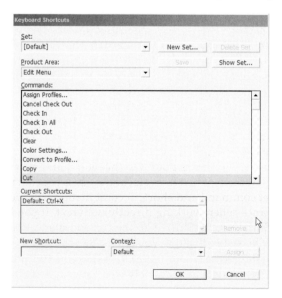

From the Product Area dropdown menu select Edit Menu, which lets you view and customize commands on the application's Edit menu. Click Cut in the Commands list. Its shortcut—Cmd+X/Ctrl+X—will appear in the Current Shortcuts field beneath the list. Don't like that shortcut? Click Default: Cmd+X or Default: Ctrl+X to highlight it, and then click the Remove button. InDesign will promptly notify you that you cannot modify the Default set of keyboard shortcuts and ask whether to create a new set for your customizations. InDesign can contain multiple keyboard shortcut sets. In fact, if you look toward the very top of the dialog box, you'll see that it already had three—Default, Shortcuts for PageMaker 7.0, and Shortcuts for QuarkXPress 4.0. If you're migrating to InDesign from PageMaker or QuarkXPress, using one of those sets can ease your transition. In the QuarkXPress set, for instance, object-arrange commands such as Bring Forward, Bring to Front, Send Backward, and Send to Back use XPress's familiar F5 shortcuts instead of InDesign's shortcuts, which use the left and right brackets ([ ]). Of course, InDesign isn't PageMaker or QuarkXPress, so not every command or keyboard shortcut from one has a place in the other; the shortcut sets are not total conversions but helping hands.

To create your own set, click the New Set button and name the set, or begin a change and answer Yes when prompted. Go ahead and create a new set now, just to practice while you go through the rest of this section. While working in your set, remember to save it from time to time with the button at the top. If, after working through this chapter, you elect to eject the shortcut set, simply choose it in the Set drop-down list and click the Delete Set button.

Returning to modifying the Edit ➤ Cut command, let's say that, instead of removing the default shortcut, you'd like to add a second shortcut. You'd like both Cmd+X/Ctrl+X and Cmd+Shift+X/Ctrl+ Shift+X to effect a cut. In that case, to add a shortcut, position your cursor within the New Shortcut field at the bottom of the dialog box and press the new shortcut. (Note to Windows users: You cannot use the Windows key as a modifier within the application.) Beneath the field you should see a warning that Cmd+Shift+X/Ctrl+ Shift+X is already assigned to the Normal Horizontal Text Scale command. If you click the Assign button, you'll strip Normal Horizontal Text Scale from the shortcut and assign it to Cut.

To the right of the New Shortcut field is Context. Every keyboard shortcut can be targeted to certain types of tasks. You could, for example, bind Cmd+Shift+X/Ctrl+Shift+X to Edit ➤ Cut only when working with tables. While working with text, with XML selections, within alert and dialog boxes, in the new Presentation mode, and in all other circumstances, it will not invoke the Cut command. In fact, if you set the Context field to Table now, you'll see that the Currently Assigned To notice no longer says Normal Horizontal Text Scale. That's because the shortcut is bound to that command only in the context of working with text. The horizontal scale of text is irrelevant to XML code, dialog boxes, and the structure of tables, and that command and shortcut combination has been assigned to function only where it *is* relevant—when working directly with text. If you left Context set to Table and assigned Cmd+Shift+X/Ctrl+Shift+X to the Cut command, *that* would apply only when working with tables. The same shortcut would still invoke Normal Horizontal Text Scale when working with text. In other words, the same keyboard shortcut can be *used six times over* for different commands in different contexts.

There are only so many keys on the QWERTY keyboard, only so many modifiers and combinations of keys, so customizing keyboard shortcuts in InDesign often entails sacrificing keyboard access to one command for another. By the same token, just as you can add multiple shortcuts to Cut, other commands already have multiple shortcuts. Do they need two (or three)? Probably not, which means their extras are fair game for commands that don't have any. Other commands have shortcuts you'll never use; put those key combinations to better use. If you use the Gradient Feather effect often, give it a keyboard shortcut (it doesn't have one by default, although the Drop Shadow command does—Cmd+Shift+M/Ctrl+Shift+M).

The Product Area drop-down list mirrors the structure of menus but includes a lot more, even commands not found on the menu bar. Object Editing, for instance, includes all sorts of align, distribution, scale, and nudge commands that simply don't have counterparts on any menu and would normally require mouse work. Explore the dialog box, changing and testing shortcuts, until you have all your most-used commands shortcutted and InDesign works your way.

The folks at Adobe did a great job in setting keyboard shortcuts on the commands most used by the average InDesign user, but they had to leave it up to you to tailor the program to *your* unique workflow. Keyboard shortcuts, various panel arrangements and customizations, even customizable menus are available to tailor the program to you. Use them.

Menus

Yes, you read me right: In InDesign CS3 and later you can customize menus. Photoshop CS2 (and its now-retired protégé ImageReady CS2) introduced the idea of customizable menus. Odd as it may sound, it's a pretty cool idea. Do me a favor: Select Window ➤ Workspace ➤ New in CS5. You'll likely be prompted to save your current workspace; answer in the affirmative. Now, return to the Window menu. Notice anything? Check out the File menu. You should see quite a few commands and submenus highlighted in a pleasing blue (see Figure 1.12).

FIGURE 1.12
Menu highlighting
in use to show off
new commands
and upgraded
areas of CS5

Now, go to the Menus command at the bottom of the Edit menu to open Menu Customization (see Figure 1.13). Similar to customizing keyboard shortcuts, you have sets to create and choose from and two categories of menus—Application Menus, those that appear within the menu bar at the top of the InDesign window, and Context & Panel Menus, which are the flyout menus on panels as well as those menus that appear when you right-click (Control-click for you single-button Mac mouse users) something. Every menu in InDesign can be customized. Pick one. Click the arrow to the left to expand the menu, showing commands and submenus in the order in which they appear on the menu itself.

If there's a command that you never use, one you'd like out of your way, click its eyeball icon in the Visibility column. The menu command or submenu will disappear from the application as if it didn't exist. To highlight a menu like those that turned blue in the New in CS5 workspace, change the color in the third column. Sorry, no custom colors, just the basic rainbow red, orange, yellow, green, blue, violet, and gray (for rain clouds, I assume).

Why would I want to remove some commands? you might ask. Well, the vast majority of InDesign users never use everything in the application. Do you do any XML work? If not, you can hide the XML-centric commands and unclutter the interface a little.

Next, I'd expect you to ask, *Why would I want to color-code my menu commands?* As you saw Adobe do with its set, color-coding menus is a great way to learn new features and commands. It can also help in memory: *Where do I set the options for an inline graphic so that it has vertical spacing? Oh, duh! Here it is: Anchored Objects on the Objects menu. I colored it red last time I used it six months ago so I'd remember where to find it again.*

For you production managers, editors, and other team leaders, customizing menus presents a new level of production control through customized workstation installs without messing with installer scripts or disabling plug-ins. Check out the sidebar "Customizing InDesign to Easily Create Workflow-Focused Workstations" to see how I helped the editor of one small newspaper keep her staff focused and her layouts clean and press ready.

FIGURE 1.13
Customizing menus

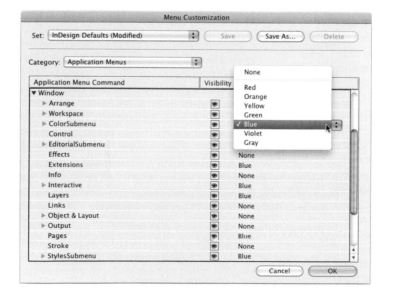

InDesign can function, to one degree or another, absent any of the nonrequired plug-ins. Therefore, if some or all of the people in your workgroup have no need of something like, say, hyperlinks and the Hyperlinks panel or type on a path, you can save (a little) system overhead and tidy up the InDesign interface a bit by disabling the plug-ins that add those functions.

CS5

In past versions, plug-ins were managed from the Configure Plug-Ins dialog box. As of CS5, however, Adobe has unified the management of plug-ins and extensions across all Creative Suite applications into the Adobe Extension Manager, an app that ships with the Suite and constituent products (see Figure 1.14). You can launch Adobe Extension Manager from its application icon or from within InDesign via Help ➤ Manage Extensions (Windows) or InDesign ➤ Manage Extensions (Mac). In Adobe Extension Manager, select InDesign CS5 from the Products list to view a list of plug-ins and extensions installed in your copy of InDesign. Plug-ins and extensions are listed with their versions and authors, if known, and may be selectively disabled by unchecking the box in the Enabled column. Already disabled plug-ins show an empty box in the Enabled column and can be toggled back on with a click in that box. Required plug-ins, those that cannot be disabled without destabilizing InDesign and triggering a planet-wide seismic catastrophe even John Cusack couldn't escape, appear with a padlock icon to the left of their names, and their Enabled column checkboxes are unalterable. To *delete*, not merely disable, a noncritical plug-in, select it and click the Remove button that appears to the right of the plug-in author's name.

FIGURE 1.14
Configuring InDesign plug-ins via Adobe Extension Manager CS5

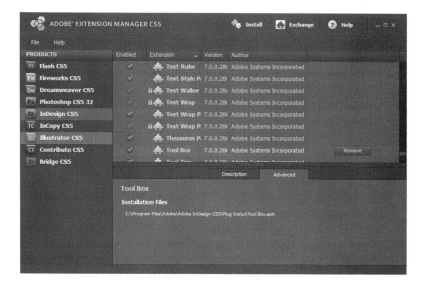

Disable any plug-ins neither you nor InDesign need to do your job; you'll have a leaner InDesign with less demand on your system RAM. If you're not entirely sure what a plug-in does, highlight it; at the bottom of Adobe Extension Manager you can view a description and advanced information about any selected plug-in. Although the resulting description isn't guaranteed to be illuminating, it might offer some clues. Unfortunately, Adobe Extension Manager typically offers much less information about plug-ins and their dependencies than the much more verbose Configure Plug-Ins utility it replaced. Ah, progress!

When in doubt about what a plug-in does and whether you need it, try disabling it and look for the absence of what you think it does. *Why would I want to disable some plug-ins?* For many of the

same reasons you'd want to disable some menus—a cleaner display, the aforementioned smaller RAM footprint, and to limit workstation installs to only what is required of the user's workflow. If your team works in a strictly print workflow, for instance, and never exports to HTML or Flash, you can remove commands, panels, and everything else to do with hyperlinks, rollover buttons, sound and video, HTML export, and so on. I can tell you from personal experience that using Extensions Manager to disable things like the Tools panel (`Tool Box.apln`) on someone else's computer is also an amusing practical joke. Just be kind enough to let the victim in on the joke before too long (or leave this book nearby opened to this page and I'll take the blame).

Workspaces

Now that you have InDesign customized to your personal work habits, with this panel stacked over here, another dozen panels collapsed to icons in a dock, three more stacked, and several panels hidden, menus color-coded and customized, and keyboard shortcuts totally customized, it's time to scare you: Everything you just did will evaporate the first time InDesign's preferences get corrupted. They get corrupted often—no more so than other applications', but that's too often.

All your customizations are saved into the application preferences, a flimsy little ASCII text file with all the resiliency and tensile strength of wet newsprint. Sneezing too hard in the general direction of your computer could tear and corrupt the preferences. Then where would you be? That's right, trying to remember all the original keyboard shortcuts while stumbling all but blind through the original configuration of panels. Of course, there's a solution to prevent the loss of your customizations. And, I'll explain that solution in detail in the sequel to this book, *Mastering InDesign CS5 for Print Design and Production Rebooted*, due out from Sybex next year. Don't let your preferences get corrupted before then.

Just kidding. I was doing an impression of a typical local news anchor—*Tune into our six o'clock broadcast to find out what's killing area children and could be killing your child right now!* (Yup, tune in at least three hours after your child has been presumably slain to learn that children are being given two desserts in the school cafeteria on Fridays.)

InDesign has, for several versions now, had the ability to save panel (previously palette, lest we forget the tragedies of yesterday) arrangements as *workspaces*. Workspaces are so much more, though: They save menu customizations, keyboard shortcuts, *and* panel arrangements. It's the last part that's the most important because, while you can save and restore sets of keyboard shortcuts and menus, workspaces are the only way to record panel arrangements.

When we looked at menu color-coding a few pages ago, the New in CS5 option you chose from Window ➢ Workspaces was a workspace. You may have noticed that loading it also rearranged your panels. If you missed that, load up New in CS5 again from Window ➢ Workspaces. Note the dock on the right wherein several panels have been hidden and replaced by others not shown after first installing InDesign. The Essential workspace will return everything—shortcuts, menus, panels—to out-of-the-box InDesign.

Anytime you customize InDesign, save your workspace by choosing Window ➢ Workspaces ➢ Save Workspace. Supply a name, and your workspace will be added to the Workspaces menu ready for instant restoration in the event of a Preferences corruption and subsequent reset or if you change things around to fit a particular project.

That brings me to another key point: You can have many, many workspaces. Sometimes you need these five panels showing, some projects require those six others, and yet other types of projects require a dozen or more, all with options showing. Make workspaces for each of your typical types of projects. Strictly print projects, for instance, aren't likely to need the Hyperlinks panel,

whereas creating a publication that will be distributed only on the client's website as a PDF *does* need Hyperlinks and probably doesn't need the Separations Preview and Trap Presets panels. By employing multiple, project-specific workspaces, you can further reduce panel clutter by limiting the application to only what the one type of project needs, without the chore of having to manually open, close, and arrange panels every time you switch to a different task or project.

InDesign in Your Pocket

Or, *InDesign on a Stick*—a USB stick/thumbnail drive/flash drive. Although you can fit InDesign and all its component plug-ins on most portable USB flash drives, it won't run from there. (Well, I'm sure somebody could get it to run, but I think that would violate the EULA.) What I mean by the title of this section is taking *your* InDesign in your pocket, your unique configuration and work habits, and sitting down at any workstation and, in 30 seconds or less, making any copy of InDesign CS5 work exactly like InDesign on your main computer—complete with panel arrangements, keyboard shortcuts, menus, and even your own autocorrect settings and Find/ Change queries.

It's exceedingly simple, really. First, make sure you've created a new keyboard shortcut set, a new set of menus, and a new workspace. Create and save them in their respective manners. Nothing here is permanent, so please don't feel pressured to create the perfect workspace or customize everything right now. Just do something simple for each, save the set, and close InDesign.

Now, open a Finder or Explorer window and navigate to the following InDesign folder. Note that, if you can't get to the folder, if it's marked as protected or hidden, or you just can't see it, check out the sidebar "Are Your Files Hidden?"

Mac: `[your user name]/Library/Preferences/Adobe InDesign/Version 7.0/en_US/`

Windows 7/Vista: `Users\[your user name]\AppData\Roaming\Adobe\InDesign\InDesign CS5\Version 7.0\en_US\`

Windows XP/2000: `Documents and Settings\[your user name]\Application Data\ Adobe\Adobe InDesign CS5\Version 7.0\en_US\`

ARE YOUR FILES HIDDEN OR RESTRICTED?

By default, Windows (all recent versions) hide certain folders and files to protect them. Unless you (or your IT department) have specifically told the operating system to show those files to you, you may not be able to interact with them. First, you'll need to unprotect and/or unhide these files. Here's how.

1. On the Start menu, select Control Panel, which will either open a new Explorer window showing your Control Panel folder or list the contents of the Control Panel folder directly in a submenu on the Start menu. In either case, choose Folder Options, which opens the Folder Options dialog box.

2. Go to the View tab.

3. In the Advanced Settings section, select the Show Hidden Files and Folders radio button under Hidden Files and Folders. To also see file extensions, deselect the check box beside Hide Extensions for Known File Types. Click OK. You may need to restart Windows for the changes to take effect.

Within those folders, you should see a subfolder for `Workspaces`. Open that, and you'll find an XML file of the workspace you just created. Go back up to the `Menu Sets` folder to find your recently created menu set. At the same level as both of those folders, you'll find others, called `InDesign Shortcut Sets`, `Autocorrect`, `Find-Change Queries`, `Glyph Sets`, `Print Presets`, `Preflight Presets`, and more. Note that you may not see all of those folders; they're created the first time you save a customization in that respective area of InDesign. If you've not yet created Autocorrect replace pairs, saved Find/Change queries, or created a custom Glyph set, you won't have folders for them. All of these folders store personal, per-user settings that are machine and even platform independent. You can pick up these files by copying the entire `Version 7.0` folder, carry them to any other installation of InDesign CS5 on the same platform (Windows or Mac), copy them to the same locations on the new machine, and have access to them at that workstation just as you would your own. When you launch InDesign, your copied workspace will be on the Window ➤ Workspaces menu, your keyboard and menu sets in the Keyboard Shortcuts and Customize Menu dialog boxes' Sets drop-down lists, and your Autocorrect, Find/Change, and Glyphs sets where they belong (I cover each later in this book). In fact, if you're handy with scripting, you could probably write an AppleScript or VBScript or BAT file that, upon execution on a target workstation, copies the `Version 7.0` folder from the USB drive to the hard drive.

You can even store your portable InDesign settings on your iPod, which, if you didn't realize it, can hold any type of data, not just music and videos. *That* would sell a few copies of this book! I can see the cover line now: *Run InDesign from Your iPod!* I'll have to talk to my publisher's marketing team.

Customizing Application Defaults

Is there a way to change the default font/swatches/hyphenation options/whatever? Collectively, it's probably the most common question I'm asked. Answer: *Yes*. If you can change the font family and style in the Character panel, you can change the default font. Likewise with creating new default swatches and removing the swatches with which InDesign ships. In fact, if you can do almost anything, you can make it the new default. Just do it with all documents closed.

Open InDesign without a document and look at the panels. If an option is grayed out, you can't change its default. If it isn't grayed out, well…there you are. Do you want hyphenation turned off by default instead of on? Uncheck the Hyphenate box on the Paragraph panel (choose Show Options from the panel flyout menu if you don't see it). To remove swatches you rarely use, open the Swatches panel and delete them. Add new swatches you use regularly—like corporate colors—by adding them to the panel with all documents closed. Every new document from that point forward will use only the swatches you see there, or will leave hyphenate unchecked, or whatever change you want to make.

To change the default font, open the Character panel and change the font. Done. Well, not entirely. You see, InDesign has a default paragraph style. When you change type options on the Character or Paragraph panel, you are indeed setting new defaults. However, you aren't changing the default styles, which can lead to problems later on if you reapply the default styles to text. If you're sure of your new font (or other type styling defaults), make the changes in the Character and/or Paragraph panels, and then open the Paragraph Styles panel. Highlight the Basic Paragraph style, choose Style Options from the panel flyout menu, and then repeat your changes there, making sure to save the style. Now your changes will survive a reapplication of the style.

Experiment with different controls and options. You can set new defaults for a great many things when no documents are opened.

Here I should note three important points:

◆ After setting your new defaults, you should close and restart InDesign to commit those changes to the InDesign preferences saved on your hard drive; if InDesign crashes before you've closed it, you'll lose those changes.

◆ Similarly, unlike workspaces and keyboard shortcut sets, your newly set defaults are part of the application preferences and can't be saved out to external files. Thus, if your preferences become corrupted and you have to reset them by holding Cmd+Opt+Ctrl+Shift/ Ctrl+Alt+Shift while launching InDesign, your typeface, hyphenation, and any other new defaults will be reset to the factory defaults.

◆ You should also realize that setting new defaults makes them the defaults only for new documents—existing documents will use the defaults set at the time of their creation.

SHARING CUSTOMIZATIONS

Many of the customizations we've covered in this chapter can be easily shared with others in your workgroup. Things like workspaces, keyboard shortcuts, autocorrect pairs, find/change queries, and more can be shared and standardized across your team. In Chapter 14, "Collaboration," you'll learn how; you'll also learn about the more powerful means of document and page collaboration available with InDesign CS5.

The Bottom Line

Organize Panels and Use the Panel Docks   Docks and other options make organizing panels in the workspace easier than ever before.

> **Master It**   Beginning with the default workspace, open all the panels you expect to use in most projects and close those you won't. Now, using grouping, stacking, docking, or just free-floating panels, arrange the panels to fit your work style, and leave yourself as much room to work on documents as possible.

Customize Keyboard Shortcuts   Adobe couldn't assign a keyboard shortcut to everything—there just aren't enough keys—so it did its best. Many of your favorite commands may not have shortcuts or may have shortcuts you dislike. You can add or change keyboard shortcuts for any command in InDesign.

> **Master It**   Just for fun, create keyboard shortcuts for each of the object effects—Basic Feather, Bevel and Emboss, and so on.

Remove Parts of InDesign to Create Lean, Workflow-Specific Installations   By customizing menus and disabling plug-ins, you can easily remove features and functions of InDesign not required by your workflow. Doing so streamlines the interface, reduces errors, and ultimately increases productivity among workflows that do not require the entirety of InDesign.

> **Master It**   To test your hand at removing features from InDesign, find all the features that are new or improved in CS5 and hide their menu commands. Then, color green the first 10 still-enabled menu commands about which you'd like to learn more. Finally, disable the plug-ins that show panels you or your team members aren't likely to need.

Change the Default Font, Colors, and More   Out of the box, InDesign CS5 uses Minion Pro 12/14.4 pt as the default text style and includes swatches for process magenta, cyan, and yellow and RGB red, green, and blue. These defaults are fine if your average document uses 12/14.4 Minion Pro and only solid process or RGB colors. But, if the average document you create requires another typeface, size, leading, other colors, or virtually any other option different from the defaults, change the defaults and save yourself some time

> **Master It**   Think about the documents you create most often. What is the type style—font family, font style, size, leading, and other formatting attributes—you use more than any other? Make those your new defaults. Do the same with your swatches, eliminating any colors you rarely use while adding those you use frequently.

Carry Your Personalized InDesign Work Environment in Your Pocket or on Your iPod   From freelancers brought into agency offices to assist with crunch time to students working in school labs, from round-the-clock production teams where different shifts use the same equipment to those dedicated enough to bring work home, seldom do creatives work solely on a single machine anymore. Creative and production personnel who switch computers waste a significant portion of their time customizing the InDesign environment of each computer on which they work even for a few minutes. To save time, nearly everything customizable about the InDesign CS5 working environment is portable. Customize one copy of InDesign, and carry your unique environment with you, making you instantly productive at any workstation.

> **Master It**   After arranging your panels and customizing your keyboard shortcuts and menus, it's time to take your InDesign workspace with you. If you have a USB flash drive, an iPod, a smart phone, or even just a floppy disk handy, copy the files containing your customized environment to the storage device. Now, if a second computer is available with InDesign CS5 installed, install those files to that computer and set up InDesign CS5 your way.

Chapter 2

Text

Like most layout applications, InDesign operates on a content-to-container premise. Everything within InDesign is either content—text and imagery—or a container to hold text, imagery, or another container. At the lowest level, the pasteboard is a container that holds everything you might place in InDesign. Then there are pages and layers—more containers—and *then* the real content enters the picture—text and imagery.

In this chapter, you will learn to

- ◆ Create and fill text frames
- ◆ Span and split columns
- ◆ Format text frames
- ◆ Format paragraphs
- ◆ Compose paragraphs

Text Frame Basics

Whether imported from an external document or typed directly into InDesign, text is, by definition, content. Therefore, it must be contained by a frame.

Creating Text Frames

The most basic text holder is a rectangular frame, and the easiest way to make one is to click and drag with the Type tool. As soon as you let go of the mouse, your text frame will be fixed and an I-beam cursor will be activated inside it, ready to accept your words of wisdom. You can then type something into the new frame. Figure 2.1 shows my words of…well, not wisdom, surely. Let's say my words of satire.

You can also make text frames that aren't rectangular. If that's your goal, don't start with the Type tool. Instead, grab one of the shape tools—the Ellipse tool or Polygon tool, both hiding behind the Rectangle tool five down from the Type tool. Draw the shape you want, and then click inside the shape with the Type tool. Whatever the shape, it will instantly be converted into a text frame, ready to accept typed, pasted, or placed text. You can even draw a new shape with the Pen or Pencil tool—as long as you create a closed path; a simple click inside with the Type tool converts the path to a text frame. You can even thread any or all of these shapes together or with rectangular text frames.

Text frames can be created anywhere—on the page, on the pasteboard, overlapping both. Once created, they can be moved by selecting them with the Selection tool (the black arrow) and dragging. Resizing is just as easy: Once selected, a text frame will display its nine control corners—four at the corners, four more at the centers of each side, and the last in the frame's middle. Dragging all but the center point will resize the frame. Dragging the center point will simply move the frame.

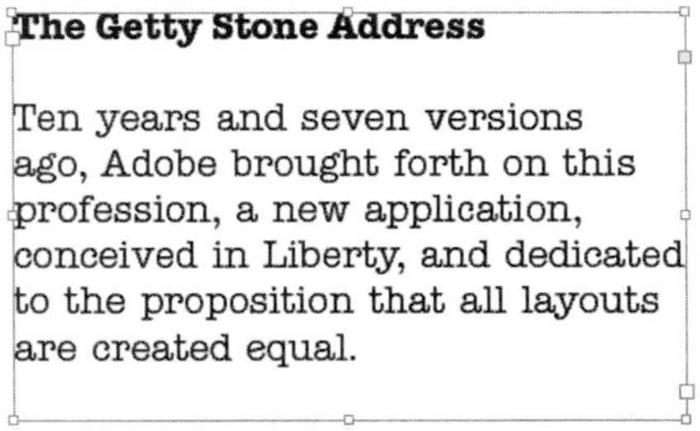

FIGURE 2.1
A newly created text frame containing text

The Getty Stone Address

Ten years and seven versions ago, Adobe brought forth on this profession, a new application, conceived in Liberty, and dedicated to the proposition that all layouts are created equal.

Notice as you resize the frame with the Selection tool, the text wraps to accommodate but does not resize. In a short while, we'll get into the different ways to style and format text. For now, it's more important to cover the ways in which text makes it *into* InDesign.

Getting Text into Text Frames

On many occasions, you'll know exactly what to type into a newly created text frame. On others, you won't. While you're waiting on a client, editor, or copywriter to provide the text for a layout, for example, you'll need to employ dummy text while you design. It's what we call *greeking* or *For Position Only (FPO)* text; it enables you to work out the placement and style of type ahead of having genuine content.

IMPORTING A TEXT FILE

Typing directly into InDesign is one way of getting text into your layout, and many people do it just that way. Most of the time, for longer text anyway, you'll write copy outside InDesign and import it. If you work on a publication or in another collaborative environment, odds are good that someone else will write the copy and you'll have to place and style it. Let's use the old standby Lorem Ipsum to simulate such tasks.

1. Create a new text frame with the Type tool. Just like last time, you'll immediately have an I-beam cursor ready to type—don't.

2. Instead, choose File ➤ Place (Cmd+D/Ctrl+D).

3. In the Place dialog, navigate to wherever you copied the Chap02 files from the book's download page.

4. Inside that folder, highlight the file lorem.txt and click Open. Five-hundred-year-old nonsense should fill your text frame (see Figure 2.2).

You've just imported an *ASCII* text file, and it doesn't look too bad. Now repeat the process with the bad-lorem.txt file. Not so nice, is it?

FIGURE 2.2
The venerable
Lorem Ipsum fill-
ing a text frame

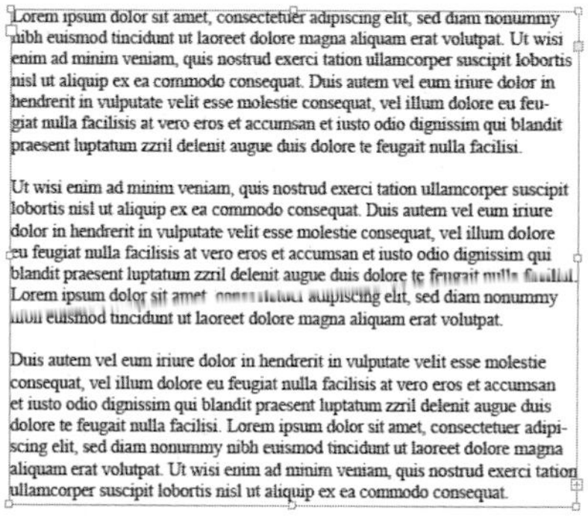

TEXT IMPORT OPTIONS

The text in `bad-lorem.txt` is roughly equivalent to what you might get from an email message or something typed directly into Windows's Notepad or Mac's TextEdit. Lines are short
and, instead of wrapping dynamically, contain hard line breaks. Choose Type ➤ Show Hidden
Characters to see what I mean; it reveals all the nonprinting characters (what QuarkXPress calls
"invisibles," if you're migrating to InDesign from that application). Figure 2.3 shows what you
should be seeing, although the width of your text frame may alter the view somewhat.

FIGURE 2.3
Show Hidden
Characters reveals
just how bad
`bad-lorem.txt`
really is.

Email and plain-text editors have a tendency to break lines of type after a few words by inserting a hard carriage return, as signified by the *pilcrow*, or paragraph mark (¶). They also don't like to
use real tabs because tab characters are not always compatible with the ASCII text format. Because
email and plain-text editors lack paragraph-spacing capabilities, vertical white space between paragraphs is usually accomplished by using multiple carriage returns—a *major* typesetting no-no.

As you might expect, all this makes for some very ugly copy and could be a lot of tedious
cleanup work for you, the InDesign user. Ten years ago, you would have had to go through the
text manually deleting the extra carriage returns, replacing the faux tabs with a smack of the
keyboard Tab key, and, one line at a time, rejoining all the lines of a paragraph. Fortunately,
InDesign was built with an automated way to clean up most of this mess.

1. Create a new text frame with the Type tool.

2. Choose File ➤ Place, and once again highlight `bad-lorem.txt`, but *don't* click the
   Open button yet.

3. Toward the bottom of the Place dialog is a check box labeled Show Import Options. Check that, and *then* click Open. Up will pop the Text Import Options dialog (see Figure 2.4). What does it all mean?

FIGURE 2.4
The Text Import
Options dialog box

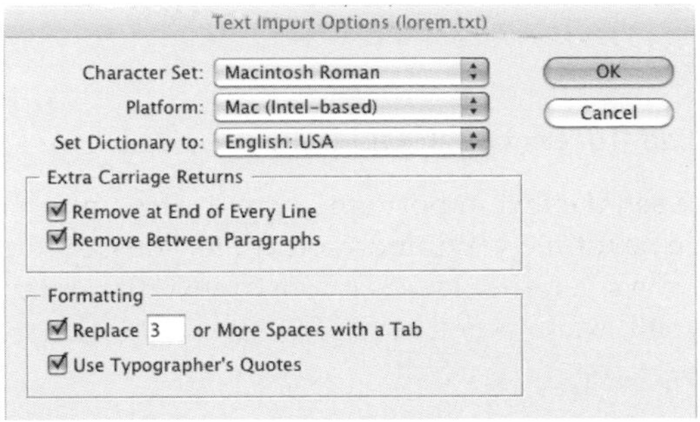

Character Set Every text file has a character set associated with it. Character sets are dependent on human-written language—such as Cyrillic, Turkish, Chinese, or Latin—and machine-written language or the operating system. Because the character set is nearly always encoded in the header of the text file, which InDesign reads, it's usually best to stick with InDesign's suggestion unless you know for certain that the default choice is incorrect.

Platform Was the file created on Windows or Mac OS? This is important because the default character sets of the two differ, and a wrong choice could lead to characters, or *glyphs*, exchanging for something unexpected. If you get strange characters in your imported text, try reimporting but switch the Platform setting. Again, though, InDesign usually picks up on the correct platform.

Set Dictionary To For spell checking and hyphenation purposes, choose the language of the text.

Remove (Extra Carriage Returns) at End of Every Line When dealing with a file like bad-lorem.txt, this is the most important setting. Turning this on will strip out all the extraneous carriage returns breaking lines within a paragraph. Manually removing them would be the bulk of the tedious cleanup, so be sure to check this option when importing most ASCII text files or content saved from text-only email.

Remove (Extra Carriage Returns) Between Paragraphs Fairly self-explanatory, this option will search out any instance of two or more consecutive hard returns and replace them with one return, readying the text for proper paragraph differentiation through indents or paragraph spacing above and/or below.

Replace *X* or More Spaces with a Tab In bad-lorem.txt, as is common with output from plain-text editors, tabs are not real tabs but consecutive spaces. This option will search out the specified number of spaces and replace them with real tabs. In the bad-lorem.txt file itself, I've set most paragraphs to begin with five consecutive spaces, but leaving the default value of 3 in place will also do the trick.

Use Typographer's Quotes Quotation marks look like (""), while ("") are marks that signify inches in distance and scale measurements or minutes in written-out time notations or global positioning coordinates. Plain-text files, with their extremely limited glyph set,

rarely contain the former. Consequently, quoted text is encased in inch marks. Turning on the Use Typographer's Quotes option will replace inch marks with real quotation marks. It will also replace foot or hour marks (') with genuine apostrophes ('). It's on by default and should stay that way unless you're importing a document containing measurements, time notations, or geographic coordinates.

4. Check all four of the check boxes in the Text Import Options dialog and click OK. Bad-lorem.txt should import looking a lot less bad.

Once set, the text import options will remain in that state—they're what we call *sticky* settings. So next time you import a text file, you can uncheck Show Import Options in the Place dialog. However, should you import a text file containing a list of items or structural dimensions, you'll want to revisit the Text Import Options dialog and disable some of the options there to avoid mangling your copy.

WORD IMPORT OPTIONS

Importing plain-text ASCII is a once-in-a-while thing at best. Most InDesign users get the majority of their copy from *rich-text* word processors like Microsoft Word. Rich text is a far more robust file format than plain text and rarely suffers from forced line breaks every 80 characters. In fact, Rich Text Format, *RTF* for short, can support paragraph spacing, tabs, typographer's quotes, text formatting like italic, bold, and underline, and even style sheets (more on those in Chapter 13, "Efficiency"). Thus, RTF files have a different set of options for importing.

Word's native DOC and DOCX files are based on RTF, and the two behave nearly identically with regard to placement in InDesign. Thus, we'll work with a Word DOC file. To get started, create a text frame. Choose File ➤ Place, and select the loremWord.doc document. Make sure Show Import Options is checked before clicking Open. Up will pop the Microsoft Word Import Options dialog (see Figure 2.5). Here's what the options you'll see mean:

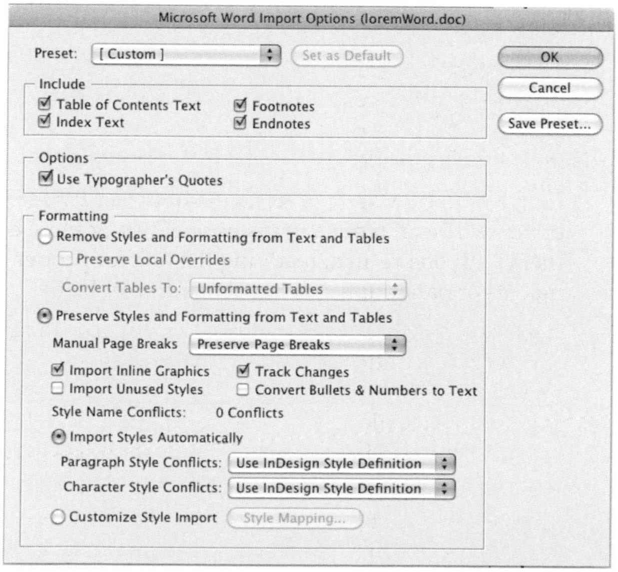

FIGURE 2.5
The Microsoft Word Import Options dialog

Preset   Although your only current option here is likely [Custom], through the Save Preset button on the right it's possible to save the selection of options as a *preset*. Once saved, a set of import options can be reactivated by choosing the preset from this dropdown menu. If you import Word or RTF files and even occasionally require different options, it's worth it to save a preset or two.

(Include) Table of Contents Text   Word can generate dynamic, hyperlinked tables of contents based on headings or other styles used in a given document. InDesign can import the *text* of those tables of contents, but it *cannot* import it as dynamic or hyperlinked. For instance, if in Word the heading "Scumdot Tests on the Linotype 1500" appears on page 57 but upon import into InDesign winds up on page 63, the TOC will still read 57 and will not automatically update itself.

Only new tables of contents created using InDesign's built-in TOC generation can create references relevant to text on InDesign pages.

(Include) Index Text   As with a table of contents, Word and InDesign can both dynamically generate hyperlinked indexes, but a Word-generated index will survive the import only as unremarkable static text.

(Include) Footnotes and Endnotes   Unlike its treatment of a table of contents or an index, InDesign *will* preserve the dynamic nature of Word's footnotes and endnotes. Footnotes and their references will be imported and, if they differ from the footnote settings in the InDesign document, renumbered in accordance thereto. Endnotes will be inserted as formatted text at the end of the imported story.

Use Typographer's Quotes   Just as with plain-text import, this option will convert inch and foot marks into quotation marks and apostrophes, respectively. Again, this can be a gotcha if your document contains legitimately used marks for measurements, time, or geographic coordinates. Generally I leave this option off, which, when I tell people that, generally raises an eyebrow in surprise. The reason I leave the Use Typographer's Quotes option turned off is because Word and every other word processor already uses typographer's quotes (sometimes called "smart quotes"), converting straight marks to proper quotation marks and apostrophes. Thus, if a foot/hour or inch/minute mark is within the incoming Word document, it's almost certainly there intentionally.

Remove Styles and Formatting from Text and Tables   Because Word documents are fully rich text, the text in them can be **emboldened**, *italicized*, <u>underlined</u>, ~~struck through~~, and even a ***<u>combination</u>*** thereof. If the author of the Word document knew what he was doing, you'll probably want to leave this radio button set on Preserve Styles and Formatting from Text and Tables. If, however, the Word document author went format crazy, choosing to remove styles and formatting (along with unchecking Preserve Local Overrides) will strip off all the formatting and styles, importing clean text ready for proper formatting in InDesign.

PLACE INTO MIDDLE

Need to place an external text document into the middle of the text already in a frame? Just put the cursor in the right spot and import with Show Import Options checked. Remove styles and formatting, and the inserted text will automatically inherit the style and formatting of the text into which it's inserted.

Preserve Local Overrides   When Remove Styles and Formatting from Text and Tables is selected, this option becomes available. Off, it completely wipes all formatting from imported text—bold text is unbolded, italicized type is straightened, and so on. Check it, however, and all the styles will be wiped away but individual text-formatting options like bold, italic, underline, and so on will survive the import.

Convert Tables To   (Accessible only if Remove Styles and Formatting from Text and Tables is selected.) If the imported text contains tables, how would you like them treated? Would you prefer them imported as InDesign tables (Unformatted Tables), or would you rather convert them to tab-separated text (Unformatted Tabbed Text), which can then either be formatted as such or manually converted to an InDesign table?

Preserve Styles and Formatting from Text and Tables   All text formatting and assigned styles are preserved. This option is on by default and required for any of the following choices to be accessible.

Manual Page Breaks   Word, InDesign, and most other word processor and page layout applications offer the ability to insert break characters that stop text anywhere on the page and jump it to the next page before continuing. The three options in this dropdown offer the choice of keeping page breaks as defined in Word, converting Word's page breaks to InDesign column breaks—instead of picking up on the next page, the text will start up again in the next column of a multicolumn InDesign layout—or dumping Word's page breaks altogether.

Import Inline Graphics   Generally a bad idea from a print professional's perspective, Word has the ability to *embed* graphics and imagery directly in the flow of text. Typically, graphics inserted in this manner do not link to their original files; they're contained entirely within the Word document. Employing this feature is a very common practice among Word users inexperienced in professional print workflows. Checking Import Inline Graphics will bring those embedded images into InDesign as embedded, *anchored objects* (which are discussed in Chapter 6, "Objects"). Unchecking it will flush those images out of the text as if they never existed.

Import Unused Styles   Like InDesign, Word allows for reusable paragraph and character styles. Lower in the dialog you'll decide what to do with styles assigned to text in the Word document, but this option applies to styles that are *not* used but are *available to be used* within the Word document. In most cases you want this option unchecked to avoid cluttering your InDesign document with Word's numerous default and user-created styles.

Enabling it, however, is a nifty way to populate an InDesign document or template with styles already defined in a Word document or template—for example, when your company is dropping Word entirely and moving to an all InDesign and InCopy editorial workflow. See the sidebar "Power Tip: Rapid Style Import" for uses of this feature.

Track Changes   In previous versions of InDesign this option did absolutely nothing. Now, as you'll read in Chapter 14, "Collaboration," InDesign does internal change tracking. If you're importing a Word or RTF document that was set in Word to track changes and includes some edits, comments, and changes, selecting this option will preserve those accountable changes in InDesign's native format. Text deleted in Word will carry into InCopy as deleted (struck through), and inserted text will be highlighted.

Convert Bullets and Numbers to Text   Should the bullets and numbers in Word's dynamically created lists continue to be dynamic, updating as necessary (especially numbered lists), or should they be converted to regular, editable text for selection and manual styling? Checking this option affects the latter.

Style Name Conflicts   A yellow caution sign appears if both the Word and InDesign documents contain styles with the same names (for instance, if they both contain a "Heading 1" paragraph style). To the right of the caution sign the number and type of conflicting styles are noted. The next few fields determine how those conflicts are resolved.

Paragraph and Character Style Conflicts   Choose whether to use InDesign's style definitions, disregarding Word's; redefine the InDesign styles to match those coming from Word; or add the Word styles as new styles automatically named to nullify the conflict.

 Real World Scenario

POWER TIP: RAPID STYLE IMPORT

Although you generally want to leave the Import Unused Styles option off in the Microsoft Word Import Options dialog, it does present an incredibly useful shortcut that can save hours or even days of work.

For instance, collaborative publishing workflows such as book, newspaper, and magazine teams usually consist of one or more writers creating original content in a Word template and designers accepting writers' Word files for placement into InDesign. The Word template from which writers create their chapters, articles, ad copy, and other text invariably contains a set of styles they are required to use—headlines must be assigned the "Head" style, kickers the "Kicker" style, bylines the "Byline" style, and so forth.

Suppose your publication is in the middle of a redesign or migration and you need to rebuild your publication template(s) in InDesign. You *can* manually re-create all the styles needed to format stories, *or* you could simply import the writers' Word templates while checking the Import Unused Styles option. That would import all the styles from the Word documents, even styles like "Sub-sub-list" that are only occasionally used. The styles will still need to be *updated* in InDesign to make them native, but that's just a simple matter of opening them and glancing through all the options. It's much faster than creating all those styles again from scratch.

Sometimes InCopy stands between Word and InDesign, with editors taking original content Word files into InCopy and then furnishing revised InCopy stories to InDesign layout artists. InCopy, which is effectively InDesign for editors and without frame-creation tools, has the same Microsoft Word import options. Thus, the same power tip applies if your editors are taking the Word files into InCopy instead of you taking them into InDesign.

Customize Style Import   Checking this option and clicking the Style Mapping button opens the Style Mapping dialog (see Figure 2.6), wherein all the styles in both documents are listed side-by-side. An entry of [New Paragraph Style] or [New Character Style] denotes the lack of conflict and that a new style will be created in the InDesign document to match the Word style. Any conflicts—where both columns have a nonbracketed style entry—can be resolved by clicking the style name in the InDesign Style column. A dropdown menu will appear showing all styles present in the InDesign document, allowing a custom mapping from the Word style, as well as conflict-resolution options matching those from the previous dialog's dropdowns. The button at the bottom of the Style Mapping dialog tells InDesign to create new, similarly named styles based on the incoming, conflicting styles.

New to CS5 is the ability to create a new paragraph or character style right from the Style Mapping dialog. Depending on whether the incoming style is a paragraph or character, the last option on the list of InDesign styles will be New Paragraph Style or New Character Style. Choosing the option launches the New Paragraph Style or New Character Style dialog, where you can define and name a brand-new style to which to map the incoming style.

Save Preset (button)   As you can see from the length of my walk-through, there are quite a few decisions to be made when importing Word documents. The options you choose may be the same for every subsequent Word document you ever import, or documents from different sources or for different purposes might require alteration of these settings. If you anticipate more than a single setup—or you merely wish to ensure you don't lose your Word import option customizations, save a preset by clicking this button, naming the preset, and clicking OK. Thereafter, all your settings are ready for instant reapplication from the Preset drop-down menu at the top of the dialog.

FIGURE 2.6
The Style Mapping dialog helps to resolve style conflicts between incoming Microsoft Word documents and existing InDesign layout content.

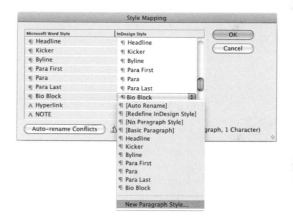

In this example, we want to select Preserve Styles and Formatting from Text and Tables and Use Typographer's Quotes. Everything else is irrelevant to this particular file—an article.

Click OK on the Microsoft Word Import Options dialog, and the Word document will flow into the text frame exactly as our prior documents did. Note that it's already formatted with type and paragraph styling.

TEXT COPY AND PASTE

You can also copy text from just about anywhere to paste into InDesign. As long as what you copy hits the operating system's clipboard as text (as opposed to outlined type or an image), InDesign will take it on paste. Text can also be copied *from* InDesign into most other text-handling applications, although how much of the styling survives the paste depends on the target application.

BUZZWORD IMPORT

If you've never heard of it, *Buzzword* is Adobe's browser-based word processor (see Figure 2.7). It's not InCopy or Microsoft Word by any means, but it's still a decent word processor. Among its good points are collaboration on the file by any number of users; easy lists, including to-do-

style, checkable items; rudimentary change tracking and commenting; and platform independence because it's browser-based. Buzzword is a free (as of this writing and for several years prior) part of Acrobat.com. Many people love it for quick document collaboration or shared idea lists—yours truly among them.

FIGURE 2.7

Adobe Buzzword

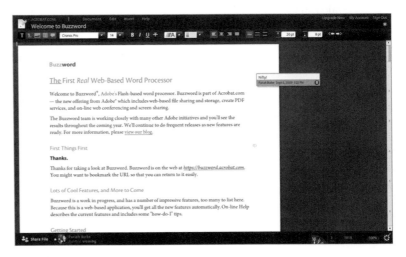

Getting content out of Buzzword has always been fairly easy. You can print directly from it, as well as export the Buzzword document to PDF, Word DOC, Word 2007 DOCX, RTF, zipped HTML, TXT, Open Office format OpenDocument ODT, and, most recently, e-book standard ePUB files. Now in InDesign CS5 you can even directly import a Buzzword document. You won't need to export the document to an intermediary format, though you will need a live Internet connection.

Choosing Place from Buzzword from the File menu will first ask you to sign into your Acrobat.com account (I mentioned it was free, right?). Once that's done, the Place Buzzword Documents dialog will present you with the list of Buzzword documents you've created or been invited to as a collaborator (see Figure 2.8). You can select one or multiple files to place as separate assets (hold the Cmd/Ctrl key to select multiple documents in the list). If the document you want isn't in the list, select the Paste URL option at the top of the dialog and, in the box beside that option, enter the document's URL.

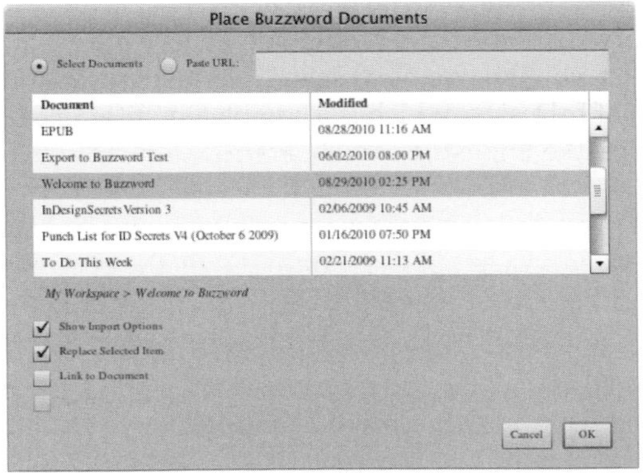

FIGURE 2.8

Placing a
Buzzword
document

There are four options at the bottom of the Place Buzzword Documents dialog. Here's what they mean:

Show Import Options   If enabled, this option will open the Buzzword Import Options dialog. As you can see in Figure 2.9, this dialog is virtually identical to the Word Import Options dialog discussed in the last section. The only difference is that Buzzword Import Options lacks several of the options in the Word version.

FIGURE 2.9
Buzzword Import
Options is a subset
of Word Import
Options.

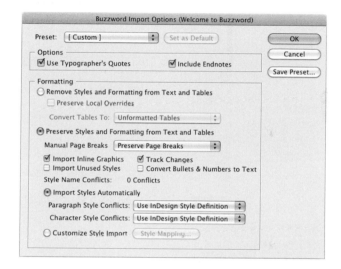

Replace Selected Item   Just like when placing through the File ⟩ Place dialog, if you already have a story selected while importing, enabling this option will replace the selected story with the incoming Buzzword story.

Link to Document   As the name implies, this option will link to the Buzzword story such that changes made to the document in Buzzword will motivate InDesign to ask you to update the document. The option is disabled by default, resulting in the imported Buzzword text being disassociated from the online original; changes made to one will have no connection to the other. Electing to link to the Buzzword document, however, offers the distinct advantage of ensuring that your InDesign layout always contains the most up-to-date content from the shared document.

Apply Grid Format   Would you believe me if I told you this option does nothing? It doesn't. In fact, you'll never see it selectable, just grayed out. It's accessible only in the Japanese version of InDesign, which is a completely different product, not just an interface language choice like English, Spanish, French, and other interface language options available in your copy of InDesign. In InDesign J, as the Japanese edition is called, the Apply Grid Format option enables the user to import the Buzzword content into a J Grid, which is the Japanese layout equivalent of a text frame. Why the option is visible in the non-Japanese editions is simple: It's an oversight; Adobe forgot to hide it.

Now, if you're sitting there staring at my screenshot of the dialog but can't find the Apply Grid Format option in your live version of the dialog, then you know someone at Adobe cured the oversight in an a later update to InDesign, hiding that superfluous option.

PLACING WITHOUT A FRAME

It happens all the time: You're working away, on a roll, and press Cmd+D/Ctrl+D, grab a text file, and realize you forgot to first create a frame. Well, unlike in QuarkXPress, you need *not* have a frame in order to place content. True, all content must be within a container, but InDesign is savvy enough to make the container *while* you place the content. Give it a try.

1. Deselect all objects by clicking an empty area of the page or pasteboard.

2. Choose File ➤ Place, and select a textual file—one of the sample documents from this chapter should suffice. Hit OK.

   Back in the document, you should notice a new type of cursor—a loaded cursor (see Figure 2.10). It even has a preview of the text you're about to place!

FIGURE 2.10
Yet-to-be-placed text documents create a loaded cursor and preview of the text.

Layering It On Thick With a little effort toward breaking old habits of saving file after file for each variation,

3. With the loaded cursor, click and drag out a rectangular area. The story will place, giving you both content and container in one swift action.

You can keep going like this, placing content without pre-created frames, throughout the entire document.

Which textual file formats can InDesign place within text frames? Plenty! Table 2.1 shows you.

To place content from a WordPerfect file, use RTF. WordPerfect and all other word processors can export to RTF with minimal loss of features and formatting; many word processors even save directly into RTF without the need for a second, proprietary format.

TABLE 2.1   Textual file formats supported by InDesign

FILE EXTENSION	DOCUMENT DESCRIPTION
.icml	InCopy CS4–CS5 documents
.incd, .incx	InCopy CS2–CS3 documents
.incd	InCopy CS stories
.doc, .docx	Microsoft Word (versions 2–2007)
.xls, .xlsx	Microsoft Excel (versions 4–2007)
.rtf	Rich Text Format

TABLE 2.1   Textual file formats supported by InDesign   *(CONTINUED)*

FILE EXTENSION	DOCUMENT DESCRIPTION
.txt	Plain text
.txt	Adobe InDesign Tagged Text
[no extension]	Buzzword documents (via File ➤ Place from Buzzword)

FILL WITH PLACEHOLDER TEXT

Now that you know how to place text, there's an even faster way to fill a frame if all you need is FPO copy. Create a new text frame with the Type tool. With the I-beam cursor in the frame, go to the Type menu and, second from the bottom, choose Fill with Placeholder Text. The text frame will pack with gibberish FPO copy.

Fill with Placeholder Text automatically fills a text frame, however large. It also uses whatever typeface, size, style, and paragraph settings are currently in effect. For instance, if 12/14.4 pt Myriad Pro is the default type setup, Fill with Placeholder Text will fill the frame with 12 pt Myriad Pro on 14.4 pt leading.

InDesign's default placeholder text closely approximates real text with variable-length words, lines, and paragraphs. It's all still gibberish, but it *could* be real copy. If you'd rather it be some *other* kind of gibberish, like Lorem Ipsum, the Declaration of Independence, or Elmer Fudd reciting act 4, scene 1 of Shakespeare's *Macbeth* ("Doubwe, doubwe, toiw and twoubwe"), changing InDesign's default placeholder text is a breeze. Place the text you'd like to use in a plain-text file named Placeholder.txt, and save it into the InDesign folder. On Windows, you'll find the InDesign program folder in the following path (if you chose the default location during installation):

    C:\Program Files\Adobe\InDesign CS5

On Windows 7 or Vista 64-bit that folder is here:

    C:\Program Files (x86)\Adobe\InDesign CS5

On Mac, it's here:

    Applications/InDesign CS5

COUNTING WORDS IN A TEXT FRAME

Editors and writers with whom you work frequently measure text by word count. *How many words fit in this part of the page? Can you find a place to slap in this 700-word article?* Of course, that means designers have to build and style text frames to hold a specified number of words.

When you're dummying up a layout with FPO copy, how can you know how many words fit in a given frame—and, thereby, how many frames are required per page, how many pages to carry an article of set length, and so on? Don't go running back to Word. InDesign actually has a pretty good word counter. It's called the Info panel (see Figure 2.11).

FIGURE 2.11
The Info panel counting characters, words, lines, and paragraphs

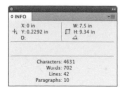

Select the Type tool, and put the cursor anywhere within a text frame's copy; don't highlight the text. The bottom of the Info panel will change to count characters, words, lines, and paragraphs throughout the entire story. Any figures after a plus sign (+) are *overset*—not visible in any text frame. The counts include text in any linked frame, on any page, and count everything in the story regardless of style—headlines, kickers, bylines, run-in captions, and so forth—but not text in other frames not threaded with the current story's frames.

To find out how many characters, words, lines, and paragraphs fit within a single text frame or paragraph, highlight the text in question. Statistics on the Info panel will revise to reflect only the highlighted text. In Figure 2.12, for instance, you can see the statistics for the first body copy paragraph of loremWord.doc.

FIGURE 2.12
Counts for a single paragraph in the shown story

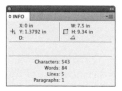

If you'd like a somewhat more visual word counter, one that appears in the text itself and survives printing or export to PDF for the benefit of writers, editors, or clients, check the Chap02 folder again. In addition to the files we've worked with so far, I've included Copyfit.txt, which contains only five-letter words and marks every 25th word with a running count, up to a total of 1,000 words.

TEXT FRAME OPTIONS

Setting up multiple columns, changing *insets*, and once in a while even mucking with the vertical justification within the frame are all things you can accomplish from within the Text Frame Options dialog (and sometimes other places as well).

With a text frame selected, press Cmd+B/Ctrl+B, or choose Text Frame Options from the Object menu (see Figure 2.13).

Check the Preview box at the bottom and you'll be able to watch how the text frame reacts to column changes live.

The Number field is, obviously, the number of columns. Regardless of the number here, you're dealing with only a single text frame. Because InDesign merely divides a single frame into internal columns, you can resize the frame (outside the Text Frame Options dialog), and all columns will contract or expand as needed.

And that's a nice segue into…

What is the purpose of the Width field? Good question. Change the number of columns by clicking the up/down-arrow buttons while watching the Width field. Notice how the width changes?

Right: InDesign is maintaining the width of the frame and the width of the gutter and altering the column width to account for the column count.

FIGURE 2.13

The Text Frame
Options dialog

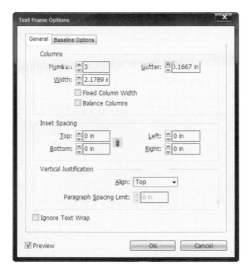

Let's say you didn't want that. Let's say you know for certain you need 1.75-inch-wide columns, but you aren't sure how many will fit in your layout. Check the Fixed Column Width box. Now, instead of the column width being variable while the frame width is fixed, the opposite is true: Columns will always be 1.75 inches, and the text frame itself will expand or contract horizontally to accommodate the specified number of columns.

If you manually resize the text frame on the page with Fixed Column Width checked, the frame will resize only in whole column increments. This is a stellar way to redesign templates for multicolumn publications.

Most of us have heard the space between pages referred to as the gutter. InDesign tries to eliminate confusion by stating that *gutter* is the distance between columns, and that the inside margins and spine make up the area of binding or the space between pages in a spread.

When setting column gutters, more is more (within reason). A common mistake is to set gutters that are too slender in an attempt to fit more copy on a page. Don't fall into that trap.

Gutters separate columns of text. That separation—and thus gutters—is absolutely critical to document readability. If a gutter is too narrow, the reader's eye will jump across the gutter and run together two disconnected sentences. Readers also have a difficult time coming back from wayward excursions to other columns to find the beginning of the actual next line—it will be twice as hard if they aren't reading the leftmost column and have to contend with too-narrow gutters on both sides of what they're reading.

Want a rule of thumb? Column gutters should *never* be less than the point size of the typeface, but even better is 150% to 200% of the type size. Anything more than 200% to 250% begins to disconnect columns.

CS5

If you're upgrading to CS5 from a previous version, you might not notice the unassuming Balance Columns option shyly situated beneath the Fixed Column Width option. Balance Columns is a powerful new feature in InDesign CS5. If the last column in your multicolumn

frame is a little short, immensely preferable to leaving a huge white gap is to shorten the height of all the columns to achieve a common bottom. Formerly you had to do this manually, adjusting the height of the multicolumn text frame until all the columns' last lines lined up. Checking Balance Columns does it automatically.

INSET SPACING

Indents push text selectively—a paragraph pushed in here and there, but not everywhere—while *insets* push *everything* in uniformly. If you want to indent a kicker paragraph or body copy, leaving subheads out to the margin, employ paragraph indents (see later in this chapter). However, if you've given your text frame a background color or stroke, you want to make sure no text bumps up against the edge, so set an inset (aka *internal margins,* frame margins, frame/box padding, and border spacing). You can see the difference between indent and inset results in Figure 2.14.

FIGURE 2.14
A text frame with inset (inner blue border) and indented text. (See it in the color insert section of this book.)

The four fields can be set to push in from the four sides independently—say, to give only top or bottom inset while leaving left and right sides flush—or, by checking the chain-link option, all four can be made uniform. In the latter case, altering the value of one simultaneously changes the other three.

Only a single inset field will be available if you're working with nonrectangular text frames.

It absolutely kills me when I see professionals not using insets, opting instead to layer a text frame atop an empty colored or stroke frame—and I see it often. Why would someone do that? Because that's the way they've done it for years. (Oh, how I abhor that justification!)

Text frames can be filled with color—CMYK, RGB, Lab, spots, tints, even gradients—they can be stroked with any style or color, they can have drop shadows and other effects, and the frame fill and stroke opacity and blending modes can even be set independently of text opacity and blending mode. Most of these options have been available since InDesign 1.0. Creating two objects to do the job one is capable of doing doubles the work necessary to create the same effect and doubles the work of maintaining it. It's half as much work to move or resize one frame than it is two. Say it with me: *Working efficiently gives me more time to be creative.*

InDesign, unlike some other programs, *does* adjust column width (or column count if you're using fixed column widths) to compensate for inset adjustments. So, there's no reason to go back to the two-object tango.

VERTICAL JUSTIFICATION

When there isn't enough copy to fill a column or frame, where do you want the text to be—the top of the frame/column, the bottom, centered, or spread out and vertically justified? That's the question asked by this option. Figure 2.15 shows the four possible options.

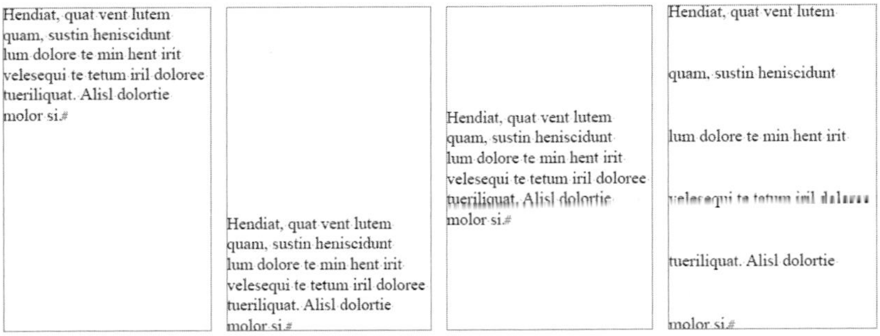

FIGURE 2.15
Examples of vertical alignment options, left to right Top, Bottom, Center, and Justify (without paragraph spacing limits)

Hendiat, quat vent lutem quam, sustin heniscidunt lum dolore te min hent irit velesequi te tetum iril doloree tueriliquat. Alisl dolortie molor si.

Hendiat, quat vent lutem quam, sustin heniscidunt lum dolore te min hent irit velesequi te tetum iril doloree tueriliquat. Alisl dolortie molor si.

Hendiat, quat vent lutem quam, sustin heniscidunt lum dolore te min hent irit velesequi te tetum iril doloree tueriliquat. Alisl dolortie molor si.

Hendiat, quat vent lutem

quam, sustin heniscidunt

lum dolore te min hent irit

velesequi te tetum iril doloree

tueriliquat. Alisl dolortie

molor si.

If you choose Justify from the Align list, the Paragraph Spacing Limit measurement field activates. When it's set to 0 inches, anything is possible—a single line could appear at the top of the frame and another single line at the bottom. To take more control over the situation, to tell InDesign that you want no more than *X* inches inserted between paragraphs and lines within paragraphs, set the measurement here. If there aren't enough lines to fill the space without violating your spacing limit, InDesign will align to the top and spread down as far as it can without violating the limit you set.

CS5

If you've used vertical justification in earlier versions of InDesign, you know that vertical justification wasn't possible in non-rectangular text frames. That's been fixed in CS5. Now you can vertically justify text in *any* frame—rectangular, round, polygonal, Pen-drawn, and so on.

FASTER COLUMNS AND JUSTIFICATION

If all you need to do is change the number of columns or the vertical justification, you needn't go all the way into the Text Frame Options dialog. These settings are probably on the Control panel in a very simplified form. I say "probably" because it depends on your screen size and your Control panel options. The number of columns is always accessible on the Control panel in Paragraph mode. Vertical alignment buttons appear, however, only if the option is enabled in the Customize Control Panel dialog and if your screen is set wider than 1,024 pixels. All the default Control panel options are included within the first 1,024 pixels. After that, InDesign includes additional options you might find useful from time to time. Among those that appear when you have a text frame selected with the Selection tool are the Number of Columns field and buttons to change vertical justification modes, as shown in Figure 2.16.

FIGURE 2.16
Number of columns and vertical alignment options on the Control panel

Column Spanning

CS5

Figure 2.17 shows an editorial-style page layout common to numerous types of publications both editorial and marketing. It's a basic two-column layout with a headline, deck, and byline that span both columns.

The layout consists of a single story set in two threaded text frames:

◆ The first contains the headline, kicker, and byline, set as a single column.

◆ The second, a double-column text frame, contains the rest of the story.

It's a standard layout used thousands of times a day by production artists across the globe. The problem with it is that there are two objects. Every formatting or copy change to the headline, the kicker, or the byline could change the depth (height) of those three elements. If one or more of those paragraphs increase in depth—say, the kicker wraps to a third line because another couple of words are inserted—the byline will get pushed down into the two-column text frame. If one or more of those paragraphs decrease in depth, some of the body copy will get sucked up into the first frame, resulting in one or more lines of body copy spanning the full width of the page instead of staying in half-page columns.

Fixing either situation is just a matter of resizing the top text frame, right? Wrong. To maintain the proper vertical spacing, *both* frames must be resized to accommodate changes in the needed depth of the upper one. Two objects to manage.

True, there is a fairly easy workaround. Instead of reducing the height of the body copy frame to accommodate the upper frame, leave the larger lower frame the full height of the page margins. Place the spanning frame atop it, and give that frame a text wrap so that it pushes body copy out of its way. Then, when the upper spanning frame is resized, it automatically pushes the body copy out of the way and maintains the same vertical spacing between the byline and the first line of the story. Of course, that still means you must manually size the upper frame in response to increases or decreases in the depth required by each paragraph.

Now that we have InDesign CS5, there's an easier way still, one that completely eliminates the need to resize *any* text frame. Moreover, it can be applied and controlled with paragraph styles, making it infinitely more versatile than two separate frames could ever be.

It's called column spanning, and it is glorious.

Spanning All Columns

Take a look at the same content in Figure 2.18. Would you believe that it's a single text frame, part one column, part two column? It is. It looks exactly the same as the two-frame layout—even the baselines line up (I did them on opposite pages of a spread). Well, it does in Preview mode and when printed or exported; with the frame edges shown you can see that it's only a single frame, while the former version was two frames.

Figure 2.18

Single and double columns in a single text frame

Here's the Article Headline

Nis eosti ut aliqui omnisi idelect emperum faccus ipsa doluptatisto moluptiae cum aut qui atur, quia eniet hicatquam quiditatint.

Pariah S. Burke

Kerro et ea que num ut et ut rem corerios enis alitatur sincid expliqu iatem. Ut vendere pra incid quisquo quodi dunt et quate volore, seque qui consed expedis molores sitatiaestia que se porerfe rciiscillut laccusantiis re que es mi, nonse numque est, sim volorep eratem. Mo dolo voluptatis debis ellaborum quas abo. Oviduci deserunt, te nobisqui iundign ienime venda qui dolorit odiosam facepre peribus, temporro ma estius, cuptas am fugia nonseditisin reptatist, apelique qui ab illuptae voluptibus evelist modicimi, accupta tionsequi accat.

Parum aut as et vendi asi odipsunt.

Ucium incimol oreriti nvenihi liciae. Lupicipic tem nat atquiam num in experum vollaborpost aut ventis expella erisci odit, ullabore odisquo onimpe riorior esciuntia volupti usaerum rem. Ur aut qui sunt la num re volor audant eleseni-menit lab iunt ut fugiaerunto occum di ut at.

Ra doluptur? Qui quunt ut lab iur? Quid que vel ex ero ommodit aut doluptas ea quo qui arum in consernatur at occum quis aut at moluptatias maion conectem aut lique pelest, conse voluptaquia soluptuscium sus am ne inulpa quo eaquis dolore aut quis eatur ad et am, sum rera venimi, simin non nustium dolum quia voluptiam, to tem sunt lant as et archici enissit, nat aliatec tiaspel issit volupti ossimus, optae mo volupta dolorpores simpele stiur? Luptas que invel mi, inim ius et ipsam nit unt et a nis ipsapit quuntium et am que poriberia alit estion paria es re, sitio quam, optaturis ipide pra pa autas sa corror mi, cus sent faccus, aut int aspicius, evenda sit, in rest as evelles dolo blaccus tinciandior repeditio culles atiae volorit assundia volupti busaes rectorum et ut ium nit fuga. Nequam quam, simus rem ipsapienis etur as aut que exero et ut voluptaepere odigenis niam volendus maio dolorep udipis aut pos eost, tem aspidero quisque con ni tent pe prem quia pa venda demporro et quodi autatinto eaquam ut eturibus et diatur re suntiunt de ipit opta quid ma vent poriost, num eos moluptae incid quaecte ntusam voluptas ex etus nate nossime etur aut que num eius.

Hent quae voluptas suntia veri blabo. Dita nihilist ad exceris siniend emporporeic testotatiis dit ea quat.

Tiandis serecero et hillis pa proratur sum imus nos eos venda

pedisci liauta dessitaque nullaborum eos est molor sum sequunt rest, nis dolorro vidisquis doloreperum quunt eni quam ipitia idi am non pero molum explant emporestis si dent ommolum quodipsam quam faccus derfers perferi di quas pla voloriporibus dusci sectem ea comnimin coresto quae pera si sit asitis ute doluptiandit volupta tatiis re volor re moluptatest, coreium rehenem nossita velendame perfera quam solupti alibus mil inia volorepera doluptam sum que pliaturita non cum fuga. Feritiis eos ut et inumquam adigento te que comnis sam ent vene ped qui tet eaquam, iusandi aut mi, ab int omnihit as eatquis eos endeseque restiatquam aut ea qui ut archille-niet ipid quam, sum, sum quiatus amusame sus im rerum net repe earcilluptio quaerepediae seque sitatis autemost occaero venimoluptia con ra sitat expe nem et adis estioreiciis desciur estrum es dolore pratiur?

Ficillesere eum quias ditiniendam fuga. Ria con reperer ovidia pedit incitio mos atem harum voluptatur moditat uribus eos ut qui is explabore niaepudaerum estiiste officatet molorem eicia voluptin pra cum faccabo riatumquibus enimpos aceprae resti arum est at aliquodit arum rem nonetur andipit atecessum voleniet volenti il exceper rovitatur, venis rem venient, sincto ius dolupta quiatum, utenduntur?

At ratior sitat. Danim rem. Et ate dunt et, illaceaquis vendit venest optatib usanda pariatum quia doloritatium dolorepe-rum et andipsa nduciis porem. Ut repedi susaepro beaqui quo ipsam rae cor sedia natquis eos qui consequi dolorep rovi-duciet estrumq uatium vel ipsam, quasi sus aboreriae sunde coneste conecat iaerumqui ratia venditi beatur, consequi dolupti aspel it omnisqu iamenis il ex escienda sero enda aut quiditi tem volupta tendis volor moluptaquia et modit et, odip-sundiam venis ressi optaqui auda voloresti dolor maiorporpos velenisquost volor aut plautempor ape volum natur rempore, arumqui a con conserspic te nusam que nis aut fugiatquos ent vellibusto totat pel milique quiatatem est aut estias dis alique maio conserciis quatus evelenimus.

Em eum nia vollectur, auda comniam venia aut vendis ipsa-mentist que niscima quis sant faccum quos adis molut quide-rume conection pa sumquiae possi dolupta etur simint, officiet volor modi voles ea quistotam, samusa conecto ribus.

Why don't you give it a try:

1. On a blank page, create a text frame that fills the margins top to bottom, left to right.

2. If you already have a suitable editorial-style story ready, place that into the text frame. Otherwise, whip up something with FPO or dummy copy like I did. Include a headline, a kicker paragraph, and a byline above the body copy.

3. Select the frame (or just leave the Type tool cursor in it somewhere) and press Cmd+B/ Ctrl+B to open the Text Frame Options dialog.

4. Set the text frame to 2 columns and click OK. The entire story—including the headline, deck, and byline—should reflow into columns.

5. Highlight the headline, deck, and byline, and from the flyout menu on either the Paragraph panel or the Control panel in either text mode, choose Span Columns. Up will pop a dialog remarkably identical to the one in Figure 2.19.

FIGURE 2.19
The Span Columns
dialog

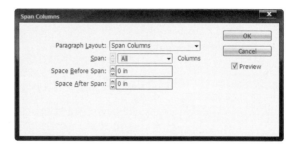

6. Change the Paragraph Layout dropdown field from Single Column to Span Columns, and then change the Span field to All. Click OK.

Ta-da! Your headline, deck, and byline will now be set as single column, the width of the entire text frame, spanning the body copy columns, which will move down just as if they were in a separate frame. But they aren't in a separate frame. Add text to your kicker so that it fills another line or two; the multicolumn section will move down again, automatically accommodating the greater space required for the kicker. You could even increase the number of columns in the frame; the top lines will stay spanning them all. You have one text frame to manage, and it updates automatically just by your setting one or more paragraphs to span columns.

SPANNING SOME COLUMNS

Let's try something a little more challenging. Instead of spanning all columns, span just some of them:

1. Begin the same way, creating a margin-to-margin-to-margin-to-margin text frame containing a headline, kicker, byline, and body copy.

2. This time, set the frame to 3 columns.

3. Highlight the headline, kicker, and body copy, and once again choose Span Columns from the flyout menu on the Paragraph or Control panel.

4. Set the Paragraph Layout menu to Span Columns.

5. Instead of choosing All in the Span field, choose 2 and click OK.

You should get the result I did (see Figure 2.20). All right, well, I also set the spanned paragraphs to align right.

FIGURE 2.20
Spanning some but not all columns yields an interesting effect.

Here's the Article Headline

Nis eosti ut aliqui omnisi idelect emperum faccus ipsa doluptatisto moluptiae cum aut qui atur, quia eniet hicatquam quiditatint.

Pariah S. Burke

MORE ABOUT COLUMN SPANNING

We kind of breezed through the Span Columns dialog. There wasn't much to see, but I do want to talk briefly about the fields.

◆ Of course, the Paragraph Layout dropdown menu is where you chose Span Columns, which activated all the functionality. Set that field back to Single Column to turn off column spanning. The third option, Split Column, is a whole other feature, one I'll discuss in just a few pages.

◆ The Span field's dropdown includes options to span All or 2–5 columns. If you have a 6-column layout, are you out of luck? No. Just type 6 into the field, or use the up- and down-arrow buttons beside the field. The items on the dropdown list are merely to give you the most common settings in a clickable place.

◆ Spanning columns works with and respects paragraph spacing you may have set on either or both the spanned and nonspanned paragraphs. It also has in the Space Before Span and Space After Span fields the ability to apply some extra vertical space just between spanned and nonspanned paragraphs, for maximum comfort.

There are a few things you should keep in mind as you work with column spanning.

Subheads Can Be Spanned   Any paragraph can span columns, not just paragraphs at the start of a story. You could, for example, set a subhead halfway down the page to span all columns, which is a really cool look most designers avoided (until now) because the labor of managing the multiple text frames necessary to create the effect was prohibitive (see Figure 2.21).

FIGURE 2.21
Spanned para-
graphs may appear
anywhere in the
story, not just at
the top or bottom.

There are a few things you should keep in mind as you work with column spanning.

Spanning Balances Columns Above and Below   When you span paragraphs in the middle of a page (or, at least, paragraphs that aren't the first or last on the page), the columned text above and below the spanned paragraphs balances to *only* above and *only* below (see Figure 2.22). Note the flow of text I've diagrammed around the spanned subhead. All copy that appears before the location of the subhead in the story is balanced across the three half-page columns above the subhead, while all text after the subhead is below it.

FIGURE 2.22
A diagram of the
flow of copy when
bisected by a
spanned paragraph

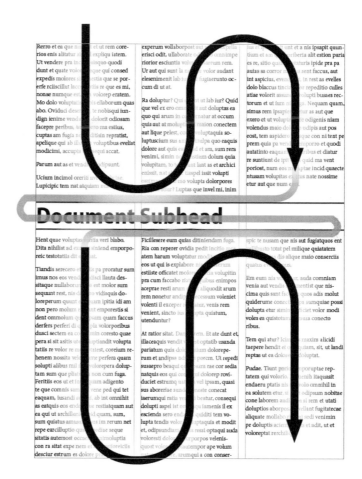

FIGURE 2.22
A diagram of the
flow of copy when
bisected by a
spanned paragraph

This could be potentially very confusing for readers whose instincts tell them to continue reading from the lowest point in a column, at the bottom of the page, up to the top of the next column nearest the top edge of the page. Help readers avoid confusion by creating clear separation between the upper and lower portions, associating the subhead more directly with the lower portion.

After the Span   When spanning fewer than all the columns, the next nonspanning paragraph always begins below the last spanning paragraph. Because English-speaking people read left to right, that fact can occasionally leave a reader confused, searching *beside* the spanned area for the first line of the following paragraph instead of *below* the spanned area.

Try using paragraph spacing, wider gutters, rules, or other tricks to help guide readers from the spanning paragraphs to the correct starting point in the nonspanning.

Spanning from the Left   Column spanning always spans paragraphs from the leftmost column. If, for example, you set the first paragraph of a story to span only two columns of a three-column text frame, you can't make it span the center and the right columns; it will

begin spanning the left column and then move toward the right one column at a time. Even with spans lower down on the page, perhaps not even in the first column, InDesign will try its hardest to begin the span in the leftmost column.

The only time it doesn't succeed in doing that is when the column-spanning paragraph is so far down in a column that InDesign can't fit the before- and after-span paragraphs above or below the spanned paragraph.

Span in Paragraph Styles   The new Span Columns pane in the Paragraph Style Options dialog contains options identical to those in the Span Columns dialog (see Figure 2.23). Thus, whether and how many columns particular paragraphs span, as well as the vertical spacing before and after a span, can be saved as part of a paragraph style for rapid reapplication to other text or universal adjustment of any spanning paragraphs.

FIGURE 2.23
Span Columns
controls in the
Paragraph Style
Options

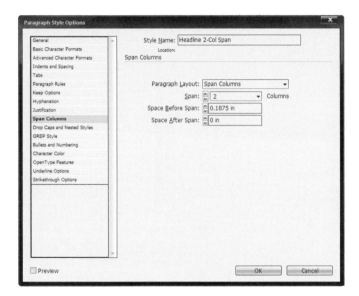

Quick Column Spanning   On the Control panel, in Paragraph mode, are quick controls to save you a trip to the Span Columns dialog once in a while (see Figure 2.24). You can't control the spacing before or after here, nor can you type in a custom number of columns to span, but the control's dropdown presets are useful in many common situations.

FIGURE 2.24
The Span Column
controls on the
Control panel in
Paragraph mode

Splitting Columns

The opposite of spanning columns, though managed in the same places—the Span Columns dialog, the Span Columns pane of the Paragraph Style Options, the Span Columns control on the Control panel—is column *splitting*.

How often have you found yourself faced with the dilemma of a bulleted or numbered list of items where the items themselves are so short they leave gaping white holes on the right? How do you deal with those situations? Do you leave the items short and suffer the unnatural white space? Do you create multiple frames, breaking before the list, setting the list in a larger number of columns in its own text frame, only to pick up the main copy in a third frame? Figure 2.25 demonstrates the problem, then the usual multiframe workaround, and finally the solution available with column splitting.

FIGURE 2.25

A list of short items leaves awkward white space (left). One solution is to use multiple frames with differing column counts (center). The best solution is to use column splitting (right).

Column splitting works very much like column spanning but in reverse; instead of reducing the number of columns of selected text relevant to surrounding text, you're increasing the number of columns. Give it a try:

1. Create a story that includes several paragraphs of multiple lines each.

2. In between two paragraphs, create a list of items and format it as a bulleted list.

3. Select the list items and, from the flyout menu on the Paragraph or Control panel (in Paragraph mode), choose Span Columns.

4. Set the Paragraph Layout field to Split Column, and turn on Preview.

5. In the Sub-Columns field increase the number of columns until all your list items fit nicely, without awkward white space. Click OK.

That's all there is to it. Of course, there are a few other options in the Span Columns dialog we could look at:

Space Before/After Split   Like the Space Before/After Span fields, these two fields offer some much-needed vertical cushioning before and/or after the splitting paragraphs. Whereas paragraph space before or after can often supply ample vertical spacing between spanned and nonspanned paragraphs, it's often more difficult to get the right paragraph spacing between split and nonsplit paragraphs without a good deal of manual tweaking. Therefore, the Space Before/After Split fields are quite useful.

Inside Gutter   Because the Split Column function adds columns, you need to create gutters between those columns (see Figure 2.26). This field allows you to set the gutter distance.

Note that the gutter is only between columns, not before the first column or after the last. InDesign also won't show you guides representing the split column gutters as it will with normal column gutters.

FIGURE 2.26
Split columns with inside gutters diagrammed

Outside Gutter The Outside Gutter is very much like a text frame's inset. To get just the right look for your split columns, you might want to push them inward a bit, giving them a left and right indent (see Figure 2.27). That's where the Outside Gutter field comes in. It applies a uniform left and right indent. Then equal-width columns are produced from the space remaining after the Outside Gutter measurement has been subtracted from the overall split column area. As with inside gutters, there are no guidelines to reveal the presence of outside gutters.

FIGURE 2.27
After applying a small Outside Gutter value, the split columns push inward from the borders of their containing column (outside gutters diagrammed).

Paragraph Formatting

Now that you have the hang of placing text and working with basic frames, let's get down to what you can do with it.

Most paragraph formatting is controlled via the Paragraph panel (Window ➤ Type & Tables ➤ Paragraph). Figure 2.28 shows the complete Paragraph panel after choosing Show Options from the panel's flyout menu.

Alignment

Along the top row are buttons for the nine types of paragraph alignment possible within InDesign:

Align Left

Align Center

Align Right

Justify with Last Line Aligned Left

Justify with Last Line Aligned Centered

Justify with Last Line Aligned Right

Justify All Lines

Align Toward Spine

Align Away from Spine

Setting aside the last two for a moment, the first three are self-explanatory. The middle four, the justify options, often cause confusion, however.

FIGURE 2.28

The Paragraph panel

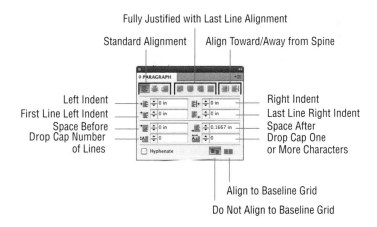

Fully Justified with Last Line Alignment

Standard Alignment | Align Toward/Away from Spine

Left Indent — Right Indent
First Line Left Indent — Last Line Right Indent
Space Before — Space After
Drop Cap Number of Lines — Drop Cap One or More Characters

Align to Baseline Grid
Do Not Align to Baseline Grid

FLUSH, RAG, RAGGED, QUAD?

If you're reading this book, you know at least one of those terms—probably a couple. Did you know they all mean effectively the same thing? The first time I heard *quad right*, I was a newly hired layout artist coordinating a job with my firm's service bureau for the first time. As is typical of print production, the new guy was quizzed. I passed with flying process colors until the prepress operator asked me if the copy was *quad left* or *quad right*. That phrase tripped me up.

The flush edge, to which text aligns, is also known as the *quad*. Thus, left aligned is *flush left* is *quad left*; right aligned is *flush right* is *quad* right. Opposite the flush edge is the *ragged* or just *rag* edge, referring to the fact that it isn't a clean, flush edge as it would be in full (both side) justification.

Fully justified text can be referred as such, or as *flush left and right*, just plain *flush*, *forced*, *forced justified*, *no rag*, and, just once by a New Zealander, *double-clean* type.

Saying text is *forced quad right* is to say that the paragraph is fully justified—both left and right—but also specifically qualifies the last line as aligned to the right.

The middle four alignment buttons, which justify entire paragraphs to both flush left and flush right (full justification), differ only in their treatment of the last line of the paragraph. As you can see in Figure 2.29, that can be a dramatic difference.

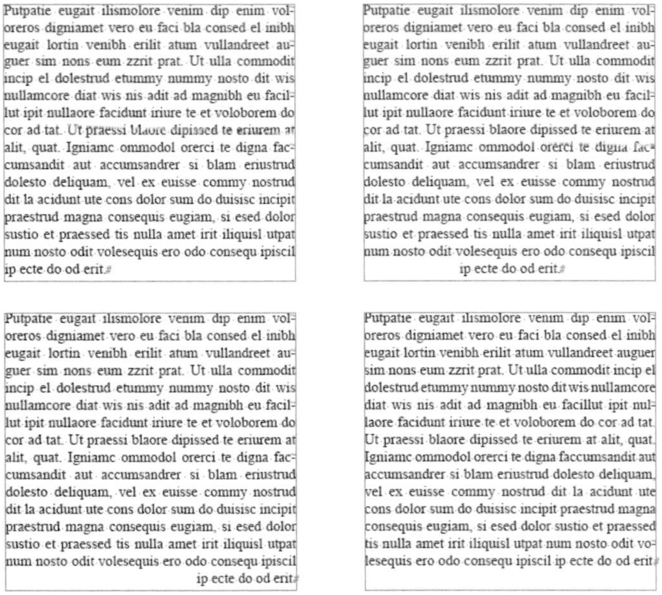

FIGURE 2.29
The same text block justified with differing last line options

Putpatie eugait ilismolore venim dip enim voloreros digniamet vero eu faci bla consed el inibh eugait lortin venibh erilit atum vullandreet auguer sim nons eum zzrit prat. Ut ulla commodit incip el dolestrud etummy nummy nosto dit wis nullamcore diat wis nis adit ad magnibh eu facillut ipit nullaore faciunt iriure te et voloborem do cor ad tat. Ut praessi blaore dipissed te eriurem at alit, quat. Igniamc ommodol orerci te digna faccumsandit aut accumsandrer si blam eriustrud dolesto deliquam, vel ex euisse commy nostrud dit la acidunt ute cons dolor sum do duisisc incipit praestrud magna consequis eugiam, si esed dolor sustio et praessed tis nulla amet irit iliquisl utpat num nosto odit volesequis ero odo consequ ipiscil ip ecte do od erit.

Putpatie eugait ilismolore venim dip enim voloreros digniamet vero eu faci bla consed el inibh eugait lortin venibh erilit atum vullandreet auguer sim nons eum zzrit prat. Ut ulla commodit incip el dolestrud etummy nummy nosto dit wis nullamcore diat wis nis adit ad magnibh eu facillut ipit nullaore faciunt iriure te et voloborem do cor ad tat. Ut praessi blaore dipissed te eriurem at alit, quat. Igniamc ommodol orerci te digna faccumsandit aut accumsandrer si blam eriustrud dolesto deliquam, vel ex euisse commy nostrud dit la acidunt ute cons dolor sum do duisisc incipit praestrud magna consequis eugiam, si esed dolor sustio et praessed tis nulla amet irit iliquisl utpat num nosto odit volesequis ero odo consequ ipiscil ip ecte do od erit.

Putpatie eugait ilismolore venim dip enim voloreros digniamet vero eu faci bla consed el inibh eugait lortin venibh erilit atum vullandreet auguer sim nons eum zzrit prat. Ut ulla commodit incip el dolestrud etummy nummy nosto dit wis nullamcore diat wis nis adit ad magnibh eu facillut ipit nullaore faciunt iriure te et voloborem do cor ad tat. Ut praessi blaore dipissed te eriurem at alit, quat. Igniamc ommodol orerci te digna faccumsandit aut accumsandrer si blam eriustrud dolesto deliquam, vel ex euisse commy nostrud dit la acidunt ute cons dolor sum do duisisc incipit praestrud magna consequis eugiam, si esed dolor sustio et praessed tis nulla amet irit iliquisl utpat num nosto odit volesequis ero odo consequ ipiscil ip ecte do od erit.

Putpatie eugait ilismolore venim dip enim voloreros digniamet vero eu faci bla consed el inibh eugait lortin venibh erilit atum vullandreet auguer sim nons eum zzrit prat. Ut ulla commodit incip el dolestrud etummy nummy nosto dit wis nullamcore diat wis nis adit ad magnibh eu facillut ipit nullaore faciunt iriure te et voloborem do cor ad tat. Ut praessi blaore dipissed te eriurem at alit, quat. Igniamc ommodol orerci te digna faccumsandit aut accumsandrer si blam eriustrud dolesto deliquam, vel ex euisse commy nostrud dit la acidunt ute cons dolor sum do duisisc incipit praestrud magna consequis eugiam, si esed dolor sustio et praessed tis nulla amet irit iliquisl utpat num nosto odit volesequis ero odo consequ ipiscil ip ecte do od erit.

If you choose Justify All Lines, watch the last line carefully. It will be spaced out to fill the width of the column regardless of its content; if there's only a single word on the last line, the characters of that word will be pushed apart to fill the space. You can often see similar results in newspapers, when a narrow, fully justified column contains a line wherein neither the previous nor the next word was able to squeeze into the line and only a single word is stretched to fill the entire width of the column.

When the *Paragraph Composer* is active instead of the *Single-Line Composer*, InDesign will attempt to compensate for short last lines in paragraphs set to Justify All Lines. Often, as in Figure 2.29, word and character spacing throughout the rest of the paragraph will be adjusted to completely absorb the last line, resulting in better last line appearance but with potentially tighter tracking and word spacing throughout the entire paragraph.

ALIGNMENT RELATIVE TO SPINE

The Align Toward Spine and Align Away from Spine options are phenomenal inventions for anyone who deals with facing-page, bound documents. The first button aligns text in the direction of the spine; the other aligns away from it. On a left-read page, text aligned toward the spine will be flush right; move the same text frame over to the right page in the spread, however, and the text will automatically jump to be left aligned.

Technical books, catalogs, magazines, reports, newspapers, and numerous other multipage publications often set heads, subheads, captions, photo credits, pull quotes, and, especially, header and footer slugs to align toward or away from the spine. When pages get pushed around or text reflows due to an addition, omission, or formatting changes, designers have typically had to go in and swap alignments manually. No more. Just choose one of these two buttons, and text will swap its flush edge all by itself as it moves from a left- to a right-read page and vice versa.

Left and Right Indent

Indents push the entire paragraph inward from the frame edge. Use these for selectively control-ling the width of paragraphs. Do not, however, use indents if you want to push all text in the frame inward from the frame edge because you've filled or stroked the frame. Instead, use frame insets, which we discussed a few pages ago.

POWER TIP: CLICK ICONS TO SELECT FIELD CONTENTS

In many of InDesign's measurement fields, including the indent fields on the Paragraph panel, you can click and drag to highlight or select the contents and then type over the contents to change. But there's a faster way. Click the icon to the left of the field. For instance, in the Left Indent field, click the little icon to the left of the up/down arrows. That will automatically select the content of the field without the often hit-or-miss click-drag selection method.

Like most of InDesign's fields, the Left and Right Indent fields can be controlled by typing in values, by using the up/down arrows beside the field, or by using the keyboard arrows. With the cursor in the field, pressing the up- or down-arrow key on the keyboard will increase or decrease the indent by predefined increments (by 0.625 inch each if your document is set to use inches as its measurement, by 1 point if using points, and so forth). Holding Shift while pressing the up- or down-arrow key will adjust the indent by larger increments (0.25 inch or 10 pt).

Separating Paragraphs

When setting stories of more than a single paragraph, you must somehow signal to the reader that one paragraph has ended and another begun. There are various ways to do that, including drop caps, rules, and outdents (where the first line is farther left than the rest of the paragraph). Vastly more common are two other methods: vertical spacing between paragraphs and first-line indents. Which of the two you choose depends on your design—they can sometimes be com-bined successfully, too.

First-line indents require less space typically, allowing a few extra lines of copy to fit on a page, but the trade-off is less white space and fewer places for the reader's eye to rest. Figure 2.30 shows both first-line indents and paragraph spacing. Notice where the same bold phrase appears in both as well as the difference in visual density between the two sets of copy. In the example, the first-line indent is 2 ems (24 pts for 12 pt type), while the paragraph spacing in the second frame is 10 pts.

Below the left and right indent fields in the Paragraph dialog (Figure 2.28) is the First Line Left Indent field, which controls the indentation value of just the first line of selected paragraphs. This field accepts positive measurements as well as negative measurements up to the inverse of the Left Indent field. Negative values, of course, create hanging indents (see Figure 2.31).

As you can see in Figure 2.31, indenting the whole paragraph a certain amount and out-denting the first line using a negative value in the First Line Left Indent field enables margin heads, resume-style entries, and custom bulleted or numbered lists. InDesign includes a more automated way to make bulleted and numbered lists, which we'll go through in detail in Chapter 8, "Stories"; knowing how to do it manually, however, is important for those times

when the built-in Bullets and Numbering just doesn't cut the mustard (for example, when you want to adjust the baseline shift of a single bullet or number character).

If you're accustomed to doing hanging indents in Microsoft Word, we should go through it in InDesign—it's a whole different animal.

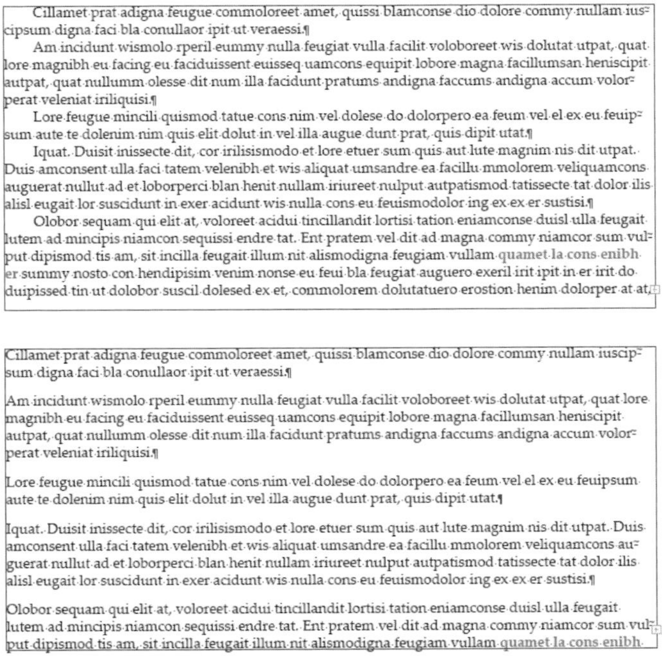

FIGURE 2.30
Above, first-line indents used as paragraph separators; below, vertical spacing after paragraphs

FIGURE 2.31
Positive left indents coupled with negative first-line indents create hanging indents for lists, stylized pseudo run-in and margin heads, or, as in this case, resume entries.

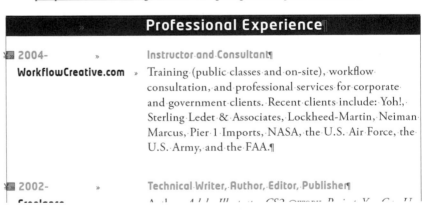

In Word's Paragraph dialog, on the Indents and Spacing tab, indentation is handled through three fields. Left and Right work the same as in InDesign, but the Special field, a dropdown list, determines whether the first-line indent value (the measurement field to the right) is positive or negative by the option chosen. Selecting First Line from the list creates a positive indent where the first line pushes into the paragraph. Selecting Hanging pushes everything *but* the first line

inward, creating an outdent on the first line. InDesign simplifies the process (thus making it less obvious) by eliminating the Special menu and allowing the First Line Left Indent field to accept either positive (indent) or negative (outdent/hanging) values.

Referring back to the resume example (Figure 2.31), the settings I used for the body paragraph hang the employer name out to the left while indenting the rest of the paragraph. Between the employer name and the job description is a tab whose stop was set to mirror the left indent value—1.625 inches. Note that, in my resume entry, the left indent is 1.625 inches while the first line is only –1.5 inches. The difference of 0.125 inches leaves enough room for the custom bullet, which is an anchored graphic frame (indicated by the yen symbol [¥]).

The Left and Right Indent fields accept only positive values, while the First Line Left Indent field will accept either. A negative value for the first line may be up to the value of the Left Indent field. You can't, say, set a –2-inch first line when the left indent is only 1 inch. Nor can you pull the entire paragraph beyond its frame's (or column's) borders by setting left or right indents to negative values. Word will let you do that, but InDesign content can't violate the boundaries of its container (paragraph rules are an exception, as you'll see later in this chapter).

When setting positive indents on the first line of body copy paragraphs, the rule of thumb is that the indents should usually be one to two em spaces, with an *em* space being equal to the font size. Thus, the indent on 10 pt type should be 10 or 20 points. Of course, this is only a best-practice guideline, and larger or even smaller indents may be dictated by style, column width, and typeface.

Book publishers tend to follow the 1- to 2-em rule for most of their titles but will deviate when a template's style warrants it. Magazine and newspaper publishers usually follow the same rule. Copywriters tend to stick with the Tab key in Word, which inserts an indent on the default half-inch tab stop. Indeed, almost exclusively because of the hack of tab indents in Word and typewriters before it, many people believe bigger is better, that any indent less than one-half inch is unprofessional and that one-inch indents are often preferable. Professional designers know better.

Instead of, or in addition to, indents, spacing between paragraphs creates breathing room. The two fields in the next section of the Paragraph panel control the spacing above and below paragraphs, with similar vertical measurement controls to the indents' horizontal controls.

InDesign suppresses spacing before paragraphs that appear at the top of a frame or column as well as spacing after paragraphs at the bottom of a frame or column.

Last Line Right Indent

The Last Line Right Indent field, which controls the indentation on the last line of a paragraph, works identically to the First Line indent with positive values beginning at the right edge.

Depending on the work for which you employ InDesign, you may use this field constantly or never.

It's most often useful for catalogs, classifieds, directories, price lists, and other list-style copy where paragraphs are fully justified and the last line ends with a particular type of information—a SKU, phone number, accreditation acronym, price, or similar bit of information. I've used it in a "magalog"—or "catazine"—style entry complete with *Sky Mall*-like hyperbolic copy (Figure 2.32). There, the paragraph is justified with last line aligned right. A tab separates the end of the copy from the SKU (no tab stop customization needed because of the alignment). Once tabbed out, the SKU pushes 0.2 inches in from the flush edge with the Last Line Right Indent field. As small and simple a trick as it is, that little bump of white space attracts the reader's eye—even more so than emboldening the SKU.

Finally, Start Paragraph defines where new paragraphs may begin—anywhere, only in the next column, next frame (for *threaded* frames), on the next page, or on specifically the next odd or even page. Why is this option useful? Headings. Tables. Charts. Figures. More.

For instance, perhaps you have a Chapter Heading style and every paragraph with that style, every top-level heading, should begin a new chapter or section of the document, beginning with a fresh, right-read (odd-numbered) page. Just set the Start Paragraph value to On Next Odd Page and save it in the Chapter Heading style. Every chapter heading will then automatically jump to a new right-read page, without you having to manually break the text flow or insert break symbols. And, because you didn't manually do anything, it can be overridden later from the Keep Options dialog with minimal effort.

Efficiency and creative freedom at once. You gotta love it when those two come together.

Highlight Composition Violations

As noted previously, hyphenation, justification, and keep options are guidelines, not rules. InDesign may have to violate those guidelines to adhere to higher-priority ones. Although you must place your trust in InDesign, there's no need to do so blindly.

On the Composition pane of the Preferences (see Figure 2.43) are options to highlight instances wherein InDesign had to ignore or violate hyphenation and justification and keep options, instances of custom tracking or kerning, and any text defined as a font or glyph that you don't have installed.

FIGURE 2.43
Composition highlight options in the Preferences

Text highlighted in yellow (see Figure 2.44 and its counterpart in the color insert) indicates an H&J or keep violation, with light, medium, and deep yellow indicating the severity of the violation, from mild through severe. Custom kerned or tracked text highlights in a pleasing sea foam green, while instances of font and glyph substitution, being the most troublesome, highlight in pink.

FIGURE 2.44
Composition violations and substitutions highlight in different colors and shades to indicate which rules are being violated as well as the severity of the violation.

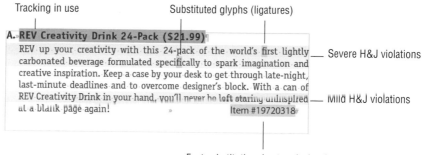

Tracking in use

Substituted glyphs (ligatures)

Severe H&J violations

Mild H&J violations

Font substitution due to missing font

Paragraph Rules

Paragraph rules are not for separating every paragraph in a story, but they can make headings and other separations clearer and more creative. As you'll soon see, they also have tremendous decorative value.

Rules (lines), like paragraph backgrounds, are another of those things people believe can only be done with separate objects. Instead of assigning rules that flow with type automatically, sizing and coloring to match as appropriate, many are stuck in the old days when their only option for paragraph rules was to draw a rule or box as a separate object placed behind or near the text frame. That just isn't so. Virtually anything that can be done as a separate object rule can be done as *part of* the text with paragraph rules.

The major benefits of using paragraph rules instead of Line or Rectangle tool objects are obvious: better alignment; adaptability to text color, size, and indentation changes; the ability to flow with text; and, of course, one object to move and resize instead of two.

Gateway to all this is the Paragraph Rules dialog (see Figure 2.45) on the Paragraph panel flyout menu. It creates rules (and boxes, dots, squiggles, and more) above and/or below—and even behind or beside—paragraphs.

FIGURE 2.45
The Paragraph Rules dialog

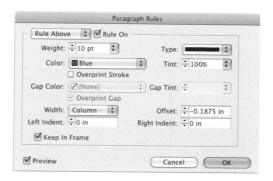

Rule Above/Below (dropdown) Choose whether to enable and edit rules above or below. Both may be activated and customized independently.

Rule On Is the rule on or off?

Weight The stroke weight of the rule. Choose a preset value from the dropdown, or enter a custom value by typing over the contents of the field.

Type Matching the styles on the Stroke panel, these are the available rule stroke styles, including solid, multiple lines, dots, dashes, hash marks, and more.

Color In addition to Text Color, which keeps the color of the rule in synch with the color of the text to which it's assigned, any swatches on the Swatches panel are available in this list. Tints of swatches may be defined in the next field, but to assign a custom color, you'll need to exit the dialog, mix the color, and create a swatch before returning to Paragraph Rules.

Tint A percentage of the Color field's ink. Note that this is *not* transparency. A 0% tint is not transparent; it's paper color.

Overprint Stroke This option is available if the stroke color is set to anything except Text Color, None, or Paper and chooses between *knocking out* any ink beneath the rule or *overprinting* it. The latter option, with the box checked, could result in color mixing. For instance, a cyan rule overprinted on a yellow background will mix the two inks, resulting in a green rule when printed.

Gap Color, Tint, and Overprint These fields remain disabled until you choose a rule type inclusive of gaps—dashed, dotted, hashed, diamond, multiple strokes, and so on. These fields control, respectively, the color of the spaces between the primary stroke color, the tint of that color, and whether it overprints or knocks out background colors.

Width If Width is set to Column, the stroke will span the width of the column regardless of the length of the text line—a single letter could have a stroke that spans the entire single-column page. Conversely, setting the width to Text rules only over (or under) the text itself; the rule will not continue across the column in the case of a short line of text or a single letter.

Offset Rules above begin drawing upward from the baseline of the paragraph's first line of text. Rules below grow downward from the baseline of the last line in the paragraph. Offset is a vertical adjustment of the rules in the direction they normally grow. Thus, a positive offset pushes a rule above higher and a rule below lower. Negative offsets pull rules toward and potentially behind text. Both rules above and below are *behind* text and will not mask the type to which they're assigned.

Left & Right Indent Positive values will push rules inward from column or text edges (depending on the Width setting). Unlike text indents, the rule indent fields can accept negative values, allowing rules to be pushed beyond the borders of text frames, which opens numerous creative possibilities.

Keep In Frame When a rule above is applied to the topmost paragraph in a frame, the rule can sometimes bleed out of the top of the frame or escape it entirely. Checking Keep In Frame puts a leash on the rule so it can't leave the yard.

Paragraph rules make excellent section and content separators, as you can see in the examples in Figure 2.46 (below and in the color insert) where level 1 headings carry different styles of rules above and/or below.

FIGURE 2.46

FIGURE 2.46
Paragraph rules attached to headings help organize and separate data.

The Bottom Line

Create and Fill Text Frames   Setting type is InDesign's primary function, and it performs that function better than any other application. The fundamental building block of type in InDesign is the text frame container and the text content.

> **Master It**   Create a new text frame, and then place the flawed text file, `bad-lorem.txt`, into it. Clean up the resulting text to make it readable. When finished with that, place the document `loremWord.doc` into the same text frame after the first imported document.

Span and Split Columns   The ability to set some paragraphs to span or split columns, reaching across multiple columns in the same text frame or further dividing areas of a frame to a greater number of columns, is a huge time and effort saver. Previously designers had to create multiple frames to answer these needs, resulting in significant time and effort spent creating all those frames, and even more when modifying them for every little change.

> **Master It**   Create an editorial-style page layout complete with headline, kicker, and by-line, all spanning two-column body copy. Do it in one text frame.

Format Text Frames   Correctly formatting and configuring text frames will save effort and time not only now but also every time a frame or its content changes.

> **Master It**   Using the text frame created in the previous exercise, convert it from a single column into three, with a 0.25-inch gutter. At the same time, give the text some breathing room by setting top and bottom insets of 0.1667 inches and no inset on the sides.

Format Paragraphs   Paragraphs must be separated and styled to enable legibility and facilitate readability. That can be accomplished through alignment, indents, paragraph spacing, and drop caps.

> **Master It**   Continuing with the multicolumn frame of placed stories, let's make them readable. In the first full paragraph of each story, add a drop cap of two to three lines. Separate the same paragraphs from anything that may come before with a comfortably large paragraph space before. Give the rest of the paragraphs a correct first-line indent and, to control runts, a last-line right indent. Because we have three probably narrow columns, let's make clean, ragless paragraphs.

Compose Paragraphs   Paragraph composition is essential to good typography. A poorly composed paragraph is one of those things that both trained and untrained eyes immediately notice—even if unconsciously—and that marks the document as the product of an amateur. From this book you should learn first that efficiency and economy of motion equate to more creative time, second that coffee is your friend, and third that practicing good paragraph composition is very, very important to the quality of your documents, your clients and employers, and the future marketability of you as represented by your portfolio.

> **Master It**   Undoubtedly by this point you have three columns of unsavory composition. You may have widows and orphans, paragraphs may be split all over the place, hyphenation may be off or run amok, and word and letter spacing could be just horrendous. Even if it isn't that bad, you have some areas in your document that need work.
>
> First, duplicate the text frame and work on the copy, keeping the original above or beside it as a reference.
>
> Begin the cleanup by asking InDesign to highlight problem areas and violations. Then, working through the highlighted text and keeping an eye out for problems InDesign didn't notice, employ the skills you learned about paragraph composition to eliminate all runts, widows, and orphans; then optically align hanging punctuation and tweak hyphenation and word and letter spacing.

Chapter 3

Characters

InDesign is the world's most advanced typesetting platform. The only other applications that even come close are Illustrator and Photoshop, and only because they follow InDesign's lead. In fact, type set in InDesign is almost as good as type set in movable type. The few sacrifices you make by setting type in InDesign instead of in lead tend to be balanced by the time savings—you can set much faster than one page every four hours—and by the lack of ink perpetually embedded under your fingernails.

In this chapter, you will learn to

- ◆ Format characters
- ◆ Transform characters
- ◆ Insert special characters
- ◆ Work with OpenType font features
- ◆ Use the Glyphs panel

Formatting Characters

Now that you know how to get text *into* InDesign, let's talk about what the world's greatest digital text-handling platform can *do* with it.

The Character Panel

Let's start the character-formatting discussion by walking through the Character panel (Figure 3.1), which contains most character-level style options. Many of the Character panel's options and fields are replicated on the Control panel in Character mode—and a few are more easily accessible via the Control panel—but we'll focus first on the Character panel and then cover the differences on the Control panel.

FIGURE 3.1
The Character panel

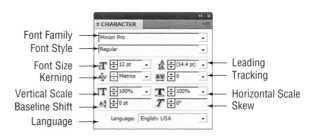

Font Family
Font Style
Font Size
Kerning
Vertical Scale
Baseline Shift
Language

Leading
Tracking
Horizontal Scale
Skew

If it isn't showing, open the Character panel from Window ➤ Type & Tables ➤ Character, or press Cmd+T/Ctrl+T. If you see only six fields in your Character panel, choose Show Options from the panel's flyout menu.

Font Family and Font Style

Most fonts are actually families of typefaces that include a roman, normal, or regular typeface and other variations such as italic, oblique, bold, semi-bold, medium, light, condensed, and countless other possibilities. When styling type, the first option is choosing the appropriate type family.

Clicking the arrow reveals a scrollable dropdown list of all font families installed on the system (see Figure 3.2), including sample text set in the family's default typeface, which is usually the roman, normal, or regular style. Some sample text examples may be boxes, which indicate that the font doesn't include the letters *S*-a-m-p-l-e; this is sometimes the case with symbol or dingbat typefaces.

FIGURE 3.2
The Character panel's Font Family field dropdown list displaying font families and samples

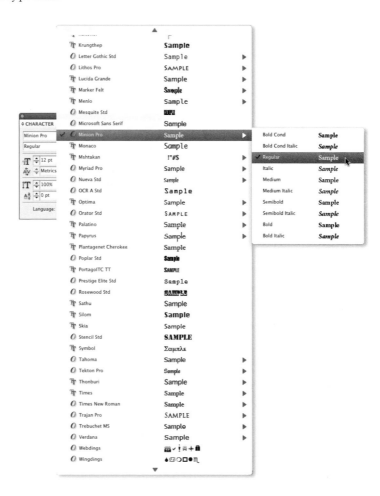

When you have more than one font in the family installed, you'll see an arrow to the right of the sample text. The arrow is a submenu displaying sample text in all the fonts in the family.

Note that, in an appalling case of discrimination, Adobe did not give the family samples submenu to users of InDesign on Windows! It's Mac only. Instead, Windows-based designers are stuck first selecting the font family and *then* looking at the individual font previews via the Font Style field or using the Type ➤ Font menu (see Figure 3.3). There, each family is listed with a flyout displaying all the fonts and sample text—in one place.

FIGURE 3.3
The Type ➤ Font menu shows not only font families but each individual font within a family.

The two types of horizontal space adjustment work hand in hand and are cumulative. For instance, if you've applied a kerning of 200 to a pair of glyphs and then tracked them in –200, the result will be no space between them. Apply a positive 200 tracking and they'll be 400 units (⁴⁄₁₀ of an em) apart. It's important to understand that concept because, even when tracking letters far apart or close together, you still need kerning to ensure that they are *not* really exactly the same distance apart and thus they *look* as if they are.

In Figure 3.7, the upper word has no kerning at all—it's set to 0. The bottom uses Metric kerning, so the relative spacing between these characters is adjusted to compensate for the negative space created by their forms. Both words have been tracked out to a positive value of 600. Which of the two looks like it has the more uniform spacing? Right: the lower one.

FIGURE 3.7
Both words have been tracked out to 600 (⁶⁄₁₀ of an em), but the top uses 0 kerning whereas the bottom uses Metric kerning.

A V A L O N

A V A L O N

If, when tracked, text doesn't look right, it might be one of those rare occasions for zero kerning. The preceding sample was not such an occasion. You now know how to make ultra-loose heads, but when else might you use tracking? When is it more than a special effect? Actually, it's used often but much more subtly.

Large type, such as might be used in headlines, often needs to be tracked together—sometimes by a large degree—for maximum effect. Conversely, dark, shallow, or thick-stroked typefaces at *small* sizes often need a little positive tracking to improve readability. The same is true of small-cap or all-cap type in any typeface within body copy.

Typefaces such as Americana have a lot of space built into their glyphs. They have tall x-heights (the height of the lowercase *x* in relation to the height of the uppercase *X*), spindly strokes, and wide, open *counters* (the holes in letters such as *O, P,* and *C*). All that extra space inside the glyphs themselves can, at certain point sizes, render too much white space. Tightening the tracking slightly in those cases can improve the overall readability.

FITTING MORE TEXT THAN WILL FIT

Stop me if you've heard this one. A man walks into a design studio with two pages of single-spaced, typed copy for his one-page, one-sided flyer. He hands the pages to the designer and says, "Put these in my flyer along with my logo, tagline, and pictures of my product. Oh! And don't forget to put my website address in really big type. And, I don't want the flyer to be cluttered. I hate cluttered design."

(What? You were seriously expecting a punch line?)

I'm asked all the time what's the best way to squeeze text into a space too small to fit it. My first (and second) answer is always, "Edit down the text and cut out the fat."

When trying to squeeze more text into a space than would fit at an appropriate size and style, your first, second, and third options should *always* be to cut copy. Get a real, edumacated editor involved to decide if the copy communicates only the required points. Or if it over explains. Or if it has any parts irrelevant to the direct purpose of the layout.

Assuming you've cut every word you can, you have polished copy, and you still can't fit it, there are a few typesetting tricks you can try. Keep in mind that these are intended to help fit an extra line or two, not another half page.

Reduce font size in fractional points.   *Must* the type be 12 pt? Would 11.75 or 11.5 pt be just as legible?

Look for a condensed or compressed version of the typeface.   Many sans-serif typefaces—such as Futura, Grotesque, and most flavors of Helvetica—have styles drawn to be legible and readable at 75% (or even less) the width of the full-sized, regular versions.

Swap paragraph spacing for indents.   Paragraphs must be separated somehow, providing a visual indicator where one ends and another begins. If the method you've chosen is vertical spacing before or after a paragraph, try eliminating that and indenting the first line instead.

Try tightening the tracking a slight amount.   Of course, how effective it—or any of these tricks—is depends entirely on the font, point size, and amount of text being tracked and fit. However, I have seen a tracking value of only −2 applied to a whole page of type allow another half dozen lines of text to fit on the page. Just don't go overboard trying to fit type; if the tracking is too tight, if there isn't a comfortable amount of horizontal white space, no one will read your text.

Reduce the horizontal scaling.   As with tightening the tracking, a little goes a long way, and a little more is terrible. In my experience, knocking horizontal scaling down 3% can create a lot of extra space and is unnoticeable—as long as all text of the same typeface is scaled. Never scale just a couple of words up or down because beside unscaled text in the same typeface and size, it *will* be noticeable. If you're using a sans-serif font, you can scale even more—sometimes to only 80% of the original width—without it looking like you were squeezing. Headlines and other large copy can also be scaled more than body copy without significant impact on readability.

Tighten the leading.   I want you to know that I sat here, staring at this sidebar for 10 minutes and debating with myself if I should include this option—and then *another* 10 minutes of debating when updating this book to the current version. Reducing the amount of leading is the first thing everyone thinks of when they want to squeeze more text into a space, and I don't want to be construed as an advocate of tightening the leading. In fact, I'm the opposite: I believe strongly in open leading because, relative to text style, leading is the single greatest factor in a person's decision to read or not read a document.

If the leading is too tight, it creates a dark, intimidating page that people resist reading. Writers or designers who create to please their egos instead of their audience invariably disagree with my position, convinced that their words or choice of fonts and pictures, respectively, will outshine and override any other document characteristics and draw in the would-be reader. These are the people who set 12 pt type over 13 or 13.5 pt leading.

If you need a little space and nothing else will work, try dropping the leading down 1%, 2%, or 3%. *Never* set body copy leading to less than 115%, and only go that low when the glyphs themselves have a lot of white space built in and have a shallow x-height. Leading is like tipping a waitress or waiter: 15% of the bill is not the *most* you should tip; it's the *least*. And, 120% leading is not the *most* for body copy; it's the *minimum*.

Try combinations of these tricks if you still can't fit all your copy. If you find yourself using more than two of these techniques concurrently, *don't*. Rethink your design and/or cut down the copy. If those are out of the question, if you can't redesign or cut copy, at least make sure your name is never associated with the final design.

paragraph edges. Conversely, skewing the text frame itself via the Transform panel changes the *area* into which text flows *and* slants the type simultaneously. Both have been skewed by –15°.

When will you use the Skew field? If you have any taste whatsoever, almost never. Like baseline shift, extreme values here can create extreme effects—and one in a million projects will warrant such—but its primary use is for subtle correction. Sometimes the italic or oblique style of a given typeface is too extreme and needs to be scaled back with a negative skew. Sometimes symbols or dingbats need a little slanting this way or that.

Use Skew with caution. After I tell you about the Language field, I'll explain Skew's most obvious purpose and why and when you should, and shouldn't, use it.

FIGURE 3.14
Skewed type in
an unskewed
frame (left) and
unskewed type in
a skewed frame
(right)

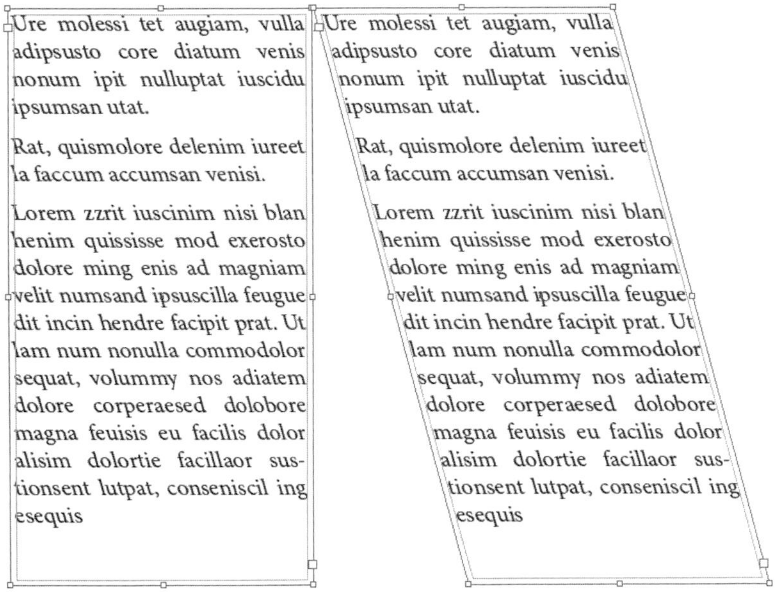

LANGUAGE

Right up front, so you don't get your hopes up: *InDesign does not translate text from one language to another.* Every time I introduce the Language field in person, via webcast, or even in writing, someone always gets excited about the prospect of InDesign automatically translating the text. Unfortunately, it doesn't. That's sadly not the purpose of this field.

If not translation, what's the purpose of this field, and why is it a character-level attribute? As always, good questions.

InDesign is fully, wholly, unlimitedly multilingual. If it can be typed, InDesign will type it. And not just languages based on the Roman alphabet. You can type Japanese, Korean, Vietnamese, Chinese, Russian, Czech, Arabic, Hebrew, and even Klingon (more about that strange idea later) as long as you have a font with the appropriate character set. You don't need to buy a regionalized version of InDesign just to set type in a language other than English. In fact, the only substantive difference between InDesign's English, Eastern European, Japanese, and other regional versions is their user interface—Russian designers get menus, keyboard

shortcuts, and so on in Cyrillic, while Americans, Brits, Mexicans, Italians, and so on get Roman characters in English, Spanish, or Italian.

Because any regionalized version of InDesign can hold text from any known (or future) human written language and because even fastidious Italian writers sometimes make typos, InDesign includes the ability to spell check and/or hyphenate the most common world languages. If, for example, you're designing an antidrug pamphlet to be distributed throughout Texas, you're required to produce the same information in both English and Spanish. Assuming you're putting the copy in both languages on the same pamphlet, a spell check run in your English copy of InDesign will seize on just about every Spanish word. If you have dynamic spell checking enabled, your pamphlet will become a sea of red squigglies. So, instead of dealing with that nightmare and the added complication of no hyphenation or possibly wrong hyphenation, select the Spanish portion and set the Language field on the Character panel to Spanish. Your red squigglies will disappear, and words at the end of lines will correctly hyphenate.

You can tell InDesign to use any one of 39 different spelling and hyphenation dictionaries on selected text, including separate dictionaries for U.S. English legal and medical terminology. Because language is a character-level attribute instead of restricted to the frame or story as it is in other layout applications, multiple languages or language variants (e.g., English: USA: Legal) can be contained in the same frame and even the same paragraph. This is a huge benefit to anyone who routinely sets those types of multilingual documents in which each English paragraph is immediately repeated in Spanish, French, Vietnamese, or another language. Instead of setting each language in its own frame and having to adjust *all* the frames for every little formatting or copy change, placing them in the same text frame causes the entire story to adapt automatically to changes.

Using the Language field is easy: Just highlight text, and choose the appropriate language from the dropdown menu. Once that's done, InDesign will automatically change dictionaries when looking at hyphenation or when running a spell check on the text, paragraph, story, or document. Text defined as English: USA (the default) will be compared against the English: USA dictionary, a sentence in the middle of the same paragraph set to Norwegian: Nynorsk will be compared against that dictionary, an English medical term among *that* against yet another dictionary. *Très bien, mesdames et messieurs.*

Character Transformations

InDesign includes much more control over character attributes than the basic styling options on the face of the Character panel, but they're scattered about.

Change Case

Anyone who imports and sets text written by clients or other noneditorial personnel will understand what I mean when I say that sometimes you need to change the case of text.

Largely because of single-font typewriters, but perpetuated by laziness in the early days of computers and now by habits developed in Internet communications, a large percentage of the business world believes all caps equals emphasis—and CONTINUE to type anything of REASONABLE IMPORTANCE in all caps despite the obvious Bold and Italic buttons in Word. Professional type designers recognize that all caps is usually not the best way to convey emphasis, and they're often left retyping the all caps words in imported documents. A word here and there isn't bad, but when an entire line is set in all caps…. Oh, the inhumanity!

If CS5 is the first version of InDesign you've used, rejoice; you needn't retype any longer. If you've been using InDesign for a couple of versions, you're already aware that it's always had commands to change the case of selected text, right? No? Oh. Well, now you are. Microsoft Word has the same commands on its Tools menu, by the way.

Highlight any text in your document and go to Type ➤ Change Case. There you will find four options: Uppercase, Lowercase, Title Case, and Sentence Case. Respectively, they transform text into all caps; all lowercase; title case, where the first letter of every word is capitalized; and sentence case, where only the first letter of every new sentence is capitalized. With text selected, an even faster way to get to the commands is to right-click (or, if you have one of those insipid single-button Mac mice, Control-click) and select Change Case from the context-sensitive menu.

Changing case is not an effect; the text is really changed. Fresh text typed into the middle of transformed type won't inherit the transformation. These commands can be undone with Cmd+Z/Ctrl+Z, by selecting another Change Case command, or by simply typing over the transformed text.

Cleaning Up after Change Case

A common scenario: A designer is faced with a story containing multiple heading levels, all of which the author set in all caps. The final design, however, will use other formatting and title case for headings. Correcting the problem is not terribly difficult—select each heading one at a time and choose Change Case ➤ Title Case. However, what if there are acronyms in the headings? Maybe it's a regional sales report with headings like "Year-End Spending, USA Offices," "Year-End Profit, UK Offices," and so forth. Maybe it's a government or government contractor report that, like all such reports, speaks in acronyms more often than complete titles. Changing the case will incorrectly change the case on all the words that should be all caps.

Simple: Change the case, then undo the damage by running Find/Change from the Edit menu. Enter in the Find What field the incorrect case word now littered throughout the document (e.g., *Nasa*), and the correct capitalization in the Change To field (*NASA*). Check the Case Sensitive and Whole Word options, and then run the change operation. Repeat as necessary for other common erroneous capitalizations.

Although a great help, the Change Case commands are not perfect. Sentence case, for example, doesn't do proper names, acronyms, or initials. If the letters of acronyms or initials that begin a sentence are not separated by periods (as in the case of, say, *NASA*), the Change Case ➤ Sentence Case command will convert all but the first letter to lowercase (*Nasa*), which, of course, is a major faux pas. Proper names that don't start a sentence will be rendered in lowercase— an even bigger faux pas. Articles like *a*, *an*, and *the*, which typically shouldn't be capitalized in titles (there are exceptions) *will* be capitalized by InDesign, which means manually fixing those. Fortunately, InDesign *does* understand that a stand-alone *I* should be capitalized.

These four simple case commands have saved many a typesetter hours of retyping work and countless typos caused thereby.

...avorite corporate newsletter, I used the following styles (illustrated below,

...s and resources within the same PDF were done in blue, with a dashed

...wned resources such as intranet systems (the Acme Customer First Order

...ocuments on the company's public website (the newsletter's first-quarter

...een and given a double underline.

...uch as those for the *Albuquerque Gazette* review and the partner's site,
...away from company-controlled materials, are styled with a single, solid
...red to closely approximate familiar Web hyperlink formatting.

...n Same Document

...tranet/Company Controlled

...xternal Resource

...TER MODE

...ere an easier way to get to commands such as Superscript,
..., Underline, and Strikethrough? Buttons! *That's* what would be
...those commands, on or off. Wouldn't that be cool? Adobe thought
...ure 3.18).

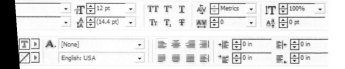

...he Character panel you can also do from the Control panel,
...dozen buttons for commands otherwise stuck two clicks
...ut menu. And, new in CS5, you can even set text fill and out-
...rol panel. Note the type color swatches nestled between the
...tyle fields. Even some of the Paragraph panel options are there,
... left, right, first line, and last line indents.
...he Control panel automatically switches into Character or
...en the two, click either the A button or the ¶ button, respec-
.... In Paragraph mode, some character-level settings are avail-
...mily, Font Style, Font Size, Leading, and even buttons for
...mall Caps, Underline, and Strikethrough.

Never separate either a superscript or subscript glyph from the preceding glyph it modifies; there should be no spaces between them.

Grammar—that is, the *Chicago Manual of Style*, 15th Edition—dictates that a sentence's ending punctuation must always supercede superscript, superior, or subscript notations, even though doing so may look odd. Even odder in appearance could be the result of following the rule of placing a footnote or endnote notation *before* a dash, for example: "Paul Revere's famous mid-night ride[1]—actually the work of two men[2]—occurred in April, 1775." Whether your publication follows the *Chicago Manual of Style* or another style guide with different rules, mitigate unusual superscript and subscript placement results with kerning.

For more on superscript and subscript, especially how OpenType fonts can make them look a lot better, see the section on OpenType later in this chapter.

NO BREAK

The last option on the Character panel flyout menu is No Break, a useful albeit oft-forgotten little command. Highlighting a word and applying this command will prevent InDesign from hyphenating that word if it appears near the end of a line—extremely handy to prevent accidental hyphenation of a proper name.

Many large organizations and government contractors have style guides dictating that certain phrases cannot be wrapped such that part of the phrase appears at the end of one line while the rest wraps to the next line. Others must deal with setting personal names with prefixes (e.g., *Mrs., Dr., MSgt.*) or suffixes (e.g., *Jr., III, DDS*); grammatical style strongly favors keeping prefixes on the same line with first names and suffixes with last. Applying the No Break command to multiple, concurrently selected words will ensure that spaces and punctuation between them cannot be interpreted as a breaking point to wrap the line.

Be careful with No Break, however, because it could create some rather large and ugly gaps at the end of a line. If you're using forced justification, where both the left and right edges are flush, instead of a big gap at the end, you'll get horribly large gaps between words and possibly even between characters in the same word.

Setting an entire paragraph to No Break will tell InDesign to never break a line anywhere. InDesign will do as you tell it, too, *oversetting* the entire thing until such time as you resize the text frame to accommodate the entire passage on a single line, which may not be possible. If you accidentally do this, back out with Undo. If that's not an option, click in the box with the Type tool, press Cmd+A/Ctrl+A to select all (it will select even overset text you can't see), and toggle No Break off again.

UNDERLINE

Think you know all about underlining text, that there's no reason to read this section? Well… uh. You could very well be right. *But*, skim it just in case. You can do much more with InDesign underlines than you might think.

In its most basic form, the Underline command from the Character panel flyout menu will underline selected text with a thin stroke the same color as the type. Open the Underline Options dialog from the same menu, however, and you get a lot more options (see Figure 3.16).

CASE EFFECTS

Choosing Change Case ➢ Uppercase will transform text to full uppercase. Any mixed case used for proper names, acronyms, initials, prepositions, or whatever will be completely and forever lost. Moreover, spell check will read the words as all uppercase, which may cause it to flag misspellings. A less drastic, impermanent option to *transforming* type to all uppercase is to use the all caps *effect*, which creates the appearance of all caps but doesn't actually alter the text.

On the Character panel's flyout menu are two case effects: All Caps and Small Caps. The former will make text *look* all uppercase, but in the background it will keep it in whatever case it was before the effect was applied. Editing the text in story editor will also reveal its real case. Small Caps will leave all capital letters as such but convert all lowercase to smaller versions of the capitals. If the typeface in use is an OpenType font with genuine small caps built in, those will be used; otherwise, InDesign will fake it by scaling capital letter versions down to 70% of their cap height.

As a general rule, the height of small caps should be identical to the height of the lowercase letters in the same typeface (the x-height). Rarely does the default of 70% correctly hit that mark. In fact, most designers change the default small cap height to from 80% to 85% of the cap height when first setting up InDesign. To do that, open InDesign's Preferences and go to the Advanced Type pane. There, beneath Superscript and Subscript, is the size of small caps relative to cap height. Up that to 85% and try it out. If the results aren't perfect, come back and tweak it.

Like most other things in the Preferences, the Small Cap percentage is a document-level attribute. Setting it to 85% for the current document will not change it in the next document you create; it will default to 70%. To effect the change for all future documents, set it with all documents closed.

Exporting or copying the text out of InDesign to another application such as Notepad or an email client, for example, will result in a reversion to mixed case.

SUPERSCRIPT AND SUBSCRIPT

Super- is a prefix meaning above, beyond, on top. *Sub-*, the antonym of *super*, is a prefix meaning below, a part of, or under. Superscript glyphs are printed aligned to or partly above the cap height of text and subscript glyphs partly below the baseline.

Typically approximately two-thirds (58%–67%) the size of the text's cap-height, superscript notations are raised up such that their baselines are between 33.3% and 67% higher than the baseline of surrounding text. Subscript notations are the same size and usually rest on baselines offset by the same amount in the negative (–33.3% to –67%). Super- and subscripts are often numbers or letters, but either can also be a symbol. Figure 3.15 shows a few examples of both in use.

Let's walk through the figure line-by-line as we discuss superscript and subscript.

The first five lines of the figure include superscript characters. The first two are mathematic examples, using superscript to denote *power of*, or multiply the preceding number by itself *this* many times. Einstein's most famous formula, energy equals mass multiplied by the square root of the speed of light in a vacuum, is the first example.

Most text typefaces include the Trademark symbol (™) drawn so that it's proportional to the rest of the typeface in its proper superscripted size and position. Most also include a Registered

Trademark symbol (®), but few include the symbol used when the text or artwork is a protected mark denoting a service, the Service Mark (SM). When it's required, and a font doesn't have it, you'll need to manually create it by using superscript.

FIGURE 3.15
Examples of superscript and subscript

$E = mc^2$

Writing 5^5 is the same as saying five to the fifth power.

WorkflowNetwork.com^SM

They graduated 1st, 4th, and 23rd in their class, respectively.

Meet me at 4:30^PM

H_2O can be expressed also as O_1H_2 or even HOH

According to Dr. H. Harold Vilmark[4], a celebrated professor…

Void where prohibited by law[1].

Next in the figure are mixed alphanumeric ordinals, those handy little notations that represent ordinals like *first* as *1st*. Stylistically, you can use either lowercase or uppercase ordinals.

Finally in the superscript category, for those not yet comfortable with the much more efficient 24-hour clock (I dig efficiency), are time notations. Grammatical and design style rules for setting a.m. and p.m. are pretty loose. Your organization may follow a style guide that dictates their usage and style; if not, you have options. For instance, am, from the Latin *ante meridiem* meaning before midday, may be written with periods (a.m.) or without (am). The same applies to p.m., *post* meridiem, after midday. Both a.m. and p.m. can be styled in a number of ways—as superscript, as lowercase, or as small caps. Never should they be set in full caps.

My recommendation is to small cap if you don't superscript. If you do superscript, capitalize am and pm. I also recommend dropping the periods and the space between the time and its notation in either case, but especially if you superscript. (Of course, if you simply abandon the whole 5,000-year-old a.m./p.m. thing and go with a simple 24-hour clock, all this mess clears up instantly.)

On the next three lines of the figure, we have subscript.

In the chemical formula for water, 2 denotes the number of hydrogen atoms required in the formula and should be subscript. Placing it above, superscripting, would be mathematical instead of chemical and would effectively say multiply hydrogen by hydrogen, which is just mind-boggling to even consider.

InDesign has its own footnote system (see Chapter 8), and you shouldn't have to manually set their reference numbers. Regardless, footnotes are *usually* set as superscript, but can occasionally be subscript, as I showed with the 4 on the second to last line and the dagger on the last line of Figure 3.15.

To apply either superscript or subscript, select the appropriate menu item from the Character panel flyout menu. The selected text will then be scaled and its baseline offset by the amounts specified in the Advanced Type pane of InDesign's Preferences.

Real World Scenario

UNDERLINE STYLES FOR HYPERLINKS

Let's assume you've just landed a plum job as the creative director for your company's newslette[r]. The newsletter, which is distributed to employees, clients, and vendors, is 10 years out of dat[e], and your first task as creative director is to redesign it from scratch. To save money and make t[he] newsletter more digestible, the company also wants you to move it from paper to PDF.

PDF's ability to contain live hyperlinks will definitely help you exploit the power of the newslett[er], but how much thought have you given to the types of hyperlinks you may employ? There are ma[ny] different types of hyperlinks a typical corporate e-newsletter may contain—links to pages with[in] the same PDF, links to the company website and documents thereon, as well as links to outsi[de] resources and partner websites. How are your readers to know which link will do what?

Take a cue from better Web publishers and use different underline styles to instantly identify yo[ur] publication's different types of hyperlinks.

1. Place or type your text—including the hyperlink candidate.

2. With the Text tool, highlight the text to be linked and that will be underlined to show the link

3. Open the Character panel, and from its panel flyout menu, select Underline Options towa[rd] the bottom. This will open the Underline Options dialog box.

4. Turn on Preview on the right, and then check Underline On. You should immediately see yo[ur] selected text underlined.

   If you've used paragraph rules or at least strokes, the controls in this dialog should be famil[iar]. Weight is the thickness of the underline, with a dropdown list of common sizes, or you may ty[pe] in any value. Offset is how far below the baseline the underline should begin. Again, you m[ay] choose a common preset value from the dropdown list or type in your own. Both the Weight a[nd] Offset value fields may also be controlled with the Up and Down arrow keys. Type is InDesig[n's] stroke types—identical to the Stroke panel. Any preexisting swatch may be used as the color of underline, or it may be left at its default, which is the same color as the text. Choosing any swa[tch] but (Text Color) None and Paper will enable the Tint field. Gap Color and Gap Tint activate on[ly] the underline type is one that includes gaps of some sort—anything but Solid, really. Gap col[or] take the place of having to layer multiple objects to achieve a two-tone dotted stroke.

5. Set up your external hyperlink underline how you like. Most users are accustomed to a so single underline that is the same color as the text (which you should change from black contrasting color like blue, green, or red). When ready, hit OK. Don't forget to actually ass the URL on InDesign's Hyperlinks panel.

Creating the hyperlink underline may not be tough, but it is tedious if you have more than a cou of external hyperlink underlines to format. Save yourself some time and make a character style this particular underline. Thus, underlining more text is simply a matter of highlighting and t clicking the style entry in the Character Styles panel.

Set up your other underlines' styles the same way, making character styles for each of them, Make them all obviously hyperlinks by changing their text and underline colors from the col the surrounding copy, but don't go overboard. Thin single, double, dashed, or dotted lines ten serve readers well.

All this raises the question, *Do you really need the Characte[r]* panel *does* serve as a full replacement for those dedicated pa them and save some much-needed screen real estate is up t

Special Characters

On the Type menu are a couple of submenus that make ins ous sizes and types of spaces much easier than using diffi

Insert Special Character

Skipping the Markers section, which we'll cover in later c dashes, quotation marks, and other marks accessible from Table 3.1 is the first, the Symbols menu.

Special characters will insert using the type style in e cursor is resting among text styled as Myriad Pro Black S choose Type ➢ Insert Special Character ➢ Symbol ➢ Co Copyright symbol drawn into the Myriad Pro Black Sem ing. If the requested symbol (or space, as below), wasn't nothing will insert or, with low-quality fonts, you'll get the symbol as another font that *does* have the requested

TABLE 3.1: Symbols

MENU COMMAND	SYMBOL	DESCRIPTION
Bullet Character	•	A bullet, middl
Copyright Symbol	©	The good old C
Ellipsis	…	The ellipsis is dots smaller t
Paragraph Symbol	¶	More correct denotes a ha paragraphs.
Registered Trademark Symbol	®	Used when a
Section Symbol	§	The double-
Trademark Symbol	™	The standa registratio

The Hyphens and Dashes menu begins with E undoubtedly familiar. The latter pair, Discretionar

A discretionary hyphen is, at most times, an invisible character—a marker really. Placing a discretionary hyphen in a word not at the end of a wrapping line of text has no apparent effect. With Show Hidden Characters active, you'll see it marked as invisible (see Figure 3.19), but the word won't hyphenate—unless InDesign decides it needs to wrap the line somewhere around the word containing the discretionary hyphen. When that happens, InDesign will hyphenate and wrap the word where you specified, even ignoring whatever syllabic breakdown is included in the dictionary for the same word. In this way, you can tell InDesign, *I know better than you, and I want this word broken at this point if it must break.* You can even put multiple discretionary hyphens in a single word, which is useful for longer or ad hoc compound words whose syllables or parts you want broken a certain way.

FIGURE 3.19
A discretionary hyphen, visible when hidden characters are shown

Amalgamated·the·flav

Nonbreaking hyphens, as the name implies, are the opposite of discretionary hyphens. They *do* show a hyphen, but InDesign will *not* wrap at the point of the hyphen.

Take a compound word like the partners' names in *Auchman-Reynolds Holdings*. It's a proper name, and it's extremely bad form to break the two constituent partner names apart across lines. Generally speaking, leaving a larger than normal right-edge gap is preferable to breaking a compound proper name (we already covered ways to tweak surrounding text and mitigate the damage). Because, as typed, that's a normal, visible hyphen in there, and InDesign looks to hyphens as the first obvious break point when *Auchman-Reynolds* won't fit on one line, InDesign will break it after *Auchman-*. To prevent that, replace the normal hyphen with its nonbreaking variant, and InDesign will never break the two words apart. It may still try to break *Auchman* or *Reynolds* syllabically—that's where the No Break command on the Character panel comes in—but it won't sever the two at the hyphen—well, almost never. If a column is too narrow to fit the entire *Auchman-Reynolds* on a single line, leaving InDesign stuck between oversetting the text or breaking it at the hyphen, InDesign will choose the latter option despite the nonbreaking hyphen.

Next on the Insert Special Character menu is the Quotation Marks submenu (see Table 3.2).

TABLE 3.2:   Quotation marks

MENU COMMAND	SYMBOL	DESCRIPTION
Double Left Quotation Marks	"	Left or opening curly quotes or typographer's quotes.
Double Right Quotation Marks	"	Right or closing curly quotes or typographer's quotes.
Single Left Quotation Mark	'	Left or opening single quotation mark.
Single Right Quotation Mark	'	Right or closing single quotation mark. Also called an apostrophe.
Straight Double Quotation Marks	"	Inch or minute hash mark.
Straight Single Quotation Mark	'	Foot or second hash mark.

Punctuation Space The width of the typeface's period. This is often used in place of a hair space when the hair and thin spaces are too narrow.

Flush Space This is a very important type of space. It's a variable-width space that widens to fill the last line of a justified paragraph. Normal composition would, in this case, either leave text flush to the left (possibly creating orphans) or, when the last line is set to full justification, stretch the spaces between all words until the line is filled. However, inserting a flush space causes all *other* words' spaces to remain constant while the flush space is expanded to consume whatever emptiness remains. If you've ever tabbed out the last line to flush-right alignment—say, to insert an endmark to close a magazine article—the flush space can and should take the place of the tab.

OpenType

The final frontier of cross-platform, multilanguage, and advanced typography has been tamed. OpenType fonts fix most of the woes of digital typography—and open entire worlds of typographic freedom and control.

What Is OpenType?

OpenType was conceived and developed as, and *is*, a complete replacement for all other font formats—for use with nearly all current and *future* written languages.

Earlier we talked about font glyph tables—how every letter, numeral, mark, and symbol has a slot to hold it in the font table. TrueType and PostScript fonts have a limit of 256 unique glyphs—256 slots in their font tables. With Latin-based languages having only 26 capital and 26 lowercase letters, 10 numerals, and about 60 common punctuation marks and symbols, 256 works. Oh, wait. That's just for English, which doesn't have any accented characters in its normal written language. We can't forget about French, Spanish, Italian, and Portuguese. Then there are *ligatures*. There are more symbols, too, such as the Euro, which isn't in either the Type 1 or TrueType specifications because it didn't exist when they were written. Hmm.... A font table of 256 glyphs is starting to look cramped.

Even squeezing all those in, non-Latin character sets don't fit into the 256-glyph tables of Type 1 and TrueType fonts. Completely different fonts will need to be designed and distributed for Swahili, Chinese, Japanese, Korean, Vietnamese, Russian, Hebrew, Arabic, and so on.

Even if non-Latin languages are of no consequence to your work, small caps, discretionary ligatures, swashes, alternative glyph versions, and several differently styled sets of numerals *should* be. Oh! Then we're going to need bold, italic, bold italic, and roman styles of the main typeface as well as such styles of small caps, discretionary ligatures, swashes, alternative glyph versions, and several differently styled sets of numerals. And those are just the basics; we haven't even touched on other weights like light, medium, semi-bold, heavy, extra bold, and black or different scales such as condensed, semi-condensed, extended, semi-extended....

How many fonts *does* one designer have to manage these days? It's starting to get complicated, isn't it?

Raise curtain. Cue OpenType.

Whereas a Type 1 or TrueType font can hold only 256 characters, OpenType's *Unicode* font table has 65,536 predefined slots. Allow me to put that in perspective. A single font can contain the complete glyph sets from Arabic, Armenian, Bengali, Braille embossing patterns, Canadian Aboriginal Syllabics, Cherokee, Coptic, Cyrillic, Devanāgarī, Ethiopic, Georgian, Greek, Gujarati, Gurmukhi

(Punjabi), Han (Kanji, Hanja, Hanzi), Hangul (Korean), Hebrew, Hiragana and Katakana (Japanese), International Phonetic Alphabet (IPA), Khmer (Cambodian), Kannada, Lao, Latin, Malayalam, Mongolian, Myanmar (Burmese), Oriya, Syriac, Tamil, Telugu, Thai, Tibetan, Tifinagh, Yi, and Zhuyin (Bopomofo). Even *after* all those are added, there's room for several languages yet to be included (übergeeks are seriously considering adding Star Trek's Klingon and two Elven scripts from J.R.R. Tolkien's *Lord of the Rings* trilogy), thousands of variations of other characters, and a "private use" area for approximately 130,000 nonstandard custom or regional characters.

Let's scale the discussion down to a typical, English-language document. One OpenType font can contain the complete upper- and lowercase alphabet, plus several versions of each, including sets drawn as small caps, swash caps, and other derivations. Maybe, in an invitation like Figure 3.21, you'd rather use something with a few more touches of style than the one for the example on the left. The one on the right uses the same two OpenType fonts—Arcana GMM Std and Adobe Caslon Pro—but with slight differences owing to alternate glyphs in those fonts.

FIGURE 3.21
The same typefaces, using alternate glyphs contained in their OpenType character sets

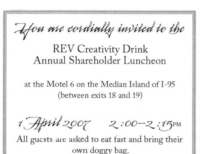 

Subsequently we'll get into how to apply different OpenType effects and to access all the glyphs in a particular font. Before we do, there's one other thing I'd like to note: OpenType fonts are completely cross-platform, unlike Type 1 or TrueType fonts (Mac OS X can use Windows TrueType fonts but not vice versa).

Cross-Platform at Last

The same OTF file Dad uses on his iMac can go to cousin Charlie's Windows 7 computer. *Yeah, so? What does that mean to me?*

It means no more empty boxes in place of copyright symbols. No more text reflow when a Windows-based designer sends a document for touch-up and RIP (raster image processing) on a Mac. No more having to whip out Fontographer or FontLab to violate your font license by converting your Mac-based colleague's fonts just so you can touch up a couple of text frames.

OpenType fonts are 100% cross-platform—the only place Windows or Mac matters anymore is your personal preference. InDesign documents are cross-platform. Images such as TIFF, JPEG, EPS, and even PSD and AI have been reliably cross-platform compatible for years. The last impediment to creative document operating system homogeny was platform-dependent fonts. OpenType knocks down that barrier, allowing any creative person—Windows or Mac—to work with colleagues on either without fear that something in the document will change from one computer to the next. In fact, OpenType even works on most Unix-based operating systems (though InDesign doesn't).

Upgrading to OpenType Fonts

Adobe OpenType fonts are all identified on Font Family and other menus by either *Pro* or *Std* after the family name, which differentiates them from Adobe Type 1 fonts. Pro OpenTypes are those that take advantage of the larger OpenType font table, including a larger set of special characters, while Std (standard) typefaces are merely those that Adobe converted directly from their earlier Type 1 incarnations without adding additional glyphs.

Unfortunately, Adobe's lead has not been followed by every type foundry, some of which have not altered their font names at all from TrueType or Type 1 through OpenType versions. TrueType and Type 1 are dying (not dead), so keep your eyes open for new OpenType versions of old favorites. As soon as you replace a Type 1 or TrueType font with an OpenType version, pull the other versions out of your active fonts and stash them away somewhere, to be used only for older document compatibility.

Using OpenType Features

Support for OpenType fonts is built into Windows 2000, Millennium Edition, XP, Vista, and Windows 7 and, on the Mac, into OS 9 and X. Therefore, every application that runs natively in those environments recognizes and can use OpenType fonts without special add-ins.

InDesign 2.0, released in January 2002, was the first application in the world to use OpenType fonts' extended features. Its brethren Illustrator and Photoshop quickly followed suit, and a couple of years later, so did QuarkXPress.

On the Character panel's flyout menu, the OpenType menu grants access to toggles that turn on or off various OpenType features (see Figure 3.22). Highlight text on the page, navigate through the Character panel flyout menu to the OpenType submenu, and click the appropriate command to enable or disable its effect. Features encased in brackets ([]) are not present in the currently selected font.

FIGURE 3.22
The OpenType menu, showing options for Adobe's Caflisch Script Pro OpenType font

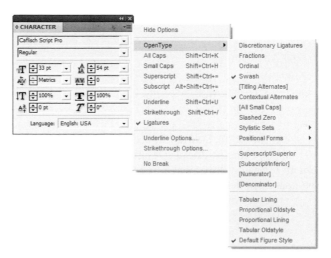

DISCRETIONARY LIGATURES

Ligatures are special glyphs drawn to avoid awkward pairings of letters. For instance, in Figure 3.23, pairings such as *ff, fi, fl,* and others awkwardly collide with each other. The upper teardrop of the *f* in *fi,* for instance, collides with the dot in the *i.* Consequently, type designers long ago developed special glyphs called ligatures that, like the lower set in the same figure, combine the two characters into a single, more elegant shape. Standard ligatures are turned off or on via the Character panel flyout menu's Ligature command. It's on by default, which is a good thing.

FIGURE 3.23
Certain character pairings cause awkward collisions (top) that are resolved by ligatures (bottom).

Standard ligatures are nothing new—they've been in digital fonts for decades and lead or wood fonts for centuries. But, two aspects *are* new to OpenType.

A ligature has traditionally been a single character; the *ffi* ligature, for example, ceased to be *f-f-i.* Running a spell check on a document containing ligatures invariably flagged words containing ligatures as misspelled. No longer. Not with OpenType.

It comes down to the difference between characters and glyphs. A character is, well, a character—letter, number, punctuation, symbol. A glyph is any form a character or another mark might take. In OpenType, the dot over the lowercase *i* is actually contained within a different table cell from the stalk of the letter. Every time InDesign or another OpenType-aware application draws an *i,* it's actually combining two cells in the table to form a single character. When the *i* is part of an *fi* ligature, the dot is simply left off. The *ffi* ligature is actually three separate cells—the *f* twice, or as in the preceding example, two different versions of an *f,* depending on the typeface and usage, and the *i*'s stalk—combined into a single glyph. (The examples in Figure 3.23 are set using the Adobe Caslon Pro Regular typeface.)

While ligatures *look* like a single character, and in most ways *act* like one as well, they are not (see Figure 3.24). Behind the scenes, the technology built into OpenType still understands that *ffi* is *f-f-i*—and so does InDesign's spell checker. You can even copy text containing ligatures from an InDesign document and paste it into applications that don't comprehend ligatures, like Web-based applications such as Twitter, Facebook, or WordPress; upon pasting, the ligatures will disappear, revealing the separate *f-f-i* characters. This is a function of OpenType itself, not InDesign, although a robust OpenType interpretation engine is required for an application to correctly understand and use glyphs.

Because of all the extra room afforded by OpenType's Unicode font table, additional ligatures beyond the most common appear in some OpenType fonts (see Figure 3.25). Pairings like *ct* and *st,* for example, can be joined with what are called discretionary ligatures—ligatures that you may or may not want to include. Other discretionary ligatures are variations on the default, obligatory ligatures. They add a nice touch once in a while, but they aren't for every document.

FIGURE 3.24
OpenType tech-
nology forms the
ligature glyph
from three sepa-
rate parts, which
always retain their
constituent select-
able forms.

FIGURE 3.25
Discretionary
ligatures (bottom)
stylize the appear-
ance of some char-
acter pairings.

ct st fh fi fl ff ft

ᑫ ſt fh fi fl ff ft

FRACTIONS

How much can OpenType really improve fractions? For many years, most fonts have shipped with common fractions built in— ¼, ½, ¾. Yes, they have, and those are great until you need something like ⅔, ⅒, or ⁵⁄₆₂₁. At that point, what have you typically done? Right: You superscript the numerator and subscript the denominator, adjust their baseline shifts, and then kern them together with a standard slash (/). It's a hack, but it's served us well over the years in lieu of anything better. Predictably, OpenType does it better without hacks (see Figure 3.26).

FIGURE 3.26
Typed numbers
and slashes before
using the Open-
Type ➤ Fractions
command (top) and
after (bottom).

1/4   1/2   1/3   5/8   1/288   5/621

¼   ½   ⅓   ⅝   ¹⁄₂₈₈   ⁵⁄₆₂₁

Assuming you're using an OpenType font that includes them (my examples use Adobe Myriad Pro and Adobe Caslon Pro, both of which do), you may have two complete sets of numerals in addition to the full-size set—0–9 as numerator and 0–9 as denominator (see Figure 3.27). These

will be numerals located respectively in the upper-left or lower-right corner of the font table cell; they are already in the right place for a fraction and don't need to be super- or subscripted. More important, they'll be drawn with stroke weights that match or complement full-size numerals and other glyphs in the font.

FIGURE 3.27
Adobe Caslon's different numerals. Top to bottom: standard full-size, numerator, and denominator, all shown at 30 pt.

0	1	2	3	4	5	6	7	8	9
0	1	2	3	4	5	6	7	8	9
0	1	2	3	4	5	6	7	8	9

As you can see in Figure 3.28, creating fractions with the age-old superscript and subscript workaround merely reduces the size of the numerals. Their stroke weights scale proportionately, making the digits obviously scaled and looking rather spindly and out of place compared to surrounding text. Additionally, the separator between them is a slash, not a *solidus*. Some would argue as vehemently against that incorrect glyph usage as I do against using three periods instead of a correct ellipsis.

FIGURE 3.28
(Top) Fractions faked with superscript, subscript, baseline shift, and kerning. (Bottom) Proper fractions using numerals drawn to be numerators and denominators, as well as proper solidi.

3¾ Tbsp.   1½ cups   5⁄9 inch
3¾ Tbsp.   1½ cups   5⁄9 inch

Compare the two lines. Which set of fractions looks out of place? Which matches its surrounding text? Here's a more pragmatic difference between them: For just three sets of fractions, it took me almost four minutes to set all the numbers as superscript or subscript and adjust their baselines and kerning—and I used keyboard shortcuts to speed up that work versus doing it via menus and the Character panel fields. Even having to make three trips to the OpenType menu, creating the proper fractions took me less than 10 seconds.

Not only do OpenType fractions yield better typography, but they're also faster and easier. Just type your fractions, highlight all three parts—numerator, slash, and denominator—and select Fractions from the OpenType menu. InDesign and the font take care of the rest.

As in ligatures, all the characters in a fraction remain individually editable. Did you mean to type *5/8* instead of *5/9*? No problem: Select the *9* and type over it.

Figure 4.1 should look familiar to you no matter how long you've been out of school. Our world (and James Cameron's) is divided into three dimensions, or planes:

◆ Left-to-right, horizontal position, and object width are plotted on the X-axis.

◆ Top-to-bottom, vertical position, and height are plotted on the Y-axis.

◆ Front-to-back, depth, relative distance, and what we often call *stacking order* are plotted on the Z-axis.

FIGURE 4.1

All vector artwork exists in three-dimensional space, along the X-, Y-, and Z-axes. You can also see it in color in the color insert section of this book.

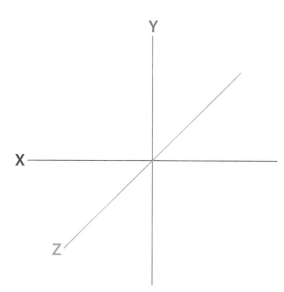

Describing the volume of a cube, for example (see Figure 4.2, which is also in the color insert in [wait for it] color!) entails asking three questions: How wide is it along the X-axis, how tall along the Y, and how deep along the Z? This is why, in places like the Transform and Control panels, you have positional fields for X and Y.

If you have a box handy, grab it. Each surface or face of a box is a plane: It exists solely along one of the three axes. Stick six planes together—top, bottom, right side, left side, front, and back—and you have a three-dimensional solid; and if the sides and planes are all equal, it's a cube. The place where each plane intersects with another is called a *vertex*.

When you're examining a real-world object like a box, planes and vertices are what define the volume and shape of an object. Talking about vector drawing, however, is slightly different; it's not the faces and sides that matter but the *corners*. Consider Figure 4.3, the same cube drawn with its faces unfilled. It still has planes; they just aren't filled with color (color you can see in the color insert).

Even with this *wireframe* cube, the vertices, the lines connecting the corners, are secondary to the importance of the corners themselves. The corners truly define and describe the shape of the object.

Vector shapes are formed by the relationship of corners—*anchor points*—and the lines that connect them—*path segments*. Together, anchor points and path segments form *paths*. Every path must have at least two anchor points (i.e., to begin and end the path) and a path segment connecting the two points. Closed paths are those that have no discernable start or end point—a complete circle or square, for example—while open paths are incomplete, with obvious start and end points.

FIGURE 4.2
A cube exists
on all three axes.

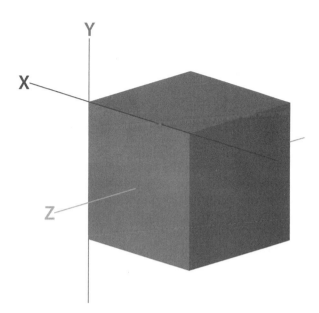

FIGURE 4.3
A cube without fills
reveals the corners
and vertices that
define its shape.

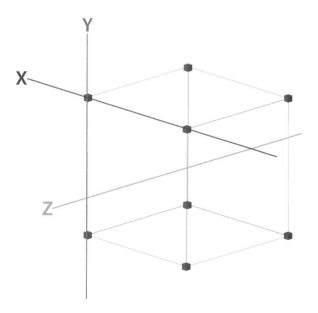

Because anchor points exist in three-dimensional space along the X, Y, and Z planes and not within a fixed-resolution grid, the relative size of the planes —and anything on them—can be scaled up or down infinitely without losing quality in the drawing. Although they appear to be squares of a certain size onscreen, anchor points don't have a size; zoom in or out and anchor points remain the same size. They're only rendered in squares because our monitors interpret data through a grid of pixels.

The cube we looked at earlier has volume because a computer draws a connection *between* the coordinates. Like the coordinates themselves, the connections have no inherent *volume*, width, height, or depth; they're just lines drawn between points on the three planes. Volume is created by the relationship between points on all three planes, and that relationship is relative. A square is a square because four anchor points are equidistant from one another. Move all four the same distance downward and the object is still a square. Enlarge the square and it's still a square, with anchor points at the exact same *relative* distance from one another.

You see, resizing vector artwork isn't really resizing. It's more like zooming in or out in three-dimensional space. Shrinking an object down to half of its size is like zooming out to view a document at 50%, like seeing the object from farther away. The object and all its detail are intact, even if they aren't discernable from that distance.

This is the essence of vector—total independence from any concept of resolution or image quality. If you're new to vector, that can be a difficult notion to wrap your mind around—at first.

Drawing Paths

Drawing in InDesign is accomplished with a number of tools—many the same as in Illustrator, Photoshop, and other applications—and any discussion of them must begin with the Pen tool.

The Pen Tool and Straight Paths

Let's start exploring the Pen tool by drawing a simple path with two anchor points joined by a straight path segment:

1. Using the Pen tool, click once and release somewhere on the page—do not drag.

2. Move over a few inches and click again. A straight path segment should connect the two anchor points.

If you see only a faint blue line for the path segment, you don't have a stroke color assigned; press D to activate the default black stroke color. If that still doesn't do it, check the Strokes panel to ensure that it has a weight. In the end, you should have what I have (Figure 4.4).

FIGURE 4.4
A straight path, consisting of two anchor points joined by a straight path segment

Now, try making a perfectly level horizontal line:

1. If your rulers are not showing, make them show with Cmd+R/Ctrl+R.

2. With the Selection tool, click the horizontal ruler and drag a guide down to an empty area of the page or pasteboard.

is because, as the first point, it could have only
second anchor point, however, you are con-
t also a potential path segment to the right.

same procedure. Instead of deselecting
ase an inch or two away to create a third

ragging, the resulting second path seg-
point to the left.
nts attached to it—in this case, one to the
diate off points at any angle. That path
hor point. Because a path segment must
gets *two* curve handles—one for each
vious the first curve is created by the
anchor point in position 2 on the right.
side of an anchor point, and when you

o curve handles. The handle you *didn't*
ing S-curve—and the other, the one
on the right. Creating the third anchor
gment. The second segment was a bowl
point and thus didn't add any curva-

ging the curve handle corresponding

can see there are four anchor points
number required to create a perfect
geometry involved limits the way

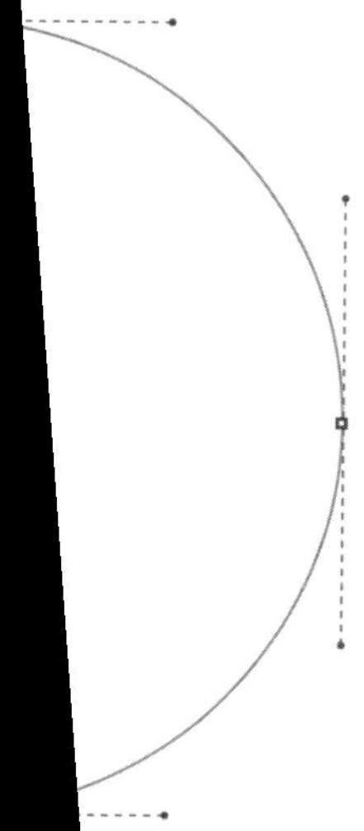

The Pen Tool and Curves

Anchor points control the angle of path segments. Wherever a path must change its direction, it's the anchor point that actually does the work. The same is true of path segment curvature.

Every anchor point has the potential to curve the path segments on either or both sides of it. Consider the S-curve in Figure 4.7. Note the two distinct curved parts in the *S*, one up, one down. The divider line shows which curve is being generated by which anchor point.

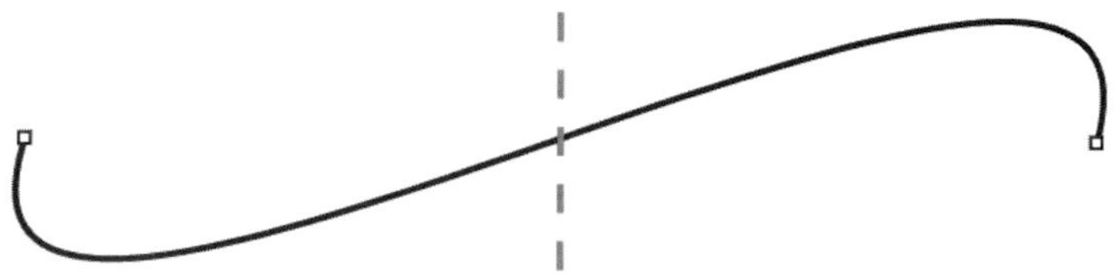

FIGURE 4.7 In this simple S-curve, the curve on the left is created by the anchor point on the left, and the curve on the right by the other anchor point.

Introducing curvature is simple: Instead of clicking and releasing with the Pen tool, click and *drag*. As soon as you begin to drag, the anchor point goes from being a plain anchor point to a smooth anchor point and *curve handles* or *direction lines* appear (see Figure 4.8). The angle and length of curve handles control the direction and depth of path segment curvature. Drag a handle straight down, and the resulting curve will be symmetrically bowl-like; drag a handle down and at an angle, and the resulting curved path segment will be asymmetrically deepest in the direction of the curve handle and shallow on the end farther from the curve handle.

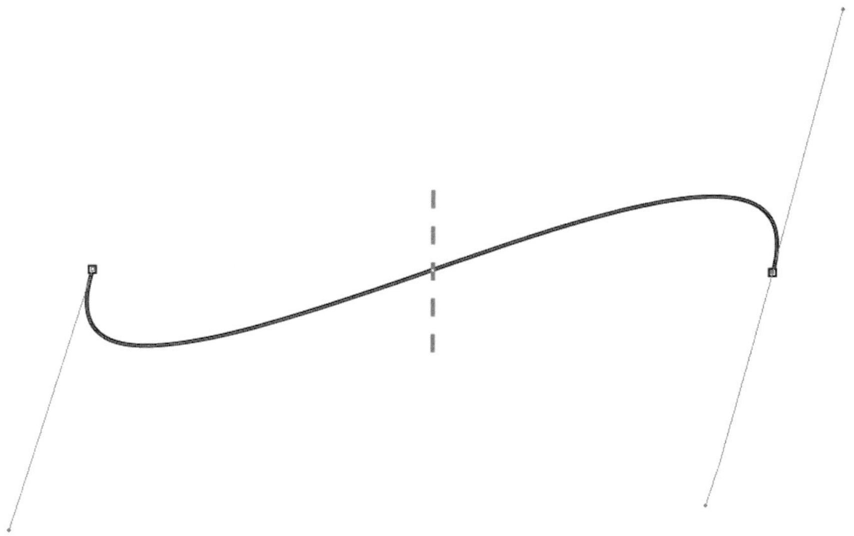

FIGURE 4.8 The same S-curve, showing the curve handles that define its curvature

3. Switch to the Pen tool and make the first anchor point by clicking directly on the guide.
4. Move over a few inches and, again, right on the guide, click to make your second anchor point.

   As your cursor approaches the guide, you'll enter the *snap zone*, the area within a few pixels of a guide that will cause the cursor to jump toward the guide. You'll know when your cursor snaps to guide by the change in appearance from a nib with an X to a nib with an empty arrowhead. If the snapping bothers you, turn it off by toggling off View ➢Grids & Guides ➢ Snap to Guides.
5. To fully appreciate your new path, hide guides with the Cmd+;/Ctrl+; keyboard shortcut.

Now, let's try the next step and create a rectangular path:

1. Either on a new layer (with the last hidden) or a different area of the page or pasteboard, drag *two* guides from the horizontal ruler, leaving a few inches between them.
2. Do the same from the vertical ruler, defining a roughly square shape with the four guide lines.
3. Working counterclockwise from the bottom left with the Pen tool, click the bottom-left intersection of guides, exactly where they cross; then click the bottom right, the top right, and finally the top left.

   At this stage you should have what appears to be a backward C. This is an open path because it has start and end points.
4. Let's close the path: With the Pen tool still selected, click again on the bottom-left corner, directly on the anchor point already there. As you get close to the anchor point, the cursor will change from just a pen nib to a nib with a circle (see Figure 4.5).

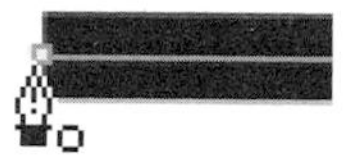

FIGURE 4.5 When closing a path, the Pen tool cursor picks up a small circle icon indicating a change in function from continuing a path to closing a path.

Now, all on your own, try drawing a triangle. Or how about a six-sided polygon, like a stop sign. Everywhere you want a path to change direction, insert an anchor point. Anchor points control the direction of each subsequent path segment.

Let's try one more exercise, this time using one of my sample files.

From the project files available on the book's download web page, open `pathtrace01.indd`. You'll see the single-page document in Figure 4.6. It contains two layers: The upper one, "Trace on This Layer," is for you to trace the content of the lower, locked layer, "Original."

FIGURE 4.6
Hey, if I didn't think InDesign was cool, would I write a book about it? No, of course not. Instead, I'd publish a website comparing it to its leading competitor (wink).

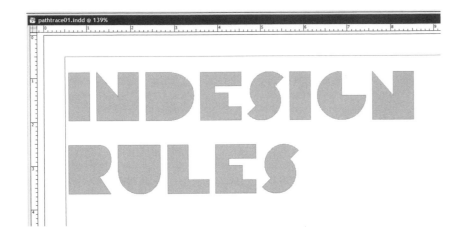

Follow these steps:

1. Using the Pen tool, trace the rectangle of the *I* until you have a closed path.

2. Once the *I* is finished, open the Swatches panel and fill it with a color other than orange so you can see how close your tracing was to the original.

3. Begin tracing the *N*. Once it's finished, give it a fill color, too, and move on to the *D*, the *E*, and so on until you've traced every letter of both words.

    Be careful to simply click and release to create a new anchor point; don't click and drag. See how close you can approximate the curves of the *D*, *S*s, *G*, *R*, and *U* using only straight path segments.

Getting a feel for the Pen tool and how to think about shapes by considering the placement of their anchor points? Starting to feel confident drawing straight-segment paths with the Pen tool? Good. Now, let's move on to what straight lines can't do.

FLATTENING: CURVE OR TRANSPARENCY?

By drawing rounded edges using straight path segments, you performed rudimentary curve flattening. When a document moves through a *RIP (raster image processor)*, all vector objects are converted to raster pixels or dots so that a print output device can create halftones of the image. Because pixels and halftones are fixed resolution and grid based (with a pixel or dot being either wholly on or wholly off), a curve, which might only partially fill the pixel or dot, must be converted to a series of straight lines that are more easily fit into a grid. They're usually very tiny lines, but straight nonetheless. This is the process of curve flattening.

Before *alpha transparency* made its way into *PostScript 3*, when a print professional used the word *flattening*, it was in reference to curve flattening. Now it's generally used in reference to transparency flattening—another matter entirely. Although curve flattening is still as relevant, it's stable and, after 25 years, predictable. Transparency flattening in the print workflow, however, has more recently been the major source of concern, innovative workarounds, expletives, and empty bottles of Pepto-Bismol.

UNWIELDY AND INCONSISTENT TERMINOLOGY

Plain anchor points, *corner anchor points*, and *smooth anchor points* are unwieldy. No, not the points, the terms themselves (some people would argue that the points are even less wieldy than the names). Those are the official names Adobe InDesign gave them, but they're all just anchor points. Also, when anchor points appear at the beginning or end of an open path, Adobe often refers to them as end points. Although that makes sense, it's yet another term for effectively the same thing: an anchor point.

To make matters much worse, the names of anchor points and other vector drawing-related user interface elements are inconsistent across Adobe applications. For instance, in InDesign an anchor point that has no curvature and no direction lines is called a "plain point"; an anchor point with independent direction lines is called a "corner point." Adobe Illustrator and other dedicated vector-drawing applications, however, from which InDesign got these tools and conventions, don't have "plain points." In fact, they refer to points without direction lines as corner points; anything *with* direction handles is a smooth or curve point. Even within InDesign itself the terms are used inconsistently. In the InDesign User Guide you'll often find instances of what InDesign usually calls "plain" points called "corner" points.

And, it's only InDesign that calls the curvature angle and depth-controlling lines that emanate from anchor points "direction lines." Traditional vector-drawing tools refer to them as "curve handles," often shortened simply to "handles."

Although the subject of this book is obviously InDesign, very few InDesign users don't also make use of other creative professional applications. Thus, despite InDesign's desire to have its own special lingo for long-established drawing constructs—lingo, I might add, that changes between versions and is inconsistently used even in different areas of the same version—I'll use the industry-standard lingo throughout the rest of the book. As you learn those terms, also keep in mind InDesign's unique corresponding terms, which you'll see from time to time in the application itself, often in pop-up tooltips.

Really, to understand this stuff, you have to do it. Let's give it a shot with another sample file I provided. From `http://www.sybex.com/go/MasteringInDesign`, open `pathtrace02.indd`. There's the S-curve. Let's trace it:

1. With the Pen tool, click the first anchor point (marked with the faded number 1) and drag down toward the solid number 1, trying to match your curve handle to mine. When you release the mouse button, you should see just an unassuming little anchor point. You've created curvature in the anchor point but not yet a path segment to show it off.

    Remember, although anchor points hold all the data, that data is invisible until a line is drawn to display it.

2. Repeat the procedure with the second anchor point, clicking and dragging again, following the point near the number 2. This time, as soon as you click the Pen tool onto the page, you'll notice the path segment. Dragging the curve handle around a bit will enable you to experiment with the depth and location of curve to fine-tune it.

    Did you notice any difference on your second anchor point? As soon as you create the second anchor point, defining that the path goes to the right from the first point, only one curve

---

In the circle, each anchor point side. Creating a perfect circle requ identical; a variance would distor up and down (90°) or flat (0° rota points themselves sit—Y or X, res

From the book's download pa the circle diagram there using th drew to close the circle.

How did it turn out? If it's no takes practice. Mastering the Pe other things in InDesign. Really tracing going pretty well, hide scratch. If not, practice some m

Forget to close a path or nee the last anchor point on the pa and resume drawing. Using th

Pen Tool Aspects and I

Like the pantheons of ancient manifest themselves in more the almighty Pen tool, like Z powers if not faces.

CONVERTING ANCHOR POINT

As you saw, path segments of an anchor point, and it w if you don't *want* curvature straight one?

High atop Mount Olym while drawing faster than

1. With the Pen tool, s ing. Make your firs

2. Before making the what happens. Not sor? That's the con anchor point from

3. Click the second a sponding to the p

4. Now, click away t with a straight pa

The same holds true if you start with a straight path and corner anchor point and need to make the next segment curved—click the last point and drag to expose the curve handle.

In its full Zeus incarnation, the Pen tool may appear to many as the Convert Direction Point tool, which is behind the Pen tool on the Tools panel. In this full manifestation, clicking a point will convert *both* sides of it, stripping away or granting curvature to the path segments of both sides simultaneously. As with the convert anchor point variant of the Pen tool, when going from corner to smooth anchor point with the Convert Direction Point tool, click and drag out a bit to reveal the curve handles. Later in this chapter we'll get into manipulating those curve handles after creation or initial conversion.

ADDING AND REMOVING ANCHOR POINTS

Another common consideration in drawing vectors is whether a path has too many or too few anchor points. To alter this, we have two more aspects of the Pen tool that render paths as malleable as the clay from which Jupiter, king of the Roman gods, purportedly formed mortal men and women.

Because each anchor point is plotted on the three-dimensional graph of X-, Y-, and Z-axes, and because each anchor point contains angle and curvature data, paths require computer processors to work out the math. Overly complicated paths and excessive anchor points cause slow screen redraws when scrolling and longer print times. Unnecessary anchor points in a path can also create an aesthetic issue: unwanted changes to the path directions or curvature. Check it out:

1. Select the Pen tool.

2. Move your cursor over a path segment, maybe around the middle between two anchor points. Notice the little plus sign added to the cursor?

3. Click, and a new anchor point is inserted at that point in the segment. The new anchor point can then be manipulated with the Direct Selection tool (we're getting to that) to alter the path at that point.

4. To infuse curvature in the same action, click and drag.

Removing extraneous points is just as easy: Position the Pen tool cursor over an anchor point instead of a path segment—presenting a nib with a minus sign—and click. With the anchor point and its associated angle or curve control removed, the path segments on either side will merge and adapt to account for the excised point. Consider the path smited.

If you need to add or delete more than a few points in a path, it's often more efficient to use a tool dedicated to the task. Once again behind the Pen tool on the Tools panel are other faces of the god: the Add Anchor Point tool and the Delete Anchor Point tool. Like Zeus in toga, in winged-helmeted battle armor, or in sandals and Golden Fleece, they're still the same formidable Pen tool, with the same powers.

DRAWING PERFECTLY STRAIGHT PATH SEGMENTS

Few know that the Pen tool can make perfectly straight, level lines without using guides. Unlike the other two incarnations of this same tool, the Pen tool in straight line mode doesn't just pick up slightly different cursors; it can do the job wearing its own face or a completely different one.

If you didn't draw your ellipse in exactly the dimensions you require, it can easily be resized via the Control or Transform panels like any other object. Or, if you know in advance the needed dimensions of the elliptical frame, there's a faster way. Instead of drawing and then resizing, grab the Ellipse Frame tool and click and release on the page instead of clicking and dragging. Up will pop a dialog with two simple options: the required width and height of the frame; set them and click OK.

Now you can fill the elliptical frame with color, imagery, or text (try text with the Justify All Lines alignment for an interesting effect).

POLYGON FRAME TOOL

With elliptical frames behind us, let's get into something more interesting: polygon frames (Figure 4.14). They're even more impressive in the color insert.

FIGURE 4.14
All of these objects were created by starting with the Polygon Frame tool.

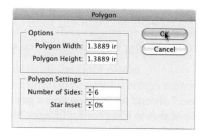

As with the Ellipse Frame tool, selecting the Polygon Frame tool and clicking the page or pasteboard brings up an options box. This one has the same height and width fields, but also two others (see Figure 4.15).

The Number of Sides field should be self-explanatory. In the percentage-based Star Inset field, though, you determine how deep those sides are set. A value of 0% means the polygon's sides will be flush with the outer diameter—a four-sided polygon would therefore be a perfect rectangle.

FIGURE 4.15
The Polygon Frame tool options dialog

Want to make a classic five-pointed star? Use the Polygon Frame tool with five sides and Star Inset value of 50%. How about the foundation shape for an official seal? Pick a high number of sides—maybe 25—and an inset of 5% to 10%. One of the most common uses I have for the Polygon Frame tool is creating equilateral triangles (three sides, 0% inset) that I'll often use as the starting point for more complex shapes, patterns, or even bullet glyphs.

Any time a polygon has an inset, InDesign automatically creates a second set of anchor points—the first for each apex, the second for each nadir. By starting with the Polygon Frame tool and manipulating the anchor points with the Direct Selection tool, Convert Direction Point tool, or other path modification tools, you can quickly create numerous complicated shapes.

Shape Tools

On the Tools panel next to the frame tools are the shape tools. They are the Rectangle, Ellipse, and Polygon tools. They are *exactly* like their matching frame tools. They're so identical, in fact, that they're superfluous—or the frame tools are. Six of one thing, half dozen of the other.

In InDesign, a frame is a frame is a frame. Shape objects are frames, and frames are shapes (and they are all paths). The only visual difference between them is the diagonal, intersecting lines in frames; they don't mean a thing. Don't believe me? Try it:

1. Draw a frame using one of the frame tools.

2. Beside it, draw a shape with one of the shape tools.

3. Now, select the Type tool (press T for expediency).

4. Click in the frame and start typing.

5. Okay. Now, with the Type tool still selected, click in the shape and start typing. Any difference?

Like most desktop layout programs, InDesign is built on the concept of the relationship between container and content. Everything you can create or place in the application is either content or a container to hold that content. Vector paths automatically form containers the instant the paths are closed. Because both frames and shapes are paths, they are both containers. Moreover, either may contain any of the following: fill colors (solid or gradient), images, text, vector objects, and even other containers.

So, you might ask, *If frames and shapes and their respective tools are identical, why do they both exist? Why not just have one set of tools and be done with it?*

The original intent of having both frame and shape tools was to distinguish between graphic frames, text frames, and vector design elements that wouldn't hold content. A noble intent, but it was quickly defeated by practicality; it's a lot faster to just select a frame and get to work than it is to select a frame and make an inconvenient trip to the Object ➤ Content menu before doing anything worthwhile.

The reason these redundant tools persist is simple hand-holding. Until just the last two versions, InDesign was locked in mortal combat with archrival QuarkXPress, another desktop publishing tool that *does* draw a distinction between frames (called boxes there) and shapes. In that veteran layout application, picture boxes may hold only graphics; to put text in them, you *must* first convert the container to a text box via menu commands. As you saw in InDesign, however, the only action required to convert a graphic frame to a text frame is to click in it with the Type tool. InDesign keeps the two sets of tools on hand as a learning aid for QuarkXPress converts. That's it, plain and simple. Eventually, in some later version of InDesign, the two sets of tools will merge, probably when Adobe wants to add another tool to the panel that isn't as easily relocated as the Measure tool.

FRAME-FIRST LAYOUT

Although there are still two sets of tools, they can be useful for frame-first (or box-first) layout work where an entire page's frames are created and placed ahead of their content. Because the frame tools have the big *X* through them, they provide a visual differentiation from tools that create decorative vector shapes. Having the obvious difference makes it easier and faster for others in the workflow to run through a page, flowing in text or dropping in images with less likelihood of accidentally putting one where the other should be.

If you draw one type of object—a shape to be a decorative vector object or a frame to hold text or a graphic—and later change your mind, there's no consequence to leaving them as they are. However, should you wish to be precise, you *can* convert one into another. Just select the object and choose one of the three types from the Object ➤ Content menu. The only time you really must do the conversion is if you've begun with a text frame but now wish to fill it with a placed graphic.

The Object ➤ Content commands will work only if the frame or path is empty. If you already have text or imagery in there, you'll need to delete it prior to converting the content type. To wipe existing text or imagery out of a frame, switch to the Text or Direct Selection tool, respectively, select the frame content, and press Delete or Backspace.

Reshaping Shapes

Creating shapes is only half the deal. It also helps to know how to *re*shape them.

Having begun with a standard rectangle, you may realize you'd prefer to have a rectangle with rounded corners. It can certainly be done with the Add Anchor Point tool, Delete Anchor Point tool, Convert Anchor Point tool, a few guides, and some careful path editing. Or, you could save yourself some work and simply use the menu command that does it automatically.

Near the bottom of the Object menu is a submenu, Convert Shape, that offers instant conversion of closed and open paths to any of nine shapes:

Rectangle	Inverse Rounded Rectangle	Polygon
Rounded Rectangle	Ellipse	Line
Beveled Rectangle	Triangle	Orthogonal Line

Give 'em a try:

1. Draw a shape—rectangle, ellipse, or polygon—select that shape with the Selection tool if it isn't already selected.

2. Choose Object ➤ Convert Shape ➤ Triangle. Faster than you can say it, you have a triangle.

3. With the same shape selected, choose Object ➤ Convert Shape ➤ Orthogonal Line. (An *orthogonal* line is one that is perfectly aligned to either the X-axis or Y-axis, horizontal or vertical, respectively.)

4. For real fun, grab the Pencil tool and draw a quick spiral in an empty area, then choose Object ➤ Convert Shape ➤ Inverse Rounded Rectangle.

Check *that* out, man! It doesn't matter how many anchor points were in your starting path or how many are required for the finished path, InDesign adds or removes as part of the process. With these commands, the only thing InDesign cares about is the overall size of the original object—more precisely, the bounding box area. If you start out with a 1 × 1-inch square and convert it to a triangle, you'll get a 1 × 1-inch triangle. The same is true when beginning with a 1-inch long line.

By now you should be asking, *How do I change the number of sides and indention in the Object ➤ Convert Shape ➤ Polygon or the radius of the rounded corners made by Object ➤ Convert Shape ➤ Rounded Rectangle?* And that would be a great question.

First, the number of sides resulting from a command to Object ➤ Convert Shape ➤ Polygon is whatever the current settings are for the Polygon Frame tool or the redundant Polygon tool:

1. On the Tools panel, select the Polygon Frame tool from behind the Rectangle Frame tool and double-click the Polygon Frame tool icon itself.

2. Up will pop the Polygon Settings dialog, where you can set the number of sides and the star inset.

Whatever options you set here are set for all future polygons—those created with the Object ➤ Convert Shape ➤ Polygon command, the Polygon Frame tool, and the Polygon tool.

Now, the way to determine the corner radius of rounded and inverse rounded rectangles is not the same—there isn't a rounded rectangle tool to double-click. Instead, those commands take their settings from the current Corner Options settings. In fact, the Rounded Rectangle, Beveled Rectangle, and Inverse Rounded Rectangle on the Object ➤ Convert Shape submenu are just shortcuts to the same features in Corner Options.

CS5

CORNER OPTIONS DIALOG

About halfway up the Object menu from Convert Shape is Corner Options, which is dramatically improved in InDesign CS5. Select—or draw—a rectangle and select Object ➤ Corner Options. You'll see a dialog like Figure 4.16.

FIGURE 4.16
The Corner
Options dialog

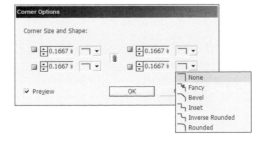

Each corner may be controlled separately, applying a different effect and/or radius. If the Make All Settings the Same button is active, depicting an intact segment of chain links, a change to one corner's options will reflect in the other three corners' options as well. Rendering the Make All Settings the Same button inactive, and thus causing it to display a broken chain link icon, enables individual alteration of each corner. Thus it's easy to round on the top-left and bottom-right corners, to have different radii per corner, or to use different effects on each corner. Corner Options are also live vector effects, meaning no permanent damage is ever done to your object, and you can always return to the Corner Options dialog to modify or remove a previously applied corner effect.

From the dropdown menu beside each corner you may choose Fancy, Bevel, Inset, Inverse Rounded, Rounded, and, of course, None for no alteration of the shape's corners—the last so you can remove previously applied corner options.

A Corner Option size equal to or greater than half the length of an object's side will completely round (or concave, or bevel, or whatever) that entire side. For example, if you apply a 0.5-inch rounded corner to a 1×1-inch square, you will convert the square into a circle. Putting the same rounded corners on a 4×1-inch rectangle will round the short sides, creating a pill shape.

Corner Options is not limited to rectangles. It can be applied to any vector shape—triangles, hexagons, 50-pointed stars, or whatever you like. The only difference is that, when applying corner effects to objects that have greater or fewer sides than four, you may only apply the same effect and radius to all corners; you cannot control corners individually. Naturally, it has no effect on ellipses, lines, and other objects devoid of corners. And, Corner Options cannot be used on placed images per se, but as you probably recall, placed objects are *content*, not containers. When an image is placed in InDesign, a container frame is automatically created, and that frame *is* a vector path and thus eligible for Corner Options. See Figure 4.17 for a few different things you can do with InDesign's Corner Options (see them in living color in the color insert).

FIGURE 4.17
Corner Options can do some nifty things.

WHEN INDESIGN CAN BE FASTER THAN ILLUSTRATOR

Interestingly, InDesign's Corner Options and convert to shape commands are sometimes faster than drawing the same object in Illustrator, which doesn't have such automated commands. Because InDesign and Illustrator are siblings, vector paths may be copied from one to the other and worked on in either. So, if you can't remember how to make a rounded rectangle in Illustrator, or if you want a 50-pointed star with beveled corners or a triangle with fancy corners, feel free to save yourself some forehead bruises by doing it in InDesign and then copying and pasting into Illustrator.

CS5

LIVE CORNERS EFFECTS

You may have noticed a new addition to bounding boxes surrounding rectangular paths. When a rectangular shape, frame, or even text frame is selected with the black arrow Selection tool, it displays in the upper-right corner a yellow box not unlike a control corner or a text frame's in and out ports (see Figure 4.18). Clicking the yellow box switches the path into Live Corners editing mode, with yellow diamonds in the corners. If you don't see that yellow box, choose View ➤ Extras ➤ Show Live Corners. If you don't see that yellow box in the grayscale figure, check its counterpart in the color insert.

FIGURE 4.18
A frame complete with the yellow box to enter Live Corners editing mode (left), and Live Corners controls in action rounding a rectangle in Live Corners editing mode (right)

In Live Corners editing mode, dragging a yellow corner control changes the radii of all four corners equally. To alter just one corner, press Shift before you begin dragging the corner control, and hold it down until you release the mouse button. To change the radius of the corner effect, drag a yellow diamond toward the center of the path. You can also change the shape of corners—cycling through Fancy, Bevel, Inset, Inverse Rounded, Rounded, and None—by holding Option/Alt and clicking a corner control. To change the shape of one corner individually, Shift+Option-click/Shift+Alt-click the corner control.

The Corner Options fields on the Control panel can help you precisely control the radius of one corner or all four at once (see Figure 4.19). Hidden within the Control panel is even a handy shortcut to the Corner Options dialog. Pop it open by holding Opt/Alt while clicking the icon beside the Corner Radius field in the Control panel.

FIGURE 4.19
Corner Options fields on the Control panel

As the name implies, Live Corners effects are *live*, meaning they can be edited (or removed) at any time. Applying corner effects is not a permanent alteration of the path shape, as would be a pathfinder operation (next section). Corner Options and Live Corners effects are effects, which change the *appearance and behavior* of a path without actually *altering* the path. That also means you can resize a path without distorting the corners! Unlike Illustrator, InDesign does not have an Expand command, so you cannot convert the corner effect to an actual path transformation—not that you really need that ability with the average corner-effected InDesign object.

There are two caveats to keep in mind as you work with Live Corners:

◆ Live Corners works only on *corners*, anchor points without curvature; you won't see any result if you try using them on smooth or curve anchor points from which extend curved path segments.

◆ Similarly, you may not see the result of Live Corners even if they work if your path has no fill and stroke or has a stroke too small to see at your current zoom level.

If you think Live Corners isn't working, ensure first that your path uses corner anchor points, and then try giving the path a fill color or gradient and/or increasing the weight of the stroke on the Stroke or Control panel.

MERGING, DIVIDING, AND OTHER PATHFINDER FUNCTIONS

You can make basic shapes. You can draw any other shape you need with the Pen and Pencil tools. You can even convert one shape into another and mess with its corners. But can you combine two separate shapes or knock one out of the other? That's what we're about to do:

1. Using one of the shape or frame tools, draw a rectangle.

2. Beside it, draw an ellipse.

3. Fill and stroke both shapes, but make sure to give them different colors.

4. Now, drag the ellipse until it partially overlaps the rectangle—about halfway should do nicely.

5. Select both shapes, and go to Object ➤ Pathfinder ➤ Add. You should get the result shown in Figure 4.20.

FIGURE 4.20
When two overlapping paths (left) are given the Pathfinder command to add, they merge into a single, amalgamated path (right). See them in two other colors in the color insert.

The Add command merges the two paths into a single, amalgamated shape. Click Undo, and try the next command on the Object ➤ Pathfinder menu, Subtract. Where the ellipse overlapped, the rectangle should now be bitten off. Undo again and try Object ➤ Pathfinder ➤ Intersect. You should have left only where the two shapes overlapped, wiping away any overhang.

Exclude Overlap is the opposite. It leaves the overhang and cuts out the area common to both shapes.

Lastly, Minus Back is the inverse of Subtract. Instead of knocking the front object out of the back, it punches the back shape out of the front. Figure 4.21 (and the same in the color insert) shows a few results from using Pathfinder commands.

FIGURE 4.21
Shapes resulting from using the Pathfinder commands

Add　　Subtract　　Intersect　　Exclude Overlap　　Minus Back

As you try out the Pathfinder commands, notice what happens to the fill and stroke colors of the resulting object, whether the front or rear object's colors are retained by the new shape. In most cases, the front object's attributes are retained. It's the opposite for Minus Back, though. And, it's not just fill and stroke colors that are assigned to this new *compound shape*. Object effects, drop shadow, transparency, and so forth assigned to the dominant path are retained by the resulting compound shape.

Also noteworthy is the fact that Pathfinder commands can be run on any ungrouped vector object—even text frames. Give it a shot with the ellipse and rectangle. Choose Object ➤ Pathfinder ➤ Intersect, grab the Text tool, and click inside the compound path; start typing. Want text that defines a shape or flows through a shape more eye-catching than a rectangle (see Figure 4.22)? Well, then, *there* you go.

FIGURE 4.22
Use Pathfinder commands for creative, eye-catching (or, in this case, gaudy) text frame shapes.

COMPOUND PATHS

Any time a Pathfinder command results in a shape that is more than a single, continuous path, you get what's called a *compound path*. Although *compound shape* is merely a descriptive term for a shape that is more complex than a rectangle, ellipse, or polygon and, in the grand scheme of things, hasn't much of a meaning, *compound path* is a more important term because it refers to a certain type of path. A compound path is a new, more complex type of path with different considerations than those for a simple, continuous path. It's multiple separate paths behaving as one.

Here's another opportunity to understand by doing:

1. Draw a perfect circle (you know two ways to do that quickly), and fill it with a solid color but without a stroke.

2. Atop the circle, create a five-pointed star that is larger than the circle (see Figure 4.23), and give it, too, a solid color fill and no stroke color.

FIGURE 4.23
We'll create a compound path by starting with a star overlapping a circle (see the color version in the color insert).

3. Select both the star and circle and go to Object ➤ Pathfinder ➤ Exclude Overlap. Your result should be similar to mine (Figure 4.24 and in the color insert), with the overlapping area knocked out and the resulting shape acquiring the star's fill and stroke attributes.

   A. Look closely at this new object, and select it with the Direct Selection tool; you'll notice all the anchor points throughout.

      See all those different shapes in there? All the separate filled areas? There's no way that object is a single continuous path. It can't be—it has 10 different filled areas, 10 different closed paths. That, ladies and gentlemen, is a compound path—multiple paths behaving as one.

B. Try changing the object's fill color—all areas will change simultaneously.

In many cases, you'll find that's the desired result. When it isn't, when you want to separately color the shapes in this compound path, remember this crucial piece of information: Move on to step 4.

FIGURE 4.24
After the Path-
finder ≻ Exclude
Overlap command,
a compound path
remains.

4. Although this will work however you've selected the compound path, let's keep it selected with the Direct Selection tool so we can more closely observe the changes to the object as we choose Object ≻ Paths ≻ Release Compound Path.

Do you see the difference? It's subtle.

A. Undo the last command and look at your compound path star. Where's the object center point? Right: in the center of the star.

B. Now press Cmd+Shift+Z/Ctrl+Shift+Z to redo the Release Compound Path command. Where is the center point now? Uh-huh. That's right: There isn't 1, but *10*.

All the shapes have been released to individual paths, with their own centers and their own independent paths. They can even be moved or edited independently if you wanted to do that (but not now).

5. Deselect all, and then select one of the star points. Give it a fill color. Good.

6. Now give the next star point a different color. Keep going until you've filled all five. Figure 4.25 (and the full-color version in the color insert) shows how my star looks so far (it also shows the center points and paths, in case you need to see them).

FIGURE 4.25
After releasing the compound path, each path is individually editable.

7. For this particular project, we don't want all the star points to be different colors, though. We want them the same color. In fact, we want the remaining circle sections to also match each other, but not with a solid color fill; we want them to have a radial gradient (see Figure 4.26). See what you can do to match your circle sections to mine.

   No luck on getting the circle parts to fill with a radial gradient like mine in Figure 4.26? Let me guess: You got a separate radial gradient in all five sections, didn't you? That's because we haven't done step 8 yet.

   Applying a gradient, object effects, and a few other things to multiple paths applies a new instance to each path. To get the desired effect for this project, we can't have separate paths. We need a compound path—but only of the circle pieces, not the star points, too, or we'll end up back at the same problem we faced in step 3.

8. Select all five sections of the circle and go to Object ➤ Paths ➤ Make Compound Path. Now we've turned these separate paths back into a compound path, which means they'll once again behave as if they were one path. Try giving it a radial gradient fill now. Better results, right?

9. Go ahead and deselect the circle parts compound path and select the individual star point paths.

10. Make a compound path of them as well, just for efficiency and expediency.

11. Now assign their fill color; I went with a solid red, but you're free to use any color or even another gradient if you like.

FIGURE 4.26
My star finished.
Yours will look
like this, too, after
a few more steps
(see the color
insert for a full-
color version).

What else can you do with compound paths? You can use them as containers for placed images:

1. Select your circle sections compound path.

2. Choose File ➤ Place, and import a photo. It will place right into the compound path.

Think about the possibilities that opens up for creative image frame shapes and vector elements.

Compound paths can also hold text, although the shapes we have with this star would be better suited to containing decorative text rather than copy you expect to be read. Click in it with the Text tool and start typing to see what I mean.

Of course, being a container, a compound path can hold other containers. Experiment and you'll come up with some really interesting ideas!

Now that I've told you where to find the Convert Shape and Pathfinder commands on the Object menu and you've gotten fairly comfortable with them, it's time to tell you that they are also available as buttons on the Pathfinder panel, available from Window ➤ Object & Layout ➤ Pathfinder. Accessing the controls from the Pathfinder panel is much easier than from the above-mentioned menus. The reason I didn't mention the panel earlier is because using the menus—indeed, this entire chapter—is wax-on/wax-off training. It's important that you learn things in a certain order and that you learn the more difficult ways of doing things before the easy, Daniel-san.

Editing Paths and Shapes

Creating paths? Check. Making shapes? Check. Reshaping them? Check. Now, what does an InDesigner do to gain total control over paths?

11. You saw what happened when you used the Convert Direction Point tool on an anchor point. Don't click this point. Instead, click *and drag* the little dot on the end of one curve handle to move it independently of the other curve handle. What you've done is sever the dependency between the two curve handles, enabling them—and their corresponding path segments—to be individually manipulated.

FIGURE 4.30
Converting the bottom point to a corner anchor point turns the curves it previously held into angles.

12. Switch back—fully—to the Direct Selection tool. The anchor point should remain selected.

13. Now grab one of the curve handles and drag it upward and inward toward the point. Keep dragging until you get a nice, smooth arc in the path segment on the same side of the formerly top anchor point (see Figure 4.31).

FIGURE 4.31
So far, so good with the disconnected curves

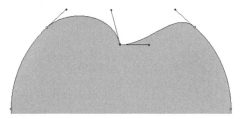

14. Do the same with the curve handle on the other side.

15. Now, we need to do something about those anchor points on the sides. Let's use the drag-selection method again to grab both of them at once. Click your Direct Selection tool a little ways off to the left, on the paper, and drag a selection rectangle rightward that covers both side—but no other—anchor points. Those two should become solid and all other anchor points hollow.

We'll get into scaling and transformations in a subsequent chapter, but let's jump ahead anyway.

16. Up on the Control panel, the third column of measurement boxes is the scale percentage fields. Just to their right is a tiny chain link icon. If that icon is a complete chain link, click it to break the chain link between X and Y scale percentages. Also click the center reference point in the Reference Point Proxy grid of nine points on the left end of the Control panel.

17. Now, set the X, upper, percentage to 90%. The shape will suddenly reduce its girth like cinching a belt (see Figure 4.32).

18. You have the basic shape now, so one at a time, select the side anchor points and adjust their curve handles to restore smooth, full curves to our shape.

FIGURE 4.32
After we scale the points, our shape is a little distorted.

Yes, I had you draw a heart. I *know* how corny and cliché and *almost* useless it is for you to know how to draw a heart in InDesign, of all programs. We're far enough into the book that I hope I've earned from you a little more patience, a little faith—at least enough to ask you to read a couple more paragraphs. This is important, and I beg of you, don't put the book down just yet. We've been through so much together; let's not end it on this note.

You're still here. *Thank you*. Here's what I need to tell you, and what I think you need to hear. True, we drew a heart. But, what we drew is nowhere near as important as all the things you learned from it. Specifically, you learned the following:

◆ How to select anchor points by clicking them with the Direct Selection tool, and how that tool's cursor changes as it approaches anchor points and curve handles. You can also select multiple, noncontiguous points by holding Shift as you click each one after the first.

◆ How to select one or more anchor points by dragging a selection area with the Direct Selection tool. That's crucial because the need to select and work with more than a few anchor points simultaneously is frequent.

◆ How to move anchor points with the keyboard—another crucial skill. They can also be moved with the mouse, of course, and if you hold Shift while you move them, their motion will be constrained to vertical (90°), horizontal (0°), or another increment of 45°, depending upon the direction of movement.

◆ How to change the Convert Direction Point tool into the Direct Selection tool temporarily, which saves trips back to the Tools panel.

◆ How to adjust anchor point curvature for a desired result.

◆ Reinforcements to skills you learned earlier, like adding anchor points to a path, converting anchor points from smooth to corner, and converting an anchor point so that its curve handles moved independently of one another instead of in tandem.

◆ What most would consider an advanced power tip—that anchor points in a path can be transformed with scale percentages the same way complete paths and objects can be transformed. Here's one better: It isn't just scaling. You can rotate, shear, and precisely position anchor points, too. We'll dive deep into those features in a later chapter, though.

There, that's my justification for the nearly unforgivable act of asking a professional such as yourself to draw a heart. It *was* a heart, true, but a simple heart brought so much knowledge and understanding. Can you forgive me?

Scissors Tool

Remember the Erase tool? The Scissors tool is *almost* like it in a different form. It's actually closer to the Paths commands, which are next, and why I saved discussing the Scissors tool until now.

When you break a path by dragging the Erase tool across a path segment, a gap occurs. That's why the Erase tool is meant to be smudged *along* a path instead of *across* it. To precisely split or *cut* a path without erasing parts of it, use the Scissors tool either on anchor points or on path segments. Clicking a path with the Scissors tool cuts it in that spot, creating two anchor points that rest atop each other. To split a closed path into two separate objects, use the Scissors tool twice. Try it out:

1. Draw a square and give it a solid color fill and contrasting stroke color.

2. Select the Scissors tool from the Tools panel and then *walk*, don't run, back to your square and click the top-left corner. Apparently, nothing should happen.

3. Again, move over to the bottom-right corner of the square and snip again with the Scissors.

4. Put the Scissors tool away and choose the Selection tool.

5. With that implement, click the top-right corner of the square and drag it away half an inch or so. If your scissor work was precise, your square should become two separate, but open, triangular paths like mine (see Figure 4.33).

FIGURE 4.33
Before snipping with the Scissors tool (left) and after (right)

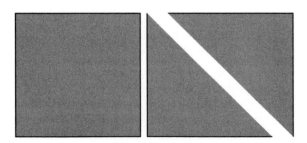

SELECTIVE SIDE-STROKING SCHEME

Observe the stroke on your pair of triangles. See how there's no stroke on the long edge of either path? That indicates that they're *open* paths, and this becomes an ultra-slick trick for applying strokes only to certain sides of an object!

The Scissors tool can split a path into two (or more) distinct paths, as you just did, but it can also be used to merely open up a path, say to reshape with the Direct Selection tool or expand it with the Pencil tool. Don't think of this tool solely as a device to turn one object into multiple objects. In fact, if you try to scissor a path containing text into two, it will fail. The first scissor will work, opening the path, but the second just doesn't—and with no warning from the otherwise prolific alerter InDesign.

If the path you divide includes a placed image, *all* resulting paths will contain copies of the same graphic, which can be a good thing or a bad thing. If the Links panel reports an external file as persisting in the document despite all attempts to remove it, look for any shapes that might have been split from others with the Scissors or Eraser tool or the Path commands.

PATH AND ANCHOR CONVERSION CONTROLS

If, like Medusa, you find that the gods aren't as benevolent to you as they should be, and you'd rather avoid paying alms to the various alternate incarnations of the Pen and Pencil tools, you can achieve many of the same results using menu commands and buttons.

On the Object ➤ Paths menu you'll find commands to Join, Open, Close, and Reverse paths. Similarly, the Object ➤ Convert Point menu includes commands to convert a select anchor point to a Plain, Corner, Smooth, or Symmetrical point. The revamped Pathfinder panel (Window ➤ Object & Layout ➤ Pathfinder) even includes buttons that match these commands (see Figure 4.34).

FIGURE 4.34
The Pathfinder panel

Here's how to use the Pathfinder panel's Paths buttons and matching Object ➤ Paths commands:

Join Path   Select two open paths and use this button to have InDesign automatically draw a path segment connecting the two closer end points, thus combining the two paths into a single, open path. Repeat this procedure to join the opposite ends of the formerly separate paths into a single closed path, if desired. Path segments generated by the Join Path command will inherit curvature from smooth anchor points; when connecting corner points, the generated path segments will be straight lines between two end points.

11. Once you've tweaked the paths to your satisfaction, select all the initials with the Selection tool and combine all three paths into a single path with the appropriate command on the Pathfinder panel or the Object ➢ Pathfinder menu.

12. With the permanently fused initials path selected, choose File ➢ Place and import an image, as I've done in Figure 4.38. Resize and move the placed image, if needed, with the Direct Selection tool as you would the content of any other container.

13. Finish off your logo with a tagline, additional elements, or whatever else is needed.

FIGURE 4.38
Letters have become a graphic frame into which you can place an image (see also the color version in the color insert).

Maybe you don't need a personal logo; maybe you already have one and you're happy with it. Where else might this technique prove useful? What about the masthead for a magazine or newsletter? Cover art for a book or annual report? If you have any symbol fonts like Zapf Dingbats, MiniPics, Wingdings, Webdings, or even Windows's Marlett, you have ready-made clipart in them that can be turned into truly unique graphic or even text frames in a snap. Figure 4.39 shows a few things I've created with this technique.

FIGURE 4.39
A few other ideas for type converted to frames (for a color version, take a look at the color insert)

The Bottom Line

Draw Precise Paths with the Pen Tool Precision drawing, the ability to create any shape, requires mastery of the Pen tool.

Master It Reopen pathtrace01.indd from the files that you downloaded from the Web. Instead of tracing it with merely straight path segments, use what you've learned about corner anchor points and smooth anchor points to trace it faithfully—straight where needed, curved where needed. Set the fill for your traced letters to contrast with the original orange ones, and when you've finished tracing, zoom in to examine how closely you were able to come to the original shapes.

Draw Paths Freehand with the Pencil Tool   The Pen tool is synonymous with precision and the Pencil tool with freedom. Sometimes, quickly drawing something with a natural feel is more important than precision.

> **Master It**   Open a new document and, using the Pencil tool, draw your own cartoonish self-portrait. Get it all sketched out before worrying about the paths themselves. Once it's done, go back with the Smooth tool and, if needed, the Erase tool to clean it up.

Combine and Subtract Shapes, and Convert from One Shape to Another   Many complex paths begin with simple geometric shapes. Indeed, most objects you create in InDesign will *be* simple geometric shapes, alone or compounded with other shapes.

> **Master It**
>
> 1. Draw three shapes—a circle, a triangle, and a square—each exactly 2 inches in diameter.
>
> 2. Convert the triangle and square to circles.
>
> 3. Manually position the circles into a rough triangular formation. Each circle should overlap its neighbors, with all three overlapping in the center. Select all three.
>
> 4. Exclude the overlaps.
>
> 5. Release the compound path, and fill each resulting shape with color individually.

Apply Live Corners Effects   InDesign's new Live Corners is a dramatic improvement over the already pretty good corner effects in earlier versions. With it you can drag to create and edit different types of corner effects and/or use the Corner Options dialog for even greater precision. The Live Corners effects in InDesign are so advanced that many Illustrator users create corners in InDesign and then paste them into Illustrator.

> **Master It**   As a demonstration of what Live Corner Effects can and cannot do, create three paths and apply Live Corner Effects to them. One of those paths should show corner effects, while the other two objects should be examples of two circumstances in which Live Corner Effects produces no—or no visible—result.

Modify Any Vector Artwork   Precision drawing mastery requires precision path editing.

> **Master It**   Beginning with a pentagon, employ the Convert Direction Point tool and Direct Selection tool to convert the straight segment shape into a five-pointed star with concave sides like this:

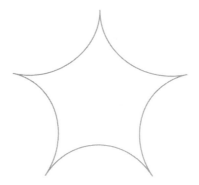

Turn Type into a Container to Hold Images or Text Strictly speaking, the technique of converting readable type into frames should be used infrequently. When used on symbol font glyphs, though, it's a great way to make short work of creating complicated shapes for use as frames or merely decorative elements.

Master It Using a font installed on your computer—preferably a symbol font—locate a suitable glyph using the Glyphs panel. Set and style it on the page and convert it to frame. Fill the frame with text—your own or InDesign's placeholder text.

Chapter 5

Images

InDesign's greatest strength, the area in which it towers head and shoulders over all challengers, is its type-handling and -rendering features. Fortunately, it's just as good with imagery—especially in CS5.

In this chapter, you will learn to

◆ Place image assets

◆ Import images without the Place command

◆ Preview and organize files with Mini Bridge

◆ Manage placed assets

◆ Go native in your workflow

◆ Create and use Live Captions

Placing Assets

> *Picture pages, picture pages, now it's time for picture pages, time to grab your crayons and your pencil....*
>
> —Bill Cosby, the Captain Kangaroo *show*

Images, like text, are content and must be encapsulated within containers—frames. And as with text, you have a choice as to when and how you create the frame: Frames can be created manually and later filled, or you can skip that step, letting InDesign create the frame automatically upon placement of an image.

Frame-First Workflow

A *frame-first workflow*—also called forms-based, templated, box-first, or grid-first workflow (this last is technically erroneous because all layouts should begin with a grid regardless of the way assets are placed)—begins with the containers and fills them with content later. You already know about working frame-first if you've ever used QuarkXPress, which *only* works frame-first.

Solo designers and graphic design studios with varied clients and projects won't often employ frame-first workflows simply because most of their client assignments begin after content has been created; they're hired to lay out that content. Creatives working in publishing houses, corporate

design departments, and other environments with a narrower focus are often required to design templates and layouts at the same time other departments or agencies are creating the content.

A product catalog, for example, is typically built on a rigid grid. The layout artist knows in advance approximately how many products she must list and the target page count. From there, she can extrapolate the number of products each page must contain and thus the amount of space each product entry is allowed for copy and imagery. Until the photogs and copyeditors turn in all the material, the layout artist can't place actual content, but she can build templates in preparation for that moment. Figure 5.1 shows what one catalog page template might look like before content is available.

FIGURE 5.1
A typical catalog page built frame-first

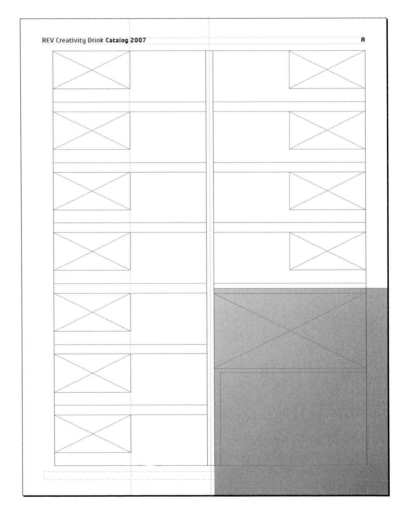

Here, 11 product photos (the frames with diagonal crossbars through them) and their accompanying textual descriptions (the empty frames surrounding the image frames) are arranged and ready to receive content. In the lower-outside corner (lower-right on this right-read page), a featured

product will benefit from a larger image and more copy atop a colored background. Thus, each page can comfortably carry a dozen products. The designer has done the math—probably with *FPO* images and text—and determined the appropriate size at which the average product photo and its description should lay out. When photos are ready, they will be fit into the waiting image frames; the same for copy in its frames. Until the product shots and copy arrive, this page is finished.

That's frame-first page construction—building spaces ahead of content.

Go ahead and build a quick frame-first layout similar to the one in Figure 5.1. Don't get overly concerned with the text frames. You'll need two or three at least, but don't spend too much time styling them.

Ready? Let's go through the various ways to fill those image frames.

Image Import Options

The most common method of importing an image is via File ➤ Place (or the Place shortcut of Cmd+D/Ctrl+D)—just as with placing text documents. Basic asset placement you already know, so we'll skip the beginner-level stuff and dive right into the various types of image assets InDesign will import and the options available for each. So, go ahead and open the Place dialog. Which types of images *can* InDesign place within frames? Plenty! Table 5.1 shows them.

TABLE 5.1:   Graphic file formats supported by InDesign

FILE FORMAT	DOCUMENT DESCRIPTION AND SUPPORTED CHARACTERISTICS
TIFF, TIF	Tagged Image Format; supports single page, compressed or uncompressed
GIF	Graphical Interchange Format; supports single frame
PNG	Portable Network Graphics; supports single-frame, alpha transparency
JPG, JPEG, JPE	Joint Photographic Experts Group
PDF	Portable Document Format; supports layers, multiple pages (one page per import), alpha transparency
AI	Adobe Illustrator document; supports layers, alpha transparency
PSD	Photoshop document; supports layers, layer sets, alpha transparency
EPS	Encapsulated PostScript
PICT	Macintosh vector/raster hybrid
WMF	Windows Meta File vector/raster hybrid
EMF	Enhanced Windows Meta File vector/raster hybrid
FLV, F4V	Flash Video movies; shows only poster frame on the page but plays in the Preview panel and on export to interactive PDF or SWF

TABLE 5.1: Graphic file formats supported by InDesign *(CONTINUED)*

FILE FORMAT	DOCUMENT DESCRIPTION AND SUPPORTED CHARACTERISTICS
MP4	H.264-encoded movie; shows only poster frame on the page but plays in the Preview panel and on export to interactive PDF or SWF
MOV	QuickTime Movie; shows only poster frame on the page but plays in the Preview panel and on export to interactive PDF (legacy video format; support for this format is being phased out)
AVI, WMV	Windows video formats; shows only poster frame on the page but plays in the Preview panel and on export to interactive PDF (legacy video format; support for this format is being phased out)

Because InDesign doesn't draw as much of a distinction as other applications do between *types* of content—text, imagery, even audio and video media—the Place dialog will automatically show every importable file type. Even if you have a graphic frame selected, InDesign will present textual documents as place options. Remember, a container is a container, and content is content; InDesign's frames can hold any type of supported content.

At the bottom of the Place dialog is the same Show Import Options check box we examined while working with ASCII and Word documents. The import options themselves, however, are quite different.

BASIC RASTER IMAGES

When you're importing basic raster or bitmap images like JPEGs, GIFs, and TIFFs, the Image Import Options dialog contains two panes (see Figure 5.2). The first, Image, offers the option of applying an embedded Photoshop *clipping path* (if included in the image) to crop the image content. If the image contains *alpha channels*, one may be chosen here as well.

FIGURE 5.2
Image Import
Options

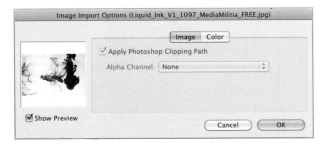

Alpha channels are extra channels in the image to define transparency or a selection. Every time you use Quick Mask mode to paint a selection, for example, Photoshop creates a special alpha channel called Quick Mask (see Figure 5.3). Save a selection from Select ➤ Save Selection in Photoshop, and you're really creating a new channel that, upon placement of the image into InDesign, can be selected on the Image tab as the alpha channel—only the areas selected in the original marquee will appear while the rest is hidden.

FIGURE 5.3
The Channels panel in Photoshop CS5 displaying a saved selection channel (Non White Areas) and the temporary Quick Mask channel created while in Quick Mask mode

The other tab available when you're importing basic bitmap images is Color, which enables you to specify an *ICC color profile* and *rendering intent* specific to the image (see Figure 5.4). Oh, yes, InDesign can manage the color of every placed image independently of one another and of the entire document. For more about per-image color management or color profiles, check out Chapter 10, "Preflight."

FIGURE 5.4
Importing an image offers individual color management of the image independent of the document or other images.

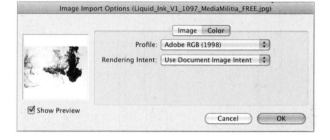

PNG

When you place a PNG in InDesign, you'll get the same Image Import Options dialog with the same Image and Color tabs as with other raster formats, but you'll also get a third tab (see Figure 5.5).

FIGURE 5.5
Image Import Options, PNG Settings

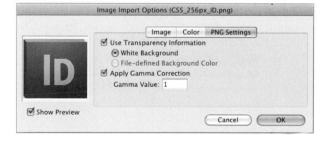

Because PNGs have alpha channel transparency—effectively, if you can create the transparency effect in Photoshop, PNG will display it that way—your first option is what to do with the background. If you'd like to preserve the transparency, check Use Transparency Information.

With that on, InDesign needs to know how to mix semitransparent areas—on white or on the background color defined in the image. For example, do you want this 50% opaque blue mixed with white so it looks 50% opaque blue, or should it mix with yellow so the result is green? Of course, if you use only PNGs created by Photoshop, Illustrator, and other Adobe products, you won't have to worry about the background color option. PNGs created by Adobe software don't have available background color definitions, and the only option is white.

Apply Gamma Correction allows you to compensate for the fact that PNGs are usually slightly off in their *gamma* ranges. If you placed a PNG and a PSD of the same image side-by-side—indeed, if the former was *made from* the latter—the PNG will look a few shades darker. It's just a PNG thing, homey. P-N-G representin', yo! By adjusting the gamma correction here, you can compensate for the inherent darkness of the PNG.

EPS

Let's just run through the EPS Import Options (see Figure 5.6) and how InDesign handles placed EPS files.

FIGURE 5.6
The EPS Import
Options dialog

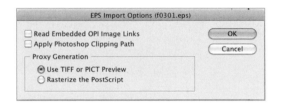

EPS is a simplistic format, and it has few options on import.

It can contain a vector clipping path and an *OPI* link. OPI stands for Open Prepress Interface, which is a process by which a low-resolution or FPO image is temporarily substituted for the high-resolution, final image. For instance, if you're doing the layout on a magazine article while the real photos are still out at the color correction house, you can use a picture of a LOLcat as FPO and then embed in the EPS a statement that links to the predetermined path and filename of the final image. At some point—conversion to PDF, print from InDesign, or in RIP—the final image will be sucked in via the OPI link to replace the FPO image, but retaining the position, scale, and crop settings of the FPO.

If yours is among those workflows using OPI, make sure to check the Read Embedded OPI Image Links option. That will tell InDesign to maintain the link to final assets, which enables their inclusion when you're printing directly from InDesign and maintains the links when InDesign content is exported or sent to RIP.

EPS files are pure PostScript code. Thus, in order to render them to screen, an application must contain—or have access to—a PostScript interpreter. Without an interpreter, you get a gray box with no idea of what's actually in the image. Until the last couple of versions, that's what you'd get if you placed an EPS image into Microsoft Word.

Twenty years ago, when Adobe was still building support for PostScript, few applications could render EPS files natively onscreen. They printed beautifully to PostScript printers, but that wasted a lot of paper because creatives moved an EPS, printed a proof, moved it a little more,

printed another proof, and so on. To compensate, Adobe enabled EPS files to generate and carry low-resolution raster preview images, first in the Mac-native PICT format and then on Windows as well with TIFF-based previews. With the embedded raster previews, more applications are able to display something other than a gray box without the need for their developers to pay Adobe for a PostScript license. (That's something they don't like doing, as evidenced by the Font Wars of the early 1990s, which began and begat the TrueType font format, because Microsoft and Apple no longer wanted to pay licensing fees for Adobe's PostScript interpreter, which was required to render Type 1 PostScript fonts on the screens of Windows and Mac computers.)

When you create an EPS in Illustrator or Photoshop, for example, you're asked whether to include a preview and, if so, whether it should be black and white (a 1-bit, no-shades-of-gray B&W) or color and whether any empty space between the EPS artwork and the rectangular bounding box that contains it should be rendered as transparent or white. Pay particular attention to that last statement because it's the cause of a lot of cranial injuries due to repetitive wall and desk impacts.

Take a look at Figure 5.7, which is Illustrator CS5's Save As EPS Options dialog. You can see the Preview Format dropdown, which is where you choose color or black-and-white raster preview images. Just below that are radio buttons to make the background transparent or opaque (white). If the creator of the EPS chooses Opaque, when you place that EPS into InDesign, *it will have an opaque background*. Former QuarkXPress users will immediately jump to the conclusion that the frame containing the EPS is defaulting to filling with white (paper color in InDesign), which XPress did until version 7. Naturally, they'll click the None color swatch to clear it. When that doesn't work, the forehead-to-desk percussion usually begins.

FIGURE 5.7
Illustrator CS5's EPS Options dialog appears when you're saving a document as EPS.

If you happen to find yourself unable to explain a white background on an imported EPS… well, there's the explanation. Pull the EPS into Illustrator and resave it with a transparent preview background.

Or, you could always just chuck the preview entirely and tell InDesign to build its own by selecting Rasterize the PostScript. It won't *really* rasterize the image itself; you'll still get crisp vector output. This option only creates a new preview proxy for onscreen viewing. Moreover, InDesign's proxy creation is usually better than the previews embedded in the EPS files themselves. I usually check Rasterize the PostScript for all my EPS imports.

If you infrequently work with EPS images and are prone to forget little details like how to overcome a white background, I humbly suggest you dog-ear this page. A concussion is not a laughing matter.

PSD PHOTOSHOP DOCUMENTS

InDesign can place native Photoshop PSD documents and Illustrator AI documents (see the following section for the latter). You don't *need* to save Photoshop documents to TIFF or Illustrator artwork to EPS in order to place them into the page layout application anymore!

As with other image formats, the Image Import Options dialog for PSD files includes Image and Color tabs to access alpha channel transparency and color management, respectively. It also includes a Layers tab (see Figure 5.8).

FIGURE 5.8
Importing a layered PSD enables the Layers tab in Image Import Options.

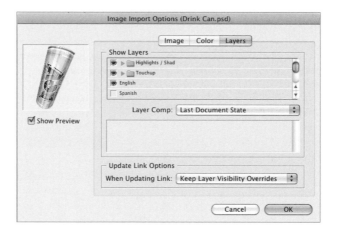

Here you can see a multilingual product shot mocked up in Photoshop. In that application, I used layers to set the label text in English, Spanish, French, Italian, and German without resorting to five separate PSD documents that I'd have to tweak and touch up to match client change requests. All the common image elements—the 3D can, the highlights and shadows, the logo— are contained on their own layers used globally in all language versions; only the variable text is separated onto individual layers.

In the top section, Show Layers, I can turn the PSD image's layers on and off individually. If I needed to place the version of the can en Español, all I'd have to do is turn off the English layer and turn on the Spanish. It even correctly interprets Photoshop's layer groups; thus I can hide or show an entire range of layers with a single toggle of the eyeball. Even better, InDesign has *Layer Comp* control.

Real World Scenario

CREATING LAYER COMPS IN PHOTOSHOP

What are layer comps? They're snapshots of the state of layers in a Photoshop document—which are on, which are off, their blending modes, and their positions. For instance, let's say in Photoshop you have a five-layer document. Everything looks good, but you'd like to experiment a little, maybe try a different arrangement of objects, maybe see how changing Layer 3's blending mode from Hard Light to Difference would affect the overall design. You want to play around a bit but not lose your way back. Undo will only save you so many times. You could make a history state snapshot, but that's a little risky. Duplicating the image would work, but it would also leave you with multiple separate files if you decided to retain the variants—maybe to show the client the customary (and often ill-advised) three versions of a design. Instead of creating multiple copies of the same document, make a layer comp:

1. Open the Layer Comps panel in Photoshop (Window ➤ Layer Comps).

2. With all the layers of the first version on and set the way you want, create a new layer comp by clicking the button at the bottom of the panel.

3. Name it something like **First Version**.

4. Start moving and changing things.

5. When you have another design you like, create a second layer comp.

6. Keep going until you have all the designs and layer comps you want.

   Now, in the Layer Comps panel, you should note that only one layer comp is visible at a time.

7. Click the empty box to the left of First Version, and *that* layer comp will become the active one, with only its constituent layers active and set the way they were in the beginning.

8. Turn on Second Version, and the layers will shift again. At the bottom of the panel there are even left and right arrows to cycle up or down through all the layer comps.

Voila! Multiple designs and variants in the same Photoshop document.

Layer comps track layers, not the image data on them. Layer visibility, position, blending mode, transparency, and effects *are* tracked and managed via layer comps, but if you swipe a paintbrush across a layer or fix a typo in a text layer, that change ripples through all comps. If you need to modify the actual content of a layer, duplicate it and make the duplicate part of the next layer comp.

I've used layer comps on numerous projects, including the drink-can design, for multilingual work. More often, I've used it for variations and managing multiple but closely related assets as a single entity—for instance, color and grayscale versions of the same image in one PSD. In Photoshop, layer comps enable efficiency by reducing the number of documents and thus the amount of duplicate layer-based data that must be managed across all those documents. Carrying them through to InDesign offers the same advantages—one asset to update instead of four or five, one file to package and send to press instead of four or five. You get the point.

Upon placing a PSD with layer comps into InDesign, you have access through the Image Import Options dialog to those layer comps in the Layer Comp dropdown list. Just pick one and go.

The Last Document State option imports the image however it was last saved in Photoshop—including which layer comp was chosen and which layers were on. Editing the image in

(File ➤ Export, choose EPS, JPEG, SVG, or PDF format), there are significant drawbacks to that method. Specifically these:

◆ It's one-page-at-a-time export. If you need images of every page of a 32-page publication, you have to repeat the process—go to the page, ensure it's the current page, select File ➤ Export, set the format to EPS, name the file, click Save—32 times.

◆ It's one-page-at-a-time import. To place those 32 pages, you have to do it 32 times.

◆ Exporting pages creates a whole new file—more assets to manage, more likelihood of missing or corrupted files, and more potential RIP problems.

◆ Exported pages are copies, not the original pages. If the actual layout of the page design changes—say, at the last minute the cover photo for the next issue changes—you must rebuild and replace the EPS of pages, again, one at a time.

◆ Exported images are EPS, an obsolete format, although InDesign does a great job with EPS previews, as do recent versions of QuarkXPress. Even QuarkXPress, the application that pioneered the methodology, didn't, prior to version 6.5, include a screen preview that could be considered reliable relevant to the print output.

Most of us have learned as a matter of necessity to work around the drawbacks, but now, why bother? InDesign solves all these drawbacks and problems:

◆ *Problem:* It's one-page-at-a-time export. *Solution:* There is no export; just save the source INDD document.

◆ *Problem:* It's one-page-at-a-time import. *Solution:* Importing InDesign INDD documents is exactly like importing PDFs, with an identical dialog and the ability to import one, all, or a range of pages, which will place sequentially from the on-deck place queue just as with multipage PDFs.

◆ *Problem:* Exporting pages creates a whole new file. *Solution:* There is no export and no additional assets to manage.

◆ *Problem:* Exported pages are copies, not the original pages. *Solution:* There is no export. When the source INDD changes, update linked assets to reflect those changes in the placed instance(s) within the current layout.

◆ *Problem:* Exported images are EPS, an obsolete format. *Solution:* There is no spoon, Neo.

You can place one InDesign document inside another, although you cannot do a "hydra import," an asexual import wherein the *same* InDesign document is placed back into *itself* as an asset. If that's what you need, consider your options. Longer documents can, for other reasons as well, often benefit from being split into multiple files coupled by an InDesign Book. With a Book tying them together, styles and swatches can remain synchronized, as can page and section numbers, and all documents in the publication can be printed, packaged, and exported to PDF simultaneously, just as can a single document. If a Book doesn't makes sense for your document, yet you still need to place a page from the current document as an asset on another page, save the asset version as a separate, complete copy of the document. Then, if the source page changes in the final deliverable, just make a new copy of the master document, overwriting the asset ver-

sion, and update links. That is still more reliable and faster than taking the route of export to EPS, JPEG, SVG, or PDF; it does result in a larger package for print, though.

Multiple Asset Place

Multiple concurrent asset placement works not just with multiple pages of one PDF or INDD but with a whole set of images—you can even mix imagery and text!

Let's jump right into a hands-on exercise:

1. Ready a folder of images and textual documents. You're welcome to use the resource files found in other chapter folders on this book's download files. The key is that they must be copied to the same folder.

2. Press Cmd+D/Ctrl+D to open the Place dialog, and navigate to the folder of images and/ or textual documents.

3. Select up to 10 of the files in the list (you can use more than 10 files; I just don't want you bogged down trying this hands-on exercise by having to place 40 or 50 images).

   On both Windows and Mac, select sequential files in a list by clicking the first, and then, while holding Shift, clicking the last. All those between will be added to the selection. To highlight nonsequential files, or to selectively remove certain files from the group, hold Ctrl (Windows) or Option (Mac) while clicking the undesirables.

4. Got your files selected? Good. Let's speed this up by *unchecking* Show Import Options, and then click OK. For textual documents like Microsoft Word and RTF files, InDesign might take a moment to process styles in the document.

   You'll be deposited back into your document with a loaded cursor and preview image. Just to the right of the cursor itself, within the thumbnail, will be a number in parentheses. This is the number of on-deck files waiting to be placed.

5. Click once inside the first image frame on the page—it will fill with the image you just saw thumbnailed, and the next image in the stack will appear in thumbnail. Click the next frame to fill it, too.

   If you encounter a text document, which will be obvious by the first few words appearing as its thumbnail, click a text frame instead.

6. Before placing the third image, look at it. It's not the one you *want* to place third, is it? (Humor me.) The order in which a filesystem sorts the list in the Place dialog does not always match the order in which you'd like to place the images. In some cases, you know which goes where, but sometimes it's just easier to change the order of the images to be placed and queue up a different one.

   How? The Up arrow and Down arrow keys on your keyboard. Try them out to cycle forward and back, respectively, in the stack of on-deck assets to be placed. The thumbnail preview will show what's in front, what will be deposited in the layout upon the next click.

7. Go ahead and fill the rest of the frames until you've emptied the place queue.

There are a few other things you should know about multiple-asset place. When you have just one asset to place, pressing Esc will clear the place cursor and return you to an unloaded cursor. With multiple assets loaded in the cursor, however, Esc clears only the frontmost (displayed) asset; the rest of the stack remains. If you want to clear out of a loaded queue of 20 pictures, switch tools by choosing one on the Tools panel.

When you turn off Show Import Options, the last selected options for a given file type are used. For instance, if, when placing a single PDF, you choose to import all pages and then, on a subsequent place operation, disable Show Import Options and place multiple assets including a multipage PDF, you'll place each page of that PDF in turn. The on-deck count *does not* add in the number of PDF pages; instead, it counts the PDF itself as one asset regardless of its page count. For example, if you place a 100-page PDF and a PSD, the on-deck count will list only 2 even though it will place 101 individual images.

Drag and Drop

Everyone uses File ➢ Place (or Cmd+D/Ctrl+D), which is the least efficient of the methods in versions prior to CS3. Now, with the ability to place multiple assets concurrently, the Place command has suddenly become extremely useful again—more so in some scenarios than this next method. Still, drag-and-drop asset placement has its own significant advantages, especially when you need only a few images from a folder of assets or if you need several assets across multiple folders.

Have you heard of Adobe Bridge (see Figure 5.11)?

FIGURE 5.11
Adobe Bridge digital asset manager

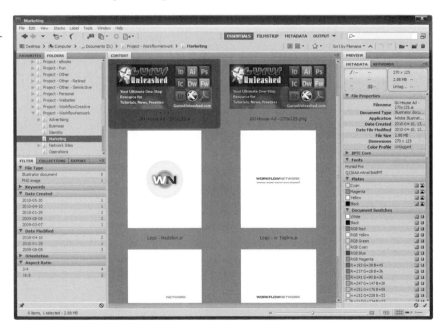

Adobe Bridge is a mid-level desktop digital asset manager (DAM) included as part of Creative Suite and with any stand-alone CS5-version application. I'm not going to devote a lot of time to discussing it because (a) I have limited page count in this book, and (b) I can probably talk my

publisher into letting me write a separate Adobe Bridge book in which I'll have several hundred pages to really go into all its cool, efficiency-building features. Suffice it to say, Bridge is pretty darn cool, with a lot of hidden features and nuances that can really speed up your work and take some of the focus off the tools and put it where your attention belongs—on your designs.

What I *do* want to talk about here is that Bridge is a visual DAM, allowing you to manage your assets by actually *seeing* them instead of trying to remember in the Place dialog the differences between photographs labeled `prodshoot070419-0067.jpg` and `prodshoot070419-0068.jpg`. With Bridge and other DAM software (like Apple's iPhoto, Extensis's Portfolio, Cerious Software's ThumbsPlus, and others), you can view thumbnails of your images, zooming in or out as needed, and manage them visually—move, delete, duplicate, reorganize, and so on.

You're Holding the Proof

Incidentally, Adobe Bridge was integral to the creation of this book by managing all my screen shots in various versions and states, the sample files destined for the download Web page, all my make-readies for the screen shots, and pictures of my wife and daughter, which I like to look at every so often while working.

One advantage Bridge has over the competition is that it will thumbnail not just graphics files; it also shows previews of Photoshop, Illustrator, Acrobat, Microsoft Office, and even InDesign documents. (Note that in order for Bridge to display thumbnails of Adobe application files, they must have an embedded preview image, which is an option in the Save As dialog or Preferences for each application.)

Although ThumbsPlus won't do InDesign documents, PDFs, and Office files, it *will* show thumbnail-sized previews of fonts—TrueType and OpenType but not PostScript. Bridge won't do fonts at all, leaving you to the horrid little preview windows of modern font managers.

Getting back to the main point of placing images, you can drag and drop directly from Bridge (or any of the aforementioned DAM utilities) into InDesign. Choose the *picture* you want to place, not the filename.

Position the Bridge window such that you can see your InDesign layout simultaneously (multiple monitors help); then drag an image from Bridge and drop it atop a frame in InDesign. Voila! Placed image.

Working content-first, you can even place multiple images simultaneously, though not into preexisting frames. Select the images in Bridge using Shift (sequential) or Cmd/Ctrl (nonsequential); then, in one motion, click an already selected image and drag it out of Bridge and over an empty area of the InDesign document. All the images selected in Bridge will stack up on a loaded cursor, ready to place as linked assets in InDesign. Note that, when using drag-and-drop image placement, InDesign will use the previously chosen or default import options for each file type; you won't see an Import Options dialog.

Because Bridge can also manage textual files—PDFs, Word documents, TXT files, RTF files, InCopy INCX documents, and even other InDesign INDD documents—they can also be imported via drag and drop.

Any other DAM application that affords the user drag-and-drop file-management capability can also be used in the same manner, as just described. iPhoto on Mac OS X is great for

Illustrator). InDesign, however, doesn't have a 3D Revolve effect, has no concept of lighting—three-dimensional or otherwise—and just doesn't get it. Consequently, you might expect that copying the 3D object from Illustrator and pasting into InDesign would result in just the original path, sans 3D, in InDesign. Fortunately, if that's what you expected, you'd be wrong.

In Figure 5.16, you can see three versions of an urn:

◆ In Illustrator, I drew a relatively simple path (highlighted on the left) and revolved it into a 3D urn. This is a live effect—I can change the path at any time and the 3D Revolve effect will update the three-dimensional shape to match my changes.

◆ The center version is the same object copied from Illustrator and pasted into InDesign. Notice how it looks identical? What really happened is that the 3D effect was converted to flat paths, maintaining the object's appearance by sacrificing the reality.

◆ If I ungrouped the paths in InDesign, I'd be left with hundreds of little slivers, which you can see as individual paths in the picture on the right. That one is the object copied in InDesign and pasted back into Illustrator. The ability to edit the 3D shape easily is gone; if I needed to change the shape or color of the urn, I'd have to spend hours doing it.

In this case, I'd re-create the object from scratch, hoping I remembered or could re-create the exact 3D Revolve settings, light source positions, and so on. Odds are, it would take me less than five minutes to re-create the urn; with something complicated, though, I could be looking at hours or days worth of redrawing time just because I thought copy and paste would be faster initially.

There's the pro *and* the con: You can copy native objects from Illustrator and have them become native objects in InDesign—no rasterization. Draw a couple of rectangles or stars in Illustrator, paste them into InDesign, and you can edit their paths further there. You can also change their colors and transparency, move around the constituent objects in a group pasted in, and so on. However, if you get something InDesign doesn't understand—like the 3D urn—InDesign will *make it understandable* and could thereby reduce or eliminate your ability to later edit the object.

TROUBLESHOOTING: PASTE FROM ILLUSTRATOR CREATES A FLAT IMAGE

If, when you copy something from Illustrator and paste it into InDesign, you get only a flat image without individually editable paths, the problem is not within InDesign, although that would be a logical assumption. In Illustrator, on the File Handling & Clipboard pane of that application's Preferences, are options for how data is copied to the system clipboard: as PDF (flat with transparency support) or AICB (individual paths, but no transparency). If, when you paste from Illustrator, the result is flat artwork without editable paths, you're dealing with PDF-format clipboard contents when you want AICB (Adobe Illustrator Clip Board).

If you change the setting in Illustrator and the problem persists, check that you haven't overridden InDesign's default pasting format. In the Preferences, on the Clipboard Handling pane, the top option, Prefer PDF When Pasting, should be unchecked.

Ideally, leave both Copy As PDF and AICB options checked. What occurs then is that Illustrator copies to the clipboard as *both*, allowing the destination—the paste into—application to select which format it supports. InDesign will choose AICB, thus accepting paths and individual objects, while applications that don't understand AICB will take the PDF-format content.

FIGURE 5.16
The same 3D
shape as drawn
in Illustrator
(left), as pasted
into InDesign
(center), and
then as copied
from InDesign
and pasted
back into Illus-
trator (right)

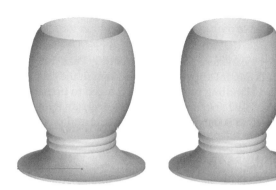

My rule of thumb is, if it takes more than one minute to draw in Illustrator, I'll save the AI file and place it rather than copy and paste to InDesign. (I'm fast with Illustrator; if you aren't, maybe try five minutes as a rule.) I would much rather retain editability of a drawing than worry about managing one more external asset.

The same is true of Photoshop images. While you can copy and paste from Photoshop to InDesign, and it's great for little bits here and there, you lose a lot. The first to go is transparency; pasted images are flattened onto a white background. Not even InDesign's Object ➤ Clipping Path ➤ Option command will get rid of the white. The same is true if you drag one or more layers from Photoshop and drop them into InDesign.

Other things to watch out for include transparency—Illustrator transparency flattens upon paste or drag into InDesign—and color. Both Illustrator and Photoshop support color models InDesign does not, like Web-Safe RGB, HSL, and Grayscale. The latter will become tints of process black (the *K* in *CMYK*), while the former two will convert to the RGB color space. Spot colors survive unless they're from a library InDesign doesn't have, such as VisiBone2, in which case they're converted to the nearest match CMYK process values. Simple Illustrator gradients—linear, radial—will convert to InDesign gradients and may be edited after paste, but more complicated ones or gradient meshes become individual vector paths in InDesign (think of the urn). Illustrator patterns become embedded EPS images and are no longer editable.

Objects or elements coming into InDesign via paste or drag and drop will be permanently converted, whereas placed assets only *appear* within InDesign using that application's supported color models; the actual colors and spaces will survive unchanged inside the external assets and thus through to output. This can also be a gotcha: An image saved in *HSL* (Hue, Saturation, Luminosity) will look RGB in the layout, enticing you to forget that the asset is not RGB, and may later cause problems with a RIP that doesn't know how to convert from HSL. Live Preflight will pick up on the color space and alert you, though, so keep an eye out for it.

Text from nearly any application—including Photoshop and Illustrator—can be pasted into (or from) InDesign, though, by default, text will lose its formatting upon paste. Back on the Clipboard Handling pane of InDesign's Preferences, you can change that behavior by toggling the setting for When Pasting Text and Tables from Other Applications to All Information instead of the default Text Only.

Every instance of a linked asset is listed on the Links panel, with its location within the layout on the right. Possible locations are page numbers (1, 2, 3, and so on); *PB* for pasteboard, denoting that the asset is not within a page and will not print; and a master page prefix (e.g., A, BB, CCC, DDDD) indicating that the asset is on that master page and thus shows on any body pages to which that master page is assigned. Multipage assets like PDF or INDD files will include not only the filename but also the asset page in use. For example, `bio_RailMagnor.pdf:2` denotes that I've placed page 2 of that PDF asset.

As you might suspect from the hyperlink-esque appearance of the locations, clicking one jumps you within the document to that asset—a quick way to inspect an asset in context without the inconvenience of hunting it down.

You can even sort the list of links in various ways. Click the page-like icon above the page number column to sort by page number; click it again to reverse the order. Or sort by filename by clicking the Name label on the left. Again, a second click reverses the sort order. To sort only assets with problems—such as missing 📷 or out-of-date ⚠ images—to the top of the list, click the caution sign header.

Link Panel Buttons

Beneath the list of assets, toward the right, are three highly useful buttons…and one you could do without.

Relink   Click the Relink button ⟳ to open a file import dialog that will replace the selected asset with a new file or with the same file in a new location. If InDesign loses track of a file, such as can happen if the asset moves to a new location or was contained on removable media that is no longer accessible to the computer, the Relink button will help you make the world right again.

Select multiple Links panel entries the same way as you would files in a list—by holding Shift for contiguous selection or Cmd/Ctrl for noncontiguous. Once selected, multiple assets can be relinked in one operation, which is actually useful much more often than it may sound.

First, there's the obvious usage of replacing a bunch of images with newly updated versions: for instance, replacing last season's catalog photos with this season's.

Next, it's useful for OPI workflows. A bunch of low-resolution images may be linked instead to their high-resolution counterparts one at a time in rapid succession.

Most often, though, the ability to replace a bunch of linked assets at once is used to fix the result of renaming or moving images or their folders. When you hold Option/Alt while clicking the Relink button, InDesign will seek to relink all missing assets, assuming there are any; otherwise it does nothing. When the Locate dialog appears, select the first image to relink to and click Open; then the Locate dialog will reappear immediately, ready to relink to the next missing asset. It's a fairly quick process of fixing broken links.

Quickest yet is that InDesign can *automatically* relink all the subsequent missing links if they're in the same location. Let's say all your images were in the `Product Shots` folder on your desktop. Now, further on in the production process, you've moved the InDesign document and `Product Shots` folder to the server. Naturally, InDesign lost track of the images in that folder, so you need to relink all of them. Option-click/Alt-click the Relink button to pop open the Locate dialog, wherein you'll navigate to the folder containing the first missing file. When you select the first missing file, before clicking the Open button, enable the option

Search for Missing Links in This Folder, and then click Open (see Figure 5.20). Assuming some or all of the other assets InDesign can't find are in that same folder or in a subfolder, InDesign will automatically relink to them without further effort on your part.

FIGURE 5.20
The Locate dialog searching for missing linked assets

When you fix a broken link or replace one asset with another, the replacement is made within the existing frame, and it preserves frame attributes such as scaling and crop data. In fact, the new image will be inserted at the same size as the replaced image. If you don't want that to happen, open InDesign's Preferences and, on the File Handling pane, uncheck Preserve Image Dimensions When Relinking.

While we're there, let's briefly define the other options in that section of the File Handling Preferences pane:

♦ Check Links Before Opening Document causes InDesign to check the integrity of every linked asset when you open the InDesign document. If you know your assets are all in order, or you'd rather check them on the Links panel manually, or if you'd just like to speed up the document-opening process, uncheck this option.

♦ Find Missing Links Before Opening Document causes the alerts to you of missing assets at document-open time. This option is available only if the one above it is turned on.

♦ Create Links When Placing Text and Spreadsheet Files will create links to, rather than embed, Word DOCs, TXT files, and even Excel spreadsheets if enabled.

♦ Default Relink Folder offers you two options: Most Recent Relink Folder (the default) and Original Link Folder. Which you choose determines where InDesign looks for missing links.

Go To Link   Go To Link ↗🖹, which is the button I think we can do without because we already have this functionality in the asset page numbers, will jump the document window to display the selected asset, which is extremely handy for figuring out just what the previous designer (or you) was thinking when placing a particular image.

Update Link   When an external asset has been modified outside InDesign, it's said to be modified or out of date and shows in the Links list a yellow caution sign. The asset isn't missing—InDesign has already found it—but the version as seen on the page isn't the latest version. Selecting such an out-of-date asset (or several of them) and clicking the Update Link button 🔄🖹 reimports the assets, refreshing their representations on the page with the latest versions. Refresh all out-of-date assets by Option-clicking/Alt-clicking the Update Link button.

Edit Original   The last button on the Links panel, Edit Original 🖊 is an incredibly useful, timesaving command. Very simply, it opens the linked asset in the application that created it. To touch up a PSD, for instance, you needn't launch Photoshop, go to File ➢ Open in that application, and then browse for the correct image. Edit Original does all that in one step, from within InDesign. Once you've completed editing in Photoshop (or Illustrator, or another InDesign document, or…), simply save the asset and close the editing application. Edit Original waits for that to occur and automatically updates the link inside the InDesign document to reflect your new changes.

If you'd rather edit a particular file in a specific application, an application that *isn't* set to be the one to open that type of file, select the file to edit and, from the Links panel flyout menu, go to the Edit With submenu and select an application. InDesign will then tell the operating system to launch that application with the selected asset loaded.

CS5   You can even run Edit Original on multiple assets at once! Just select the desired assets and click the button; they will then all open in their creating applications or the applications configured to edit them.

CS5   ## Link Info

The lower half (give or take) of the Links panel is the Link Info section (see Figure 5.21). If you don't see it, double-click any linked asset or click the tiny arrow in the bottom-left corner of the Links panel to show it. If you're updating from CS3, the Link Info area replaces the Link Information dialog and lists valuable metadata about an asset, different sets of data for different types of assets. You'll find basics such as filename and path, file size and type of file, creation and modification dates, and the date it was placed in the InDesign document as well as some fields whose purpose may be less obvious:

Figure 5.21
The Link Info
section of the
Links panel

Page   The page on which the asset is used. The value displayed here is identical to that in the top half of the Links panel and is therefore redundant.

Status   The status of an asset is in terms of how it relates to the InDesign document. In addition to the yellow caution sign or red dot that appears in the upper half of the Links panel for, respectively, outdated or missing assets, this field will explain a little more verbosely than an icon what's wrong with an asset. If the asset isn't missing and is up to date, the Status will be listed as OK.

Path   A handy little field, here is the full path to the asset. You can right-click the Path field and choose a command to copy the path, with or without filename, to the clipboard, ready to paste into another application's Open dialog.

Copy Asset Metadata

Right-clicking different fields in the Link Info section of the Links panel enables you copy the values of those fields to the clipboard. Information like the creation, modified, or place dates and times, the path to assets, the name of the layer on which an asset resides, and much more can be copied from the panel and pasted just about anywhere within or without InDesign. You can even right-click and choose Copy All Link Information, which copies *all* the metadata shown in Link Info, including field names and field values. That data can then be pasted into a text frame for cataloging images for OPI or other uses or pasted into a spreadsheet or database program for asset management and classification purposes. You can also access the *XMP metadata* for placed assets that support XMP metadata on the same context-sensitive menu.

Layer Overrides   Relevant only to layered PSD, PDF, INDD, and AI files, this field states whether you've shown or hidden any layers or layer comps to make the placed image differ from the state of the external file.

Creator   Which application created an image is sometimes useful information to know, particularly if you're experiencing a problem with that image. For instance, if you have a misbehaving EPS file, being informed via the Link Info that the EPS was created in Freehand 1.0 (circa 1992) could explain the problem and suggest a course of action—in this case, open the Freehand EPS in a recent version of Illustrator and do a Save As to rewrite and modernize the PostScript code comprising the EPS.

Layer   The Layer metadata notes on which of the InDesign document's layers the asset was placed.

Transparency   If an asset uses alpha transparency in some way, it will be noted here. A few years ago, that was extremely valuable information for the designer to have because some RIPs had trouble processing natively transparent images. Consequently, designers would have to note transparency usage and flatten transparency prior to output. Now it's not a very big deal for designers, but press and prepress personnel still frequently use that information to diagnose issues in customer files.

ICC Profile   Does the asset have an embedded ICC profile? If so, the profile will be noted in this field.

Linking vs. Embedding

When you embed assets in a layout, you put all your eggs in one basket, as my grandmother used to say. If *one* file gets corrupted, *all* your work is *gone*.

Embedding assets is tempting, and I see many new creatives opting for it. They're tempted by the fact that embedding means fewer—or no—external assets. They like the idea of having just one file to move around, never having to worry about network paths remapping or forgetting to copy a PSD from this other folder onto their USB drives to work on the layout at home.

Sure, a layout with all or a significant portion of its imagery and copy embedded is easier to deal with, easier to manage, and easier to send to a thumb drive or DVD-ROM, but it's emphatically not worth the risk. Eggs. Basket. Splat. Weeks of work oozing out all over the linoleum.

I like being right as much as the next guy, but I *hate* being proven right on the linking-versus-embedding debate. It truly saddens me when somebody comes up to me long-faced at a conference or on Twitter and begs me to help him fix a corrupted document wherein he has embedded all his images. Sure, I know a few tricks I can try (most are somewhere in this tome), but it's a rare occasion when they work; if all the safeguards have failed, there just isn't much to be done to resurrect a truly corrupt INDD. At that point, it's a matter of re-creating the document. If all the assets are external, the work is a *lot* less than if they were all embedded and must also be re-created from scratch.

If *that* doesn't dissuade you from embedding assets, maybe this will: Remember the urn? If you embed, you potentially lose the ability to quickly and easily edit original artwork. Images placed as links and then embedded *can* often be extracted back to an editable state, but artwork brought in via paste or drag and drop from an application is instantly frozen into EPS or TIFF format—good-bye live effects, good-bye layers, good-bye to a lot of stuff.

Opinions differ on the linking-versus-embedding debate. Some—including a few other InDesign gurus—say embedding is fine, that there are enough safeguards in place with InDesign's SavedData and extremely stable file format. In my experience, having done page layout and compositing for all these years, having looked into the faces of misty-eyed owners of unopenable documents, and having researched enough technical support cases wherein months' worth of work was lost due to a simple power surge or mistimed network backup, embedding anything that will take longer than five minutes to re-create—cumulatively—is, in my opinion, a bad idea.

Eggs. Basket. Splat.

Fitting

Relating content to its container is accomplished through a process called *fitting*.

Is the entire image displayed at 1:1 scale, or is it cropped? Is the frame larger than the content to provide a colored border? When you place an asset, are you working frame-first or content-first, and is the frame already the needed size? All these questions—and more—are a matter of fitting. InDesign naturally contains features and commands for fitting that have been standard in layout applications for years, but it also introduces some new ones.

FITTING COMMANDS

InDesign's fitting commands are found in not one, not two, but *three* locations—the first two are the Object ➤ Fitting menu and the Fitting submenu on the context-sensitive menu available

when you right-click a frame with content. In past versions of InDesign, these two menus differed. The context-sensitive version was a subset of Object ➤ Fitting, containing only the most common fitting commands. To much rejoicing, the context-sensitive menu now offers rapid access to *all* the fitting commands (see Figure 5.25).

FIGURE 5.25
The Fitting menu and commands (as shown from the context-sensitive menu)

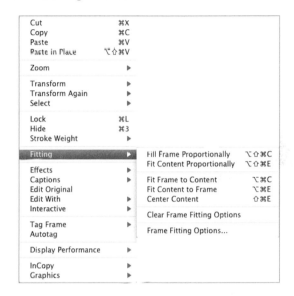

In addition to finding them on the menus, you'll find them as convenient buttons on the Control panel (see Figure 5.26); they appear on the far right anytime a frame is selected.

FIGURE 5.26
Fitting command buttons on the Control panel

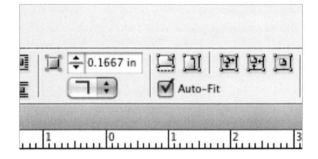

A fourth means of access, keyboard shortcuts, also exists for all the fitting commands, but because they tend to be three- or four-key commands, it usually takes less brain power and finger acrobatics to use the Control panel buttons or right-click to access those fitting commands you use infrequently.

Let's quickly run through the fitting commands.

Fit Content to Frame   Stretches or shrinks imagery to fill in the full area of the frame. This command may result in distortion of the image to accommodate the frame dimensions.

Fit Frame to Content   Resizes the frame up (decrop) or down (crop) to match the dimensions of the content (either imagery or text). Use this when you want 100% of your content showing but without excess or empty frame area around it.

Center Content   Aligns the content to both the horizontal and vertical centers of the frame without resizing either frame or content. Center Content is a quick way to begin a framed picture effect wherein a color-filled frame is larger than its content image.

Fit Content Proportionally   Uniformly scales the content in an attempt to fill the frame. Scaling stops when it fills *either* the horizontal or vertical dimension of the frame; thus the image is not distorted, but empty frame space may endure along the other axis.

Fill Frame Proportionally   Uniformly scales the content to completely fill the frame *without* stopping at the smaller of the frame's horizontal or vertical dimension. Instead, scaling continues until *both* dimensions are filled, stopping at the larger second dimensions and often cropping the image. For instance: Placing a 1×2-inch image inside a 2×2-inch frame and choosing Fill Frame Proportionally will scale the image up 200% (resulting in a 2×4-inch image), filling the horizontal 2-inch dimension and cropping the vertical by 50% (2 inches).

It's important to remember that fitting occurs relative to the actual frame dimensions. By default, strokes assigned to frames straddle the frame path. For example, a 4-point stroke puts 2 points inside the frame and 2 points outside. In that scenario, the 2 points of stroke inside the frame will cover 2 points of the content all the way around.

While you may be tempted to resize the frame to account for stroke weight, don't. It will throw off your measurements and scaling, something you'll have to wrestle with every time you resize, alter fitting, or scale the frame and content. Instead, use the Stroke panel to move the stroke to outside the frame instead of the default middle (straddle) alignment.

FRAME FITTING OPTIONS

The last option on the Fitting menu is Frame Fitting Options (see Figure 5.27). Please do *not* skip this section assuming you already know about this dialog or can intuit it simply from the screen shot or by trying it yourself. While that may be the case, the most powerfully productive use of Frame Fitting Options is *hidden*. I don't want you to miss that.

FIGURE 5.27
Frame Fitting
Options dialog

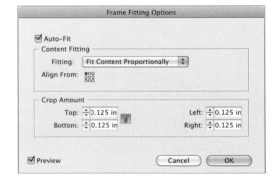

Without Frame Fitting Options it takes a lot of work to do something as simple as using the frame to crop out a border embedded in an image. You have to either measure the width of the border and then subtract twice that width from the frame's width and/or height or zoom way in, turn on high-quality display, and manually reshape the frame and refit the content over several steps. Either way, if either the frame or the content has to later change size, you're forced to do it all over again. Anyone who has arranged a series of photos from various sources knows this toilsome process.

Thankfully, it's no longer necessary.

Frame Fitting Options has crop boxes with a live preview. They work just like other measurement fields in that you can type in a value and use the increase/decrease arrow buttons or, with the cursor in the field, even the Up and Down arrow keys on your keyboard. The chain link button between the Top and Bottom and Left and Right crop fields links all four together—changing the value in one alters all four to match. (Good-bye image border.)

In the middle of the dialog, the Alignment From Reference Point Proxy alters the alignment of the image within the frame. This can operate alone, simply altering where an image falls within its frame, but it also affects how the image reacts to cropping operations.

Positive cropping values pull the content *toward* the selected reference point, while negative cropping values push the content *away*. In Figure 5.28, for example, you can see the different alignment and cropping result of the same image and frame using positive (left) and negative (right) cropping values. In both of these, the content is aligned to the top left; changing the reference point dramatically alters the cropping results (see Figure 5.29).

FIGURE 5.28

At left, a frame and image cropped to positive 0.75 inches all the way around; at right, the same frame and image with negative cropping of the same amount. Both are aligned to the top-left reference point.

FIGURE 5.29

Using a positive 0.75-inch cropping value, different alignment reference points dramatically alter cropping results. From left to right: aligned to bottom right, center, and middle top.

Now, I promised you a hidden feature. I'm a man of my word, so here it is, in a hands-on exercise:

1. Still have your catalog template with the empty frames? If not, go ahead and create about a half-dozen empty picture frames.

2. Select all those empty frames and go to Object ➤ Fitting ➤ Frame Fitting Options.

3. Break the Make All Settings the Same chain link, and set Top and Left crops to **−0.25** inches.

4. Set the reference point to the top-left corner, and set Fitting to Fit Content to Frame. Click OK.

5. Deselect the frames, and go to File ➤ Place.

6. Select a number of images roughly equal to the number of frames and import them.

7. Once you have a loaded cursor, place the images one at a time into the frames you just modified. You should immediately notice the fitting effects.

Let's assume you have a series of product shots all from the same manufacturer or photog. They were all taken amid a sea of white backdrop and drape, with the products always the same distance from dead center.

Your first option is to take them into Photoshop, crop or trim them, and then save a new set of images. The drawbacks to that are as follows: It's more work for you—you'll probably have to do at least some fitting and cropping in InDesign regardless; it creates another set of digital files to track and manage; and should substitution of products occur or new versions of the photos be delivered to you, you'll have to do both the Photoshop and InDesign work again. Your second option is to place the unaltered photos into InDesign and, through fitting and cropping, get them just right.

By presetting your Frame Fitting Options—fitting and/or cropping—you can prep for the most common tasks required by your series of product shots, making the cropping, fitting, and alignment all part of the placement process instead of an extra step you must do to each afterward. They won't all be perfect (unless you're incredibly lucky), but performing a few touch-ups here and there is much more efficient than repeating the same settings for the majority of your photos each in turn.

Even without alterations to the cropping or alignment, the ability to preset fitting is a huge time-saver. You can fill an entire frame-first catalog layout with images all fit proportionally within their frames in seconds!

Auto-Fit

Introduced in InDesign CS4, the Auto-Fit control automatically makes images scale with their containers. Most of the time when you resize a graphic frame, you want the image inside to resize as well. This has always entailed switching to the Scale tool (which, honestly, most people forget is even there) or, more commonly, holding Cmd/Ctrl while dragging one of the frame's bounding boxes. Activating the Auto-Fit command from the Control panel or any other place you can find the standard Fitting commands negates the need to remember to press Cmd/Ctrl

before resizing a frame. It automatically scales the image inside to match the resizing frame. Moreover, Auto-Fit honors whatever fitting option you've chosen. For instance, if the image is set to Center Content, resizing the frame automatically scales the image and preserves the width of the border-like distance between the image and frame edges.

PROPORTIONAL ASSET PLACEMENT

InDesign CS4 added another nice little touch to fitting graphics and media files upon place. After selecting one or more assets for placement in the Place dialog, when you click and drag to define the area for the graphic frame, InDesign will limit the frame to the proportional dimensions of the image—and then drop in the image scaled to fit proportionally. For example, if you're placing a 2×1-inch image, the rectangle you drag to create the frame will always be twice as wide as it is tall, in perfect proportion. As an added bonus, the image itself automatically fits proportionally to the frame.

Live Captions

CS5

Live Captions is a new feature in InDesign CS5, one that can make almost any InDesign user's job easier. Unfortunately, Live Captions also has some major flaws.

Image Metadata

The ability for images (and other documents) to contain metadata in the same standardized format isn't new; it's been around for about a decade, as have databases that can extract and use that data. The ability to actually *do* something with that metadata beyond simply cataloging and searching through documents *is* new to CS5. Look at an image in Adobe Bridge, for example (see Figure 5.30), specifically at the Metadata panel (if it isn't showing, activate it from Window ➤ Metadata Panel). The billion and sixteen fields available in the collapsible sections are the image's metadata.

The RAW image I have selected includes RAW and EXIF camera data such as the Focal Length, Max Aperture Value, and whether the flash fired during the shot. That information is useful for generating Live Captions if I'm producing a catalog of photographs or a contact sheet. The DICOM section is applicable to medical imagery in patient records or for publication in medical journals or circulars. The other sections—Audio, Video, and Mobile SWF—are relevant to multimedia content and thus not germane to this discussion. Most often, InDesign users like us will want to generate Live Captions from a different section of an image's metadata—the IPTC Core metadata.

IPTC is an abbreviation for the International Press Telecommunications Council. The IPTC Core data is the basic, central set of information used for editorial or general imagery within XMP (Extensible Metadata Platform), the XML-encoded layer of textual information that enables images to contain metadata, and for that metadata to be read and extracted by a wide variety of systems, software, and devices that exist now or will be invented in the future. IPTC Core metadata includes fields to define the source, subject, copyright holder, license, description, and classification of a photo. This information can be edited through Bridge's Metadata panel, in Photoshop with the File ➤ File Info command, or through a variety of other applications and processes that enable access to image (or other document) XMP metadata.

FIGURE 5.30
An image and its metadata displayed in Bridge CS5

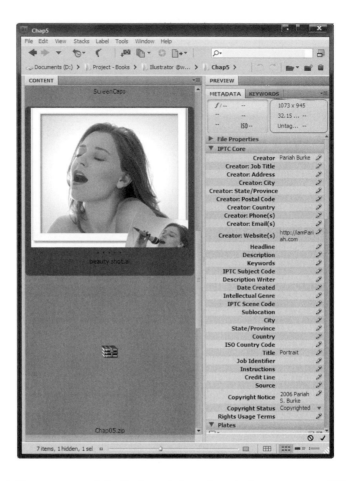

By way of example, let's say you work in the layout department of a newspaper. When the section editor buys a digital photo from a photo journalist, the photog would almost certainly have pre-filled the IPTC fields regarding the creator, copyright and licensing, creation date, and the location where the image was shot. The editor will then likely fill out a few more fields—Headline, Description, Keywords, Description Writer, Provider, Source—and, depending on the rights purchased from the photographer, may alter the values of the Copyright Notice, Copyright Status, and Rights Usage Terms fields. All that information is now part of the image, saved within the image's XMP metadata. All of it is also eligible for inclusion in the layout automatically via InDesign's new Live Captions feature.

Creating a Live Caption

There's still much to discuss with Live Captions, but let's set aside the ins and outs for a moment to try it, er, live.

1. Open Bridge CS5 and, within it, navigate to and select any TIFF, PSD, or other image format that supports metadata.

2. On Bridge's Metadata panel, expand the IPTC Core section (see Figure 5.31). If you don't see the Metadata panel, turn it on by choosing Window ➤ Metadata Panel.

FIGURE 5.31
The Metadata
panel in Bridge CS5

3. Within the IPTC Core metadata fields, find the Credit Line field and enter your name.

4. Click the image thumbnail again, whereupon Bridge will prompt you to apply the changes you've just made. Apply them.

5. Place the image into InDesign via one of the many means.

6. Right-click the image and, from the context-sensitive menu, choose Captions ➤ Caption Setup. That will open the Caption Setup dialog (see Figure 5.32).

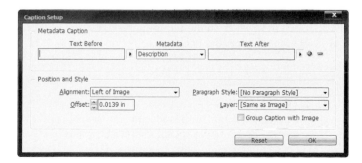

FIGURE 5.32
The Caption Setup
dialog

7. We'll go through every option in the Caption Setup dialog shortly. For now, leave every field as is except the Metadata field. Change that to Credit, an option about midway through the list of metadata fields, right after Swatches Used. When you click OK, nothing will apparently happen.

8. Right-click the image again, and now choose Captions ➤ Generate Live Caption. You will now have a small text frame bearing your name at the bottom of the image, as I have mine in Figure 5.33. You've just created a Live Caption.

FIGURE 5.33
My Live Caption showing the contents of the image's Credit field

At this point you might be saying to yourself, *Caption I get, but what's the "live" part of it?* Allow me to show you:

1. Return to the image in Bridge.

2. Change the name in the Credit Line field to someone else's name and reapply the change.

3. Switch back to InDesign, and, on the Links panel, note that the image with which you've been working is now listed as in need of an update.

4. Update the link, and watch what happens to the content of the text frame beneath the image. It should update to reflect the new name you entered in Bridge. Thus, the caption is live according to the value of the image's metadata field.

Now try this:

1. In Bridge once more, find a different image.

2. In that second image's IPTC Core Credit Line metadata field, enter your name again and apply the change.

3. Place that image into InDesign directly beside, but not touching, the first image.

4. With the black arrow, select the text frame under the first image and move it beneath the second image, careful to ensure that the text frame *does* touch the second image. Note that the text inside the frame will now be your name as listed in the second image's Credit Line metadata.

Live Caption frames contain special text markers rather than actual text. Those markers look up the information from the specified metadata field in whatever asset they touch, returning the value in the field. Thus, when you moved the Live Caption text frame from one image to the next, it read the different data embedded in the second image and displayed it.

If, instead of a name, your caption frame changed to say <No Intersecting Data>, then that's because the frame wasn't touching the second image after you moved it. Live Captions must actually touch the assets from which they read. That makes them reusable, copy and paste-able. It also might mean that your text winds up too close to the image itself. If so, use frame inset spacing to give the caption frame a little padding (see Chapter 2, "Text").

When the caption frame is in the right place but is requesting metadata that hasn't been added to the image, the Live Caption will display <No data from link>.

Live Caption Options

Live Captions offer plenty of options if you know what you're looking at. Getting back to the Caption Setup dialog, let's run through the options there (see Figure 5.34).

FIGURE 5.34
The Caption Setup dialog

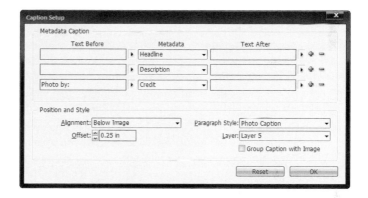

Text Before/After   Enter in the Text Before and/or Text After fields any static text you'd like to flank the metadata. For instance, if using the Credit metadata, you might want to set the Text Before to "Photo Credit:" or "Illustration by". You can paste into these fields, but the arrow to the right of each field offers quick access to the most common symbols—symbols like Copyright and Trademark, em and en dashes, and the entire contents of the Type ➢ Insert White Space menu.

Metadata   The Metadata dropdown list is where you choose which metadata from the asset you want to expose in the caption. Not every image will contain data in all the fields listed, of course. In addition to what you'll find in Bridge's Metadata panel, you'll find other common metadata available to you, including instance-specific metadata such as the page on which an image appears in the current document, its dimensions, the actual and effective PPI, and much more.

Add/Remove Rows   To the right of the Text After field are unlabeled plus and minus buttons that, respectively, add or remove rows of data. You can retrieve several pieces of metadata—each with an optional text before and/or after—simply by adding new rows. There are two caveats here, though. First, each row becomes its own paragraph in the Live Caption text frame; you can't place two pieces of metadata on the same line. Second, every row *must* contain a metadata field. You can't, for example, have one line that contains only the contents of the Text Before field and no metadata.

I have figured out a workaround to these limitations, though. See the "Multiple Captions" section that follows.

Alignment   From the Alignment field you can choose to have a Live Caption generated below, above, or on either side of the image. Choosing to put it on one of the sides rotates the frame so that the text is 90° or 270°, which is perfect for many publications' photo credits, copyright notices, and other types of captions.

Offset   This handy field creates a frame inset on the edge of the text frame bordering the image. In other words, it gives your captions some breathing room so that they aren't flush against the image they describe.

Paragraph Style   Choosing a paragraph style from this dropdown list, or creating one with the New Paragraph Style option at the bottom of the list, automatically assigns a style to the text in Live Captions so that you don't have to go back and do it manually.

Layer   This is a stroke of brilliance on Adobe's part. Many designers prefer to put their captions on a layer separate from the images and other text. This is especially useful when the images have text wrap assigned to them and when the Text Wrap Only Affects Text Beneath option is enabled on the Composition pane of InDesign's Preferences. In such cases, placing captions automatically on a layer above images with text wrap insulates the captions from the wrap settings so that they, too, aren't pushed away from the image.

To place captions on a specific layer, select any available layer in the dropdown list. You may also choose Same As Image, which puts captions on the same layers as the images from which you generate them, regardless of whether those images are all on one layer or on dozens. The final option, Active Layer, puts captions on whatever layer happens to be active in the Layers panel.

Group Caption with Image   This check box option automatically groups the caption and its image to make repositioning easy and free of the risk of disassociating a Live Caption text frame from an asset.

Multiple Captions

Instead of putting multiple pieces of metadata into a single Live Caption text frame, you might find that you want to create multiple Live Caption text frames. For instance, you may want along the bottom one frame that contains what is traditionally considered an image caption, the content of the Description or Headline field, and then running vertically up one side you might also want to credit the photographer. You can certainly do that and more. Every image has four sides, all of which may have separate caption objects; you could even add additional captions beyond four. The only requirement is that the caption frames touch the image they describe.

To create a second (or third or fourth or…) Live Caption text frame, simply repeat the creation process: Define the caption setup; then choose Generate Live Caption from the Captions submenu on the context-sensitive right-click or Object menu.

Static Captions

Live Captions update their metadata markers to reflect the metadata in an image. And, of course, they must touch the image they describe. What if you don't want the metadata updated

or you want to move the caption frame away from its image? In those cases you'd want static, not live, captions. There are a couple of ways to create them.

First, of course, is the Generate Static Caption command on the Captions menu, immediately below the Generate Live Caption command we used previously.

Next, you can convert any Live Caption text frame into a static, non-updating caption by right-clicking it and choosing Captions ➤ Convert to Static Caption. That option is also available on the Object menu under Captions. This command will convert the Live Caption text frame into a standard, nondynamic text frame, freezing all of the content and rendering it normal, editable text. Thus, no matter where you move the frame, even over another image, the text inside it will not change.

You can also automatically create static captions at the moment you place images into InDesign. In the Place dialog there's a new check box, Create Static Captions (see Figure 5.35). Activating that option while placing images will, after your image lands on the page, automatically generate a static caption text frame equal to the width or height of the image frame, directly below, above, or beside the image frame. Where the caption frame is created and what metadata it contains is determined by the last options you set in Caption Setup. Perhaps, needless to say, creating static captions at place time also works with multiple images—place 10, 20, or 30 images all in one shot, and InDesign will automatically generate static captions for each of them. Just think about how easy that function could make your next catalog, directory, or membership directory project!

FIGURE 5.35
The Create Static Captions option in the Place dialog

Live Captions Limitations

You may recall from the beginning of the section when I said that Live Captions contains major flaws. Here's where I'm going to detail them. Bear in mind, I think Live Captions is a great first try, but out of the box, it's not fully ready for production use.

NOT LIVE LIVE CAPTIONS

The metadata may be live, but that's it. Let's say you filled a page with 10 or 20 pictures—maybe it's a contact sheet, a catalog, or a membership directory—and to each you added a Live Caption text frame. Those Live Captions consist of some text before and a metadata marker for the images' Description fields. You proof the client. The client comes back to you saying, "This is great, but in addition to the picture descriptions, let's also add in the Capture Date." Capture Date is another available metadata marker.

Effecting that change shouldn't be a problem, right? Just select all the Live Caption text frames and return to Caption Setup, adding in a second row of data. The problem is, when you click OK after making that change, *nothing will happen*. You see, Live Caption text frames, once created, are not connected to the Caption Setup dialog. They will not update to reflect changes in that or any location. Instead, you have to make your changes in Caption Setup and then regenerate all new captions, deleting the old ones. If you don't delete the old ones first, you'll wind up with multiple caption frames stacked atop each other, probably showing different data.

There is no way around this built into InDesign. Fortunately, I have a workaround, though it is nowhere near as efficient as it would be had Adobe made Live Captions objects live.

Live Caption text frames can be reused, as you saw in the exercises; just move them onto different images to reflect different metadata. That behavior enables you to make your work with Live Captions much more efficient. Instead of re-creating each Live Caption for each instance in a document or in multiple documents, now or in the future, build up a library of Live Captions objects (File ➤ New ➤ Library). Each time you create a new Live Caption configuration, add a frame containing that configuration to the library. Thereafter, when you need the same Live Caption again, don't re-create it; just drag it out of the library and onto an image.

LEGACY METADATA

I was the one to discover the following limitation of Live Captions, and I genuinely felt bad when I brought it to the attention of Chris Kitchener, Adobe's Senior Product Manager for InDesign, a week after InDesign CS5 shipped.

Remember what I explained about the IPTC Core metadata, that it's the international standard for general and editorial-related metadata within images? Guess what InDesign *doesn't* use: the IPTC Core metadata. In addition to the instance-specific and EXIF photo metadata you'll find available for use in Live Captions, you'll also find fields like Credit, Headline, Description, Country, and so on. These fields are not part of IPTC Core. Rather, they're from an old, deprecated set of metadata Adobe itself (via Bridge and elsewhere) lumps together under the heading of Legacy Metadata.

In other words, that shiny new copy of InDesign CS5 in your hands, with its glisteningly fresh Live Captions feature, is using metadata fields that haven't been widely used in years—since before CS5 was even on the drawing board.

Take a look at Figure 5.36, which is the interface for managing image (or any document's) metadata, by selecting File ➤ File Info from within InDesign, Photoshop, Illustrator, and other Adobe applications. If you compare the fields on the Description, IPTC, IPTC Extension, and other tabs to the fields available for selection within Caption Setup, you won't find many matches.

FIGURE 5.36

The File Info XMP metadata dialog opened from File ➢ File Info

Screenshots RAW NEW.psd

| Description | IPTC | IPTC Extension | Camera Data | Video Data | Audio Data | Mobile SWF |

Document Title: Mastering InDesign, Screenshots Chapter 5

Author: Pariah S. Burke

Author Title:

Description: Screenshots for use in Chapter 5 of the book Mastering InDesign CS5 for Print Design & Production, by Pariah S. Burke (Wiley, 2010)

Rating: ★ ★ ★ ★ ★

Description Writer:

Keywords: InDesign; Bridge; Photoshop; Mastering

ⓘ Semicolons or commas can be used to separate multiple values

Copyright Status: Copyrighted

Copyright Notice: Copyright 2010 Pariah S. Burke

Copyright Info URL: http://iamPariah.com   Go To URL...

Created: 2010-09-08 – 18:27:04   Application: Adobe Photoshop CS5 Windows

Modified: 2010-09-09 – 11:21:04   Format: application/vnd.adobe.photoshop

Powered By
xmp

Preferences   Import... ▼   OK   Cancel

Instead of the IPTC Core and other modern metadata fields accessible from within Adobe's main applications, including InDesign itself, Live Caption uses the Legacy Metadata fields (see Figure 5.37). Getting to those fields is tricky:

FIGURE 5.37

The Legacy Metadata fields exposed in Bridge CS5

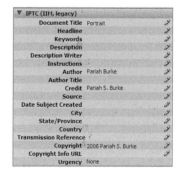

▼ IPTC (IIM, legacy)

Document Title	Portrait
Headline	
Keywords	
Description	
Description Writer	
Instructions	
Author	Pariah Burke
Author Title	
Credit	Pariah S. Burke
Source	
Date Subject Created	
City	
State/Province	
Country	
Transmission Reference	
Copyright	2006 Pariah S. Burke
Copyright Info URL	
Urgency	None

1. Open Adobe Bridge and select a file whose Legacy Metadata you'd like to edit.

2. Choose Preferences from the flyout menu at the top of the Metadata panel.

3. Switch to the Metadata pane of Bridge's Preferences, and, in the list on the right, locate and place a checkmark beside IPTC (IIM, legacy), which is between the File Properties and IPTC Core sections (see Figure 5.38).

FIGURE 5.38
Exposing the Legacy Metadata fields for editing within Bridge

4. Click OK, and you'll now see the IPTC (IIM, legacy) section in the Metadata panel. Those field names match the names of those available for use as Live Captions. Edit them as needed.

It's important to note that several Legacy and IPTC Core fields are linked—enter data into the Legacy Author field, for instance, and the same data populates the IPTC Core Creator field. Thus, you *could* ignore the Legacy fields entirely, using just the IPTC Core fields in the File Info dialog or Bridge. You would, however, need a map or scorecard to figure out which fields in one set map to another, the metadata fields InDesign actually uses. Fortunately, I've provided just such a scorecard. You can download it free of charge from `http://iampariah.com/projects/other-projects`.

SINGLE-LINE CAPTIONS ONLY

As I noted before, each row in the Captions Setup dialog becomes its own paragraph and may contain only a single metadata marker. Moreover, every row must contain a metadata marker, even if you want only static text in a paragraph by itself.

You *can* build multiline captions where some lines have only static data, but doing so is a hack, a workaround, not an intended function of Live Caption. To create a caption like the one in Figure 5.39, where a line of static text exists on a line by itself, you have to fudge the Caption Setup options. Basically, you must define each non-metadata-only line by filling in the Text Before and/or Text After fields and by choosing from the Metadata list a piece of metadata from a field into which you've entered a space. For instance, in that figure, I've selected the Edited By field. In Bridge's Metadata panel I set the image's Edited By field to include just a space and nothing else. Thus, when the caption is generated by InDesign, it *looks* like the top line doesn't have any metadata, when, in fact, it does (note the space).

FIGURE 5.39
A multiline Live
Caption

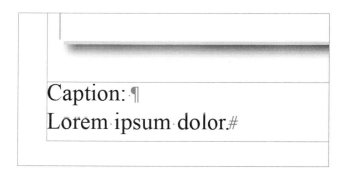

ONE STYLE

As you may have surmised already, only one paragraph style can be applied to a Live Caption text frame, inclusive of all paragraphs within that frame. You can't automatically make the first row of data *this* paragraph style and the next *that* style. You also can't apply character styles automatically. For instance, you couldn't have "Photo Credit" assigned a different character style than the photographer's name that follows it.

I don't have a direct solution to these limitations, but I do have some techniques that, depending on the situation, might help.

First, if you want to style words differently, such as in the case of something like a photo credit, use Nested Styles or even GREP Styles (both discussed in Chapter 13, "Efficiency").

If it's multiple paragraph styles you need, setting a multirow Live Caption (or static caption) with different paragraph styles, there isn't much you can do. If it's a couple of captions here and there, styling them by hand would probably be the most efficient method. However, if you're looking at many captions that require styling, I would suggest employing Find/Change to search for words common to all the lines that need a new paragraph style and to apply the appropriate paragraph style to them. Remember that assigning a new paragraph style to any part of a paragraph automatically applies it to the entire paragraph.

The Bottom Line

Place Image Assets Focusing on efficiency with this version of InDesign, Adobe seeded numerous tiny improvements in the task of placing image assets.

> **Master It** Create a frame-first layout containing 6 to 10 image frames. Preset the blank Frame Fitting Options to Fit Content Proportionately, and then, using any folder of images available, import and place, in one operation, all the images needed to fill the frames.

Import Images without the Place Command Drag and drop enables visual selection and import of image assets, while copy and paste, under the right conditions, offers a more natural way of moving assets from one place to another in the same document or between InDesign and other applications.

> **Master It** Create another empty frame layout similar to the previous one, and then, using Adobe Bridge and ensuring that both Bridge and the InDesign layout are visible onscreen, visually choose and place image assets from within Bridge to fill the empty frames.

Preview and Organize Files with Mini Bridge   Mini Bridge is a panel-based tool integrated into InDesign and Photoshop to make the tasks of asset previewing, sorting, classification, and selection as easy and as integrated into the document-production experience as possible.

Master It   Within Mini Bridge, navigate to a folder of images or other thumbnail-eligible documents. Once there, peruse the contents of the folder in Review mode, rejecting some and adding others to a new collection.

Manage Placed Assets   Getting image assets into the layout is only half the job; you must also know how to manage—and even replace—assets once they're on the page.

Master It   Use one of the two documents created in the preceding "Master It" exercises, and, without using File ➤ Place, drag and drop, or even copy and paste, replace three of the images (in the same frames) with other assets. If you have Photoshop and/or Illustrator installed, choose another image already placed on the page and edit the image itself in Photoshop or Illustrator *without* opening the application from the Dock or the Start menu.

Go Native in Your Workflow   InDesign can place native Photoshop PSD documents and Illustrator AI documents. You don't need to save Photoshop documents to TIFF or Illustrator artwork to EPS in order to place them into the page-layout application anymore. Instead, go native with PSDs and AIs, keeping your work in one file instead of a pair of raw and intermediary files. Being able to control the visibility of layers and layer comps directly within InDesign makes going native an even more compelling prospect.

Master It   If you have Photoshop and/or Illustrator, look among their respective samples for layered files or create your own. Now place those images into InDesign at least twice per image, using the Layer Options to vary the look between the instances of the same image.

Create and Use Live Captions   Despite its rather significant flaws, the Live Captions feature can make almost any InDesign user's job easier.

Master It   Find a handful of photographs—preferably work-related photos, but snapshots from your digital camera will work in a pinch—and, in Bridge CS5, fill in their metadata. Include the appropriate creator credit, copyright information, and an image description, what we typically think of as a caption. Next, place those images into InDesign while simultaneously generating static captions containing all of the metadata you just defined.

Chapter 6

Objects

If there's a "coolest subject" in this book, this is the chapter most likely to contain it. In fact, many of the topics covered in this chapter could fit that description—at least from a standpoint of creativity and creative productivity. If production efficiency or collaboration is the coolest subject to you, well, I have whole chapters about those, too.

As with drawing in InDesign, the name of the game when applying transparency and effects to objects is efficiency through doing as much as possible *within* InDesign, resorting as infrequently as possible to creating objects in Photoshop. If you've been in the layout game for any length of time, you know how often it was necessary to design whole pages in Photoshop just to enable object interaction, and if you know that, you also know how problematic late changes became. Each release of InDesign empowers you to do more in the layout itself, retaining all the freedom of InDesign objects, and without rasterizing.

In this chapter, you will learn to

- Use attribute-level transparency and object effects
- Design custom stroke styles
- Create mixed ink swatches and share swatches
- Work with anchored objects
- Set type on a path
- Employ the Gridify behavior of common tools
- Use the Gap tool
- Create and transform objects with the help of Smart Guides

Transparency and Effects

InDesign 2.0 introduced transparency to desktop publishing applications in 2002. Finally, two objects blended together without having to rasterize them in Photoshop. Objects—text, paths, even placed image assets—could be rendered less than opaque, and they could be blended together using familiar Photoshop blending modes such as Multiply, Screen, Exclusion, and others. A new world of creative freedom and efficiency exploded.

Since then we've been given the ability to create drop shadows natively in InDesign, and they are pretty cool (if overused), as well as a plethora of other transparency-based effects that are *really* cool.

Attribute-Level Transparency

Object-level transparency means that an entire object—simultaneously and equally the object's contents, fill color, and frame and stroke color—may be blended with its background by changing opacity and blending mode. With an image in a frame, for example, setting a 50% opacity made the frame, its stroke, fill color, and the image inside the frame semitransparent all at once. If you wanted a fully opaque frame stroke over a semitransparent image, you had to stack two objects—the first, the strokeless image frame, and above it, an empty, stroked frame. That was object-level transparency.

InDesign, like Illustrator before it, now has attribute-level transparency—the opacity and blending mode of the fill, stroke, and contents can all be set independently of one another. It's all done through the Effects panel (see Figure 6.1). Open the Effects panel by choosing Window ➢ Effects.

FIGURE 6.1

The Effects panel

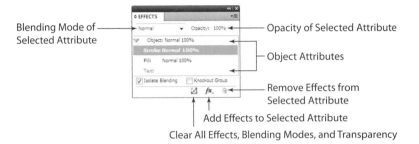

Blending Mode of Selected Attribute

Opacity of Selected Attribute

Object Attributes

Remove Effects from Selected Attribute

Add Effects to Selected Attribute

Clear All Effects, Blending Modes, and Transparency

The Effects panel has the Blending Modes dropdown menu and the Opacity field, which accepts input via typed-in values or adjustments to the Opacity slider by clicking the arrow button to the right. The middle section of the panel asks the tantalizing question, *Which attribute do you want to blend, to render semitransparent?*

By default, Object is selected, meaning opacity or blending mode changes will apply to the entire object. To change just one attribute—the stroke, fill, or text—select that attribute beneath Object prior to altering the blending mode or opacity percentage. Each attribute may have its own settings, and all may be modified within the same object if so desired. Thus, as you can see in Figure 6.2, with its opaque text, 50% opaque stroke, and Color Dodge blending mode fill, each attribute may be blended independently within the same object instead of stacking multiple objects that must be individually (and often laboriously) altered for a change request.

FIGURE 6.2

This rather gaudy image clearly demonstrates the separate transparency effects on each of the object's attributes. See the color insert section of this book to fully appreciate the image.

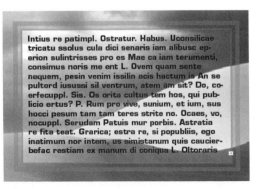

You might notice that the attribute-level options mention nothing about changing the opacity of images inside a graphic frame. That's because the option isn't there. That function is a hidden, secret trick. (You might want to either dog-ear this page or write the trick on a sticky note to affix to your monitor.) To change opacity settings or effects on an image independently of its containing frame's fill and/or stroke, you must select the image itself with the Direct Selection tool, the white arrow. It's *then* that the Effects panel will reveal control over the placed image (see Figure 6.3). Using the black arrow Selection tool accesses only the container, not its content. It makes sense, logically, that Adobe would divide the scope of the Effects panel along the line drawn by the Gemini-like Selection and Direct Selection tools—logical, but far from obvious.

FIGURE 6.3

The Effects panel managing a placed image once the image has been selected with the Direct Selection tool

Isolate Blending, a check box at the bottom of the panel, allows you to specify that objects with transparency blend only within their group, appearing opaque in relation to objects below that. Electing to enable Knockout Group (the other check box) knocks the selected object out of the ink of objects below, thus preventing blending and overprinting that might cause, through the non-opaque nature of printing ink, a blending regardless of the Isolate Blending choice. If you don't see either of these check boxes, choose Show Options from the Effects panel flyout menu to reveal the lower portion of the panel.

Effects

Attribute-level transparency is only one-half of the transparency possible in InDesign. As cool as that is, it's the attribute-level Photoshop-like effects that really widen one's eyes and tug up the corners of one's lips.

Start by creating an object; then, on the Effects panel, click the *fx* button at the bottom, which pops up a menu. Choose Drop Shadow to begin. If you're familiar with Photoshop's layer-style effects, the basic controls of InDesign's Effects dialog will be instantly familiar (see Figure 6.4). Even if you aren't a Photoshopper, you should find the controls and options intuitive.

The first thing to note is the dropdown menu in the top-left corner. As with the Effects *panel*, the Effects *dialog* effects (man, I wish Adobe had created more distinction in the names) are attribute level, meaning that the entire object as well as just its stroke, fill, and text can have their own individual effects. Text inside a frame, for instance, can have a drop shadow and bevel while its frame has an inner glow and is 75% opaque, and the stroke… The number of possible permutations of 9 effects, 15 blending modes for many of the individual effects, and all those effects and blending modes applied separately across the four object attributes is a dizzying venture into mathematical probabilities. And, they all interact to create a gestalt potentially as visually rich (or garish) as anything that could be created in Illustrator with the Appearance panel.

So broad and varied are the possibilities of the Effects dialog that the only way to really come to understand them is to experiment on your own. Therefore, I'll explain some of the options and discuss the effects themselves just a little, leaving you to explore by yourself after that. Make sure the Effects dialog is open to follow along.

FIGURE 6.4
The Effects dialog with intuitive controls

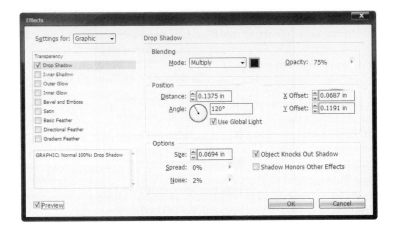

DROP SHADOW

In addition to X and Y, horizontal and vertical, Offset distance fields, Drop Shadow has a much more intuitive Angle spinner to accomplish the same thing. You don't have to estimate the conversion between the angle of the light source and horizontal- and vertical-axis-oriented coordinates. Just drag the rotating spinner or type in the angle degree in the field to the right. Even better, all effects can be oriented according to the same light source with the Use Global Light check box (more on Global Light in a few pages).

When InDesign draws a drop shadow, it does so *behind* the object as well as whatever portion of the shadow is visible beyond the area of the object. If the object fill or stroke is less than opaque, you'll see the drop shadow through it. More important, even if the object itself *is* opaque, even if you *can't* see the shadow through it onscreen, you could find the reverse is true upon printing. As you know, printing ink isn't truly opaque; black ink is close, as are several types of spot inks, but cyan, magenta, and yellow especially tend to allow ink beneath to shine through. Thus, applying a black drop shadow to a yellow-filled object, for instance, will often result in a yellow-tinged black object or a messy near-black green. Checking Object Knocks Out Shadow prevents drop shadows from showing through both onscreen and in print by knocking the shape of the object out of the shadow. The shadow itself will therefore be only around the edges of the object, not behind as well. Figure 6.5 shows the difference between Object Knocks Out Shadow on and off (see the color insert for a full-color version of Figure 6.5).

Shadow Honors Other Effects is a choice between adapting the shadow to reflect shape and transparency changes introduced by other effects (option checked) and ignoring them, drawing the shadow solely based on the real object or attribute shape (option unchecked). For instance, say you've added an outer glow effect as well as the drop shadow to a simple square. With Shadow Honors Other Effects unchecked, the shadow draws only in the shape of the path, the square. Conversely, with Shadow Honors Other Effects checked, the shadow will expand to incorporate the shape of the outer glow as well as the original square.

When InDesign draws a drop shadow, it begins feathering from the start to the end of the shadow—from the original object shape out to the end of the shadow. This creates a soft, feathered shadow, but you don't always want a soft, feathered shadow. Optically, the sharper a drop shadow, the harsher the light and the closer the object is to its background. To effect sharpness, use the Spread percentage field, which pushes the opaque area of the object shape out farther into the shadow area to reduce feathering in the edges.

Noise adds digital, random noise to a shadow, making it appear less smooth. Why on earth would you want to do *that*? For realism, of course. Other than glass and Mr. Clean's head, few things in nature are perfectly smooth. Adding a little noise—say, 1% to 3%—makes a shadow more believable, usually without being consciously noticeable to the viewer. Continue increasing the noise percentage to roughen the shadow—try 90% to 100% for an interesting mezzotint effect.

To change the color of the drop shadow, click the color swatch between the Blending Mode and Opacity fields. Black is the default, but other colors offer tremendous creative opportunity. Don't be afraid to experiment. These are all nondestructive, live effects, meaning they can be changed or even turned off at any time without consequence.

Inner Shadow

Inner Shadow has options similar to those of the Drop Shadow effect but places a shadow within the object or attribute rather than without. It has the effect of making objects and text appear cut out of, or sunken into, the background (see Figure 6.6). Like the Drop Shadow effect, Inner Shadow has a noise percentage. It substitutes choke for spread, however, but the effect is the same, with opaque shadow pushing inward to reduce the feathering in shadow edges.

Figure 6.6
Inner Shadow can be used to create a letterpress effect.

OUTER GLOW

Blending mode, opacity, color, size, noise, and spread work as they do in Drop Shadow and Inner Shadow effects. The Technique field offers two options: Softer and Precise.

A softer outer glow spreads outward smoothly from the *sides* of a shape. Color does not emanate from corners, which results in corner rounding or softening; the farther outward the glow is pushed via the Size field, the softer the corners. Selecting the Precise option *does* use the corners, radiating the glow outward equally from the total area of the shape. Thus, though the corners would necessarily be somewhat rounded, even an extremely large outer glow on a square would look like a square.

INNER GLOW

The Inner Glow effect pane is very much like the Outer Glow pane, with all the same options plus one extra: Source. The glow is placed inside the object or attribute, and the Source field chooses whether the glow shines inward from the edges or outward from the center.

Note that Technique has the same Precise and Softer options it has with Outer Glow, but they work a little differently. With Softer, the glow radiates evenly from (or to, depending on the Source option) all sides and corners, leading to a soft, rounded glow deeper in the corners. Electing Precise, however, draws the glow from (or to) the sides without overlapping at the corners, thus creating distinct rays of color (see Figure 6.7).

FIGURE 6.7
Both objects have the same Inner Glow effect, including a source of Edge. On the left, Technique is set to Softer; on the right, it's set to Precise.

BEVEL AND EMBOSS

You can add depth to text and objects with bevel and emboss effects. Angle and Altitude control the apparent depth of the three-dimensional effect, while Highlight and Shadow set the colors, opacities, and blending modes of the colors to reveal the dimensionality. Style choices are as follows (refer to Figure 6.8):

FIGURE 6.8
Styles, from left to right: Inner Bevel, Outer Bevel, Emboss, and Pillow Emboss

Inner Bevel   Places the bevel within the confines of the shape or attribute

Outer Bevel   Grows the bevel outward without impinging upon the fill of the object or attribute

Emboss   Colors part of the object itself as well as the area outside the object to create the effect of the shape rising up from, or sinking into, the page

Pillow Emboss   As the name implies, re-creates the effect of stitching a pattern into a satin pillow, where the stitch sinks into the page but the area within and without is raised

The Direction dropdown menu determines whether the shape rises up in relief from or, like intaglio, sinks down into the page.

SATIN

Satin creates a satiny sheen effect by infusing color into the shape from opposing corners and sides.

BASIC FEATHER

This effect softens and fades out the edges of the object or attribute, allowing it to taper into background objects. The options here are simple and sparse because the feather softly grows inward uniformly from all edges. Choke, as in other effects, controls the spread of the nonfeathered area and its balance with the feathered edges. The Corners dropdown offers three choices: Sharp, Rounded, and Diffused. Respectively, they feather inward preserving the points of corners, round corners before feathering inward, and, with Diffused, feather inward in a vaguely rounded way.

DIRECTIONAL FEATHER

To sharpen the feather or to feather edges to different degrees, use the Directional Feather effect. Feathering from the top, bottom, left, and right may be controlled together or individually by depressing or releasing, respectively, the Make All Settings the Same chain link icon between them. The angle twirler sets the direction into which the feather radiates—the direction of fade between the object and its background—and should be used in conjunction with the widths.

The Shape dropdown menu allows you to choose from where the fading begins—the First Edge Only, the Leading Edge, or All Edges. On simple objects like squares and circles, the choice you make in the Shape field is irrelevant; there will be no difference among the three. However, in the case of a shape with corners or points placed at different depths within the overall area of the shape, something like a star, for example, the Shape setting determines which edges fade initially (see Figure 6.9).

FIGURE 6.9
A star with the same width Directional Feather effect with, left to right, the Shape field set to First Edge Only, Leading Edge, and All Edges

GRADIENT FEATHER

From the perspective of both creativity and, especially, productivity, the Gradient Feather effect is worth more than all the rest put together. Graduating a solid color into no color is a very, very common task for many designers and layout artists—something we've faked for decades with a color-to-white gradient blend. The white, of course, was still fully opaque, making it impossible to allow background objects to shine through and blend with the gradient. Blending modes could make some gradients mix well with some backgrounds, but it was hit or miss. Most of the time, getting a gradient or any object to blend gradually with objects behind required doing it in Photoshop with layer styles or in Illustrator with opacity masks. Now it can be done directly in InDesign (see Figure 6.10).

FIGURE 6.10
Examples created with the Gradient Feather effect (also in living color on the color insert)

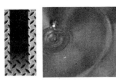

The Gradient Feather works exactly like the Gradient panel. Instead of working with color stops that blend one into the other, you're working with *opacity* stops, levels of opacity, that blend into one another. A black stop is 100% opaque, a white 0% opaque. Click an opacity stop—or click on an empty area beneath the gradient ramp to add a new opacity stop—and then set the opacity in the Opacity field. The object or attribute will respond by becoming more or less opaque in the corresponding area.

Both linear and radial gradients are supported, with angles on the former just like a normal color-to-color gradient. Additionally, the same manual control given to color-to-color gradients via the Gradient tool on the Tools panel is offered through the Gradient Feather tool, accessed by clicking and holding the Gradient tool in the Tools panel. Just like its counterpart, the Gradient Feather tool determines the placement, compression, and angle of a gradient feather defined through the Effects dialog. Where you click with the Gradient Feather tool is the start of the feather, and, after dragging, where you stop is the end of the feather.

More about Effects

When an object or one of its attributes has one or more effects applied, a special *fx* icon appears beside the object or attribute on the Effects panel (see Figure 6.11).

FIGURE 6.11
The *fx* icon on Fill indicates that it has effects applied.

MOVING AND REPLICATING EFFECTS

Given the fact that effects are attribute level, it's a common mistake to apply an effect to, say, the fill when you meant to apply it to the entire object. Rather than undoing all your work in the Effects dialog and trying to re-create it for the correct target, simply change the target of the effect. Click the *fx* icon beside the attribute in the Effects panel, and drag it atop a different attribute. For example, if you applied effects to the fill but they were intended for, or you'd like them applied to, the whole object, drag the *fx* from beside Fill, and drop it beside Object. Done. The effects will move from one to the other.

To *copy* the effect to another attribute without removing it from the first, hold Cmd+Option+Shift/Ctrl+Alt+Shift before selecting the fx icon. Then, upon dragging, you'll see a hand cursor with a plus sign in it indicating that the effects will be copied and not moved.

Now, to copy the same effect to a completely different object, it's very much the same. Select the object with the effects—the source object—and drag the *fx* icon from beside that object's attribute entry on the Effects panel. Drop the icon directly atop the target object. It will apply the same effect to the same attribute, meaning that if you drag a Stroke effect from the source object, it will be a Stroke effect in the target object. This is for ad hoc effects replication or for use between objects whose other characteristics vary. The easiest way to apply the same effects to multiple objects is to create an object style, which we'll discuss in Chapter 13, "Efficiency."

Effects can be removed in several ways, the easiest two of which are to drag the *fx* icon to the trashcan icon at the bottom of the panel and to select the attribute on the Effects panel and choose Clear Effects from that panel's flyout menu.

GLOBAL LIGHT

Effects like shadows, glows, beveling and embossing, and so on are lighting effects. They're meant to bring the illusion of three-dimensionality to a two-dimensional medium by faking the effects of light cast on volumetric objects floating in 3D space. The illusion works only if the effects follow the basic logic of consistent light sources. In other words, if your drop and inner shadows are being cast about in different directions, if they don't line up with the highlighted and shadowed surfaces of your bevels, you can't sell the illusion. The viewer will be yanked out of the perception of 3D space into the reality of flat ink on flat paper.

If your design has—or should have—multiple light-directed effects, determine where the light source is relative to the document and the objects. Decide in your mind where you are placing the imaginary light bulb that illuminates your objects and casts those shadows and reflects in those highlights. Once you see in your mind's eye the light bulb dangling in place near the document, tell InDesign where you've hung it by selecting Global Light from the Effects panel's flyout menu (see Figure 6.12).

FIGURE 6.12
The Global Light
dialog

The Global Light dialog has but two options—Angle and Altitude—with one informing the document lighting effects' direction and the other the intensity of the light. It's always the same

wattage bulb (Energy Star–compliant, environmentally friendly, of course), but its effect on the document becomes more intense as the altitude decreases. Both fields accept typed-in numeric values in degrees, but a more intuitive way to alter both is to drag the light source crosshair in the dial. Dragging it around the dial changes the angle, and dragging the crosshair toward or away from the center dot alters the altitude, descending or ascending, respectively. If you've already created effects on objects, and if, in the individual options for those effects, you checked the Use Global Light option, then changes made in the Global Light dialog will alter all those effects while you watch (turn on Preview, of course).

Using effects with a global light has a slight drawback: uniformity. True, uniformity is key to maintaining the illusion of dimensionality, but being *too* uniform will ruin it just as quickly as not being uniform enough. It's a delicate balance. The problem with global light is that it sets all light-directed effects to use *exactly* the same angle and altitude.

Let's say you have a row of blocks. (I don't know why you'd have a row of blocks. It's just an example.) Let's also say that you've decided your light source hangs just a little lower than the top-left corner of the first block at around 35° to 45° altitude. In reality, the closer an object is to a light source shining on it, the more severe the highlighting and the sharper and shallower the shadows cast by the object. As objects move away from the light source, highlighting becomes less intense and shadows lengthen while their edges diffuse. This is true whether the light is pointed straight down to form a circular light area or angled to form conical light. Unfortunately, InDesign's understanding of lighting is very simple—and I mean beyond the facts that there's only one possible light source and no way to shape the light. Distance from the light source is not among the factors considered by InDesign when it's creating light-directed effects. In fact, InDesign considers every object to have its own companion light source; the global light is just aligning all the objects' individual light sources to the same location relative to each object. The object farthest from the light source you imagine will be influenced exactly the same by the global light source, with identical effect angles and intensities, as the object closest to your imagined light source. Take a gander at Figure 6.13 to see what I mean. Notice how the highlights and shadows of the objects on the left are identical despite logic dictating that they should all vary dependent upon their distance from, and angle in relation to, the light source on the left. Which of the two sets looks more realistic?

FIGURE 6.13
InDesign's Global Light creates light-directed effects that are unrealistically uniform. An InDesign-created set of drop shadows (left) versus a set manually tweaked to reflect real-world perceptions (right). (Check the version on the color insert to really see the difference.)

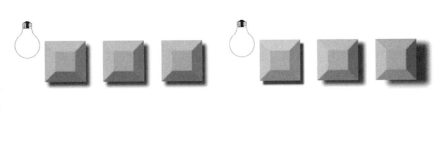

The advantage to using the document's global light settings to inform effects is simple to grasp: Every such effect, on every object or attribute to which it has been applied, can be altered document-wide from the single location of the Global Light dialog. With global light, efficiency and productivity are a trade-off with realism and accuracy. Efficiency is a powerful motivator, and I'm not implying otherwise—you know how much I value creative efficiency—but if you want realism, if you really want to sell the illusion of dimensionality, don't rely on the document global light. Use it, certainly, but deviate when logic or the laws of physics dictate.

As you saw in the right image in Figure 6.13, realism dictates that light-directed effects adjust their angle, length, and depth in correspondence with the objects' position and distance in relation to the light source. With objects closer to the top-left page light source, I shortened and sharpened their shadows, gradually lengthening and softening the edges on other object shadows as they moved away from the light. Moreover, objects that were not directly in line with the light source—such as the bottom-left and top-right corners—required that the shadows rotate. How? Simple: I drew imaginary lines (light rays) from the light source to the corners of the objects. Shadows don't cast *toward* a light source, so if the light struck a particular side, I pushed the shadow away from that edge, casting it off the opposing side.

I started with a global light but tweaked the settings per block to create a realistic environment. The rest was basic geometry and a lifetime of familiarity with Thomas Edison's invention. I'd use the same method to determine the location of highlights and shadows on beveled or embossed objects.

Creating realism is time consuming, of course. Anyone who has ever watched a "Making Of" DVD featurette knows that. When you're making changes to objects with realistic characteristics, it can take even longer to maintain or adapt the reality to the changes, so quality becomes a trade-off with speed. I won't presume to tell you where to draw that line, when to set a document global light and be done with it, and when to start tweaking angle spinners and Spread fields. Some jobs demand speed and "good enough" quality, others the extra mile even with the extra time it will take to run that far.

Strokes

If you're in the game, then the stroke's the word.

— *Billy Squier*

If you've used InDesign or any layout or illustration application for more than a few minutes, you have the basics of strokes and the Stroke panel. Let's talk about those things that you may not have heard, the things about which I often get questions from experienced InDesign users. Figure 6.14 is the Stroke panel with options shown (from the flyout menu). With a tip of the hat to Billy Squier, let's briefly go through each section. Don't take no rhythm; don't take no style.

Weight   The stroke thickness, expressed in whole or partial points (e.g., 1 pt or .333 pt).

Cap   When open paths terminate (as opposed to a closed path like a circle that has neither a start nor an end), how should their ends look? That's the question posed by these three unassuming buttons. Your options are Butt Cap, Round Cap, and Projecting Cap, and their resulting effects on paths are exactly what the buttons depict.

FIGURE 6.14
The Stroke panel

Miter Limit　When a path makes a corner, InDesign has to decide what to do with the stroke on the outside of the turn. It must consider whether the stroke color should keep going in the same direction until it reaches a point, even if that's a great distance off, or if the stroke should be clipped somewhere before it reaches a point. The Miter Limit field sets the clipping boundary; when a stroke reaches that limit, InDesign will cut down the path (see Figure 6.15).

FIGURE 6.15
 A sharp corner results in a long spike in the stroke (left), and a miter limit clips the stroke (right).

Many people think the Miter Limit field is measured in points. It's not. It's in multiples of the stroke weight. Thus the default miter limit of 4 is four times the stroke weight; a 1 pt stroke weight begets a 4 pt miter limit. Using defaults, InDesign will clip the stroke with the join type option if the stroke reaches or extends beyond 4 pts long. If you're getting too many mitered corners when you want sharp, up the miter limit.

Join　Join is the shape of corners in paths, either Miter Join (sharp, single angle), Round Join, or Beveled Join.

Align Stroke　These three buttons determine where the stroke falls relative to the path. Paths themselves have no thickness—they're just the connections drawn between two points plotted on the X and Y axes. Because they have no thickness, the stroke must align somehow to the path. As you can see in Figure 6.16, where that is has a great effect on the results. You can choose

◆　Align Stroke to Center, straddling the path such that a 20 pt stroke puts 10 pts inside and 10 pts outside the path

◆　Align Stroke to Outside, putting the entire stroke outside the path and thus keeping the fill color, image, or text unimpinged upon

◆　Align Stroke to Inside, putting the entire stroke inside the path to encroach upon and perhaps obscure part of the shape fill

FIGURE 6.16:
Left to right:
stroke aligned to
center, outside,
and inside.

Type   The Type menu contains the different styles of stroke available, including a single solid stroke, picture-frame-like multiple-line strokes, and several varieties of broken strokes—these last will get more interesting in three more paragraphs.

Start and End   Need an arrowhead or other stroke adornment? Although not as robust as Illustrator or other drawing and flowcharting software, InDesign can do basic flowcharting and diagramming arrows. The start is the first anchor point you created in drawing your path, and the end the last. A little-known feature is the ability to reverse the direction of arrows without a return to the Stroke panel—to do it, if you choose, with a keyboard command.

Let's say you have a straight-line path drawn left to right to which you've applied a start of an arrow and an end of a circle. The arrow, therefore, is on the left and the circle the right. If you need it the opposite way, you can go back to the Stroke panel, exchanging the start and end adornments; you can also flip the path or rotate it, but that becomes problematic if the path is already at an angle. Instead, select Object ➤ Paths ➤ Reverse Path. The direction of the path will be reversed, just as if you drew it right to left, and the start and end will transpose without altering the position or rotation of the path itself. If you need to do that frequently, assign a keyboard shortcut to the Reverse Path command in Edit ➤ Keyboard Shortcuts.

Gap Color and Gap Tint   When you choose any stroke type other than Solid, Gap Color lights up. The gap is the space between multiline, dashed, dotted, slashed, or other broken stroke types. In addition to coloring the positive parts of the stroke, the Gap Color dropdown allows you to select a swatch to color the negative spaces between. Once a gap color is chosen, Gap Tint activates to fine-tune the gap color. In other words, if you want effects like those in Figure 6.17, you don't have to overlay multiple objects.

FIGURE 6.17
Gap colors create the effect of multiple objects overlaid without doubling the work to create and manage them. (See the full-color version in the color insert.)

Custom Stroke Styles

When you select Dashed, the last option in the Type menu, additional fields appear at the bottom of the Stroke panel (see Figure 6.18) to define a custom dashed stroke. Using points or any measurement system InDesign understands, enter dash and/or gap widths (as many as three pair) for exactly the dashed stroke you need. Above the Dash and Gap fields, choose how the dashed stroke handles corners to (try to) avoid weird bunching of, or gapping in, dashes.

FIGURE 6.18
Defining a custom
dashed stroke

When the Dash and Gap fields don't offer enough control, or to create a stroke comprising something other than rectangular dashes, select Stroke Styles from the panel flyout menu. You'll see listed there the multiline stroke styles. Click the New button to open the New Stroke Style dialog and build your own stroke style (see Figure 6.19).

Changing the Type field sets the tone for the stroke and the rest of the options.

FIGURE 6.19
The New Stroke
Style dialog

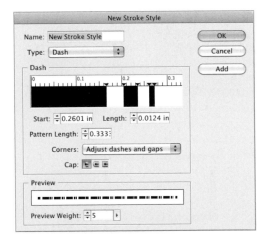

Dash   Figure 6.19 shows the version of the New Stroke Style dialog that occurs when you choose the Dash type. Within the horizontal ruler you *draw* the dashes as black blocks; negative spaces between the blocks are gaps that will appear in the stroke. At the bottom of the dialog, the preview keeps your stroke in perspective, at the weight you choose in the bottom field.

To draw a new dash segment, simply follow these steps:

1. Click in an empty space in the ruler section—either within the ruler itself or in the drawing area below it.

2. Once a dash segment is begun, drag the arrows above it, within the ruler, to resize the dash. You can also use the Start and Length fields for precision sizing.

    ◆ If the pattern is too short or long at its default one-third inch, change the Pattern Length field. Even if the pattern is a good length at its default, you may want to adjust it to take up any excess empty space at the end of the pattern, which will become a gap before the pattern repeats.

    ◆ Note the presence of Cap and Corners adjustments to precisely control the ends of dashed strokes and how dashes behave at angles.

    ◆ A custom stroke must begin with a dash (or dot or stripe); it cannot begin with a gap. Additionally, each stroke is limited to five dash segments. If you genuinely need something more complicated than five dash segments, use Illustrator to create and apply the custom stroke as a new brush style, and then copy the stroked object into InDesign as a vector path.

3. When you're happy with your new custom stroke style, give it a name at the top, and then click either OK, to save the style and close the New Stroke Style dialog, or Add, which also saves the style but leaves the dialog open and ready to create additional styles.

Dotted   Of the two default dotted stroke styles—Dotted and Japanese Dots—many designers prefer to use the latter because of its narrower gaps between dots (see Figure 6.20). Tightly spaced dots are more aesthetically pleasing when used as, for example, text separators in horizontal paragraph rules and vertical *drop rules* and cell borders in tables.

FIGURE 6.20
InDesign's default dotted styles: Dotted (upper) and Japanese Dots (lower)

Real World Scenario

CUSTOMIZING THE DOTTED STYLE

Personally, I often find even the Japanese Dots style a little loose for my tastes—particularly when using a 25% to 50% black dotted stroke close to text. Other times, say, with a custom two-color frame border, Dotted is spaced too tightly. Choosing the Dotted style from the Type menu opens a horizontal ruler similar to the one offered for new Dash type strokes, but there are no lengths; just click within the ruler to place a dot, and click and drag a dot to reposition it. The Center field aligns the center point of the dot to a place on the ruler.

Stripes   Multiple line strokes like Thick-Thick, Thick-Thin-Thick, and so on are Stripe types. Choosing Stripe from the Type menu activates unique fields and a vertical ruler (see Figure 6.21). Click and drag to draw a stripe. Rather than absolute placements within a fixed-width pattern, stripes are set in the style based on percentage of height. For example, a stripe of 10% will be 1 pt in a 10 pt stroke or 10 pts in a 100 pt stroke.

FIGURE 6.21
Drawing a Stripe
stroke style

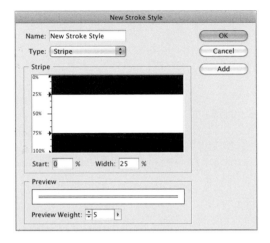

Your new stroke styles will be available from the Type menu on the Stroke panel and also from anywhere stroke styles are selected—paragraph rules dialogs, underline and strikethrough options, and more. Through the Stroke Styles dialog, they can also be saved to, and loaded from, disk for sharing with colleagues.

Swatches

Wait! Don't skip ahead! I'm not going to waste your time with a Swatches panel walk-through or by explaining how to use and create swatches. Plenty of InDesign 101–style books will tell you about that, and if you're reading *this* book, you've long since graduated from InDesign 101. This section isn't about the basics of working with swatches. In the first half of this course we'll discuss advanced swatch work like *mixed ink* swatches and mixed ink groups, and then we'll talk about sharing and working efficiently with swatches.

I expect everyone to be prepared at the start of each section with a sharpened No. 2 pencil, a three-ring binder, and InDesign CS5 opened on his computer.

Mixed Inks

Mixed ink colors are the result of mixing one or more spot colors with process inks or of mixing two spot colors. You may know of them under another name: tint build or multi-ink colors; the latter is what QuarkXPress calls them. Mixing inks allows you to coax a larger selection of colors and tints from a minimum of inks (read *more creativity, lower production cost*).

Creating Mixed Ink Swatches

If, after reading the preceding paragraph, you're feeling as confused as an Obama economic adviser, don't throw in the towel just yet. The best way to understand mixed inks is to make a mixed ink, so let's do that.

Mixed inks must contain at least one spot color, and that spot color must already be on the Swatches panel. The first step, therefore, is to make a spot color swatch.

1. From the Swatches panel flyout menu, select New Color Swatch. In the resulting dialog, set Color Type to Spot, and from Color Mode, choose any spot color library like PANTONE Solid Coated (PANTONE+ if you've upgraded to the 2010 PANTONE PLUS Series of digital color libraries that replace the older PANTONE Matching System libraries).

2. When the colors load, pick one and click OK.

3. Now that you have a spot color swatch created, the New Mixed Ink Swatch command will be selectable from the Swatches panel menu. Choose it and up will pop the New Mixed Ink Swatch dialog (see Figure 6.22).

FIGURE 6.22:
The New Mixed Ink Swatch dialog

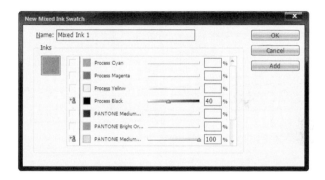

4. Click in the empty box to the left of the spot color you just created to start, and then choose one of the process inks to mix in.

5. Beside each ink name is the ink's tint ramp and a tint percentage field. Try dragging the tint sliders while watching the preview swatch on the left. Notice the new colors created by combining the two inks?

   Depending on the spot you chose, chances are good that some of the colors you can mix up with only two inks would have otherwise required additional spots to print. That would be more plates (read *additional RIP time and film charges*) and more inks (read *more cycles through the press and additional per-ink setup charges*).

6. Once you have a new color you like (keeping in mind that what you see onscreen may not be accurate), give it a name more explanatory than the default *Mixed Ink 1*; then click OK to save the swatch and close the dialog or Add to save the swatch and leave the dialog open ready to create more mixed ink swatches. Of course, you can use more than two inks as long as at least one is a spot color.

CREATING MIXED INK GROUPS

The only real drawback to creating a mixed ink according to this procedure is the tedium of it, the need to manually commingle the inks to create a new mixed ink swatch. If you wanted to, say, get all possible combinations of two inks in 10% increments of both tints, you'd have to manually create all those new swatches by changing percentages and then clicking Add. That isn't particularly difficult, just tedious. Wouldn't it be great if InDesign found all the possible combinations for you? That's exactly what mixed ink *groups* do.

Select New Mixed Ink Group from the Swatches panel flyout menu to open the dialog shown in Figure 6.23 and its counterpart in the color insert. As with the New Mixed Ink Swatch dialog, add an ink to the mix by clicking in the blank space at the left. Now, instead of specifying a tint percentage to make the mix, set a *range* of tint percentages and let InDesign create each individual mix and swatch. Let's do it, starting from an opened New Mixed Ink Group dialog:

FIGURE 6.23
Create many mixed ink swatches at once with New Mixed Ink Group.

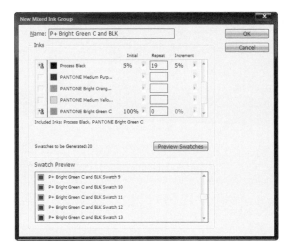

1. In the Initial column, set the starting tint percentage for each ink. For this exercise we want to add varying stages of black to the spot color, so set the initial tint of the spot to **100%** and Process Black to **5%**, the lowest desired mix value.

   The first mixed ink swatch will have these initial tints and will grow from there toward greater tint percentages. Because the spot begins at 100%, only black's contribution will increase while the spot remains constant at full ink density.

2. The Repeat field is the number of color steps and the number of swatches to create, starting at the initial value. Because we want to add black in 5% increments up to 100% black plus 100% spot, set the Increment field to **5%** and the Repeat field to **19** (100% divided by 5% equals 20 steps minus the initial 5% step). The spot will stay constant at 100%; thus its Repeat field should be 1, disabling the Increment field as well.

   Notice that below the ink selection area is a running count of the number of swatches to be created. Each ink you add, each repeat value, increases that number exponentially. Always check the count before hitting OK to make sure a typo or incorrect value hasn't set you up to generate too many swatches.

3. Click the Preview Swatches button to see the results of the mixed ink group without committing them to the document's Swatches panel. Swatch names are determined by the Name field at the top of the dialog, with *Swatch X* appended.

4. If the swatches meet with your approval, click OK and watch the Swatches panel populate.

In addition to the various Swatch X mixed ink swatches (identified by the double ink droplet icons), you'll have a mixed ink group swatch identified by a stamp-like icon (see Figure 6.24). You see, all those swatches you just made are still a dynamic part of the mixed ink group—change the group, change all the swatches. Save the cheerleader, save the world.

FIGURE 6.24
Creating a mixed ink group results in all of these mixed ink swatches (also on the color insert).

You *can* change individual swatches, to adjust the mix percentages, for example, or to convert the group swatch into a standard spot or process swatch. But, to change the colors in all the swatches in the group—for instance, to replace one spot or process color with another across all the grouped mixed inks—edit the group, not the swatch. Instead of editing the swatch, double-click the mixed ink group swatch itself (hold Cmd+Option+Shift/Ctrl+Alt+Shift while double-clicking to edit without applying the swatch to the selected object and without making it the default for new objects). That will get you to the Mixed Ink Group Options dialog (see Figure 6.25), where you can rename the group, convert mixed ink swatches to process colors (note that this is irreversible), and disable or replace one or more inks in the mix (note that you must always have at least two colors in the mix, and at least one must be a spot). When you click OK, all the swatches in the group will update to reflect the changes.

FIGURE 6.25
Editing a mixed
ink group in the
Mixed Ink Group
Options dialog

If all you want to do is replace a color in a mixed ink group, there's an even faster way. When, on the Swatches panel, you delete a normal spot or process swatch used in a mixed ink or mixed ink group, InDesign will ask you to choose a color with which to replace the one you're deleting. Your choice will update all mixed ink and mixed ink group swatches that included the replaced color.

Managing Swatches

I'm sure you already know that you can drag and drop swatches in the Swatches panel list to reorder them, just as I'm sure you're perfectly aware that you can rename swatches by editing them (Cmd+Option+Shift+double-click/Ctrl+Alt+Shift+double-click). There are some other things that you may not know, however.

SELECT ALL UNUSED

This command on the Swatches panel flyout menu selects all swatches that aren't currently used by some object in the document. Once they're selected, just click the trashcan icon at the bottom of the panel to delete all unused swatches in one fell swoop. Leaving unused swatches in a document has no practical effect—you won't, for instance, get extra plates during separation just for having swatches in the panel. It is a usability issue and productivity issue, however. It's just easier to work with a Swatches panel uncluttered by the extraneous results of past experiments.

ADD UNNAMED SWATCHES

Add Unnamed Swatches is kind of the opposite of Select All Unused. In the course of designing, we don't always create swatches for every color we mix on the Colors panel and elsewhere. Often, colors are created on page 2 and forgotten about by page 6; when page 8 rolls around, the color is created again ad hoc with hopefully the same mix as other instances. Selecting Add Unnamed Swatches from the Swatches panel flyout menu creates swatches for all in-use colors in the document that don't already have swatches. It also associates the source objects with the swatches, making color replacement as easy as deleting the swatch and choosing a substitute.

MERGE SWATCHES

In the Swatches panel, select any two or more swatches, and then choose Merge Swatches from the panel menu. What happens is not really a merge—you won't get green by using the command on blue and yellow swatches. Instead, it's more of a replacement.

Let's say you have three color swatches—red, blue, and yellow—all in use as the fill colors for different objects. Selecting them in the Swatches panel in order—first clicking red, then blue, and finally yellow—and executing the Merge Swatches command will simultaneously delete the blue and yellow swatches and fill all blue and yellow objects with red. The first swatch you click, regardless of its actual order in the list, becomes the surviving replacement color. Merge Swatches is a handy way to replace colors with a minimum of fuss—particularly for those of you who are cleaning up someone else's document in preflight.

UNDELETABLE SWATCHES

A very common frustration is ending up with swatches that you can't find in use anywhere and can't be deleted no matter what you try. This problem is nearly always caused by a color embedded in a placed asset—particularly vector assets. See the sidebar "Finding the Unfindable Swatch, Deleting the Undeletable Swatch" for a real-world strategy to deal with this problem.

FINDING THE UNFINDABLE SWATCH, DELETING THE UNDELETABLE SWATCH

Most often, a swatch that cannot be deleted in InDesign is actually contained within a placed EPS, PDF, AI, or other image asset. InDesign can place and modify such assets within the context of the instance on the page, but it cannot *edit* the asset itself, cannot change the EPS, PDF, AI, or what have you. Therefore, InDesign can't delete or alter swatches that may be in the asset. Worse, you often can't even *find* where the color is used. Often this happens because the path carrying the offending color is hidden behind other paths, or, even more common, there is no path, just a single anchor point.

In vector drawing, a single anchor point is considered an object just as surely as a complex path. As an object, the anchor point may have a fill and/or stroke color assigned to it even though there isn't a path to make either fill or stroke visible. One errant click of the mouse in Illustrator or another program can create an orphaned anchor point, and thus an orphaned color instance, resulting in an undeletable color swatch in InDesign. Because these orphaned anchor points are invisible, they're also often impossible to find—unless you know to look for them and *how* to look.

FIND THE IMAGE

First, in InDesign, identify the image that is the source of the undeletable color swatch.

1. Save a copy of the document—never perform troubleshooting on the original.
2. Remove all unused swatches from the Swatches panel to narrow the possibilities and make cleanup easier.
3. Go back to the first page of your document containing placed assets, and select and delete all placed assets.
4. Select all unused swatches again with the appropriate Swatches panel command. Is the ostensibly undeletable swatch among those highlighted as unused? If not, move on to page 2, deleting all placed assets and then selecting all unused swatches. Keep repeating this seek-and-destroy process until the swatch *does* get selected by the Select All Unused command, and then move on to step 5.

   When removing all objects and then selecting unused swatches causes the undeletable swatch to be flagged as not in use, you will have found the page containing the swatch. The next step is to narrow that down to the exact image.

5. Press Cmd+Z/Ctrl+Z to undo the deletion of all of the page's objects, and then, one at a time, delete each placed asset object and choose Select All Unused from the Swatches panel flyout menu. Eventually, the undeletable swatch will be among the selected, identifying the exact image that contains it.

6. Press Cmd+Z/Ctrl+Z again to restore the image you just deleted, and keep it selected.

7. On the Links panel (Window ➤ Links), the asset will also be highlighted. Click the Edit Original button at the bottom of the Links panel, the button that looks like a pencil, which will open the application registered on your system to edit such imagery—Illustrator for vector or Photoshop for raster, for example.

Note: If the undeletable swatch is not contained within a linked asset, if it's instead within objects or imagery that were *pasted* into InDesign, the Links panel will not help you. Instead, copy the asset and paste it back into the application that created it. Make the necessary changes, and then copy and paste back into InDesign.

IF THE EDIT ORIGINAL COMMAND OPENS PHOTOSHOP…

1. Open the Channels panel in Photoshop (Window ➤ Channels).

   RGB, Lab, and process colors created in Photoshop do not generate swatches upon import of the image to InDesign. Only spot colors, created on separate channels, create InDesign swatches. Therefore, your undeletable swatch will be a separate channel beneath the Red, Green, and Blue channels or Cyan, Magenta, Yellow, and Black channels. That channel's name will be the same as the title of the InDesign swatch.

2. Turn off all channels except the offending spot color channel by clicking the eyeball icon beside each of the other channels. When only the spot color channel is visible, its contents will render onscreen in black rather than in the actual color.

3. Examine the image data there. Do you need it? Should it remain a spot color, generating a new plate upon separation output from InDesign or the RIP? If your answer is yes, close everything and go back to your original InDesign document to keep working. If no, if you don't want the spot color, decide whether you want that image data at all.

   ◆ To keep the image data but convert the spot color into the nearest equivalent mix of process inks (or RGB), highlight the spot channel and choose Merge Spot Channel from the Channels panel flyout menu. The image data on the spot channel will become part of the CMYK or RGB channels, approximating the original spot color as closely as those color models allow. Note that Merge Spot Channel is not available for images in Lab mode. If your image is in Lab mode, you'll need to first convert it to RGB or CMYK with the appropriate command on the Image ➤ Image Mode menu.

   ◆ If you decide you don't want the spot color or the image data on the channel, select the spot channel and drag and drop it atop the trashcan icon at the bottom of the Channels panel.

4. Save the document and close Photoshop.

   Because you used InDesign's Edit Original command, InDesign will automatically update the placed asset without further action required. When you reopen your original document, of course, you'll be prompted to update the image with a single button click. In both the original and temporary troubleshooting copy, the formerly undeletable swatch should now be deletable.

IF THE EDIT ORIGINAL COMMAND OPENS ILLUSTRATOR...

Illustrator is much more like InDesign than like Photoshop in terms of color handling and swatches. You won't find a Channels panel, for instance. Instead, you'll need to locate the path or anchor point containing the unwanted spot color swatch:

1. On Illustrator's Swatches panel you'll find the offending swatch (hint: spot color swatches appear with a black dot inside a white triangle in their lower-right corner). With no objects selected, choose from the Swatches panel the spot color swatch of which you want to rid yourself.

2. Go to Select ➤ Same ➤ Fill Color. Illustrator will then select any and all paths (and orphaned anchor points) filled with that color. If nothing was selected, move on to step 3; otherwise, skip down to step 4.

3. If trying to select objects with the offending swatch as their fill produced no results, then it isn't being used as a fill color. Try looking for it as a stroke color with Select ➤ Same ➤ Stroke Color.

4. Examine what was selected and decide whether to delete or recolor it.

   ◆ If you decide that you don't need the selected items, press the Delete key on your keyboard. Poof! Problem solved.

   ◆ However, if you decide you *do* want the selected paths, you just don't want them to use a spot color ink, convert the spot color to CMYK or RGB. Double-click the swatch in the Swatches panel and, in the Swatch Options dialog, change Color Mode to CMYK or RGB and then the Color Type field to Process Color.

   Note: Even if you did get hits on the fill color, it's a good idea to go back and look for any paths with that stroke color as well.

5. Save the document and close Illustrator.

   Because you used InDesign's Edit Original command, InDesign will automatically update the placed asset without further action required. When you reopen your original document, of course, you'll be prompted to update the image with a single button click. In both the original and temporary troubleshooting copy, the formerly undeletable swatch should now be deletable.

Note: Illustrator artwork can contain both embedded and linked raster images and even other vector art files. It's entirely possible to have a Russian doll of images—one image placed into another, which is placed into another, and another, and so on. If you determine that the unwanted swatch is within a linked asset rather than the Illustrator document itself, use the Edit Original command on Illustrator's identical Links panel, and then follow the same procedures for whichever application opens.

IF THE EDIT ORIGINAL COMMAND OPENS ANOTHER APPLICATION...

Most raster image editors will conform at least loosely to the Photoshop directions, and most vector drawing applications to the Illustrator. Use those as guides within the unique environments and user interfaces of whichever applications you employ to edit raster and vector artwork.

Other times, swatches are rendered undeletable because of file corruption, which is regrettably very common with documents converted from QuarkXPress, PageMaker, or even earlier versions of InDesign. The best way to counter file corruption is to force a complete rewrite of the document code:

1. Choose File ➢ Export and save a copy of the document as an InDesign Markup IDML file—a special, pure XML copy of the document.

2. Close the original INDD document, and open the IDML version.

3. Choose File ➢ Save As and save the document back to a normal INDD InDesign document.

4. Try deleting the offending swatch.

Of course, the four magic swatches whose names are bracketed—None, Paper, Black, and Registration—can never be deleted by design.

Speaking of swatch issues upon converting documents from QuarkXPress…

SWATCHES FROM QUARKXPRESS

When opening a QuarkXPress version 3.3 to 4.1 document in InDesign, swatches convert faithfully, with a few notable exceptions:

White QuarkXPress doesn't have a swatch named Paper. Instead, it has White. Upon converting the XPress document to InDesign, you'll often have both Paper and White. In theory, leaving the White swatch in use shouldn't hurt; in practice, though, it has been known to confuse some RIPs. The solution is simple: Delete the White swatch. If it's in use as a fill or stroke color, InDesign will prompt for a swatch with which to replace it. Choose Paper.

Multi-Ink Colors to Mixed Ink Colors The two are nearly identical with one difference: QuarkXPress allows multi-ink colors without the inclusion of a spot color while InDesign's mixed ink colors require a spot. Multi-inks *with* a spot will convert just fine into mixed inks. Multi-inks *without* a spot will become standard process color swatches.

Color Library Colors Colors from QuarkXPress's color library are converted to process swatches based on their CMYK values.

HSB and Lab Colors QuarkXPress HSB and Lab colors are converted to RGB colors in InDesign.

Sharing Swatches

The ability to share swatches—between documents, between applications—makes for fewer trees sacrificed to scribbling down color formulas. Whether it was eco-conscience or a desire to shave just a little more time and effort off designers' project work, Adobe has made accessing and sharing color swatches between applications easy within the Creative Suite.

IMPORTING SWATCHES FROM OTHER DOCUMENTS

On the flyout menu of the Swatches panel, the Load Swatches command enables importing swatches from any preexisting InDesign document or template. Just choose the command, select the document, and click Open; all that document's color swatches will import to the current document. You can import swatches from InDesign INDD documents and INDT templates, Illustrator AI and EPS files, and Adobe Swatch Exchange ASE files.

If you want to import swatches from other documents selectively instead of all at once, follow this procedure:

1. Choose New Color Swatch from the Swatches panel flyout menu.

2. In the New Color Swatch dialog, select the last option in the Color Mode dropdown, Other Library. A file dialog will appear.

3. Choose from the Open a File dialog any of the file types InDesign supports for swatch import—INDD, IDML, INDT, AI, EPS, or ASE—and click OK. The swatches in the chosen document will appear in the swatch list of the New Color Swatch dialog.

4. Choose the swatch to import, and click OK or Add.

MAKING NEW DEFAULT SWATCHES

If you work in an in-house design, production, or press services department, or if for some other reason you find yourself regularly working with the same colors, the Load Swatches command can make your brand identity colors the defaults for all new documents. Open InDesign *without* opening documents, and load up swatches from a previous document. They will populate the Swatches panel (delete any you don't regularly need). Close InDesign to commit the changes, and then, in every future session of InDesign, every new document you create will automatically have your corporate colors ready and waiting on the Swatches panel.

SHARING SWATCHES WITH OTHER APPLICATIONS

An Adobe Swatch Exchange (ASE) file is a universal swatches format that works with InDesign, Illustrator, Photoshop, and Fireworks. Each of those applications can export its native Swatches panel to Adobe Swatch Exchange; the swatches can then be brought into the others with the Load Swatches or New Color Swatch (and counterpart) command. In InDesign just choose Save Swatches from the Swatches panel flyout menu and save the ASE file somewhere where the rest of the Creative Suite applications can find it.

Using ASE files is a great way to ensure consistency between original art—from raster to vector, print layout to Web layout—and even for the future. What I mean by that is this: I recommend to my freelance and agency clients that deal with multiple clients (and multiple brand color sets) that they create an ASE file for every client and multiple-document project as part of the initial job setup. Either the production manager or one assigned creative generates the necessary swatches from the client specs, creates the ASE, and makes it part of the core project files alongside other core files like the client's logo, signature fonts, and so on. After the initial work is completed, when follow-up jobs come in for the same client, any member of the design team can import the swatches from the ASE and get right to work without having to dig through other document Swatches palettes to identify which are the brand identity colors and which are only specific to a particular document or project.

VIEWING SWATCHES—WITHOUT OPENING OR IMPORTING

I have to say, as simple a thing as it is, the ability to view a document's colors in Adobe Bridge—without opening the document—strikes me as among the best arguments for using Bridge. If all you want to do is see which colors a document uses or grab a couple of color formulas, there's no longer any need to load the creating application and open the document, or even import swatches.

You're probably managing your digital assets in Bridge anyway, so just select the desired document and look to the Metadata panel on the left (see Figure 6.26). Among the expandable sections are Plates (not for INDD files), which shows all the process and spot inks in use, and Document Swatches (for INDD files), which displays all swatches used in the document. Because the default name of custom swatches is the formula (e.g., *C=66 M=69 Y=0 K=0*), you don't have to open the document to obtain a custom color formula. Nice, huh? Just remember to go by the color formula rather than the color appearance. The swatch Bridge displays may be nothing at all like the color in the document; if you compare Figures 6.24 and 6.26 on the color insert, you'll see that the spot colors in Bridge's Document Swatches panel look nothing like they do in InDesign. For instance, PANTONE Bright Green C looks cyan in Bridge, and the mixed ink swatches all turned black.

FIGURE 6.26

The Metadata panel in Adobe Bridge shows the selected document ink plates and document color swatches.

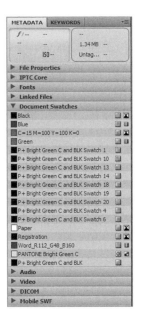

Anchored Objects

Adobe calls graphics and other objects that maintain their position relative to a place in the text regardless of where that text flows *anchored objects*. I call them tethered objects. After all, anchoring something is to stop it from moving. Anchored objects move—they follow the text describing them, jumping pages all by themselves if the text to which they're attached jumps to other pages. That's the behavior of a tethered object, not an anchored. Regardless of the semantics, anchored objects is one of the most time-saving features ever added to a layout application.

Here's a scenario: Imagine a typical business report—let's say an annual shareholders' report. The majority of the document is a single story, flowing from page to page to page. At various points in the main narrative, copious photographs, charts, graphs, and maybe some pull quotes are required to support the main text. In the typical workflow, these supportive materials (for simplicity's sake let's refer to them collectively as images) are placed into the document independent of the text frame, maybe floating out in the margins, maybe over the text itself and with

a text wrap. Somewhere in the text are references to most images—for example, *See Chart 16*—to give them context. If editorial or style changes force text to reflow, moving image references to different pages, the layout artist must manually go back and, one at a time, move the images as well. If a major reflow change occurs early in the document—say, page 5 of 350 pages—that artist is looking at days of doing nothing but repositioning images to follow their references.

That's a huge commitment of valuable creative and production time. Anchored objects reclaim that time, turning the act of repositioning 345 pages of images from days of tedious work into minutes of minor cleanup.

You see, instead of letting images float free in frames disconnected from the main story, images can be tethered to a specific place in the text with an invisible marker character called an anchor. That anchor is fixed in the text after *this* word or before *that* character, and it behaves like any other character, albeit invisibly. When text reflows, the anchor marker flows with it, dragging the image frame (or additional text frame) along. Anchored objects will *always* appear on the same page as the text that describes them (if you choose; you can also make them appear on the opposite page). InDesign will move them for you as the text moves. You can even force them to jump from the left to the right page and vice versa, changing position relative to the spine and page edge, if the anchor marker flows to the other side of the spread.

Anchoring Your First Object

Let's go hands-on, anchoring an object to text.

If you're already comfortable with threading text frames, something we'll get into in Chapter 8, "Stories," go ahead and set up your own facing-pages document with three to five pages and a single story running between them in a series of two- or three-column frames. If you prefer, I've already created such a document in this chapter's folder at `http://www.sybex.com/go/MasteringInDesigncs5`, and you're welcome to use it. Just open `Anchored Objects Text.indd` and turn to page 2 in that document.

1. With your text ready to go, find a place on the first page of the story about midway down the first column. Highlight two words, and give them an obvious and contrasting color like blue, green, red, or orange.

   The color isn't necessary to create anchored objects, of course; we're just doing it as part of this exercise solely so we can easily pick out the location of the object anchor we'll insert momentarily.

2. Deselect the text and text frame, and place an image, any image, into the document.

   I'm going to use the infamous Photoshop sample file `Ducky.tiff`, found in the Samples folder under the installation folder of Photoshop CS3 or before (Ducky was sadly retired in CS4). If you chose a large image, scale it down to about the width of a single column of the text.

3. On the Text Wrap panel (Window ➤ Text Wrap), choose Wrap Around Bounding Box to push text out of the way of the image.

   Again, although you may elect to use a text wrap on a real project, we're doing it now just to simplify this exercise—it's easier to watch the colored tracking text if it isn't hidden behind the image.

4. With the image still selected, cut it with Cmd+X/Ctrl+X, and switch to the Type tool by pressing T.

5. Insert your cursor between the two words you colored and paste with Cmd+V/Ctrl+V. You should see something like what I have in Figure 6.27 and its full-color twin in the color insert.

FIGURE 6.27
After pasting the image into the text

Wait, you might say. *That's just a simple inline graphic.* Correct, we've just inserted an inline graphic, which is nothing revolutionary. What *is* different, however, is how InDesign has redefined the role of inline graphics.

6. After pasting, your image frame should still be selected. If it isn't, grab it with the black arrow Selection tool, which will select the image and its frame (the Direct Selection tool will select just the image inside). The frame is the key part of this. Now, choose Object ➢ Anchored Object ➢ Options to open the initial, deceptively simple view of the Anchored Object Options dialog (see Figure 6.28).

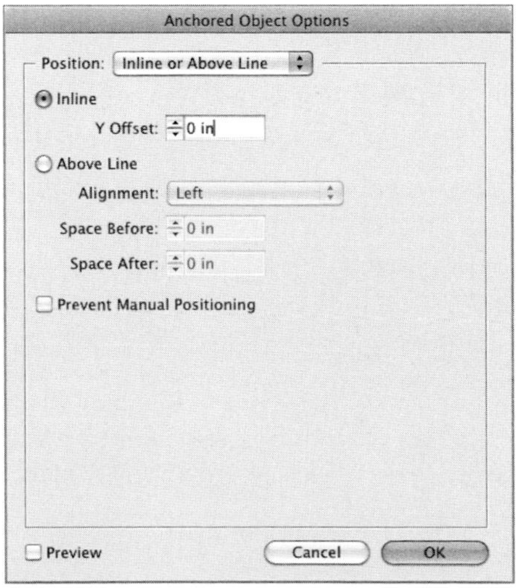

FIGURE 6.28
The Anchored Object Options dialog

With Position set to its initial value of Inline or Above Line, examine the Anchored Object Options dialog for a moment, and its functions should be easily gleaned. If not, don't sweat it; after this initial exercise, we'll go through what everything means.

7. For now, check the Preview box at the bottom, and arrange the dialog onscreen such that you can clearly see it and the image we're working with.

8. Now, set the Position field to its other option, Custom. Your image should jump similarly to mine (see Figure 6.29 and, to keep track of the red text, the version in the color insert).

FIGURE 6.29
After changing the Position field from Inline or Above Line to Custom, my image jumped out of the flow of text.

Ullaorero commolesenim zzrit wismodipit ad exeraestrud magnit nullan eu feugiam inciliq uipsum velese modolut ut vulputat. Im exeriure modolut la adigniat. Ut wis atio odit loborem quat in henibh ectem nis nosto del illa feuipit loborerit lor acing esto del ectem do odipis nummodolore consecte facipsummy nit alisim erate faccumsan utat, vel doloreet laortiscil ullam, quamcorem eu feugait la ad eu faciduisim zzriure faciniamcore digna cor ipsusto consequat, sequipisim dolutat.¶

Ut nibh elenim vel dolent iliquamcor iuscinibh et dolorpe rcillum venis nos nos ad magnisim nustion relit nis aciduip ex etum del ex ex eu feuiscil

Ud te dolobore corper adipsustrud euipsusto commy nonulla faccummy nullam, cons alis dipit, quissit am quat, quipsumsan hent atie min ullaor suscipis adio con ulputat. Ullaor sed molortie feu facilla augait la feuipsustio con et la alissit utem deliquatem dipsumsan utpatio odolore tisi eugiamet dolenibh exercipit am am ipsum eum dignim doloborem nummod erilit pratie magna con velenim delenim dolore tiscipisl estis etumsandit prat. Lorer in volore delendre magna ad mod minci bla feum delit nullam duis am acinis alit loreet nons nismodio odiam nulla faciduis aciduim diat. Met praesequat nusci blaoreet nonsequate vullum nosting

9. Check the Relative to Spine option at the top, but leave everything else at its defaults. Click OK.

10. With the Type tool, return to the story a paragraph or so *above* the colored text. Begin typing. It can be anything you want, just as long as you add a few lines or a new paragraph. We don't want so much new copy that the colored text goes into the next column, not yet. As you insert new text, as the colored tracking text is forced to move down the column, you should see the image move down to follow.

Congratulations, you've just made your first anchored object, an image that will follow a specific place in the text without ever needing to be manually repositioned.

11. Zoom to the point where you can see the entire spread onscreen.

12. Insert a lot more text, enough to push the colored tracking words to the next page across the spread (copying and pasting paragraphs will be much faster than typing).

Where did your image go? Right. It not only followed the text; it swapped sides of the page. That was the effect of the Relative to Spine option I had you check a moment ago. The anchored object alignment was relative to the spine—in this case, using defaults, it was positioned away from the spine. Thus, when the text jumped from a left-read to a right-read page, the anchored object swapped sides of the paper to stay in the outside margin away from the spine.

Now that you have the basic how-to of anchored objects down, pick your jaw up off the floor, and let's dive a little deeper into this tremendous time-saver.

Anchored Object Anatomy

As I noted before, anchored objects are thus called because they're poorly named—er, I mean, because they anchor to an invisible marker character within the text. If you look at hidden characters by choosing Show Hidden Characters from the bottom of the Type menu and zoom in on the words we colored, you'll see a yen symbol (¥) between the words, at the spot where we pasted the image frame (see Figure 6.30).

FIGURE 6.30
The anchored object marker appears as a yen symbol (again, see the color insert).

Ut·nibh¥elenim·vel

The anchor marker won't print, of course, and doesn't cause any additional spacing. Otherwise it's treated like any other character. You can select it, delete it (which deletes the anchored object, too), copy it (which copies the anchored object, too), and paste it (which, you guessed it, pastes the anchored object, too). Wherever that marker goes, so too goes the anchored object.

Because the anchor marker is treated like text, once it's highlighted, you can adjust its kerning, leading, or baseline offset, changing the anchored object in the process.

How can you distinguish an anchored object from a stand-alone object? Simple: Look for the anchor at the top of the object frame (see Figure 6.31). It's important to note that you can anchor *any* type of object. It can be a filled image frame like the one we just inserted, a filled text frame (for pull quotes, for example), an empty frame, a set of grouped objects (very useful for anchoring a photo *and* its caption or photo credit), or even a vector path you drew in InDesign.

FIGURE 6.31
An anchored object displays the anchor icon along its bounding box.

To convert an anchored object into a stand-alone object, select the object and choose Object ➤ Anchored Object ➤ Release. The object will remain but will no longer be tethered to the text.

Inline Anchored Object Options

Let's go back to the Anchored Object Options dialog (select the object and choose Object ➤ Anchored Object ➤ Options), and go through first the Inline or Above Line options. Figure 6.32 is that view again.

Inline Y Offset   When you choose Inline, you're telling InDesign that the image should remain on the same line as its marker, at the same horizontal place as the marker, be that the first character in the paragraph, the last, or in the middle of a sentence three lines deep (see Figure 6.33 and the version in the color insert). Therefore, your only option here is how far vertically to move it— think of the Y Offset field as baseline adjustment for the anchored object. Positive values move the object's baseline (bottom edge) up from the baseline of surrounding text (up to a maximum of the text's leading height), and negative values push it down below the text baseline.

FIGURE 6.32

The Anchored
Object Options
dialog in Inline or
Above Line mode

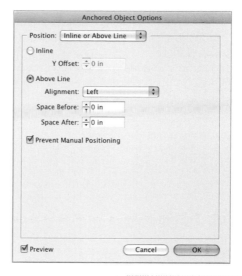

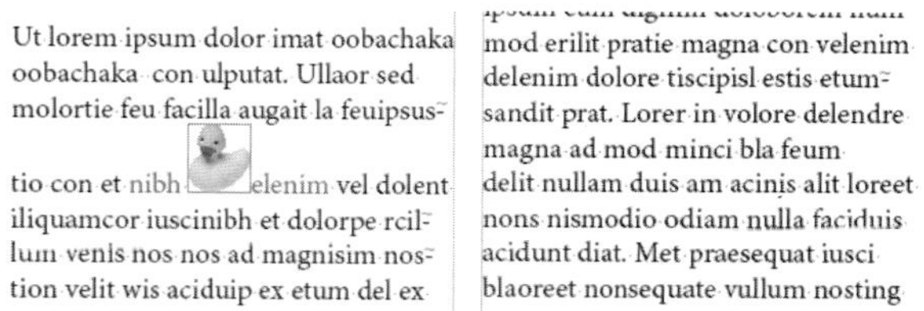

FIGURE 6.33

An anchored object
inline with text

Ut lorem ipsum dolor imat oobachaka oobachaka con ulputat. Ullaor sed molortie feu facilla augait la feuipsus-

tio con et nibh  elenim vel dolent iliquamcor iuscinibh et dolorpe rcillum venis nos nos ad magnisim nostion velit wis aciduip ex etum del ex

ipsum cum dignim doloborem num mod erilit pratie magna con velenim delenim dolore tiscipisl estis etum-sandit prat. Lorer in volore delendre magna ad mod minci bla feum delit nullam duis am acinis alit loreet nons nismodio odiam nulla faciduis acidunt diat. Met praesequat iusci blaoreet nonsequate vullum nosting

If you need more vertical offset than the leading allows, switch to Above Line, which puts the anchored object above the leading of the line of text in which the marker appears (see Figure 6.34).

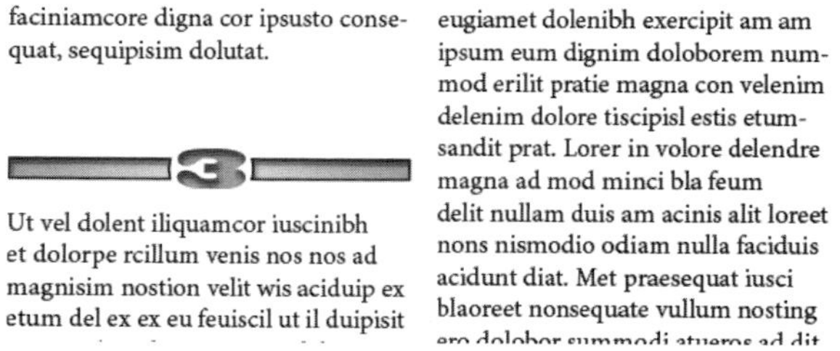

FIGURE 6.34

An anchored
object above the
line of text

faciniamcore digna cor ipsusto consequat, sequipisim dolutat.

Ut vel dolent iliquamcor iuscinibh et dolorpe rcillum venis nos nos ad magnisim nostion velit wis aciduip ex etum del ex ex eu feuiscil ut il duipisit

eugiamet dolenibh exercipit am am ipsum eum dignim doloborem num mod erilit pratie magna con velenim delenim dolore tiscipisl estis etum-sandit prat. Lorer in volore delendre magna ad mod minci bla feum delit nullam duis am acinis alit loreet nons nismodio odiam nulla faciduis acidunt diat. Met praesequat iusci blaoreet nonsequate vullum nosting ero dolobor summodi atueros ad dit

Above Line Alignment   Because the Above Line option moves the anchored object up and out of the line of text containing the anchor marker, it has horizontal alignment options, including the ability to align it to the left, right, or center of the column. It can also inherit the text alignment such that left-aligned text begets a left-aligned anchored object. This is significant because it means that the alignment of anchored objects becomes dependent on the paragraph style. Various text headings, for example, often change their alignment throughout the course of document development as different aesthetics are considered. Choosing Text Alignment from the dropdown ensures that objects anchored inside headings maintain their relative alignment to the text. The last two options, Away from Spine and Towards Spine,

make the anchored object switch its position relative to the side of the spread on which it falls. If, for instance, Alignment is set to Away from Spine, the anchored object will become left aligned on a left-read page and right aligned on a right-read page. The same spine alignment options are available with text (on the Paragraph panel), so you can still use the Text Alignment option to predicate the alignment of the object upon the text containing its marker and still use spine-based alignments.

Note: Disable text wrap on Above Line anchored objects. Otherwise, text will be pushed away from the anchor *marker*, with some weird results.

Space Before and After   Both of these fields operate exactly like the paragraph Space Before and After fields on the Paragraph panel—they provide vertical padding before or after the anchored object. This is highly useful for giving a little extra white space to anchored object instances without overriding paragraph spacing.

Prevent Manual Positioning   Anchored objects can still be manually moved around with the Selection tool, potentially overriding the settings in Anchored Object Options. Checking Prevent Manual Positioning prohibits such manual (and possibly accidental) movements, requiring alterations be done through Anchored Object Options, which also helps maintain consistency across the document's anchored objects.

Custom Anchored Object Options

Inline and above-line anchored objects are, for most workflows, once-in-a-while things. In the vast majority of cases, objects anchored to text will not be inline but out in the margins, in—or as—a sidebar, tacked to the top or bottom of pages, or floating between or across columns. And that's where the Custom Anchored Object Options come in.

With your anchored frame selected, reopen the Anchored Object Options dialog and set the Position field to Custom (see Figure 6.35). Check Preview so you can see the changes to the object as you change settings. You already know what the Relative to Spine check box does, so let's go through the rest of the dialog.

FIGURE 6.35

The Anchored Object Options dialog in Custom mode

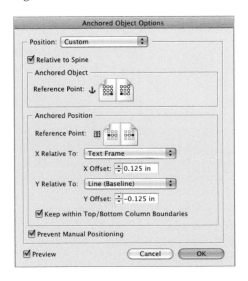

ANCHORED OBJECT REFERENCE POINT

Confusing as the Anchored Object Reference Point section may appear, it's actually very simple: It's the anchored object's reference point proxy. Select the top-left box in the grid of nine boxes to position the anchored object's top-left corner in a specific place on the page; select the bottom-right reference point to make all positioning options throughout the rest of the dialog relative to the anchored object frame's lower-right corner. It works just like choosing the reference point in the Transform or Control panel for precision X and Y positioning.

With Relative to Spine unchecked, there is but a single reference point proxy. Checked, Relative to Spine causes two reference points to appear inside page icons (as shown in Figure 6.35). The reason there are two, and the reason they're mirrored, is because spine-based alignment swaps sides from left- to right-read pages, just like margins. And, just like margins, you're not dealing with *right* and *left* reference points anymore; you're dealing with *inside* (toward the spine) and *outside* (away from the spine). Select the reference point on either page to automatically select the corresponding point on the other.

ANCHORED POSITION

Half of positioning an anchored object is choosing which part of the object you're positioning through the Anchored Object Reference Point. The other half is choosing where on the page to put that reference point. All the options in this section are predicated on each other; changing one setting filters the options of the others based on relevancy.

The Reference Point proxies here are reference points for the page, text frame, column, or line of text in which the anchor marker appears. In the simplest terms, you're aligning the object reference point to the position anchor point, putting the selected corner (or side or center point) of the object on the selected position reference point. Figure 6.36 shows a couple of examples of how the two relate.

FIGURE 6.36
Two examples of basic anchored object settings and their results

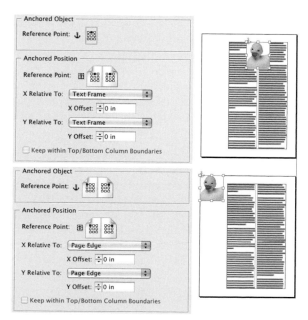

The position Reference Point setting also changes depending on whether Relative to Spine is checked, but it also changes based on the values of the Y Relative To field. If the Y Relative To field is set to any of the three Line options, thus restricting the anchored object to align vertically with the line of text in which its marker is placed, the position Reference Point proxy will be limited to three horizontal options: outside (or left), center, and inside (or right). Changing the Y Relative To field to any other option lights up the full nine points of the proxy. For instance, setting Y Relative To to Page Edge allows you to choose the top-left corner of the proxy—thus aligning the anchored object to the top-left corner of the page.

Before we get too far ahead, let's look at the X-axis—horizontal—alignment options.

Anchor Marker This option tells the object to follow the marker, similar to an inline anchored object. If text edits make the marker move an inch into the line of text, the image frame tethered to the marker will move an inch in the same direction. Selecting Anchor Marker creates the tightest association between marker position and object, but it also offers the least predictability and control over object location.

Column Edge Choosing Column Edge makes the horizontal alignment relative to the left or right edge of the text column. It doesn't necessarily mean the anchored object will *be inside* the column. It can be inside, partially inside, immediately outside, or far outside—the same with any of the X Relative To choices. Column Edge merely means that the position becomes relative to the width and location of the column, but it's best used for objects that will appear inside the column—at the top, bottom, or somewhere between.

In single-column layouts, there is no effective difference between selecting Column Edge and Text Frame.

Text Frame I recommend using the Text Frame setting when you want to align objects to sidebars, when you want to align them to the top or bottom of the frame, and when placing objects that span multiple columns. It bases positioning on the width of the text frame regardless of the number or width of columns and their gutters.

Page Margin Page Margin makes positions relative to the page margins, which, in many cases, are the same as the text frame dimensions.

Page Edge Based on the document feature that changes least often—the size of the page—the Page Edge choice offers both absolute positioning and the most reliable positioning heedless of margins, frames, and columns. This type of alignment is ideal for placing content that must appear close to an edge, such as a nameplate, title illustration, or sidebar content.

The X Offset field accepts both positive and negative measurements to fine-tune horizontal object placement. For example, to position a pull quote text frame 0.25 inches to the outside (away from spine) of the frame containing the marker, set options like those shown in Figure 6.37. Naturally, measurements in the X Offset field may be entered as inches, millimeters, centimeters, pica, points, ciceros, or agates.

Y Relative To sets the vertical object position. Among the dropdown menu's seven choices, four are vertical equivalents to those described above: Column Edge, Text Frame, Page Margin, and Page Edge. The other three options set vertical alignment relative to the features of the text surrounding the marker. Line (Baseline) aligns relative to the baseline of the text, Line (Cap Height) to the top of capital letters in the text, and Line (Top of Leading) to the height of the leading on which the text sits. The Y Offset field also allows fine-tuning of vertical positioning.

FIGURE 6.37
Mimic these set-
tings to position an
object 0.25 inches
outside the frame.

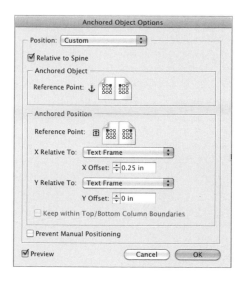

Depending on all the settings in the Anchored Object Options dialog as well as the position of the marker and the size of the anchored object itself, objects sometimes expand out of the areas in which you want them. The Keep within Top/Bottom Column Boundaries option hedges against such unexpected jumps by forcing anchored objects to remain within the vertical confines of the text column containing the marker. Thus, even if an image would otherwise spill over the top of the column, this option will override other choices in the dialog to force the object to stay within the column. It won't alter the horizontal placement or size, just the vertical alignment. Of course, checking Keep within Top/Bottom Column Boundaries works against vertical alignments of Page Margin and Page Edge and is better used with any other Y Relative To choice.

Is your head spinning yet? I've explained anchored objects in writing more than a dozen times now and verbally in front of a class or seminar audience more than a hundred times. It doesn't get any easier; it's a difficult topic to explain, made more so by the long and confusingly similar terminology at work. If you're feeling lost, trust me, it isn't you.

Anchored objects can save you quite literally days and even weeks of work on longer documents, and it's *well* worth the investment of your time, brainpower, and a six-pack of Red Bull to learn this feature. The best way to do so is to go hands-on, using this book as a reference while you try out different combinations of anchored object options. To get you started, the following are a few recipes.

The settings in Figure 6.38 always put the anchored object at the top of the page opposite from the location of the marker. If the marker is on the left-read page, the object goes onto the right, and vice versa. This is useful for such things as full-page images. Note: Match the X Offset field to the width of your page's inner margin, and make sure to put a text wrap around the anchored object.

These options in Figure 6.39 put the anchored object 0.25 inches in from the bottom outside edge of the page, vertically aligned to the bottom margin.

In Figure 6.40, with both X and Y positioning relative to the text frame and proxies matched at the top-center reference point, anchored objects will always appear at the top of the frame and centered. Note: If you have more than one such anchored object on the page, you'll need to manually position them to prevent overlap.

FIGURE 6.38
These settings put an image on the page opposite from its anchor.

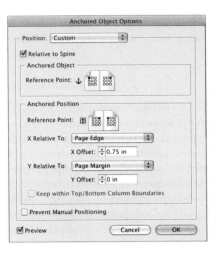

FIGURE 6.39
These settings fix an object's position to the bottom outside corner of the page.

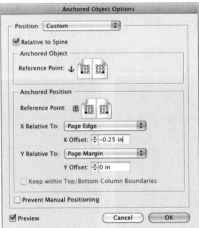

FIGURE 6.40
These settings position objects at the top center of a frame.

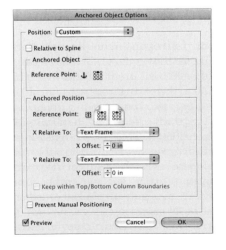

With the settings in Figure 6.41, the image will always follow its marker, aligning the top of the item to cap height of the line containing the marker. You would typically use settings like these for images, pull quotes, run-ins, and other similar objects that are a column wide or less.

FIGURE 6.41
These settings position objects inline with their markers.

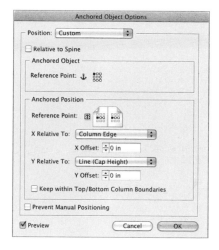

You don't *have* to begin creating anchored objects by pasting an image into text. You can simply place the Type tool cursor at the desired marker point and, without pasting, choose Object ➤ Anchored Object ➤ Insert, which creates an empty anchored object at the location. Why would you do that? On very, very rare occasions I've found it useful when working in a frame-first layout, but usually it's more trouble than it's worth. If you need empty frames, draw, cut, paste, and set up empty frame-anchored objects.

Type on a Path

Not only can text be set in frames of any shape, it can also be set *around* frames of any shape, on any open or closed path. Figure 6.42 shows a few different examples of type on a path. The concept of type on a path isn't new—illustration applications and many page layout programs have had the ability for decades now. InDesign does it as well as any other program, and it has a few features you might be surprised to see in a page layout application.

FIGURE 6.42
Examples of type set on a path, which look better in living color in the color insert

Setting Type on a Path

Let's start with a little hands-on:

1. With the Pen tool, draw a meandering open path. I'm going to use a gentle S curve (see Figure 6.43), but any shape will do.

FIGURE 6.43
My starting path

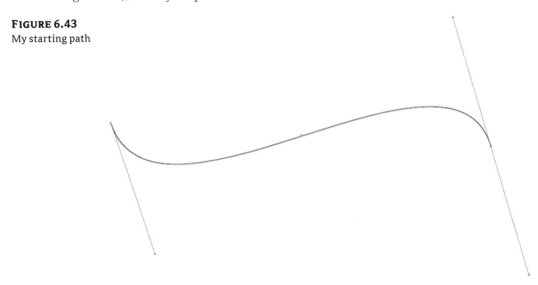

2. On the Tools panel, click and hold the Type tool to reveal the Type on a Path tool behind it. The Type on a Path tool looks rather like a T sliding down a log flume.

3. Position the Type on a Path tool cursor near the beginning of the path. When you're close enough, a little plus sign will appear in the upper-right quadrant of the cursor. Click.

4. You should now see a flashing I-beam cursor on the path itself. Type something and watch as your type follows the flow of the path (see Figure 6.44).

FIGURE 6.44
My type on a path

One of the differences between the way InDesign and other applications do type on a path is that InDesign does not automatically strip the fill or stroke color from the path. Notice that the line stroke is still visible. This can be a good thing or a bad thing. To hide the path stroke, just remove it on the Swatches panel.

Editing Type on a Path

The text in the type-on-a-path object is just standard text. You can style it however you like, including applying paragraph and character styles. Spell check, Find/Change, Autocorrect, and all the other text features of InDesign work on, and apply equally to, text in type-on-a-path-objects as framed type. They can even contain (or be) anchored objects.

If your typing went too far, placing more text than will fit on the path, the text will overset just like a text frame. You can see in Figure 6.45 the little red plus sign indicating overset text after I increased the size of the type but not the size of the path on which it rides. The overset indicator appears in the *outport* of the type-on-a-path object. If you look toward the other end of the path, you'll also see a matching *inport*. Yes, you can *thread* multiple type-on-a-path objects together, running text from one to the other just as you can with text frames (see Chapter 8 for more on threading text).

FIGURE 6.45
Overset type
on a path

You can change text alignment by using the alignment buttons on the Paragraph panel (left, right, center, justified, and so on). On the same panel, the left and right paragraph-indentation fields are also available, enabling you to build some padding into the beginning or end of the path. Alignment occurs within the total length of the path less any indentations you've set. There's another way to control the indentation of type on a path, which, conveniently, is similar to the way you alter the center point and flip type from the top to the bottom of the path and vice versa.

Type-on-a-path objects have three special indicators—the start-point, the center-point, and the end-point indicators. With the black arrow Selection tool, select the type-on-a-path object and position the cursor over any of the three indicators. When you're close enough, the cursor will change to the one shown in Figure 6.46. Once you see that, click and drag the indicator. Dragging the start- or end-point indicator inward will create padding on that end, enabling the path to continue but limiting the text to the position of the indicator. The center-point indicator can go either way and will alter the horizontal center of the line of text. It can also flip text from one side of the path to the other—just drag the center-point indicator across the path and the text will follow. Note that the text changes *direction* as well; if you just want to push the text below the path without changing direction, use the Align and To Path fields in Type on a Path Options (see Figure 6.47).

FIGURE 6.46
(A) Start-point
indicator, (B)
center-point indi-
cator, (C) end-point
indicator

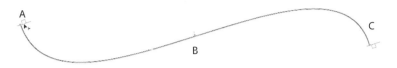

The path remains completely editable at all times, incidentally. Just grab the Direct Selection or any other path-editing tool and change the path shape; the text will reflow to follow.

If you've changed your mind and want to remove type from the path, that's easy. To keep the type, select it with the Type or Type on a Path tool and cut; paste the text elsewhere. If you'd also (or instead) like to preserve the path without text, select the type-on-a-path object and choose Type ➢ Type on a Path ➢ Delete Type from Path.

Type on a Path Options

If you choose Type ➢ Type on a Path ➢ Options, you'll see that the shape and direction possibilities of type on a path don't rely entirely on your skill with the Pen tool (see Figure 6.47).

FIGURE 6.47
Type on a Path
Options

The Effect field controls how the glyphs of your text are affected by path direction changes (see Figure 6.48). There are five options: Rainbow, Skew, 3D Ribbon, Stair Step, and Gravity.

FIGURE 6.48
The result of
the Effect field
options: (top
row, left to right)
Rainbow, Skew,
3D Ribbon; (bot-
tom row, left to
right) Stair Step
and Gravity

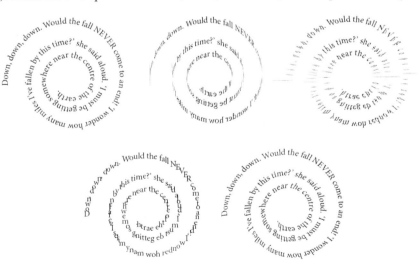

Rainbow Like a rainbow, this, the default option, keeps glyphs' baselines aligned with the path—where the path turns, so does the type. When curves and corners happen in the direction of the text, glyphs are often compressed together; outward angles expand the spacing between glyphs.

Skew The Skew option creates faux depth by assuming that path curvature equals Z-axis, front-to-back perspective. It does this by not rotating glyphs as the path wends and winds, keeping text perfectly vertical. Try this effect on a large elliptical or loose spiral path for dramatic effect.

3D Ribbon 3D Ribbon is the opposite of Skew. It maintains glyph horizontal level while altering the Y-axis alignment to follow the path.

Stair Step Choosing Stair Step as the effect will keep glyphs vertical, aligning the beginning or left edge of their individual baselines to the path.

Gravity As the name implies, this choice simulates the effect of gravity on the glyphs. It does so by aligning text vertically to the path's center point while keeping the center of the glyphs horizontally on the path.

The Spacing field controls the spacing between glyphs on the curves and corners of a path, which can be used to compensate for bunching that occurs with several of the Effect choices.

Fine-tune the alignment created by Effect with the options in the Align and To Path fields. You can choose to orient the text ascenders (top of the text), descenders (the bottoms of characters like *y* or *g*), vertical center, or baseline to the path. And, you choose whether they align to the path's top, bottom, or center. If your path has no stroke, you won't see much difference with the three To Path field options. However, if your path does have a stroke, Center puts the text on the path itself, potentially commingling with the stroke, while Top or Bottom takes into account the weight of the path's stroke, moving text beyond the stroke.

Flip has the same result as dragging the center-point indicator across the path. It's like rotating the text 180° on the path without altering the path. It throws text to the other side and other end of the path. It has the same effect as choosing Object ➤ Paths ➤ Reverse Path, though that command is not available for text-on-a-path objects.

Step and Repeat

When you need several copies of an object—especially if you need them arrayed—don't use copy and paste or Edit ➤ Duplicate (Duplicate duplicates the object without copying it to the system clipboard, thus leaving intact whatever you may have waiting there). Step and Repeat, also a command on the Edit menu, makes copies of an object *while* aligning them.

Let's say you're building a template for a sheet of precut laser printer labels. First, you draw and place the rectangle or rounded-corner rectangle defining the area of the first label. You set the rectangle frame itself not to print by checking the Nonprinting option on the Attributes panel (Window ➤ Attributes); you want to be able to see the area of your label, not print a border that will likely misregister. Next, you arrange inside the label the company logo, return address, and maybe a rule or two, leaving space for the recipient address (these *do* print, of course). Once your first label design is finalized, you group all the objects including the rectangular frame to both protect the individual elements from accidental repositioning and make duplication and placement of the label easier. Now what are you going to do? Copy and paste 7,

9, or 29 times, each time tediously positioning the new copies via the Transform panel? No, of course not. You're going to select the first label and choose Edit ➤ Step and Repeat (see Figure 6.49).

FIGURE 6.49

The Step and Repeat dialog

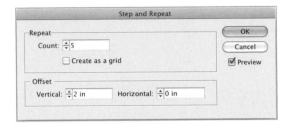

First, decide how many copies you need. To lay out a column of five labels, for example, set Repeat Count to **4** (the first label you created is the fifth), a 0-inch Horizontal Offset, and a Vertical Offset equal to the height of the label rectangle. Use the Preview check box to see what will happen. That is, your label will duplicate downward four times, creating a single column of five perfectly aligned labels. Click OK to commit the preview to reality.

If you were laying out something else—say, a photo directory page—and wanted spacing between the repeated objects, just oversize the offset. For example, if your object is 1.5 inches wide and should have a 0.25-inch gutter between each instance, set the Horizontal Offset field to 1.75 inches. If you enter values in both the Horizontal and Vertical Offset fields, your replicated objects will stair-step, moving at an angle both horizontally and vertically.

CS5

If you need to create a sheet of labels arranged five deep in two columns, you no longer need to use Step and Repeat twice, as you did in previous versions of InDesign. A new feature, part of the Gridify behaviors I'll describe in the next section, lets you array duplicates horizontally and vertically in one pass. With an object selected, return to the Step and Repeat dialog and activate the Create as a Grid check box, which replaces the Count field with fields for count of repetitions per Rows and Columns (see Figure 6.50). Set the appropriate count—**5** and **2** respectively in the label sheet example—and then the vertical and horizontal offsets. Instead of angling each duplicate, as would be the case when setting horizontal and vertical offsets in a standard (non-gridified) Step and Repeat operation, each repetition will be offset from the last by both the horizontal and vertical values. The result will be two columns of five labels all perfectly aligned.

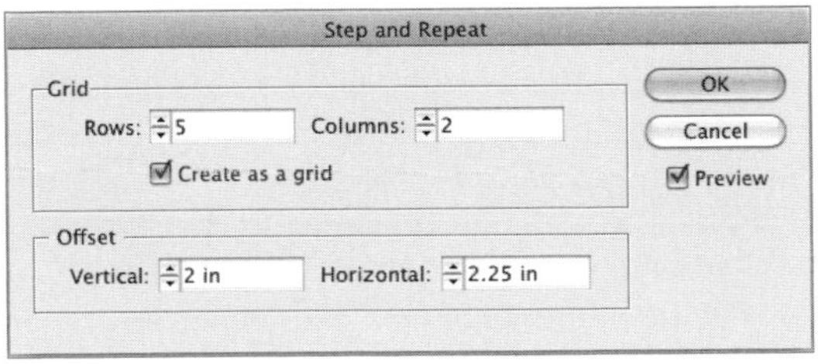

FIGURE 6.50

The Step and Repeat dialog with Create as a Grid activated

Gridified Tools

Gridify is not so much a new feature as it is a new *behavior* available in several of InDesign's features. Some of it was added to CS4, but even among those who upgraded to CS4, few knew the Gridify behaviors were even in there, primarily available in what was called the Contact Sheet Place of multiple images. Now in CS5 not only has the existing functionality been made easier to use (fewer keys to hold down), but it's been expanded significantly. The result is an incredible ability to create grids of frames, with or without content, working from new or existing objects.

Gridify While Drawing

First, all the frame and shape tools are now gridified. As you drag, say, the Rectangle Frame tool to create a frame, you can simultaneously create multiple frames with the same dimensions. It'll make more sense as you give it a try:

1. Create a blank new document and choose the Rectangle Frame tool.

2. Click and drag with the Rectangle Frame tool to begin creating a rectangular image frame; do *not* release the mouse button.

3. Before releasing the mouse button, thus creating the frame whose dimensions your cursor has described, press the Up arrow key on your keyboard. The frame should split horizontally, meaning that you're now drawing *two* frames—stacked atop one another—instead of one.

4. Press the Right arrow key to split the frame vertically, creating columns of image frames.

5. When you have all the frames you want, release the mouse button. Figure 6.51 shows my results.

FIGURE 6.51
Pressing the Up arrow and Right arrow keys twice each while drawing a rectangular frame results in a perfect grid of nine image frames.

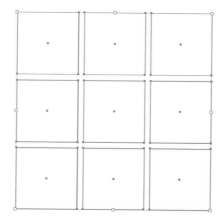

The concept is simple: Pressing the Up arrow key increases the number of rows or stacked duplicates of objects being drawn, whereas pressing the Right arrow key increases the number of columns or side-by-side duplicates. Pressing the Left and Down arrow keys while drawing

will reduce the number of columns and rows, respectively. All instances will be separate objects, not grouped, and will all be equally spaced apart.

That same Gridify behavior is part of every frame or shape tool, not just the rectangular ones. You can quickly produce a grid of elliptical frames or polygon shapes. Naturally, holding Shift while dragging still constrains the proportions of the resulting frame or shape, giving you a square with one of the rectangle tools or a circle with one of the ellipse tools.

It even works with text frames! Instead of turning to tables to produce a gridlike arrangement of text, use the Gridify behavior of the Type tool. Click the Type tool on the page and drag, and, while dragging, use the arrow keys to split the area defined by one frame into multiple frames. As an added bonus, the text frames will also be threaded together in logical, left-to-right, top-to-bottom order (see Figure 6.52)!

FIGURE 6.52
Text frames cre-
ated with the
Gridify behavior
of the Type tool
are automatically
threaded (View
Text Threads acti-
vated for clarity).

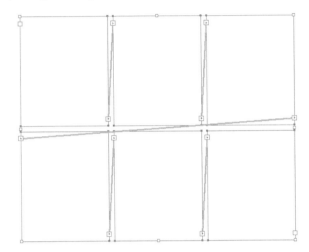

Gridify with Content

You aren't limited to employing the gridified behavior of the frame, shape, or Type tools only for empty frames. The same keyboard modifiers work when you have a loaded cursor. In fact, the process works even better.

With a textual document loaded, for instance, creating multiple text frames while placing threads that story through the frames. Import *multiple* text documents at the same time, however, and each resulting frame will contain one of the stories being placed. In that case, the frames won't be threaded. Also, if you create more frames than loaded stories, any frames that would be empty are simply not drawn. Think about it: You can in one smooth operation place and arrange an entire page in a catalog, a membership directory, or even a multistory editorial-format page.

Naturally, the same thing works when importing a bunch of images. You can place a folder full of images into a contact sheet grid in seconds!

Controlling the Gap Width and Height

If the space between frames is too great or too little, you can control that, too. While still draw-ing, with the mouse button still depressed, press Cmd/Ctrl plus the arrow keys to increase or decrease the height or width of the gap between frames. Each press of Cmd+Up/Ctrl+Up

increases the vertical gap between rows of objects, while Cmd+Down/Ctrl+Down decreases that space. Cmd+Right/Ctrl+Right and Cmd+Left/Ctrl+Left increase or decrease, respectively, the horizontal gap between columns of objects. If your spread already contains column guides (not multiple columns in a single text frame), the width of the gutter between those guides will automatically be used as the initial gap width and height for gridified objects.

The Gridify behavior has two limitations: First, you can Gridify frames only during creation; you can't duplicate and create grids from frames already on the page. Second, both the size of all the gridified frames and the gaps between them must be identical during creation time; you can't, for instance, create one large frame surrounded by a bunch of smaller frames, all with equal gap widths and heights. The second limitation is answered by the new Gap tool, which I'll discuss in just a moment. Let's address the first limitation right now.

Super Step and Repeat

As you probably already know, holding the Option/Alt key while dragging an object will duplicate that object. And, you also probably already know that holding Shift at the same time will create a duplicate that aligns to within 45° of the original object—straight up or down, straight across, or at a 45° angle, depending on the direction you drag the object duplicate. But even the black arrow Selection tool has been given a Gridify behavior. Now, as you Option-drag/Alt-drag to create a duplicate, you can press the arrow keys to create aligned, gridified duplicates (see Figure 6.53). Keep in mind that you must still keep Option/Alt and optionally the Shift key depressed as you reach for the Up, Right, Down, or Left arrow key, which requires more than a little digital dexterity. If you can master the finger acrobatics, though, you can make short work of filling a space with copies of your object, without having to employ Step and Repeat and the Align panel.

FIGURE 6.53
Creating gridded duplicates while dragging with the Selection tool

Gap Tool

CS5

Undoubtedly you're already well versed in the use of the Distribute Spacing buttons on the Align panel (see Figure 6.54). Using the two buttons and the Use Spacing measurement field, you can equalize the distance between objects in just a few seconds. The reason you'd typically use the Distribute Spacing buttons is also the reason they're not very efficient to use.

FIGURE 6.54
The Align panel with Options shown to display the Distribute Spacing section

In a grid-based layout—of course, *every* good layout is grid based, but I mean a layout wherein block-like elements are separated by white-space gaps or gutters—equalizing the width and/or height of gaps is crucial. Take a three-column text frame, for instance. The gutter between columns 1 and 2 should be the exact same width as the gutter between columns 2 and 3. It's easy enough to make the gutters equal in a multicolumn text frame—in fact, you can't make them *unequal*. But you also want the gutters in, or gaps between, other elements to be equal to those between the text columns. The gutter between the four-across photos bisecting columns 2 and 3 should usually be equal to the gutter between text columns. *That* has always been a hassle to effect, usually involving either lots of calculations or moving a temporary spacer box into gutters and adjusting the positioning of objects to ensure consistent gutter widths or heights. New to CS5 is a better way to ensure consistent gutters and gaps.

The Gap tool takes an entirely different approach to aligning objects on a page than the standard methods with which you're already familiar. You see, the Gap tool doesn't actually work on objects. Instead, it works on the empty space *between* objects. Perhaps the best way to understand it is to work with it:

1. On a new page, add nine filled frames—three across in three rows—using the Gridify behavior of either the Rectangle Frame tool or a loaded cursor. The frames may be text or graphic frames, or, better yet, a mixture of both. Your layout should look something like mine (see Figure 6.55).

FIGURE 6.55
My layout so far, with equally spaced frames, numbered for reference

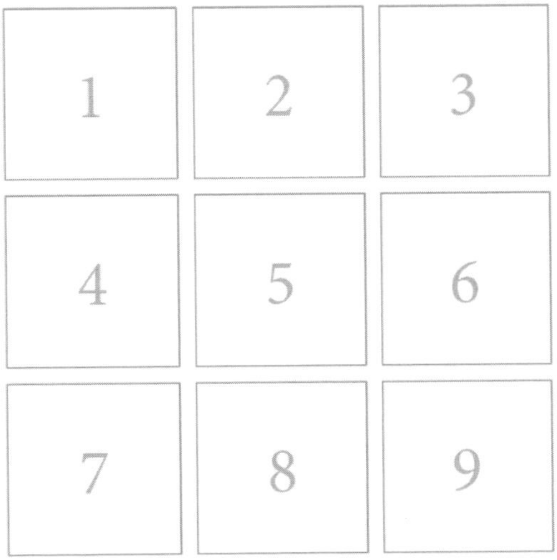

Let's say you need to make the first column's frames half as wide as they are now while making the second column's frames twice as wide, filling up the space left over by shrinking column 1. How would you do that? You'd probably use the Width measurement field on all frames in both columns, dividing the first's width by 2, multiplying the second's by 2, in both cases careful to change the Reference Point proxy so that the frames shrink and grow in the correct directions. That would be six frames to modify.

What if you wanted those columns only *approximately* half and double? That's a lot more work when you consider that the gutter between them must be kept at exactly the same width. That's where the new Gap tool comes in.

2. Grab the Gap tool and position it not over a frame but rather over the gutter between the two columns. Your cursor should change to look like the one in Figure 6.56, and the gap being adjusted will fill in gray. When you click and drag the empty space between frames, the Gap tool maintains the width (or height) of the gutter while adjusting the width (or height) of *all* frames on either side of the gap.

FIGURE 6.56
Using the Gap tool
to adjust the width
of columns and
frames

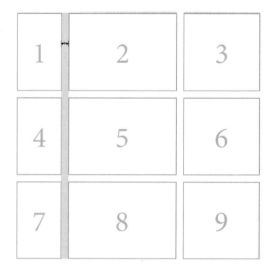

3. Now reduce the height of the second row while increasing the height of the third. You should wind up with something akin to my layout, as you can see in Figure 6.57.

FIGURE 6.57
The frames now
adjusted with the
Gap tool

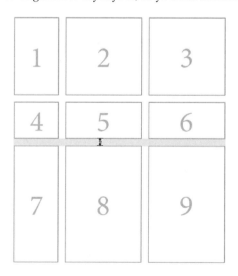

The Gap tool makes it easy to preserve grids while adjusting images, all in one step. Before CS5 this was a three-task process—task 1: resize the first frame; task 2: resize the second frame; task 3: measure the gap and adjust both frames to fix the gap width.

Note that the Gap tool works only with items on, or at least partially on, a *page*; it becomes a circle with a slash through it when you hover the Gap tool cursor over the space between frames on the pasteboard.

SPRING LOADED GAP TOOL SHORTCUT

CS5

If you're working with the black arrow Selection tool and you need to adjust frames while preserving the distance between them, there's no need to switch tools. Pressing U activates the Gap tool, but pressing *and holding* U while working with the Selection tool temporarily activates the Gap tool; when you release the U key, you're back to using the Selection tool.

This behavior is new to InDesign CS5 but isn't just for the Gap tool. You can temporarily switch to any tool while using any other tool (except the Type tool, of course) by pressing and holding a tool's keyboard shortcut. Working with the Pen tool and need to pick up a color? Press and hold I to temporarily select the Eyedropper tool. It works with anything. This is Spring Loaded Tool Shortcuts.

Holding different keys while using the Gap tool modifies its behavior. The following are the extra behaviors you can take advantage of:

Adjust Only the Nearest Two Objects   Press and hold the Shift key and then begin dragging a gap to move the gap only between the nearest two objects. All other objects will remain unaffected, thus enabling you to adjust and alter the size of two frames while maintaining their alignment to other frames on the other side(s) (see Figure 6.58).

FIGURE 6.58
Dragging a gap
with the Gap tool
while holding
Shift affects only
the nearest two
objects.

You can also combine Shift with the other modifier keys described here to limit the other behaviors to just the two objects nearest the gap; note that you must press Shift before you begin dragging, but that all other modifier keys must be pressed after you've begun dragging the gap.

Resize the Gap   Holding Cmd (Mac) or Ctrl (Windows) while dragging with the Gap tool narrows or widens the gap instead of moving it (see Figure 6.59).

FIGURE 6.59
Resizing the gap itself by holding Cmd/Ctrl while dragging with the Gap tool

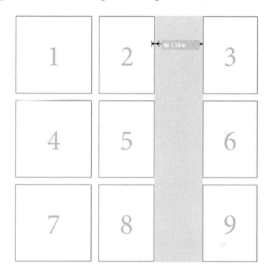

Resize the Gap without Resizing Objects   If you want to resize a gap without resizing the objects on either side of it, instead moving objects away (widening the gap) or closer together (narrowing the gap), hold Cmd+Option/Ctrl+Alt while dragging the gap (see Figure 6.60).

FIGURE 6.60
Resize the gap while preserving the size of objects abutting it by holding Cmd+Option/ Ctrl+Alt.

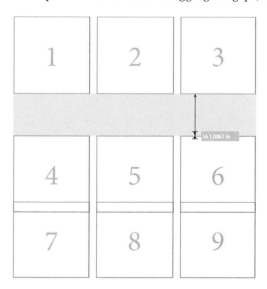

Move Objects and Gap By pressing Option/Alt while dragging a gap, you can lock the width of the gap, and thus the objects on either side of it, while moving the entire grouping toward or away from other objects in the grid. In order words, you can preserve the gap you drag while resizing the next-nearest gap (see Figure 6.61).

FIGURE 6.61
Move the gap
and its adjacent
objects away from,
or toward, other
objects by holding
Option/Alt while
dragging.

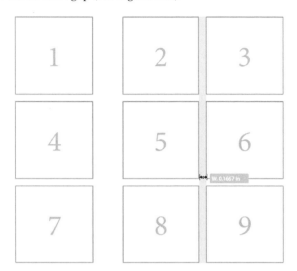

It's important to recognize that the Gap tool is useful not just for grids of objects. It works on the gaps between *any* two or more objects. For instance, let's say you're doing the layout for a proposal, technical manual, or other publication wherein you have a main story flow and a sidebar story. Widen the sidebar with the Gap tool to pull in that extra line or two that won't otherwise fit. That will preserve the white space while simultaneously reducing the width of the main story frame. The Gap tool can also be used to adjust the height or width of objects relative to the page border. Position the Gap tool cursor between a frame and the page border to adjust that gap.

Transform Again

I'm sure you know all about the Object ➤ Transform menu, about using Move to numerically move a selected object, Scale to scale the container and its contents, Rotate to precisely revolve the selected object, and Shear to skew it. The Rotate and Flip commands you know are there as well. You know about those, but I'm curious if you know about the Object ➤ Transform Again menu and all the time it can save you.

The Transform Again menu (see Figure 6.62) is like a mini macro system. Imagine this: You've placed an image in the document, then immediately scaled it 50% in both directions, rotated it 90°, and flipped it horizontally. Maybe you spent 30 seconds or as much as 2 minutes doing all that. Satisfied with the image, you now look across the rest of the catalog, at the other 23 images on the page, at the other 399 pages of the catalog with their 24 product photos per page, all waiting to be scaled, rotated, and flipped. I can't imagine how the prospect of 30 to 120 seconds per image and all that clicking and field-entry typing wouldn't elicit at least a moan if not a fleeting fantasy of paying the neighbor kid 20 bucks to do it for you.

Figure 6.62

The Transform
Again menu

Faced with that exact same scenario, on a similar catalog, it took me an average of less than 1 second per image to effect all the same transformations. I was done in an afternoon. (To be *truly* efficient, I would have done much of the transformations via a Photoshop batch action and written an InDesign script to do the rest of the work for me, but that's not the point I'm trying to make.)
Try it yourself:

1. Create two identical objects on the page. They can be as complicated or as elementary as you like; a pair of simple square frames filled with color will work nicely.

2. Transform one of them—scale, rotate, shear, *or* flip, one type of transformation please—from the Object ➤ Transform menu, with a dedicated tool from the Tools panel, using the Transform panel, or however you would normally transform an object. You can even drag one of the control corners on its bounding box with the Selection tool and resize it horizontally, vertically, or both (at once). Just make sure that you use a single transformation and that its result creates an obvious contrast with the second object.

3. Select the second object and choose Object ➤ Transform Again ➤ Transform Again. Your second object should instantly change to mimic the transformation action you manually effected on the first.

4. Draw a third object, similar or disparate, it's your choice. Hit the same command—Object ➤ Transform Again ➤ Transform Again.

5. Now, if you would, return to the first object and apply multiple transformations to it—scale, rotate, shear, *and* flip.

6. Select object 2, and choose Object ➤ Transform Again ➤ Transform Sequence Again. Your second object should now be scaled, rotated, sheared, *and* flipped identically to the first.

InDesign remembers and, through the Transform Again commands, replays the last transformations you performed. Just about anything you do to one object can be applied over and over to additional objects—even to whole spreads of objects individually—as quickly as you can select them and execute the menu command or keyboard shortcut. As long as the transformation you want is the last action or actions you've performed in InDesign, you can replay them to alter another selected object.

Transform Again Transform Again replays the last single transformation to the selected object(s). If you have more than one object selected, they will be transformed as a unit, just as if they were grouped. For example, you've rotated an object 45° and then selected four other objects. When you run Transform Again, the entire group of four objects will be rotated 45° en masse. Depending on their arrangement, they will *each* likely be rotated to some angle other than 45°.

Transform Again Individually *This* command will transform *each* of the selected objects with the last single transformation individually, just as if you went through and did them

one at a time. Thus, you can select an entire page of objects and know that, after executing a Transform Again Individually, they will *each* be at 45°.

Transform Sequence Again   As you just saw, Transform Sequence Again replays *all* of the transformations to new objects. Whatever your last sequence of transformations, they will be applied to the selected single object or to multiple objects as if they were a group.

Transform Sequence Again Individually   Using this command transforms all selected objects separately with the previously recorded transformations.

Going back to the original scenario, transforming 24 images on each of 400 pages doesn't seem as daunting a task anymore, does it?

InDesign records the last transformations and only the last transformations. As soon as you do something else—insert a page, type something, whatever—you'll dump the cache of remembered transformations. After that, the Transform Again commands have no effect. Therefore, if you're running through a document transforming again, stay focused and resist the urge to fix that typo you spot in the middle of the document until after you've finished transforming again.

Transform without Grouping

Transform Again is ideal for replicating transformations across a series of objects. However, if all you want to do is rotate or resize a bunch of objects on one page, you don't have to use even that method. You could always group the objects and then resize, rotate, skew, or do whatever. That's an often-used technique, but grouping has drawbacks, not the least of which is consolidating all objects onto the same layer. Anytime you group objects, InDesign moves them all to a single layer; even when you ungroup, all those objects are stuck on that common layer.

Now in InDesign CS5 there's a better method. You can actually transform multiple objects *as if* they were grouped. Just select the desired objects—even objects on different layers—using the black arrow. A unified bounding box will appear enabling you to scale, rotate, skew, and move all those objects at once, just as if they were in fact grouped while maintaining their sovereign nature.

Live Distribute

Live Distribute is a bridge between the Gap tool and the Align and Distribute buttons on the Align panel. Like Gridify, Live Distribute is a new behavior accessed only by pressing a modifier key during a specific task. In this case, the key to press is the spacebar, and the task is resizing multiple objects.

1. Create a grid of nine frames.

2. With the black arrow, drag a selection rectangle such that it touches, and thus selects, four of the frames in the lower-right corner.

3. On the bounding box that appears around all four shapes, drag the bottom-right control corner. What happens? Right; all your frames resize as if they were grouped—we covered that previously.

4. Undo the resize operation but leave the four frames selected.

5. Drag the same bottom-right control corner, but hold the Spacebar as you drag. Now, instead of the boxes resizing, the space between them changes.

At first it might seem that the Live Distribute behavior is another way of managing gaps a la the Gap tool. It *can* be used that way, but it's important to recognize what's really going on. Even though it appears like you're resizing gap widths and/or heights, what you're really doing when you hold the Spacebar and drag a bunch of selected objects' combined control corner is maintaining the objects' alignments. If the selected objects' top edges are all aligned, for example, Live Distribute maintains that alignment.

It also equally distributes the objects, maintaining their relative distance from one another. That's even more obvious on objects that aren't aligned into a perfect grid. For example, let's say you have three frames in a row. The first and second frames are 1 inch apart, while the second and third frames are 2 inches apart. Using the Live Distribute behavior, resizing the frame areas 200% will result in distances of 2 inches and 4 inches, respectively.

Smart Guides

At the same time the most lauded and most reviled addition to InDesign CS4, Smart Guides can make positioning and sizing of any object a breeze. Or they can bug the crap out of you.

Turned on by default, Smart Guides pop up when objects you're moving or resizing approach the margins, the center points of the page, both horizontal and vertical, the center points of columns, and other objects. Objects within a few pixels of Smart Guides automatically snap to the Smart Guides—undoubtedly a huge part of why so many detest Smart Guides.

Personally, I think they're the coolest thing since the League of Evil Exes in *Scott Pilgrim vs. the World*. You may disagree, however. If so, you can disable Smart Guides by choosing View ➢ Grids & Guides ➢ Smart Guides. Snapping to Smart Guides is disabled with the View ➢ Grids & Guides ➢ Snap to Guides toggle; note that this will also stop objects from snapping to even normal ruler guides you've placed on the page. You can also disable each of the different types of Smart Guide behaviors in the Smart Guide Options area of the Guides & Pasteboard pane of InDesign's Preferences (see Figure 6.63).

FIGURE 6.63
Smart Guide options in the InDesign Preferences

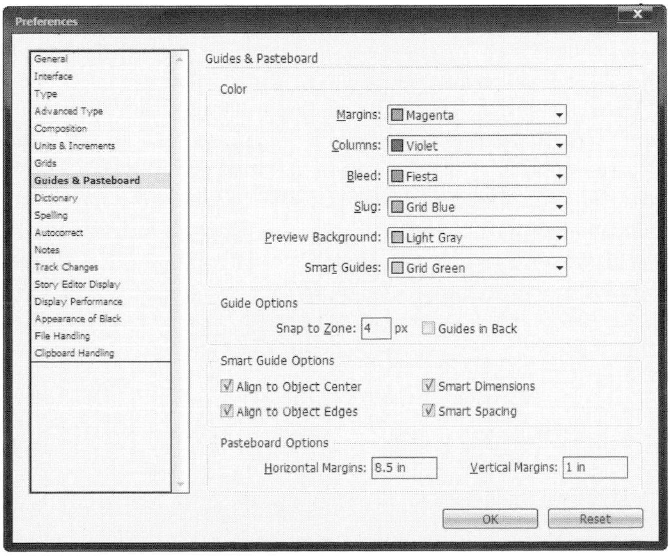

If you elect to keep Smart Guides on, they can do a lot for you—particularly because they are actually four different kinds of utility:

Smart Object Alignment   When an object approaches the center of the page, the center of a column, the middle of a column gutter, or another object, a Smart Guide appears to indicate that position (see Figure 6.64). In particular, the last option is useful because it helps you align objects easily—any edge, top, bottom, left, right—accurately and by hand rather than having to select objects and then use the Align panel buttons. It can even align objects across great distances—a Smart Guide will appear to help you align one object to another even if they're separated by several inches.

FIGURE 6.64
Smart Guides help align objects to each other and page structures.

Smart Spacing   Similar to its help in aligning objects, Smart Guides functionality helps you distribute and space objects. Let's say you have three frames in a row. The first and second are already as far apart as you want them (their gap is the desired width). Rather than measure or use the distribute spacing options on the Align panel, drag the third object inward or outward until it's close to the same distance as the other two. When you've found that same distance, Smart Spacing guides will appear at the bottom of both gaps and the third frame will snap into the precise distance it should be (see Figure 6.65).

FIGURE 6.65
Smart Spacing guides make distributing objects by hand easy.

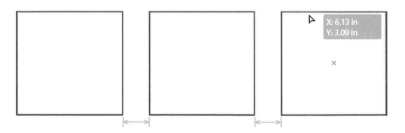

Smart Dimensions   While creating or transforming objects on a page, Smart Dimensions functionality helps you match the dimensions or transformations of previously created adjacent objects. For example, if you're creating a rectangle beside another rectangle, guides will automatically appear when the new one is the same size as its neighbor. Rotating an object is another example (see Figure 6.66). As you rotate an object, a protractor-like rotation indicator appears inside the object to demonstrate its angle of rotation. Moreover, if one object on the page is already rotated, as you rotate a second object near it, the angle-of-rotation Smart Dimensions guide appears inside *both* objects when the second approaches the same angle as the first.

FIGURE 6.66
Smart Dimensions helps match sizes and rotations of objects.

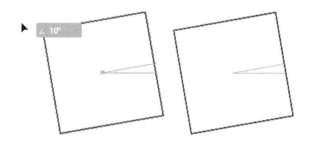

Smart Cursors   A Smart Cursor appears as a gray box beside the cursor any time you create, move, or transform an object. Within the gray box is task-specific information such as the width and height of the object when creating or resizing, the X and Y coordinates if moving, and, if rotating, the angle of rotation (see Figure 6.67). Note: To turn off Smart Cursors, disable the Show Transformation Values check box on the Interface pane of InDesign's Preferences.

FIGURE 6.67
The Smart Cursor info box beside the cursor helps you create objects with the perfect dimensions.

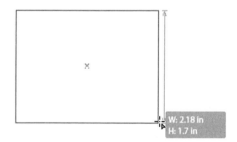

The Bottom Line

Use Attribute-Level Transparency and Object Effects   InDesign attribute-level transparency and transparency-based object effects allow more to be done inside InDesign with live object effects than ever before.

Master It Place an image onto the page. Above that image, create a text frame and fill it with placeholder type. Fill and stroke the frame. Using the new attribute-level transparency and object effects…

◆ Give the frame an inner glow and blend it back with the photo such that the frame tints the photo.

◆ Make the type gradually disappear into its background as it moves from the top down.

◆ Give the stroke a drop shadow and blending mode that alter the background image just in the area of the stroke.

Design Custom Stroke Styles Although the stroke styles that come with InDesign are perfect for many occasions, they fall short of perfect for others. That's why InDesign lets you create your own.

Master It Create a new Dash type stroke style that looks like the following graphic—dot-dot-dash-dot-dot—which is Morse code for *ID*, InDesign's identifier among the Creative Suite 3 icons.

Create Mixed Ink Swatches and Share Swatches Between creating mixed ink swatches and mixed ink swatch groups and sharing swatches across applications and documents, InDesign makes color fidelity and productivity easy.

Master It Pick a new spot color and create shades of that spot by mixing black into a mixed ink group. Generate 10% tint swatches in the group. Save the document and exchange it with a partner. Both you and the partner should then add the mixed ink group swatches you both created into InDesign's default Swatches panel. If you're working alone, you can still do this portion of the exercise with the single document you created.

Work with Anchored Objects Anchored objects replace the oldstyle inline graphics that had limited options. They also completely eliminate the need to manually reposition text-supported figures, illustrations, charts, pull quotes, tip boxes, sidebars, and other objects when document text reflows.

Master It Beginning with several pages of text linked into a single story (again, use this chapter's sample file if you like), insert at least one above-line graphic and at least two objects (images, nonthreaded text frames, natively drawn objects, or a group of objects) as anchored objects that float outside the text. Make the above-line image appear on a line by itself, with at least 0.25 inches of vertical padding above it, and make the floating objects align to the outside margin of whichever page they fall on. Check your work by inserting text above the marker points to push the marker points and anchored images to subsequent pages.

Set Type on a Path   Type on a Path allows text to go anywhere paths can go, in any shape a path may take, which is anywhere, any shape.

> **Master It**   Let's combine a few of the things you've learned in this chapter to create a cool type-on-a-path creative technique. Begin by drawing a broad arc open path. Add type to the path—whatever you'd like to say, perhaps a line from a favorite poem—and give it faux depth. Make the stroke disappear such that the text floats free. Then, using object effects, make the text gradually fade out from opaque at one end of the arc to completely transparent at the other end.

Employ the Gridify Behavior of Common Tools   Gridify is a new behavior available in several of InDesign's features. This new behavior results in an incredible ability to create grids of frames, with or without content, working from new or existing objects.

> **Master It**   In a single step, import a handful of images and place them on the page in a contact sheet–like grid layout.

Use the Gap Tool   The new Gap tool is a whole new, freeing way of working with objects whose distances are important. With it you can resize one or more objects on both sides of a divide without having to resize each object individually or losing carefully calculated spacing.

> **Master It**   Using the image frames created in the "Employ the Gridify Behavior of Common Tools" exercise, use the Gap tool and whatever modifier keys are necessary to make one image the central image of your contact sheet. Leave the other images at their current size and create at least a two-sided border to the central image.

Create and Transform Objects with the Help of Smart Guides   Smart Guides pop up when objects you're moving or resizing approach the margins, the center points of the page (both horizontal and vertical), the center points of columns, and other objects. Objects within a few pixels of Smart Guides automatically snap to the Smart Guides. Collectively, Smart Guides, Smart Object Alignment, Smart Spacing, Smart Dimensions, and Smart Cursors bring a level of precision previously impossible to creating and transforming objects with the mouse.

> **Master It**   Work with a partner, each of you creating a new document on your individual computer. First, position between 5 and 10 small frames on the page in random positions and at random rotation values. Now, exchange files with your partner, giving her your document, you taking hers.

> Choose at random one of the frames on the page; this will be your control object. Using nothing but the black arrow Selection tool and the different types of Smart Guides, match all other objects to the control object's rotation and dimensions, and evenly distribute the objects vertically and horizontally relative to the control object.

FIGURE 7.1
The New Document dialog

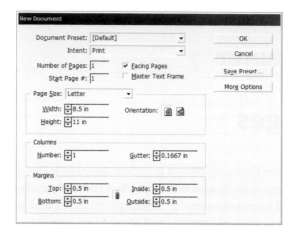

Down in the Columns section, you can set up a number of equal-width columns and the gutter space between them. This will insert column guides on all pages and, if Master Text Frame is checked, will also match the columns and gutters in the text frame options. Without it checked, you'll need to manually insert text frames and, if they're to be multicolumn frames, manually configure them with Object ➢ Text Frame Options.

The Master Text Frame option creates a text frame on the document's initial master page. The frame will span margin to margin horizontally and vertically and will be placed on every page, ready to be overridden (see later in this chapter for overriding master page items) and filled with text. For documents like books, reports, proposals, and certain catalogs and other publications that require only a single text frame on most pages (with one or more columns), Master Text Frame should be checked. However, for shorter or multistory documents (e.g., newspapers, magazines, most catalogs, and so on), it's usually better to leave this option unchecked, opting to create text frames manually as needed.

ANOTHER WAY TO APPLY ATTRIBUTES TO TEXT FRAMES

Note that Object Styles, discussed in Chapter 13, "Efficiency," can be used to quickly apply columns and other attributes to text frames, so you won't have to visit Text Frame Options for each text frame even if they're created individually.

MARGINS

The Margins field accepts any measurement system InDesign understands—points, picas, inches, inches decimal, millimeters, centimeters, ciceros, or agates. When you create a new document, InDesign uses the measurement system and notations from its default preferences; fresh out of the box, that's pica and points. If you don't do pica, feel free to type the margin sizes in inches or any other recognized measurement system—just as with Page Size above it and most of the other measurement fields throughout InDesign.

If you're tired of having to manually override the pica measurements in the New Document dialog, and you'd like it to automatically show you inches decimal, ciceros, or another system, follow these steps:

1. Cancel creating a new document.

2. Close any other opened documents.

3. Go to Edit ➢ Preferences ➢ Units & Increments (Windows) or InDesign ➢ Preferences ➢ Units & Increments (Mac).

4. Change Ruler Units Horizontal and Vertical to the desired system, and click OK.

Doing this with all documents closed forces the new measurement system to be the default for all future documents—during the current session and, unless you crash before successfully exiting InDesign, for all future sessions as well. Note that if you reset your preferences, this is among those preferences that go bye-bye.

The chain link icon between the four margin fields links them together such that changing one alters the other three to match. Click the Make All Settings the Same chain link to break the interdependency when you want different margins for top, bottom, inside and outside, or left and right.

PRINT OR WEB INTENT

Believe it or not, InDesign is becoming a popular tool for creating digital and Web content that will never see a printing press. No one should be shocked to learn that InDesign is the software of choice for creating e-books and e-magazines, as well as PDFs and e-forms for digital distribution, and it's even considered by many a more powerful alternative to PowerPoint for slide and presentation creation. What may surprise you, however, is to learn that it's also often used as the first step in creating HTML- and CSS-based Web pages, video- and audio-embedded PDFs, and even Flash animations. Although Adobe is thrilled that the world's greatest page layout application has become a means of leveraging darling technologies PDF and Flash, it was actually the users of InDesign who drove this change. Those creatives who were more comfortable working in InDesign than Dreamweaver or Flash began finding ways of using InDesign as a substitute for those applications. Consequently, Adobe has added more and more Web and Rich Internet Application (RIA) features with each new version of InDesign.

Of course, *this* book is about print design and production in InDesign, which is still the primary purpose of the application. It'll focus on the print-related features, but the other growing use for InDesign was worth mentioning, particularly because the New Document dialog box now asks you to choose between creating documents for print and for the Web.

The Intent field contains two values: Print and Web.

Print Setting Intent to Print prepopulates the rest of the New Document dialog fields with typical print-project page sizes and options, using pica or whatever you've specified as your preferred measurement system.

Web Electing Web for the document intent changes the measurement system to pixels, switches the document color blend space to RGB, and sets up for a digital document.

Note that, other than the ruler units switching over to pixels, there is no true difference between setting the two intents with regard to the available options. You could set Intent to Web and still choose Letter from the Page Size dropdown menu, and still configure bleed and slug areas. Although a Web intent sets the document blending space to RGB rather than CMYK—a Print intent chooses CMYK—the option can be changed once the document is created from Edit ➤ Transparency Blend Space.

FACING VS. NONFACING PAGES

If you have the concept of facing and nonfacing pages down cold, skip this section. Many, many people—including experienced InDesign users—have questions about the distinction and repercussions between checking that box beside the Number of Pages field. It's to them that this section speaks.

Facing pages are any bound document that will have *left-read* or *verso* and *right-read* or *recto* pages; there's a spine between the pages, and they face one another (see Figure 7.2). If you're *duplexing*, printing on both sides of a page, you probably want to check the Facing Pages option at the top of the New Document dialog. Because facing pages swap edges, odd-numbered pages in English texts are always right-read (pages are to the right of the spine or binding edge) and even-numbered pages are left-read. Their margins also swap. Page 1's right margin becomes page 2's left margin and vice versa. Therefore, calling the margins *left* or *right* is only accurate half the time. Instead, *left* and *right* become *inside* and *outside*. Inside margin measurements control the distance from the spine (the bind edge), whereas outside margins specify how far content appears from the trim edge. InDesign will automatically flip the margins between odd- and even-numbered pages—swapping left for right, right for left—between pages.

FIGURE 7.2
Facing pages (left) are for bound documents, while nonfacing (right) are for single pages or documents that will all have a common bind edge.

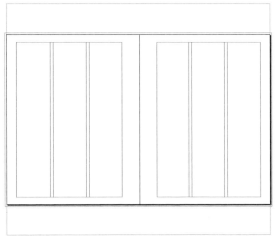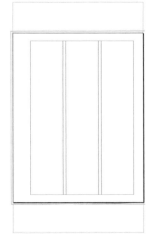

When Facing Pages is checked in the New Document dialog, the Margins section shows Inside and Outside fields. Uncheck it and you'll see the field labels change to Left and Right.

You'll want nonfacing pages for any document in which all pages will have a common bind edge. For instance, you might be creating a report where only the right-read pages will be printed upon, leaving their backs blank. That's a common scenario for velo-, GBC-, spiral-, three-ring-, or

even staple-bound documents and reports around an office or courtroom. Deposition transcripts and other evidentiary documents, for instance, are typically one-sided, nonfacing pages.

How do you know if the person before you created the document with facing or nonfacing pages? Simple: Look to the Pages panel. A document created with facing pages will have page icons set two-up on the spine (see Figure 7.3) instead of spineless singles. Even a one-page document displays the difference—page 1 of a facing pages document will be to the right of the spine. Also note the position of the *A* master page identifier. It's positioned on the outside edge of facing pages but centered on nonfacing.

FIGURE 7.3
On the Pages panel, facing pages (left) and nonfacing pages (right)

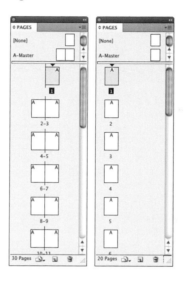

If you (or the client) decide to change the layout of a document from facing to non or vice versa after you've already begun working, fret not. File ➤ Document Setup contains that and most of the other options from the New Document dialog—including the Start Page # field that is new as of CS5. You might probably also need to adjust the margins, which can be done through Layout ➤ Margins and Columns.

RULER ORIGIN

Ruler orientation is also affected by choice of facing or nonfacing pages. Although you can override this in Edit ➤ Preferences ➤ Units & Increments, by default InDesign orients the horizontal ruler's zero-point to the top-left corner of the spread. Thus, in an 8.5×11-inch document of nonfacing pages, the right edge of every page is at 8.5 inches. With facing pages, though, only even pages and page 1 end at 8.5 inches. Page 3 and all odd pages (except page 1) *begin* at 8.5 inches (the spine) and end at 17. Positioning an object onto the right page of a spread using the Control or Transform panel, for instance, requires X positions greater than 8.5 inches.

The Origin field in the Units & Increments Preferences can change the horizontal ruler behavior (see Figure 7.4). Spread is the default and works as described previously, beginning at the top left of the left page and growing across the entire spread. Page restarts the numbering for each page—at the spine, the right-read page starts over again at 0 inches. Finally, setting the Ruler Units Origin to Spine orients the ruler zero-point on the spine itself; pages

to the right of the spine get positive measurements while pages to the left of the spine have negative measurements emanating from the spine.

FIGURE 7.4
The three Origin settings alter the orientation of the ruler's zero-point—its origin. Top to bottom: Spread, Page, and Spine.

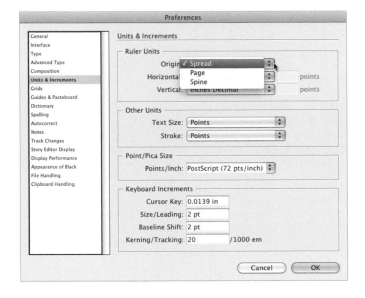

PAGE LAYOUT

If you graphic designer readers are considering skipping this section because you believe bleeds and slugs are in your print service providers' sphere of concern rather than yours, *don't*. Failure to create proper bleeds is among the most common reasons why designers' printed output is flawed and service providers charge for cleanup time or simply kick the job back as unacceptable.

You print providers shouldn't skip this section either. While I doubt I'll teach you anything you don't already know about bleed, live area, and slugs and why they're important, you might learn a different way to explain these concepts to designers so *they* get it. (Feel free to distribute copies of this book to your designer clients. Sybex has very attractive volume discounts. <wink>)

Bleed is when artwork or text runs to the page trim edge. The cover of this book is a good example. Notice how the ink bleeds off all four edges of the cover leaf. The bleed *area* is how far *beyond* the page ink must extend in order to safely ensure against slivers of plain paper appearing in the finished piece should pages misalign on the cutter.

Let's define the terms we're talking about visually. In Figure 7.5 (and its more easily understood counterpart in the color insert section of this book) you can see a trifold brochure I designed for a client as well as different marks and guides (I've removed some marks to make my point easier to discern). On the very outside, the blue guide box is the *slug* area. Inside that, with the artwork running right up to them, are the red bleed area guides. Next, the paper edges—turned green in the figure for easy identification—are the trim, the expected final paper size post-print, post-trim, post-finishing. Finally, within the page are the magenta margin guides that form the document *live area* (sort of). The white area beyond is, of course, the pasteboard.

FIGURE 7.5

A document showing slug, bleed, trim, and margin guides

SLUG

Slug is a nebulous term that can be applied to a lot of different things. In my travels and more than two decades in the business I've noted its usage change regionally and by specialization within each of the print, prepress, and design industries. Quite a few people use the term slug to reference headers and footers or parts of them, like the page number. (The page number is properly called a *folio*, not to be confused with *folio* referencing a folded sheet of paper comprising two leafs or spreads.) In this context, slug refers to any information that must accompany a design through prepress and print but that will be trimmed off during finishing.

What should you put in the slug area? Whatever the designer or print service provider may need: Job name, job number, document title, InDesign filename, client name and contact info, date, designer's name and contact info, color bars, short knock-knock jokes for your service provider's amusement—anything *can* go in there. What *should* go in there is whatever is needed by the designer, the prepress bureau, the printer, the finishing and bindery service, and whoever will retain the film or plates generated from the artwork (if there are film or plates). It's a great place to put special instructions to providers down the line, too. For instance, if your job contains a spot color used as a placeholder plate for a varnish, in addition to setting up the ink properly in Ink Manager, note in both the job ticket and the slug area which ink is the varnish. Even if the prepress and press operators miss the note on the job ticket, they'll see it in the slug because the slug will output to every piece of film and every printed page. If you're running film for the job, include enough information that, a year or five down the road, you'll be able to immediately identify the job, client, designer, and corresponding digital document. Many a

wasted hour has been spent at swapping sheets of film on a light table trying to figure out which page 14 cyan plate goes with which page 14 yellow, magenta, and black plates.

Before sending a job to press, *I* typically add one small table into the slug area above the page and another table below. In the top, I include the job name as given to my print and finishing providers, the page number, the date, my account number(s) at the service provider (for proper billing and tracking), my name and contact information (so a RIP or press operator can immediately call or e-mail me without having to wait for a trip to the customer database), and any special instructions echoed from the job ticket. Within the lower table is information for *my* reference, including internal job name and number, client name, digital document title and filename, and authoring application and version. I often send PDFs to press, so I want to know on the film if I should be searching archive DVD-ROMs for an InDesign, QuarkXPress, Illustrator, or some other type of document and what version of that software I used in case whatever version I'm currently using has trouble translating from older ones (InDesign had that problem with version 1.0 and 1.5 documents). Knowing the authoring application and version can also help my prepress provider understand the document and any unique RIP considerations (once in a while it's a factor, even with properly made PDFs). Of course, I put all this information on the master page rather than doing it manually page by page.

MARKS AND SYMBOLS

Marks and symbols like crop marks, bleed marks, and registration marks vital to the proper output of your job will, by definition, wind up in the slug area.

Setting up a slug area is simple. When you're creating a new document (or later in Document Setup), clicking the More Options button reveals the Bleed and Slug area (see Figure 7.6). The chain link button on the right will mirror all four sides' measurements, which is usually not necessary. In most cases, you want to put all your slug information on one or, at most, two sides of the output. Your service providers will often add additional marks and symbols or their own tracking information, and you want to leave them space in which to do so. Additionally, because the slug will print on film and paper, too generous a slug area can unnecessarily enlarge the required substrates, potentially increasing the cost of the job and killing more trees than necessary. Slug areas should only be large enough to hold the required information comfortably.

FIGURE 7.6
The Bleed and Slug area of the New Document Setup dialog with More Options shown

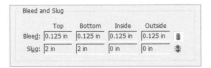

When exporting a PDF for press, you'll want to ensure that the PDF includes the slug area. As you can see in Figure 7.7, the Marks and Bleeds pane of the Export Adobe PDF dialog has an Include Slug Area check box at the bottom. Check that for press output, but uncheck it when publishing a PDF to your website or intranet for digital distribution.

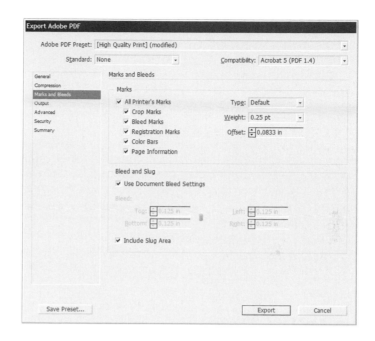

The Print dialog's Marks and Bleed pane has the same box (see Figure 7.8) if you're output-ting straight from InDesign or printing to PostScript. When printing to a desktop printer, you typically want to print only the trim size, so uncheck it. However, if you'd like to scale the entire design to include the slug, bleed, and any marks, check the appropriate options, and then, on the Setup pane, activate the Scale to Fit option. Note that the entire output will shrink down to fit within the chosen paper size (and respect any *rebates*), including the slug and so forth.

FIGURE 7.8
Check the Include
Slug Area box
when printing
final output or a
complete proof
inclusive of the
slug, bleed, and
printer's marks.

In both locations you can also add needed marks and symbols via the Printer's Marks check boxes as well as control type, weight, and offset (distance from artwork) of the crop, bleed, and registration marks.

BLEED

Bleeding designs are run on sheets larger than the intended deliverable page size and then trimmed in very large stacks on a guillotine or other type of cutter. Cutter operators are punctilious (they have to be; they have 10 fingers relying on their attention to detail). Still, they're human (as evidenced by the number of cutter operators at annual conventions answering to the nickname of "Lefty"). Moreover, sheets of paper have a tendency to shift ever so slightly as a blade is rammed down through a stack. Even a one one-thousandth of an inch shift can leave an ugly white strip down one or more sides of an edge-to-edge print piece that didn't account for such possibilities. That would ruin an otherwise beautiful design. Hedge against this common problem by drawing beyond the trim. Don't stop image frames or filled objects at the page edge; keep them going out ⅛ inch. Look at Figure 7.9, the same document with and without bleeds. See the difference? The one that extends the art to fill the bleed area can't be marred by paper slivers; if the cutter is off enough to cause slivers with an ⅛-inch bleed, the operator will send the job for a print rerun anyway.

FIGURE 7.9
The same full-bleed design *without* the safety net of extending artwork out to the bleed area (left) and *with* (right). Also see the full color version in the color insert.

Create a bleed guide around any side that will run ink up to the trim edge—it's usually easier to just set up a four-sided bleed guide even if fewer edges will bleed. When sending a bleeding document to press, *always* bleed the artwork. Get the desired bleed area size from your print service provider; when in doubt, use the industry standard ⅛ inch or 0.125 inch. Then, as you design, account for the bleed area by extending objects and colors out to the red bleed guide. If you use a background image, crop it at the bleed guide, not at the trim. Depending on the image, that may require you to enlarge it in InDesign or even go back to Photoshop or Illustrator and add more space around the focal point of the picture. As you get in the habit of using bleeds and bleed guides in InDesign, you'll learn to plan for the bleed when prepping artwork.

As you noticed in the preceding text, adding, resizing, and outputting bleed to print or PDF is controlled in the same place as whether to include the slug area. You have additional control over bleed, however (see Figure 7.10). You can use the document bleed settings as defined in New Document or Document Properties, or you can override them (or correct for their absence)

by specifying new bleed values in the Bleed and Slug section of the Print or Export to PDF Marks and Bleed panes.

FIGURE 7.10

Bleed controls in the Print dialog's Marks and Bleed tab

LIVE AREA

Similar to bleed, live area compensates for paper shifts on a cutter, but on the *inside* of the trim. If pages or the blade slips during a cut and a bleeding print shows paper along one edge, it therefore follows that the opposite edge of the page will *lose* some of its artwork. It's even more important that the design elements critical to communicating the message of a design be inset from the trim edges than it is that background colors extend out beyond. You don't, for instance, want the last digit of an ad's call-to-action phone number or Twitter ID chopped off. (I've seen that exact thing, actually, within an ad in a major, one million-plus circulation magazine; the client showed it to me when I was hired to take over from the firm that had created and placed that ad.)

The buffer space of the live area is, like the bleed buffer, typically ⅛ inch or 0.125 inches. It can vary, though. Product packaging labels and low linescreen boxes, for example, often need 0.25 or even more distance between trim and live area (and trim and bleed). Consult your print service provider.

I wish I could show you a dialog where you can create a live area guide (orange would be a nice choice in guides), but I can't. InDesign doesn't have such a feature, although I keep lobbying for one. Instead, Adobe considers the margin guides to define the live area despite the fact that they default to half an inch around all four sides instead of an eighth of an inch. Margins *can* be used to represent the live area—it makes sense in some respects given the way Adobe built InDesign's Margins feature—but there are some drawbacks to it as well.

InDesign allows you to put anything you want within, outside, or crossing the margins—so does every other professional layout application and most consumer-grade layout tools as well. Margin guides, in fact, matter very little in InDesign. The only place they really have an effect is in automated text frame creation.

When you check the Master Text Frame option while creating a new document, the resulting master page text frame will be sized and placed according to the margin guides. When you're autoflowing multipage placed text, new text frames will also be generated according to the area defined by the margins. Other than that, their function is primarily as a visual guide to you. It's the automatic text frame sizing that also foils their use as live area guides. A live area should be, under most conditions, 0.125 inches in from the trim edges all around. If you use automatic text frames, though, that puts text flush with the live area guides. That's not so much a problem for printing—the live area guides define the minimum area that you can be sure will print and cut intact—but more of a design issue. Copy running flush or too close to the edge *looks* bad. Readers need white space along the edges of paper to grip the page or book as well as to give their eyes a place to rest.

So, what's the verdict? Margins as live area guides or not? If every page will be manually created with individually placed frames, then you should be good to go using margin guides as live area guides. If you're using any kind of automatic text frame creation (master text frame, auto-flowing text), then don't use margins as live area guides. Instead, do this:

1. Select Ruler Guides from the Layout menu and change the color to something other than the defaults: Cyan (guide color), Magenta (margin guides), Violet (column guides), Fiesta (bleed guides), Grid Blue (slug guides), White, Light Gray, and Black (see Figure 7.11). Personally, I like green for my live area guides because it stands out against most colors without being too similar to other types of guides.

FIGURE 7.11
Ruler Guides options enable changing guide color.

2. Go to the document master page(s) for the document and drag horizontal and vertical guides from the rulers for each edge (four for nonfacing documents, eight guides for both pages in the spread of a facing-pages document). Notice how they're now green.

3. Unlock guides by unchecking the View ➤ Grids & Guides ➤ Lock Guides toggle command.

4. Using the Control or Transform panel, position unlocked guides 0.125 inches in from the page edges on all outside edges; with bound documents, you'll probably want more space on the bind edges. Those guides will define your live area.

5. Deselect all guides with Cmd+Shift+A/Ctrl+Shift+A and return new guides to their default color (Cyan) with Layout ➤ Ruler Guides again.

With separate live area guides, you can now use the margin guides for their intended purpose—limiting content and enabling white space. As you design, keep all important elements inside the green guides, extend all bleeding objects out to the bleed guide, and you'll be safe from misaligned cuts.

Still, it seems like a lot of work to set up bleed, slug, and especially live area guides for every new document, doesn't it? Wouldn't it be cool if there were an easier way? There is.

Reusable Document Setups

This section is about efficiency. As I've said before, if you need to do something more than once, do it *only* once and automate it. InDesign has numerous automation-enabling facilities for many common tasks, including reusable page setups.

DOCUMENT PRESETS

At the top of the New Document dialog (File ➤ New ➤ Document) is the Document Preset drop-down menu (see Figure 7.12). By default, it contains only [Default] and [Custom]. The latter is intended just to be a visual cue for you the InDesign user. Change anything below and the preset becomes [Custom]; you do not need to preselect [Custom] in order to make any changes below it.

FIGURE 7.12

The New Document dialog's Document Preset menu showing a few presets I created

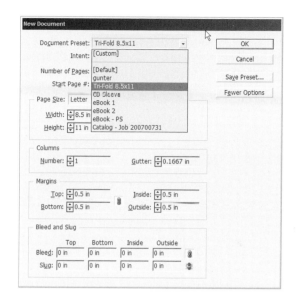

If you *more often than not* have to change something from its default in the New Document dialog—maybe your typical document is tabloid sized, includes a standard-sized bleed, has multiple columns, or needs something other than a half-inch all-around margin—set it up just once and build a preset. Every subsequent document you create will then not require all the manual settings; you'll be able to select it from the Document Preset menu and have all your options applied. Just set the options once, click the Save Preset button, and give the preset a name in the Save Preset dialog that pops up. Upon clicking OK, you'll find your custom preset below [Default] in the list, ready for two-click setup of your next document. Build presets for all the different types of documents you create at least once in a while.

PAGE SIZE PRESETS

The Page Size list contains the most common paper sizes customers told Adobe they use. Among them are standard U.S. letter, legal, and tabloid sizes; British A4, B5, and other standards; compact disc and 3.5×2-inch business card sizes, and common screen-resolution measurements like 800×600 and 1024×768 pixels. If the list isn't inclusive of your most common page sizes, tell Adobe; maybe a future edition of InDesign will include your favorite page sizes. Until then, you can manually override them by changing the width, height, and/or orientation below the dropdown menu, or you can add your own common sizes to the Page Size list.

CS5

A WHOLE NEW WAY TO ADD CUSTOM PAGE SIZES

You may recall that in previous versions of InDesign you could add custom page sizes to the New Document dialog by editing the New Doc Sizes.txt file in a text editor. No more. As of CS5, that file no longer exists, and all custom page sizes are added directly in the New Document dialog box.

CS5

To add your most commonly used page sizes, choose the last option in the Page Size menu, Custom Page Size, which will open a new dialog (see Figure 7.13). Set the width, height, and orientation in the appropriate fields, give your custom page a name unique from others in the Page Size menu, and click the Add button. Rinse, repeat if you want to add more than one custom page size, or click OK to commit the changes and close the dialog.

FIGURE 7.13
The Custom Page
Size dialog.

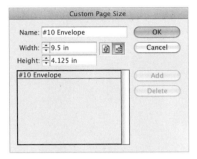

Deleting an unused custom page size later requires a return to the Custom Page Size dialog. Select the unwanted size in the list and click Delete to get rid of it.

DOCUMENT TEMPLATES

Neither document presets nor custom page sizes can save your manually created live area guides, but a template can. In fact, a template can save everything to do with a particular document—paragraph, character, table, cell, and object styles as well as swatches, dictionary spelling and hyphenation exceptions, columns, and master pages, among other things. I always recommend templates for workflows that frequently employ the same or similar document layouts and styles. Cumulatively, templates can save a massive amount of time over setting up documents manually, and they can be passed around the office or posted on a shared server for simultaneous use by everyone. Templates, in fact, are the key to consistent style usage among workgroups (more on that in Chapter 13).

If you've set up trim area guides or any other document feature likely to be reused on the same page size in the future, save it as a template. Just go to File ➤ Save As, and change the Save As Type dropdown to InDesign CS5 Template. The resulting file will have an .indt extension instead of .indd and will have a slightly different icon. For all intents and purposes, it's just a standard InDesign document with the sole exception that the .indt extension triggers a slightly different behavior when File ➤ Open is used. Instead of opening the template itself, InDesign will create a new, untitled document based on that template—a duplicate—and will not open the original template directly. In the new document you'll have everything you had in the template—paragraph, character, table, cell, and object styles as well as swatches, dictionary spelling and hyphenation exceptions, columns, and master pages, among other things.

The trick is in the way the Open dialog works. Note the three Open options at the bottom (see Figure 7.14). Original opens the original file, whether an InDesign document, template, or Interchange Format INX file. Copy generates on the fly an unsaved duplicate of the selected document; the original is left untouched, but InDesign creates a new document faithful to the original in every respect. Finally, Normal says to use whichever is the default behavior for the specific document type—INDD, INX, and IDML documents open originals, INDTs create

copies. Normal is the default, which means that, when designers in your workgroup need to create new documents from your template, they won't be editing the template itself. To do that, you must deliberately choose to open the original. Note that when you're opening documents created in a previous version of InDesign or created in a compatible version of PageMaker (6.0–7.0) or QuarkXPress (3.3–4.1 and QuarkXPress Passport 4.1), a copy will be created regardless of the Open radio button choice. In such cases the copy will bear the advisory "[Converted]" as part of the unsaved filename in the document title tab.

FIGURE 7.14
In the Open a File dialog, the Open radio buttons determine whether the original will be opened or a new copy created.

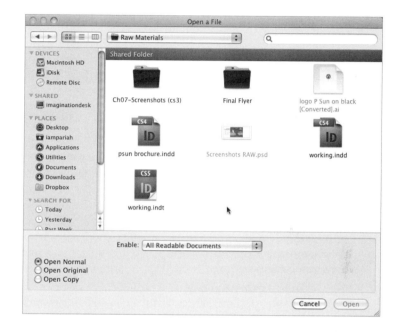

A template-based workflow is the ideal for any periodical and is usually more efficient and leads to fewer content-destroying mistakes than opening the previous issue's files, resaving as the next issue's files, and then replacing content. I've seen few other workflows wherein at least one document setup is reused that doesn't also see a benefit from employing templates.

Layout Adjustment

This isn't strictly a master page thing, but layout adjustment is most often used in conjunction with master pages, so it makes the most sense to bring it up here.

After initially creating the document, you can change its type—facing or nonfacing—as well as the paper size and orientation with File ➤ Document Setup. Using Layout ➤ Margins and Columns, you can also alter the margins, number of columns, and column gutter width. Finally, on master pages, margin guides can be manually dragged to new positions (if unlocked). None of these changes will adapt your page objects to the new conditions. If you want your text frames to expand or contract to fit new margins or to automatically reduce or increase the number of columns they contain according to changes you've made in Margins and Columns, or if you want other objects to adjust to the new document layout without you having to do it all by hand, turn to Layout Adjustment on the Layout menu (see Figure 7.15).

FIGURE 7.15
The Layout Adjust-
ment dialog

Layout Adjustment does a decent job of reformatting page (and master page) objects to conform to new document conditions such as new page sizes and orientations and margin and column guide relocation. Frames will be moved and resized as needed to adapt to the new layout if Enable Layout Adjustment is activated prior to making the layout change. Here is what the options mean:

Snap Zone   The maximum distance an object must be from one or more margin or column guides or the page edge to be a candidate for repositioning or resizing with Layout Adjustment. For instance, with a value of 0.25 inches, a master text frame directly on four margins will be adjusted, but a graphic frame 0.5 inches from the nearest guide will not be adjusted.

Allow Graphics and Groups to Resize   Vector objects, frames, and groups of objects will be repositioned by Layout Adjustment regardless of whether they fall within the snap zone. This option determines whether they may also be scaled to better fit. For instance, if converting an 8.5×11-inch document from portrait to landscape, if enabled, a full-page background graphic frame will follow suit to become 11×8.5 inches with its content scaled accordingly.

Allow Ruler Guides to Move   Manually created ruler guides—column center points, for example—can be moved to maintain their relative position to margin and column guides with this option checked.

Ignore Ruler Guide Alignments   Throughout working on a document, we often create numerous ruler guides that are not significantly related to the layout. Because layout adjustment considers all guides in its calculations, these nonessential guides can cause it confusion, leading to improperly adjusted layouts. Checking this option tells InDesign to ignore them, factoring in only page edges and column and margin guides when repositioning and scaling objects.

Ignore Object and Layer Locks   This option is an easier alternative to digging through all the layers and objects on the Layers panel looking for little padlocks. Enabling this will reposition and/or scale objects regardless of their individual or layer lock statuses.

Managing Pages

Once you have a document created and have begun laying out the design, you'll need to insert, delete, duplicate, rearrange, and even import the occasional page.

Pages Panel

The hub of page management activity is the Pages panel (see Figure 7.16).

The first thing you'll notice is that each page icon in the panel is a thumbnail of the actual content of the page—master pages, too. You won't spend a great deal of time guessing on which page you placed that picture last week because you can see the contents of all pages in the Pages panel's thumbnails. In addition to page contents you'll see a couple of other things in page icons.

FIGURE 7.16
The Pages panel

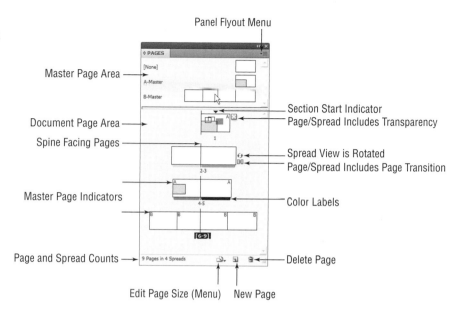

Panel Flyout Menu

Master Page Area

Document Page Area

Spine Facing Pages

Master Page Indicators

Page and Spread Counts

Edit Page Size (Menu)   New Page

Section Start Indicator
Page/Spread Includes Transparency

Spread View is Rotated
Page/Spread Includes Page Transition

Color Labels

Delete Page

Master page indicators (the little *A*s in the figure), appear in the outer top corner on facing pages and top center on nonfacing pages. Master page indicators communicate on which master page a document page is based—by default *A-Master*.

CS5

Colors can now be assigned to page icons to categorize or differentiate them from one another. By right-clicking a page icon and accessing the Color Label submenu, or by selecting the page and choosing the Color Label submenu from the Pages panel flyout menu, you can assign one of 15 colors to a given page or spread. Color labels display as horizontal bars beneath the page icons (see Figure 7.17 and the color version in the color insert). Master pages can also be color coded and set to cause document pages based on them to coordinate.

FIGURE 7.17
Assigning color labels to individual pages

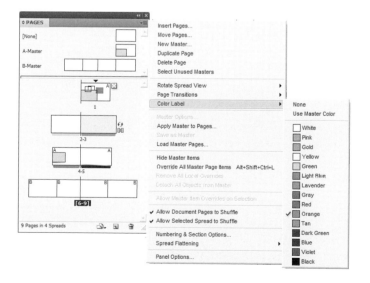

Why would you want to use color labels for pages? Quite a few potential uses immediately spring to my mind:

◆ Maybe you label incomplete pages in red as a cue to return to them.

◆ When using assignments in a document (see Chapter 14, "Collaboration"), page color codes can be coordinated with user colors to provide a visual, thumbnail map of assigned pages and to whom those pages belong.

◆ Periodical designers might label all their ad pages in one color, feature content in another color, and department pages in a third.

◆ Periodical production editors might use some of the available 15 colors to do away with external flatplan tracking for different states of creation, approval, and sign-off on pages and bring all that functionality directly into the publication files, tying it directly to the pages, where it can be used most efficiently.

Customizing the Pages Panel

In its default view, the Pages panel shows masters at the top in small icons and documents in medium icons at the bottom. Both grow vertically, which, especially in the lower section, leaves a lot of wasted horizontal space. A lot of customization is possible, though, as you can see from just a few possible configurations in Figure 7.18. You can change the size of pages and master icons from extra small to jumbo, show them horizontally or vertically, and change which is on the top. Those sentimental for PageMaker can tear the panel away from the dock, align it across the bottom of the InDesign window, and set pages to show horizontally rather than vertically.

FIGURE 7.18
Pages panel options offer flexible arrangements.

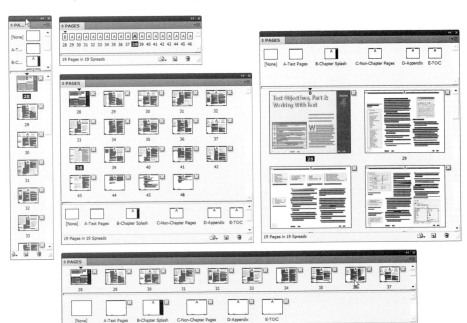

All this customization is available in the Panel Options dialog (see Figure 7.19), which is the last item on the Pages panel flyout menu. The final option, a dropdown menu titled Resize, defines which section, if either, is fixed height. When one is chosen as fixed, resizing the panel alters the other section. Setting both to Proportional will resize them equally. If you long for the good-old days when master page identifiers were easy to read and pages were just plain white (and, when selected, blue) icons, or if rendering page thumbnails slows down your system, uncheck Show Thumbnails for pages and/or masters.

FIGURE 7.19
Panel Options
dialog

The Icons section of Panel Options offers three choices: Transparency, Spread Rotation, and Page Transitions.

Transparency   The first, Transparency, if enabled will cause the display of a small checkerboard icon beside any page containing transparency. That can take the form of an imported graphic containing transparency; an object, including frames, text, and vector paths, that is set to less than 100% opaque; or the use of transparency effects like a drop shadow, outer glow, or feather. This option is disabled by default because nowadays sending transparency to press doesn't require any extra thought or preparation. A few years ago, however, it could be an issue depending upon the RIP system your output providers used. Then, enabling an indicator of transparency was highly useful, and was enabled by default.

Spreads   Spreads can be turned 90° clockwise or counterclockwise, as well as 180° to flip them upside down (see "Rotate Spread View" later in this chapter). Although the Pages panel will not show page icons as rotated—because they aren't rotated, Rotate Spread View changes only their *view*, not the actual spread rotation—enabling the Spread Rotation check box adds another icon, two arrows chasing each other circularly, beside a spread to indicate the rotated view.

Page Transitions   Page Transitions is a presentation feature that enables wipes and other slideshow-like page transitions. In Chapter 9, "Documents," we'll talk about Page Transitions. Using a page transition on either page in a spread, and then enabling the Page Transitions icon in the Panel Options, places a third, roughly *H*-like icon beside the spread's page icons.

Inserting Pages

Here is a refresher on the familiar ways to add pages to a document:

Adding a Page At the bottom of the Pages panel, the Create New Page button adds one page at a time to the end of the document or, if you have a page selected, immediately after the selected page. New pages adopt the master assigned to the last or selected page—for instance, if page 5 of a five-page document is assigned to master page A (and includes the *A* indicator), new pages will also be assigned to master page A.

Alternatively, Cmd+Shift+P/Ctrl+Shift+P has the same effect as the Create New Page button.

Layout ➤ Pages ➤ Add Page also adds one new page at the end of the document, assigning the same master page as the last in the document.

Adding Several Pages at Once The Insert Pages command on both the Pages panel flyout menu and the Layout ➤ Pages menu offers insertion of multiple pages at once at a specific location in the document (e.g., before or after page *X*) and choice of the master page to which to assign inserted pages (see Figure 7.20).

FIGURE 7.20

Insert Pages dialog

Although not new, this method demands more explanation than a quick bullet point. Dragging either the name or icon(s) of a master page down into the Pages panel has two possible effects. Dropping it on top of an existing page will apply the master page (or blank [None] master) to the document page. If a page belongs to master page A, dropping B on it will remove all the non-overridden A master page items and apply all the features of B. Dropping B onto a page already assigned to B will reapply the master page items of B; all overridden items will remain in place, of course, but the originals as they appear on the master will also appear.

The other behavior of dragging and dropping master pages is to insert new pages. *Where* it inserts them is a matter of hand-eye coordination. Dropping a master onto a blank area of the pages section, such as below the icons or in the empty space to either side, will insert new pages (based on that master) at the end of the document. Putting them anywhere else—like trying to insert a new page between pages 2 and 3—is where all those hours spent playing "Halo" pay off. It requires the same skills as rearranging pages, so read on, McDuff.

Rearranging Pages

Managing page order is also done through the Pages panel. To move a page, simply

1. Click on and highlight its icon.

2. Drag it to the new location.

To select an entire spread,

1. Either click the page numbers below the icon, or click on one side and then Cmd+click/Ctrl+click on the other. Once selected, they'll drag as one.

MANAGING PAGES | 295

2. Select a range of sequential pages like files in the file system—click the first and then Shift+click the last. Use Cmd+click/Ctrl+click for nonsequential pages.

Where they land when you drop them is the tricky part:

Moving Pages to the End Like inserting master pages, dragging existing pages and dropping them at the bottom of the stack or out in the empty space will relocate the pages to the end of the document. The cursor will be a hand without adornment.

Moving Pages to a Specific Location Dragging near to the outside edge of an existing page will show a bold vertical line (see Figure 7.21) indicating that the page(s) will be inserted before (bar to the left) or after (bar to the right) that location. The cursor communicates this fact as well, as you can see.

FIGURE 7.21
Inserting pages to the left of page 36 displays a specific cursor and a thick insertion point bar.

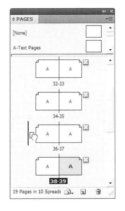

Moving Pages between Other Pages By default, dropping pages between two pages in a spread shuffles everything down in spreads. For example, dragging page 6 and dropping it in between pages 2 and 3 will make 6 the new 3 (a right-read page), push 3 down into the 4 position (a left-read page), and cascade similar order and side changes throughout the remaining pages. When inserting masters or moving pages between two in a spread—hovering the cursor over the spine between page icons—a subtle shift left or right changes the cursor and the insertion point. A pixel or two to the left of the spine inserts to the left, inserting in place of page 2; to the right leaves page 2 alone to insert ahead of page 3 (see Figure 7.22). It's tricky and made more so the smaller your page icons, thus my analogy to video game reflexes.

Alternatively to dragging and dropping, you can use the Move Pages command on the panel flyout menu or Layout ➤ Pages menu.

In the Move Pages dialog (see Figure 7.23), specify a page number, page range, or nonsequential pages to move and then a destination—after or before the page number in the next field or to the start or end of the document. The Move Pages (pages to be moved) field accepts an amazingly flexible range of inputs. You can enter a single page number, of course, or a page range separated by a hyphen (e.g., 4-9), nonsequential pages separated by commas (e.g., 3, 6, 1, 9, 366), or a mixture of both (e.g., 1-3, 87-109, 6-12, 5, 20-21). The order in which pages are entered in the Move Pages field will determine their order after the operation, and they'll be renumbered accordingly.

FIGURE 7.22
A few pixels deter-
mine whether
pages will insert to
the left of the spine
or the right.

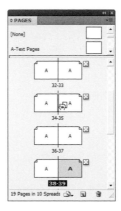

FIGURE 7.23
The Move Pages
dialog

If you're proficient in first-person-shooter video games, you should do well with drag-and-drop management on the Pages panel. However, if "Bejeweled" is more your speed, use the Insert Pages and Move Pages commands.

Single-Page and Multipage Spreads

Once in a while, there's a need for spreads consisting of more than two pages. Often multipage spreads were used as a workaround for InDesign's former inability to accommodate pages of different sizes in a single document. Creating three-, four-, or five-page spreads could create the effect of large, foldout-style covers or inserts. Often, this workaround created more problems than it was worth. Two 8.5×11-inch pages on the same side of the spine may *look* and behave *onscreen* as a single 11×17-inch page, but a RIP still sees them as separate 8.5×11-inch pages. It takes extra effort and planning on the RIP operator's part to ensure that the pages print as a single unit. The new Page Size feature, by contrast, really does create a single page, and the RIP recognizes it as such; thus there is less opportunity for mistakes and bad film.

When you do have a legitimate need for spreads of more *or less* than two pages—for instance, to force a new right-read or left-read page without its opposite—InDesign *can* accommodate you, although it's not obvious how.

Previously I stated, "By default, dropping pages between two pages in a spread shuffles everything down in spreads." That behavior is called *shuffling*. Inserting a page—new or from elsewhere in the document—forces all subsequent pages to shuffle down while maintaining two-page spreads. Drag and drop as long as you like; you'll never get a third page on a single spread. At least not as long as the Allow Document Pages to Shuffle command is active on the Pages panel flyout menu. Turn off that command, and you can build multipage spreads like some of the ones you see in Figure 7.24. If you need to override just a single spread—a trifold cover or centerfold, for example—but want the rest of the pages to shuffle with page order

changes normally, leave on Allow Document Pages to Shuffle. Instead, highlight a specific spread and turn off Allow Selected Spread to Shuffle, which is also on the Pages panel flyout menu. Now, just drag new pages from the master pages section above or existing pages from elsewhere in the list and then drop them directly to the side of the desired spread.

FIGURE 7.24

Spreads of more than two pages are possible once Allow Document Pages to Shuffle has been disabled.

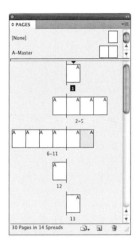

Note that this is also a gotcha: Turning off shuffling often leads to spreads *unintentionally* greater than two pages. If that happens to you, *don't try to fix it by moving pages again!* Although moving pages back *should* repair any damage done, one of InDesign's quirks is that it doesn't, especially not when one or more of the pages contains objects that cross the spine. Often these get left behind or shoved out onto the pasteboard. Instead of manually moving pages back, immediately *undo* the move operation that resulted in the unwanted spread. Even if you've saved the document, InDesign will step backward through the operations with Cmd+Z/Ctrl+Z—as long as you haven't *closed* the document since performing the operation.

Moving Pages between Documents

No way!

Yes way, Ted!

InDesign has the ability to move pages between InDesign documents with ease. Having multiple page sizes in a single layout has been characterized for decades as the Holy Grail of desktop publishing, therefore the ability to merge and move pages between documents must be a quest of almost equal glory. King Solomon's Mine? Let's go with that.

Astute observers would note that there's one field in the Move Pages dialog I didn't discuss yet: the Move To field (see Figure 7.25). Via Move Pages, you can tell InDesign to move them to any other opened document. Just choose the desired destination document from the Move To list, and then all the options above it will become germane to *that* document rather than the current. You can, say, move (copy really) pages 10–20 from Document A to the beginning, end, or a specific location within Document B. Checking the Delete Pages After Moving option *really* moves them from one place to another instead of just copying.

FIGURE 7.25
The Move Pages
dialog moving
pages to another
document

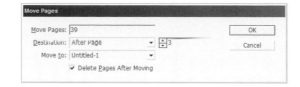

If you'd prefer to do it visually, to select pages based on their thumbnail previews instead of trying to recall which page numbers you need, you can drag and drop pages from one document's Pages panel into another document as easily as rearranging pages intra-document. Bring the source document to the foreground and arrange it so that you can see the destination document as well (employ the Arrange Documents menu on the toolbar for this). Select and drag the needed pages on the Pages panel, and drop them over any visible portion of the destination document window. The Insert Pages dialog (see Figure 7.26) will instantly pop up, asking where you'd like the dropped pages placed. It will also give you the option of deleting them from the source document.

FIGURE 7.26
The Insert Pages
dialog

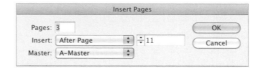

Duplicating and Deleting Pages

Sometimes, you don't want to create new pages or move them from other documents. Sometimes you just want to make a copy, and sometimes you want to destroy. Here's a quick refresher of the various ways in which to accomplish those tasks.

◆ Drag the icons of one or more pages and spreads from the list in the Pages panel atop the Create New Page button to duplicate those pages and all their contents to the end of the document.

◆ With one or more pages or spreads selected, choose Duplicate Page, Duplicate Pages, Duplicate Spread, or Duplicate Spreads from the Pages panel flyout menu, Layout ➢ Pages menu, or context-sensitive menu available by right-clicking a selected page icon.

◆ With pages or spreads selected, click the Delete Selected Pages trashcan icon at the bottom of the panel. If the page contains objects, you'll be prompted to confirm your decision.

◆ Drag the icons of one or more pages and spreads from the list in the Pages panel and drop them onto the trashcan icon at the bottom of the panel to delete them. If the page contains objects, you'll be prompted to confirm your decision.

◆ With one or more pages or spreads selected, choose Delete Page, Delete Pages, Delete Spread, or Delete Spreads from the Pages panel flyout menu or context menu available by right-clicking a selected page icon. If the page contains objects, you'll be prompted to confirm your decision.

◆ From the Layout ➢ Pages ➢ Delete Pages command, you can access the Delete Pages dialog, which, like the Move Pages dialog, enables entry of single, sequential, nonsequential, or mixed page numbers for page deletion.

Objects and Rearranged Pages

When moving, duplicating, or deleting pages, it's important that you know how InDesign determines to which page an object belongs. If, for example, you've created a background color wash across a spread, what happens to the graphic frame if the right-read page is moved to another place in the document? Will the frame move with that page and suddenly appear behind both it and its new mate, or will it remain behind with the original left-read page and adorn *its* new mate? If a page is deleted, what happens to the graphic frame?

The rules by which InDesign conducts itself in determining object-to-page relationships, and thus what happens to objects when pages are rearranged or deleted, are pretty simple. If you're coming from proficiency in QuarkXPress especially, it's important to recognize that InDesign and XPress differ in their most fundamental definition of object placement, which creates different, almost opposing rules for handling the object-to-page relationship with regard to page movement. In QuarkXPress, *everything* is relative to a fixed origin point of the top-left corner; objects *always* belong to the page on which their top-left corners fall. Thus, even if an 8.5-inch-wide box's origin is only 0.001 pt to the left of the spine, deleting the left-read page also deletes the box.

InDesign determines ownership by the center point instead of the top-left corner. If the center of a frame is on the left-read page, the object belongs to the left page; if the center is 0.001 pt to the right of the spine, it belongs to the right-read page. If the object is perfectly centered on the spine, left wins. In that case, moving or deleting the right-read page keeps the frame in place, allowing it to cover the new right-read if shuffling is enabled or spill out onto the pasteboard if shuffling is turned off.

In the event of a mixed-master spread, wherein one page is assigned to one master page and the other page to a different master, objects from *both* master pages will apply. If any of those objects span the spine, they will apply to *both* left- and right-read pages in the spread.

Page Size, Orientation, and Rotation

The Holy Grail of desktop layout has been found, but not by Indiana Jones.

Since long before computers, there has always been a need to create documents that include multiple page sizes or orientations. With the rise of *VDP* and digital-to-press output making high-quality, one-off productions an affordable option, multiple page sizes and orientations in documents have become more common and more desirable. But the software had never caught up with the need. QuarkXPress, since version 6.0, has done multiple page sizes in one "project," but it's not truly the same thing. You see, QuarkXPress merely allows multiple, disconnected layouts to be saved in the same file—it's an MDF, a multiple document format, similar to the way Excel allows multiple spreadsheets to be saved in a single Excel document. QuarkXPress, even in the latest version as of this writing, still won't allow two or more differently sized pages in a single, continuous layout.

Multiple Page Sizes

CS5

Sip from the Holy Grail of desktop layout and revel in the divine power to create a single document containing multiple page sizes and/or orientations (see Figure 7.27). You can have an 8×11-inch document wherein the occasional page is an 11×17 foldout. You can create a half-page inside cover fold right beside the full-size front cover. You can design an entire stationary kit—letterhead, envelope, business card, and rolodex card—all in the same document. You can do anything you can imagine, with any number of equally or differently sized pages.

FIGURE 7.27
Multiple page sizes in a single document are now a reality.

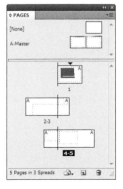

To change the size of a page, select its thumbnail in the Pages panel, and from the bottom of the Pages panel, beside the New Page button, click the Edit Page Size button. A menu will pop up offering the same paper sizes as in the New Document dialog—including any custom page sizes you've built (see Figure 7.28). Select a size from the list, and your page will adjust to that size. If what you need isn't in the list of preset sizes, choose Custom Page Size to define a new one. Margin and column guides will also adapt to match, though the Pages panel thumbnail will not—not accurately, at any rate.

FIGURE 7.28
The Edit Page Size button menu

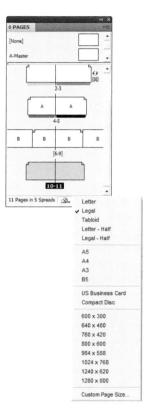

The Pages panel icons are weird and do not correctly display the sizes of pages. For instance, you could have the left page of a spread set as 17×11-inch portrait-rotated tabloid size and the right a 3.5×2-inch business card, but the Pages panel will display them both as the same height, with the business card being wider than the tabloid! Obviously, Adobe hasn't yet finished polishing the Holy Grail. (They should have just bought PageControl from me; we had proper Pages panel display and more figured out years ago.)

If you'd rather use a more hands-on and visual method of altering the sizes of pages, grab the new Page tool from beneath the Direct Selection tool on the Tools panel. With it you can select a page *in the document* rather than on the Pages panel. With the Page tool active, the Control Panel switches into Spread mode, displaying controls relevant to page size and orientation (see Figure 7.29). First are fields for the X and Y coordinates to reposition the selected page relative to other pages in the spread. Next are Width and Height fields for manually defining the dimensions of the page, as well as a dropdown menu of preset page sizes, and buttons to switch the page

orientation from portrait to landscape or vice versa. You can also enable layout adjustment right from the Control panel such that when a page resizes, its contained objects move to accommodate the new dimensions. Additionally, you can turn on Objects Move with Page, which relocates the page's objects to match changes in the X or Y page position fields; if that option is cleared, any objects on the page will remain at the page's previous location. The final option is Show Master Page Overlay, which, as you might infer, shows a translucent overlay of the assigned master page and its objects to help you better align and size the selected page.

FIGURE 7.29
The Control panel in Spread mode, showing options while using the Page tool with or without a single page selected (top) and with two or more pages selected (bottom).

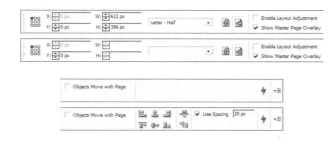

Select any two or more pages with the Page tool as you'd select any other types of objects (by Shift-clicking), and the Control panel will change to include standard align and distribute spacing buttons from the Align panel. With these you can precisely align all the pages in a spread, whether they're of the same or different sizes.

Master pages, too, can be resized just as can document pages. Thus it's easy to create masters for your foldouts and other atypical page sizes in your document.

WHICH PAGE SIZE?

Note that when you apply or reapply a master to a resized document page, you'll be prompted to make a choice between using the master page size and keeping the current document page size.

Mix Portrait and Landscape

The Edit Page Size menu and Page tool are useful even if you don't need to resize pages but just want to work on one or more pages as landscape without having to rotate every object you create, your monitor, or your head 90°. To rotate one or more pages in a spread, select them with the Page tool, and then select the appropriate orientation button from the Control panel, either Landscape or Portrait. Alternatively, you could use the Edit Page Size menu on the Pages panel, open the Custom Page Size dialog, and select from the orientation buttons there. Because you won't change paper sizes, printing won't require an additional paper tray on your desktop printer or special RIP settings before sending to a printing press.

Rotate Spread View

Rotate Spread View changes the *perceived* rotation of spreads onscreen (whole spreads, not individual pages) but doesn't actually rotate those pages. Although the ability to actually rotate a page or all the pages in a spread may seem to invalidate the need for the Rotate Spread View function, there's still a separate and distinct need addressed by this feature. Rotating all spreads is useful for projects such as wall calendars where pages display at the top and bottom rather than left and right, and selectively rotating a spread here and there is a more convenient and rapid way of working on centerfold posters and other rotated materials without having to selectively rotate each page or spread. Moreover, when you use the Page tool or Edit Page Size menus to change the orientation of pages, they still align in horizontal spreads, with left- and right-read pages. To work on upper- and lower-read pages, like the aforementioned calendar and similar layouts, you must use spread rotation.

To use this feature, select one or more page icons in the Pages panel, and choose your rotation from the Rotate Spread View submenu on either the View menu or the Pages panel flyout menu (see Figure 7.30). Selecting one page in a spread will rotate the view of the entire spread, even if other pages in the spread are not selected. You can rotate the spread view 90° clockwise or counterclockwise, as well as 180° to flip it upside down. Revert spreads to their default left-to-right rotation with the Clear Rotation command on the same menu. Note that the Pages panel will not display spreads rotated; the only indicator you will get is a rotation icon beside rotated spreads if that option has been activated in the Pages panel's Panel Options.

FIGURE 7.30

The Rotate Spread View menu on the Pages panel flyout menu

Master Pages

And now, without further ado, I humbly present to you master pages.

Master pages are like templates within the document. Anytime you need the same element on multiple pages, put it on a master page. Things like headers, footers, background art, page borders, and more—anything that repeats on more than one page—belong on a master page. So

do many text frames when more than a couple of pages use the same size, number of columns, and text frame options. It isn't a new concept—all the major layout applications have had master pages since the late '80s. Despite the ubiquity of the feature, surprisingly few creative pros know how to use them or just how significant master pages can be in reducing repetitive work. Repetition kills productivity, creativity, and imagination. No other single feature saves as much time and frustration as master pages.

Assigning a master to a document makes all the objects on that master page appear on the document page, but those objects technically don't exist on the document pages themselves. That's both a huge pro and a small con to using masters. The pro is that the same object can appear on literally thousands of pages, but only a single object *instance* must be created or altered in order to effect a change across all pages. If your client says that the folio you placed on the top outside corner of every page must be moved to the bottom center of the pages, you only have to make the change once per document. The con—a minor inconvenience really—appears when you need to change or do away with just a single object instance here and there on document pages. In that case, you must override the master page object. We'll cover all of that—without lingering too long on the basics—in this section.

Master Page Setup

At the top of the Pages panel is the master page section. With any new document, you'll have [None], which is a blank master, and the default A-Master, which is also initially blank. A-Master is one you can edit and on which you're supposed to put repetitive elements if your document contains them—just double-click A-Master to edit its page (nonfacing document pages) or spread (facing pages). [None] is for those times when, while working with master pages that contain objects, you need a new page devoid of all the master page items.

In InDesign, each master name has what Adobe calls a prefix, an identifier (the *A*), and a name (*Master*). Most people don't realize that neither is fixed.

Document pages display the identifier of the master page to which they're assigned as a symbol on the page icon. *A, B, C*, and so on are fine in many cases, but they're effectively meaningless. When you have multiple master pages handling different types of content, it can make your work less confusing to use something more meaningful than single-letter identifiers.

Select A-Master on the Pages panel and then Master Options from the panel's flyout menu. In the Master Options dialog (see Figure 7.31), the Prefix field can hold up to four alphanumeric characters. Instead of *A, B, C*, why not have prefixes that *really* communicate something about each page?

- How about *Ad* for pages based on the full-page ad master, which doesn't include headers, footers, or folio?

- *Dept* would be a great designator for magazine department pages.

- In catalogs, what about *12UP* for those pages featuring 12 products and *6UP* for pages where half as many products get twice as much room?

- Working with multilingual documents? Use *ENG, ESP, FRA, ITAL, DEU, RUS, ELV, PORT, BS*, or other prefixes to instantly label pages in the Pages panel according to the languages of their copy and master items.

- Numerous types of documents use several variations on column grids for variety, so why not prefix their masters with *2COL, 3COL*, or *6COL*?

FIGURE 7.31
Master Options
enables turning
arbitrary default
identifiers and names
into something that
makes sense for your
document.

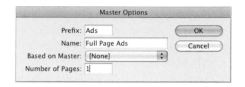

The only requirement is that the combination of prefix and name be unique. Although InDesign will let you assign the same prefix to multiple master pages, don't do it. How will you know which document page belongs to which of the three *B*-prefixed masters?

When you can't fully communicate the function of a master in only four characters, come up with a meaningful acronym, abbreviation, or shorthand for the prefix, but use the Name field to better explain it—like a kicker lends meaning to a headline. In that field, you have a potential 100 characters with which to name the master. An obtuse prefix like *BPx2*, which may be perfectly logical to you, may just drive the already distressed new guy to tears. So, explain the prefix with a meaningful name like *Back Page Spread*. Depending on the width of your Pages panel and the display options for the masters section, only part of the name may show; mouse over it to read the whole thing in a tooltip.

Master pages can be anywhere from 1 to 10 pages wide. If you happen to need that trifold (or decafold) cover or centerfold, you can build a master page to manage its common elements, and each page of a master spread can be a different size and orientation.

Overriding Master Page Items

Here is one of the most often cited frustrations for recent QuarkXPress-to-InDesign converts. You see, in QuarkXPress, items placed on master pages are added to their document pages as normal objects, just as if they were created on the document page itself rather than the master to which it's assigned. You can select objects added by masters, delete them, transform them, and do anything else you like to them with impunity and with no barrier whatsoever. As you might expect, the QuarkXPress behavior leads to frequent accidents. An errant click here or there can make one page's master page objects different from another's, defeating the purpose.

InDesign doesn't automatically make master page objects selectable and changeable on document pages (hence the aforementioned frustration arising out of confusion). If you want to override a master page object, turning it into an object on the document page itself, you must hold Cmd+Shift/Ctrl+Shift while clicking on the object. *Then* you can do whatever you need—type into it, place an image inside it, move or transform it, and so on.

Note that overriding a master page item raises its placement in the stacking order *above* non-overridden objects. For instance, if you stacked a red frame above a blue frame on the same layer on a master page, overriding the blue frame on a document page would bring it forward, in front of the red. If necessary, counter this behavior by using layers on the master page, placing the red frame on a higher layer than the blue. Overriding the blue in that case retains the correct stacking order.

Another way in which InDesign differs from QuarkXPress is that InDesign's master pages *can* use layers. XPress's can't. There, only document pages are allowed layers—at least, as of the time of this writing, when QuarkXPress 8 is the most recent version.

If you want to override all the master page items on a particular document *spread*—note that I didn't say *page*—the fastest way to do it is with the Override All Master Page Items command on the Pages panel flyout menu and the context-sensitive menu that appears when you right-click a page icon.

Master page items overridden on the document page are not *completely* disconnected from their masters. Only the attributes you've specifically changed are overridden, while all other attributes remain tethered to their master page originals. For example, let's say you overrode and then moved the blue frame. If you later go back to that master page and fill the original frame with yellow instead, all instances of that object—including the overridden one—will change to yellow. The inverse is also true: If you override the frame and change its color on the document page while leaving its position on the page unchanged, moving the master page object and changing *its* color will move the overridden version as well, but it will not alter its color because that was the overridden attribute. Stroke, effects, scaling—everything that you don't specifically override—remain linked to the master page instance.

If you want to break *all* the links between the overridden object instance and its original, making it totally independent from later master page changes, choose Detach Selection from Master in the Pages panel flyout menu. Use Detach All Objects from Master on the same menu to break the link between all overridden master page objects on the spread; non-overridden objects will be unaffected by either command.

Restoring Master Page Items

So, you've gone just Cmd+Shift-clicking/Ctrl+Shift-clicking all over the place, overriding master page item after item, with absolutely no regard to your or your coworkers' safety and well-being. Now, after sobering up, you realize you want back the emotional security of objects linked to their master page instances and safely locked from accidental alterations. It happens. We all initially get drunk on the power of Cmd+Shift-click/Ctrl+Shift-click. Fortunately, it's an easy fix.

Restoring Master Page Items while Retaining Overrides If you want to *keep* all overrides *and* restore master page items too, drag the master page from the top of the Pages panel and drop it again on the document page(s). You can also use the Apply Master to Pages command. Use caution though, because this will also break the link between overridden items and their master page instances, rendering them completely and solely document page objects.

Removing Selected Local Overrides To return only certain objects to the full control of the master page, removing any overrides and returning the object to a locked status and the master stacking order, select the object(s) and choose Remove Selected Local Overrides from the Pages panel flyout menu.

Removing All Local Overrides If you want to return the *entire spread* back to its master page state, tossing out any changes you've made to overridden objects, use the Remove All Local Overrides command from the Pages panel flyout menu.

Text Frames on Master Pages

In the New Document dialog, you're given the option of Master Text Frame. Checking that option will automatically create a text frame on the A-Master master page; the frame will fill the page both horizontally and vertically within the margins. If you increased the number of columns in

New Document from one, the frame will have that number of columns and use the gutter width options chosen. Everything else will be left according to the *Basic Text Frame* object style.

To use that text frame on a document page, Cmd+Shift-click/Ctrl+Shift-click to override it, and then double-click again to enter typing mode; start typing.

Master page text frames can be threaded across the spread—the frame on the left page can be linked to the one on the right (or vice versa for Japanese, Hebrew, or other right-to-left printed languages), and text will flow smoothly between them once overridden. When placing text documents, however, you'll need to manually link frames on different spreads. The easiest way to do that is to start by overriding the first instance and then place your long text document into it. Click the red, overset outport on that frame and move on to the next page or spread (create pages if necessary). This time, don't hold any modifier keys while clicking; just click within the area of the frame. InDesign is smart enough to pick up on what you want to do, and it will simultaneously override the text frame *and* flow your loaded text into it. Keep moving through the document, one page at a time, until your story is completely visible.

Page Numbers

To insert page numbers on a master page (or on a document page for that matter), create a text frame or insert the cursor in an existing text frame. Then, choose Type ➢ Insert Special Characters ➢ Marker ➢ Current Page Number. On a master page, you won't actually see a number there, of course. Instead, you'll see the master page's own prefix identifier—*A, B, 12UP,* whatever—but jump to a document page assigned to that master and you'll recognize that it's really a page number. You can't type page number markers directly because they're *markers,* special placeholders created with powers and abilities far beyond those of mortal men.

While you're in the Marker menu, take note of the other markers you can insert. Next and previous page numbers are for jumplines, which we'll cover in Chapter 9. Section markers print on a document page the prefix of the section or chapter under which the page falls. Section prefixes are defined via the Layout ➢ Numbering & Section Options command, which we'll also discuss in Chapter 9.

Nested Master Pages

Consider this: You're laying out a 320-page visually rich proposal that will be printed in 4-color and perfect bound in hardcover. There are several chapter-like sections, with chapter-like titles, stylized initial pages, and special, uniquely formatted "summation" pages at the end. The last section of the book is the proposed contract. Naturally, in a book that large, there's also a table of contents and some front matter pages. Let's examine how such a book's outline and layout plan might look (see Figure 7.32).

According to that outline, you'll need to design several types of pages. Most will be used for more than a single page, so you'll naturally turn to master pages. Now, you *could* design every master to be self-contained, manually creating the folios and other elements on every different master. If changes are needed, doing it in only 4 or 5 places *is* much better than doing it in 320, but having to make changes in only *1* place is better than 4 or 5. For that, we'll turn to nested master pages.

The cover, back cover ("bacover" in industry jargon), and "Contract" pages have no common elements, so we don't need masters for them; they'll get tagged with [None].

Now, look at the rest. What common element appears on all other pages? The folio, page numbers in different formats. So, the very first step is to set up the first master page as a two-page

spread, each page containing just a single, small text frame, the one to hold the page number. Let's set the prefix of that master to # and its name to *Page No. Only*. That's done. Document section numbering options will take care of changing between Roman and Arabic numbers where appropriate (see Chapter 9).

FIGURE 7.32

A book outline and layout plan

1. Cover
2. Guts
   A. Front Matter
      i. Contact Info
         No head/foot
      ii. Foreword
         Folio (Roman Upper), section title in right head
      iii. Statement of Readiness
         Folio (Roman Upper), section title in right head
   B. TOC
      Folio (Roman Upper), section title in right head
   C. Chapter 1
      i. Chapter Intro Page
         Folio, begins on right-read, no head; image & gradient BG
      ii. Content Pages
         Folio, chapter title in right head, firm name in left head, preparer/sales rep name & phone in left foot
      iii. Summation
         Folio, no chapter title, firm name in left head, preparer/sales rep name & phone in left foot
   D. Chapter 2
      i. Chapter Intro Page
      ii. Content Pages
      iii. Recap
   E. Chapter 3
      i. Chapter Intro Page
      ii. Content Pages
      iii. Recap
   F. Contract
      Folio (Page X of Y) and contract title in right head
3. Bacover

What are the next most common elements? Well, the headers and footers are, but some pages require only certain ones and not others. The best way to handle those is to create several master pages that can be applied as needed to the different types of content pages—front matter sections, the TOC, chapter content pages, and chapter "summation" pages. However, instead of duplicating the masters and still ending up with several instances of each header and footer to update in the event of a change, which we could easily do with the Duplicate Master Spread command on the Pages panel menu, we'll nest one more level and save ourselves some time down the line.

Let's create a new master page:

1. Use the New Master Page command on the Pages panel flyout menu.

2. For its options, set a prefix of **Base**, a name of **All Heads/Foots**, number of pages **2**, and—and this the crucial part—set the Based on Master dropdown to **#-Page No. Only**.

That founds master *Base* on master #, incorporating all the latter's elements into the former without duplicating, and if the page number text frames are moved or otherwise

changed in their original location on #, that change will automatically roll through Base and all other document and master pages assigned to Base.

3. Click OK, and you'll see the magic page number codes appear exactly as you drew them on the first master.

4. Now set up your headers and footers. Because each chapter or section will have its own unique head on the right-read page, draw and style the frame, but leave it empty.

At this point, you should have two master pages. Note that the icon beside Base shows the # identifier, signifying that it's based on, and using the elements from, the #-Page No Only master.

Now, let's create masters to handle the unique variants of Base, those that omit either the footer or one head or another:

1. Create a new master with **FM** as the prefix, **Front Matter** as the name, based on **Base-All Heads/Foots**, and **2** pages.

   You should see an exact duplicate of Base, including the elements incorporated from #, but the FM icon now shows Base—we're nested two levels deep now. Front matter pages (except for "Contact Info," which has no heads or foots) should display only the folio and right head, which leaves the left-page head and footer as extraneous.

2. One at a time, hold Cmd+Shift/Ctrl+Shift as you click either the header or footer text frame with the Selection tool to override the item.

3. Now delete and repeat the process with the other frame. Once those frames are gone, the FM master is finished.

Build a new master also based on Base-All Heads/Foots for the chapter introduction page master, and then remove the unneeded elements by overriding and deleting them, and add the missing objects like the image and gradient background.

Make another master also based on Base-All Heads/Foots for Chapter 1. This one *will* have all headers and footers, so you don't want to delete anything. You do, however, want to override the right-read page's header and fill in the Chapter 1 title, as well as include a vertical colored bar (because we're color-coding the sections of this proposal). When finished,

1. Choose Duplicate Master Spread from the Pages panel's flyout menu.

2. Change the prefix and name to reflect Chapter 2.

3. Edit the chapter title text frame on the top of the right-read page to be the Chapter 2 title and add its colored vertical bar.

4. Repeat the duplication steps for the remaining chapter.

If you didn't care to color code each chapter, if you wanted only the chapter number in the header, you could do that with just a single master page for all chapters and by inserting a section marker at the appropriate place in the header on the master page. Through the settings in the Numbering & Section Options dialog, you could also have configured the automatic inclusion of chapter names without manually inputting them, but that's a level of complexity to leave out until we've gone over the Numbering & Section Options dialog in Chapter 9.

Because chapter "summation" pages don't have chapter titles, you can employ just a single additional master page based on Base-All Heads/Foots with overridden and removed elements

for all instances of such pages. "Contract" pages should get their own, top-level (not based on another master) master page because they don't share any of the common elements of Base or even #. In the end, you should have eight master pages, although they won't indent on the Pages panel; if they did, their nesting would make them look like this:

#-Page No. Only

    Base-All Heads/Foots

        FM-Front Matter

        CH1-Chapter 1

        CH2-Chapter 2

        CH3-Chapter 3

        SUM-Summation

CON-Contract

As you lay out the various pages, assign them their particular master pages. With the exception of pages based on the CON-Contract master, which is entirely self-sufficient, only a single instance of page numbers must be changed in order to effect that change throughout every page in the document. Common headers and footers are the same—one object change affects all dependent masters and document pages. Believe me, it's a lot more complicated to *read* how to do it than to *actually* do it hands on (thus the step-by-step instruction I hope you'll follow). Try out nested master pages a few times within your documents; distill your multipage documents down to the most common elements, and break those out into nested master pages. An outline and layout plan like the one just shown will help you visualize the division of master pages and their objects the first few times thinking through it. You'll soon recognize how much faster and more efficient you can make tomorrow's work with just a little planning and effort today.

Creating Masters from Document Pages

This one happens to me often: Working content first, you start up a new document, place in a good portion of your content, and begin the layout. Either you want to experiment a little and work out the design before moving to master pages or you don't initially think you'll have common page elements and need a master page only to later realize that you do, in fact, need a master page. The result is that you lay out a perfect master page with all the required elements, but you do it on a document page. What now?

You *could* cut all the objects and then use Edit ➤ Paste In Place to get them onto a master—and that works too. The drawbacks to that method are that you have to remember to paste in place (Cmd+Shift+Opt+V/Ctrl+Shift+Alt+V) instead of the much more habitual normal Paste (Cmd+V/Ctrl+V), and it works well only when the master page is already blank. Otherwise, you have to first select all, delete, and then paste in place. Easier is to just select Save as Master from the Pages panel flyout menu. Instantly it creates a new master page using the default prefix and filename. Even cooler, if the document page you choose as your source is assigned to a master already, the new master will also be based on the same master, creating instant nesting.

Color Gallery

On the following pages, you will find color versions of some of the figures in this book.

 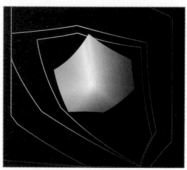 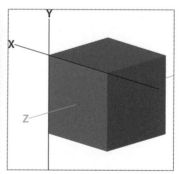

Text

Working with text is the core function of InDesign. Chapter 2, "Text," discusses how to get text and tables into InDesign from external sources like Word, Buzzword, Excel, and other applications, as well as how to format and arrange text into paragraphs, columns, and tables.

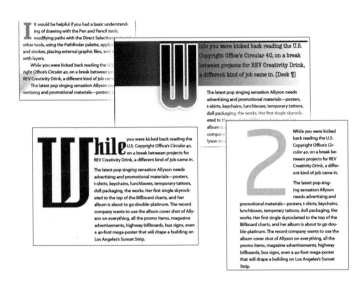

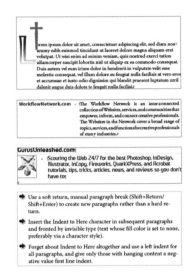

Tracking in use   Substituted glyphs (ligatures)

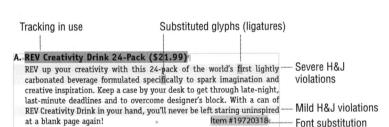

A. REV Creativity Drink 24-Pack ($21.99)

REV up your creativity with this 24-pack of the world's first lightly carbonated beverage formulated specifically to spark imagination and creative inspiration. Keep a case by your desk to get through late-night, last-minute deadlines and to overcome designer's block. With a can of REV Creativity Drink in your hand, you'll never be left staring uninspired at a blank page again!

Item #19720318

— Severe H&J violations

— Mild H&J violations
Font substitution due to missing font

TOP LEFT: Drop cap effects made easy. **TOP RIGHT:** Examples of practical uses of Indent. Top to bottom, custom drop caps, hanging subheads or descriptors, inline graphics, and custom bullets. **MIDDLE LEFT:** Composition violations and substitutions highlight in different colors and shades to indicate which rules are being violated as well as the severity of the violation. **MIDDLE RIGHT:** A text frame with inset (inner blue border) and indented text. **BOTTOM LEFT:** Paragraph rules attached to headings help organize and separate data.

Drawing

Chapter 4: "Drawing," explains how to draw, modify, combine, and separate vector paths in InDesign. The following figures are from that chapter, largely from the step-by-step tutorials and examples of what you can create in vector artwork using InDesign's built-in tools.

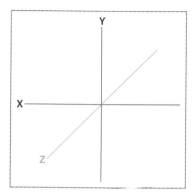 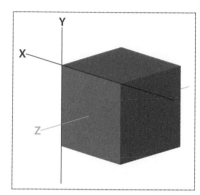 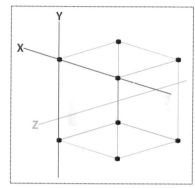

LEFT: The X-, Y-, and Z-axes. **CENTER:** A cube exists along on all three axes. **RIGHT:** A cube without fills reveals the corners and vertices that define its shape.

LEFT: Shown in gray is the first path, with the second in red. The original image is hidden in this figure for clarity. **CENTER:** My Pencil tool–traced hairpiece, shown filled in red. **RIGHT:** The bangs piece (filled in blue) should merge with the main hairpiece in the drawing.

79%
people
aged 19-30
like beveled
corners

Mastering InDesign CS5 for Print Design & Production

Author: Pariah S. Burke | Publisher: Sybex

www.iamPariah.com | www.WorkflowCreative.com | www.WorkflowNetwork.com

Corner Options can do some nifty things.

All of these objects were created by starting with the Polygon
Frame tool.

LEFT: A frame complete with the yellow box to enter Live Corners Editing mode (left), and Live Corners controls in action rounding a rectangle in Live Corners Editing mode (right). **RIGHT:** When two overlapping paths (left) are given the Pathfinder command to add, they merge into a single, amalgamated path (right).

Add   Subtract   Intersect   Exclude Overlap   Minus Back

Shapes resulting from using the Pathfinder commands.

These images from Chapter 4 show the results of using a compound path.

ABOVE: Another example of converting text to image-filled frames. **LEFT:** Letters have become a graphic frame into which you can place an image.

Objects

In Chapter 6, "Objects," we looked at many of the coolest features of InDesign, including transparency and effects, using and creating custom strokes, making mixed ink swatches and groups, inline and anchored objects, working with type-on-a-path objects, using Step and Repeat to quickly fill a page, using the new Gridify behavior of many tools, using the new Gap tool, transforming again and without grouping, Live Distribute, and the convenience and precision of working with Smart Guides.

InDesign's Global Light creates light-directed effects that are unrealistically uniform. An InDesign-created set of drop shadows (left) versus a set manually tweaked to reflect real-world perceptions (right).

LEFT: This rather gaudy image clearly demonstrates the separate transparency effects on each of the object's attributes. **RIGHT:** The same object (set to 50% opacity for clarity) with the same drop shadow. At left, Object Knocks Out Shadow is on, and at right, it's off.

LEFT: Gap colors create the effect of multiple objects overlaid without doubling the work to create and manage them. **BOTTOM:** Examples created with the Gradient Feather effect

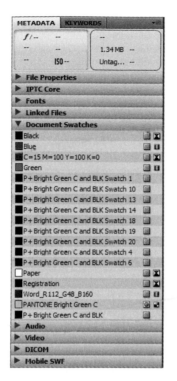

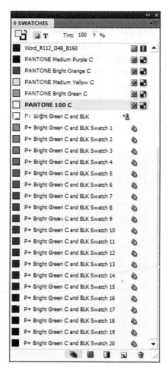

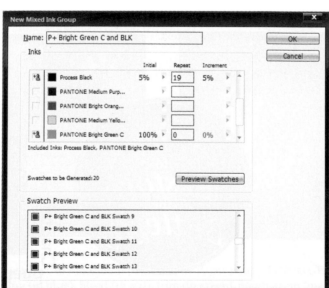

TOP LEFT: The Metadata panel in Adobe Bridge shows the selected document ink plates and document color swatches. **TOP RIGHT:** All of these mixed ink swatches result from creating a mixed ink group. **BOTTOM:** Create many mixed ink swatches at once with New Mixed Ink Group.

Preflight

The following figures are from Chapter 10, "Preflight," which discusses color management, color gamuts, transparency flattening, and more.

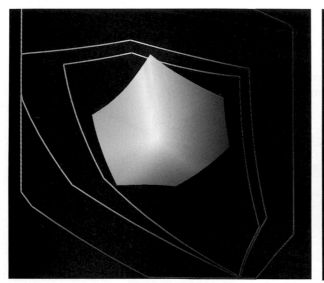
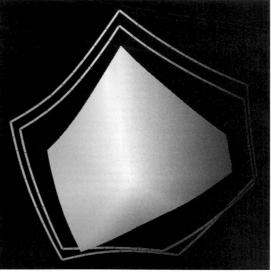

LEFT: What are color gamuts? Here are the color ranges contained within four common ICC profiles (all but the front are outlined). From the outside in: ProPhoto RGB, AdobeRGB (1998), sRGB, and U.S. Web Coated (SWOP) v2. **RIGHT:** Three common CMYK color profile gamuts. From the outside in: U.S. Sheetfed Coated v2, U.S. Web Coated (SWOP) v2, and U.S. Sheetfed Uncoated v2.

Original (Proof Colors off)

Europe ISO Coated FOGRA27
(simulating paper color and black ink)

U.S. Sheetfed Uncoated v2
(simulating paper color and black ink)

The same document with different proof profiles selected.

Three transparent objects interact. Flattened, three have become seven color-centric chunks (bottom).

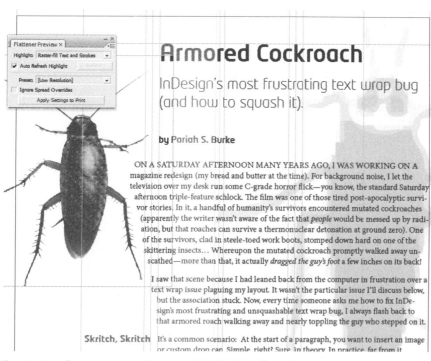

Previewing flattening on a document highlights affected areas and dims nonaffected areas.

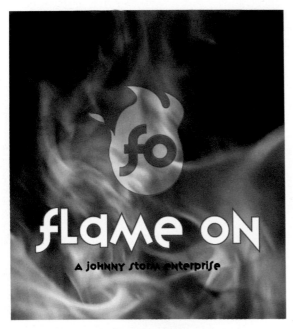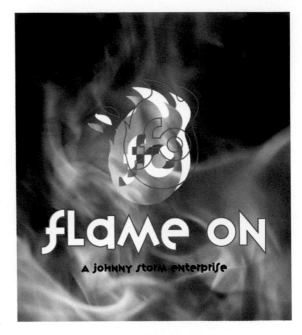

Pre-flattening (left) and post-flattening (right).

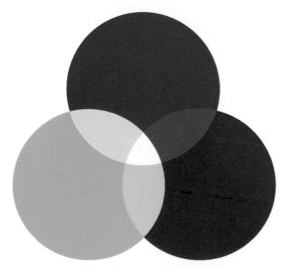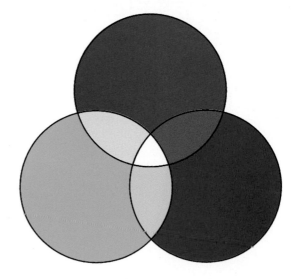

Pre-flattening (left) and post-flattening (right).

Print

The following figures are from Chapter 11, "Print," which discusses printing InDesign documents, creating imposed printer's spreads, managing inks, and packaging documents.

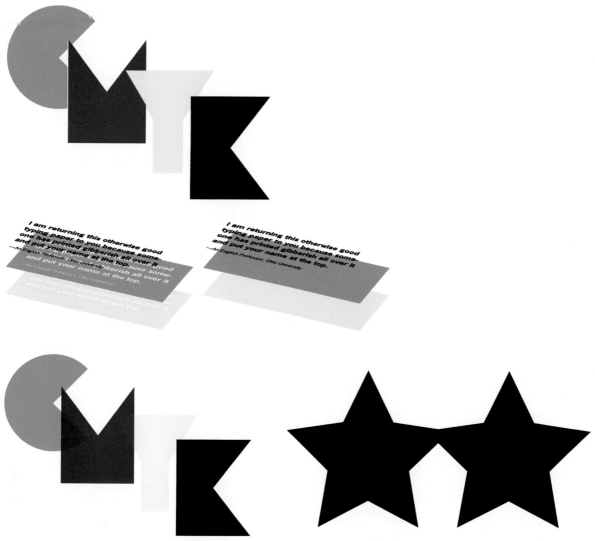

TOP: Slight misregistration in the magenta plate causes a sliver of white between inks (assuming the image was printed in registration, that is). **MIDDLE:** Text knockouts out of background color (left) and the same text set to overprint (right). **BOTTOM:** At left, overprinting all four colors creates undesired mixes. Center, a 100% black ink star, and right, a rich black star—a mixture of all four process inks.

Efficiency

In Chapter 13, "Efficiency," we focused on those techniques and workflows we hadn't had a chance to discuss earlier in the book, as well as tips and processes that help you work smarter and not harder with text, tables, and objects.

Chapter 1 My father's family name being Pirrip, and my Christian name Philip, my infant tongue could make of both names nothing longer or more explicit than Pip. So, I called myself Pip, and came to be called Pip.	MY FATHER'S FAMILY NAME BEING PIRRIP, AND my Christian name Philip, my infant tongue could make of both names nothing longer or more explicit than Pip. So, I called myself Pip, and came to be called Pip.
*M*y father's family name being Pirrip, and my Christian name Philip, my infant tongue could make of both names nothing longer or more explicit than Pip. So, I called myself Pip, and came to be called Pip.	My father's family name being Pirrip, and my Christian name Philip, my infant tongue could make of both names nothing longer or more explicit than Pip (*see* www.Domain.com). So, I called myself Pip, and came to be called Pip.
My father's family name being Pirrip, and my Christian name Philip, my infant tongue could make of both names nothing longer or more explicit than Pip. So, I called myself Pip, and came to be called Pip.	1 ....My father's family name being Pirrip, and my Christian name Philip, my infant tongue could make of both names nothing longer or more explicit than Pip. So, I called myself Pip, and came to be called Pip.

This figure from Chapter 13 demonstrates uses for character styles.

Collaboration

The following figures are from Chapter 14, "Collaboration," which helps you build an effective, efficient workflow for collaborating with other designers, editorial personnel, and yourself.

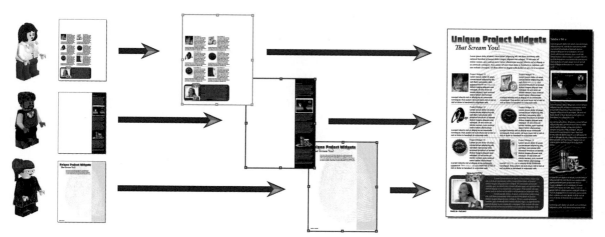

Diagram of a Placed Page Collaboration Workflow in use on a single page.

Flowchart of a common periodical publication workflow.

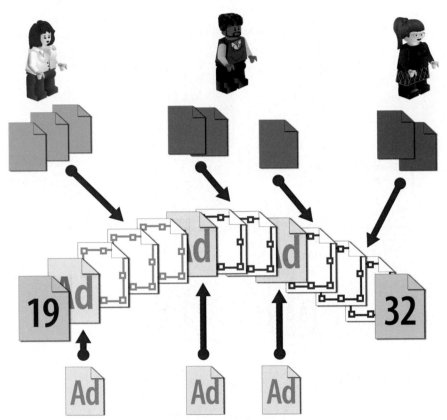

Diagram of a Placed Page Collaboration Workflow in a multipage document.

Master Page Power

Oh, yes, there's yet more power at your fingertips. The following commands are all located on the Pages panel flyout menu.

Apply Master to Pages   When you need to apply a master page to more than one or two pages at a time, don't use the drag-and-drop method. Instead, use Apply Master to Pages. Just select the master to apply, and then enter one or more page numbers individually, sequentially ranged (e.g., 1–10), comma-separated non-sequentially (e.g., 5,3,1), or a mixture of both (e.g., 4,1–2,7–8,5).

Load Master Pages   An incredibly powerful feature almost on a par with the ability to move pages between InDesign documents, Load Master Pages allows you load the masters from another InDesign document into the current one. In the event of a naming conflict—if they both contain *A-Master*, for example—InDesign will prompt you as to whether the inbound masters should replace the current document's masters of the same names or whether the inbound ones should be automatically renamed, thus retaining current and new. Renamed masters will follow the default *A, B, C* prefixing scheme.

Allow Master Item Overrides on Selection   On by default, this option appears while you're working in the master pages. It's what enables objects on the master to be overridden and modified on document pages. To ensure that even a Cmd+Shift-click/Ctrl+Shift-click can't accidentally override a master page item, select one or more objects on the master page spread and disable this command.

Disabling the ability to override master page objects is a gotcha, though, too. Many a desk (and forehead) has been dented while trying to answer the question, *Why, why,* why can't I edit my master page items? If you disable this feature, write yourself a note *in the document* and set the note to not print.

Hide Master Items   Want to work on document pages without seeing the master page items? This command will do that. This, again, is another gotcha. Write yourself a note if you turn it on.

The Bottom Line

Create Pages with Bleed, Slug, and Live Areas   Properly setting up a for-press document involves more than choosing paper stock and ink colors. To ease the burden of setting up pages, InDesign includes ways to automate creation of similar documents after the first.

Master It   Examine this book's cover. Don't redesign it, but set up a new, blank InDesign document as if you were designing the cover for this or another Mastering series book. Include the appropriate features—bleed, slug, and live areas—and create reusable cover presets and a template.

Manage Pages in and between InDesign Documents   Any multipage document requires familiarity with the Pages panel and related features. Working *well* with multipage documents requires practiced proficiency.

Master It   Create two new InDesign documents of one page each. Now, using the skills learned in "Managing Pages," insert four additional pages in each document for a total of five pages each. In very large type (at least 200 pts), manually label each page with a text

frame containing the page number; do not use the Current Page Number marker. In the first document, preface page numbers with the Roman numeral I, and in the second with II, such that pages are numbered I1, I2, I3, I4, I5 and II1, II2, II3, II4, II5. Save both documents. Copy all five pages from the II document into the I, and then arrange pages in order such that page II1 follows I1, II2 follows I2, and so on.

Create Documents with Multiple Page Sizes and Orientations   The ability to produce documents that contain multiple page sizes is a crucial new feature of InDesign CS5 that dramatically alters and streamlines a fundamental workflow of workarounds that has existed since the introduction of desktop layout applications more than 25 years ago. Learning to utilize this new functionality is critical for learners to be efficient in the production of many types of documents today; moreover, the ease with which multiple-page-size documents can now be created will undoubtedly inspire an even broader range of such documents to become commonplace.

Master It   Utilizing the multiple page size and orientation features of InDesign CS5, create a stationary kit for yourself, your freelance business, or a fantasy business you might some day like to have. One per page, include a 3.5×2-inch business card design, an 8.5×11-inch letterhead design, a 4 ⅛×9 ½-inch standard #10 envelope design, and a fourth page. The fourth page may be any type of identity material you like, for instance a Rolodex card, a CD/DVD label, a mailing label, or some other type of page that you might commonly use to promote your business—be creative!

Master Master Pages   Master pages are the key to efficient initial layout and especially document revisions. Mastering their use is essential for design that uses common elements across multiple document pages.

Master It   Refer back to the hands-on instruction in the section on nested master pages. Follow the instruction in that section to build all the master pages required for the proposal project. Check your results against mine. Once you have the master pages built correctly, use the other skills learned in this chapter to add document pages (a few for each proposal section or chapter) and to assign to them the appropriate master pages.

Chapter 8

Stories

Now that you've mastered setting and styling type on a page, it's time to think bigger—about writing, editing, and flowing text across multiple pages. It's time to think about *stories*. A *story*, as InDesign uses the term, is a complete segment of text of any length. The main narrative that flows across 500 pages of a book is a story, but so is the single-line caption under a picture. As you were taught in freshman English, stories have a beginning, middle, and end; in InDesign, a story has a beginning—its first or only text frame—and an end—the last line of the end of the continuous flow of text. (The middle isn't particularly important to InDesign.)

In this chapter, you will learn to

◆ Thread and unthread text frames and flow text

◆ Create bulleted and numbered lists

◆ Write and word process in InDesign

◆ Reference different places in the document with footnotes, endnotes, and cross-references

◆ Fix, find, and change text and more

Threading and Unthreading Text Frames

Although these days more and more people are turning to InDesign for the purposes of designing slideshow presentations, e-forms, website wireframes, Flash animations, and various one-page layouts like posters and business cards, the vast majority of InDesign documents still fit the profile of multiple pages with one or more text *threads*, articles, or stories running throughout those pages. Any time text flows continuously from one frame to another, the story, and thus its containing frames, is said to be threaded (linked, for you QuarkXPress converts).

If CS5 is your entry into the world of InDesign but you're familiar with page layout in general, be aware that there are several distinct differences between InDesign and other layout applications when it comes to threading text. In that regard, InDesign works more like PageMaker than QuarkXPress, but it has, in some respects, improved over the methods employed by both of those other layout applications. In other respects, it's less friendly and more work to flow a multipage story in InDesign.

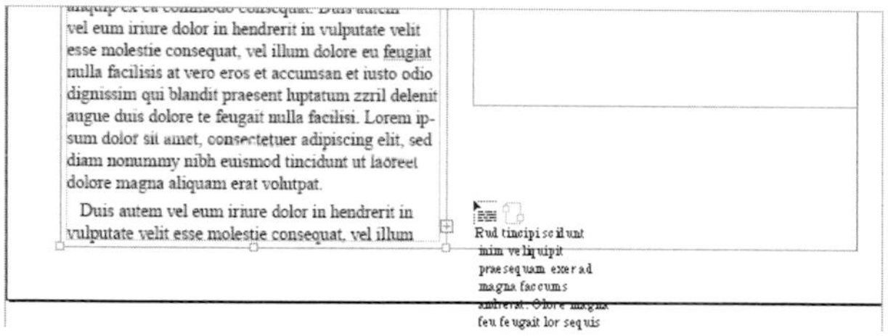

FIGURE 8.2

After clicking the overset indicator in the out port, you'll get a loaded cursor.

After threading the two frames, note the changed states of their in and out ports (see Figure 8.3). Frame 1's in port is still empty because it begins the series, but now its out port, instead of showing the red plus overset text symbol, displays a blue, outward-pointing arrow indicating that the text threads out to another frame. Similarly, the in port of frame 2 indicates that it is receiving text from a previous frame in the series. Thus, at a glance, you can discern whether a frame is threaded and, if so, whether it is the first, last, or another frame in the series.

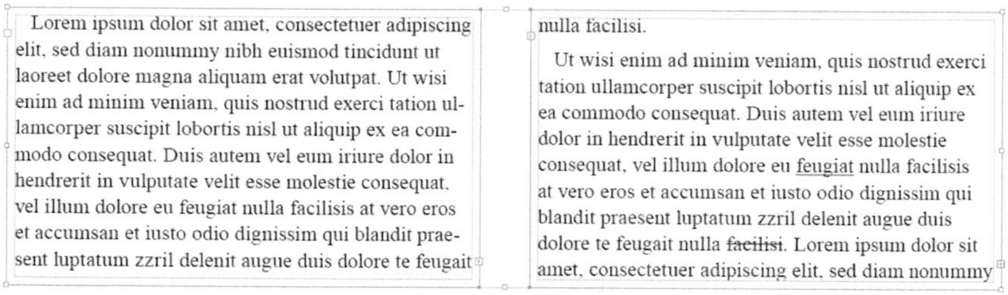

FIGURE 8.3

In and out ports of threaded frames display blue arrows indicating direction of story flow.

If your story must occupy more than two frames, there's a faster way to link them than successively loading up from out ports. During or after clicking the first frame's out port but prior to clicking into the second frame to begin the thread, press and hold Option/Alt. Indicated by a semi-autoflow cursor above the loaded preview (see Figure 8.4), you'll now be able to thread into the second and successive frames simply by clicking into each of them once. For instance, if I was going to thread the same story through the two main text frames and then into the small graphic frame in the bottom right of the page (refer back to Figure 8.1), I'd click frame 1's out port to load the cursor and then, while clicking frame 2, hold Option/Alt, which flows my copy into frame 2 but also leaves me with a loaded cursor so I can immediately click frame 3 and thread into that as well. If I had to thread across multiple pages of pre-created frames, I'd use the same method.

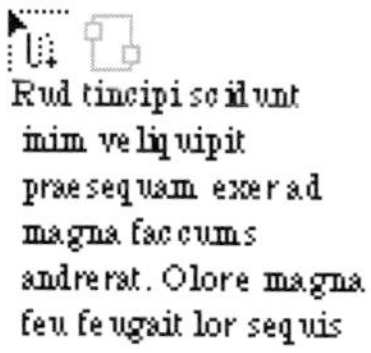

FIGURE 8.4

Multiple-frame linking is quickly accomplished in semi-autoflow mode as indicated by this cursor.

THREADING WITHOUT PRE-CREATED FRAMES

When you're working content-first or find yourself with a longer-than-planned story to place, you'll want to know how to create and thread frames all in one action. It works the same way as placing a document without having made frames to hold it in advance. Click once on the out port of a story frame, and then, using the loaded cursor the same way you would when initially placing text, draw a rectangular area to become the next frame in the chain. InDesign will simultaneously create the frame, flow the next part of the story into it, and thread the frame with the first. Hold Option/Alt while drawing subsequent frames to do all that plus leave the cursor loaded and ready to create even more frames.

In addition to drawing frames, you can simply click and release within the page to have InDesign automatically make a text frame that fits horizontally within the margin and/or column guides. With a single-column page—one containing no column guides—clicking with a loaded cursor will create a text frame as wide as the page margins. Among column guides on multicolumn pages, however, it will create one, single-column text frame only as wide as the column. If you want multiple columns in single text frames, you'll need to manually resize and configure text frames after creating and threading. The height of the resulting click-to-create text frames is the point of click down to the bottom margin. Thus, if you click around the vertical midpoint of a page, the resulting text frame will cover only the bottom half. Click at the top margin guide to create a frame of full page or column depth.

THREADING UPON IMPORT

The methods discussed thus far work when threading text already in the document as well as when initially importing text, either with or without frames pre-created. After selecting the text document in the Place dialog and clicking OK, you'll have a loaded cursor. At that point, if you have frames pre-created, holding Option/Alt while clicking inside the first frame will fill the frame with text and return you to a loaded cursor ready for placement into—and threading with—subsequent frames. The same holds true if you haven't any pre-created frames: Hold Option/Alt while drawing your first frame, and you'll still have the loaded cursor waiting to draw, place into, and thread with additional frames.

THREADING WITHOUT TEXT

When you work frame-first, building your layout as boxes in advance of content availability, but know you'll need to thread a story between multiple frames, pre-thread the empty frames. The procedure is the same—click on the out port of frame 1 and then anywhere in frame 2 and so on. You'll see the same telltale port arrows, and when you place, paste, or type a story into the first frame in the chain, it will automatically flow between them without the need for you to manually thread at that time.

THREADING TIPS

You can thread together any empty containers capable of holding text. You can incorporate not only rectangular text frames but also elliptical, polygonal, and starred. If you make a mistake working frame-first—say you put an image frame where you wanted a text frame—don't stop threading just to convert the frame from the Object ➢ Content menu. Instead, simply click in the image frame with the loaded cursor. InDesign will convert it to a text frame, place the story

inside, and thread it to the previous frame all in one step. Even path text (aka text on a path) objects can be threaded from one to another or back and forth with frames.

Often you'll want to ensure that stories always break at a certain point and jump to the next frame in the thread. While you *could* use the time-honored (and wasteful) method of manually resizing frames to force appropriate jumps, that creates a lot of work for you during initial layout and often more if the copy is edited again. Instead, use a frame break. Before the line that should begin a new frame, select Type ➤ Insert Break Character ➤ Frame Break to insert the special frame break marker. No matter how that story composes, the text after the break marker will always jump to the next frame in the chain.

As I'm sure you can imagine, frame breaks, if forgotten, can be a gotcha as well. If you get in the habit of working with Show Hidden Characters (bottom of the Type menu) turned on, you'll never be left scratching your head about why a giant white space appears at the bottom of a frame. (Well, almost never. Look for overly zealous paragraph-keeps options and for text-wrapping objects on other layers, too.)

Viewing Threads

In addition to the information conveyed by the in and out ports of frames, it's often helpful to be able to see a more pronounced indicator of threading between frames. Activating View ➤ Show Text Threads displays lines between out ports and in ports, enabling you to follow the flow of a story from frame to frame, page to page (see Figure 8.5). This is similar to the way QuarkXPress shows linkage but with the distinct advantage of not locking you into keeping active a tool that can't edit anything while you examine the linkage. The Show Text Threads command can stay on while you use any other tool or modify the story, frames, or pages however needed. As long as one (or more) text object in the thread is selected, the thread indicator arrows will appear on all text objects in that thread.

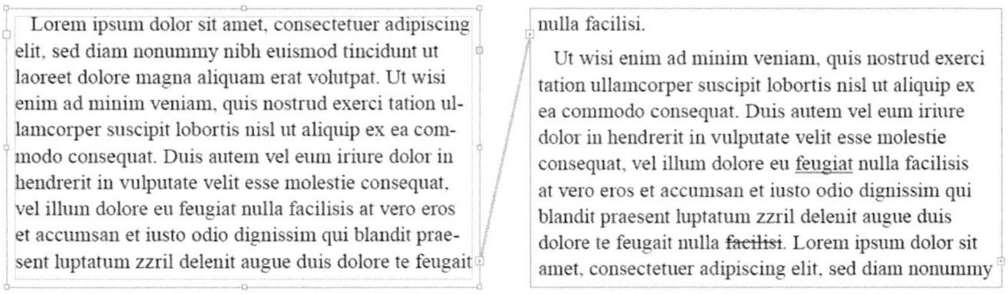

FIGURE 8.5
With text threads shown, lines link all the frames in a threaded chain.

Managing Threads

Already got a threaded story and need to insert, move, or unthread frames? Here's how.

UNTHREAD TEXT FRAMES

Like assembly, disassembly doesn't require a special tool. To stop a thread, reeling in the story from all subsequent frames into which it flows, just double-click the out port of the first frame—or the last frame you wish to stay threaded. (You could also double-click the in port of the first frame to be unlinked.) The story will remain threaded up to that point (unless you spooled it back into the very first frame in the thread). Frames that were previously part of the thread down the line won't delete; they'll be left in place, empty and unthreaded. This last is an important thing to note

because threading accidents sometimes happen wherein pre-created frames are inadvertently threaded into the wrong story. Unthreading the frames reverses the error but leaves the frames ready to accept new content so you don't have to manually draw new ones.

REMOVING FRAMES FROM A THREAD

Probably the most frequent calamity when threading frames in InDesign is creating too many frames while autoflowing a story. That's sort of like the fact that, between *Superman II* and *Superman Returns*, there were two other Superman movies that should never have been made (*Superman III* with Richard Pryor and *Superman IV: The Quest for Peace*) and just about everyone wishes could be unmade. For example, you may have a three-column layout wherein the outside column isn't for the main story but for sidebar content. When autoflowing, InDesign will create a threaded text frame between every pair of column guides inside the margins, including that sidebar column. (Ideally, you want to set your document margins such that the sidebar appears outside them, but that's not always feasible.) In that common scenario and others, you might want to remove a frame from the middle of a threaded series without breaking the rest of chain.

Simple: Select the offending frame and press Delete or Backspace. The frame will disappear, and text it held will flow into the next frame in the thread. Bye-bye Richard Pryor and his evil computer, bye-bye Superman crusading for nuclear disarmament, and hello respectable Man of Steel continuity.

After eliminating any unwanted frames, just make sure to check the end of the story; you'll probably have overset text because of the reduction in space.

ADDING FRAMES INTO A THREAD

Adding a new frame into the middle of an existing thread is almost as easy as removing one. After drawing the new frame, click the out port on the threaded frame ahead of it, and then click inside the new frame to bring it into the chain. You would think that you'd then have to complete the connection by going from the new frame's out port to the next frame in the chain, but, happily, you'd be wrong. InDesign takes care of that automatically. Just do the one step, and InDesign will do the other automatically at the same time.

DUPLICATING FRAMES IN A THREAD

When you cut, copy, or duplicate frames in a thread, you will *not* be working with the same story upon paste (or duplicate). Instead, InDesign will create a perfect replica of the frame, with identical text, but *outside* the original thread. If you cut, thus removing the frame, the remaining frames in the thread will heal the breach and flow text between them—without actually cutting out the text that was in that now-removed frame. Copying or duplicating leaves the original thread intact but creates a new, isolated frame containing just the text it originally held, without the preceding or following parts of the story.

Autoflowing Text

Autoflowing is the process of pouring text into threaded frames without manually clicking a loaded cursor into each one. InDesign has autoflow but also several other methods of flowing threaded stories. When you're working with multiple frames, modifier keys, in addition to clicking, determine which method occurs.

TABLE 8.1: TEXT FLOW OPTIONS AND THEIR CURSORS

CURSOR	MODIFIERS	EFFECT
	(none)	**Manual Text Flow:** Threading frames one at a time, loading up the cursor from an out port, and clicking inside or drawing another frame.
	Opt/Alt	**Semi-Autoflow:** When you hold Opt/Alt while clicking inside the second frame, this option threads in that frame but keeps the cursor loaded and ready to link to and/or draw subsequent frames.
	Shift	**Autoflow:** Places the entire story without leaving any copy overset, adding pages and frames as needed.
	Opt+Shift/Alt+Shift	**Fixed-Page Autoflow:** Flows the story through any existing pages and threaded frames but will not create additional frames or pages if needed (any leftover text will be overset).

When you pre-link empty frames and then place, paste, or type text into them, you're performing a sort of manual fixed-page autoflow ("mo' flow") because you manually created the connection only to later reap its benefit quasi-automatically. True autoflow creates frames and pages where none existed before, although, as pointed out in the section "QuarkXPress vs. InDesign" above, it has its limitations. Then there's Aunt Flo, who sends you nice sweaters on your birthday. But, I doubt she uses InDesign.

Any of these flow methods can be used in either content-first or frame-first layout and during either initial document import or threading from an existing text frame.

REVERSING THE FLOW

If you have a frame selected and the Replace Selected Item option checked in the Place dialog, an incoming story will automatically flow into the selected frame. From there you can begin flowing using one of the flow options above. If you didn't want the story to fill the selected frame, just undo (Cmd+Z/Ctrl+Z), which will get you back to a cursor loaded with the unplaced story.

Autoflow in Master Page Frames

If you begin a document by checking the Master Text Frame option in the New Document dialog (see Figure 8.6), InDesign will create on the master page or pages a text frame than runs margin to margin horizontally and vertically. Note that, unlike prior editions of InDesign, the Master Text Frame option is now *not* enabled by default. Choosing multiple columns in the Columns section of the New Document dialog in addition to electing to create master page text frames does two things. First, it places ruler guides on the page to define the columns. It also makes the master text frame a multiple-column frame just as if you set it up manually in Object ➤ Text Frame Options.

FIGURE 8.6
The New Document dialog

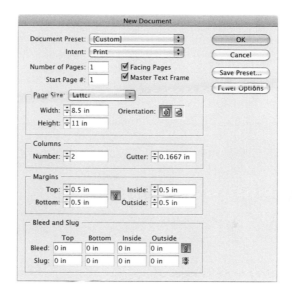

Master page objects are locked in InDesign so they can't be accidentally messed with (this is a good thing), so overriding the master text frame on the first page of the document requires Cmd+Shift-clicking/Ctrl+Shift-clicking it. Once it's overridden, you'll be able to type or paste into the now document page text frame.

You do not need to override the master text frame when *placing* a story, however, to get autoflow et al. to work. That used to be a problem in earlier versions of InDesign but no longer. Instead, just place the story by clicking your loaded cursor—with or without flow control modifier keys—within the area of where the unoverridden master text frame will be, which, unless you changed something since creating the document, fills the page margins. InDesign will, in one step, override the master text frame and place your story into it. If you use autoflow or fixed-page autoflow, InDesign will override and flow text into any subsequent master text frames, threading them one after the other.

Using master text frames is the ideal way to lay out multipage documents that consist primarily of one continuous text story. They aren't the way go, however, for documents like newspapers or newsletter that typically present multiple stories per page; in those cases, you'll want to use single-column text frames on pages with multiple columns created by column guides rather than by using a master text frame. When it's appropriate, though, using master text frames has the distinct advantage of enabling modification of all frame instances from the single master page representative (or two representatives in facing pages documents). To modify the story frames—say, to change the number of columns, vertical alignment, inset, background color, or other options—you have only to change the attributes of the master page text frames on which all story frames are based.

Incidentally, master text frames in facing pages are automatically threaded across a spread upon creation. Thus, once manually overridden, text will flow freely from the master text frame on the left-read page to the one on the right-read. They are not, however, linked spread

to spread; pages 2 and 3 link together, as do 4 and 5, but 3 does not thread to 4. If you aren't autoflowing your story, you'll need to manually thread into and out from each spread. If you *are* autoflowing your story using Smart Text Reflow (see below), then the master page text frames *will* thread spread-to-spread.

Smart Text Reflow

Since CS4, InDesign can also automatically add and remove pages as you place, type, or edit text, and even as you change the font size or other formatting that causes text to recompose. Begin typing in a text frame and, as you reach the end of the text frame, InDesign can create a new frame and page, threading it with the last one, without the need for you to reach for the mouse. The feature is called Smart Text Reflow.

It works not only when making changes to text content or formatting directly in the document, but also while placing stories from external documents. Unless you've changed the Smart Text Reflow preferences (covered below), the way to use it when placing is to place the story into an overridden master page text frame (of any number of columns). InDesign will then automatically add pages of threaded master page text frames, including their column settings, until the entire story is laid out. Thus, in many, many situations, Smart Text Reflow supersedes the flowing options discussed previously. Some creatives, particularly those who work on single-story documents such as books, catalogs, and directories, might find Smart Text Reflow the only method of flowing text feature they need.

Smart Text Reflow is on by default but can be disabled or controlled in the Type pane of the Preferences (see Figure 8.7).

FIGURE 8.7
Smart Text Reflow options in Preferences, on the Type pane

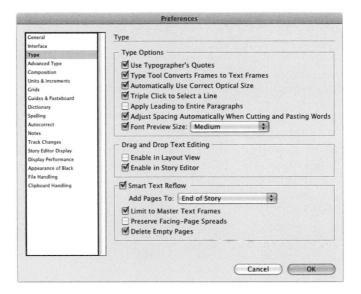

Smart Text Reflow   Enabled by default, Smart Text Reflow can be turned off entirely by clearing the checkbox.

Add Pages To   Choose where new pages will be added when needed, either to the end of the story (the default), the end of the section, or the end of the entire document. The last option is useful when working on stories that jump to the end of the document, such as in a magazine. More about jumping stories in the next few pages.

Limit to Master Text Frames   When this option is enabled, Smart Text Reflow will add pages only when you're working in master text frames, those created on document pages as a result of checking the Master Text Frame option in the New Document dialog or that you've manually created on master pages.

If Limit to Master Text Frames is disabled, then new pages will be added (and removed) when needed by *any* text frame, not only those based on master page frames. In such cases, the new, automatically generated text frames created on new pages will be single-column and fill the areas of the page margins. This would be the case even if you were writing or editing inside a multicolumn text frame when your actions triggered Smart Text Reflow to create the new page(s).

As a very wise precaution to prevent every text frame from spontaneously generating pages every time something goes overset, Adobe built in a fail safe: When Limit to Master Text Frames is disabled, Smart Text Reflow will activate and create new pages only when the source frame—the one into which you're typing or editing content—is already threaded to at least one other text frame. In other words, if you accidently overset text in the (typically unthreaded, standalone) photo credit text frame attached to a photo, you won't have to worry that InDesign will just start growing pages.

Preserve Facing-Page Spreads   This option is disabled if your document does not use facing pages. If it *does* use facing pages, then this option prompts you to consider whether Smart Text Reflow should add a single page or a full spread every time it must create pages. If enabled, this option will create a full spread every time Smart Text Reflow adds pages. If it's disabled, Smart Text Reflow will add only one page at a time, which may result in your subsequent pages shuffling, causing left- and right-read pages to swap sides.

Delete Empty Pages   Just as Smart Text Reflow can *add* pages when your text needs more room to grow, it can also *remove* pages left empty by text omissions, edits, or formatting. Enabling this option will do just that, but it will only remove pages if the Smart Text Reflow-created frame is the only document-level object on the would-be-removed page—master page objects don't count against the ability to delete pages.

Remember that the Smart Text Reflow settings, like most preferences, are document-level settings. Enabling, disabling, or changing Smart Text Reflow will apply only to the currently active document. To make it apply to all future documents, close all documents and then make the preference changes.

Jumplines and Carry-Overs

Of course, threaded text doesn't necessarily follow one page after the other. Magazines, newspapers, newsletters, magalogs, and numerous other types of publications often include more than one story per page, and they and other types of documents often jump several pages or sections between pages of one story. Directing readers between nonconsecutive frames in a thread is the job of *jumplines* and *carry-overs*—the former telling the reader where the story goes, the latter telling the reader where the story came from.

InDesign can do forward jumpline (e.g., "Continued on page *X*") and backward carry-over (e.g., "Continued from page *Y*") editorial directives, and both with total freedom and auto-updating numbers. In fact, they're accomplished with whatever text you insert plus tiny little text markers for the actual page numbers. Creating a jumpline or carry-over is incredibly easy:

1. To create a jumpline, create a new text frame to hold only the jumpline itself, and type and style the text of the jumpline—for instance, "Continued on page" or "Story continues page". Don't insert a number where a number should go; we'll do that momentarily.

2. Move the jumpline frame such that it overlaps, at least a little, a threaded frame (see Figure 8.8).

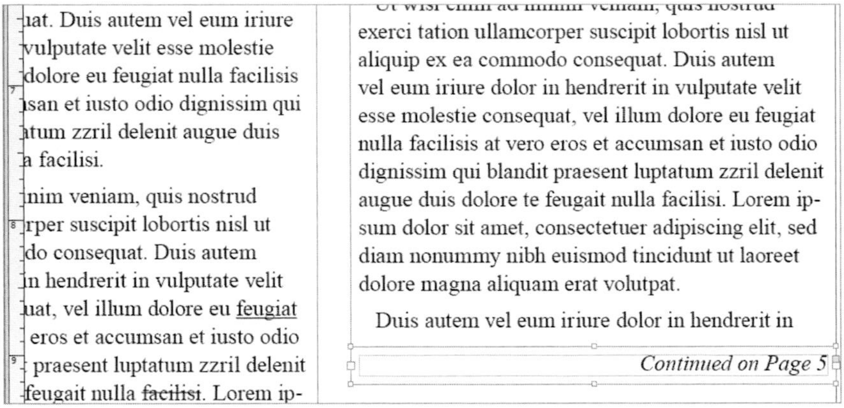

FIGURE 8.8
A jumpline directs readers to the next frame in the thread.

3. Now switch to the Type tool, place the cursor at the end of the jumpline text, and choose Type ➤ Insert Special Character ➤ Markers ➤ Next Page Number, which will insert the number of the page on which the next frame in the thread appears. And, if you reorder pages or move around frames, that page number will automatically update to reflect the new location of the next threaded frame.

4. To create a carry-over, a backward jumpline that explains from whence the story continues, follow the same procedure, aligning the carry-over text frame such that it touches the jumped-to frame, but use the Type ➤ Insert Special Character ➤ Markers ➤ Previous Page Number command.

Either continue line marker may be used inside the actual story as well, which is useful for references to sidebar material and other objects tethered to a particular place in the copy as an anchored object. For instance, you could say "Reference the chart on page *X*," which will reference whatever page the chart happens to land on, even if it's the current page.

In most cases, it's not a good idea to put continue lines inside the text they reference because the continue lines themselves are then subject to reflow. It's rather embarrassing to jump a story from page 10 to page 38 and, two paragraphs into the latter, see "Continued on page 38."

Lists, Numbers, and Bullets (Oh, My!)

InDesign includes a robust set of bulleted and numbered list functions, including the ability to stop and restart numbering as well as continue numbering across different stories and even different documents in the same book. In fact, CS5 brings InDesign closer than ever to advanced list and numbering power formerly reserved for the highly technical and less-than-creative pro-friendly world of technical publishing applications like FrameMaker and Ventura Publisher.

Bullets

InDesign has an extremely advanced and flexible implementation of bullets. They go far beyond circles, disks, and rectangles and are customizable and editable in ways other software hasn't even dared to imagine.

With text selected, choose Bullets and Numbering from the flyout menu of either the Paragraph panel or the Control panel in paragraph mode to access the Bullets and Numbering dialog, which controls a remarkable number of options (see Figure 8.9). Select Bullets from the List Type dropdown list to light up most of the options below it.

FIGURE 8.9
Bullets in the Bullets and Numbering dialog

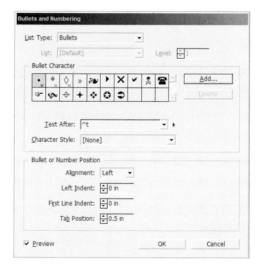

The Bullet Character section looks rather like the Glyphs panel's Recently Used list, doesn't it? It should—it functions much the same way. Out of the box, InDesign has five default bullet characters—the standard bullet glyph, an asterisk, a lozenge (the hollow diamond), the right-pointing double-angle quotation mark (often used by the Brits as quotation marks), and a nice fleuron from the Adobe Jenson Pro typeface (if you don't have Adobe Jenson Pro installed, that glyph becomes a double-accented A). To use one of these as your bullet, click your choice. Odds are, however, that you'll rarely use the latter four—they just aren't that stylish.

Clicking the Add button lets you pick any glyph from any installed font on your system as your bullet character. If you want a square bullet, find a font containing a square. If you want to make bullets out of dollar signs, you can do that, too. The Add Bullets dialog is nearly identical to the Glyphs panel (see Figure 8.10). At the bottom, choose the font family and style, and then, from the glyph table above, select the desired bullet glyph. If you want just one bullet, click OK, but if you want to explore your bullet glyph options, maybe across multiple fonts, click Add instead. The Add button adds the selected glyph to the Bullet Character list but doesn't close the Add Bullets dialog. Careful: It's easy to lose track of time in Add Bullets; at some point, you will have to get back to work.

FIGURE 8.10
Add Bullets looks and works like the Glyphs panel.

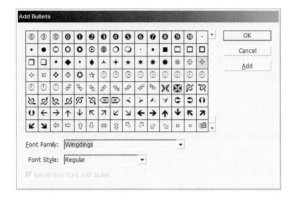

The Remember Font with Bullet check box lights up when you have selected a common glyph like a letter, number, or standard punctuation mark. Let's say you've decided that the *at* symbol (@) in BlackOak Std would make a swell bullet glyph. With Remember Font with Bullet *unchecked*, the @ will *not* be in BlackOak Std if the list text itself isn't. Instead, the bullet will set in the typeface of the list text. In many cases, that's exactly what you want. In this example, however, you want to make sure that @ bullet is always BlackOak Std regardless of the list text typeface—currently or after future changes—so you'll check the option.

Continuing with Figure 8.9, after choosing your bullet glyph, there are still plenty of options to consider:

Text After   The text, symbol, or marker separating the bullet from its list item. The default ^t is the universal code for a tab character, but the field will accept just about anything you can type. If you want a *leader* instead of a tab, type periods, hyphens, or underscores in the Text After field. To the right of the field is an arrow that will reveal a pop-up menu of common symbols and spaces. You can even combine several symbols, spaces, and manually typed glyphs to create a very intricate separator between bullet and text.

Character Style   Bullets can be assigned to any pre-created character style, which lets you become far more creative with InDesign bullets than you can elsewhere. In most applications, for instance, a bullet must share all the styling attributes of the list text it identifies; there simply isn't a way to change even something as simple as the bullet color—at least, not without converting the bullet to editable text, thus losing all the benefits of automated

bulleting. Using a character style, however, you can control every character-level attribute of the bullet independent of its accompanying text. Character color, point size, horizontal and vertical scaling, underline, strikethrough, skew, baseline shift—it's all open for customization. If you forgot to pre-create a character style for your bullet, don't cancel out of Bullets and Numbering. Instead, choose New Character Style from the bottom of the Character Style menu and whip up what you need. The ability to create a new character style right there is new to CS5.

Alignment   This option has little effect on bullets, which tend to align the same regardless of this setting, but three options—Left, Right, and Center—become important when creating numbered lists, particularly when the numbers grow beyond single digits.

AN ARSENAL OF FREE BULLETS

Explore your font collection via the Glyphs panel to look for potential bullet characters to draw on in future projects. You can find some surprisingly good bullet candidates hidden among letters, numbers, and punctuation, particularly in OpenType fonts.

Naturally, you'll want to also check any symbol or dingbat fonts in your collection. Look carefully in your font library; some of the best bullets come from often-overlooked sources. On Windows, for instance, is a typeface named Marlett. It's the font from which the operating system pulls user interface symbols like the *X* on the application close button in the top-right corner, as well as the minimize, maximize, and restore button labels. Those likely won't become your favorites for bullets, but other symbols in Marlett might, like right-angled triangles (arrows) pointing left, right, up, and down, as well as several types of boxes, check marks, and other symbols. Other gold mines of great bullets could be slumbering undiscovered on your system as you read this.

If you've exhausted Marlett, Zapf Dingbats, Wingdings, Wingdings 2, Wingdings 3, Webdings, and other symbol fonts that typically come preinstalled with Mac OS X, Windows, or Microsoft Office, you'll find an arsenal of free symbol fonts online. Think about it: For your next Halloween-themed report or design, you could use jack-o'-lanterns, witches, or tombstones as your bullet characters, or how about shamrocks as bullets in your March sales papers? Every year, for most of the major American holidays—Halloween, Thanksgiving, Christmas and Hanukah, Valentine's Day, St. Patrick's Day, the 4th of July—I collect tons of free holiday-related fonts and make them available for download individually or as a group from one of my publications, *Designorati*. Although there are plenty of blood-dripping, romantic, or snow-covered Latin fonts for typing text, each holiday's collection also includes a variety of symbol fonts ready to be used as bullets or converted into graphic or text frames (see "Technique: Convert Text to Image-Filled Frame" in Chapter 4: "Drawing"). Just visit www.Designorati.com and use the search box to find "free fonts" or the name of the specific holiday whose fonts you're after.

Indents   Like paragraph indents, the Left Indent field controls the overall left indent, while First Line Indent alters just the first line left indent. The first line is the one carrying the bullet or number glyph. To hang list items such that their bullets or numbers stick out farther left than all other lines in the item, set Left Indent to a positive value and First Line Indent

to an equal negative value. Note that these fields are mirrors of their counterparts on the Paragraph panel—changing values in one place changes values in the other.

Tab Position   If the Text After field includes a tab (^t code), the Tab Position field sets the tab stop or how far rightward of the bullet or number the text of the item begins.

After defining the bullet (or numbering) options once, you can quickly reapply them without having to return to the Bullets and Numbering dialog. Choosing either Apply Bullets or Apply Numbering from Type ➤ Bulleted & Numbered Lists will reapply the last-used options for those adornments. If you've yet to configure bullets or numbers in this session of InDesign, the defaults will be used. The same is true of the easier method of executing the Apply Bullets and Apply Numbering commands, using the buttons on the Control panel in Paragraph mode (see Figure 8.11). Unfortunately, there is no analogue on the stand-alone Paragraph panel.

FIGURE 8.11
The Control panel in Paragraph mode, with the Apply Bullets and Apply Numbering buttons highlighted

Of course, the best way to reuse bullet and numbering options is to add them to paragraph styles. We'll talk more in depth about paragraph styles in Chapter 13, "Efficiency," but you can see in Figure 8.12 that the interface for defining them within a paragraph style is identical to the Bullets and Numbering dialog.

FIGURE 8.12
Configuring bullets and numbering in a paragraph style in the Paragraph Style Options dialog

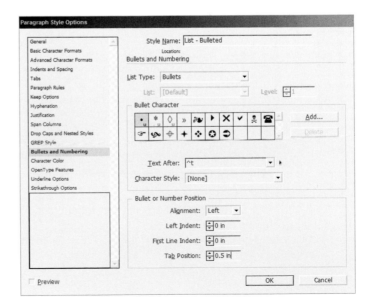

Numbering

Setting List Type to Numbers replaces the Bullet Character section of the Bullets and Numbering dialog with options specific to organized lists (see Figure 8.13).

FIGURE 8.13
Options for a numbered list

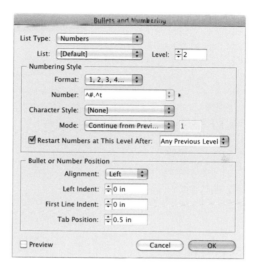

The numbering options are as follows:

Level (Upper section) When multilevel, outline-style, hierarchical, or nested numbering is created, the Level field determines to which level of numbering the selected text will belong and which of the options below it are applicable. For instance, in Figure 8.14, you see several levels of numbering.

FIGURE 8.14
A multilevel numbered list

```
1.  Articles
       A.  SECTIONS
              i.    Features
              ii.   News
              iii.  How-To
              iv.   Reviews
       B.  SUBJECTS
              i.    InDesign
              ii.   QuarkXPress
              iii.  InCopy
              iv.   Plugins/Xtensions
              v.    Creative Suite 3
2.  Tips & Tricks
       A.  CLASSIFICATION
              i.    Tip O' the Day
              ii.   Subscribers
       B.  TOPICS
              i.    InDesign
              ii.   QuarkXPress
              iii.  InCopy
              iv.   Photoshop
              v.    Illustrator
              vi.   Acrobat/PDF
3.  Special Content
       A.  Polls
       B.  Contests
       C.  Weekly Giveaway
```

Format   The Format field sets the type of numbering to be used. Options are Arabic, Arabic with leading zeroes, capital Roman, lowercase Roman, uppercase alphabetic, and lowercase alphabetic.

You can also choose none, which completely removes enumeration, leaving only the glyphs after the numbers (if any), kind of like bullets.

Number   Referring back to Figure 8.13, combined in this field are the functions of Bullet Character and Text After. Displaying the number requires the presence of the ^# code preceded or followed by whatever you like—a period, a number symbol (#), a tab, or any one of several types of spaces or leader symbols in the menu to the right. You'll find on the Insert flyout menu (the arrow) the Insert Number Placeholder submenu, which lets you insert a number of any level up to, and inclusive of, the value in the Level field above, as well as chapter numbers, which are set in Numbering & Section Options (see the appropriate section in Chapter 7, "Pages").

Mode   Mode offers the option of continuing numbering from a previous number or manually setting the start-at number in the field on the right. The advantage to the latter is that numbered lists can be stopped, followed by unnumbered paragraphs or sections, and then the numbering can pick back up again with the next logical digit.

Restart Numbers at This Level After   If Mode is set to Continue from Previous Number, this check box and dropdown list pair will activate. When working in multilevel numbering, this option says, "When a list item of this level appears after a higher-level item, restart numbering." For example, let's say we're defining level 3 numbering. Checking Restart Numbers at This Level After and setting the dropdown to Any Previous Level will cause level 3 list items to begin numbering anew at *1* after every level 2 item.

After I introduce the Lists feature, the sidebar "InDesign Numbering Shaves Weeks off Book Production" will explain how to use the numbering and list features.

Lists

InDesign includes paragraph, character, object, table, and cell styles. While they were obviously on a roll, giving users reusable styles for everything requested (well, almost; Live Caption settings aren't included in any of the former styles), they could have also added List styles. Fortunately for us, they didn't. I mean, do we really need another panel? Adobe's accommodating mood did introduce reusable list management, but they leveraged existing technologies to do it.

Since their introduction, bullet and number paragraph attributes have been part of Paragraph styles, thus making them reusable and easily manageable. As numbering capabilities deepened in successive InDesign releases, they are still primarily managed in Paragraph styles, but the Lists feature augments styles.

Choosing Type ➤ Bulleted & Numbered Lists ➤ Define Lists opens the Define Lists dialog (see Figure 8.15). In this interface you create, edit, delete, or load from other InDesign documents or templates the lists, but you'll actually use them in the Bullets and Numbering dialog.

FIGURE 8.15
The Define
Lists dialog

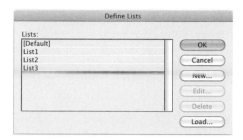

Clicking the New button to begin a new list (see Figure 8.16) offers three options, the first of which is the name by which you'd like to refer to the settings. The other two are what enable such important things as figure, caption, table, chart, and other types of numbering outside consecutive paragraphs of list items.

FIGURE 8.16
The New List
dialog

Consider figure numbers in, say, a technical book about InDesign for real-world print professionals. It's important for reading comprehension and reference (and writing, artwork creation, editing, compositing…) that figures throughout the book be numbered. But, in nearly all cases, the figures and their captions will be laid out in frames totally disconnected from the body copy and each other in unthreaded frames. Therefore, it isn't possible to just pull up Bullets and Numbering, set a couple options, and expect InDesign to handle the figure and caption renumbering if I relocate this section from Chapter *X* to Chapter *Y*.

That's where the Continue Numbers Across Stories list option comes into the picture. When the resulting list definition is used within the Caption paragraph style, every caption in the current chapter will be automatically numbered by InDesign, and those numbers will dynamically update if figures and their captions are reorganized.

Checking Continue Numbers from Previous Document in Book accomplishes the same thing between chapters. For example, I set my numbering options to include the chapter number as well as the figure number, update the Caption paragraph style to reflect that change, and then never have to manually update a figure number again. How much time would that save in compositing a book like this? (Well, seeing as I'm still writing it and don't yet know how many figures I've got, I don't know for sure how much time it would save the compositor or me [and I forgot to ask with the last edition of the book]; let's just say it would save lots of time.)

In other types of documents, figures and captions might not need numbering. Perhaps tables, charts, or some other type of content must be numbered sequentially even if they don't adjoin.

Often one or more such numbered items will be incorporated into the document's table of contents or an appendix, increasing the importance of numbering them. Combining the new Lists function with numbering and paragraph styles, *all* of these types of content and more can be numbered by InDesign.

 **Real World Scenario**

InDesign Numbering Shaves Weeks off Book Production

Not long ago I was asked to design a template for a book publisher (not this book or this publisher, regrettably). In addition to the usual specs and goals, I was tasked with automating or at least streamlining as much of the compositing and layout process as possible. Because the publisher's typical authors are themselves designers and software experts, the publisher allows authors to do their own initial composition and layout, with the need for only oversight and minor error correction in-house. While that decision enables the publisher to realize tremendous savings in both book production time and budget, it added to my task one wrinkle: I couldn't employ third-party plug-ins or even custom scripts.

Book authors worked in InDesign or InCopy, manually numbering figures, captions, and tables. If one such figure, caption, or table was moved, cut, or added during editing and author review stages, it meant someone would have to manually renumber all those subsequent figures, captions, or tables. Guess who that would be left to—right, yours truly, the layout guy.

Although the compensation for all those hours fixing numbers would have probably made a sizeable down payment on a new Harley for me, I realized that it would also leave me so busy fixing numbers I'd never have time to ride the hog. So, I updated the book template to do figure, caption, and table numbering dynamically.

For the Figure Caption, Table Title, and Chart Title paragraph styles, I defined lists that continued across stories and used ^H.^#.^t (Chapter Number.Instance Number.[Tab]) as the number. With the correct chapter number defined for each chapter in Layout ➤ Numbering & Section Options, and all chapters collected into an InDesign book, every figure, table, and chart self-numbered with no manual numbering required by the other authors and editors or production. Additionally, because all the individual chapter InDesign documents were managed through the Book panel, even the occasional chapter reordering wasn't an issue because InDesign will update chapter numbers—and thus all dependent numbered items—automatically.

InDesign also enabled easier creation and management of the paragraph styles governing numbered lists in the body copy itself. That template has three levels of hierarchical lists, progressively moving down through Arabic numerals, capital letters, and lowercase Roman numerals. In the earlier, nondynamic versions of the InDesign and InCopy templates, each list was a separate and independent style, and they were dumb lists. Every time an author needed to return to first-level list items from second- or third-level, she would have to first apply the paragraph style and then manually change the Start At (number) field in Bullets and Numbering. For example, if the author created a list like the following, simply numbering the second top-level item required several manual steps. If the author later had to add, remove, or reorder the list items, almost every item had to be manually tweaked with a trip to Bullets and Numbering and the Start At field.

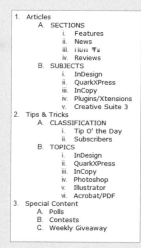

In the new book template, however, all I had to do was configure each of the three list paragraph styles to continue numbering from the previous instance of the same level (the Mode field in Bullets and Numbering) and to restart numbering for the sublists (the second and third levels) after any previous level. The only downside to these options was that the directive to continue numbering from the previous instance of the same level meant that, if a list on page 25 contained five top-level items, a completely separate list on page 100 would begin numbering at item 6. That, of course, is a simple fix: The Restart Numbering command begins the numbering over again at 1 (or I, i, A, or whatever). For the authors (and compositor on occasion), one command, usually executed from a keyboard shortcut, is easier, faster, and less distracting than opening the often-closed Paragraph panel, choosing Bullets and Numbering from the flyout menu, changing the Start At field, and hitting OK.

All the authors had to do was apply paragraph styles as they wrote in InDesign or InCopy because I had built the styles to handle numbering automatically (and many were nested, automatic application styles, too, but that's a topic for Chapter 13), saving significant time at all stages, especially in post-editing production. Instead of the usual technical book publishing turnaround time of 3 to 12 weeks, this publisher's books go to press within *days* of the completion of final editing.

Overriding Bullets and Numbers

At some point you'll probably need to restart the sequence of list item numbering. You'll find the Restart Numbering command in three places: on the Paragraph panel flyout menu (and mirrored on the same menu on the Control panel in Paragraph mode), in Type ➤ Bulleted & Numbered Lists, and on the context-sensitive menu that appears when you right-click within numbered text. With the text cursor somewhere inside the list item, execute that command and numbering will restart at 1, 01, A, a, I, or i, as configured.

The Convert Bullets to Text/Convert Numbering to Text command lets you break down dynamic bullets or numbers into standard, editable text. Using live or dynamic bullets and numbers, you have through character styles and the various other options in Bullets and Numbering tremendous control over the appearance of the bullet or number glyphs themselves.

They are not editable text, however, and are excluded from spell checks and find-and-replace operations. When you need those functions or unadulterated styling power without lengthening your Character Styles panel, Convert Bullets to Text/Convert Numbering to Text will convert dynamic, auto-updating bullets or numbers to standard, editable glyphs. The appearance of the bullets or numbers remains intact, including any indents, but they will no longer update, and you can now edit them as you can any other text in a frame.

Word Processing

Did I catch you by surprise earlier when I mentioned authors writing books in InDesign instead of writing them in Word? Really, there's no reason a competent InDesign user shouldn't write directly in InDesign. If the concept of writing in the layout raises an eyebrow, then perhaps you'd entertain using InDesign's built-in word processor in lieu of the page. And, if you're so old school that you bristle at the very idea of using a layout application for word processing, perhaps you'll consider Adobe's Best Kept Secret 7.0 for the task.

Add and Remove Pages as You Type

Smart Text Reflow all by itself makes InDesign usable as a word processor. Think about it: In Microsoft Word, Google Docs, or any other word processor (are there others?), pages are automatically added or removed as you type. Unlike former editions of InDesign or current versions of other page layout applications—even former editions of InCopy, which is an editorial word processor—you don't have to use a panel, menu, or toolbar command to insert or remove pages; they just appear and disappear as needed. Well, now InDesign (and InCopy) can do that same thing. So, if you want to sit down and just start typing a document in InDesign, *you can*. Well, sort of. You have to set it up properly, but that's not hard. Just make sure you do the following in your document, and then InDesign can be your total Word replacement:

1. Enable Master Text Frame in the New Document dialog.

2. Turn Smart Text Reflow on, and enable the Limit to Master Text Frames and Delete Empty Pages options.

    Remember, if you set these options with all documents closed, they'll be enabled by default for all new documents you create.

3. Cmd+Shift-click/Ctrl+Shift-click inside the margins of your document's first page to override the master text frame.

4. Begin typing in the now-overridden master text frame.

The advantages of typing directly in InDesign are numerous and significant. To name just a few,

◆ There's the fact that you'll get accurate line breaks, seeing your text *exactly* as it will print while you type.

◆ You have full formatting control in InDesign and the ability to pre-load all the paragraph styles and character styles you'll need.

◆ You don't have to import text and then go through converting the source application's styles to InDesign styles the way you have to with Word.

- InDesign includes change tracking features nearly on par with Word's.
- You're already comfortable with InDesign and know where to find everything.

Story Editor

If you'd rather not write directly in the layout, InDesign has a built-in text-only word processor. Story Editor is an alternate view on a given story, isolating text from layout. Figure 8.17 shows the Story Editor side-by-side with the layout view of the same story. Editing either instantly updates the other.

FIGURE 8.17
Story Editor (right) editing the text of the frame in the layout (left)

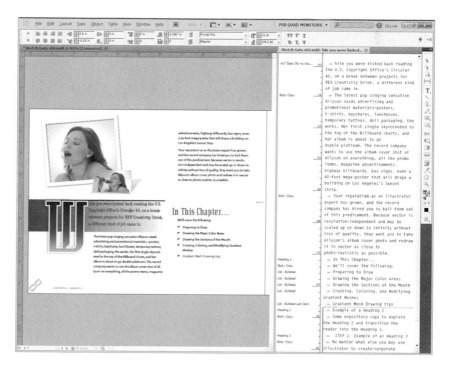

To open a Story Editor view, select a text frame or place the Type tool cursor inside it, and choose Edit ➢ Edit in Story Editor, or press Cmd+Y/Ctrl+Y. If you highlight text prior to opening the Story Editor view, that same text will be highlighted in Story Editor. If your InDesign layout window is maximized, so will be the Story Editor window that pops up. Rest easy; the layout is still open behind it. Cmd+Y/Ctrl+Y is a toggle that will open Story Editor view from layout view or layout view from Story Editor view. Additionally, you can restore or resize the Story Editor window to be less than the full application window size. Both views can be tiled side by side if you like, too.

Because Story Editor focuses on the copy, it displays only the most basic of formatting—italic, bold, and bold-italic—all other formatting, including typeface, size, leading, indents, and so on, is hidden. Objects like anchored or inline objects and tables, as well as special types of text such as variables, hyperlinks, footnotes, tracked changes, and many other types are called out in the flow of text by special markers; you can see those different types of markers in Table 8.2.

TABLE 8.2: OBJECT AND SPECIAL TEXT INDICATORS IN STORY EDITOR

IDENTIFIER	OBJECT OR SPECIAL TEXT
inserted	Inserted Text (Change Tracking Enabled)
deleted	Deleted Text (Change Tracking Enabled)
newold	Replaced Text (Change Tracking Enabled)
moved	Moved Text (Change Tracking Enabled)
▶◀	Note
1 Footnote text	Footnote
accumulated	Hyperlink
⊚	Hyperlink Text Anchor
Since the conceptual planning <OV> steps for a project like t	Cross-Reference Source Text
⋏	Index Marker
👁	Hidden Conditional Text
Creation Date⟩ Created: 2006-07-23	Variable
X Tag1⟩	XML Tag
▼⊞	Table
⚓	Inline or Anchored Object

Text and tables can still be styled and formatted within the Story Editor, and paragraph and character styles still applied—indeed, all the panels, tools, and menu commands relevant to text are as accessible in Story Editor as in layout mode—but their effects won't befog the purely word processing view. Line breaks, hyphenation, and composition are also not accurate—this is copyediting, not galley proofing—and text is displayed in a single column as wide as the Story

Editor window (less the Style Name column on the left). As a performance boost that saves time, InDesign holds a queue of updates—if you type quickly into the Story Editor view, the text will appear or change there instantly, but there may be a slight pause before the layout is updated to reflect the changes.

Although you won't see the *effect* of paragraph styles, the left column, in addition to providing a scale of column depth in the document measurement system (inches, points, millimeters, or whatever), lists beside each paragraph the style assigned to it (see Figure 8.18). Thus, at a glance, you can discern the formatting of the paragraph. And that's a very good thing because sometimes those paragraph style tags are your only visual cue that a new paragraph has begun. Unfortunately, Story Editor still doesn't have other common paragraph break cues like whitespace indents or paragraph spacing, which, until you get used to it, could make you resort to the abominable practice of double returns between paragraphs. Choosing View ➤ Story Editor ➤ Show Paragraph Break Marks turns on the weird quadruple braces you see at the beginning of each paragraph, but sometimes they're more confusing and visually cluttering than not having any indication of paragraphs breaking.

FIGURE 8.18
Story Editor communicates copy-specific information.

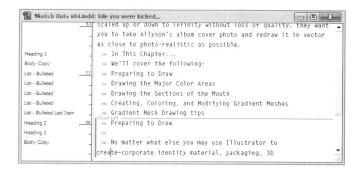

One exceptional feature of Story Editor that layout view simply can't match is the ability to see and edit overset text. Any copy that won't appear on the layout is still present, but called out, in Story Editor with the *overset* marker and red border down its left side. Even better, the depth ruler in the Style Name column continues measuring overset text so you can see exactly how many column inches are yet needed to lay out the rest of the story.

CUSTOMIZING STORY EDITOR

Story Editor is designed to be used. Despite the fact that they still won't put in decent paragraph stop and start indicators (like an option for vertical whitespace display-only tabs), Adobe wants you to be able to write and edit copy comfortably. That doesn't always mean black, 12 pt, Letter Gothic STD type on a white background. In the Preferences, on the Story Editor Display pane, are options to completely customize the word processing experience to your unique comfort level (see Figure 8.19). A few themes are preconfigured, or you can set your own font, size (via a dropdown menu of common sizes or by typing in a specific point size), line spacing, and text and background colors. The anti-aliasing method can also be changed, as can the size and shape of the cursor.

Of course, InCopy can open its own ICML file format, as well as Microsoft Word DOC files, ASCII text, Rich Text Format, and other common textual document formats, but it can also open InDesign documents. Because it lacks layout tools, frames cannot be moved or modified in InCopy, but their contents—text and, optionally, imagery—can, which is what enables offloading editorial work from design and production to the editorial department. Editors who want to proof or even edit copy within the final layout can do so through InCopy's layout view (see Figure 8.21). The document in layout view is 100% accurately copyfit.

FIGURE 8.21
Layout view enables InCopy editors to proof and work within the final layout, without overloading them with InDesign's full tool set.

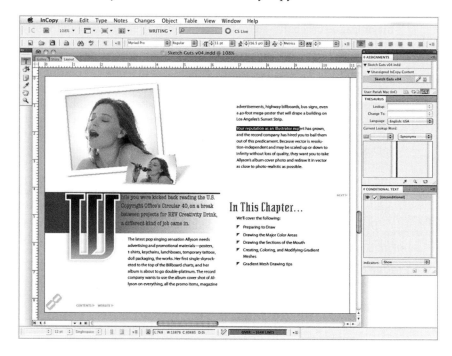

Finally, galley view is a combination of both other modes (see Figure 8.22). It's a story editor but with accurate line breaks, hyphenation, composition, and copyfitting.

Working together, InDesign and InCopy fill both sides of the design-editorial dynamic, allowing one department to concentrate on its specialty and allowing the other group to do the same. Native editing of both applications' files in the other, live copy and layout update links between them, and for more robust needs, the ability to assign frames, pages, and spreads to specific InCopy users are the reasons InCopy is rapidly supplanting Microsoft Word in collaborative publishing workflows. If you're part of such a workflow, whether design and editorial are at the same or different sites, migrating writers, editors, and proofers to InCopy could be the most valuable idea you gain from this book. I say that with all sincerity, and I have the experience migrating numerous publishing clients to back up the claim.

We'll talk more about the way InDesign and InCopy can work together in Chapter 14, "Collaboration."

FIGURE 8.22
Galley view presents accurate copyfitting in a familiar word processor environment.

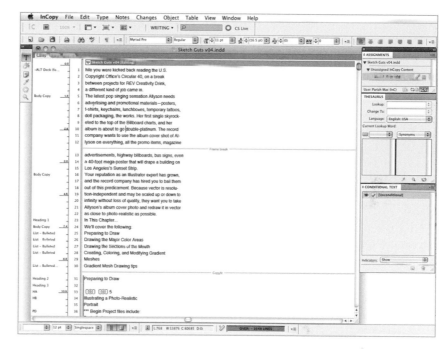

Referencing: Footnotes, Endnotes, and Cross-References

Technical publications, instructional tomes (like what you're reading right now), scholarly works, trade journals, and other types of longer documents often include the need to cite sources, provide additional information outside the main flow of copy, or reference one part of the document in another. These are common and fundamental functions of working with stories, and InDesign handles them very, very well. Well, okay, except in the case of endnotes, which it doesn't officially do but which you can make InDesign do.

Footnotes

Footnotes are citations or resources placed at the end of a column or page and referenced from within the text of that column or page. Figure 8.23 shows a typical footnote.

FIGURE 8.23
A footnote

> Ut wisi enim ad minim veniam, quis nostrud exerci lobortis nisl ut aliquip ex ea commodo consequat. Duis autem hendrerit in vulputate velit esse molestie consequat, vel illum facilisis at vero eros et accumsan et iusto odio dignissim qui l zzril delenit augue duis dolore te feugait nulla facilisi. Lorem consectetuer adipiscing elit, sed diam nonummy nibh euismo dolore magna aliquam erat volutpat.[1]
>
> 1   Mary had a little lamb. It was salty.

Inserting a footnote is easy. Position the cursor in the text immediately after the word or phrase to reference the footnote, and then select Type ➤ Insert Footnote. Using the current footnote options, a new footnote reference will be added to the text at that point and the footnote itself at the bottom of the column; your cursor will stand ready to type the footnote.

While in the footnote frame, you can jump back to the footnote reference point by using the menu command Type ➤ Go To Footnote Reference.

The easiest way to edit footnotes and their reference numbers is in Story Editor, where they magically appear together. In Figure 8.24, you can see both collapsed and expanded footnotes in their colored boxes. To collapse or expand, just click the colored part of the footnote box. To collapse or expand all footnotes at once, choose Collapse All Footnotes or Expand All Footnotes from the context-sensitive menu or from the View ➤ Story Editor menu.

FIGURE 8.24
In Story Editor, footnotes appear inline with their reference numbers.

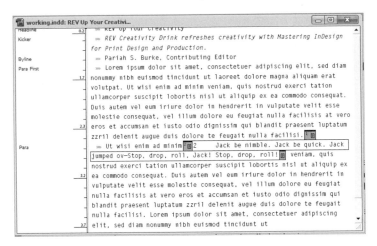

Footnotes are anchored to their reference numbers. If text reflows, moving the reference to another column or page, the footnote follows to the bottom of that column or page. Similarly, pasting or dragging text containing a reference to a different place in the same document takes the footnote with it. The same occurs when pasting or dragging into a different document, with the added benefit that both the reference and footnote itself will pick up the footnote formatting options in effect in the new document.

Deleting a footnote is even easier than inserting it—delete just the reference number and the entire footnote goes along with it. (This is undoable if you accidentally delete the reference number and footnote.)

You *can* delete the footnote number or other identifier at the beginning of the footnote itself, but you really shouldn't—readers match the reference to the footnote by that mark. If you've deleted the number and want to reinsert it, position the cursor ahead of the footnote and choose Type ➤ Insert Special Character ➤ Markers ➤ Footnote Number.

FORMATTING FOOTNOTES

Extensive footnote formatting controls are available from Type ➤ Document Footnote Options. The first tab of Footnote Options, Numbering and Formatting, is largely concerned with the appearance and sequence of footnotes (see Figure 8.25).

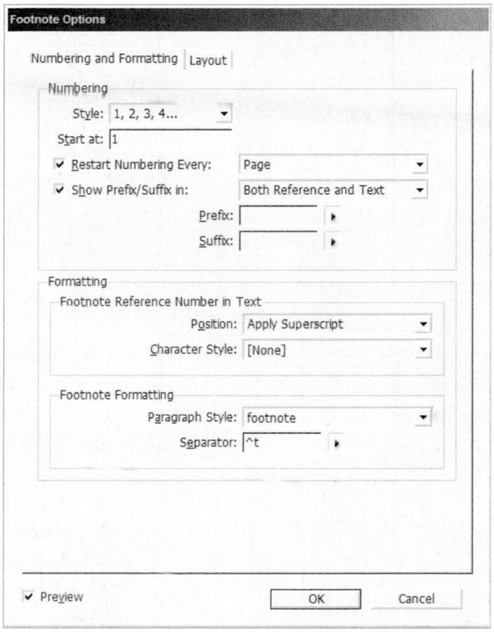

FIGURE 8.25
Footnote Options
Numbering and
Formatting tab

FIGURE 8.25
Footnote Options
Numbering and
Formatting tab

What does it all mean?

Style   Footnotes may take on numerous styles, including the most common Arabic numerals; the second most common, a system of symbols including the dagger (†), double-dagger (‡), and so on; incrementing asterisks; Roman numerals in both cases; and alphabetic enumerators in both lower- and uppercase.

Start At   InDesign automatically increments footnote numbers in the same story and renumbers them to reflect additions, deletions, and rearrangement of footnote references. By default, the first footnote in the story will begin with *1* and ascend from there. In cases where a single chapter or document comprises more than a single story, you'll want to either manually choose the starting number in the Start At field or set an appropriate Restart Numbering Every option.

Restart Numbering Every   Depending on the type of document being written or laid out, you may want footnotes to continuously increment throughout the whole document or just per section, spread, or page. For the former, leave Restart Numbering Every unchecked. However, to start the footnote reference numbering over at the Start At value for every section, spread, or page, check this box and choose the appropriate divider in the dropdown menu to the right.

Show Prefix/Suffix in   Between the check box, dropdown list, and specific Prefix and Suffix fields, you can add brackets [], parentheses (), hair spaces, thin spaces, or custom glyphs to either or both the footnote reference number and footnote text. The spaces in particular are handy when footnote references are rendered in a typeface that makes them too close to preceding or succeeding glyphs.

Footnote Reference Number in Text In the Position dropdown, determine if you'd like to format footnote reference numbers in the usual fashion of superscripted numbers or if you'd like them subscripted or even rendered as normal position, full-size numbers. Publications and associations vary in how they like footnote reference numbers presented.

By creating beforehand and assigning here a character style, every aspect of reference numbers' appearance is open to customization distinct from surrounding copy.

Footnote Formatting Footnotes themselves are paragraphs and can be styled while editing. Here, though, you have the ability to specify a particular paragraph style to set the majority of global appearance options. In the Separator field, enter the glyph(s) or mark(s) to divide the identifying reference number from the footnote text it keys. The default, ^t, is code for a tab.

On the Layout tab, more advanced formatting as well as footnote placement is stipulated (see Figure 8.26).

FIGURE 8.26
Footnote Options
Layout tab

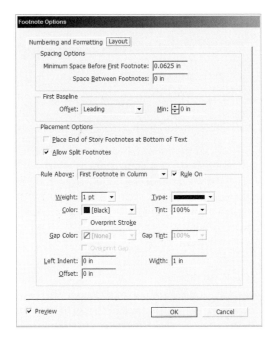

Spacing Options Enter in these fields the amount of vertical spacing between the end of the story column and the first footnote as well as the amount of vertical paragraph space separating multiple footnotes from each other. The latter option has no effect with single footnotes.

First Baseline Baseline offset sets the vertical distance between the baseline of the first line of footnote text and the (by default ruled) top of the text frame holding footnotes. Control text baseline offset using the same options as in normal text frames—by ascent, cap height, leading value, x-height, or a fixed amount. The Min field refines Baseline Offset values of Leading or Fixed by specifying the minimum amount of space between the top of the line and the baseline of its text.

Place End of Story Footnotes at Bottom of Text   This option specifies where footnotes appearing in the last frame of a threaded story appear. In all frames but the last, footnotes are placed at the bottom of the column in which their reference numbers appear. In some publications and according to some style guides, however, it's preferable to place all footnotes from the last *frame* of a story not at the bottom of each column but beneath the last column. Checking this option sets the latter condition.

Allow Split Footnotes   When footnote text outgrows the amount of space allotted to hold footnotes, how should it be handled?

◆ Checking this option splits long footnotes across columns (and perhaps even pages), creating effectively threaded footnote frames at the bottoms of successive columns.

◆ Unchecking Allow Split Footnotes can force InDesign to move the *body copy* line of text containing the footnote reference number to *its* next column, which could result in large, multiline gaps at the bottom of main story columns. If the resulting gap is too large, InDesign will instead overset the footnote text.

One way to help control footnote cohesion is to ensure that you've assigned to it a paragraph style with appropriate keeps options defined (e.g., keep X number of lines together or keep all lines together).

Rules   Mirroring the options of a paragraph rule above the paragraph, this section lets you create visually interesting separators above the first footnote section and/or above all footnote sections (for split footnotes). To disable the rule entirely, uncheck the Rule On box.

In addition to all the formatting options in Footnote Options, you can still manually and individually style footnotes. For instance, you could select the footnote text (press Cmd+A/ Ctrl+A with the cursor inside a footnote to select the entire text of just that footnote) and apply character styles, font or color changes, or anything else you can normally do with text.

You can also manually style the footnote reference numbers, but it's a much better idea to do it in Footnote Options with character styles. Even doing it that way, though, styles will be lost if you clear overrides and character styles in the paragraph containing the footnote reference.

Cross-References

Cross-references connect two points in a document and direct readers from one point to a different place in the same document. For instance, you could tell readers to "see Table 8.1" or "read up on endnotes on page X," thus directing them from point A, the location of the directive, to point B, the referenced content. If you're working in a book file (see Chapter 9, "Documents," for coverage of book files), a cross-reference can point readers to a place in a different file or chapter in the book, which is a separate InDesign file, but a book will ultimately be presented as a single printed or electronic document. (Like that clever use of a cross-reference to another file in this booked document to prove the point right there in the sentence *saying* how you can create a create a cross-reference to another file in a booked document?)

There are two parts to a cross reference:

◆ The *destination text* is the place to which a cross-reference refers, such as Table 8.1 in a reference to "See Table 8.1."

◆ The second part is the confusingly named *source cross-reference*, which is the text referring to some other text, for example, the "See Table 8.1" directive itself.

Since the conceptual planning steps for a project like this are sparse, it affords us a unique and excellent opportunity for a primer on copyright for the creative professional—which is exceedingly relevant to this project ("Copyrights are, as the plurality of the name implies, more than a single right." on page 10).

CROSS-REFERENCE TO A TEXT ANCHOR

What you've just created may be exactly what you'd like to see. We'll get into formatting and changing the content soon. For now, though, let's say instead of linking to a full paragraph, you wanted to reference a specific word or location within a paragraph. Here's how you do that (and why the Cross-References panel is conjoined with the Hyperlinks panel).

1. Within a text frame, place your cursor at the point to which you want to link, the destination text, immediately before the first word of the desired destination text.

   Alternatively, you can highlight a selection of text and make that entire selection the destination text.

2. Choose New Hyperlink Destination from the Hyperlinks/Cross-References TomKat panel flyout menu. That will open the New Hyperlink Destination dialog (see Figure 8.30).

3. Set the Type to Text Anchor and give the destination a name; this can be either the destination text itself or some other name that will help you identify the destination. Click OK.

   It will appear as if nothing has happened; you will not see an entry for the hyperlink destination in either the Hyperlinks or Cross-References panel.

FIGURE 8.30
The New Hyperlink
Destination dialog
creating a new Text
Anchor for a cross-
reference destination

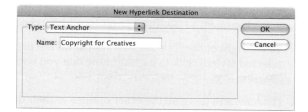

4. Back in the document proper, find a location in a story where you want to insert the source cross-reference that directs readers to the destination we just defined. Place your type cursor where you'd like the source cross-reference to appear.

5. At the bottom of the Cross-References panel, click the Create New Cross-Reference button.

6. This time, choose Text Anchor from the Link To dropdown menu.

    The Destination section of the dialog will change to provide access to the destination document and any text anchors defined in that document (see Figure 8.31).

FIGURE 8.31
The New Cross-Reference dialog when Text Anchor is chosen from the Link To menu.

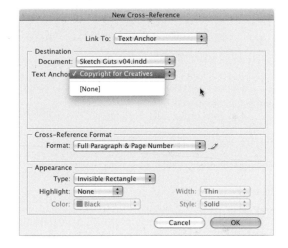

7. Choose the document you're currently editing from the first menu, and then from the second choose the text anchor you just made a few steps ago.

8. Again, leave all the other options at their defaults and click OK.

    The resulting source cross-reference will look like the last one, a page number following a quote of the entire destination text paragraph. This time, however, it will reference the location of the text anchor, not the entire paragraph.

Cross-Reference Formats

Cross-references can be presented in many, many different formats—that is, what parts are shown, how much of the destination text is quoted, if any, what numbers—page, chapter, section—appear, and so on. The required format of cross-references is usually defined by a publisher's or organization's style guide. Check yours ahead of time to get off on the right foot. If you don't currently have a style definition for cross-references (or footnotes and endnotes), many publications defer to the *Chicago Manual of Style*, or you could always make up your own style rules.

In the New Cross-Reference dialog, in the Cross-Reference Format area, the Format dropdown menu offers a number of preconfigured cross-reference formats:

◆ Full Paragraph & Page Number

◆ Full Paragraph

♦ Paragraph Text & Page Number

♦ Paragraph Text

♦ Paragraph Number & Page Number

♦ Paragraph Number

♦ Text Anchor Name & Page Number

♦ Text Anchor Name

♦ Page Number

If none of these suits your purposes, click the pencil icon to the right of the Format field and define your own format.

This book, for instance, uses quite a few cross-references that point you to figures, tables, other chapters, and occasionally something else. Typically those cross-references are in formats other than those available by default in InDesign. For instance, when I ask you to read more about a mentioned subject in another chapter, I usually do so by saying "(see 'Section Name' in Chapter X, 'Chapter Name')." Unfortunately, InDesign can't automatically include the chapter name in a cross-reference for me. Thus I have to do those manually. But, if I wanted something along the lines of "(see 'Section Name' on Page X in Chapter Y)," well, InDesign can do *that* for me, though that isn't one of the predefined formats. I'll have to build that format myself (see Figure 8.32).

FIGURE 8.32
Building a custom format in the Cross-Reference Formats dialog

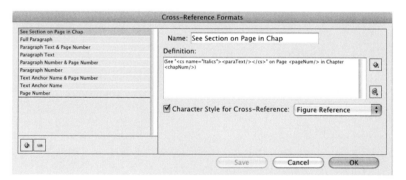

On the left in the Cross-Reference Formats dialog is the list of defined formats. Clicking the plus sign beneath that list creates a new format, which you can name on the right. Also on the right is the format definition, created by adding and arranging *format building blocks*. Format building blocks are the, uh, building blocks of a format. Each building block presents some kind of data—a chapter number, the page number, the paragraph text, a portion of the paragraph text, and so on. You string building blocks together (often with normal text) to produce a format that results in the source cross-reference.

The menu to the right of the Definition field is where the building blocks are stored (like the big can that held all your Lincoln Logs). Adobe didn't see fit to give that menu a name (there's no name in the documentation and no tooltip appears when you hover over it), so I hereby dub it the Building Block menu. Click the Building Block menu to reveal your choices of building blocks;

click a building block and its code will be inserted into the Definition field at the location of your cursor. Table 8.3 gives you a list of the building block names as well as their codes and functions.

TABLE 8.3: CROSS-REFERENCE FORMAT BUILDING BLOCKS

NAME	CODE	DEFINITION
Page Number	`<pageNum/>`	Inserts the page number of the text destination.
Paragraph Number	`<paraNum/>`	Inserts the number of the text destination paragraph when the text destination appears within a numbered list.
Paragraph Text	`<paraText/>`	Inserts the text of the destination paragraph, without a number, when the text destination appears within a numbered list.
Full Paragraph	`<fullPara/>`	Inserts the text of the entire paragraph in which the text destination resides.
Partial Paragraph	`<fullPara delim="" includeDelim="false"/>`	By specifying a delimiter in the `delim=""` section (e.g., an em dash or period), this building block inserts the text of the destination text paragraph from the beginning until it encounters the specified delimiter. The delimiter itself is not included by default. To include the delimiter, change `includeDelim=` to `"true"`.
Text Anchor Name	`<txtAnchrName/>`	Inserts the name of the text anchor defined on the Hyperlinks panel.
Chapter Number	`<chapNum/>`	Inserts the chapter number of the destination text.
File Name	`<fileName/>`	Inserts the filename of the cross-reference destination document.
Character Style	`<cs name=""></cs>`	Assigns a character style to other building blocks or text in the current format definition. To use, name an existing character style between the quotation marks in `name=""`, and place the building block(s) and/or text to be given that character between the tags; for example: `<cs name="Bold">This will be bold</cs>`.

In addition to the building blocks themselves, you can type in just about any text—including carriage returns to force source cross-references onto their own lines or push text after them down into its own paragraph. There's also a special characters menu, the @ symbol menu, that

will help you insert marks, glyphs, and whitespace that are a little more difficult to type into the Destination field.

The Character Style for Cross-Reference option lets you assign a character style to the format. Just pick a character style from the list, or choose New Character Style to whip one up right then and there. Note that the style you choose (or create) will apply to the *entire* format, start to finish, all of its text and building blocks. To style only a portion of a format differently than the rest, use the Character Style building block, which lets you wrap text or other building blocks in different character styles. You can even use multiple Character Style building blocks to completely customize the look of your source cross-reference.

Once you've defined a format you like, click Save to save it and remain in the Cross-Reference Formats dialog, ready to build more formats, or click OK to save and quit. Your new format will now appear on the Format menu of the New Cross-Reference dialog.

Formats are document specific—if you define custom formats for the current document, you won't have those same formats in others or new documents you create. You can load formats from one InDesign document into another with the Load Cross-Reference Formats command on the Hyperlinks/Cross-References panel flyout menu. Also, if you want have your new formats on hand for all new documents, without the need to load them each time, build your formats (or load them in) with all documents closed. Then they'll be part of InDesign and automatically included in each new document you create.

CROSS-REFERENCE APPEARANCE

In addition to assigning a character style to your cross reference (or parts of it with the `<cs name="  "></cs>` building block), the Appearance section of the New Cross-Reference dialog lets you define the physical, non-character-level appearance of the source cross-reference Figure 8.33):

FIGURE 8.33
The Appearance section of the New or Edit Cross-Reference dialog

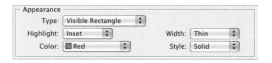

Type   Your choices here are Invisible Rectangle or Visible Rectangle. The former doesn't create a box around the source cross-reference and, consequently, disables rectangle stroke appearance options Color, Width, and Style. Visible rectangles or highlights (just below) are particularly useful in electronic documents to help readers recognize that the cross-reference is actually a hyperlink to the location it describes.

Highlight   When a reader clicks the cross-reference hyperlink in an electronic document such as a hyperlinked PDF, he expects to see something happen, some visual feedback that he's clicked something. This is a basic tenet of hypertext and e-publication user experience design; it's why hyperlinked text on Web pages changes color and why 3D beveled buttons inset or depress when clicked. You have four choices on this menu.

None   No on-click effect will occur. On a slow system or when the hyperlink is bad (such as if the destination text or text anchor to which it links was deleted), the user

will have no feedback to tell him he's done something or that the document should have done something.

Invert   The area of the cross-reference hyperlink will invert its colors, swapping black for white, red for green, and so on.

Outline   An outline will appear around the cross-reference hyperlink once clicked but then disappear again after the link has been followed.

Inset   The cross-reference hyperlink will appear to inset or recess into the page, much like a beveled button appears to press into the page when a user clicks it.

Color   When Visible Rectangle is selected from the Type menu, choose here the color of the rectangle's stroke. The rectangle will encompass the entire cross-reference hyperlink in its default, non-clicked state.

Width   Set the width of the visible rectangle around the hyperlink. Choices are limited to Thin, Medium, and Thick, which are relative to the zoom level of the document and not configured to be specific weights measurable in points.

Style   Rectangle strokes may be Solid or Dashed.

Although cross-reference appearance options can't be saved in paragraph styles, the appearance options you choose remain in effect for the current document until you change them. Thus new cross-references you create will automatically inherit the appearance as you last set it.

EDITING CROSS-REFERENCES

Cross-references can be edited at any time. Double-clicking the cross-reference's entry on the Cross-References panel opens the Edit Cross-Reference dialog, which is identical to the New Cross-Reference dialog, enabling you to change what the cross-reference links to, its format, and its appearance.

To delete a cross-reference, select its entry in the Cross-References panel and click the trash icon at the bottom of the panel or drag the cross-reference to the trash icon. Upon deletion of the cross-reference, the source cross-reference text *remains in the document*, converted to plain text. This can be a pro or a con. The con is, if you wanted the cross-reference gone completely, you now have to find that now-standard text source cross-reference and manually delete it. On the other hand, if you want to keep a cross-reference but one that isn't dynamically updated and managed via the panel, you have it; deleting the entry on the Cross-References panel leaves the text as it was last written, page number and all, but as nondynamic text.

You can also directly edit even dynamic, functioning source cross-references just like other text. However, if the cross-reference is updated or relinked, your manual styling gets reversed faster than Conan O'Brien's *Tonight Show* contract.

CROSS-REFERENCE WARNINGS AND FIXES

Cross-references and their source text automatically update page numbers, chapter numbers, and so on to reflect changes to the destination text or its host document. However, if the destination text's paragraph has been edited, InDesign considers the cross-reference out of date. In such cases you'll see a yellow caution sign appear beside the cross-reference in the Cross-References panel. Preflight and Live Preflight will also warn that one or more cross-references

However, it also means that, should you use the same word in another document, spell check will once again call into question the competence of your third grade teacher.

Language   The Language dropdown list is not the complete list you'll find at the bottom of the Character panel. This one is filtered down to just the dictionaries in use in the current document. If a word somewhere in the story is assigned to the German: 1996 Reform dictionary, that will appear as a target language here.

Dictionary List   Choose from this list whether you want to see below and edit words you've added to the dictionary, words you've removed from the dictionary, or words you've ignored via the Check Spelling Ignore All button. I love the last option because sometimes you click Ignore All overzealously. By choosing to edit that list in the Dictionary dialog, you can tell InDesign to stop ignoring the word.

Word   Depending on which dictionary list is active, here is where you type the word to add to, remove from, or ignore in the dictionary. It's also where hyphenation exceptions are specified (we'll get to that in just a moment). Note that the Case Sensitive check box at the bottom is often important when adding words.

HYPHENATION EXCEPTIONS

Entering a word as unadorned text—like `alliteration`—leaves the hyphenation to InDesign's internal and somewhat sensible syllable sensing system. Believe it or not, it's actually pretty good. Sometimes, though, InDesign's hyphenation choices don't jibe with yours. In those cases, you'll need to override it. At the very least, you may want a preview of how InDesign will hyphenate. Clicking the Hyphenate button will give you that preview. Thus, after you type in *alliteration*, the Hyphenate button will transform it into *al~lit~~er~~~a~tion*.

Confused? Allow me to explain.

You see, InDesign sagaciously understands that there's a difference between discretionary hyphens—potential breaks in words at the end of a line of text—and always-visible hyphens in compound words like *single-page*. Thus, entering an actual hyphen in the Word field makes that hyphen *always* appear in the word—there's nothing discretionary about it. Discretionary hyphens are represented by tildes (~), and the number of tildes prioritizes hyphenation. In the example *al~lit~~er~~~a~tion*, InDesign will first try to break the word between *er* and *a*. If that isn't feasible, it will attempt to break between *lit* and *er* before breaking at the single-tilde points. Tildes equal hyphenation priority; the more tildes, the more InDesign will seek to break the word at that point. If, in some crazy layout, InDesign has to break the same word multiple times, it will do so according to the priority established by the tildes if possible.

To override InDesign's idea of hyphenation priority, change the number of tildes. The Word field is entirely editable, so you can add or remove tildes to your heart's content. If, for example, I wanted to ensure that *alliteration* was only hyphenated at one point if at all, I could enter this: *alliter~ation*.

To prevent hyphenation of a word altogether, remove the tildes throughout, but precede the entire word with a tilde, like so: *~alliteration*. If InDesign can do anything but break the word, it will therefore leave it intact. Note that, if InDesign has no other choice, it will still break the word according to its internal understanding of syllables. For instance, if you set *alliteration* in a column too narrow to hold the entire word, either InDesign will break it despite a directive to the contrary, or it will elect to overset the rest of the story beginning with that word. Which is chosen is primarily based on how nice you've been to InDesign lately.

SHARING DICTIONARIES

Using the Import and Export buttons in the Dictionary dialog, it's easy to share dictionaries between users. If you work solo on disparate projects, you'll probably have little use for this. But, if you're a member of a workgroup that regularly uses custom words or hyphenation exceptions, the ability to export dictionaries to text files and import from the same is a huge time-saver.

As one means of improving workflow efficiency, I always recommend that workgroups assign one member as the Keeper of the Lists. If your group deals with the same nondictionary or special hyphenation rule words again and again, designate someone to maintain in her copy of InDesign (or InCopy, since dictionaries can be shared between them as easily as between installations of InDesign) all the proper names, acronyms, and other special words and hyphenation exceptions needed by the typical documents produced in the workgroup or department. Every time that list updates, the Keeper of the List should export her list to a central repository—probably the file server—and alert the rest of the group to reimport the master dictionary list, merging it into their existing dictionaries. Using this method, no one in the group need suffer delays in a spell check run with stops on the CEO's name, the *camel case* product name (e.g., InDesign), or the contracting government agency's acronym.

Dynamic Spelling

Dynamic spelling is what we humans do; InDesign does dynamic spell *checking*. Semantics aside, activating this feature by choosing Edit ➤ Spelling ➤ Dynamic Spelling tells InDesign to check spelling in the layout (and story editor) without having to wait until it's time to run Check Spelling. Dynamic Spelling will run through the document, comparing text already in the document against the dictionary as well as doing the same on the fly as you type.

Misspelled words will be underlined with a red squiggly line whereas capitalization errors will be underlined with squiggly green lines (see Figure 8.38). Right-clicking (Control-clicking for you single-button-mouse Mac users) on a word bearing such an underline offers suggested alternates as well as the ability to ignore the word, add it to the dictionary, and open the Dictionary dialog.

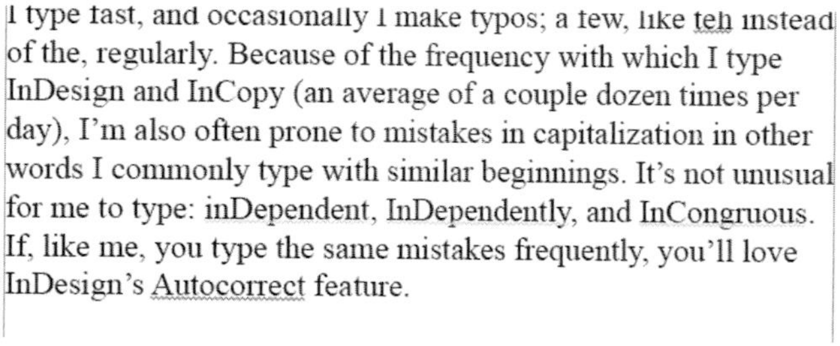

FIGURE 8.38
With Dynamic Spelling active, misspelled words are underlined and spelling-specific options replace the normal context-sensitive menu.

I type fast, and occasionally I make typos; a few, like teh instead of the, regularly. Because of the frequency with which I type InDesign and InCopy (an average of a couple dozen times per day), I'm also often prone to mistakes in capitalization in other words I commonly type with similar beginnings. It's not unusual for me to type: inDependent, InDependently, and InCongruous. If, like me, you type the same mistakes frequently, you'll love InDesign's Autocorrect feature.

Autocorrect

I type fast, and occasionally I make typos; a few, like *teh* instead of *the*, regularly. Because of the frequency with which I type *InDesign* and *InCopy* (an average of a couple dozen times per day), I'm also often prone to mistakes in capitalization in other words I commonly type with similar beginnings. It's not unusual for me to type *InDependent*, *InDependently*, and *InCongruous*. If, like me, you type the same mistakes frequently, you'll love InDesign's Autocorrect feature.

Enabled with the Edit ➢ Spelling ➢ Autocorrect command but edited in the Autocorrect pane of Preferences, Autocorrect replaces one word with another as you type. The options are simple. In the Autocorrect Preferences, click the Add button to open a dialog where you can enter the misspelled word for which InDesign should search and the correction with which to replace it (see Figure 8.39). The Misspelled Word field accepts letters, numbers, and basic punctuation but not spaces. The Correction field, however, *does* accept spaces, which enables you to fix oft mistakenly combined words—for instance, *atleast* should be *at least*.

To fix my occupational hazard *InD-* and *InC-* capitalization errors, I enable the check box at the top of the pane, Autocorrect Capitalization Errors.

Edit autocorrect pairs you've already created by double-clicking a row in the list.

If you're like most people, you're hoping I won't say what comes next: Autocorrect is not retroactive. It replaces as you type but won't touch text already in the document. Nor will it fix mistakes in placed or pasted text. To change those, you need Find/Change.

FIGURE 8.39
Adding an Autocorrect rule, with the Autocorrect Preferences pane behind it

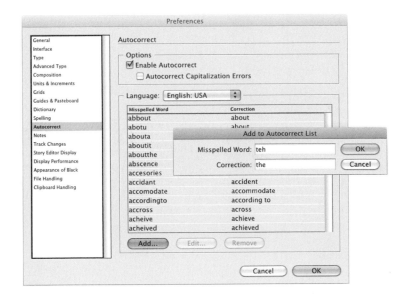

Find/Change

Far from the average application's Find/Change utility, InDesign's is a powerhouse with the ability to save and reuse searches, search across multiple documents simultaneously, and, best of all, use GREP expressions for remarkable search-and-replace capability using pattern matching.

Open Find/Change from the Edit menu with or without an object or text selected. At the top are several example queries. Adobe saw fit to preload the Query dropdown list with high-utility examples such as replacing two carriage returns (common in placed stories) with the single carriage return required by clean, professional layouts, replacing hyphens and double-hyphens with en and em dashes, and more (see Figure 8.40).

To save your own query for later reuse, click the disk icon beside the list. Prune the list with the trashcan delete button.

FIGURE 8.40
Preset saved queries
in Find/Change

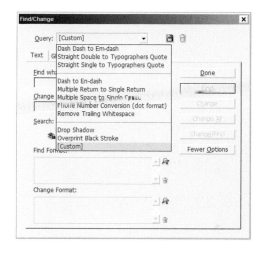

TEXT

Each of the tabs in the Find/Change dialog does something a little different, so let's start with
the Text tab (see Figure 8.41):

FIGURE 8.41
Find/Change Text tab

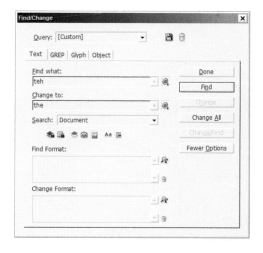

Find What and Change To   Enter in the Find What field the text to replace and in the
Change To the text to replace it with. Both fields have dropdown lists of recently used previous values as a convenience. Additionally, both fields have Special Characters menus to the
right (see Figure 8.42). Using these menus, you can search for just about any text you can
imagine, including symbols, dashes, every type of space and break InDesign can insert, and
even wildcards like any digit, which finds any number between 0 and 9, any letter—*A–Z*,
a–z—and any character whatsoever—from letters to numbers, punctuation to dingbats.

FIGURE 8.42
The Special Characters menu for the Find What field

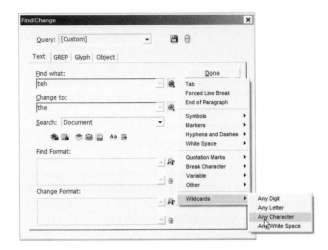

FAMILIAR METACHARACTER SEARCH CODES

Items from the special character menu are inserted as caret code metacharacters similar to the codes in Word. If you're familiar with Word, however, be advised that they are not always the same codes. For instance, ^t is a tab in both, but a manual line break (aka forced line break), which breaks the line but not the paragraph, is ^l in Word and ^n in InDesign. I caution you to become familiar with InDesign's unique Find/Change codes rather than typing in your commonly used Word Find and Replace codes.

Search   Select what you'd like to search—selected text (if any), the current story, from the cursor to the end of the story, the entire document including all stories and frames, or all stories and text frames in all open documents.

Include Locked Layers   Check this to *search* text on layers locked in the Layer Options dialog (see Figure 8.43). Even with it checked, you cannot *replace* text on locked layers. Unlock the layer prior to running Find/Change.

FIGURE 8.43
Close-up of the find options buttons

Include Locked Stories   This option searches for, but will not replace, text among stories that are locked because of being checked out (by other users) in InCopy workflows or version-control software like the now defunct Version Cue.

Include Hidden Layers   On nonvisible layers, you *can* search *and* replace, but the layer will not be made visible. When you're performing an incremental search and replace using the Find or Change button instead of Change All, the search text will be highlighted on the hidden layer without making the layer visible—basically, you'll see a highlight with nothing highlighted.

Include Master Pages   Check this option to also search and replace through objects contained on master pages.

Include Footnotes   Check this option to also search and replace within footnote text. To search for footnote reference numbers, choose that option from the special characters menu under Markers.

Case Sensitive   When this option is disabled, the contents of the Find What text triggers matches regardless of capitalization. For instance, a search for *InDesign* with Case Sensitive disabled will also find *indesign*, *INDESIGN*, and *Indesign*. With the option enabled, only instances of *InDesign* would be found.

Whole Word   Whole Word will find only exact, whole word matches to the Find What text. This option is disabled by default, meaning that a search for *red* will find not only the whole word but also where *red* appears in other words, such as in *appeared*, *redefine*, and *colored*.

More/Fewer Options   Show or hide the Find Format and Change Format areas.

Find Format and Change Format   Using the Specify Attributes to Find button to the right of the Find Format and Change Format fields enables you to replace any possible character or paragraph formatting attribute, including predefined character and paragraph styles, fonts, colors, indents, OpenType options, bullets and numbering, drop caps, and any other style attribute you may have applied to text and now want to use to narrow the search, add to Find What text, or replace with another (or no) attribute. To remove formatting options from the search or replace criteria, click the trashcan icon beside the appropriate field.

Find/Find Next   Find the first instance of the search text matching the Find What field, with the formatting and search options specified, if any. InDesign will highlight the found text and await further instruction. Once the first instance is found, this button changes from Find to Find Next.

Change   Replace only the selected instance with the Change To field contents.

Change/Find   Replace the selected instance and immediately find the next.

Change All   Automatically find all instances of the Find What text and replace with the Change To text.

GREP

Just in case you're not an über l33t Unix geek, GREP is an acronym (and resulting command) from that world meaning "Search *g*lobally for lines matching the *re*gular *e*xpression and *p*rint them [to screen]." (I suppose GREP is easier to remember than the full acronym for the directive—SGLMREPT). Despite its intimidating meaning and origin, GREP is incredibly powerful,

allowing you to search for and replace just about anything you could possibly type in InDesign with a tremendous number of variables.

The GREP Find/Change tab is very similar to the Text tab, as you can see in Figure 8.44. On the Text tab, variables and metacharacters are specified using caret codes. With GREP, it's a tilde (˜) or backslash (\), but the distinction goes beyond mere syntax differences.

The difference between the normal search and/or replace with variables on the Text tab and a GREP search is the scope of variable data. On the Text tab, it's easy to search for something like *Figure* X.y. The Find What field in that case would be Figure ^9.^9, with ^9 being the code for any digit. In a GREP search, the same Find What would be Figure \d.\d. But, with GREP, you can go far beyond replacing the text and issue an order to find Figure X.y only under certain other conditions—say, only if it appears at the beginning of a paragraph, as would be the case in a figure caption but not in a reference to the figure within body copy (using an option from the Locations list in the Special Characters menu beside the Find What field).

Below the Change To field and the Search field to define scope is a subset of the Text tab's find options consisting of the buttons to search locked or hidden layers, locked stories, master pages, and footnotes. The absent options are not relevant to GREP's pattern-matching searches.

FIGURE 8.44
Find/Change
GREP tab

GLYPH

On the Glyph tab of Find/Change (see Figure 8.45), individual glyphs can be sniffed out and/or replaced—a handy utility for changing glyph typefaces or styling options or replacing a euro symbol (€) with a dollar sign ($), such as might be needed when prepping the Berlin office's European catalog for a North American release. If you know the Unicode or GID/CID code for the glyph, choose the appropriate system in the ID dropdown, and then enter the code to its right. If not, then use the arrow beside the Glyph field to pop up a mini Glyphs panel for visual searching. Set the desired Font Family and Font Style values for either or both Find or Change and go.

FIGURE 8.45
Find/Change
Glyph tab

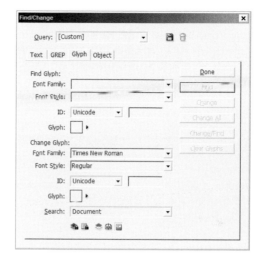

OBJECT

The Object Find/Replace tab is truly revolutionary. You can actually search and replace the graphic characteristics of objects! Want to find all frames with a .25 pt thick, 50% black stroke? No problem. Do you need to globally alter the text wrap around all inline frames? Easy as pie. Did the client come back and ask you to change every two-column text frame across the 300-page document to three columns? With Find/Change's Object tab, even that daunting task won't take more than a few seconds.

At the bottom of the Object tab, choose what to search out—text, graphic, unassigned, or all frames, and, just above it, the scope of the search (see Figure 8.46).

FIGURE 8.46
Find/Change
Object tab

The rest of the tab is all object formatting. Click the Specify Attributes button (with the magnifying glass) beside either of the Format fields to open the Find (or Change) Object Format Options (see Figure 8.47), which is virtually identical to the Object Style Options dialog. You can search for and replace any object-level attribute—including transparency and transparency effects. Days of changes can be effected in minutes. If you're management, the ramifications of this new feature should become immediately obvious to you. If you're an hourly employee, don't tell management about Object Find/Change.

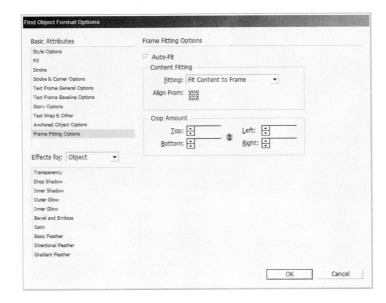

FIGURE 8.47
Find Object Format Options enables searching for any object-level attribute, including effects.

Objects created ad hoc can be assigned to defined object styles, too. Thus objects can be readied for even more expedient update.

Replacing Fonts

Although in all Find/Change modes except Object you can replace font families and styles, InDesign has a dedicated utility better suited to that purpose. On the Type menu, Find Font presents a list of all fonts in use in the document (see Figure 8.48). Not only is the user interface more conducive to the task of replacing one typeface with another, but it can optionally redefine style definitions as well—something Find/Change can't.

All fonts currently in use in the document are listed at the top, with counts just below the list. To replace one typeface with another, click on the in-use entry in the list, and then choose the font family and font style for the replacement at the bottom. If the typeface is part of a style definition (or might be), check Redefine Style When Changing All to also update the style definition. The benefits to that option, of course, are that paragraph and character styles can be used freely without reintroducing the undesired typeface, and neither will clearing overrides on text to which the styles have been defined. Once your options are set, choose what to do. The various Find and Change buttons work similarly to Find/Change. For instance, Find First will locate the first occurrence of the selected typeface, jumping the document window to display the text that is the first instance.

The text will also be highlighted. Change All will replace all instances of the typeface except those embedded in placed EPS, PDF, AI, and INDD documents, which InDesign cannot access.

FIGURE 8.48

Find Font replaces typefaces and redefines styles too.

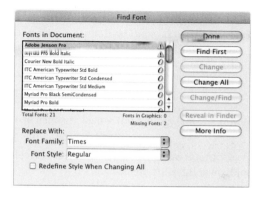

To change fonts embedded in placed assets, locate the needed images. Then use the Edit Original command on the Links panel to open the assets in their creation applications and replace the font there.

Reveal in Finder (Mac) or Reveal in Explorer (Windows) will pop open a file system window zeroed in on the folder containing the font file. This is useful, for example, when you need to copy the font for emailing, deleting, or repairing (all outside of InDesign, of course).

The More Info/Less Info button toggles the Info area at the bottom of the Find Font dialog (see Figure 8.49). In the Info section you can see important information about a given font, including its type, version, embedding restrictions, path, and, most useful of all, which paragraph and character styles include the font as part of their definitions.

FIGURE 8.49

The Info area of Find Font provides valuable insight into a font and its usage in the current document.

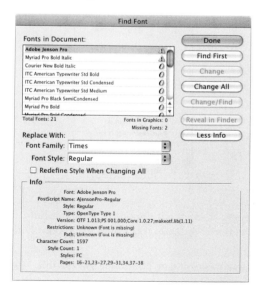

The Bottom Line

Thread and Unthread Text Frames and Flow Text   Threaded text frames are the foundation of multipage documents, and, whether manual, auto, or semi-auto, flowing text is the way to pour that foundation.

Master It   Create a new document with a two-column master page text frame and employ the skills learned in this chapter to lay out a multipage Word or other text document. There should be no overset text when you've finished.

Create Bulleted and Numbered Lists   InDesign offers creative and structural control in updated bullets and numbering features and the Lists property.

Master It   In a new document, use Lists and Bullets and Numbering to re-create the headings from this chapter's section "Threading and Unthreading Text Frames" as a hierarchical list.

Write and Word Process in InDesign   The world is changing, and writing and editing in the layout application is no longer a crazy idea.

Master It   Write content directly in a new InDesign document layout view such that, as you type and format your text, pages are automatically added and removed. If you have trouble coming up with subject matter, try perhaps a new version of your resume, your next blog post, a short essay on what you've learned from this book, or an editorial opinion arguing your side of the debate regarding whether Lindsay Lohan, Tara Reid, and Paris Hilton should be launched into deep space or fed to Godzilla.

Reference Different Places in the Document with Footnotes, Endnotes, and Cross-References   Referencing one part of a document from another and providing additional information about a subject outside the main flow of a story are important functions of a great many types of publications, both print and electronic. InDesign includes robust support for footnotes and cross-references, and, with the use of an easy technique, even endnotes can be created, though InDesign doesn't officially have support for endnotes.

Master It   Working from the document you created in the last Master It exercise, find appropriate content to add to your document as endnotes, and then create those endnotes.

Fix, Find, and Change Text and More   In addition to beefing up its already solid text support systems of spell checking, hyphenation, and Autocorrect, InDesign includes a Find/Change with incredible capabilities.

Master It   Using the two-column, multipage document created just a few moments ago, use the Find/Change features to convert the text frame to three columns with a 0.25-inch column gutter. At the same time, give the text frames a semitransparent background color (while keeping the text fully opaque) and a frame inset.

Chapter 9

Documents

Working with documents involves knowing how to move around in them, change viewing options, and compare views. Working with longer documents efficiently means mastering InDesign's unique long-document features such as indexing, creating tables of contents, and working within the time-saving and collaboration-ready atmosphere of book files.

In this chapter, you will learn to

- Interact with documents visually and change zoom level, view modes, and display performance

- Employ page transitions for PDF and SWF output

- Build and manage grids and guides

- Work with object-oriented layers

- Create and manage book files

- Index terms and create an index

- Create tables of contents

Seeing Your Work

Seeing your work is important (duh!). InDesign CS5 offers numerous ways of viewing and interacting with documents and objects to help you work as efficiently and quickly as possible.

Zooming

There are many, many (many) ways to zoom in or out in InDesign, letting you see as much or as little of a document as you need for both macro- and micro-focused work.

First, of course, is the Zoom tool (located near the bottom of the Tools panel), which, predictably, looks like a magnifying glass. Click it once to zoom in by predefined increments; Opt+click/Alt+click to zoom out by the same increments. To zoom in on a particular area, click and drag with the Zoom tool. InDesign will then fit the rectangular area defined by your dragging in the window, zooming until the width and/or height of the area fits snugly within the document view window. Clicking and dragging while holding Option/Alt has the same effect in zooming out.

Double-click the Zoom tool icon itself on the Tools panel to reset the view to 100% magnification. Double-click the Hand tool just above (or beside if your Tools panel is two columns wide) to fit the entire spread in view.

In the Application bar, just to the right of the Go to Bridge button, is the Zoom Level field. It displays the current zoom percentage, and its accompanying arrow offers a dropdown full of common preset magnification levels (see Figure 9.1). If nothing on the list suits your needs, type a custom percentage into the Zoom Level field. While working with documents in the default tabbed layout, where each document is accessible via a tab beneath the Control panel, the current view's zoom percentage is also displayed to the right of the document name in the title tab.

FIGURE 9.1
The zoom percentage field

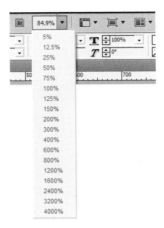

If your hands are on the keyboard already, save a trip to the mouse by using the universal zoom in and zoom out keyboard shortcuts of Cmd+/Ctrl++ (Cmd/Ctrl and the plus sign on the regular, main part of the keyboard, as opposed to the numeric keypad) and Cmd+-/Ctrl+- (Cmd/Ctrl and the hyphen) respectively. Cmd+0/Ctrl+0 fits the entire page onscreen. Other common zooming keyboard shortcuts are in the upper half of the View menu. One you won't find there is Cmd+Option+2/Ctrl+Alt+2, which toggles between the last two zoom states. For example, if you zoomed in to 800% to work on the detail of a vector path, and then pulled out to the full-page view to see the effect of your work on the overall page, pressing Cmd+Option+2/Ctrl+Alt+2 would return you to the same spot at 800% to resume your detail work.

An extra nifty bonus to InDesign CS5 is that now the zoom keyboard shortcuts work while dialog boxes are open! I can't count the number of times I've opened a dialog box only to realize I need to zoom in or out to really see the effect of the controls I'm changing. Now, instead of closing the dialog, changing zoom level, and then going back to the same dialog, you can use Cmd+/Ctrl++ and Cmd+-/Ctrl+- even while dialog boxes are opened. *Hazzah!*

CS5

BY MAGELLAN'S BEARD, WHERE IS MY NAVIGATOR PANEL?

If you're looking for the Navigator panel, which enabled you to move around and zoom based on a thumbnail presentation of your current spread, you can stop looking. It fell off the edge of the map. InDesign CS4 did away with it. And hardly anybody noticed.

Arranging Document Windows

In 2003 I worked the HOW Design Conference for Adobe. One of the sessions I attended while not working the stump-the-expert Adobe Help Booth was one in which the speaker vehemently decried the evils of multitasking. It was counterproductive, she said, and then backed up her claim with worrisome scientific evidence detailing the harmful effects of multitasking on concentration levels, productivity, and even permanent damage to our short-term memory faculties. As well meaning as the speaker was, as convincing as her evidence, I doubt anyone who heeded her advice was able to swear off multitasking for long. I would like to say I was able to, but as I write this chapter I'm also simultaneously editing another chapter, thinking about the best way to present the topic of exporting to interactive PDF in the next chapter, answering InDesign-, InCopy-, Photoshop-, and Illustrator-related questions on Twitter, trying to figure out what my wife and I are going to have for lunch today, and, in InDesign itself, I have six documents opened related to everything above except the choice of dining establishments (that's facilitated by 6 of the 30-odd tabs I have open in my Web browser). Multitasking is the way of the modern world. There's no getting away from it, even if it is bad for you—like milk, red meat, sunshine, or whatever is this week's what-you-thought-was-so-healthy-scientists-now-say-could-be-killing-you proclamation.

If you're one of the rare exceptions who has managed to eliminate multitasking (and milk, red meat, and sunshine) from her life, feel free to skip this section. However, if you're like the rest of us, doing more and more and more with less and less and less time, you'll probably want to learn about how InDesign helps you work most efficiently on multiple documents.

You probably already know that InDesign can open multiple documents at one time. It's always been what we call an MDI, a multiple document interface. Those documents can be arranged in front of one another, so that only one document appears on screen at a time, or cascaded, such that each document's window is smaller than the one behind it, showing all title bars at once. Some documents can be minimized and hidden from the screen entirely. And then there are a dizzying number of ways to display multiple documents onscreen simultaneously.

By default, all InDesign documents are opened maximized, with a tab beneath the Control panel identifying the document title and zoom percentage and containing a Close Document button (see Figure 9.2). Navigating between opened documents is simply a matter of clicking the tabs. To go back to the old style of window arrangement, where each document window floated independently of the others, choose Window ➤ Arrange ➤ Float All in Windows. Choosing Window ➤ Arrange ➤ Float in Window floats merely the active window, enabling you resize and arrange it, while any other opened documents remain maximized and tabbed. Returning to the default tabbed behavior is as simple as choosing Window ➤ Arrange ➤ Consolidate All Windows.

FIGURE 9.2

The default view of document windows is maximized and tabbed.

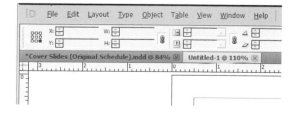

Now when you want to see multiple documents at once, which is crucial for such tasks as visually comparing document versions or dragging pages from one document into another, you'll want to use the Window ➤ Arrange ➤ Tile command. Tile will evenly divide the available application space among the opened documents; if you have two documents, they'll be side-by-side, each taking up half the available space; if you have four documents opened, they'll quarter the screen. The result will be a grid of documents, and that grid can be manually resized at your whim. Just position your cursor over the frame between document windows, click, and drag; you will simultaneously shrink the window(s) on one side of the frame while enlarging the view into the window(s) on the other side.

If the Tile command doesn't give you the most convenient layout, try the 20 different window layouts available as buttons on the Application bar's Arrange Documents menu (see Figure 9.3). You can arrange two or more document windows as rows that evenly divide the available space vertically, as columns that divide it horizontally, as evenly distributed cells in a multirow, multicolumn grid, or as a number of layouts that give more space to the selected document and divide the remaining space among the other windows. However you need to view multiple documents, InDesign can accommodate you with a minimum of work.

FIGURE 9.3
The Arrange Documents menu on the Application bar

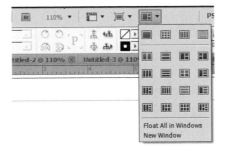

Note that if you choose a layout that contains options for fewer documents than you have opened—say, the 6-Up arrangement while you have eight documents opened—any documents that don't fit will be tabbed together with their nearest neighbor.

Multiple Windows for the Same Document

Many times it's necessary to work on multiple pages concurrently, or to at least keep another page or another zoom percentage in view while working. Just as, if not more, common is the need to preview a document in one window while working on it in another or to compare the colors on the page in two proofing modes. InDesign allows you to open the same document in multiple views, which can then be tiled or arranged, automatically or manually, just as if they were views into completely separate documents (see Figure 9.4).

To open a new document view, choose Window ➤ Arrange ➤ New Window. Arrange the windows as you like, changing zoom levels, display performances, preview modes, and pages independently of one another. Any changes to document content in one view will instantly reflect in the other.

FIGURE 9.4
Multiple windowed views of the same document, in this case, using different view modes and zoom levels

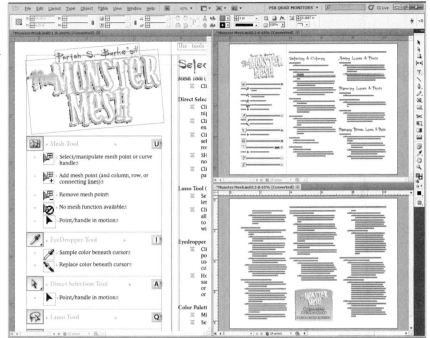

Display Performance

InDesign uses an advanced rendering engine called the Adobe Graphics Engine to create true *WYSIWYG* onscreen previews of object resolution, placement, and interaction (color accuracy depends on your hardware and color management settings). Naturally, rendering everything at true resolution and color can cause longer page drawing times, especially while moving around or zooming in and out on graphically rich pages. Most of the time, you don't need to work in true WYSIWYG; most of the time, a very good approximation of artwork using lower-resolution proxies is all you need.

DISPLAY PERFORMANCE MODES

By default, InDesign displays pages and objects onscreen as lower-resolution proxy images, which InDesign itself generates on the fly. Their positioning is accurate, but resolution, transparency interaction, color, and visual detail are diminished to reduce the work required of the video card and RAM. Balancing quality with speed, this is InDesign's Typical Display display performance setting.

There are two others (see Figure 9.5).

High-Quality Display renders everything to screen as true WYSIWYG. Do check this mode before finalizing a document, but performing all your work in High-Quality Display, especially with 300 to 1200 dpi or higher images, will lengthen the time it takes to change pages and views.

Fast Display is lightning quick because it replaces all images with gray boxes, dramatically reducing the workload of the video card when you're changing pages or views.

FIGURE 9.5
The same image as shown in the different display performance settings: (from left to right) Fast Display, Typical Display, and High-Quality Display

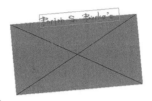

All three are found on the View ➢ Display Performance menu, as are options governing object-level display settings.

DISPLAY PERFORMANCE OPTIONS

If Typical is too mundane for you while High-Quality is just too high, you can adjust them, raising one or lowering the other, to reach that Goldilocks zone. Open up InDesign's Preferences (Cmd+K/Ctrl+K) and navigate to the Display Performance pane (see Figure 9.6). There you can change the default display performance option (at the top) or fine-tune exactly what it means to be in Fast, Typical, or High-Quality display performance mode. To change options, choose the view setting you want to tweak from the Adjust View Settings menu, and then adjust the speed-versus-quality sliders that control the display of pixel-based raster images, vector paths and type, and areas affected by transparency. Lastly, you can enable or disable anti-aliasing of the edges of type (anti-aliasing looks smoother onscreen but takes longer to draw) and the size at which, when zoomed, type will cease being shown as glyphs and simply become gray patterns.

FIGURE 9.6
The Display Performance Preferences pane

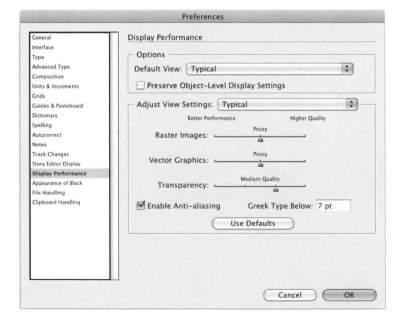

OBJECT-LEVEL DISPLAY SETTINGS

Each placed image may have its own individual display performance setting—Fast, Typical, or High-Quality Display—specific to that image and instance. Accessed from the context-sensitive menu available by right-clicking an image, this option allows you to display a single image at its true resolution (High-Quality Display) or to gray out onscreen a large or overly complicated image for faster response from the application as you work (Fast Display). Both are independent of the document-wide Display Performance setting.

In order for object-level display performance to be available from the context-sensitive menu, that option must be enabled on View ➤ Display Performance, which it is by default. To remove all image-specific display performance settings, restoring all objects to the document's setting, choose View ➤ Display Performance ➤ Clear Object-Level Display Settings.

View Modes

InDesign CS5 has five view modes accessible from View ➤ Screen Mode, the Screen Mode menu on the Application bar, and the bottom of the Tools panel (see Figure 9.7). The modes may be selected from the Tools panel by clicking and holding on the icon of the currently displayed mode, which will pop open the list of modes shown in the figure. Additionally, holding Option/Alt while clicking the display mode button will cycle through the five modes one at a time. If you have your Tools panel set to two-column display, Normal mode will be a button by itself, while the four preview modes share a place beside it. You can also simply press the W key on your keyboard (when not editing text, of course) to toggle between Normal and the last selected preview mode (except Presentation mode).

FIGURE 9.7
View modes at
the bottom of
the Tools panel

Normal   The normal working mode. Pasteboard, guides, and grids are shown, as are frame edges, text threads, and other elements if individually set to show on the View menu.

Preview   Only the page trim area is visible, and pasteboard, guides, grids, frame edges, text threads, and so on are all hidden. If an object is selected in Preview mode, its bounding box will become visible.

Bleed   Similar to Preview with the addition of including the bleed area in the view.

Slug   Similar to Preview, but includes both the bleed and slug areas.

Presentation   Choosing this mode will hide the panels, toolbars, and other "chrome" of the application, displaying pages of the current document full screen on a black background.

Presentation Mode

`CS5`

Presentation mode turns InDesign into a basic slideshow presenter. It's ideal for over-the-shoulder proofing to your boss or collaborators, or even for bypassing PDF export altogether to deliver slideshows in front of an assembly. Despite the fact that I speak at InDesign and other creative professional conferences, appear before InDesign and other user groups, and present slideshows in many of my near-weekly consulting and training engagements, I haven't actually touched PowerPoint in years. Instead, I design my slides in InDesign and then export to PDF, using Acrobat's Full Screen mode (Cmd+L/Ctrl+L) to present my slides. Now with CS5, I don't even bother with Acrobat half the time—which saves me stressful steps when fixing a typo discovered at the last moment.

If I want page transitions like a wipe, split, or fade effect, though, I have to revert to exporting my slides to PDF and using Acrobat to present them. It's lame, but Presentation mode will not show page transitions assigned to spreads in InDesign; those work only when the InDesign document has been exported to PDF or SWF (see below for more on page transitions).

Still, even without the ability to display nifty effects to move from the presentment of one page to the next, Presentation mode is very cool and very much needed. Again, you can enter Presentation mode from the various places where you can change to any view mode, but you can also use the keyboard shortcut Shift+W to toggle between Normal and Presentation modes. Table 9.1 shows the other shortcuts and controls you'll need to know to work effectively within Presentation mode.

TABLE 9.1:   Presentation mode controls

CONTROL	RESULT
Shift+W	Enter Presentation mode
Shift+W, Esc	Exit Presentation mode
B	Change the screen background color to black
G	Change the screen background color to 50% gray
W	Change the screen background color to white
Home	Jump to first spread

TABLE 9.1: Presentation mode controls *(CONTINUED)*

CONTROL	RESULT
End	Jump to last spread
Right-arrow, Down-arrow, Page Down, click	Move to next spread
Left-arrow, Up-arrow, Page Up, Shift-click	Move to previous spread

Page Transitions

When you *are* creating presentations for PDF or Flash Player SWF, or, more likely, when you're ready to embrace the undeniable future that traditional print publishing must also encompass new media output and magazines that want to survive will not plan entirely on being read as ink on paper, you may want to employ effects that jazz up the passage of one slide or page to the next. That's page transitions.

InDesign includes a dozen page transition effects, as you can see in the Figure 9.8 view of the Page Transitions dialog box. With the exception of the ubercool, almost certain to become cliché Page Turn, which creates a realistic turning of the page animation in Flash SWF only, all the page transitions may be applied to PDFs or SWFs.

FIGURE 9.8
The Page Transitions dialog box shows the available page transitions all at once.

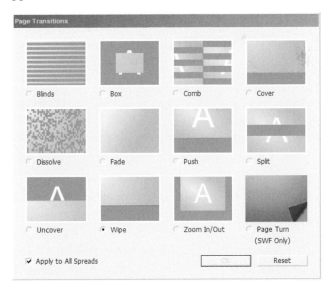

Adding page transitions to your publication is easy:

1. Beginning with a multipage document, select one or more pages in the Pages panel.

2. Either right-click a selected page and choose Page Transitions ➢ Choose, or select the same command from the Page Transitions menu on the Pages panel flyout menu. Up will pop the Page Transitions dialog.

3. Hold your mouse cursor over the thumbnail of each transition to see a short animation that previews the transition effect. When you've found one you like, select its radio button.

   You can apply a different transition to each page, or, by enabling the Apply to All Spreads option, apply your chosen transition to every spread in the document, selected or not.

4. When you click OK, you'll be brought back to the Pages panel, where a new icon will appear beside spreads that have transitions assigned them (see Figure 9.9).

FIGURE 9.09
Page Transition icons indicate that their adjacent spreads are assigned transitions.

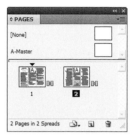

5. Now, to fine-tune the transitions, open the new Page Transitions panel by choosing Window ➤ Interactive➤ Page Transitions (see Figure 9.10). There you can also set transitions—because of the panel, there's no longer a genuine need to open the Page Transitions dialog box, but I like the dialog because it lets you see all the transitions at once rather than having to select them from a menu, like the panel's, before you can see their thumbnails and preview animations. You can change the direction and speed of transition effects with the menu options.

FIGURE 9.10
The Page Transitions panel

Again, transitions and their options can be applied to individual spreads or, by using the Apply to All Spreads command from the Page Transitions panel flyout menu, to the entire document.

6. Now export your document to interactive PDF or SWF to complete your presentation or epublication.

A few other things to keep in mind:

♦ If you'd rather not see the page transition icons in the Pages panel, they're easily disabled via the panel options (Pages Panel flyout menu, Panel Options command).

◆ You can remove individual spread transitions by choosing the None transition from the Page Transitions panel.

◆ To remove transitions from all pages, use the Clear All command on the Page Transitions panel flyout menu or on the Pages panel flyout menu in the Page Transitions submenu.

◆ Choosing Edit from the latter when a page contains a transition effect opens the Page Transitions panel.

In true InDesign fashion, there's a third location for all of these same commands, which would be Layout ➤ Pages ➤ Page Transitions. I left it unmentioned until now so you wouldn't have to read befuddling directives like "to remove transitions from all pages, use the Clear All command on the Page Transitions panel flyout menu, on the Pages panel flyout menu in the Page Transitions submenu, or on the Layout ➤ Pages ➤ Page Transitions menu."

Guides and Grids

Well-designed documents are based on grids, and grids are composed of ruler guides.

Guide Basics

If you've used InDesign or just about any other creative application for any length of time, you probably already know how to create ruler guides. Click and drag from either the vertical or horizontal ruler; wherever you release the mouse button, a guide will drop. Beyond this fundamental, InDesign has a few tricks of which you might not be aware.

Hold Cmd/Ctrl while dragging from the vertex of the two rulers to simultaneously create both a horizontal and vertical guide (see Figure 9.11). Dragging the intersection point of the rulers *without* holding Cmd/Ctrl moves the origin or zero-point of the ruler.

FIGURE 9.11
Dragging from the intersection of the rulers while holding Cmd/Ctrl creates both guides at once.

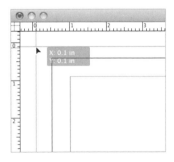

Where a guide falls depends on the location of your cursor when you let go of the mouse button. If your cursor is within a page, the guide will land on, and be unique to, that page. However, if your cursor is out on the pasteboard at the time, dropping a horizontal guide from the horizontal ruler will create a guide that spans the spread, however many pages that may be.

Guides can be hidden and shown in a couple of ways. First, of course, they disappear in Preview mode. They can also be deliberately hidden by changing the toggle command Hide/Show Guides from View ➤ Grids & Guides or by using the equivalent keyboard shortcut of Cmd+;/Ctrl+;. Additionally, because guides are considered objects of a sort in InDesign, they

are layer specific; hiding a layer on which guides were drawn hides the guides as well. Unlike Illustrator, however, after whose Layers panel InDesign's was patterned, guides are not shown as selectable objects.

By default, guides are not locked. That means that if you don't get a guide exactly where you want it upon initially dragging and dropping it from the ruler, you can simply click the guide to select it and then precisely position it using the X and Y positioning fields on the Transform or Control panels, just like any other object. You can also delete them just as easily—select the guide and press the Delete or Backspace key on your keyboard. Alternatively, dragging a guide back into its spawning ruler will also delete or unmake the guide, if you prefer a creepier way of looking at it.

You can also eradicate all guides on the current spread in one fell swoop with the WMD-like View ➤ Grids & Guides ➤ Delete All Guides on Spread command.

If you'd rather not risk accidentally moving or deleting your guides, choose the command View ➤ Grids & Guides ➤ Lock Guides. Guides can also be locked selectively per layer. To do that, select the desired layer in the Layers panel, choose Layer Options from the panel flyout menu, and activate the Lock Guides control in the Layer Options dialog box.

Guide Options

Snapping is the term given to the behavior of an object jumping toward a guide when the object is dragged to within a certain distance of the guide. By default, the distance, or snap zone, is 4 pixels. When an object is dragged to within 4 pixels of a guide, the object will jump the remaining distance and align its closest edge to the guide.

To disable snapping, choose View ➤ Grids & Guides ➤ Snap to Guides to toggle the behavior off or on.

To change the snap zone distance, go to the Guides & Pasteboard pane of the InDesign CS5 Preferences and change the Snap to Zone value (see Figure 9.12).

FIGURE 9.12
Guides & Pasteboard pane of Preferences

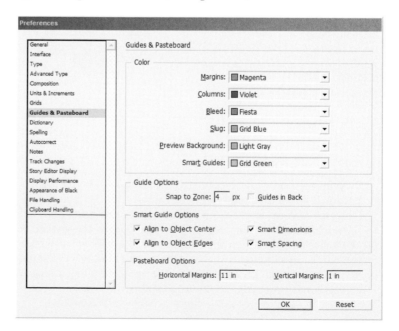

Not listed in the Preferences Guides & Pasteboard pane is an option to change the color of normally cyan ruler guides. Their color *can* be changed, however, just not in Preferences where the colors of margin, column, and other special-purpose guidelines can be set. Instead, the color of ruler guides must be set through the Ruler Guides dialog (Layout ➤ Ruler Guides; see Figure 9.13). When you're changing the color of ruler guides, any existing guides will remain unaltered; the color chosen here will apply only to guides created after clicking the OK button. That, of course, opens up lots of options to use color-coded guides for different purposes, such as setting a live area ⅛-inch inside the page trim size or having guides indicating the center of columns in one color while another color is used to define the width of columns.

FIGURE 9.13
Ruler Guides
options

The View Threshold field refers to the minimum magnification level at which guides will be visible. Thus, setting a View Threshold value of 100% means that, should you zoom out to 50% of the actual document size, ruler guides will be hidden.

Guides Manager

Similar to QuarkXPress's Guides Manager utility is InDesign's Create Guides dialog (Layout ➤ Create Guides; see Figure 9.14). Here, you can create and precisely place several ruler guides in one quick operation by specifying the number of rows (horizontal guides) and columns (vertical guides) and the distance between them (gutters). Additional options allow you to delete any guides already on the page and to limit the rows and columns to fit within the page or margins. The ability to preview via the check box under Cancel lets you proof your grid before creation.

FIGURE 9.14
The Create Guides
dialog

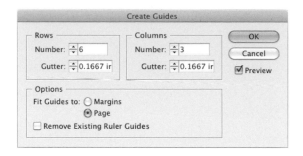

Document Grid

Document grids, like guides, are nonprinting, but they assist in precise layout composition and alignment of objects on the page. Unlike guides, both document grids and baseline grids are document-wide, nonlayered objects, meaning they appear on every page of the document and cannot be assigned to, or hidden by, a specific layer. Additionally, grids cannot be changed per master page; they are one grid per document, for every page of a document.

Working with a document grid is like working on graph paper (see Figure 9.15). It covers both pages of a spread and the pasteboard.

FIGURE 9.15
The document grid
shown

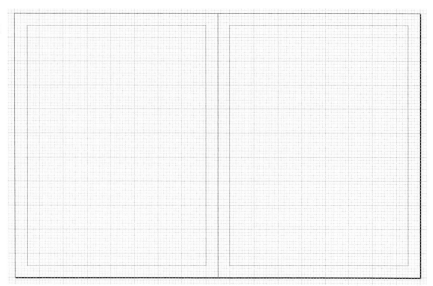

Document grid properties are controlled from the lower section of the Grids pane in Preferences (see Figure 9.16). Here, the color of grid lines can be changed, as well as the distance between cells. In the Gridline Every fields, enter the distance between grid lines, such as 1 in or 72 pt. Set the number of minor (lighter) grid subdivision lines and cells by changing the Subdivisions fields. To create subdivisions every 10th of one inch, for example, set subdivisions to 10.

Figure 9.16

Grid options

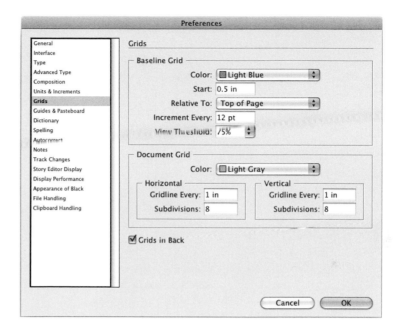

Grid measurements begin at the page edge closest to the ruler origin. Thus, if the ruler's zero-point is the top-left corner of a spread, the grid will begin counting out the Gridline Every and Subdivision field values from the top-left corner of the spread, separating the document to the right and down. For example, a Gridline Every value of 1 inch evenly divides an 11×17-inch spread 11 times vertically and 17 times horizontally. Custom or mismatched page sizes (e.g., the spread's left page is a different size than its right page) can make grids not so equally divisible. In such cases, change the ruler origin from Spread to Page or Spine in the Preferences Units & Increments pane.

When a facing-pages document includes a single-page spread, as is typically page 1, the grid will begin at the top-left edge of the page even though, in the absence of a left-read page, the right-read page does not begin at the ruler zero-point but begins instead at the spine.

By default, grids are placed furthest back in the Z-order; any object placed on the page will obscure the grid behind it. To reverse that behavior, placing the grid in front of all objects and thus always unobscured, uncheck Grids in Back on the Grids pane of Preferences.

Show or hide document grid lines, and decide whether objects snap to those grid lines, using the appropriate commands on the View ➤ Grids & Guides menu.

Baseline Grid

Baseline grids are horizontal-only rulings used to evenly array lines of text vertically. Whereas the document grid looks like graph paper, baseline grids appear to be ruled notebook paper (see Figure 9.17). Baseline grids do not extend beyond the spread into the pasteboard.

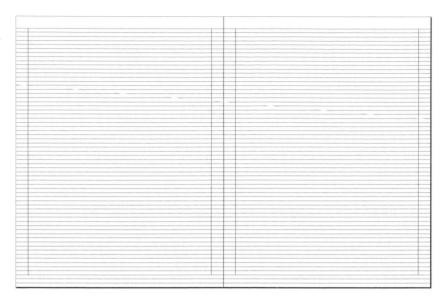

FIGURE 9.17
A document with
a baseline grid

GLOBAL BASELINE GRID

A global, document-wide baseline grid is set up in the Preferences on the Grids pane above the Document Grid options (see Figure 9.18).

FIGURE 9.18
Baseline
Grid options

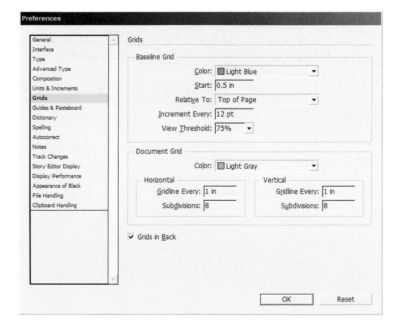

In addition to color, several settings are needed to build a usable baseline grid:

Start   Enter here as a measurement the distance to offset the top of the baseline grid from the top of the page or the top margin on the page, as specified by the Relative To dropdown.

Increment Every   The vertical distance between baseline grid lines. This should be equal to your text's leading value. Note that this field accepts any measurement notation InDesign understands—inches, points, pica, millimeters, and so on, though it will convert any value to the system it expects in this field, that being points.

View Threshold   Similar to the same option in Ruler Guide options, View Threshold sets the minimum magnification level at which baseline grid lines will be visible. Using the default value of 75%, for instance, grid lines will remain visible when zooming the document view to 75% magnification or greater, but zooming out to 50% will hide the lines for an unobstructed view of the document.

Although there is a Show Baseline Grid command under View ➤ Grids & Guides, there is not a snap-to command. Choosing Snap to Guides also causes objects to snap to the baseline grid.

PER-TEXT-FRAME BASELINE GRID

In addition to a document-wide baseline grid, each text frame may have its own unique baseline grid. Whereas a global baseline grid is ideal for balanced column text such as would be used by a newspaper or book, a single, spread-wide baseline grid has limited utility to layouts featuring columns or frames of text set on different leading values.

To use a per-frame baseline grid, select the text frame and open the Text Frame Options from Object ➤ Text Frame Options. On the Baseline Options tab, activate the frame-specific baseline grid by checking Use Custom Baseline Grid (see Figure 9.19). With the exception of the Color field, which includes the option to match grid lines to the layer color, all other options are equivalent to their counterparts in Preferences. What is unique is the top section, First Baseline, which determines how the first line of text relates to the baseline.

FIGURE 9.19
Text frame Baseline Options tab

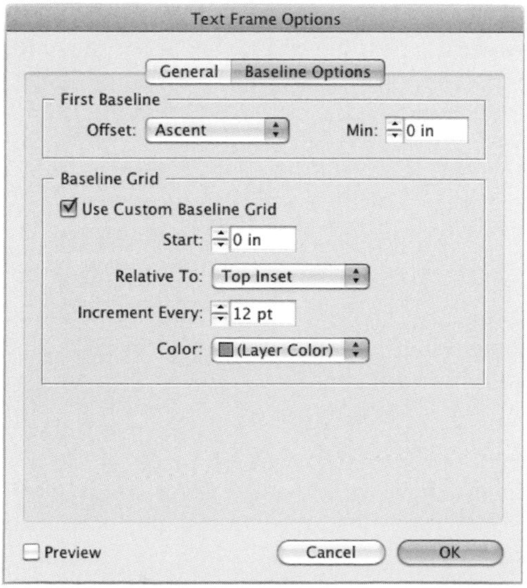

The Offset field in the First Baseline section offers five options: Ascent, Cap Height, Leading, X Height, and Fixed. Each of these changes which part of the first line of text is used to calculate the distance from the top of the text frame and thus how far the first line of text is inset from the top of the text frame.

Ascent   The top inset on the frame will extend down to type ascenders, such as in characters like *t*, *b*, and *h*.

Cap Height   The frame's top inset will extend down to the height of capital letters in the font (usually specified as the top of a capital *X*).

Leading   The distance between the top inset and the first line of text baseline will be equal to the text's leading value.

X Height   Despite the confusing use of the capital *X* in the name, this value actually uses the x-height, the height of a *lowercase x*. The top inset of the frame will extend down to the top of the lowercase *x*, with capitals and ascenders extending up and into the area of inset.

Fixed   The baseline of the first line of text will begin at the top edge of the text frame.

Figure 9.20 demonstrates the differences between Offset options when applied to the same text frame.

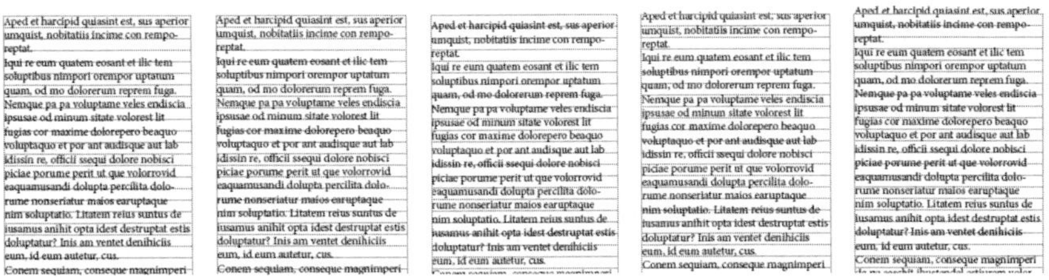

FIGURE 9.20
Different First Baseline Offset values applied to the same frame. From left to right: Ascent, Cap Height, Leading, X Height, and Fixed.

Any of the First Baseline Offset values can be adjusted for a perfect fit by modifying the value of the Min field. The value in the Min field is the minimum value for the baseline offset when the chosen Offset option's value is less. For example, if you set the Min field to 12 pt and then use the Offset Leading option, the minimum amount of vertical space given the first line will be 12 pt. If the type's actual leading value is greater than 12 pts, the leading value will be used instead.

Layers

Layers in previous editions of InDesign were simple, one-level things that were familiar to anyone who had used QuarkXPress, Photoshop since version 4, or scores of other applications. The Layers panel in InDesign CS5 got a radical makeover, though, so I'd better take a moment to introduce its new functions.

Layer Object Entries

CS5

Rather than simple layers, the new CS5 Layers panel is more akin to Illustrator's Layers panel, though still not as robust. You can still only have one level of layers—no nested or sublayers like Illustrator—but, taking after older brother Illustrator, InDesign's layers now expand to show

targetable entries for each object on the layer, on the current page (see Figure 9.21). For example, if you have a page with five text frames on it, each text frame appears as a separate entry beneath its current layer. Just click the spinner arrow beside the layer name to show or hide layer contents.

FIGURE 9.21
Individual objects on the current page can be identified and selected from the Layers panel.

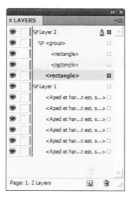

Because each object is now listed separately on the Layers panel, selecting and working with objects becomes dramatically easier—particularly if the objects overlap. Instead of risking screwing up your layout by sending objects backward or forward just to get at an object lower in the stack, click its Selection Indicator—the colored square to the right of the object name—on the Layers panel. When the Selection Indicator is filled, the object is selected and can then be deleted, moved, made semi-transparent, or whatever you want to do to it. Select multiple objects by Shift-clicking additional objects' Selection Indicators after the first. Select all objects in a layer by clicking the Selection Indicator beside the layer name itself.

You can also hide individual objects now simply by clicking, and clearing, the eyeball visibility indicator in the leftmost column of the object's Layers panel entry. Similarly, objects can be locked or unlocked by clicking in the second column of the entry. Of course, just like the old days, an entire layer, inclusive of its contained objects, can be hidden/shown or locked/unlocked by clicking within the appropriate column beside the layer name.

Change the stacking order of objects—which object is in front of other objects—by dragging object entries up or down in the Layers panel. Often this is a much faster way of reordering overlapping objects than using the Object ➤ Arrange menu commands or even their keyboard shortcuts.

To move an object from one layer to another, drag either its entry or just the Selection Indicator and drop it onto the new layer.

Quick Facts about Layers

As an experienced layout software user, you're already familiar with the basics of working with layers. Still, there a few nuances to using layers that may have escaped your notice:

◆ Unlike in QuarkXPress, master pages *can* contain layers, and they work exactly like layers on document pages.

◆ Layers are document-wide, meaning that turning off Layer 1 on page 6 turns it and any objects it contains off in all pages of the document. If any master page objects are included on Layer 1, they will be hidden from document pages as well.

◆ Holding Option+Shift/Alt+Shift while clicking the layer visibility icon (the eyeball) hides all layers except the one being clicked. Doing it again shows them all again.

◆ Similarly, holding Option+Shift/Alt+Shift while clicking the layer lock icon locks or unlocks all layers except the layer being clicked.

◆ Grouping objects that are arranged individually on several layers collects them all onto the uppermost layer. Ungrouping does not return them to their original layers.

◆ Grouped objects appear on the Layers panel as a <group> entry, which can be further expanded to enable selection and hiding of the individual objects in that group. Grouped objects cannot be individually locked or unlocked via the Layers panel.

◆ When pasting objects copied from multiple layers in the current or another document, the Paste Remembers Layers command on the Layers panel's flyout menu will faithfully arrange objects on layers as in the source. If the same layers do not already exist, InDesign will create them to hold the pasted objects.

◆ Entire layers—including all objects on them—can be defined as nonprinting in the Layer Options dialog accessible from the Layers panel flyout menu (see Figure 9.22).

FIGURE 9.22
Layer Options
dialog

◆ Guides can be selectively hidden or locked on a per-layer basis in Layer Options.

◆ Even when the layer is hidden, any objects assigned a text wrap will continue to influence type on other layers. Checking Suppress Text Wrap when Layer is Hidden in the Layer Options prevents the phantom wrapping behavior.

◆ Empty layers can quickly be selected and subsequently deleted using the Select Unused Layers command on the Layers panel flyout menu.

◆ The Merge Layers command on the Layers panel flyout menu will combine two or more layers highlighted in the Layers panel, placing all of their objects together on a single layer.

◆ Dragging an existing layer (or multiple layers) and dropping it atop the New Layer button at the bottom of the Layers panel will create an exact duplicate the layer and its objects.

◆ Right-clicking a layer in the Layers panel accesses the unique Select Items on Layer command that selects all objects contained on the target layer.

◆ Right-clicking a layer or layer object entry in the Layers panel also reveals the Select and Fit Item command, which selects the item(s) in question and zooms to fit it (or them) in the current document view.

◆ Objects on the Layers panel are given default names like <group>, <rectangle>, or, for text frames, the first few words of the frame embraced in braces.

◆ Layers and object entries on the Layers panel can be renamed by clicking twice (with a slight pause between clicks), which enables inline renaming, and then typing in a new name.

Books

InDesign is ideally suited to working with longer documents, but longer documents are not ideally worked upon as a single file. Rather, they are easier, faster, and more securely worked on by one or multiple compositors or designers as a series of files connected via an InDesign *book file*.

A book file, in InDesign parlance, is a connection between otherwise separate InDesign documents. That connection allows the multiple documents to be treated and managed as a single, cohesive document—a book—including page numbers that run sequentially from one to the next and the ability to preflight, print, and export to PDF all documents joined by the book file as a single unit.

Beginning a Book File

Create a new book file by choosing File ➤ New ➤ Book. When prompted, specify the location and name of the INDB book file. Typically, the book file should be named after the project title and saved in the same location as the documents that are or will be components of the project. When you click Save, the Book panel will appear (see Figure 9.23).

FIGURE 9.23

A new, empty book
on the Book panel

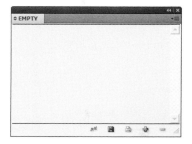

As with the Layers panel, the major area of a Book panel is a list, in this case a list of documents. Add documents to the book by clicking the Add Documents plus button at the bottom, which will generate an Open-style Add Documents dialog. In Add Documents, browse to the InDesign documents you want to add to the book. Multiple documents may be added concurrently using standard multiple-selection modifier keys such as Cmd/Ctrl to select nonsequential files and Shift for sequential selections. Click Open, and the selected document(s) will be added to the Book panel. Additional documents, including those in other folders or on other disks, can be added to the book the same way. The book file, not their respective locations on disk, ties them together.

Here are a few tips about working with book files:

◆ Although a book file can manage only a single book, any given document may belong to any number of book files.

◆ If any documents were created by earlier versions of InDesign, or are InDesign Interchange Format INX files, checking Automatic Document Conversion on the panel flyout menu will convert documents to CS5 format while adding them to the book file.

◆ Remove documents from the book by highlighting them and clicking the Remove Document minus sign button.

◆ Save changes to the book file by clicking the disk-like icon at the bottom, or choose Save Book or Save Book As from the Book panel flyout menu.

◆ To open a document that is part of a book, double-click the document in the list.

Page, Chapter, and Section Numbering

Upon adding documents to a book, the first thing you should notice is the document page numbers, which, unless you've specifically changed the section and numbering options in the individual documents, will be sequential—the numbers on the right in Figure 9.24. Each InDesign document, unless changed in the document's Numbering & Sections Options or the New Document dialog, always begins numbering at page 1. Once booked, however, only the document first in the list begins with page number 1. Each successive document then begins numbering its pages where the previous left off.

FIGURE 9.24

Documents on a Book panel automatically synchronize and increment page numbers.

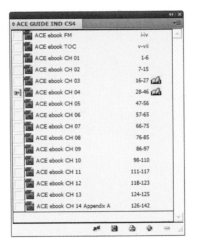

If page numbers show on the document pages themselves, placed there with the Current Page Number special character marker on the page or master page, the page numbers will update to reflect what is shown in the Book panel. If documents, and thus page numbers, are not in the correct order, simply rearrange the documents in the list by dragging and dropping. Page numbers will instantly resynchronize to match the new document order. They will also update to reflect any pages added to, or subtracted from, documents in the book.

Fine control over continuous or other page numbering begins with Book Page Numbering Options, opened from the panel's flyout menu (see Figure 9.25). In the Book Page Numbering Options dialog, Page Order offers a direct continuance of page numbering, continuing on the next odd, or next even, page, and the option to insert blank pages to help with page number jumps to odd or even pages.

Turn off Automatically Update Page & Section Numbers to stop InDesign from automatically updating page and section numbers when documents' page counts change or their order in the list is altered. With this option off, use the commands on the Update Numbering menu on the Book panel's flyout menu to manually update page and section, chapter and paragraph, or all numbers when needed.

FIGURE 9.25
The Book Page
Numbering
Options dialog

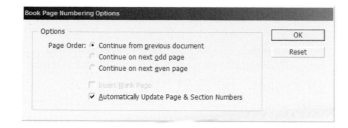

The Document Numbering Options command on the panel menu controls page numbering and section options for a highlighted document. The Document Numbering Options dialog is nigh identical to the Numbering & Section Options dialog available on the Layout menu in any single document (see Figure 9.26):

FIGURE 9.26
Document Num-
bering Options

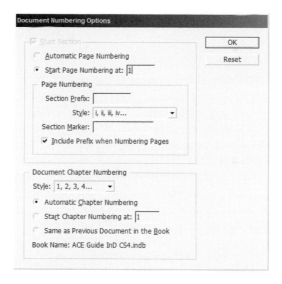

Automatic Page Numbering   Continues numbering from the previous document in the book. If the selected document is the first, it will begin numbering from page 1, subject to the other options below.

PROS AND CONS OF AUTOMATIC NUMBERING

Doing it automatically, of course, means you'll never have to worry if you've sent a publication to press and forgotten to update page numbers. The downside to automatic numbering, though, is that with a large number of documents or documents containing many pages, the automatic updating of page numbers for each page count or document order change could make you wait while InDesign repaginates the entire book.

Start Page Numbering At Choose this option and enter a number in the field to the right to begin numbering pages in the document at a certain point.

Section Prefix The Section Prefix field enables you to prepend up to eight characters—letters and/or numbers—to section numbers. For instance, you'd enter *Part-* here to create page numbering and TOC entries such as *Part-X Page Y*.

Style Choose the style for section numbers, either Arabic or upper- or lowercase roman or alphabetic.

Section Marker Documents may be divided into multiple sections—for instance, in this book, there are sections for front matter pages, the TOC, the chapters, the glossary, and the index. Each section of a publication may be numbered or formatted differently, and the page number may also be prefixed with a section-specific bit of information like *Section 1: Page 19*.

To insert a section marker in a text frame—say, in the folio beside the page number—do the following:

1. Place the Type tool cursor in the appropriate place in the text frame.

2. Choose Type ➤ Insert Special Character ➤ Markers ➤ Section Marker.

The section marker that appears will be specific to that section.

What you enter in the Section Marker field is what appears as the section marker inserted into a text frame. For instance, to identify the glossary of a book, you may enter *Glossary*. When the section marker appears on the page, it will then display as *Glossary* in the folio, header, or wherever you've placed the marker. If the Include Prefix when Numbering Pages box is checked, it will also insert the section marker as part of automatic page numbers created using Type ➤ Insert Special Character ➤ Markers ➤ Current Page Number.

Document Chapter Numbering Although a single document may contain several sections, it may contain, or be, only a single chapter. In this section, choose the format of chapter numbering, the chapter number for the current document, and whether to continue growing from, or mirror, the chapter number of the previous document in the book. The latter option is used to define two or more documents as being part of the same chapter.

Chapter numbers are made visible on the page by inserting the Chapter Number text variable (text variables are covered in Chapter 13, "Efficiency").

Synchronizing Book Styles

One of the most useful aspects of book files is the ability to synchronize nearly all styles and common elements between all documents in the book, thus eliminating inconsistencies in such things as paragraph, character, object, and table styles as well as swatches, text variables, and trap presets.

Every book must have a style source—a single document in the book file whose styles and options all other documents will adopt. Typically and by default, the first document added to the book is the style source, but that can be changed. The leftmost column in the Book panel is the Style Source Indicator column (see Figure 9.27). The style source is whichever document bears the icons in its Style Source Indicator column. To make a different document the style source, click once in the Style Source Indicator column beside the document name.

FIGURE 9.27

In this Book panel, the icon on the left indicates that the chapter 4 document is the book's style source.

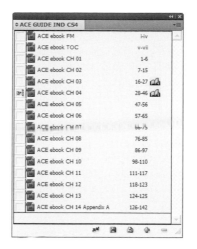

Synchronizing—copying styles from the source to one or more destination documents—is accomplished in a couple of ways. Select one or more documents in the Book panel, and then click the Synchronize button, the leftmost button, at the bottom of the Book panel. Or choose Synchronize Selected Documents or Synchronize Book from the panel flyout menu. The former appears when fewer than all documents are selected, and the latter when all or none are selected.

Set which types of data are synchronized by selecting Synchronize Options from the Book panel flyout menu. In the Synchronize Options dialog, check all types of styles and data to be matched across the documents (see Figure 9.28). Note that, by default, several available items and formats, such as Master Pages, are unchecked and thus not set to synchronize; you'll need to turn these on if you want to synchronize them across documents.

FIGURE 9.28

Synchronize options specify what will be copied from the style source to other documents in the book.

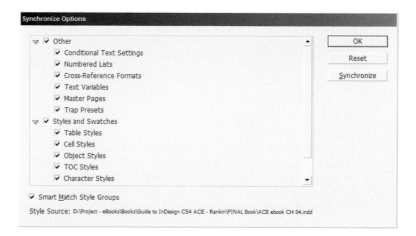

During synchronization, any conflicting or changed styles in the book documents will be overwritten by those copied from the style source. There will be no prompt or way to undo the synchronization. Synchronization may occur whether documents are opened or closed. To

preserve styles unique to a document, change style names in the document to unique names (e.g., change Body Text to Body Text Ch 3).

At the bottom of the Synchronize Options dialog is the option Smart Match Style Groups, which is checked by default. If enabled, InDesign will not duplicate uniquely named styles that have been moved into or out of style groups. For example, let's say in Document A the paragraph style Photo Credit is not in a style group, but in Document B you've moved Photo Credit into the style group Captions. If you set Document A to be the style source and then synchronize, InDesign will remove Photo Credit from the Captions group in Document B, putting it back into the top level of paragraph styles. Conversely, if you set Document B as the styles source, Photo Credit will end up in a group in Document A and all other documents, even if InDesign has to create the Captions group in documents that don't have it.

Leaving Smart Match Style Groups unchecked will create two Photo Credit styles—one within and without the Captions group. If a document already has two paragraph styles, each named Photo Credit, perhaps one in a group and one not, or both in different groups, InDesign will consider the Smart Match Style Groups disabled, even if you check it, and synch both styles named Photo Credit in their respective group locations.

Outputting Books

Although synchronizing common formatting and even structural elements between multiple documents reduces the work involved in managing and prepping for print-related documents, the ability to treat many documents as one when outputting is the largest advantage of book files. In fact, that ability alone justifies the existence and utility of book files even when you're working with documents that don't have sequential page numbers or page numbers at all. Check out the following sidebar for a real-world qualifier of that last statement.

BOOK FILE PORTFOLIO EASES PROPOSAL AND BID GENERATION AND PROVIDES A COMPETITIVE EDGE

Book files are useful for many things. For example, a designer who values economy of motion might connect a dozen separate portfolio pieces together via a book file. The portfolio documents wouldn't be sequentially numbered and certainly wouldn't want style synchronization. However, instead of opening and printing each of the 12 documents individually, documents that are most likely spread throughout numerous folders on the designer's computer, you can print the entire portfolio, exported to PDF, or packaged with a single command—possibly without opening even one of the documents.

I do this very thing, as a matter of fact. Often, as part of a project bid, I'll be asked to send samples of my previous work. Like most of you reading this, my body of work is broad and varied, but a client or prospective client needs to see only what is relevant to the project at hand. You wouldn't, for instance, send photos of product packages you've designed to accompany a proposal to design a travel agency's intranet website. Each set of work samples should usually be a subset of your entire portfolio, with pieces chosen specifically to convey to the client, *I know how to do the job you want done. See? I've done similar work before to the benefit of other clients.*

Some of my previous work is in native InDesign documents, some in QuarkXPress documents, some in Illustrator, PDF, websites, scans, image files, and so on. I include all of them in an InDesign

book file. For QuarkXPress documents I convert to InDesign just for the portfolio, for websites I take screen shots, and for all other assets; I simply place them into their own InDesign documents. All of these purpose-built INDD documents reside in a single folder with the INDB book file, but the pieces that are natively InDesign, as well as the placed assets, remain wherever they happen to live on my hard drives—client folders, other project folders, and so on; the book file will happily manage them from multiple locations. All the pieces I might want to send along with any proposal or request for samples are added to, and managed through, a single book file. When I need to print or create a PDF to accompany a proposal, I choose the relevant pieces, select them individually in my portfolio's Book panel, and then choose Print Selected Documents or Export Selected Documents to PDF from the panel's flyout menu.

For instance, if I'm proposing a magazine template design, I include only my previous magazine work; if I'm bidding on an advertising job, I include primarily ad-centric prior work; and so on. I selectively choose which pieces to include from the Book panel that includes all of my portfolio pieces. When I output, the result is a single print job or PDF, displaying only what I want included and nothing I don't, without the hassle of hunting down and printing each piece individually or converting each to a PDF and then combining PDFs.

Naturally, in addition to being less work, it's faster to open a single file—the INDB—select a few entries, and then choose one menu command, than to deal with the documents individually. Thus I can nearly always get a PDF of selected pieces in front of a prospective client's eyes while we're still on the initial phone call. And that gives me an edge over any competitors the client called before me, competitors who promised to get some samples together and off to the client the next day or even later in the same day.

With all or no documents selected in the Book panel, choose one of the following commands:

Preflight Book   This command will check all documents in the book for problems related to images, fonts, plug-ins, and so forth.

Package Book for Print   To collect all of the book's constituent documents, including their image assets and fonts, together in a single folder ready for archiving or delivery to a print provider. The INDB book file itself will also be added to the project's package folder, with links updated to point to the location of the new document copies.

Export Book to ePub   To build a single, continuous ePub format document from all documents in the book ready for consumption via an e-reader.

Export Book to PDF   To build a single, continuous PDF from all documents in the book.

Print Book   To print the entire book, one document after the other, as if all were but a single document. The printer icon at the bottom of the Book panel is a shortcut to this command.

Any of these operations can also be performed selectively, on only some of the documents within the book file, by selecting only the desired documents before executing the command. Note that when only some of the documents are selected on the Book panel, these commands change to Preflight Selected Documents, Package Selected Documents for Print, and so on.

Indexing

Another strength of book files is their ability to build a unified index of topics or table of contents incorporating information from within all the documents referenced from the book file. Of course, an index can also be built in stand-alone documents. In fact, it must begin in each document, and then, if the document is part of a book, one index may be generated incorporating keywords and/or cross-references from all chapters.

Creating Index Entries

Indexing begins by inserting invisible index marker characters and associating them with topics, or keywords, to create index entries. It's done on the Index panel (Window ➤ Type & Tables ➤ Index), which has two modes (see Figure 9.29). Both Reference and Topic modes display all indexed topics in the preview area, using alphabetic heading lists, but only Reference mode includes page numbers. Topic, by contrast, streamlines the list by leaving out page numbers, enabling faster editing of the text of topics that will appear in a generated index in the printed publication. Click the expansion triangles to spin open or closed the levels of the list. Hold Cmd/Ctrl when clicking an expansion triangle to open or close all levels below, and contained by, the current entry or header.

FIGURE 9.29
The two modes of the Index panel: at left, Reference mode; Topic mode at right

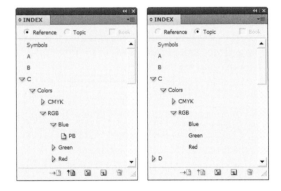

Create a new index entry by highlighting a word or phrase, or by simply inserting the cursor at the desired point in the story, and then clicking the Create New Index Entry button at the bottom of the Index panel. Up will pop the New Page Reference dialog (see Figure 9.30); if text was highlighted, it will automatically fill in the first Topic Level field. Note that the Index panel must be in Reference mode to create a new index entry; otherwise you'll be presented with the New Topic dialog rather than the New Page Reference dialog.

For a simple, single-level index, only the first Topic Level entry is needed. However, if you want to create a more detailed, hierarchical index—something like Figure 9.31—use several Topic Levels fields. For instance, to place the reference to entry Blue under the heading of Colors in the generated index, enter **Colors** in the Topic Levels 1 field, and **Blue** in Topic Levels 2. Later, when adding the references for Red, Green, Cyan, Magenta, Yellow, and Black, you'll do the same, with Colors in the Topic Levels 1 field and each color beneath in the Topic Levels 2 field. To add a third level of organization—for example, RGB or CMYK, into which each color will be distributed—place the color name in the Topic Levels 2 field and the color name, the actual reference, in the Topic Levels 3 field. The up and down arrows to the right of the Topic Levels fields alter the order of the field contents, moving them up or down in priority.

FIGURE 9.30
The New Page Reference dialog

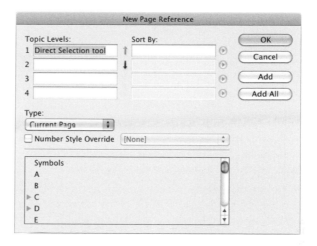

The Sort By fields enable changing the order in which topics sort in the generated index. For instance, the entry *The New York Times*, if unchanged, would sort among the Ts, which is stylistically incorrect. It should sort among the Ns (as *New York Times, The*), so in the Sort By field, enter **N**, **New**, or **New York Times**—as much text as is needed to properly sort the entry among other N entries in the index. Each topic level may have its own Sort By key of one or more characters.

FIGURE 9.31
A multilevel index (left) and the Page Reference Options entry details for one (right)

Index

C

Colors
  CMYK
    Black 2
    Cyan 2
    Magenta 2
    Yellow 2
  RGB
    Blue 2
    Green 2
    Red 2

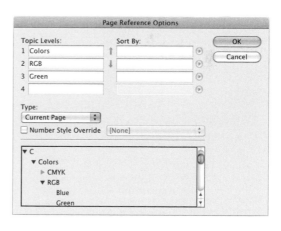

In many cases, you'll actually want to create two or more index entries for the same term, each with different Sort By options, to overcome confusion inherent in the term and help readers find the topic. Take, for example, the entry *Commonwealth of Massachusetts* in a book about politics, the law, geography, or history of New England. Most people in the United States—including most of the state's residents and former residents (which includes yours truly)—tend to look for information about the Commonwealth of Massachusetts simply by looking under M in the index. A large minority of others, those accustomed to dealing with the state's formal title, will head to the Cs. A good indexer would therefore list *Commonwealth of Massachusetts* under both C and M.

The Type dropdown list presents several options for specifying the type of reference, some of which will cause an additional field to appear beside the Type field:

Current Page   Includes beside the entry text the current, single page number on which the index marker appears.

To Next Style Change   Creates in the generated index an entry that may be a single page number or a range (e.g., *Blue 10–13*). Whether the entry is a single page or a range and, if the latter, how long the range is are determined by the distance between the marker and the next paragraph style change. For example, if the index marker is placed within a heading assigned to the paragraph style Heading 1, the index reference will continue through the last character assigned to the Heading 1 style.

To Next Use of Style   Creates in the generated index an entry that may be a single page number or a range (e.g., *Blue 10–13*). Whether the entry is single page or a range and, if the latter, how long the range is are determined by the distance between the marker and the next use of the same paragraph style. For example, if the index marker is placed within a heading assigned to the paragraph style Heading 1, the index reference will continue until the next instance of the Heading 1 style in the story, inclusive of any other paragraphs assigned paragraph styles other than Heading 1.

To End of Story   Creates in the generated index an entry that may be a single page number or a range (e.g., *Blue 10–13*). From the marker point until the end of the story will be considered one complete entry. Note that additional index entries may appear within the range as well.

To End of Document   Creates in the generated index an entry that may be a single page number or a range (e.g., *Blue 10–13*). From the marker point until the end of the document, inclusive of all stories, will be considered one complete entry. Note that additional index entries may appear within the range as well.

To End of Section   Creates in the generated index an entry that may be a single page number or a range (e.g., *Blue 10–13*). From the marker point until the end of the section as defined in Layout ➢ Numbering & Section Options will be considered one complete entry. Note that additional index entries may appear within the range as well.

For Next # of Paragraphs   Creates in the generated index an entry that may be a single page number or a range (e.g., *Blue 10–13*) depending upon how many pages the specified number of paragraphs covers. Choosing this option causes another field to appear wherein you may enter the number of paragraphs.

For Next # of Pages   Creates in the generated index a ranged entry for the specified number of pages. Choosing this option causes another field to appear wherein you may enter the number of pages.

Suppress Page Range   Creates an index entry without a page number.

The last six options on the Type menu create cross-references to other index entries, suppressing page numbers and ranges on the current entry. Cross-references are discussed further on in this chapter.

Check the Number Style Override check box and choose a character style from the drop-down menu to assign a character style to the particular index entry, enabling formatting unique from other index entries.

At the bottom of the dialog is a reiteration of the Index panel's Topic mode view for use in matching topic levels or referencing name, capitalization, and other considerations. Topics may be dragged from the list and dropped into the Topic Level fields.

The New Page Reference dialog includes four buttons: OK, Cancel, Add, and Add All. Cancel's function is self-evident, but the other three require definition:

OK   Add the current reference and close the dialog.

Add   Add the current reference *without* closing the dialog, leaving it ready for manual input of additional references to the same place in the document.

Add All   Add the current reference *and* additional, separate references for all other instances of the same word or phrase in the document. Add All is enabled only if text is high-lighted in the document and uses for every reference the same options as set in the New Page Reference dialog—the same Topic Levels, Sort By, Type, and Number Style Override options.

InDesign's Add All indexing is case sensitive, meaning that *Polyglot* and *polyglot* are consid-ered different words and different index entries. Similarly, singular and plural word forms are considered separate topics, such as in the case of *language* and *languages***.**

Once a reference has been created, it will appear on the Index panel. In Reference mode, each individual reference or instance will list its page number or range of pages (depending on the options selected in New Page Reference dialog). Instead of page numbers, some entries may display special codes indicating that they may not be included in the generated index (see Figure 9.32).

FIGURE 9.32
Index entries that
may not appear
in the generated
index

HL   Entries are contained on a hidden layer. Although the index is generated (later in this section), such entries may be included or excluded regardless of whether the text is actually visible on the page.

Master (Name of Master Page)   Entries are contained on a master page and will not become part of the index.

PB Entries are located on the pasteboard and will not become part of the index.

PN Entries are overset and do not appear on a page. Such entries can be included in the generated index, but without page numbers.

Managing Index Entries

Double-clicking the *topic*—the entry name of any level—in either mode of the Index panel opens the Topic Options dialog, which has a truncated set of options from the Page Reference Options (see Figure 9.33). However, double-clicking the *reference*—the page number beneath the topic in Reference mode—reopens the Page Reference Options.

FIGURE 9.33

Editing a topic in Topic Options (left) and editing a reference for an instance of the topic in Page Reference Options (right)

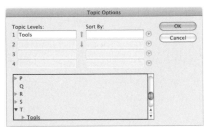 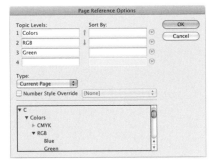

The Index panel flyout menu presents additional options for managing topics and references, including the ability to duplicate or delete them.

Choosing the Capitalize command opens the Capitalize dialog (see Figure 9.34), enabling capitalizing the first letter of the selected topic, the selected topic and any subtopics it may contain, all topics in the Level 1 position, or all topics and subtopics regardless of level. If you don't choose to capitalize, index entries will look exactly like they do in the text of the document—e.g., *cyan* will be listed in the index as *cyan* rather than *Cyan*.

FIGURE 9.34

The Capitalize dialog

In the Sort Options dialog, also accessible from the panel menu, choose the options for sorting on the list in the generated index (see Figure 9.35). Check the box beside each glyph type InDesign should consider when sorting index entries. Change their order by clicking a particular type once to highlight and then using the up or down arrows in the bottom-right corner of the dialog.

The Remove Unused Topics and Show Unused Topics commands enable cleaning up the list, though this is for your convenience only; topics added to the Index panel but not actually used in the document, perhaps because their containing text was deleted, will not be included in the generated index. Go to Selected Marker is a command that jumps the document view to focus on the instance of the index entry within the document or book.

FIGURE 9.35
Sort Options

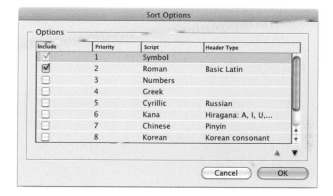

Long documents tend to generate long indices, and moving around on the Index panel requires a great deal of scrolling. To ameliorate this problem, InDesign includes a field for searching within the entries list, although it's hidden by default. At the bottom of the Index panel flyout menu, the Show Find Field command exposes the Find field at the top of the panel (see Figure 9.36). Type in all or part of an expected topic name, and click either the Find Next Entry in Panel or Find Previous Entry in Panel down or up arrows.

FIGURE 9.36
The Index Panel
with the Find field
shown

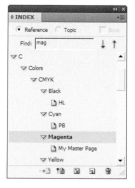

When an index entry is created, it adds into the story at the point of creation an invisible character called the index marker. As you can see in Figure 9.37, with hidden characters shown (Type ➤ Show Hidden Characters), index markers are distinctive marks consisting of two vertically aligned dots underscored by two converging, slanted marks below the baseline. It looks rather like a colon teetering atop a caret or that symbol for Earth from *Stargate*. The extra dots are the invisible characters marking spaces between words.

For all intents and purposes, index markers are text characters that can be deleted or moved like any other glyph in the story, either in the layout or in Story Editor. Indexing should be done only on final-stage or near-final-stage documents, and once references are created, text should *always* be edited with Show Hidden Characters active to prevent accidental deletion or misplacement of index markers. Markers appear *before* the word or phrase they reference. Deleting a marker removes its reference from the Index panel. Because markers are treated as their own characters, highlighting and then dragging (if drag and drop of text is enabled) or cutting only the text the Index panel references but not the index marker itself will *not* automatically move the marker as well. Instead, the text will move, but the entry reference—and thus the generated index—will point to the location of the marker, which may vary greatly from the actual location of the keyword or phrase.

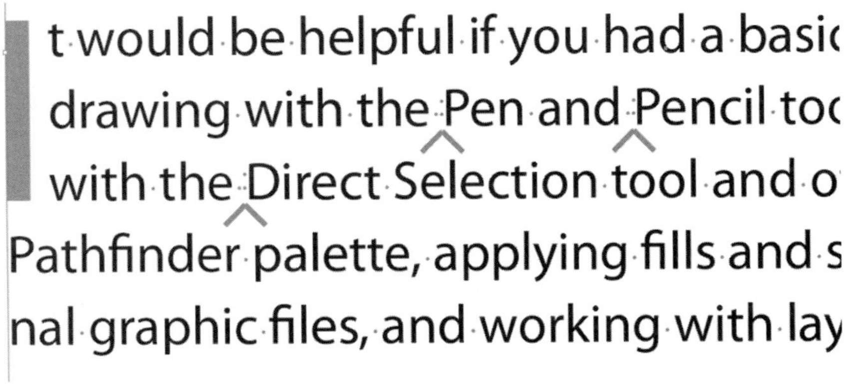

FIGURE 9.37
When hidden characters are shown, index markers become visible.

t would be helpful if you had a basic

drawing with the Pen and Pencil too

with the Direct Selection tool and o

Pathfinder palette, applying fills and s

nal graphic files, and working with lay

Cross-References

Instead of, or in addition to, listing a page number, cross-references point to other index entries. Equal or substitution cross-references are those that do not list their own page number, referring the reader to a different index entry—for example, *VDP, see Variable Data Printing*. Additional or related cross-references are those important and unique enough that they *do* list page numbers, but they also suggest to the reader additional, related information via a pointer to another index entry (e.g., *tethered objects, 192. See also anchored objects*). Both are relatively easy to create in the Index panel and have several options to choose from.

Cross-references are created the same way as normal index references—by choosing a marker insertion point, clicking the Create a New Index Entry button, and completing the options in the New Page Reference dialog. The difference is in the Type menu. Cross-references use the six options located below the line in the Type menu (see Figure 9.38). Selecting any of the cross-reference types also exposes the Referenced field. In the Topic Levels fields, set the topic(s) for the cross-reference entry itself, and then, in the Referenced field, set the separate, end-level topic to which the cross-reference will point. For example, to create an index entry that will print as *WorkflowNetwork.com 35, See also Author's Projects*, you would set Topic Levels 1 to WorkflowNetwork.com, the Type field to See [also], and put **Author's Projects** within the Referenced field.

FIGURE 9.38

Cross-reference
types in the Page
Reference Options
dialog's Type menu

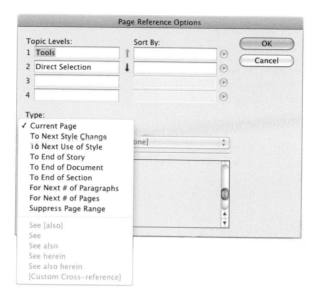

Following are the six cross-reference types:

See Produces a substitution or redirection cross-reference with no page number. Example: *InDesignVSQuark.com, See QuarkVSInDesign.com.*

See Also Produces a related cross-reference, listing both a page number for the current topic and a referral to an additional index entry. Example: *WorkflowCreative.com, See also iamPariah.com.*

See [Also] Creates *either* a See or See Also type of cross-reference depending on whether a topic or page reference is selected, respectively. This option is adaptable to changes in the topic or page reference and is therefore generally preferred to See or See Also.

See Herein Although rarely used outside legal and scientific publications, this option creates a reference to another topic beneath the level of the current topic in the hierarchy. For example, a level 1 topic of *Connect with Author* might contain a second-level subtopic for, among others, *Social Media*. *Social Media* might contain only a single, third-level topic named *Twitter: @iamPariah*. In that case, the index entry for *Social Media* itself might then forgo a page reference and simply direct readers to the *Twitter: @iamPariah* entry.

See Also Herein Similar to See Herein except that both a page number for the current topic and a referral to the contained topic are included.

Custom Cross-Reference Choosing this option activates a third field, Custom, which replaces connective cross-reference text like See, See Also, and See Herein with any custom text. In the following example, the Custom field was set to "gain efficiency by reading": *InDesign CS5 1-400, gain efficiency by reading Mastering InDesign CS5 for Print Design and Production.* Like See [Also], Custom Cross-Reference chooses whether to include a page number based on whether the cross-reference topic references another entry's topic or page reference.

Power Indexing

A few parting words about creating and managing index entries efficiently.

Add a New Reference to an Existing Topic When the topic is already listed in the Index panel and already contains references, you can create a new reference and index marker for additional locations without going through the New Page Reference dialog:

1. Place the cursor at the location for the new index marker, or highlight text.

2. On the Index panel, drag one of the existing topic references, and drop it atop the Create a New Index Entry button.

A new reference will be added beneath the topic pointing to the index marker the act creates at the cursor location or ahead of the highlighted text.

Creating Topics First Topics can be created ahead of references. With no text selected, switch to Topic mode on the Index panel and click the Create a New Index Entry button at the bottom of the panel. In the New Topic panel, fill in the Topic Levels and/or Sort By fields, and choose OK or Add. With topics pre-created, adding entry references becomes easier and more consistent.

Loading Topics If you already have the topics defined in another InDesign document, perhaps from a previously completed, similar project or from another document in the same book, choose Import Topics from the Index panel flyout menu, navigate to the InDesign document containing the topics, select, and click Open. The topics will populate the current document's Index panel.

Book Indices When the current document is part of a book, the Book check box at the top of the Index panel lights up and becomes selectable. Check the box, and the Index panel will recognize book page and section numbering options, updating the index list to include topics and references in other documents throughout the book, and generate a book-aware index.

Rapid Indexing After the initial entry reference is added, subsequent entries can be added from the keyboard easily. Just select the next word or phrase, or place the text cursor at the marker insertion point, and press Cmd+Option+Shift+[/Ctrl+Alt+Shift+[. A new reference will be created instantly, and you can move on to the next index entry. All the same New Page Reference dialog options will be reused from the last manual entry, so be wary if you set up unique options the last time.

Indexing Proper Names Proper names should typically be indexed as last name first (e.g., *Smith, John*) although InDesign indexes the typical entry exactly as it appears in the story (e.g., *John Smith*). While it can be overridden in the New Page Reference dialog either at creation time or later by double-clicking the entry on the Index panel, it's much faster to use the keyboard shortcut: Cmd+Option+Shift+]/Ctrl+Alt+Shift+].

Indexing Multipart Proper Names The previous method of indexing proper names works by placing the last word first in the entry sort order and the generated index. A name like *James Earl Jones* would thus correctly list as *Jones, James Earl*. It *won't*, however, work for multipart names like publications (e.g., *The Corellian Times*), ships (e.g., *The Millennium Falcon*), titled names (e.g., *Capt. Han Solo*), suffixed names (e.g., *Anakin Skywalker, Jr.*), and other names or phrases of more than two words where the last is not the properly listed and sorted first word. To get around this limitation, force InDesign to *treat* certain pairings as single words

by inserting a nonbreaking space (Type ➤ Insert White Space ➤ Nonbreaking Space) between the words that should not break in the story text prior to creating the index reference. For instance, insert a nonbreaking space between *Millennium* and *Falcon*, forcing InDesign to consider *Millennium Falcon* as a single, continuous word. When that happens, using the Cmd+Option+Shift+]/Ctrl+Alt+Shift+] shortcut *will* properly place the article (or title, first name, etc.) at the end of the entry, separated by a comma (e.g., *Millennium Falcon, The*).

An added benefit to using a nonbreaking space to marry multipart proper nouns is that when the noun approaches the end of a text line, InDesign will not break the name between the words; it will wrap the entire name unbroken to the next line.

Generating the Index

At any point following or during index entry definition, the index may be generated and placed like any story, in the current document or, in the case of a book, as a wholly separate document.

Select Generate Index from the Index panel's flyout menu. The Generate Index dialog has two states separated by the More/Fewer Options button (see Figure 9.39).

FIGURE 9.39
The Generate Index dialog, in initial mode (above) and with options shown (below)

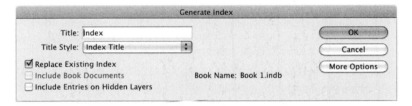

What it all means:

Title   When the index is generated and placed, it will have a title as the first line of the story. By default, the title will be *Index*, but it can be anything you like. Leaving the Title field blank removes the title from the generated index entirely, without leaving a blank carriage return where it would have been.

Title Style   Choose from this list the paragraph style for the index title (if there is a title). InDesign will, upon first generating the index, build new paragraph styles for the various parts of an index, beginning with the Index Title style. So, if you want your index title formatted uniquely, just leave the Title Style field at its default and, after generating the index, modify the Index Title paragraph style manually.

Replace Existing Index   Available if you have already generated an index at least once. InDesign does not *update* an index as might, say, Microsoft Word, which uses fields instead of story text for indices. Rather, regenerating an index in InDesign *replaces* the previous index entirely, generating a completely new story but within the same text frame(s) as the previous version.

It is because of the replacement of the previous index that you do not want to manually format text within an index story; upon regeneration and replacement, all local overrides will be wiped away. Edit the various index paragraph styles and/or use the Number Style Override option in the Page Reference Options dialog instead.

Include Book Documents   Available only if the Book option is checked on the face of the Index panel, this option will generate a single index for all documents within an InDesign book.

Include Entries on Hidden Layers   Enables including index entries whose markers are on hidden or turned-off layers.

Nested or Run-In   Indices come in two structural formats, nested, where each entry and subentry appears on its own line followed by a carriage return, and run-in, where only the top-level entry has its own line and all subentries are incorporated into it in a paragraph (see Figure 9.40).

Include Index Section Headings   Toggles whether to include alphanumeric headings such as *A*, *B*, *C*, and so on ahead of their constituent entries within the index.

Include Empty Index Sections   When Include Index Section Headings is checked, only those headings containing entries will be included. For example, if there are no index entries beginning with *A*, no *A* heading will be created. The Include Empty Index Sections check box forces the inclusion of headings—like *A*—even if there are no entries within.

Level Style   As with the title style, InDesign will generate paragraph styles titled Index Level 1, Index Level 2, Index Level 3, and Index Level 4 to format their respective levels in the generated index. If you already have one or more paragraph styles defined to use for the various levels, specify the styles here via the dropdown menus.

Index Style   Change the formatting of various elements of the index from these four options. For instance, to make page numbers green and bold while their corresponding reference text is black and not bold, create a character style for bold and green, and assign it to the element in the Page Number field. Section Heading is a paragraph style, while the rest are character styles.

FIGURE 9.40
At left, a nested index places each entry on its own line. At right, a run-in index combines all lower levels of topics into a single paragraph.

Index

C

Colors
  CMYK
    Black 2
    Cyan 2
    Magenta 2
    Yellow 2
  RGB
    Blue 2
    Green 2
    Red 2

D

Direct Selection 2

Index

C

Colors; CMYK; Black 2; Cyan 2; Magenta 2; Yellow 2; RGB; Blue 2; Green 2, Red 2

P

Path; 1, 2, 4, 5, 6, 7
Pencil tool 2, 6
Pen Tool 2

S

something; paths; tools; panel 2

T

Tools; Direct Selection 2

Entry Separators   Either by using the modified Special Characters menus accessed by clicking the arrow to the right of each field or by typing directly into the fields, specify the various separators and connectors for each index element:

◆ Following Topic is a symbol or glyph to be inserted after each topic. When using the run-in index style, it's often wise to separate the topic from its subtopics and references with some form of white space—various spaces or a tab (^t).

◆ Again, more useful in run-in indices where entries appear on the same line, Between Entries creates a separator between successive entries (for example a bullet or pipette [|]).

◆ The character used between ranges of pages (e.g., *35–38*). The default symbol (^=) in the Page Range field signifies an en dash, which, rather than the hyphen, is the proper punctuation for a range of numbers.

◆ Between Page Numbers is the text between nonranged page numbers. For instance, when an index entry is listed on multiple pages such as *Sernpidal 79, 202, 206*, the comma and space are the Between Page Numbers separator.

◆ Before Cross-Reference separates an entry from a cross-reference. In the example *Belkadan. See Also Tingel Arm*, the period and space after *Belkadan* are the Before Cross-Reference field value.

◆ To end an entry, after all text, with a special symbol, space, or text, enter it in the Entry End field.

When you click OK, the Index story will be loaded into the cursor, ready for placement. It places like any other story, with the same auto-, semi-auto-, and manual-flow options. When

Paragraph Style, which will launch the New Paragraph Style dialog. Alternatively, leave the default of [Same Style] to include the same style in the TOC as on the document pages.

Page Number   Choose whether to place the page number before or after the entry text or to omit the page number entirely. With the Style field to the right, you can give the page number its own character style for customized formatting.

Between Entry and Number   The separator character or characters to appear between the entry text and its number (or number and text, if the page number is before the text). The pop-up menu to the right offers many symbols, markers, and special characters. To create a leader dot separator, specify a tab (^t) in the field and then modify the paragraph style (outside of the Table of Contents dialog) to include a leader dot separator at that tab stop. The dropdown menu at the right allows assigning a character style to the separator itself, enabling any unique styling to be applied to just the separator.

Sort Entries in Alphabetical Order   By default, and in most cases, TOC entries are sorted in order of appearance in the document. However, especially when creating documents for electronic distribution as PDFs or ePubs, this option opens numerous other possible uses for the Table of Contents feature beyond creating a standard TOC.

When InDesign generates a TOC, it creates hyperlinks connecting the TOC entries to the text they reference. Exporting to interactive PDF or ePub preserves these hyperlinks, enabling a reader of such a digital document to click the TOC entry and jump to the content. Thus, the option to sort entries alphabetically rather than logically opens the possibilities of creating vastly different lists such as lists of product names, an advertisement index, personnel referenced in the document, or even a replacement for a standard index—without having to manually create index entries. The only significant limitation to using the Table of Contents functions in place of index and other features is that InDesign's Table of Contents is dependent upon paragraph styles; it cannot create an entry from a character style or a specific word in the middle of a paragraph.

Level   In a hierarchal TOC such as the one at the front of this book, entries from each successive style are considered inferior to their predecessors—Heading 1, for instance, is superior to Heading 2, which is superior to Heading 3. The Level field defines that hierarchy. As each style is moved from the Other Styles list to the Include Paragraph Styles list, InDesign automatically assigns a successive level. If you have reordered the Include list by dragging and dropping, you will also need to change the level for each affected style.

Often successive TOC entries are indented as visual cues to the hierarchy. The Include list mimics the hierarchy by indenting styles in the list, giving *you* a visual representation of how the generated TOC may look. The Level field is nonexclusive, meaning that you are not required to have only a single level 1 or level 2 entry. If you have two or more equally important styles, they can all be set to the same level.

Create PDF Bookmarks   Similar to the way each entry on the page itself will be hyperlinked to its content, InDesign can automatically generate PDF bookmarks, which are hidden until PDF or ePub export time. Adding these, and choosing to include bookmarks when exporting to PDF, creates something akin to Figure 9.43—a Bookmarks panel sidebar TOC-style list of topics that, when clicked in a PDF or ebook reader like Acrobat or Adobe Reader, become hot links and jump the reader to the referenced content.

FIGURE 9.43
The TOC-style bookmarks in this InDesign-created document were built by checking the Create PDF Bookmarks options in the Table of Contents dialog.

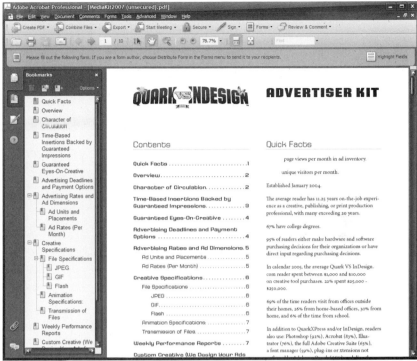

Replace Existing Table of Contents If you have previously generated and placed a TOC, this option will replace (not update) it. When using the Table of Contents to build separate styles of tables, you want this option unchecked. The option is active only if you already have a TOC in your document.

Include Book Documents When generating a TOC for documents managed through an InDesign book file, check this option to generate a single TOC that points to all instances of the included paragraph styles in all documents within the book. If you aren't working with a book, this option will be grayed out.

Run-In By default, all TOC entries are given their own line, with a carriage return at the end. An alternate style is to use the run-in method that, like the same option within an index, separates only by top-level styles. All entries lower in the hierarchy than the top will be placed together in a paragraph (see Figure 9.44). You could even run-in the top-level headings if you wanted. Merely check the Run-In option for each heading style you'd like to appear as semicolon-separated, rather than paragraph-return-separated, entries.

Include Text on Hidden Layers Choose whether to include in the TOC text that appears on hidden layers. This is useful if you're creating an index to advertisements or advertisers in your publication, for instance, and you've put the display names of those items on a hidden layer that readers won't see.

FIGURE 9.44
Left, a standard hierarchical TOC places each successive level of entry on its own line. A run-in version (right) places only the top level on its own and bunches lower levels together in paragraphs.

Contents

Quick Facts 1
Overview 2
Character of Circulation 2
Time-Based Insertions Backed by Guaranteed Impressions 3
Guaranteed Eyes-On-Creative 4
Advertising Deadlines and Payment Options . . . 4
Advertising Rates and Ad Dimensions 5
  Ad Units and Placements 5
  Ad Rates (Per Month) 5
Creative Specifications 6
  File Specifications 6
    JPEG 6
    GIF 6
    Flash 6
  Animation Specifications: 7
  Transmission of Files 7
Weekly Performance Reports 7
Custom Creative (We Design Your Ads for You) 7
Terms & Conditions 8
Insertion Order 9
Diagram of Ad Units & Placements 10

Contents

Quick Facts 1;
Overview 2
Character of Circulation 2
Time-Based Insertions Backed by Guaranteed Impressions 3
Guaranteed Eyes-On-Creative 4
Advertising Deadlines and Payment Options . . . 4
Advertising Rates and Ad Dimensions 5
  Ad Units and Placements 5; Ad Rates (Per Month) 5
Creative Specifications 6
  File Specifications 6; JPEG 6; GIF 6; Flash 6; Animation Specifications: 7; Transmission of Files 7
Weekly Performance Reports 7
Custom Creative (We Design Your Ads for You) 7
Terms & Conditions 8
Insertion Order 9
Diagram of Ad Units & Placements 10

Numbered Paragraphs This option tells InDesign how to handle paragraphs that have been numbered through the List and Numbering functions. Note that InDesign does not recognize numbers that have been converted to standard text and will include them in the TOC regardless of this setting. The options are as follows:

Include Full Paragraph Lists the text in the TOC exactly as it appears on the page, with all text automatic numbering intact. For example, the ninth table in a chapter whose number is defined within the paragraph Numbering options to include the prefix *Table 9* and whose table caption is *Four-Star Coruscant Cantinas & Tapcafs* will list in both the main story and the TOC as *Table 9.9 Four-Star Coruscant Cantinas & Tapcafs.*

Include Numbers Only Ignores the text in the paragraph and includes only the automatic number and any prefixes. For example, to include a TOC entry for *Table 9.9* without the table's caption, choose Include Numbers Only.

Exclude Numbers Includes in the TOC the text of the paragraph but not the automatic number. The TOC output using the previous example would therefore be simply *Four-Star Coruscant Cantinas & Tapcafs.*

Click OK to return to the document with a loaded cursor ready to place the TOC story, which may be placed and flowed like any story. If any stories in the document contain overset text assigned to the included styles, you will be prompted after clicking OK whether to include those overset instances in the TOC.

Unlike an index, a table of contents doesn't have its own panel. Also unlike an index, you needn't go through the entire generate process to update a TOC. Instead, select a text frame holding the TOC style, and choose Layout ➤ Update Table of Contents. Shortly, an alert dialog will inform you that the table of contents has been updated successfully.

When creating a comprehensive TOC for book documents, it's often better to place the TOC into its own self-contained document and to add that document to the Book panel.

The Bottom Line

Interact with Documents Visually and Change Zoom Level, View Modes, and Display Performance   InDesign provides numerous means of changing the way you interact with documents, how fast they move, how you see them, and what you see.

Master It   Open any InDesign document containing text and images on the same page. Open three different views of the same document, arranged simultaneously onscreen, zooming all to fit the page within the document window, and compare the views according to the following options:

- View 1: Preview mode with High-Quality Display display performance
- View 2: Layout mode with Fast Display display performance
- View 3: Bleed mode with Typical Display display performance

Employ Page Transitions for PDF and SWF Output   Page transitions add pizzazz to slideshow or Flash presentations.

Master It   Open or create a set of slides in InDesign, one per page, and assign a different page transition to each page. At least some of the pages should use nondefault options for those transitions. Export your slideshow to interactive PDF or SWF and test it out.

Build and Manage Grids and Guides   The foundation of any well-laid-out document is a well-thought-out grid.

Master It   Create a new document and build a grid on the master page consisting of six equal columns and three equal rows within the page margins. Once that's done, apportion the top row into three equal sections.

Work with Object-Oriented Layers   The ability to see and interact with each object on the page via the Layers panel is a potentially large time and frustration saver, particularly when compared to other methods of selecting overlapping objects. Renaming object entries in the Layers panel helps you organize your work.

Master It   Create a new document and place three similarly sized colored rectangles atop one another. The colors should be, in order from front to back, blue, red, and white. Use the Align panel (Window ➤ Object & Layout ➤ Align) to help line them up if necessary. Then, in the Layers panel, reorder the objects such that, from front to back, they become red, white, and blue, and then rename the objects to **Foreground**, **Midground**, and **Background**.

Create and Manage Book Files   Often one person finds it easier to work on longer documents by breaking them up into chapters or sections and connecting them via a book file. For

workgroups wherein different people are responsible for different sections of the document, a book file is essential to productivity.

Master It   Working alone or in a group, create at least three InDesign documents of several pages of text each. Save each document, and then create a book file to connect the documents. Finally, create a single PDF from the entire book.

Index Terms and Create an Index   An index helps readers find content. From simple keyword lists to complex, multilevel, topic-driven indices, InDesign handles them all, marrying index entries to referenced text through index markers.

Master It   Open or create an InDesign document containing a story of at least three pages in length. Working through the document, create index entries and cross-references for at least 10 words, one of which should be a word that repeats numerous times throughout the story (use a common word such as *the* if needed). Once the terms are indexed, generate and place the index story on a new page.

Create Tables of Contents   Tables of contents direct readers in logical or virtually any order to content, and InDesign's TOC options are varied and powerful for myriad uses.

Master It   Open or quickly create a rudimentary book-style document containing body text and several heading paragraphs utilizing at least two levels of headings. Create and assign paragraph styles for the body text and headings. Using what you've learned in this chapter, generate and place a hierarchal TOC.

Chapter 10

Preflight

At the end of the day, it's all about printing—more precisely, it's about *printing well and accurately*. It's about getting what you see on screen onto paper or another substrate and getting the two to match as closely as possible. Everything we do in InDesign leads up to that ultimate, defining moment when we watch with bated breath as the job rolls off the press.

Up until now, we've talked about the design functions of InDesign (with a watchful eye on the end goal). Now let's get into what happens after design, into the ramp-up to outputting a job. Preparing a job for print, ensuring the document doesn't contain errors that could alter or halt the process of printing, checking for broken links and bad fonts, managing color for accurate translation from screen to substrate—all of this and more is called *preflight*, getting a document ready for press.

In this chapter, you will learn to

◆ Configure color management on documents and images

◆ Soft proof documents to screen

◆ Configure and use Live Preflight and the Preflight panel to examine a document for problems

Managing Color

Defining and reproducing color is an area in which print design and production is ever striving for improvement. From better color management to newer, larger ink gamuts like 2010's introduction of the all-new, expanded PANTONE PLUS Series ink system, from transparency to RGB workflows, each new release of InDesign raises the bar on color creativity, control, and output. InDesign CS5 is no exception. And all of it comes down to managing the way our color-rendering devices perceive and render color.

> *The purest and most thoughtful minds are those which love colour the most.*

> *—John Ruskin (1819–1900), artist, author, poet, and art critic*

Any discussion about using and outputting color in for-print design or production must begin with a primer on color management—without a doubt the single most confusing (and by most accounts boring) subject in this exciting business of ours. I'll be concise and (hopefully) entertaining to mitigate the boredom while dispelling the confusion. At the very least, look at it this way: We're getting color management out of the way. It's all downhill from here.

On Windows XP and earlier, it's the Microsoft Image Color Management (ICM) user interface; on Windows Vista and Windows 7, the utility is Display Color Calibration (DCC). The way to get to and configure ICM and DCC has a tendency to change between versions of Windows, so rather than walk you through four or five different methods, the fastest way is for you to choose Help and Support from the right side of your Start Menu and search for the phrase "color management."

Once your monitor is calibrated, you should create an ICC profile for it (or them), which is the last step in both ColorSync/DCA and ICM/DCC. InDesign and other Creative Suite software will then pick up and use the monitor profile from ColorSync/DCA or ICM/DCC, compensating for the unique characteristics of your monitor as you work.

Both Mac and Windows color calibration utilities rely on your eyes to determine color, *gamma*, and white and black points, but your eyes aren't reliable color gauges. They can be influenced by ambient conditions like other lights in the vicinity, how long your monitor has been switched on, monitor light reflected off other surfaces, and the unique physical aspects of your eyes themselves. The configuration of rods and cones in our eyes is as unique as our retinal patterns. For instance, 10% of men and 1% of women have some form of color blindness, profound or subtle, and many never even notice it. Calibrations by eye—and the profiles created thereby— should be considered approximations, not accurate determinations of unique monitor color rendering. To get an accurate description of how the monitor interprets color, you need to take the subjective human out of the equation.

A software-backed hardware device that attaches to monitor screens is the best way to profile a monitor (and often calibrate in the same process). That device is a colorimeter. Note that device color characteristics change over time and should be profiled again often (monthly if not weekly).

To measure the color characteristics of a printer—anything from desktop to proof printer to digital press—use a spectrophotometer. This hardware device examines printed output, determining color fidelity on the printed page. If you go to your local Home Depot, you'll find a spectrophotometer behind the counter in the paint department. Although they often only know it as the "paint-matching scanner thing," the folks at Home Depot use it to extract eight-color tint formulas from paper and other physical objects.

When it comes to profiling a printer, it gets a little more complicated. You see, a printer—inkjet, laser, web press, offset press, *everything*—lays down ink that is, more or less, the same color across all jobs and production floors. Cyan, magenta, yellow, black, Pantone colors, and all the other inks we use are predictable in their color and, for the most part, identical from one shop to the next. However, ink color is not the only factor when it comes to printed color. Equally important is the color of the *substrate*, or paper stock, on which ink is printed. Cyan, magenta, yellow, and many premixed spot inks are semitransparent and are therefore tinted by the color of the substrate beneath. Laying down 100% cyan ink coverage on pure, neutral white substrate gives you pure cyan. However, putting down 100% cyan ink coverage on yellowed parchment yields a sea-foam green. If you want to *see* pure cyan atop yellowed parchment, your software has to be told that fact so it can adjust the colors to compensate for the tint of the substrate. Thus, every time you print on a new substrate, you should use a new ICC profile built specifically for that output device and substrate combination.

When you don't have direct access to the color-rendering device —for example, your print provider's devices or if you vended out your oversized scans—and therefore can't profile it yourself, ask the service provider for the most up-to-date ICC profile for the relevant device (on the substrate you've chosen). ICC profiles are just ASCII files with an `.icc` (or `.icm`) extension. They're easily emailed as attachments. Once you receive them, drop them into the correct system folder:

```
Mac: /Library/ColorSync/Profiles
Windows: \Windows\system32\spool\drivers\color
```

InDesign and other color-managed applications and technologies will automatically detect and make available in the Color Settings dialog (see below) profiles stored there, although you may have to restart the applications after installing new profiles. Once the profiles are recognized, you'll need to actually tell InDesign or whatever application you're using to use the new profiles.

By telling your creative tools about the color characteristics of your print devices, you can work in software like InDesign confident that what you see onscreen will print fairly close to the same way. Once your creative software knows your monitor, output, and input (digital camera, scanner, etc.) profiles, you will have achieved predictable color and a color-managed workflow.

(Please know that I've provided only the briefest overview of color management; entire books at least as thick as this one have been written on the subject. If you want to get serious about color fidelity in your workflow, don't stop with my introduction to the subject.)

Configuring Color Management

In the past, configuring color management seemed to require a PhD in spectrophotometry (the scientist at Adobe who taught it to me had two PhDs). It's much easier now in general, but especially if you use InDesign as part of the Creative Suite.

BRIDGING COLOR MANAGEMENT SETS

We've talked about Adobe Bridge a couple of times now, primarily in the context of asset manager. It does much more, as I intimated, and Adobe's intent is that Bridge become the central hub of your Creative Suite experience—indeed, of your entire workflow. Toward that end, color management across all individual CS5 version applications is managed inside Bridge rather than within InDesign, Photoshop, and Illustrator respectively, which keeps color display results almost identical between the individual applications.

On the Edit menu in Bridge, you'll find Creative Suite Color Settings, which opens an extremely simplified interface to apply full sets of ICC profiles and color management options to all CS5 applications simultaneously (see Figure 10.1).

FIGURE 10.1
Creative Suite
Color Settings in
Adobe Bridge

In the Suite Color Settings dialog, click one of the five friendly, plain-language sets, and then click Apply. Behind the scenes, all applications will then be synchronized to use the following color management settings:

Monitor Color   Used for onscreen and video projects without CMYK colors.

RGB Working Space	(Your monitor's ICC/ICM profile)
CMYK Working Space	U.S. Web Coated (SWOP) v2
RGB Policy	Off
CMYK Policy	Off
Profile Mismatches	Ask When Opening
Missing Profiles	N/A
Rendering Intent	Relative Colorimetric
Black Point Compensation	Yes

North America General Purpose 2   Large RGB and CMYK gamut profiles compatible with (but not optimized for) typical print output devices in North America. Will *not* warn when profiles do not match.

RGB Working Space	sRGB IEC61966-2.1
CMYK Working Space	U.S. Web Coated (SWOP) v2
RGB Policy	Preserve Embedded Profiles
CMYK Policy	Preserve Numbers (Ignore Linked Profiles)
Profile Mismatches	N/A
Missing Profiles	N/A
Rendering Intent	Relative Colorimetric
Black Point Compensation	Yes

North America Newspaper   Optimized for the most common newspaper printing settings used throughout North America. Will warn when profiles don't match.

RGB Working Space	Adobe RGB (1998)
CMYK Working Space	U.S. Newsprint (SNAP 2007)
RGB Policy	Preserve Embedded Profiles
CMYK Policy	Preserve Numbers (Ignore Linked Profiles)
Profile Mismatches	Ask When Opening & When Pasting
Missing Profiles	Ask When Opening
Rendering Intent	Perceptual
Black Point Compensation	Yes

North America Prepress 2   Similar to North America General Purpose 2 except that profile mismatches *will* generate warnings, it uses a very large RGB gamut profile, and CMYK colors in linked assets will be preserved to the exclusion of separate profiles assigned to the assets.

RGB Working Space	Adobe RGB (1998)
CMYK Working Space	U.S. Web Coated (SWOP) v2
RGB Policy	Preserve Embedded Profiles
CMYK Policy	Preserve Numbers (Ignore Linked Profiles)
Profile Mismatches	Ask When Opening & When Pasting
Missing Profiles	Ask When Opening
Rendering Intent	Relative Colorimetric
Black Point Compensation	Yes

North America Web/Internet   Uses a large gamut RGB profile purportedly representative of the color values available to the upper average of all monitors in use to access the Web. Any RGB colors will be converted from other profiles to the one defined as this set's RGB Working Space.

RGB Working Space	sRGB IEC61966-2.1
CMYK Working Space	U.S. Web Coated (SWOP) v2
RGB Policy	Convert to Working Space
CMYK Policy	Preserve Numbers (Ignore Linked Profiles)
Profile Mismatches	Ask When Opening & When Pasting
Missing Profiles	N/A
Rendering Intent	Relative Colorimetric
Black Point Compensation	Yes

If you're in or collaborating with folks in Europe or Asia, check the Show Expanded List of Color Settings Files option at the bottom of the Suite Color Settings dialog to reveal a more robust list of color settings files not limited to North American standards.

The sets shown in the Suite Color Settings dialog are the most common for those who can't (or won't) profile their devices to obtain specific ICC profiles.

I'm asked often—I mean, *very* often, *What are the default color management options I should use for _____ design work?*

My answer: *Profile your particular monitor, scanner, camera, and printers; use those as defaults.*
Them: *No, what* generic *profiles should I use?*

There are *no* "generics" in color management. Unlike air traffic controllers and pilots the world over who all speak English, there's no generic language to unite the delegates of the UN Security Council. The only way their discussions of color management work is if interpreters listen to input in native languages and then convert verbatim into the next delegate's or device's native language.

If, before you can leave this page, you absolutely *must* have something akin to "generic" settings in a process that has no definition for the word, then use one of the five sets discussed previously—whichever comes closest to describing what you're doing in InDesign and its brethren. And then hope really hard that the output comes close to the colors you envisioned.

V2 VERSUS V1?

A number of broad ICC profiles ship with Creative Suite and its constituent applications. Many of these, for instance U.S. Web Coated (SWOP), carry the v2 version number suffix. If you've continuously upgraded from earlier Adobe applications, you may also have v1 profiles hanging around. Use the v2. The v1 ones were created with older software (Color Savvy for the now defunct Adobe PressReady), whereas the v2 profiles were built using a special version of Photoshop and perform better in multistaged color conversions wherein an image is converted from one profile to another and then either back to the first or into a third profile.

Within InDesign and the other applications is a set that alleges to turn off color management. In InDesign it's titled Emulate Adobe InDesign 2.0 CMS Off. These color management off sets are a misnomer—*there is no off switch* to color management in Creative Suite. Instead, these sets will define defaults just like the rest, which, come press time and depending on your work, can cause either barely noticeable color shifts or disastrously wide spectral swings. The ostensibly off set assumes that all your RGB images were created directly on your monitor, in its color space, and that everything will be printed in the U.S. Web Coated (SWOP) v2 CMYK space. Here is what CMS Off *really* gives you:

RGB Working Space	(Your monitor's ICC/ICM profile)
CMYK Working Space	U.S. Web Coated (SWOP) v2
RGB Policy	Off (Leave it as is, without considering the source profile and without converting it to the current working space, and upon print, just convert the RGB numeric values to CMYK numeric values.)
CMYK Policy	Off (Print it as is, without considering the source or output profile and without converting it to the current working space.)
Profile Mismatches	Ask When Opening
Missing Profiles	N/A
Rendering Intent	Relative Colorimetric
Black Point Compensation	Yes

I *vigorously* advise against using CMS Off if color matters in the least to your work. Even one of the out-of-the-box presets would be a (marginally) better option.

CUSTOMIZING COLOR MANAGEMENT

Monitor Color, North America General Purpose 2, North America Prepress 2, North America Newspaper, North America Web/Internet, and all the other color management sets are just that—sets; each one is a group of preconfigured options activated all at once. Except for Monitor Color, which picks up your monitor profile from ColorSync/DCA or ICM/DCC, all the presets are based on wide gamut profiles that may or may not cause color shifts with specific devices. They don't take into account the color capture and rendering characteristics of the specific devices that created imagery or those that will put the imagery on paper. You'll want to change that fact, personalizing color management to the unique languages and dialects of your equipment.

Although you *should* be able to customize Creative Suite synchronized color management settings within Bridge, Adobe didn't get around to building that in—frustratingly, it's been omitted for quite a few versions. Instead, you have to take a circuitous route. Back in InDesign, go to Edit ➤ Color Settings. You'll be presented with a rather intimidating dialog (see Figure 10.2), but don't let it scare you.

FIGURE 10.2
The Color Settings dialog provides granular control over the ICC profiles and options in InDesign color management.

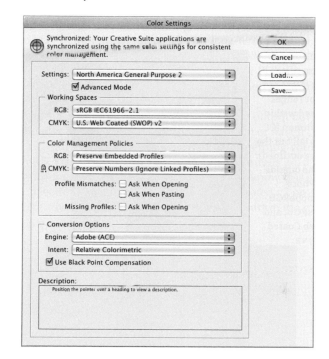

Settings

This is the list of saved color settings. The defaults examined previously appear on this list, as do the expanded list installed with Creative Suite or a CS5 application and any settings you've configured and saved. On the right of the dialog is a Save button. If you manually configure any of the options discussed below, save a set for easy access later. Saving a set also writes the settings to a file on your hard drive so it can be backed up and even shared with other users or clients.

If you've received a set of color settings from someone else and it doesn't appear in the list, use the Load button to browse for it.

Advanced Mode

Check the Advanced Mode check box to toggle display of the Conversion Options section at the bottom of the dialog.

Working Spaces

Between Working Spaces and Rendering Intent is the crux of color management and, assuming your profiles are well made, the real determination of the quality of your color output.

Use Black Point Compensation

Usually better left on, this option maps the pure black of the source profile (or working space) to the pure black of the destination profile (output device). For example, let's say you're employing a printer and substrate combination in which, after 92% gray, everything goes to pure black—the values are said to be *plugged*. Similarly, the whites *blow out* below 14% gray. (Both of these are fairly common with low- to mid-count linescreens or highly absorbent paper like newsprint.) A press or prepress operator knows about these limitations with equipment and will build them into the device and substrate-specific ICC profile. That profile will then tell InDesign that it doesn't have a full range in which to set black tones, that it really has only 78 full, 1% steps of gray between black and white, inclusive. With Black Point Compensation checked, InDesign will reset the value of pure black to 92% black—the point at which the ink will plug up to *become* full black—and adjust the white point to 14%. All the values in between will shift slightly to maintain smooth transitions. In that scenario, for example, 50% gray input will shift up slightly to maybe 52% to 56% so that it stays as the midpoint between black and white, preserving tonal range.

Restoring Color Management Consistency across Applications

If you modify the color settings in one application, the legend at the top of the dialog will alert you that the others in Creative Suite (assuming you have them) are out of synchronization. To ensure consistent color between InDesign, Photoshop, Illustrator, and Acrobat, you should mirror your settings from one to the rest. In the first three, you'll find this dialog in the same place—Edit ➤ Color Settings—and in Acrobat on the Color Management pane of its Preferences (Cmd+K/Ctrl+K). Note that Photoshop has additional controls in its Color Settings dialog, primarily dealing with gamma and spot control, while Acrobat has fewer controls than InDesign.

Per-Image Color Management

As noted earlier, each image placed, pasted, or dropped into InDesign can have its own output color profile and rendering intent. Images can come in with an embedded profile or the profile can be changed once you're in the document. Moreover, changes to an image profile within InDesign modify only the image's output from InDesign (and output from PDFs exported from InDesign); they do not alter the original asset on disk. To change an image profile and/or rendering intent, with an image selected choose Object ➤ Image Color Settings or Graphics ➤ Image Color Settings from the context-sensitive menu to access the Image Color Settings dialog (see Figure 10.5). These are the same controls you access when placing color-managed image files with Show Import Options checked.

FIGURE 10.5
Image Color Settings controls color profile and rendering intent per image

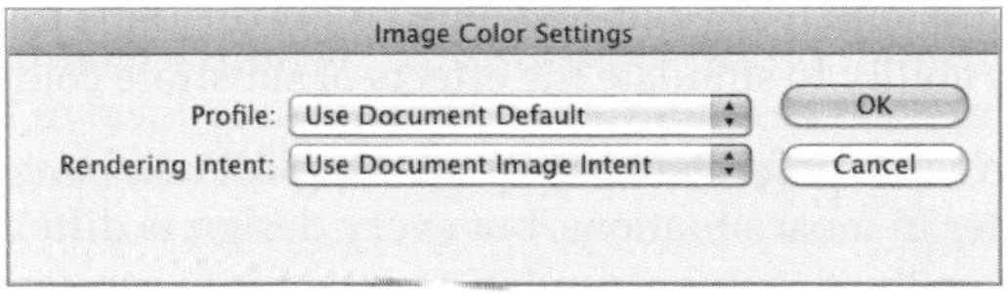

Changing Color Profiles

In Color Settings (or Bridge's Suite Color Settings), you define the color management options for the InDesign *application* and any new documents created while those options are in effect. What you do in there, however, will not alter the color management options on existing documents. To alter the working spaces, rendering intents, and so on, you need Assign Profiles or Convert to Profile, which are both found on the Edit menu below Color Settings. The difference between assigning and converting profiles is a tricky, hair-thin line.

REMOVING OR ASSIGNING DOCUMENT PROFILES

Assign Profiles (see Figure 10.6) first lets you strip off any profiles assigned to the document, including those previously assigned through this dialog, added via Convert to Profile, or in effect as the working spaces at document creation time. When you discard profiles, be careful: They will probably look fine onscreen because they'll use the current Color Settings working spaces and rendering intents while the document is opened, but the document itself will not carry those profiles with it to press or someone else's computer.

FIGURE 10.6
Assign Profiles enables removing or assigning profiles as well as different rendering intents per image type.

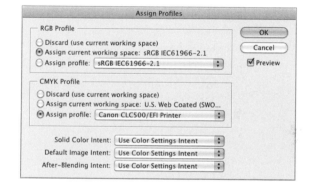

When you assign the current working space (below the Discard radio buttons) or assign another profile from the drop-down menus, the RGB and CMYK color definitions will remain unchanged, although they will appear different onscreen. Assigning a profile doesn't remap colors with a rendering intent; it effectively tells InDesign that the colors were wrong to begin with, that *these* are what they should have been.

Although the ability to both discard and assign new profiles is frequently useful, what is *really* cool about Assign Profiles is the bottom three drop-down boxes that let you set rendering by image *type*. Solid Color Intent defines the rendering intent for vector artwork, either natively drawn or imported somehow (place, paste, drop). Default Image Intent is the default raster or bitmap image rendering intent. Last, the confusingly named After-Blending Intent is the rendering intent to apply to objects that interact through transparency. For instance, if one image is overlaid on another and set to the Multiply blending mode, then the two objects will be mapped to in-gamut colors using the rendering intent specified here if different from the intent in Color Settings.

The handy Preview check box lets you see the results of your changes with the ability to hit Cancel and revert to the pre–Assign Profiles state.

CONVERT TO PROFILE

Converting a profile is the opposite of *assigning* a profile. Instead of telling InDesign *the colors were off, they should have been this,* Convert to Profile (see Figure 10.7) says, *The color definitions were right—and they look fine onscreen—but now I need them mapped to the gamut in this other color profile.* As the dialog indicates, Convert to Profile fires up the United Nations translator to convert the document's speech from the Source Space color language into the Destination Space color language.

FIGURE 10.7

In Convert to Profile, document working spaces and rendering intent may be remapped.

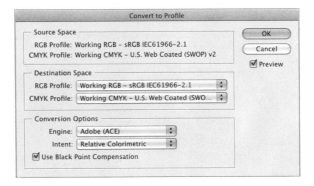

When would you use Convert to Profile? A good example is when you have to begin a project ahead of knowing how it will output and on what substrate. In that case, you'd set the document working spaces to large-gamut profiles like Adobe RGB (1998) and U.S. Web Coated (SWOP) v2. Later, once you've received the correct ICC profile for the printer and substrate, use Convert to Profile to remap the CMYK profile to that particular profile. Just be careful: Every time you convert the document profile, you're mapping colors between two separate gamuts, causing permanent, possibly destructive changes. *Once the document profile is converted, you can almost never go back.*

Proofing

Now that you've painstakingly configured your document's color management, it's time for that labor to bear fruit.

Proof Colors

There are three types of proofs in the print design and production business: *Soft proofs* display onscreen, simulating final output colors as close as RGB-based devices and a CMS can; prints sent to proof printers, those that are not the final output device, are called *hard proofs; pudding proofs* are the finished job, which we fervently hope matches the better of the other two. Because you were so punctilious in setting up your application, document, and individual image working spaces and rendering intents, you've unlocked the potential of InDesign's built-in soft proofing—Proof Colors.

Near the top of the View menu you'll find the Proof Colors command, which, if you choose it now, probably won't do much to your document. Above it is the Proof Setup menu, which lists the document CMYK profile, the working CMYK profile, and Custom. Choosing Custom opens the Customize Proof Condition dialog (see Figure 10.8).

FIGURE 10.8
Customize Proof
Condition sets
the conditions for
the Proof Colors
command.

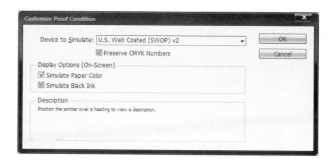

The purpose of soft proofing in InDesign is to approximate printing conditions live in
the InDesign document window, which negates the old, time-consuming trick of printing to
PostScript using a specific PPD and then distilling the PostScript file into a PDF soft proof. Instead
of using PPDs, the modern, color-managed workflow relies on Rosetta stones—ICC profiles.

The Device to Simulate menu includes all the compatible ICC profiles installed on your
system. Not just CMYK profiles, mind you; all the RGB profiles are there, too, which helps you
preview documents you'll be publishing in an electronic medium like PDF, HTML, or EPUB. In
case you feel like broadcasting your InDesign document, you can also see what it would look
like in video profiles like HDTV, PAL/SECAM, and NTSC. Actually, these are available because
InDesign is displaying every ICC/ICM profile on the system.

Selecting any profile other than the document's current working RGB or CMYK profile activates the Preserve (RGB/CMYK) Numbers check box. When Preserve Numbers is checked,
InDesign will not alter the display colors of objects drawn natively in InDesign—including
frames, strokes, text, and so on—nor will it alter the display color of images being managed by
the document CMYK working space. Images would be so managed because either they don't
have linked profiles of their own or you chose Preserve Numbers (Ignore Linked Profiles) as
the CMYK (or RGB) policy in Color Settings. Unchecking the Preserve Numbers box adapts *all*
colors to soft proof regardless of color management policies. If you'll be going to press with the
Preserve Numbers (Ignore Linked Profiles) option, then you'll probably want to leave Preserve
Numbers checked during soft proofing.

Simulate Paper Color and Simulate Black Ink read the characteristics for both as stored in the
selected device profile. When Simulate Paper Color is checked, the CMS will try to ascertain the
color of the substrate and change the white point of the image display to match. For example,
with parchment paper defined as the expected substrate for the job, all the white areas and highlights will turn yellowish tan, which will also shine through and tint areas of transparency and
non-opaque inks—cyan, magenta, yellow, and many spot colors. Simulate Black Ink, which is
automatically turned on if Simulate Paper Color is activated, uses the Black Ink Compensation
I mentioned earlier to determine the actual value of black on the specific output device and
adjusts the black point and gray values accordingly.

When you click OK, the entire document will be thrown into soft proof, or Proof Colors mode
(see Figure 10.9). You can scroll around, change pages, zoom in or out, and even continue to
work in Proof Colors mode, although screen redraws may be somewhat slower. To turn off soft
proofing, select View ➤ Proof Colors.

FIGURE 10.9
The same document with different proof profiles selected. (Also see the full-color version in the color insert.)

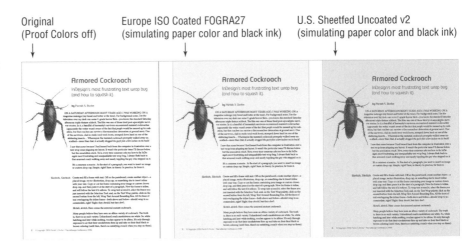

Original (Proof Colors off)

Europe ISO Coated FOGRA27 (simulating paper color and black ink)

U.S. Sheetfed Uncoated v2 (simulating paper color and black ink)

SIMULATING SPOT COLOR INKS ONSCREEN

InDesign will *try* to simulate spot color inks onscreen, but often that just isn't possible, particularly with special inks like PANTONE's pastel or metallic libraries. The limitation isn't InDesign in that case; many of those special inks just can't be rendered on a monitor in RGB. In those cases, ignore what you see onscreen and trust your swatch book. As long as you've specified the correct library and PMS color numbers, InDesign will accurately send the spot to press.

Proof Separations

Soft proofing doesn't end with simulating ink and paper colors. There's more yet to come, starting with viewing separations onscreen. If you're still printing seps to PDF, *stop*. There's a better way.

SEPARATIONS PREVIEW

I love the Proof Colors command, but Adobe's idea of putting onscreen separations into InDesign and then putting the controls for it on a panel instead of disuniting separations previews from the document in a dialog or a separate window is pure brilliance (see Figure 10.10). With these controls on a panel, the entire document can be proofed a page at a time or multiple pages at once by zooming out. Options can be changed on the fly—say, to get a deep look at just the black plate or to change the ink limit—and they can be turned off and on easily. Open the Separations Preview panel from Window ➤ Output ➤ Separations Preview.

From the View drop-down menu you have three choices: Off (the normal, working, nonpreviewed document state), Ink Limit, and Separations.

FIGURE 10.10
The Separations Preview panel

Separations

Inks are managed on the Separations Preview panel the way layers are managed on their name-sake panel. After you select Separations from the View drop-down, all inks in use anywhere within the current document will be presented as individual entries, including process and spot inks. To hide certain inks—for instance, to isolate a spot plate—click the eyeball icons beside the other inks. Activating the CMYK entry at the top of the list automatically turns on the individual Cyan, Magenta, Yellow, and Black plates. Any ink not visible will hide objects of that color in the document, which is very useful to ascertain whether Black Ink Compensation has turned black ink values into four-color rich black.

From the Separations Preview panel flyout menu you have the option to show single plates in black, meaning that, if only the yellow ink is shown, yellow objects will appear onscreen in black as if printed to film by an imagesetter or filmsetter. Turning this off displays each plate in its ink color—Yellow shows yellow objects, Magenta shows magenta objects, and so forth, like a Matchprint before compressing the color films together.

Even better, with separations preview active, hovering your mouse cursor over any object will display the ink densities for each individual color; hover the cursor beside CMYK for the combined total (see Figure 10.11).

FIGURE 10.11

Hovering the mouse cursor over an area of color within an object shows the ink densities for each ink used to create that color.

Ink Limit

To check your design's ink densities more visually, choose Ink Limit from the View drop-down, and then set the ink coverage percentage limit in the field to the right. InDesign will highlight in red any instances wherein the ink density exceeds the limit, while graying out any in-limit colors.

Proof Flattening

Transparency was one of the most difficult concepts to grasp for, well, a whole host of people and systems. RIPs were probably the most confused despite transparency being a core feature of PostScript 3. Long-time QuarkXPress users saw no value in transparency because XPress didn't do it—the attitude was, to paraphrase *Saturday Night Live*'s Mike Myers (back when *SNL* was funny), if it's na' Quarkish, it's crap. Adobe itself was 20 years late to the party and, when it did build transparency into PostScript and its applications, it had some trouble getting it just right. Despite propaganda, Adobe *did* get it right quite a few years ago. A fair percentage of change-fearing print and prepress workers were frightened by transparency and so instinctively disparaged transparency with that most vile of epithets: *It shalt not print!*

Well, Adobe *did* get it right, even QuarkXPress uses transparency (since version 7 in 2006), and, most important, *transparency does print.*

It prints natively in PostScript 3-compatible RIPs because PostScript 3, released in 1998, is built to print transparency (it's also built to handle color management internally). More than a

decade later, a few RIPs still in operation deserve walk-ons in VH1's *Stuck in the 90s* series; they still haven't updated to support PostScript 3.

If you happen to be shackled to one of these PostScript Level 2 has-been RIPs, don't fret: You can't send blended objects, drop shadows, or semitransparent strokes to RIP *directly*, but the ever-courteous InDesign knows how to handle the RIPs of yesteryear. The secret is flattening.

FLATTENING

In any layout or graphics application, including InDesign, QuarkXPress, Illustrator, Photoshop, and so on, objects are not wholly two-dimensional. They have width and height (x and y) but also pseudo depth through stacking order or z-order (z for the third-dimensional z-axis). Objects in InDesign (or another program; layers in Photoshop) are stacked atop or below one another, allowing them to be independently manipulated as opposed to a single-layer raster image where artwork really is two-dimensional on the pixel grid. As we all know, printing is a two-dimensional process: Ink sits on drums, rollers, plates, or screens and then transfers onto a single two-dimensional substrate surface: paper, cloth, plastic, or glass. Presses, printers, and imagesetters just don't do 3D—even object printers that print in revolution around a 3D package or other object are only applying 2D ink to a flat surface. A *raster image processor (RIP)* converts everything into a raster image at the output device's resolution, creating halftone dots from solid areas of color. All that text, all those carefully drawn paths, gets rasterized into the equivalent of a single-layer raster image. At some point, the stacking order of objects must be abandoned as well, incorporating or discarding areas of color blocked by objects higher in the stacking order. This is the process of *flattening*—squishing everything down to two dimensions and removing transparency.

During flattening, the notion of objects is secondary to the concept of colors. If you look at Figure 10.12, you'll see a few rectangles typical of InDesign objects at the top. They interact with one another through transparency—the green is 50% transparent, blending with the yellow; the red is opaque but has a drop shadow that forces it to blend with the yellow and green. Where areas of transparency overlap other objects, their colors mix to create new areas of color. At the bottom, flattening has carved out each distinct area of color to become its own flat, opaque, 2D object, which I've spread out so you can appreciate the effect of carving. Some—the drop shadow as well as the yellow and green rectangles it touched—are no longer vector paths; now they're raster images.

FIGURE 10.12
Top, three transparent objects interact. Flattened, three have become seven color-centric chunks (bottom). Check the color insert for a full-color view of this figure.

Depending on the types of objects and how they interact with surrounding colors, some vector objects will be rasterized as a matter of necessity. Which objects retain their resolution independence as vectors (or remain separate raster objects) and which rasterize into solid imagery is the dominion of the InDesign Transparency Flattener, which, by and large, is under your control.

Previewing and Controlling Flattening

The core of the Transparency Flattener controls is the Flattener Preview panel (see Figure 10.13). You'll find it on Window ➤ Output ➤ Flattener Preview.

FIGURE 10.13

The Flattener Preview panel

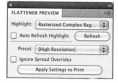

The Flattener Preview panel highlights objects containing, or affected by, transparency in red while sapping color out of the rest of the document's onscreen view. In Figure 10.14 and its counterpart in the color insert, you can see the results of highlighting raster-fill text and strokes on a document with blended mode images above or below text. By previewing the flattening before going to press, you can find and fix common problems. As you change flattening controls, the onscreen preview can be set to update with the Auto Refresh Highlight check box, or you can manually update it by clicking the Refresh button.

FIGURE 10.14

Previewing flattening on a document highlights affected areas and dims nonaffected areas.

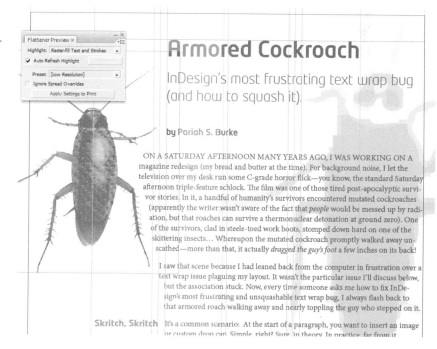

From the drop-down list at the top, choose what you'd like to see. All Affected Objects will highlight all *objects* affected by transparency; even if those objects are carved up into affected and nonaffected regions, InDesign will highlight the entire object. All Rasterized Regions shows only those areas that have had to be rasterized. All the other options isolate specific types of flattening and specific types of objects.

If a region or objects require flattening, InDesign has three methods available to accomplish it:

Clip　When it comes to the interaction of raster images and transparency, InDesign tries to accomplish flattening by making multiple, clipped copies of the images. For instance, in Figure 10.15, the logo on the left is a vector shape blended with the placed image background via 75% opacity and the Overlay blending mode. When flattened (on the right), the background becomes one raster image with the vector shape knocked out, but then two other copies of the background are included—one to fill the vector flame fill, the other to fill the vector flame outline. Each image is whole and rectangular, but each has had a clipping path applied. Moreover, the copies of the image that were colored by the overlaid logo have been recolored at the pixel level to create the pre-flattened effect. (Note that I moved the pieces for clarity. Of course, once flattened, they would align as before.)

FIGURE 10.15
Pre-flattening (left) and post-flattening (right). See the full-color version in the color insert for more detail.

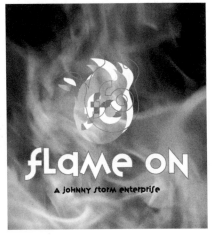

Divide　Just like the Pathfinder Divide command (see Chapter 4, "Drawing"), this primarily vector object method of flattening carves all the colors out into their separate objects. For a visual example, direct your peepers to Figure 10.16. For a full-color visual example, direct your peepers to the color insert. Pre-flattening (left), three circles overlap one another and blend together using a Screen blending mode to create seven distinct areas of color. On the right, post-flattening, three objects have become seven, with no blending (I outlined them to make the differences easier to see).

Rasterize　The last and least-desirable option available to the Transparency Flattener is to rasterize a region of transparency. When not rasterizing would make the flattened result too complicated, when it would create too many small chunks that might slow or even crash a RIP, InDesign will opt to rasterize an area. Rasterized areas become fixed resolution and can potentially output with lower quality than other areas. Spot colors forced to rasterize will convert to their nearest CMYK equivalents and may not match nonrasterized areas that use the actual spot.

FIGURE 10.16
Pre-flattening
(left) and post-
flattening (right)

 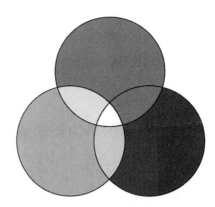

FIGURE 10.16
Pre-flattening
(left) and post-
flattening (right)

Which flattening method InDesign employs depends on the specific artwork—whether it's raster or vector, how it blends with objects above and below, the colors used, and so on—and as determined by the chosen flattener preset. Presets are managed and customized via the Edit ➤ Transparency Flattener Presets menu command and the Transparency Flattener Presets command on the Flattener Preview panel's flyout menu. In any of these places, the Preset menu lists three default, bracketed (undeletable) presets. Each contains quality decision directives and has certain uses.

Low Resolution Best for low- to mid-grade desktop ink-jet and laser printers. Text and line art, if rasterized, is fixed at 288 ppi, while gradients and meshes are rasterized to 144 ppi.

Medium Resolution Works with higher-grade or higher-RAM desktop printers and provides a fairly fast print on proof printers. Uses 300 and 150 ppi.

High Resolution The highest quality but the most complex output. Save this for imagesetters, platesetters, plateless direct-to-press systems, and high-end proof printers. Uses 1200 and 300 ppi.

The three default presets are general purpose and have large gaps between them. Ideally, you want to flatten all your for-press work with the High Resolution preset, which has everything cranked up. For most documents, that works. However, with lots of transparency on lots of pages, your RIP could error or timeout. So could a desktop printer with one of the other presets for that matter. You'll want to know how to make your own presets.

From the Transparency Flattener Presets dialog, choose New to open the Transparency Flattener Preset Options dialog (see Figure 10.17). At the top, give the preset a name you'll understand when you reopen this document six months down the road. Then, make your quality-versus-complexity decisions. It's all a trade-off.

FIGURE 10.17
Transparency
Flattener Preset
Options dialog

Transparency Flattener Preset Options		
Name: Flattener Preset 1		OK
Raster/Vector Balance: ———▲—— 75		Cancel
Rasters Vectors		
Line Art and Text Resolution: 288 ▲▼ ppi		
Gradient and Mesh Resolution: 144 ▲▼ ppi		
☐ Convert All Text to Outlines		
☑ Convert All Strokes to Outlines		
☐ Clip Complex Regions		

Raster/Vector Balance   (Slider and measurement box) Although the other options are important, the Raster/Vector Balance slider is the most important part of determining flattening quality—and how long it takes to print a document. The slider adjusts the Transparency Flattener's priorities—how hard InDesign should try to maintain vectors before electing to rasterize transparent regions. On the right, identified as Vectors, is high quality. The closer to the right you take the slider, the more InDesign will try to use the divide (on vector objects) and clip (on raster) methodologies. Additionally, the closer to the right, the more complicated the document and longer to print. Conversely, moving the slider toward the left sets a lower threshold for rasterizing transparency and results in faster prints. Every document is different, so experiment with the slider on a few jobs to get a feel for how close to the right you can push the Raster/Vector Balance slider.

Resolution   If these types of items must be rasterized, what resolution would you like? The drop-downs on these two fields offer common resolution settings, but you may also type custom values into the fields.

The values here are also used during the clipping flattening method because InDesign will downsample clipped images (that interact with transparency) to the higher resolution in the Line Art and Text Resolution field. Thus, a placed 600 ppi image with a semitransparent color box above it will be downsampled to 288 ppi resolution if the Low Resolution preset is used. If the resolution of an image is lower than the Gradient and Mesh Resolution value, InDesign may upsample images interacting with transparency to meet the Gradient and Mesh Resolution value. The upsamples are not very good, by the way, using the Nearest Neighbor interpolation method with which you may be familiar from Photoshop. In other words, *watch out*, particularly if you're working with a client's "high-resolution GIF logo from the website's home page."

Convert All Text to Outlines   Don't gloss over this one. At first glance, most design and print pros tend to think, *Oh, I know all about converting type to outlines.* That may be true for converting type to outlines in general, but do you know the unique considerations inherent in doing it during flattening? When type interacts with transparency, one of two things must happen: It gets rasterized, or, preferably, it converts to outlines and becomes part of the divide or clip flattening methods; sometimes type even becomes a clipping path and contains a section of a raster image. Those things are going to happen regardless of whether this box is checked. What this box really does is decide how the rest of the type is treated.

When type is converted to outlines, it can get heavier—thicker, boldlike—onscreen and on some low- to mid-level printers (not on imagesetters or DTP printers). If type that doesn't interact with transparency isn't outlined, if it's left as live type, then suddenly a vertical half of a paragraph or even a few letters within a word can appear bolder than surrounding text just because they had strips of blended art close to them. Conversely, when type is rasterized, it rarely gets thicker. In fact, once in a blue moon, it appears *thinner*. So converting all text to outlines might not save you from type of visually disparate weights on your desktop and proof printers. Outlined type is also slower to print.

So, which should you use—Convert All Text to Outlines on or off? I don't know. I can't see your document. Proof the flattening in the Flattener Preview panel before sending a

document to print on your desktop or proof printer. You can use different flattener presets per spread (see below), so set an overall document preset, and then spot-assign different presets to handle unique situations.

For final output, I recommend leaving this option off because I've yet to see the thickening or thinning issues appear with good-quality imagesetters, platesetters, or direct-to-press digital printers. Even though PDFs created either by printing or by exporting from InDesign do exhibit the same issues *onscreen* and in desktop or proof printers, just as they do when output directly from InDesign to desktop printers, I've never seen a PDF actually *print* thick (or thin) text to high-end devices.

Convert All Strokes to Outlines   The description and potential problems with this choice are identical to Convert All Text to Outlines except that it deals with strokes instead of type.

Clip Complex Regions   Raster images are rectangles; that's their nature. So when InDesign rasterizes a region of transparency, it creates rectangles. Sometimes, those rectangles bisect objects—it's not uncommon to observe a letter split in two, with one side remaining a vector path and the other rasterizing into a larger region. And sometimes, these are noticeable. In fact, they are *often* noticeable onscreen, on low- to mid-grade printers and in PDFs, but in the majority of such cases they are *not* noticeable on final output to a high-end output device. Still, you may want to change the way InDesign relates objects and paths to areas that must be rasterized.

Turning on Clip Complex Regions will direct InDesign to try to rasterize only up to an object's path. If it can't do that—maybe half the letter *is* affected by transparency—it will incorporate the entire path. It does this by creating more and more complicated clipping paths, which, of course, slows down the flattening process and printing.

I apologize if I left you with more questions and answers in defining the purposes, pros, and cons of the Transparency Flattener Preset Options dialog. If you've read through the rest of this book, you know there are usually rules or at least guidelines or rules of thumb. Flattening, however, is like curves or levels in Photoshop—there are no hard rules because every document is different. Flattening is a process of trade-offs, quality versus complexity. Where the tipping points occur between acceptable and unacceptable quality and acceptable and unacceptable print speeds are subjective; only *you* can determine the location of those tipping points with *your* particular documents. If you care about quality and print speed, use the Flattener Preview panel to scrutinize your document.

A Few More Words about Flattening

Flattening can be accomplished in-RIP with PostScript 3–compatible RIPs. When using older-technology RIPS, it has to be done at output time, either via printing or exporting to PDF from InDesign. You'll find the familiar list of Transparency Flattener presets on the Advanced pane of the Print dialog and the Advanced pane of the Export Adobe PDF dialog.

Acrobat version 5 and later (PDF 1.4 and later), being based on PostScript 3, natively supports transparency. There's no need to flatten prior to, or during, export to PDF when sending to PDF version 1.4 or later. However, when exporting to PDF 1.3 (Acrobat 4), flattening *will* occur, a fact

many forget and wonder why they got output looking a lot like the default High Resolution flattening preset instead of their custom preset. Exporting to PDF/X-1a or PDF/X-3 requires flattened, PDF 1.3-compatible PDFs; PDF/X-4 uses PDF version 1.4.

When working in an Open Prepress Interface (OPI) workflow, it's important to remember that InDesign flattens only what it can see. If you have the high-resolution final images available, tell InDesign where to find them so it can properly flatten at output (InDesign will then handle the OPI replacement, too). Do this in two steps:

1. Check the box Read Embedded OPI Image Links in Import Options of placed EPS files. You'll need to have done that while initially placing the graphics, or relink them from the Links panel and do it then.

2. At output time, check OPI Image Replacement on the Advanced pane of the Print or Export EPS dialog.

With both of those options checked, InDesign will handle the OPI substitution and flatten using the high-resolution images instead of the low-resolution proxies. If your workflow requires that InDesign have access only to the proxy image and that replacements cannot be made until further down the line, *do not flatten the document*—do not print, export to PDF 1.3, or export to EPS.

On the Edit menu is the Transparency Blend Space submenu. Blend spaces override swatches to maintain consistent color across a spread in the event of transparency interaction. In other words, if you choose Document CMYK as the spread blend space (Edit ➢ Transparency Blend Space ➢ Document CMYK), all colors on the spread will be shown onscreen and be sent to press as CMYK—even if you draw an RGB object, even if you use an RGB swatch. Transparency output is a spread-level consideration, and InDesign doesn't want your flattened blues to be different from one side of the spread to the next. This is a definite gotcha for those who publish to PDF distributables because an otherwise RGB document can suddenly have two CMYK pages smack in the middle. If that's you, change the Transparency Blend Space to Document RGB.

Individual spreads (but not individual pages) can be assigned their own flattening presets. On the Pages panel, select one or more spreads and then, on the Pages panel flyout menu, you'll find the Spread Flattening submenu with these options:

Default Uses the document preset, even if it has yet to be defined.

None Ignores transparency entirely and outputs opaque objects that do not blend (a bad idea unless troubleshooting).

Custom Lets you customize flattener options for that particular spread.

The only way to gauge spot color transparency interaction onscreen is with Overprint Preview on (View ➢ Overprint Preview). The same is true in PDFs. When creating PDF proofs, check the Simulate Overprint box on the Output pane of the Export to Adobe PDF dialog to better render spot color interaction with transparency.

Color, Difference, Exclusion, Hue, Luminosity, and Saturation blending modes are generally not recommended for use on or in connection with spot colors.

Preflighting

For the uninitiated, preflight is the process of checking a document for potential printing issues before printing—flight. InDesign includes a better-than-introductory preflight function that I recommend all designers use. Press and prepress shops will use a much more robust preflight system like FlightCheck, Preflight Pro, PitStop Pro, or PDF Checkup. But leaving preflight entirely to your print or prepress provider is a serious, potentially costly mistake. InDesign's preflight can identify and fix the most common problems with InDesign documents, problems designers should *never* leave to press operators or prepress operators to fix. Failing to find and fix these common problems will tick off and alienate a designer's best friends—his print and prepress providers—and often cost the designer hard currency because many providers (justifiably) charge to fix these common, easily preventable problems that are squarely within the designer's sphere of responsibility.

Moreover, I advise print and prepress shops to encourage their designer clients to learn and use InDesign's preflight before submitting files. It does help stop many of the simple, common problems with InDesign documents.

In InDesign CS4 and CS5, preflight moved from a dialog box accessed via the File ➢ Preflight command to a panel-based, always-on (by default), document-examination and error-alerting system. Packaging a document is also no longer slowed by a preflight check because preflight is always running.

Live Preflight

Looking to the lower left of any document window, between the page-navigation buttons and the horizontal scrollbar, you'll see the Live Preflight reporting section. From the moment you create a document, through everything you do inside it, InDesign is constantly examining it for common problems. It's sort of like Jiminy Cricket in those "I'm No Fool" educational films they showed in elementary school, always watching over your shoulder, acting as your conscience, keeping you safe from traffic, strangers, exposed electrical wires, and other dangers. Within InDesign, however, Jiminy Cricket is watching out for print-specific dangers like missing links, the use of unwanted color spaces, substituted glyphs, and so on.

Hopefully your documents all show a cricket-green icon followed by "No Errors," indicating that preflight found no problems that would prevent your document from printing properly. At some point, though, you're bound to see that green light burn a worrisome red. When it does, double-click it to reveal the green imp himself, the Preflight panel.

Preflight Panel

The Preflight panel, accessible by double-clicking the Live Preflight reporting section or by choosing Window ➢ Output ➢ Preflight, reports all the potential and actual dangers that could harm your print job (see Figure 10.18). Each type of problem is categorized, under COLOR for such problems as images containing RGB colors when they've been disallowed in the document, LINKS when linked assets are out of date or missing, TEXT for such issues as overset text, missing fonts, and unresolved caption variables, and IMAGES and OBJECTS for issues like hidden objects, the use of interactive elements, object-level bleed or trim issues, non-proportional scaling of placed objects, and more.

FIGURE 10.18
The Preflight panel
showing various
errors

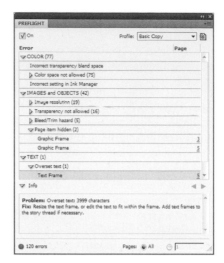

Use the Preflight panel to efficiently discover, examine, and fix problems with your document. Let's walk through the panel:

On   This check box enables or disables live preflight checking of the document.

Profile   This drop-down box enables the selection of the preflight profile against which you want to check the current document (see the next section, "Preflight Profiles"). Clicking the button to the right of the drop-down field embeds the currently selected preflight profile in the document, enabling that profile to travel with the document to output providers, collaborators, or, if you're a press or prepress operator who wants to show the designer the problems you discovered, back to the creator of the InDesign document.

Error   In this area, grouped by category of issue, are listed any and all instances where something failed the criteria of one or more preflight conditions. Each error or advisory is listed along with its page number.

◆   Click the page number once or double-click the name of the object posing a problem; the current document view will jump to display the object in question.

◆   Use the arrow buttons just below the Error area's scrollbar to move forward or back through the problems, jumping the document view to focus on each problem object sequentially.

◆   Click the object name in the Error list to load the information about the problem into the Info section below.

MORE ERRORS THAN THE EYE CAN SEE

Be careful! You may not be seeing all the problems in your document in the Error section. By default, InDesign shows you only 100 instances of each type of error. So, you might go through a document, fixing everything, only to watch more errors, things that you thought were all right, suddenly appear in the Error list as if they magically went bad. To see all the problems and advisories up front, go to the Preflight panel flyout menu and choose Limit Number of Rows Per Error ➢ No Limit.

Info In the Info area, which may be hidden by toggling the spinner arrow to the left, you'll see information relative to the currently selected problem. First, the problem is defined according to the violated preflight condition, then, labeled as Required, what the condition allows. Finally, InDesign will advise a fix for the problem.

Preflight Status (Unlabeled) In the bottom left, mirroring the display in the document window's bottom-left corner, is the count of found problems and advisories.

Pages By default, all pages of a document are compared against the selected preflight profile's conditions. However, using the radio button and field on the right, you can preflight only specific pages or ranges of pages.

Preflight Profiles

Preflighting in InDesign CS4 and CS5 is much more robust than in earlier versions. Quite a number of conditions can be checked, not all of them things you want Live Preflight to search for in every document all the time. Accordingly, you can create preflight profiles containing different sets of conditions against which documents will be evaluated. For example, when preparing a publication for print, you might want to enforce the presence and size of a bleed area, something you wouldn't do when producing documents destined only for PDF digital distribution.

THE PREFLIGHT PROFILES DIALOG

Create, delete, examine, and manage preflight profiles from the Preflight Profiles dialog box (see Figure 10.19), which you can open via the Preflight panel's flyout menu and the Define Profiles command. On the left in the dialog are the available profiles. At the very top, italicized, will be listed any profiles embedded in the current document. [Basic], as indicated by the brackets, is the undeletable, unalterable default profile below document-embedded profiles. Other profiles you create will appear beneath [Basic]. At the bottom are three buttons: New Preflight Profile, Delete Preflight Profile, and Preflight Profile Menu, which lets you export and load profiles as well as embed or unembed document-embedded profiles.

FIGURE 10.19
Defining preflight conditions in the Preflight Profiles dialog

Exported profiles are saved as IDPP (InDesign Preflight Profile) files and may be shared with other InDesign users. They can even go cross-platform; the same IDPP file exported from

Uses Transparency   Advises if any objects use transparency, which includes not only an Opacity value of less than 100% but also blending modes or transparency effects such as a drop shadow or outer glow.

Image ICC Profile   Checks against one or both criteria: Profile Setting May Cause CMYK Conversion, which will alter the CMYK colors of an image, and Any Profile Override, whereupon the InDesign user has deliberately overridden the color profile of an object. If you check Exclude Images with no Embedded Profile after the latter option, images that had no embedded profiles and were subsequently assigned to a profile by InDesign will be ignored and not generate an error for having their profiles overridden.

Layer Visibility Overrides   Reports if one or more layers have been hidden.

Minimum Stroke Weight   Useful when equipment cannot render stroke weights below a certain thickness, such as in the example of lower-resolution corrugated printing. Alerts if any strokes carry a weight below the set minimum. May also ignore all strokes except those using multiple ink colors or white.

Interactive Elements   Alerts if the document contains video, audio, animated objects, multistate objects (i.e., rollovers), buttons, or any media not compatible with Flash Player. The last option is typically the most used; when producing interactive ebook publications from InDesign, only the aforementioned types of objects are safe bets. Anything not compatible with the Flash Player may not play in the exported PDF.

Bleed/Trim Hazard   An extremely useful condition to keep for any document destined for press, this condition alerts if objects are too close to the page edge and thus in danger of being cut off in the event of a minor page shift during paper cutting. Note that if artwork is set to bleed, this condition will error for every bleeding object. If used with bleeds, check to ensure that all important data and objects are within the safety zone of the live area, but ignore warnings about objects that are supposed to bleed. You may set the size of the live area and choose whether to check the inside edge, the area toward the spine.

Hidden Page Items   Alerts if any objects are set as hidden or nonprinting.

TEXT

TEXT category conditions examine and assess text used within the document. From something as simple as ensuring that the document doesn't contain overset text to requiring that type is not set smaller than a certain size, the conditions here help you ensure that perfect type goes to press.

Overset Text   If a text thread appears within the printable area, but part of that text doesn't fit and isn't visible anywhere, this rule will issue a warning.

Paragraph Style and Character Style Overrides   This condition will alert if text assigned to a paragraph and/or character style carries an attribute not defined in the style. You can choose to ignore specific types of overrides: font styles, kerning or tracking, language, and/or color.

Font Missing   Alerts if text or a style is using a font not installed on the current system.

Glyph Missing   Produces an error on glyph substitution if a particular character, number, or symbol was used in the text but doesn't actually exist in the font assigned to that text.

Dynamic Spelling Detects Errors   Alerts if Dynamic Spelling is enabled and has identified misspellings.

Font Types Not Allowed   A powerful and much desired condition, Font Types Not Allowed offers the ability to prevent unsupported fonts from making it through to RIP. Select which types of fonts count as errors: Protected Fonts (those whose licensing restricts them from being shared to providers and that will not copy when using the Package feature), TrueType, Bitmap, Type 1 Multiple Master, Type 1, Type 1 CID, Adobe Type Composer ATC, or different flavors of OpenType, CFF, CFF CID, and TrueType based.

Non-Proportional Type Scaling   Produces an error if text has been scaled horizontally or vertically with the relevant fields on the Character panel (or equivalent fields on the Control panel's Character mode).

Minimum Type Size   Similar to the Minimum Stroke Weight condition under IMAGES and OBJECTS, this condition is typically used to prevent the omission or breakage of letterforms on equipment that cannot render stroke weights below a certain thickness.

Cross-References   Checks for out-of-date (content updated but not reflected in the cross-reference) or unresolved (cross-reference destination missing or overset) cross-references.

Conditional Text Indicators Will Print   Warns when conditional text indicators such as underlines or highlights will be visible upon printing.

Unresolved Caption Variable   When a Live Caption frame is set to display a metadata value not present in the adjacent image, or when a Live Caption frame is disassociated from an image and thus not pulling in metadata, the caption is unresolved. This condition keeps those embarrassing mistakes from going to press without alerting you.

CS5

Span Columns Setting Not Honored   In certain, rarely occurring circumstances, InDesign will be forced to ignore span- or split-column directives, and enabling this condition will produce an alert that such has happened. The situations in which this can occur are:

◆ When a span column paragraph is set to span a greater number of columns than the text frame actually contains.

◆ If the calculated width of a split column is less than 3 pts, which is the same column width limit at which any text frame will fail to compose.

CS5

Tracked Change   As a hedge against going to press with a potentially unwanted change skipped inadvertently by editorial, this condition will trigger an alert if any tracked changes remain to be accepted or rejected.

DOCUMENT

The DOCUMENT preflight conditions look at those aspects of the document outside the purview of the other categories—conditions such as requisite page sizes and counts, bleed and slug options, and whether the document contains blank pages.

CS5

Page Size and Orientation   This condition alerts if any or all of the document pages fail to conform to the specified width and height. The Ignore Orientation check box, if enabled, says it's okay if a page rotated—width and height swapped—as long as each dimension of pages matches in width and height one way or the other. Although there are many reasons you might want to check for page size during preflight, perhaps the most common I've seen is when the design is destined for something other than 8.5×11 inches, but when the designer may be rather new to working with InDesign. Novice users often just hit OK on the New Document

dialog, accepting the defaults, which are 8.5×11 inches. Remember that preflighting happens live, as the designer works, so if the Page Size and Orientation condition is activated, the red dot will appear the instant a document of the wrong dimensions is created.

Number of Pages Required   This is a highly versatile condition that could prove useful to any type of bound document design. Choices include setting the condition to warn if the document contains more or fewer than x number of pages, anything besides an exact number of pages, or a page count that is not a perfect multiple of y. The last option, when set to Multiple of 4, can warn creatives when a publication bound for press doesn't have enough pages to be printed in standard 2-on-2 spreads. Other choices area quite helpful for ensuring proper page count in light of the InDesign CS5 ability to automatically add pages instead of oversetting text.

Blank Pages   Sometimes sending blank pages to output is desired, but more often not. This condition will alert if there are any blank pages, with options to consider pages blank even if they contain only master page items and/or nonprinting objects.

Bleed and Slug Setup   Ensure that documents have your workflow's required bleed and/or slug settings by enabling this condition and setting the sizes.

`CS5`

All Pages Must Use Same Size and Orientation   This condition fires off an error if any page of the document differs in size and/or orientation (landscape or portrait) than another page in the document. It errors only on differences, rather than when something doesn't meet a specific size. For that, use the Page Size and Orientation condition.

Creating a Preflight Profile

You can tell Jiminy Cricket exactly what dangers to watch out for and which situations are safe. Begin by creating a new profile:

1. Click the New Preflight Profile button, which bears a plus sign at the bottom left of the Preflight Profiles dialog.

2. In the Profile Name field, give your profile a meaningful name. Hint: "Basic Copy" is not a meaningful name.

3. Under the heading of General is the Description field. Enter here a concise description of the purpose and function of the profile—this is especially important if you'll be distributing the profile for others to use. If you're at a loss as to what to put there, here are a few suggestions:

   ◆ An overview of the conditions evaluated by the profile.

   ◆ If you are creating a general distribution profile for your press or prepress clientele, enter here your shop's name and contact info as well as a line or two explaining the profile's general purpose, that it checks *this* and *that*.

   ◆ If the profile is specific to a particular output process—say, low-resolution, limited-color corrugated printing or plotter output—state that.

   ◆ If the profile is to be used only when producing documents of a certain type—maybe ebooks—describe the document type well enough that the average InDesign user would be able to decide for herself when it's appropriate to use the profile.

4. Now set the conditions against which InDesign should evaluate the document content. Each of the five sections—LINKS, COLOR, IMAGES and OBJECTS, TEXT, and DOCUMENT—contains in an expandable list relevant conditions. Check those you want; uncheck those you don't. When you're ready, click Save to commit your changes to the profile.

5. If you want to distribute the preflight profile to others, click the Preflight Profile Menu button to the right of the Delete Preflight Profile button, and choose Export Profile. When prompted to save the IDPP file, give it a meaningful name and save it to disk. Click OK.

You've just created a preflight profile. Now, when you wish upon a star (makes no difference who you are), InDesign will check every object and attribute of your document against the conditions you set. Like the charmingly dapper insect in his top hat and tails riding your shoulder, the Live Preflight reporting area at the bottom left of your document will light your way, giving you the green light (hopefully) or tugging at your conscience with a red light when something isn't quite right.

Preflight Options

Rather than put the preflight options in the Preferences dialog where all the other options and preferences are stored, they're hidden under Jiminy Cricket's hat, in the Preflight Options dialog box accessible from the Preflight panel's flyout menu. In Preflight Options you define the default behavior for Live Preflight on new documents (see Figure 10.20).

FIGURE 10.20
The Preflight
Options dialog box

Working Profile Choose here the preflight profile to use by default on all new documents. When the choice is anything but the default [Basic] profile, the check box below will light up, enabling you to embed the chosen profile within new documents so that the profile travels with those documents to providers and collaborators.

When Opening Documents Choose here, when opening InDesign documents, whether to use the working profile chosen above or the preflight profile embedded in those documents, if one exists. Even with the latter chosen, if the documents don't already contain an embedded preflight profile, the working profile will be substituted automatically.

Include   Set here the options for what should be checked against the current preflight profile. Of course, every object on a printable page is going to be preflighted, but do you also want Live Preflight to examine objects on hidden or nonprintable layers? How about objects on the pasteboard or objects set via the Attributes panel to nonprinting?

The Bottom Line

Configure Color Management on Documents and Images   Consistent color throughout the workflow is critical—even in grayscale jobs. With each version of Creative Suite, Adobe makes color management smarter, easier, and more consistent across the Creative Suite applications. However, the nature of color management is such that it works only if you configure it for the devices specific to your workflow.

Master It   Configure Adobe Bridge to use the ICC profiles for your monitor and printer (or other output device) across all of Creative Suite. You can profile your devices yourself using Mac's Display Calibrator Assistant or Windows's Image Color Management. If you're configuring a high-end output device such as an imagesetter or proof printer, ask your print service provider for the most up-to-date ICC profile for the device. If you choose to configure color management for your desktop printer, either profile it yourself or visit the manufacturer's website; most OEMs include free, downloadable ICC profiles. These aren't specific to your printer's unique color-rendering characteristics, but they will get you close.

Soft Proof Documents to Screen   When software makers say *What You See Is What You Get (WYSIWYG)*, it's really not, not in the case of color, not from the typical working mode of applications. That's where soft proofing comes in. Its pixel-based preview still isn't a precise representation of what you can expect with ink on paper, but when configured correctly, InDesign gets it surprisingly close.

Master It   Using one of your own documents or a sample from another chapter on this book's download page, proof the approximate expected output colors with your printer's ICC profile. Next, examine how the document will separate when sent to press and how transparency will flatten. Look for potential printing issues, and resolve them.

Configure and Use Live Preflight and the Preflight Panel to Examine a Document for Problems   Printing is about much more than just clicking the Print button. It requires planning and careful preparation. During design and certainly before output, you must make a number of design decisions critical to your artwork's printed quality. Then, when it is time to send away the job, you have options about how to do that.

Master It   Create a new, comprehensive preflight profile. Name it **Check Everything**, give it a description to reflect that purpose, and set it to check for all the available conditions.

Chapter 11

Print

The ultimate purpose of any InDesign document is to be consumed. The format in which it's consumed can vary among PDF, ePUB, HTML, and other electronic files. The most common final form an InDesign document will take, however, is ink on paper. Ink must be managed and defined, trapping and overprinting defined, and paper characteristics accounted for.

Your document may be one sheet or many, bound booklets or loose pages; it can be printed out on an ink-jet or laser printer or sent to a commercial printing press. However your InDesign document will be rendered to hard copy, it's essential that you understand the processes and controls to produce the output you envision.

In this chapter, you will learn to

◆ Manage the inks used in a document

◆ Set an object's colors to overprint

◆ Print documents with various options

◆ Produce booklets and output in printer's spreads

◆ Package documents, images, and fonts for delivery or archival

Ink Manager

The Ink Manager (see Figure 11.1), accessible from the panel flyout menus on the Separations Preview and Swatches panels and from within the Output pane of the Print and Export to PDF dialogs, enables direct management of individual inks. Each in-use ink is listed along with its type, neutral density, and trapping sequence. Icons matching the Swatches panel communicate the type of ink—such as process, with a CMYK icon ▮, or spot, with a gray circle icon ◉, or an aliased ink ⚞.

Ink Type

This field sets the trapping type for the selected ink, which can be one of four:

Normal   Use this for process and most spot inks.

Transparent   Set varnishes and die line inks with this option, which will take the selected ink out of trapping calculations, ensuring that ink beneath traps properly.

Opaque   Heavy inks like metallics need special treatment. The Opaque setting traps along the edges of the selected ink but does not trap underlying inks.

OpaqueIgnore Similar to Opaque, OpaqueIgnore is used for heavy inks and does not trap underlying colors but *prevents* trapping along the edges of the selected ink.

FIGURE 11.1
Ink Manager

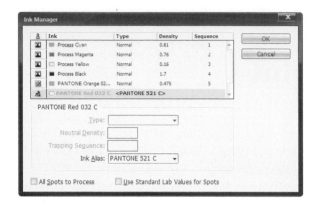

Neutral Density

When trapping is enabled, Neutral Density fine-tunes trap placement. By default, the U.S. English and Canadian versions of InDesign use standardized SWOP ink density values, but you can adjust the value here for specific press needs.

Trapping Sequence

Trapping Sequence changes the order in which inks are factored into trapping calculations (see "Overprinting and Trapping" later in this chapter).

Ink Alias

Although decreasing in frequency thanks to the efforts of, and improved communications between, Pantone and software makers like Adobe, a common problem faced by print professionals is multiple instances of the same spot color in one document. The problem is usually caused by selecting a PMS color in one application, which lists it one way (for example, Pantone 346 U), and then choosing the same color in another application whose PMS library writes color names differently (for example, PMS 346 UC). They're both the same Pantone 346 solid uncoated, but because they're named differently, InDesign, and later PDF and RIP, will output them to separate plates. As I said, this problem is improving because creative pro applications are standardizing their color library naming schemes such that applications like Photoshop and Illustrator use the exact same name. Thus, placing a PSD and an AI, both containing the same spot color defined in their native applications, into InDesign results in a single ink.

When using older imagery, however, particularly yesteryear's EPS files, you might still get two separate plates for the same color. Of course, because the colors are embedded in external assets, you can't simply delete one swatch on the Swatches panel and tell InDesign to replace it with the other as you can with objects created within InDesign. This is where ink aliases come in.

Within Ink Manager, highlight one of the repetitive spots and then, from the Ink Alias field below, choose the other instance of the spot. Aliasing is the process of saying, *Everywhere this ink appears, print this other ink instead.* At output time, InDesign will then replace all instances of one with the other, resulting in a single plate for both inks.

Real World Scenario

USING INK MANAGER TO CORRECT PHOTOSHOP CHANNEL DISASTERS

Every few months I witness or read about in online forums someone who, through some weird accident, wound up creating a two- or three-color image in Photoshop using a dozen or more channels. In the document's Channels panel, he has multiple channels (plates) for each of the two or three spot colors. Why is this a disaster? Because each of those channels will be treated as a separate plate, turning a 2- or 3-color job into a 10- or 12-color job; the price of printing goes through the roof, as does the poor pressman who has to run the thing.

The worst I ever saw personally was a two-color PSD with 14 channels for a single spot and 11 more for the second color. As near as I could figure, the designer, whom we won't call Jane because that's her real name (let's call her Mary), had mistakenly used channels like layers, creating a new channel for every new object or section of color while she painted.

When these types of Photoshop images pop up, there isn't a great deal that can be done to fix them within Photoshop. Sometimes cutting all image data off the extraneous channels one at a time and pasting onto a single target channel works; sometimes it doesn't. Splitting the image into two, one to hold each color, merging the channels down into a single channel each, and then reconsolidating the images also works once in a while. Converting the image to grayscale and then back to duotone in Photoshop consolidates the channels easily but destroys the original color separations and usually requires copious recoloring work.

I spent two solid days working on Mary's PSD, trying these methods and others, to no avail. At the time, I had at my disposal the unlimited knowledge and resources of Adobe—including the direct assistance of several members from the Photoshop development team; none of us could come up with a solution that didn't require Mary to completely repaint her artwork, which she eventually did.

Since then, InDesign's Ink Manager has provided the solution to Mary's problem via ink aliases. If you find yourself dealing with such a Photoshop document, place it into InDesign and output from there. Select one instance of each doppelganger ink as the primary, and, using Ink Manager, alias all the others to their primary. Upon output, you'll have just one plate for each color.

Often images such as those previously described are set in multichannel color mode, and InDesign does not support placing PSD images in multichannel. InDesign handles images in only the CMYK, RGB, Lab, grayscale, indexed, and bitmap color spaces (in other words, just about everything except multichannel). To get around the limitation, follow these steps:

1. Reopen the image in Photoshop.

2. On the Channels panel, create four empty new channels, and drag them to the top of the channels list.

3. Convert the document color mode to CMYK via Image ➤ Mode ➤ CMYK Color. The conversion will automatically turn the four empty channels into empty Cyan, Magenta, Yellow, and Black channels. Spot channels—the ones containing all the image data in this case—will be preserved, and upon save from Photoshop, InDesign will be able to import the image.

Note: If the image will be the only content of the InDesign document, you'll wind up outputting blank C, M, Y, and K plates. When it's time to output, disable printing of the cyan, magenta, yellow, and black inks in the Print dialog Output pane.

Converting Spots to Process

To convert all spot colors in the document to their nearest process (CMYK) mix equivalents, check the All Spots to Process box at the bottom of Ink Manager. Regardless of whether spots are embedded in external assets (e.g., a linked PDF), InDesign will, upon output, convert them to process.

To selectively convert just a single spot to process, click its icon in the ink list. When the spot icon changes to a CMYK icon, the spot is defined to convert to process.

Using Standard Lab Values for Spots

As you saw earlier in Chapter 10, "Preflight," CMYK is a very small color gamut, particularly when compared with the absolutely massive Lab gamut. Although spot color swatchbooks have always contained CMYK values for spots, enabling conversion from spot to process, this has limited the display of spot inks to their process formulas. Newer swatchbooks, such as InDesign CS4's and CS5's DIC, HKS, PANTONE, and TOYO libraries, also contain Lab values for their swatches. The Lab values enable more accurate color throughout the process via better color management and higher-fidelity spot conversions—within workflows capable of handling conversion from Lab. The Use Standard Lab Values for Spots option is off by default for backward compatibility, but if your workflow can use Lab values, turn it on.

When Overprint Preview is enabled, InDesign will automatically *display* spot colors using the Lab color model onscreen without altering output spot color values. However, Lab values *will be used* for printing and exporting if Simulate Overprint is active in the Output pane of the Print or Export to Adobe PDF dialog.

Overprinting and Trapping

On a printing press, every ink is run separately. All sheets run through on one color, go through a dryer or sit on a drying rack for a while, and are then reloaded into the press to receive the next color. With all that moving of paper, by human hands and machine grippers or rollers, you might expect that the paper could shift slightly and that ink colors might not perfectly align. And you would often be right. Paper shifts, and inks don't align—they *misregister*—which can leave ugly white gaps between areas of color such as those in Figure 11.2 and its full-color counterpart in the color insert section of this book.

Overprinting is exactly what it sounds like: making one ink print on top of another. Black, for instance, is the most opaque of the CMYK foursome and typically overprints cyan, magenta, and yellow in small areas like type, strokes, and so forth.

Trapping is the process of extending colors beyond object borders so they overlap—just slightly—to compensate for misregistration, eliminating ugly white gaps in any competently run print job. By default, InDesign keeps trapping turned *off*. It does that because most print service providers prefer to set their own traps farther down the line in a dedicated trapping application or system or in-RIP process. If that isn't the case, if you need to set traps in InDesign—maybe *you* are the print service provider reading this—InDesign has both automated and manual trapping options. The automated traps are very good, and unless you really know what you're doing, I advise leaving it to InDesign to trap.

The built-in InDesign trapping engine calculates traps on the ink level based on the neutral densities of adjacent colors and typically spreads the lighter color into the darker at any

intersection. As we discussed previously, Ink Manager offers methods of influencing the trapping engine's calculations, including how it handles special types of spot colors like varnishes, dies, and heavy inks. These types of spots in particular require an experienced hand because, in the case of varnishes and dies, there isn't a color to trap, and with heavy inks, trapping can often cause undesirable results (for example, you really don't want to mix magenta process ink with a metallic gold ink that contains real bits of metal).

Manually setting traps involves two panels: Attributes and Trap Presets.

FIGURE 11.2
Slight misregistration in the magenta plate causes a sliver of white between inks (assuming the image was printed in registration, that is).

Overprint Attributes

Overprinting ensures that there are no misregistration gaps because there are no gaps to worry about. In Figure 11.3, for instance, you can see a comparison between *overprint* and *knockout*. In a knockout, the upper shape is punched out of the color(s) below at separation time—the area filled by black text is left as holes in the cyan and yellow—which creates the obvious potential for misregistration. If the paper moves slightly on press, a white gap will appear around the edge of the text. However, with overprint, the cyan and yellow are both continuous, even where they will clearly be hidden by the black, so a slight misregistration will be impossible to detect (in this one area).

FIGURE 11.3
Text knockouts out of background color (left) and the same text set to overprint (right). See the color insert for a full-color version.

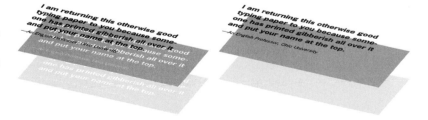

What are the drawbacks to overprinting? Why not just set everything to overprint?

Good questions. Printing ink is not completely opaque. Even black ink isn't, though it's the least transparent of the four process inks. Check out Figure 11.4, especially in the color insert. See how the colors mix in the "CMYK"? Now see how the black star on the right looks more black than the pure black one in the center? That's because I've set the box on the right to be percentages of cyan, magenta, yellow, *and* black all overlaid (rich black). Even though the black ink was printed last, putting it atop the other three, they still shine through the 100% pure black ink to tint it, er, blacker. If the colors behind the black weren't even, if they were, say, colored stripes, those stripes would show through the black by creating two-toned black (which is a really nifty effect in the right context). Now, if I had set a cyan-filled object to overprint its background instead of knocking out the background, who knows what we'd get. Put a 100% pure cyan object overprinting a 100% yellow background, and the ink colors will mix to create green. The only way to maintain the cyan is to knock out the yellow, subtracting the area of cyan from the yellow except for enough overlap to hedge against misregistration.

FIGURE 11.4
At left, overprinting all four colors creates undesired mixes. Center, a 100% black ink star, and right, a rich black star—a mixture of all four process inks.

InDesign will handle its own knockouts by default—or leave them to the RIP or trapper. Again, InDesign does a very good job of choosing when to overprint and when to knock out, but you can override the settings with the Attributes panel accessible from the Window menu. With an object selected, some or all of the Attributes panel's four check boxes will become available. Each of these options is very simple:

Overprint Fill Make the object's fill color overprint all colors that appear behind the object rather than knocking them out.

Overprint Stroke Overprint just the object's stroke.

Overprint Gap This option is enabled only when a gapped stroke style such as dashed, dotted, or hashed is chosen and when a gap color has been selected. In this case, it will make the stroke's gap color overprint background colors.

Nonprinting Why the option to not print an object was stuck in the same place as the overprint controls has always baffled me. The vast majority of designers will leave overprinting decisions to their print service providers, so they'll typically never touch the Attributes panel. However, just about everyone needs to define an object as nonprinting from time to time. Putting that particular option here means most designers can't find it when they need it.

To create an object that doesn't print—for instance, template slugs and labels or notes to yourself about the manner of document construction—select the object and check this box. To temporarily override this setting and force objects with the non-printing attribute to print, check Print Non-Printing Objects on the General pane of the Print dialog.

Overprinting controls are relevant only to natively drawn objects—paths and text—and have no effect on placed images, which are managed by InDesign's trapping controls.

A few words about overprinting strokes: Strokes straddle a path—half inside, half outside—by default. If you overprint a stroke, you will therefore overprint the colors around the outside of the path *and* overprint the fill *inside* the path, which most of the time creates the appearance of two separate strokes. To avoid this situation, set the object stroke entirely within or without the path via the Stroke panel. Also, when you have a choice between overprinting a fill or a stroke, you'll get better results in most cases by overprinting the stroke because InDesign defines the stroke as higher in the stacking order than the fill.

On the View menu is the Overprint Preview command, which simulates overprinting results onscreen. Additionally, previewing separations automatically activates Overprint Preview.

OVERPRINT PREVIEW GOTCHA

When Overprint Preview is turned on, text threads—those arrows that show you how a story flows between multiple text frames—will not show. This is true even if you have Show Text Threads enabled on the View menu. It's a common gotcha because overprinting has nothing to do with threaded text and because many people like to leave Overprint Preview always on in InDesign.

Book author, speaker, and internationally recognized InDesign dude that I am, I'll admit that this gotcha even gets me from time to time. I forget about it after a few years, which is what happened in the spring of 2010 when, during a webinar presentation in front of 124 people, I couldn't get the text thread arrows to show (it was quite embarrassing). I had completely forgotten about the fact that they won't show when Overprint Preview is enabled. Boy, did I feel silly when a member of the audience reminded me about the correlation! I knew about the gotcha, I really did, but the last time I'd actually thought about it was 2007, when I wrote the CS3 edition of this book.

Trapping

At the risk of sounding academic, Ink Manager's job is to manage ink across the entire document (or book, if multiple documents are sent to PDF or print as one unified document). The ink Type, Neutral Density, and Trapping Sequence fields control trap on an entire ink wherever it may appear and in whatever type of objects—natively drawn paths and type as well as native assets. Overprint attributes are object level, controlling fundamental trapping per fill or stroke on individual natively drawn objects. Beyond and between Ink Manager and overprint attributes are InDesign's precision trapping controls, which, again, trap based on neutral densities of inks, not objects, which accounts for objects containing multiple colors.

and have chosen a compatible printer and PPD, this is where to make your choice between the built-in trapping engine and Adobe In-RIP.

Whichever choice you make, trapping is controlled via customizable trap presets, which can be applied per page or to a range of pages via reusable, shareable trap presets.

SETTING TRAP OPTIONS

On the Window ≻ Output menu you'll find the Trap Presets panel (see Figure 11.8). In this list-style panel you'll find the default and undeletable [No Trap Preset] and [Default] presets. Presets you create are saved as part of the document, which means every new document will be devoid of your previous presets. Fortunately, you can load them into any document from any other InDesign document with the Load Trap Presets panel menu command. Choosing that command will show a File Open dialog; just navigate to and choose the InDesign document containing the presets you need to load them into the current document. If you use the same trap settings more often than once in a blue moon, or if you need to share them across your shop, stick an otherwise empty template document on the file server from which anyone can load the trap presets. Like so many other things, trap presets can also be loaded into InDesign with all documents closed to make them default parts of every new document created from that point forward.

FIGURE 11.8
The Trap Presets panel

Create new presets with the New button at the bottom of the panel or by duplicating an existing preset with the command on the flyout menu, and then modify its options with the menu's Preset Options command. The Modify Trap Preset Options dialog will then appear (see Figure 11.9). Clicking the New button while holding Opt/Alt will create the new preset and immediately open Modify Trap Preset Options for the new preset.

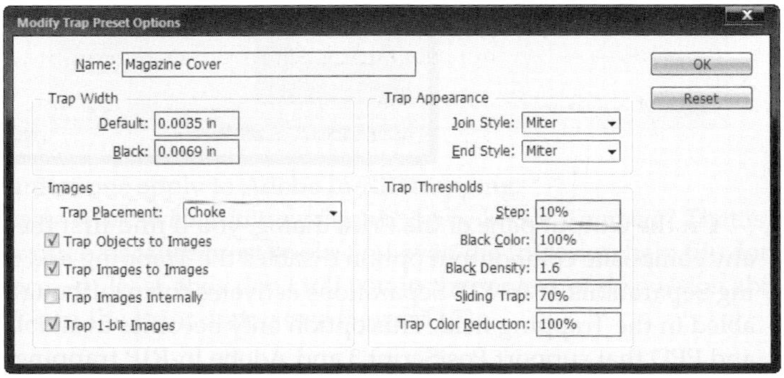

FIGURE 11.9
Modify Trap Preset Options dialog

What are the controls?

Trap Width Default & Black   The amount of ink overlap desired. InDesign's built-in trapping is limited to a maximum 4-point overlap, while Adobe In-RIP is capable of up to 8 points. Default controls the overlap for all ink colors except black, which has its own separate trap width.

Trap Appearance Join Style   Identical to the way path segments are joined via the same option in the Stroke panel, this field offers miter, round, and bevel choices to shape corner points in two trap segments.

Trap Appearance End Style   The End Style setting defines how trap lines behave at their end points. Selecting Miter keeps the lines tight and away from one another, while Overlap directs them to overlay one another.

Trap Placement   When InDesign native objects abut placed images, Trap Placement determines the location of the traps.

Center   Operates like a default stroke on a path, straddling the path edge to partially overlap the object and the image.

Choke   Overlaps only the placed image, staying outside the vector path.

Spread   The opposite of Choke, trapping based on the placed image colors, thus placing the trap inside the vector path and outside the image.

Neutral Density   Restores the default trap engine priority of spreading lighter colors into the darker regions and thus can create traps with a ragged-edged appearance, jumping from one side of the object/image join to the other.

Trap Objects to Images   This check box determines whether vector objects should use the Trap Placement choice to trap to placed images they adjoin.

Trap Images to Images   This check box specifies if images immediately adjacent to other images should trap to one another.

Trap Images Internally   This check box, off by default, asks if you would like to trap the colors appearing inside placed imagery to other colors inside the same imagery. Activating this option is recommended only for simple imagery with large areas of solid color and high contrast—business graphics, for instance—and should definitely not be used on continuous-tone photographic imagery. Trap Images Internally is subject to the limitations of the trapping engine—for example, this option will have no effect on DCS imagery, pre-separated images that contain layers for each plate as well as a composite preview layer. When enabled, this option will complicate and slow trapping calculations.

Trap 1-Bit Images   1-bit images are pure black and white. Even if tinted within InDesign, they are still treated as 1-bit images and thus need no internal trapping. If you activate this option by checking its box, such images will be trapped with adjacent vector objects using neutral density and ignoring the Trap Placement setting.

Step   Step, the first option in the Trap Thresholds section, defines what percentage of difference must exist between adjoining colors before trapping occurs. The lower the value of difference, the more traps result. Adobe recommends 8% to 20% for best trapping.

Black Color In this field, set the minimum percentage of black ink before Black Trap Width overrides Default Trap Width. The lower the value, the less black ink is required in a color before Black Trap Width takes over. The default 100% value forces only pure black to trap using the Black Trap Width.

Black Density When using dark spot colors, determine how dark the ink's neutral density must be to be considered black for the purposes of trapping and thus using Black Trap Width.

Sliding Trap When areas of variable tints such as gradients abut, trapping with a uniform color along the entire length of the gradient can cause noticeable contrast between the object and the trap. Therefore, a sliding trap adjusts the trap placement relevant to the neutral densities of colors throughout tint variances. A sliding trap begins by using a spread on the darker side. When the difference between two colors' neutral densities exceeds the percentage entered in the Sliding Trap field, the trap moves from a spread to a centerline, providing a smoother transition between colors. To force a constant spread trap that never switches, set Sliding Trap to 100%; use 0% to enforce a constant centerline trap.

Trap Color Reduction In the simplest terms, this field is the limit to how much InDesign is allowed to mix neutral densities from either side of a trap to create and lighten the trap itself. Setting Reduction to 0% prevents any reduction and sets the trap to the neutral density of the darker color, which is not necessarily the same color, just the same neutral density.

ASSIGNING TRAP PRESETS

Once you've configured the needed trap presets, it's time to assign them to pages. From the Trap Presets panel flyout menu select Assign Trap Preset to open the simple dialog shown in Figure 11.10. At the top are all the presets available. Select one, then enter a range of page numbers—or choose All to assign the same trap preset to the entire document—and then click the Assign button. The assignments section at the bottom of the dialog lists all trap assignments for reference. Presets may be applied to any page or range of pages; different presets can even be assigned to left and right pages in the same spread.

FIGURE 11.10
Assign Trap Presets dialog

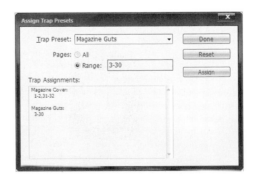

When you're synchronizing documents in books, all the trap presets from the master document will be added into the available trap presets of each document. Synchronizing will not, however, assign them. If you intend to assign the same trap preset to all pages of all documents, don't create a new one. Instead, assign the Default preset to all pages in all documents manually.

Make any changes to the Default preset in the master document. Then, when you're synchronizing, the master document version will overwrite all the other documents' trap presets, applying the new settings.

   Also important to note is that when native InDesign objects are rasterized during flattening, they usually lose overprints and traps. This does not happen for placed AI and PDF documents that include their own overprints and traps, however; those survive flattening.

Print Dialog

We've talked about most of the Print dialog already, in context. Let's quickly run through what we haven't already covered.

General

In addition to printing all pages and sequential selections from the current document, InDesign allows printing of nonsequential pages. In the Range box (see Figure 11.11), enter a sequential range as *X-Y*. If you want to print nonsequentially, use commas, like this: *2,4,6,8,10*. Maybe, with a multiple-template magazine, for instance, you want to print about 10 pages, but they're spread out in 2- and 3-page chunks across the document's 36 pages. Simple: Combine range and nonsequential like so: *2-3,8-10,20-22*. If all you need is even or odd pages, for instance when doing manual duplexing, select the appropriate option from the Sequence dropdown.

FIGURE 11.11
The Print dialog
General pane

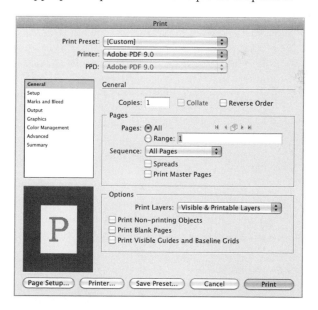

   Printing master pages is useful for quite a few things, particularly when proofing or redesigning templates.
   Under Options, you can choose to print layers that are visible (on) and not tagged as nonprinting, but you can also override layer visibility and non-printing status. I like this feature for

variations and particularly document review markups. I can feel free to mark up a document with change notes right in InDesign as long as my collaborators or I do it on a layer set to non-printing. When I *want* to print those markups or other non-printing data, the Print Layers drop-down lets me print them. Thus, through *deliberate action* I can get a hard copy of my document and markups, comments, and other non-printing data, but I don't have to worry that comments like "Were you drunk when you wrote this!?" will *unintentionally* go to press.

Setup

If you need to scale pages to fit in a smaller space, make thumbnails, or tile large pages to span multiple sheets of smaller paper, do it here instead of in your printer's setup dialog (Setup [Windows] or Page Setup [Mac] button on the bottom left). Why? Because InDesign will scale or divide the pre-processed data; leaving it to your printer scales the post-RIP imagery. You'll get better quality letting InDesign take care of it. (See Figure 11.12.)

FIGURE 11.12
The Print dialog
Setup pane

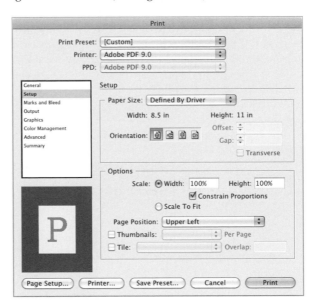

The preview on the left will update with any changes here (or elsewhere in the Print dialog), which makes it easy to adjust thumbnails, scaling, page position, and tile overlap.

Marks and Bleed

This is cool (see Figure 11.13). Want color bars? You got 'em. Want crop marks with a custom offset? There they are. Need to print a proof with custom bleed widths without messing up the document? Well then, just uncheck Use Document Bleed Settings and set the new widths. You can even print information in the document slug area.

FIGURE 11.13
The Print dialog
Marks and Bleed
pane

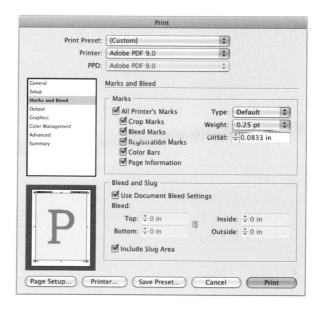

Output

We've already covered most of this pane (see Figure 11.14). The rest is as follows:

FIGURE 11.14
The Print dialog
Output pane

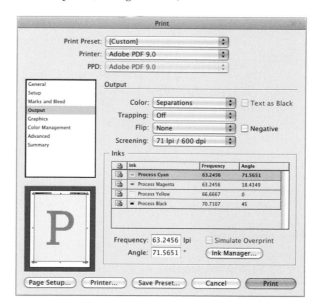

Text as Black   Prints all text in black ink.

Flip   This one tends to get some people who are used to other layout applications. Flip is how you set emulsion up or down (Flip Horizontal), but it also lets you rotate the image simultaneously.

Screening   All the screen frequencies (in lines per inch and dots per inch) available for the selected PPD.

Inks   Notice the little printer icon next to each ink? If you'd like to selectively print or omit from printing any inks, click those icons just as you'd hide layers by clicking the eyeball. InDesign makes it really easy to create your own custom comps or seps or to print without including the colors taking the place of varnishes or dies.

Graphics

See Figure 11.15. This should be called something else since there's really only one option for images, but…

FIGURE 11.15
The Print dialog
Graphics pane

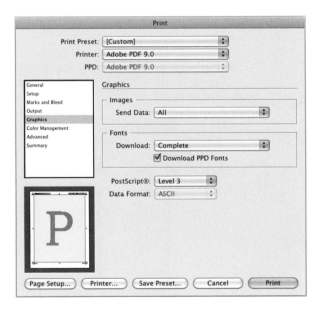

Send Data   If high-quality images aren't important to a particular proof, you can speed printing by sending subsampled, low-resolution proxies or no images at all to the printer.

Fonts   Should an entire font be sent to the printer, a subset comprising only the glyphs used in the document, or no fonts at all? The last option includes only a reference to the font in the PostScript file and is useful only when the printer has the needed fonts onboard. When you've used TrueType fonts or TrueType-flavored OpenTypes, it's generally best to download them.

Download PPD Fonts   Even if the fonts in use are printer resident, InDesign will download the fonts anyway. Typically, you want this on to guard against disparate versions of fonts causing glyph substitution or text reflow.

PostScript   The version of PostScript encoding for the printed data. This option automatically sets itself according to the highest supported level of PostScript in the output device as reported by the PPD. Some desktop printers support emulated PostScript (a PS interpreter from someone other than Adobe), which often doesn't support the full set of features for a particular PostScript level. If you experience problems printing at PostScript 3 with a device that should support it, try changing PostScript to Level 2. Similarly, when printing to a PostScript file with a generic PPD, you may need to knock the level down to PostScript Level 2 for compatibility.

Data Format   Binary has better compression and is a little faster, but it can cause problems with EPS and DCS files and may not be compatible with many output devices. I've used Binary a couple of times, but only on direct request from a service provider. I've never had trouble sending ASCII-encoded PostScript code to a wide variety of devices.

Color Management

At the top of this pane (see Figure 11.16), choose whether to print using the document working space profile or the proof profile defined in the Customize Proof Conditions dialog.

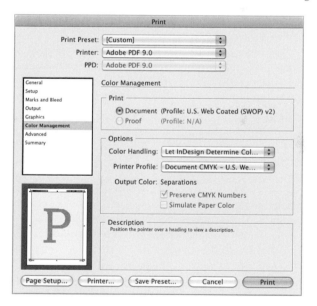

Next, depending on the printer, PPD, and output options selected, Color Handling will offer options to let InDesign handle color management or to handle it in-RIP. Choose the latter only if you have a PostScript 3-compatible RIP with onboard color management.

Finally, choose the output device's specific ICC profile. The rest of the options you already know.

Advanced

See Figure 11.17. In the OPI section, you can omit different types of proxy images from the print stream to leave just the OPI link comments in the PostScript code. Use this when OPI image insertion is to be handled further downstream.

FIGURE 11.17
The Print dialog
Advanced pane

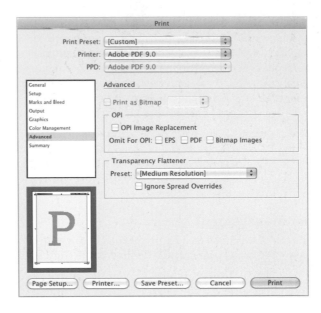

Above the omit options, OPI Image Replacement tells InDesign to handle OPI image replacement in the print stream. Leave it unchecked for an OPI server to do the replacement. In order for InDesign to take care of image replacement, the following conditions must be met:

◆ EPS images in the document must have OPI comments linking to high-resolution versions.

◆ When the EPS proxies were imported, the Read Embedded OPI Image Links check box must have been checked in Import Options.

◆ InDesign must be able to access the high-resolution images.

If the first and second conditions are met but not the third, InDesign will leave in place OPI comment links for images it can't access.

Last is Transparency Flattener presets and the ability to ignore or override spread overrides, which we discussed in depth in the "Proof Flattening" section of Chapter 10.

Print Presets

Once you've configured all your print settings the way you need them, do yourself a favor and save a preset with the button at the bottom. Next time you need the same configuration, you'll find all your arduously configured settings only two clicks away on the Presets menu.

Even better, from File ➤ Print Presets ➤ Define (see Figure 11.18), you can manage all your presets and even save them to external, shareable PRST files. Clicking New or Edit opens the Print dialog to create or modify a complete set of printing options in the familiar interface.

FIGURE 11.18
The Print Presets
dialog

FIGURE 11.18
The Print Presets
dialog

DISTRIBUTE YOUR OWN PRINT PRESET FILES

I frequently recommend to my print and prepress shop clients that they generate PRST Print Preset files for their common devices and workflows and then distribute those files to their customers as part of job preparation instructions. Save yourself—and your designer customers—some agony and delays. Just make sure to also include the appropriate PPD and ICC files.

Print Imposed Pages and Booklets

A common question I hear frequently is: *Is there a plug-in to make printer's spreads from InDesign?* The answer is: *Well, there's a* built-in *function to create printer's spreads.*

Reader's Spreads vs. Printer's Spreads

Pages are read and designed in order, of course, but they aren't printed that way. When a bound, facing-pages document is printed in signatures or leaves, the pages are not printed onto the two-up sheets of paper sequentially. Rather, pages are printed out of order so that, after the paper is folded and bound, pages *appear* sequentially (see Figure 11.19). The process of taking consecutive pages and placing them in the correct arrangement that they bind into sequential order is called *imposition*, sometimes *pagination*, and results in what is often referred to as *printer's spreads*. (By contrast, *reader's spreads* means pages printed consecutively in spreads, the way you design them in a facing-pages InDesign document.)

Every magazine, book, newspaper, or other document with a spine and more than three pages has been imposed. Usually imposition is done in prepress, after the digital files leave the designer's control and before printing. But you can do basic imposition yourself, creating printer's spreads, directly in InDesign. It's accomplished through the Print Booklet feature, whose main purpose is to enable you to print your own booklets on your ink-jet or laser printer, which is also perfect for creating an imposed proof of your folded and/or bound document before sending it to press.

FIGURE 11.19
This diagram shows a simple eight-page publication with the pages imposed into the order required to read them sequentially once the spreads are folded and bound. The pages pre-folding (left) and post-folding (right).

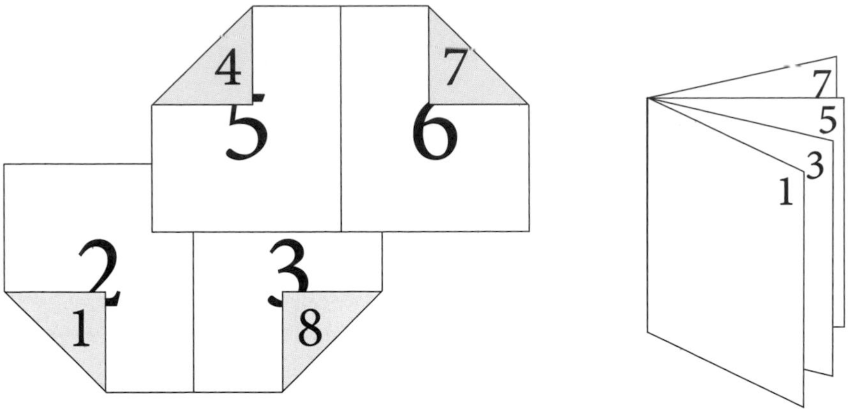

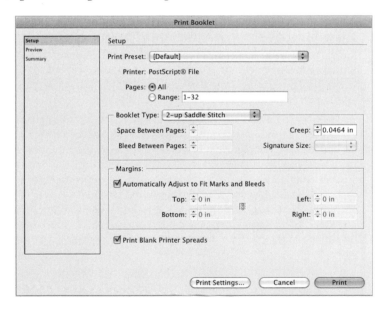

Print Booklet

If you'll be so kind as to select Print Booklet from the bottom of the File menu, you'll be greeted with the Print Booklet dialog box (see Figure 11.20). Here you can perform basic imposition. Print Booklet isn't as robust as dedicated imposition software like PREPS, Quite Imposing, or Imposer Pro, but it's perfect when you need to print only two, three, or four pages per sheet of paper. Let's run through the settings in the dialog.

FIGURE 11.20
The Print Booklet dialog

Print Preset The Print Booklet dialog doesn't replicate the standard Print dialog's options such as printer selection, PPD, color options, printer's marks, and so on. Typically you'll want to define those in advance in the Print dialog and then save all those settings as a print

preset, which you can then select from the menu at the top of the Print Booklet dialog. If you didn't create a print preset ahead of time, which is common, click the Print Settings button at the bottom to open the Print dialog and effect those changes.

PRINT BOOKLET LIMITATIONS AND WORKAROUNDS

Before we get too far into this, before I potentially build up your expectations too far, I need to state what you *can't do with* Print Booklet—and how to overcome those limitations.

First, you can't impose a document containing multiple page sizes, which is particularly disheartening because a huge selling point of InDesign CS5 is its newly native ability to allow multiple page sizes in a single document. If your document contains multiple page sizes, and you access the File ➢ Print Booklet command, you'll be rudely informed that "The active document uses multiple page sizes. Print Booklet works only with documents that use a consistent page size."

So, are you out of luck? Yes and no. You are indeed out of luck if you want to impose documents containing multiple page sizes with what you already own—that being InDesign. However, if you're not averse to spending a little more to get the functionality, pick up a copy of the plug-in Croptima InPlate from http://croptima.com. As of this writing, InPlate is running € 49.90 per copy, which is approximately $64 in U.S. dollars. Note that both the price and the exchange rate might change at any time, and both are completely outside this humble author's control.

InPlate is like Print Booklet on steroids—right, shriveled testes... er, no. I mean big muscles, no neck—including support for additional binding methods, editable and noneditable imposition PDF output, output back to an InDesign document comprising printer's spreads, imposition presets, greater control over bleeds and gaps, multiple language support, and the ability to process up to 10,000 InDesign or PDF pages at one time.

That brings up another of Print Booklet's limitations: According to the InDesign User Guide, you cannot create a PDF from imposed pages. The implication is clear: You can only send imposed pages to a printer or PostScript file. Well, that's not true.

No, you can't *export* imposed pages to PDF, primarily because you can't turn those imposed pages back into an InDesign document, which you'd need to have prior to choosing File ➢ Export. To get around that limitation, you can either use the aforementioned InPlate or simply *print* to PDF from within Print Booklet. Click the Print Settings button inside the Print Booklet dialog box to bring up the regular Print dialog box, and then set your printer to be Adobe PDF. Click OK to return to Print Booklet, and click the Print button; you'll now output a PDF. It won't be a fully editable PDF, of course, because it will be print-to-PDF rather than export-to-PDF, but it will be a PDF nonetheless—complete, high resolution, and press ready.

Pages   Just like in the Print dialog, you can select to print all pages or print any sequential or nonsequential group of pages. In this case, however, you want to *always* print sequential pages; InDesign will do correct imposition for you, but only if you feed it consecutive pages.

Booklet Type   On this menu you choose how many pages will print on each piece of paper and how they'll be imposed. You have three choices, each of which produces a very different result (see Figure 11.21).

FIGURE 11.21
Diagrams demonstrating different booklet types: A. 2-Up Saddle Stitch (32 pages); B. 2 Up Perfect Bound (32 pages); C. 2-Up Consecutive (4 pages); D. 3-Up Consecutive (6 pages); E. 4-Up Consecutive (8 pages)

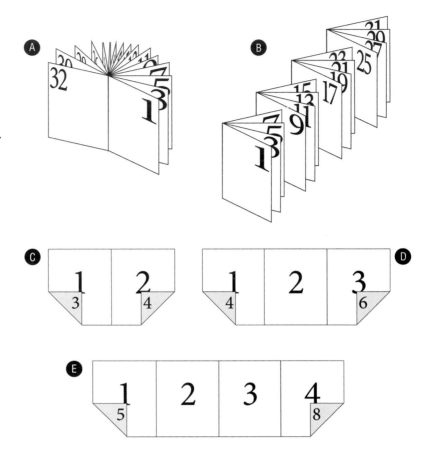

2-Up Saddle Stitch *Saddle stitching* is the bindery process in which a stack of spreads or signatures is folded in the center and stitched or stapled together. You're already quite familiar with this type of bindery—every magazine that has a centerfold, where you can see the staples or stitching in the middle or on the outside spine, is saddle stitched or saddle stapled.

This type of imposition produces spreads that are printed front and back, two pages per side, and that will be folded in the middle altogether as a stack. Saddle-stitched bindery is ideal for relatively small publications, 4–60 pages, depending on stock thickness. Beyond a certain number of spreads, folding would become untenable due to stock thickness and *creep* and would necessitate a move to perfect bound.

2-Up Perfect Bound *Perfect bound* publications are those characterized by having a distinguishable, squared spine—such as a book or any issue of *National Geographic* magazine. Many magazines and catalogs use perfect binding rather than saddle stitching or stapling for a cleaner look and the ability to include artwork or titles on the side of the publication

(the spine). The cover of perfect-bound publications is usually a single sheet of paper or other substrate folded twice, with the pages of the publication glued into its spine.

Like 2-Up Saddle Stitch, this type of imposition produces spreads that are printed front and back, two pages per side. Each page will be folded, but they won't all fold together as a stack. Rather, in perfect binding, each spread or a small group of spreads is folded individually, creating signatures, and then all the signatures are stacked together and glued along their spines.

N-**Up Consecutive** Choosing either 2-, 3-, or 4-Up Consecutive will produce pages arranged in consecutive order, two, three, or four to a sheet. This type of imposition is ideal for foldout booklets and brochures. For example, to create a trifold brochure, design six pages (three for the inside panels, three for the outside panels), with each page the dimensions of a panel, and print those six pages as 3-Up Consecutive. The result will be the trifold brochure, ready to be folded.

Booklet Page Options Beneath the Booklet Type dropdown menu are four other fields, each of which may or may not be active depending on the type of imposition chosen.

Space Between Pages (Not available with 2-Up Saddle Stitch.) Enter here a value (positive only) to create a spinal gap between pages. In perfect-bound documents, the Space Between Pages value should be the positive equivalent of the Creep field value if you are using a negative creep value (what's called "creeping in").

Bleed Between Pages (Available only with 2-Up Perfect Bound.) This is what we call a crossover, or bleeding the artwork into the spine. Typically you want the value of this field to be ¼ to ½ the width of the Space Between Pages field value. If you aren't using a spinal gap with Space Between Pages, leave the Bleed Between Pages value at 0.

Creep (Not available for Consecutive booklet types.) Outside the print world, the word *creep* can be used as a noun—for example, "I don't want that creep anywhere near my daughter"—or as a verb—as in "Watch me creep slowly to the front of the crowd." Creep, in the realm of print production, is both a noun and verb, but using the verb definition it refers to the fact that when sheets of paper are stacked and folded together, the edges of interior sheets stick out from the edges of enclosing sheets (see Figure 11.22). It's basic physics—paper has volume, and each sheet of folded paper displaces each consecutive sheet of paper folded inside it.

FIGURE 11.22
In folded pages, creep develops.

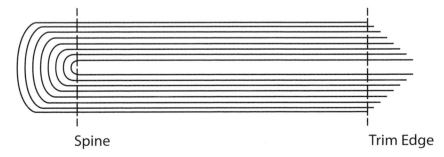

Spine   Trim Edge

As you might intuit from the illustration, creep has two very important, negative physical consequences.

First, it creates points of paper leading toward the centerfold rather than a nice flush edge. You can see this for yourself by grabbing a stack of blank paper and folding it; the open edge of each folded sheet will stick out a little farther than the sheet wrapped around it. This is no problem to fix —the outside edges of bound documents are trimmed to chop off creep and make a flush edge.

The second problem is the more severe and can't be fixed; it can only be compensated for at printing time (that would be now, in this dialog box, incidentally). As one sheet of folded paper displaces another sheet of folded paper inside it, the inner sheet gets pushed outward. That, of course, creates the aforementioned uneven edge on the outside of the publication. But it also displaces the *spine edge* of the paper the same amount. Thus, the closer you get to the centerfold of a saddle-stitched publication, the farther away the spine gets from the cover or outermost sheet. With a thick enough book, you might wind up cutting off parts of pages on inner sheets when you trim the uneven edge. Moreover, depending on the thickness of the book, content near the spine in the outer sheets, those closer to the cover, might be obscured, hidden within the spine. Unfortunately, you can find examples of both types of creep-related problems out in the real world, in even professionally produced magazines and other saddle stitched or stapled publications.

The Creep value field enables you to compensate for creep by shifting the content of pages toward or away from the spine. Outer signatures' page content is shifted away from the spine, while inner signatures' content is moved inward toward the spine. The net result is that the spine gap winds up different per signature, so when printed the spine gap and position of content *appear* uniform from page to page.

The formula for calculating creep in the Print Booklet dialog is the creep or offset value of each signature multiplied by the number of signatures, which might be easier to understand in algebraic expression: $T = C \times X$. No, math isn't my strongest subject either; fear not, this will all make sense in a minute.

A 32-page saddle-stapled document is composed of four pages printed on each signature (two printed on the front, two on the back), thus 32/4 = 8 signatures. So X, the number of signatures, equals 8. Thus the formula is now $T = C \times 8$. We have to figure out the value of C, which is the thickness of the paper.

If you happen to have a micrometer handy, you can measure the thickness of one sheet of the stock on which you expect to print. Without a micrometer there are a couple of ways you can find the thickness of the paper: You can ask your print service provider or contact the paper manufacturer; many times you can find the thickness of the paper on the paper's own packaging or in the manufacturer's catalog or website. If you don't find a value for "thickness," look for "caliper," which is the thickness of a piece of paper measured in thousands of an inch. I've supplied in Table 11.1 the caliper of a few common paper stocks; these are not exact because the caliper of paper varies between paper finish and manufacturers.

TABLE 11.1:   Average thickness of common paper stocks

BOND (LBS)	OFFSET (LBS)	COVER (LBS)	TAG (LBS)	INDEX (LBS)	CALIPER
16	40	22	37	33	0.0032
18	45	24	41	37	0.0036
20	50	28	46	42	0.0038
24	60	33	56	50	0.0048
28	70	39	64	58	0.0058
31	81	45	73	66	0.0061
35	90	48	80	74	0.0062
40	100	56	93	83	0.0073
43	110	60	100	90	0.0074
44	110	61	102	92	0.0076
53	135	74	122	110	0.0085
54	137	75	125	113	0.009
58	146	80	134	120	0.0092
65	165	90	150	135	0.0095
67	170	93	156	140	0.010
72	183	100	166	150	0.011
76	192	105	175	158	0.013
87	220	120	200	180	0.015
105	267	146	244	220	0.0175

Now that you know the thickness of each sheet of paper, you can finish the formula. Assuming we're working with standard 20 lb copy paper, the caliper is 0.0038, so plug that into the creep formula: T = 0.0038 × 8. Ergo, T, the total creep and the value to enter in the Creep field, is 0.0304. Remember to enter the *in* or " notation if your Creep field is showing any measurement other than inches.

You can enter this value as positive or negative. A positive value moves page content away from the spine, while a negative value moves page content inward, toward the

spine. The latter is called a *creep-in* or *push-in* and should be used when you've specified a positive value in the Space Between Pages field.

Now, when InDesign prints the spreads, the cover or outer two pages won't be adjusted, but starting from the inside pages of that same sheet, each sheet's content will be moved 0.0038 inches to compensate for creep. The innermost pages, those two printed in the centerfold, will be moved the full 0.0304 inches.

Signature Size   (Available only with 2-Up Perfect Bound.) Choose here the number of pages—2–32—to be printed on each sheet. If the number of document pages isn't evenly divisible by the signature size, InDesign will add blank pages to the end of the document.

Margins   Typically you'll want to leave Automatically Adjust to Fit Marks and Bleeds selected, which tells InDesign to calculate the page margins necessary to accommodate the page contents and any bleeds and printer's marks activated in the document or activated by the Print Preset. If you aren't satisfied with the results of InDesign's calculations, however, uncheck the option to gain access to the four margin fields for setting your own measurements.

Print Blank Printer Spreads   If the number of pages imposed isn't evenly divisible by the number of pages required for the particular booklet type (for example, a multiple of 4 for saddle-stitched documents), blank spread pages will be added.

At any time during setup—and frequently, as you're first learning to impose pages within Print Booklet—switch to the Preview pane to see a live rendering of signatures reflecting the options you've set (see Figure 11.23). Unfortunately, the Preview pane shows only the spreads, not the fully imposed sheet; you won't, for example, see an 8-up sheet when you've chosen 8-Up Perfect Bound. You will, however, see how each page—including blank pages—will output to printer's spreads. Just beneath the preview window is the count of spreads and to its right a slider enabling you to move spread by spread through the imposed preview.

FIGURE 11.23
Previewing an imposed spread in Print Booklet

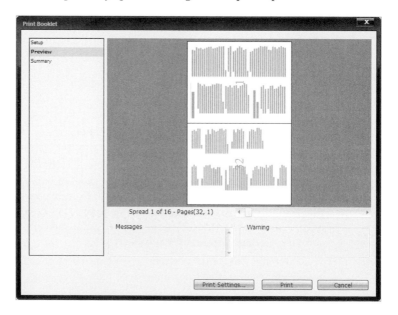

Packaging

The purpose of packaging—which QuarkXPress converts will know as Collect for Output—is obviously to send your original InDesign document (and all its required assets) to your press or prepress provider for output. Many designers and their production counterparts prefer PDFs for this purpose (See "PDF (for Print)" in Chapter 12, "Export"), though many still prefer to send (or receive) the full InDesign document.

Even if you don't send native InDesign documents (and their assets) to your print service providers, packaging a document or publication is something you're going to want to know how to do. It is nearly always the final step in document production, after printing or exporting, to archive the document and all its assets to CD, DVD, or Blu-ray for error-free reuse or reprinting in the future.

In the olden days of the wild and wooly 1980s and 1990s, we had to spend hours rifling through our hard drives, other people's hard drives, file servers, and maybe even removable media, manually collecting all the linked assets and fonts used in a single publication. Invariably, it seemed we always missed one, much to the consternation of our service bureaus. Nowadays, the software collects everything for us.

Choosing Package from the File menu initiates the packaging process, which will collect all the graphics and fonts, put copies of them in orderly folders, and create a new copy of the InDesign file (or files, if you're packaging a book) that links to the newly organized assets. Let's run through packaging, and then all will become clear, grasshopper.

The Package Report

When you tell InDesign to package an unsaved document, the first thing that will occur is that you'll be prompted to save. Next, InDesign will run a snappy document analysis. That minimal analysis was what passed in CS3 and before as the laughable built-in preflight function. Thankfully, InDesign now offers a much better preflight, which you can read all about in Chapter 10. Now this minimal analysis is referred to as the Package Report.

Summary   As you might discern from the title, this pane summarizes the more detailed data on the following panes. (See Figure 11.24.) Of note here are two things: At the top it probably states "Scope: Entire Publication," alluding to the fact that you can also package multiple documents or an entire book at once. Refer back to the discussion about books and Book panels in Chapter 9, "Documents," for instructions on packaging some or all of a book. The second thing to note is the check box at the bottom—Show Data For Hidden and Non-Printing Layers. Generally, you want this checked to make sure there are no problems with documents that create multiple versions via layers (for example, a multilingual layout) and that fonts and assets used by non-printing labels and instructions won't cause problems.

Fonts   All the fonts the document uses are listed here along with their names, types (TrueType, Type 1, OpenType, and so on), statuses (OK, missing, incomplete, embedded), and protection statuses. (See Figure 11.25.) The last item is important. If the type foundry protected its font from embedding—which *is* at the discretion of the type foundry—that font can neither be embedded in an exported PDF nor be automatically copied by the packaging process. If you have protected fonts, you'll need to coordinate with your service provider to make sure it has the same font.

FIGURE 11.24
The Package Summary pane

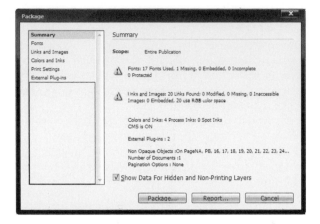

FIGURE 11.25
The Package Fonts pane

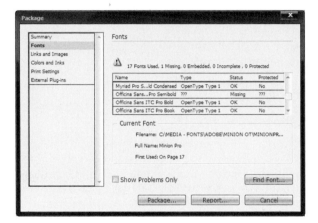

Click any font in the list to load more detailed information, including the font filename for easy hard-drive searching and the location of the font's first use in the document, into the Current Font area below. If you need to replace a font, click the Find Font button to open the standard Find Font dialog.

Links and Images   The Links and Images pane does for, uh, links and images what Fonts does for fonts. (See Figure 11.26.) You can see in the list each instance of an image, its file type and color space (RGB, CMYK, Lab), on which page it appears, its status (linked, embedded, modified, missing), and which, if any, ICC profile it is assigned or carries internally. If an image is listed as missing or modified, a Relink or Update button appears in the Current Link/Image area, which also displays other very useful information. Repair All updates all images listed as modified and helps relink all missing images more quickly than doing them one at a time.

FIGURE 11.26
The Package Links
and Images pane

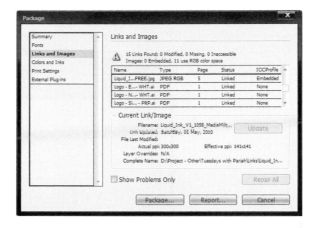

Colors and Inks   What's missing here (see Figure 11.27) is a link to Ink Manager, but, oh well. All the document inks as well as their angles and *lpi*, or lines per inch, are listed. Any aliasing you've done via Ink Manager is reflected here by notations such as "This publication contains *X* duplicate spot colors" combined with the ink list showing only the actual, aliased-to ink. Whether the color management system (CMS) is on is also noted at the top.

FIGURE 11.27
The Package Colors
and Inks pane

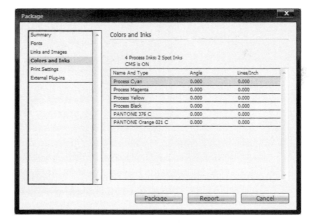

Print Settings   A list of the settings from the Print dialog or assigned print style, which is useful for making sure things like PPD and OPI are correctly set. (See Figure 11.28.)

External Plug-ins   If, in creating your document, you use or even have installed a plug-in that didn't come out of the InDesign box and your print service provider doesn't have the same plug-in, there could be trouble. At the minimum, your providers or collaborators will be annoyed by a warning every time they open the document; at the worst, they won't be

able to open or output your document. The External Plug-ins pane (see Figure 11.29) exists so you can see what nonoriginal plug-ins are installed and communicate to your providers or collaborators, whereupon all of you can work out how to handle the matter (see Chapter 1, "Customizing," for how to manage plug-ins).

FIGURE 11.28
The Package Print
Settings pane

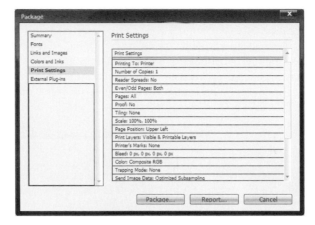

FIGURE 11.29
The Package Exter-
nal Plug-ins pane

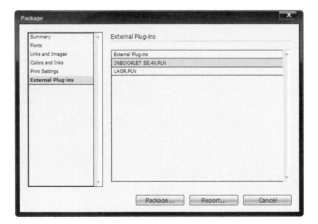

At the bottom of the Package dialog, the Report button generates a plain-text report of everything in the graphical Package Report user interface ready to email to your provider. Package moves to the next logical step and, of course, the next logical section of this chapter.

Wrapping the Package

After the package report comes a semi-useless Printing Instructions dialog. Every package operation generates an `Instructions.txt` file in the package folder. Most print service providers have their own job tickets for you to fill out—usually a PDF or HTML eform, or something you complete over the phone with your service rep. Adobe thought it would be convenient for everyone to put the designer contact information and printing instructions right in the package; it was a good idea but one that, after nearly 10 years, hasn't taken off because printers and

designers had already figured out their own ways to transmit this (and more) job information. If you want to fill this out, go for it; you're not required to enter information, just to press the Continue button. The document generated does include the package report, which can be useful to your provider, though.

Finally, we're into the Package Publication dialog, where the real action happens. It looks a lot like a save dialog (Figure 11.30), because it is. Package will create a new folder into which it will place a new copy of the InDesign document(s) and subfolders for assets and fonts. In this step, pick the location and folder name for the package. It's important to remember that you cannot choose the folder containing the current working version of the InDesign document(s) you're presently packaging. InDesign can't overwrite a file it's reading from. Create a new subfolder, or put it somewhere else. I often choose my desktop so I can then just drag the packaged folder to a DVD-R or FTP upload client and then delete it after burning the disc or transferring the folder.

FIGURE 11.30
The Package Publication dialog

At the bottom of the Package Publication dialog are your options for the package:

Copy Fonts (Except CJK)   Do you want it to grab all the fonts used by your document so they can travel, or be archived, with the document? (Hint: *Yes*, yes you do.) CJK fonts (Asian fonts) will not be copied; if your document makes use of them, you'll later have to manually grab them and copy them to the package's Fonts folder. The same is true of any fonts that restrict embedding; InDesign can't copy these, so you'll, um… have to find… your own solution for printing your document while respecting the type foundry's intellectual property and font license.

Copy Linked Graphics   Do you want it to copy all the linked images from all the hundreds of places they could have been and put them in the package's Links folder for easy travel and archival? (Same hint.)

Update Graphic Links In Package   This option updates the InDesign document(s) to point to the linked assets in the package's Links folder rather than to the originals in their various locations. Because all the linked images will wind up in a folder beneath or inside the folder containing the INDD document, this option makes the document truly portable by using relative instead of absolute file paths. If you uncheck this, every time the document is opened off a CD or DVD, all images will need to be manually relinked before the document can be used. (Word of advice: That *will* make the recipient angry.)

Use Document Hyphenation Exceptions Only   With this option *not* selected, the external user dictionary stored on your computer will merge with the document's embedded dictionary such that both will be used for determining hyphenation when InDesign composes text. When sending the job out to your service providers, they won't have access to your external user dictionary. Any relevant hyphenation exceptions stored therein won't be accessible, and text may reflow. If you've made use of a number of hyphenation exceptions, import your external user dictionary into the document's dictionary, and then check Use Document Hyphenation Exceptions Only.

Include Fonts and Links From Hidden and Non-Printing Content   Do you also want to include the fonts and imagery used only in non-active or non-printing layers? If not, then the document will continue to generate image or font missing warnings.

View Report   Launches your text editor with Instructions.txt loaded when packaging completes.

After clicking Package, you'll probably be given a friendly warning about the risk of copyright infringement when distributing fonts as part of a package. After that, sit back and let InDesign do its thing. It's a fast process, but, depending on the number of fonts, assets, and documents, you might have time to check email, pick a fight with the sales department, or scan the headlines on GurusUnleashed.com. When it's done, you'll still be looking at your original document—the unpackaged one. You'll also have a new package folder—mine was Test Doc Folder—containing a complete copy of the InDesign document, the Instructions.txt report, and two other folders. Every linked image asset will be in the single Links folder and every font in the Fonts folder. If your InDesign document includes assignments, linked InCopy documents, or linked Word or Excel files, those will be in the root folder with the INDD file. To transport the whole document and all assets to someone else, or to archive it permanently, just zip or burn the Test Doc Folder folder. You'll never deal with a link-missing warning again.

Document-Attached Fonts

CS5

New to InDesign CS5 is a highly useful nicety that works in conjunction with packaging. Package has always copied the documents fonts into a Fonts folder. Using those fonts, however, meant that whoever worked on your document would need to manually install the fonts on his system. No longer.

Now, every time InDesign opens a document, it automatically searches the folder in which the document resides for a subfolder titled Fonts. Finding such a folder, InDesign *itself* installs the fonts contained in that folder! Everyone who opens a properly packaged document, with a complete set of fonts as part of the package, will be able to see and edit the InDesign document

using those fonts, without the need to manually install them. Most people won't even notice that the document uses fonts not previously installed on their systems.

Even better, InDesign limits the use of the fonts to the document that brought them. You can have two documents open, one with an exotic font included in the package, the other a new document. That exotic font that is available for unrestricted use in the first document won't even appear on the Font Family menus in the other document. Nor can those fonts be used outside of InDesign. This document-exclusive use of the fonts is a brilliant move. It's how Adobe satisfied the piracy-hyperaware type foundries and made designers and press/prepress personnel's jobs a helluva lot easier.

The Bottom Line

Manage the Inks Used in a Document   Ink Manager enables direct and granular control over the inks used in a document, including process and spot inks, ink type, neutral density, trapping sequence, and aliasing one ink to another.

> **Master It**   Aliasing one ink to another is an important task you may have to perform from time to time, particularly if you frequently place image assets created by different individuals or groups.

1. On the Swatches panel, create two spot color ink swatches—they can be any color, from any color library.

2. Create two large rectangles on a page, ensuring that they don't overlap. Color one rectangle using the first spot color and the other with the second.

3. Print separations of the file to your local laser or ink-jet printer. If you don't have one on hand, print separations to an Adobe PDF and then view the PDF file.

4. Back in InDesign, use Ink Manager to alias the second ink to the first.

5. Now print separations again, noting the difference in output this time from the previous separations print.

Set an Object's Colors to Overprint   Overprinting is the process of setting an object's inks to print on top of any inks that may appear behind it. This results in mixing of the foreground and background colors. When the foreground color is black, the effect is minimal and may not be noticeable at all—particularly if all the black in the document always overprints ink beneath it. Overprinting cyan, magenta, or yellow, which are not as opaque as black ink, on top of one another, however, will result in color mixing.

> **Master It**   Create two partially overlapping circles, each with a fill color and a heftily weighted stroke. Set the fill of the foreground circle to cyan and the fill of the background circle to magenta. Give both a 100% black stroke color. Now duplicate the pair of circles so that you have four circles—two sets—side-by-side. Configure the first set's foreground circle such that its fill overprints and the second set's foreground circle such that its fill is a knockout. Now activate Overprint Preview and examine the difference between the two sets of circles.

Print Documents with Various Options   The Print dialog is the interface for printing documents to paper or even electronic files like PDFs or PostScript. Understanding the role of each of the panes is crucial to predictable printed output.

Master It   Open (or create) an 8.5×11-inch document and print a page or two to 8.5×11-inch paper, inclusive of all printer's marks. All marks must appear on the printed page.

Produce Booklets and Output in Printer's Spreads   Imposing pages for output into printer's spreads or a bound document is a frequent need, one that many InDesign users look high and low to fill with a plug-in, all the while missing the fact that the function is already built into InDesign. Contrary to the terms most people look for within InDesign—*impose* or *imposition*, *paginate* or *printer's spreads*—Print Booklet is the tool for the job.

Master It   Create a new 32-page document. Now use Print Booklet to set up (but not necessarily print) a 2-Up Saddle Stitch booklet from the document. Be sure to account for the correct amount of creep, assuming you'd output to 28-lb bond stock.

Package Documents, Images, and Fonts for Delivery or Archival   Packaging a document collects all the document image and font assets into folders along with a new copy of the InDesign document updated to point to those assets. Thus, packaging makes a document portable, reliant on no assets other than those in subfolders contained within the document's folder. A portable document can be easily transferred to service providers and collaborators or archived to CD or DVD.

Master It   Open any InDesign document that contains both images and text. Package the document such that it's ready for delivery or archival.

Chapter 12

Export

Printing is not the only way in which documents leave InDesign. As often as not, they're exported to PDF to stay in that format or be RIPped and printed from, to ePUB for consumption in an e-book reader, to IDML for use by earlier versions of InDesign, to XML for content repurposing, or to Flash, HTML, or JPEG for use onscreen.

In this chapter, you will learn to

◆ Export documents to IDML, XML, HTML/XHTML, and ePUB formats

◆ Generate PDFs for both print and onscreen use

◆ Export pages as images and Flash content

IDML

CS5

IDML stands for InDesign Markup Language, which replaces InDesign CS1–CS3's InDesign Interchange (INX) format files. IDML files, like their predecessor INX, are XML-based versions of native InDesign INDD documents, containing all the same features and layout specifications. IDMLs, unlike INDDs, are backward compatible. If it's necessary that designers on InDesign CS4 and CS5 collaborate, the CS5 users can export to IDML and have their documents opened and worked on by InDesign CS4. There is no need for the CS4 user to export IDML though; InDesign can always open INDD files created by previous versions.

An IDML file is a structured, tagged document, which enables it to be interpreted and processed by XML applications like databases and content management systems. It's highly suitable for this purpose, as a matter of fact, and is largely what enables automated publishing systems to excerpt, reformat, or repurpose print content to other print documents or different media.

Exporting an IDML is easy. Choose File ➤ Export, and from the Save as Type dropdown list in the Export dialog, choose InDesign Markup (IDML). There are no options to choose other than a filename. All formatting and editing ability available in INDD documents is retained in IDML files.

Another advantage to the use of IDML files is to clear out corruption in InDesign documents. File corruption, though uncommon with InDesign, does occur, particularly if the same document has been converted to and resaved within several progressive versions of InDesign. As part of the IDML export process, InDesign rewrites the entire file, changing the order of the bytes that compose the file, preserving only the file code directly related to in-use objects and constructs (e.g., styles, swatches, etc.). As a happy consequence, all the corrupt bits of code, which are usually bits of deleted objects and legacy code from when documents were converted from an older version of InDesign, are not included in the IDML. They have no place in it, so InDesign just leaves them out. This results in a corruption-free copy of the InDesign document, which may itself be opened and resaved as a new INDD InDesign document, which too will be corruption free.

XML

XML, or eXtensible Markup Language, is the great content ubiquitizer (you can quote me on that). The goal and function of XML, its raison d'être, is to separate content (text, imagery, tabular data, and so on) from its design and even its file format, thus allowing the content to be redesigned and repurposed in any imaginable way, in any media present or future. In practical terms, that means you can take a catalog or magazine laid out in InDesign, suck the data into a database, and spit it out as Web pages, ePUBs, completely redesigned PDFs, QuarkXPress tagged documents, barcodes, and whatever else you can imagine. The possibilities are completely endless because XML was designed for all the uses we can imagine now *and* everything we can't *yet* think of.

Exporting to XML begins the same way as exporting to IDML, via File ➤ Export and then choosing the appropriate Save as Type. That's where the similarities end, though. After choosing a filename and clicking the Export button, you'll be presented with the Export XML dialog, which contains two tabs, General and Images.

General Options

The General tab of the Export XML dialog contains options relative to the structure and style of the exported content (see Figure 12.1). Libraries of books have been written on XML and related subjects, DTDs, and schemas, and indeed at least one entire book has been written specifically on the subject of working with XML in InDesign; I don't have space to fully explain all of it here. Instead, I'll limit my discussion primarily to the options in the dialog, suggesting you continue learning about XML and related topics from sources such as my friends Jim Maivald's and Cathy Palmer's book, *A Designer's Guide to Adobe InDesign and XML: Harness the Power of XML to Automate Your Print and Web Workflows* (Adobe Press, 2007).

FIGURE 12.1
The Export XML
dialog's General tab

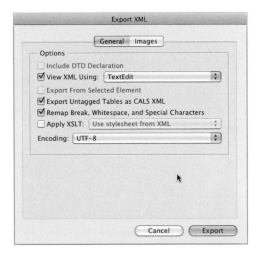

Include DTD Declaration In XML, everything has structure—text, images, tables, captions. Everything is assigned a hierarchical importance—imagine if your document was viewed in outline mode. With a magazine or newspaper article, for instance, the most important piece of content is the headline, so that starts the outline. Next in importance is the deck, which

explains the headline, so structurally that's made subservient to and one step less important than the headline. As laid out, the byline usually comes after the deck, but structurally speaking, the byline may not be the third most important piece of information. The story may have a kicker or subheads or a hook paragraph that ranks higher in actual importance than the byline; thus *they* would follow the deck hierarchically, even though something like a subhead wouldn't appear in the document as read by a human for several paragraphs. Images, even though they appear throughout the story, might be considered the least important bit of information, so they may be given the lowest priority.

The DTD, or Document Type Definition, defines that structure, the appropriate order of tags, and which types of elements are allowed to be used in the XML document. DTDs are created outside of InDesign and loaded into it (via the Tags panel flyout menu) before export to XML. If a DTD was already loaded into the document, and the document contains a DOCTYPE element, the option to include a reference to the DTD will be available.

View XML Using If enabled, this option will open the XML file for viewing within the chosen application. Additional applications can be selected by using the Other option on the dropdown menu and navigating to those applications' installation locations. These can be a browser, an XML editor, or a text editor.

Export From Select Element If you selected an element in the Structure pane, this option will be available to offer you the choice of exporting only from the selected element forward.

Export Untagged Tables as CALS XML This is a bit of a misnomer. Only tables that are themselves untagged but contained *within* a tagged text frame will be exported as CALS. Tables inside untagged frames will not be exported in the XML.

Remap Break, Whitespace, and Special Characters This option replaces these XML-invalid types of characters with their valid decimal entities.

Apply XSLT *XSLT* is the abbreviation for XML Stylesheet, which defines the transformation of the exported XML—for instance, to HTML. If the document already contains the reference to an XSLT, keep the Use Stylesheet from XML option; otherwise, browse for the appropriate XSLT to use.

Encoding The three options here—UTF-8, UTF-16, and Shift_JIS—enable you to change the character encoding of the exported XML for maximum compatibility with different systems.

Images Tab

While exporting XML from a document containing tagged images, you have the option to export the document's images as well (see Figure 12.2). At the same time you can convert them, whatever their original formats, into Web-friendly GIF and JPEG format images (why PNG, the standard of the Web and mobile media, is not an option, I know not).

Copy to Images Sub-Folder: Check one or all options to copy during export the

- Original Images, as TIFFs, PSDs, or what have you

- Optimized Original Images, the images at their original sizes converted to JPEG or GIF

- Optimized Formatted Images, the images at their dimensions as used in the document in JPEG or GIF format

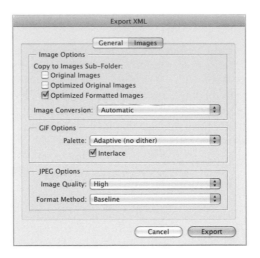

For example, let's say you placed a 10-inch square image into InDesign but reduced its size on the page to half (5×5 inches). The Original Images or Optimized Original Images option would give you a 10×10-inch image; the Optimized Formatted Images option, however, would give you a 5×5-inch image, because that's the size of the image as used in the document.

Image Conversion   This menu is available when one of the Optimized options is selected. Choices include GIF, JPEG, or automatic, which lets InDesign choose whether a particular image is better suited for GIF (large areas of color, sharp edges) or JPEG (many small areas of color, subtle color shifts). If you leave the option as Automatic, be sure to specify both GIF and JPEG options below.

GIF Options Palette   Choose the color palette to use for generated GIFs. Adaptive (No Dither) offers the fullest range of color but does not dither, which is to say that it will not smooth the edges of color transitions by mixing pixels of one color with pixels of the other. The Mac and Win system palettes each include 256 colors, like Adaptive, but are specific to the unique 256-color palette of the respective operating system. There are 40 colors that are close but not identical between the platforms. The Web palette is solely the 216 colors that do match identically between Mac and Windows computers.

GIF Options Interlace   Interlace causes generated GIF images to progressively load, creating the perception of a faster image load, although it actually takes longer for the full image to render.

JPEG Options Image Quality   As a lossy compression method, the relative size of a JPEG image is in direct relation to its quality. The higher the quality, the larger the file. Low (10%), Medium (30%), High (60%), and Maximum (100%) quality are your choices.

JPEG Options Format Method   Multiple flavors of JPEG are available. Baseline is the oldest and most commonly supported, though Progressive is widely supported in browsers and other rendering software of the last 10+ years. Progressive has the added benefit of rendering the JPEG in stages, creating the perception of a faster image load.

HTML/XHTML

A long time ago, in a version far, far away, InDesign had the ability to export *HTML*. It was a feature few used but more would have. Then, as distant cousin and HTML editor GoLive lay near death, Adobe sought to prolong GoLive's inevitable death by replacing InDesign's HTML export with a Package for GoLive command. They were not the same thing. Package for GoLive generated a specially coded PDF that was ridiculously useless, even inside GoLive, yet InDesign could no longer export HTML at all. This sour state of affairs lasted for two versions, until GoLive finally breathed its last.

Then HTML export returned to InDesign, masked as Export for *Dreamweaver*, the successor and former competitor to GoLive. Now many fear that direct export to HTML is never to come again, that InDesign users taking print content to the Web will forever have to copy and paste or learn to use Adobe's HTML editor of the day. Fear not, friend. HTML export *is* in InDesign, and it works well.

To initiate exporting the current document to HTML, choose File ➢ Export for ➢ Dreamweaver. *Wait!* I know what you're thinking, but it only *looks* like you're stuck with Dreamweaver! In fact, the Export for Dreamweaver command merely generates normal HTML and CSS that any editor can use—even TextEdit or Notepad.

General

After choosing a filename for the HTML export, you'll see the XHTML Export Options dialog, which begins with the General pane (see Figure 12.3).

FIGURE 12.3
The XHTML Export
Options dialog
General pane

Export Choose Selection if you've selected something prior to initiating the export, or choose to use the entire document.

Ordering Choose whether the exported content should be ordered in the HTML code according the visual layout of the page or with the XML structure (if any) within the document. If the document is untagged, the Same as XML Structure option will not be available.

Bullets and Numbers For bullets and numbers in the InDesign document, you may choose to have them converted to plain text or converted into the HTML-equivalent code to generate dynamic lists—unordered for bullets, ordered for numbers.

Images

On the Images pane you decide how you'd like document images handled (see Figure 12.4). The main option to concern yourself with is the Copy Images dropdown menu, which offers three choices: Original, Optimized, and Link to Server Path.

FIGURE 12.4
The XHTML Export
Options dialog
Images pane

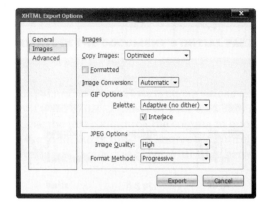

If you elect the Original option, the images will be copied exactly as they appear in the InDesign document, in their native formats such as TIFF, EPS, or PSD, none of which can be rendered by the average Web browser. Use Original only when the images in the document are already in Web standard formats: JPEG, GIF, or PNG (yes, *here* PNG is supported).

Optimized converts the document images into GIFs or JPEGs, using the same options discussed relative to the Export XML Images tab, described previously under "XML," "Images Tab." The only real difference is the Formatted check box, which preserves in the exported images transformations and formatting applied to the image inside InDesign, such as the scale or rotation of an image.

Choosing Link to Server Path from the Copy Images menu replaces the other fields with two more:

Path on Server   The path to the server folder that will house the image files.

File Extension   The extension of the final images (e.g., `.jpg`, `.gif`, or `.png`).

Note that capitalization is critical in both the Path on Server and File Extension fields: If you use a capital letter, Web browsers will look for that capital letter in the filename or path. Should you use a capital letter here but in fact use lowercase in the filename, the connection will fail, leading to a hole in the page where the image would be.

Advanced

The Advanced pane is where you specify how formatting translates between InDesign's paragraph styles, character styles, and manual formatting and HTML (see Figure 12.5), as well as other options.

FIGURE 12.5
The XHTML Export
Options dialog's
Advanced pane

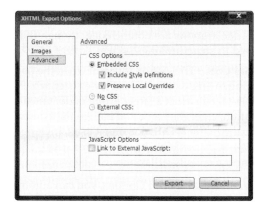

CSS, which stands for Cascading Style Sheets, is the formatting language of HTML. It defines the look of text and images in HTML documents as well as the layout of the page. You have three options:

Embedded CSS This option asks InDesign to insert into the resulting HTML document the CSS code necessary to replicate the design of the document page as closely as possible in the HTML page. Such CSS code includes text styling and formatting options and object size and positioning information. InDesign will also wrap text and objects in CSS class and ID declarations that link the wrapped items with their style sheet definitions. The two check boxes ask, respectively, whether paragraph and character styles should be written as CSS code and whether local text formatting overrides should be preserved in the HTML.

By way of example, compare the following. First is a paragraph style definition, copied from the Style Settings area of the Paragraph Style Options dialog. The second is the same style as translated by InDesign into CSS formatting.

```
Neo Tech Alt + Medium + size: 90 px + leading: 150 pt + color: [Paper] +
align: flush right - hyphenation - OT contextual alternates


{
font-family: "Neo Tech Alt";
font-weight: normal;
font-style: normal;
font-size: 7.50em;
text-decoration: none;
font-variant: normal;
text-indent: 0em;
text-align: right;
color: #ffffff;
margin: 0em;
}
```

For now, let's assume you've already made the decision to include Flash as a channel in your publishing workflow. There are two ways to get Flash content out of InDesign, or rather, there are two destinations for Flash content from InDesign. First, you can export directly to a Flash SWF (pronounced "swif"), which, like a PDF, is a ready-to-be-consumed file format accessible to the vast majority of online-connected people through ubiquitous software, in this case Adobe Flash Player, which nearly everyone online has installed. Second, and new to InDesign CS5, is the ability to export your content into a FLA file, which isn't something you'd distribute. Rather, a FLA file is intended to be opened in Flash CS5 Professional to be worked on further.

Export to Flash Player SWF

Getting to the Export SWF dialog begins the way most exports do, by choosing File ➤ Export and then selecting Flash Player (SWF) from the Save as Type dropdown menu. There are two sections to the Export SWF dialog: the General and the Advanced tabs.

GENERAL

The General tab defines the size, shape, and content of the SWF file (see Figure 12.9).

FIGURE 12.9
The General tab of the Export SWF dialog box

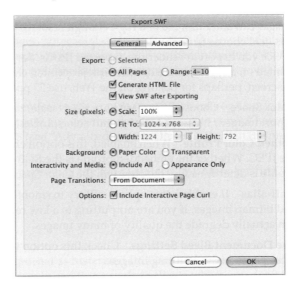

Pages   SWF files can contain multiple pages, though only the first page will be shown unless you've built in some form of navigation to transition between pages. Choose All Pages to export the selected objects, if any are selected, or choose Range to specify a range of pages.

Generate HTML File   In order for SWF files to be viewed online, they must be embedded within an HTML Web page using special code. Checking this option creates an HTML file with the proper code required to contain and play the SWF.

View SWF after Exporting   It's always a good idea to proof an exported file immediately after creating it. This option does that. If Generate HTML File is checked, viewing the file

after export will open that HTML file, with the SWF embedded in it, in your Web browser. Otherwise, the SWF itself will launch in Adobe Flash Player.

Size   Choose or type in a percentage to have InDesign scale the SWF content proportionately. Alternatively you can precisely control the size of the resulting SWF by choosing Fit To to have it fit common screen sizes. If the ideal dimensions aren't to be found there, choose the last radio button and manually enter the Width and Height values for the SWF.

Background   Choose whether the background of the SWF is Transparent or Paper Color. Note that choosing Transparent will disable Page Transitions and Page Curl.

Interactivity and Media   Include All includes all interactive and multimedia elements from the InDesign document—for instance, embedded movies and audio, rollover buttons, and animations. Appearance Only makes those elements static, as if they were simply pictures of multimedia content. Movies don't play, instead showing the current frame or "poster" frame; animations show a static object at its current place in the animation, and; rollover buttons show the current state of the buttons without the ability to change to other states.

Page Transitions   Choose from this list any page transitions you'd like to employ to jazz up the act of going from one page to the next. If you've already assigned transitions via the Pages panel or the Page Transitions panel, choose From Document at the top of the list. You can also export sans transitions by opting for None.

Include Interactive Page Curl   Available only in Flash content, a sleek page curl effect can be added to enhance the reading experience by simulating the act of pages turning for the reader instead of simply flashing from one page to the next (pardon the pun).

Advanced

Fine-tune your SWF Flash Player content with the options on the Advanced tab (see Figure 12.10).

Frame Rate   Choose the number of frames per second for animations. The higher the frame rate, the smoother the resulting animation appears, but also the larger the resulting file. Lower frame rates create smaller files but may introduce stuttering or jumping in animations.

Text   Text in the exported SWF can be live, as represented by the Flash Classic Text option, or converted to vector outlines or rasterized pixels. With pixels, the quality can degrade easily, revealing jagged edges if the SWF is scaled up or zoomed into. Outlines, as vectors, retain their quality but leave text as unselectable. Live text renders at the highest quality of the screen, at the current zoom level, but also remains selectable and accessible. I strongly recommend you keep this set at Flash Classic Text.

Options   Choosing Rasterize Pages converts the entire pages into images—text, paths, placed art, everything. Flatten Transparency keeps the appearance of the artwork but merges areas where colors or objects blend with their backgrounds. Additionally, both options remove any interactivity in the document. Unless you have a specific reason for it, I advise against enabling either of these options.

Image Handling   The Image Handling section sets the options for raster images coming from the InDesign layout to the SWF. Choose the type of image under Compression, either JPEG or the lossless PNG format, and then the output resolution in ppi. Choosing JPEG as the compression format also enables the JPEG Quality field, where you can set the quality of the resulting JPEGs.

FIGURE 12.10
The Advanced tab

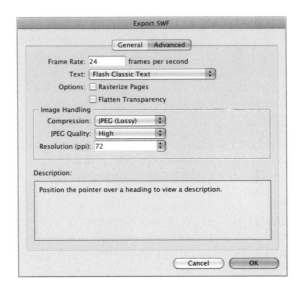

Export to Flash CS5 Professional

CS5

When your Flash content document needs more work—advanced animation, more robust interactivity, dynamic content inclusion, scripting—don't export it directly to SWF. Instead, get the design and content into Flash CS5 Professional, where that powerhouse of rich, experiential media development can help you (or a collaborator) work serious magic. Each page in the InDesign document will be translated to a keyframe in Flash.

The options in the Export Flash CS5 Professional (FLA) dialog, which you can get to via File ➤ Export and setting the type to Flash CS5 Professional (FLA), are nearly identical to, but a subset of, those in the Export SWF dialog (see Figure 12.11). They're so similar, in fact, that I'll spare you the rehashing and focus on only the differences—there are two.

FIGURE 12.11
Export Flash CS5
Professional (FLA)
dialog

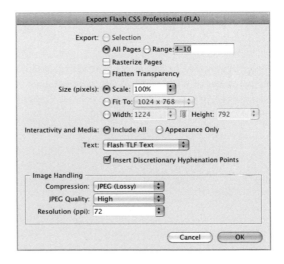

On the Text dropdown menu is one more option, Flash TLF Text. The TLF stands for Text Layout Framework, which, in Flash Professional, offers much better text-handling and formatting options. You want this on, in other words. Choosing Flash TLF Text also allows the selection of the Insert Discretionary Hyphenation Points option. It's just what it sounds like—it allows the text to be hyphenated at the end of lines.

ePUB

CS5

ePUB—which is capitalized correctly—is the evolving standard format for reflowable e-books. Unlike PDF publications, which can be richly designed, multiple-column layouts on par presentation-wise with the best print publications ever produced, and which may contain interactivity and multimedia content, ePUBs are extraordinarily simple in presentation. They may contain only a single column of copy and images inline with the copy. They cannot contain interactivity beyond basic hyperlinks, and their text composition changes with every device on which they're read—everything from a full-sized computer screen to mobile phones like the DROID or iPhone and mobile e-book readers like the Kindle and Nook.

If this sounds familiar, you must have at least looked into Web design in the 1990s; the features and limitations of ePUBs are nearly identical to the features and limitations of HTML circa 1995. In fact, ePUBs basically *are* HTML. The ePUB file itself that you'll get from InDesign is not really a file at all; it's an archive, like a Zip or Rar, and within it is contained the HTML-like text of a publication, its image assets, and a CSS file for formatting.

LEARNING ELECTRONIC PUBLISHING WITH INDESIGN

The subject of creating ePUBs—how to prepare your InDesign documents, what formatting is allowed and how to format it, ways to get your ePUBs onto devices and into their readers—is not something this book should cover. It is, after all, InDesign for print design and production. More to the point, as I write this, I am in possession of knowledge about upcoming products and add-ons to InDesign that will dramatically alter the ePUB and digital publishing processes in general. These products and add-ons have not yet been announced publicly, and only some of them will be available by the time this book hits store shelves. Consequently, even if a full coverage of ePUBs and electronic publishing were within the scope of this book, the information I could write would be outdated and largely irrelevant by the time you read it.

Electronic publication design and production with InDesign is evolving rapidly. I've built a website to evolve with it, in a fashion and at a speed a printed book simply can't match. Visit http://workflowEPUB.com to catch yourself up to the exploding electronic publishing industry, including ePUBs and other formats, and stay current.

Exporting ePUBs

Exporting a document to ePUB format begins by choosing File ➤ Export For ➤ ePUB. After choosing a filename and location to which to save your .epub file, you'll be presented with the Digital Editions Export Options dialog (see Figure 12.12), whose name owes to InDesign CS4's Export for Digital Editions command; before ePUB became the standardized name of .epub files, Adobe called them Digital Editions.

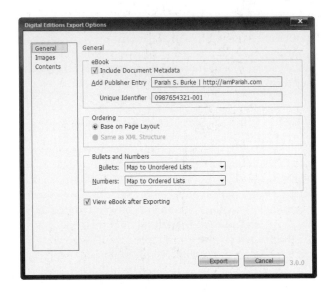

Because an ePUB is essentially HTML, many of the options in the Digital Editions Export Options dialog are identical to those in the XHTML Export Options dialog, which we discussed in detail toward the beginning of this chapter. Let's look then at just the differences and features unique to exporting an ePUB.

GENERAL PANE

Only the eBook section of the General pane is unique to ePUB export; the remaining sections are identical to their HTML export counterparts.

Include Document Metadata Choosing this option saves within the ePUB metadata such as the filename, creator, and other pertinent information added to the InDesign document via the File ➢ File Info command.

Add Publisher Entry Insert here the name and/or Web address of the e-book's publisher.

Unique Identifier In order for e-book readers to properly track and manage ePUBs, each ePUB must contain a unique identifying code. Typically this is the ISBN or ISBN-13 number of the book or the ASN number of a periodical, if one was obtained. If your publication doesn't have an ISBN or ASN, you can enter your own unique code. If the Unique Identifier field is left blank, InDesign will generate a unique ID automatically. Note that the unique ID InDesign generates will *not* be an ISBN or ASN.

IMAGES PANE

The options on the Images pane (see Figure 12.13) are identical to those on the same pane in the XHTML Export Options dialog.

FIGURE 12.13
The Digital Editions Export Options dialog's Images pane

CONTENTS PANE

The Contents pane is where the heavy lifting of building and formatting an ePUB is done (see Figure 12.14).

FIGURE 12.14
The Digital Editions Export Options dialog's Contents pane

Format for EPUB Content   Select the desired format for the ePUB output file. XHTML, the default, is the more widely used standard and can be read by nearly every e-book reader, including those built for the visually impaired. However, if you know your document is going to be consumed by the visually impaired rather than by everyone, set the format to

DTBook, which stands for Digital Talking Books, e-books specially formatted for print-disabled consumers such as those with visual or physical impairments.

Include InDesign TOC Entries   If your document has TOC-formatted styles, you can generate a table of contents automatically during ePUB output. The resulting TOC will appear at the top of the e-book, with entries hyperlinked to their destinations.

TOC Style   After you select Include InDesign TOC Entries, the TOC Style field lights up, enabling you to choose any existing TOC styles in your document. You can create TOC styles (in advance) via the Layout ➤ Table of Contents Styles command.

Suppress Automatic Entries for Documents   When creating an ePUB from a book, InDesign will insert the filenames of each chapter in the TOC. Selecting Suppress Automatic Entries for Documents omits the filenames.

Use First Level Entries as Chapter Breaks   Because the ePUB file format is in reality an archive containing other files, what is read and distributed as a cohesive ePUB may in fact be multiple text documents—for instance, one document per chapter, like a book. Activating Use First Level Entries as Chapter Breaks creates a new XHTML file for each chapter, breaking at each occurrence of the paragraph style used in the TOC as the first-level TOC entry. This option is particularly important in light of the 300-KB limit per ePUB XHTML file imposed by many e-book readers and the current ePUB file specification. By splitting a large document into multiple, chapter-specific XHTML files, e-book readers can load only one chapter at a time without impacting the human reader's experience.

Generate CSS   As XHTML, ePUB e-books must be styled through the use of CSS, Cascading Style Sheets. The options are limited, as I previously noted, to such things as type color, font family, font style, and type size, but they're better than no formatting at all. When you ask InDesign to generate the CSS, embedding the CSS formatting into the ePUB file, you have three suboptions to consider:

> **Include Style Definitions**   A style definition is the formatting to be applied to tagged text—for instance, the CSS attributes to make text a certain size or color. Check Include Style Definitions to add that formatting to the file. Once included, the styles may be further edited in Dreamweaver or other CSS or ePUB editors.

> **Preserve Local Overrides**   Include such formatting as bold, italic, or underlined text, formatting that may be not defined as part of the paragraph or character styles in use on that portion of the text.

> **Include Embeddable Fonts**   Although not every e-book reader supports the display of embedded fonts, you can embed fonts used in the document for those readers that do. Note that, just like embedding fonts into PDFs, only those whose type foundries have not specifically disallowed embedding will be included.

Style Names Only   Rather than including full style definitions, you can elect, by choosing the Style Names Only radio button, to include just the names of the CSS styles, sans formatting definitions. The idea is that you will later fill in the CSS formatting in a CSS or ePUB editor.

Use Existing CSS File   If you've already built a stand-alone CSS file to format your ePUBs—something you'll likely want to do if you publish ePUBs more often than once in a blue moon—select this option and then click the Choose button to locate your external CSS file. Upon export InDesign will wrap a copy of the external CSS file into the ePUB.

PDF (Interactive)

CS5

Exporting to PDF is a fundamental task in InDesign. PDF is, after all, the media in which most of us send documents to press and proofs to clients. In InDesign CS5, though, there's been a subtle but important change. As you may have surmised from the improved HTML, SWF, ePUB, and Flash Professional export, CS5 has a whole new focus on e-publishing. Now there are *two* types of export-to-PDF operations—exporting to Interactive PDF and to PDFs intended for print. The former, in fact, is the new default. Let's get it out of the way and then move into the export options for print-ready PDFs.

When you press Cmd+E/Ctrl+E (or choose File➤ Export), the default Save as Type for InDesign is, and always has been, PDF. Naturally you can change the Save as Type—we've done it a few times previously—but for most people, most of the time, the default PDF is what you want. In CS5, the default is a different kind of PDF, Adobe PDF (Interactive), which leads not to the familiar Export to PDF dialog box but to the Export for Interactive PDF dialog, which looks very much like the Export to SWF and Export Flash CS5 Professional dialogs (see Figure 12.15). This is because an interactive PDF is one that is intended for media-rich publications that will be consumed *as* PDFs, documents such as slideshows, kiosk presentations, e-books, e-catalogs, and e-magazines.

FIGURE 12.15
The Export to Interactive PDF dialog

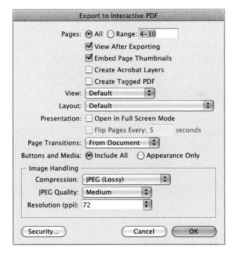

Export to Interactive PDF Options

Let's go through the options in the Export to Interactive PDF dialog.

Pages   Choose to export all pages or only some. The Range field can accept any arrangement of pages, in any order. Use hyphen-separated numbers (e.g., 2-7) to send a sequential range of pages, or comma-separated numbers (e.g., 8,6,4,2) to send nonsequential or out-of-order pages. You can also combine both methods, for example, 2-7,20,18,16,10-14.

View After Exporting   Proofing an exported document before sending it out is always a good idea. Checking this option saves you the trouble of launching Acrobat and hunting down the file you just created; as soon as the PDF is finished generating, Acrobat will launch with the file loaded and ready for inspection.

Embed Page Thumbnails Each page of a PDF may be navigated visually via thumbnails in Acrobat's Pages panel. This option creates those page thumbnails—snapshot images—of pages so that they're ready and waiting for the PDF's audience.

Create Acrobat Layers This option can create layers in the PDF from the top-level layers in InDesign. For instance, if your document is multilingual, with separate layers for English, French, and Russian text, this option will preserve those layers in the PDF document, enabling readers to toggle the various languages on or off, much like layers in InDesign or Photoshop.

Create Tagged PDF If your InDesign document contains structure tags, this option will translate them to PDF tags. Even if you didn't pre-create tags in InDesign, if Create Tagged PDF is enabled, Acrobat's Distiller engine, which is performing the export, will tag common elements in text such as paragraphs, tables, lists, basic formatting, and so on. Tagged PDFs are more accessible to persons with disabilities and are easier for PDF readers on alternate devices (i.e., cell phones, PDAs, tablets) to reflow for optimal reading.

View When a PDF is opened in Acrobat or Adobe Reader, it can be set to automatically zoom to a particular percentage or to fit one or both dimensions of the page. How your PDF looks the very first time someone sees it is important—it could determine whether the would-be reader dives right in or immediately closes the document and never opens it again. How the view is zoomed has a good deal to do with that first impression. You have several options:

Default Shows whatever the reader has set as the default view within Acrobat or Adobe Reader.

Actual Size If the page is 11×8.5 inches, for example, it'll be zoomed regardless of screen size to approximately 11×8.5 inches.

Fit Page Zooms to fit both the width and height of the document in the application window.

Fit Width and Fit Height Chops off the other dimension if necessary, and requires the user to scroll in order to see that other dimension.

Fit Visible Zooms to include the visible portion of the page in the application window.

Fixed Zoom Percentage Regardless of the screen size, this zooms to 25%, 50%, 75%, or 100% of the document dimensions.

Because of the vast difference in screen sizes, I strongly advise against using a fixed zoom percentage; instead, consider Fit Page, Fit Visible, or Fit Width.

Layout Similar in importance to View, Layout (think of it as presentation layout) determines the initial view on your document. Both the view and layout can be changed by the reader in the PDF client, but rarely does the average PDF consumer know how to do that. Thus, you should put your best foot forward with the layout. You can choose from the following options:

Single Page Shows one page at a time, jumping from the bottom of one page to the next.

Single Page Continuous Shows one page at a time, but scrolls smoothly between pages rather than jumping.

Two-Up (Facing) Puts two pages side by side in the view a la a book or magazine.

Two-Up (Cover Page) Shows pages side by side except for the first page, which is assumed to be a cover that displays solo.

The Two-Up layouts are available to choose as either standard (jumping pages) or continuous (smooth-scrolling) behavior.

Presentation   For slide show or kiosk presentations, consider presetting the PDF to Open in Full Screen Mode. This has the effect of immediately placing Acrobat or Adobe Reader into its full-screen Presentation mode, thus hiding the application scrollbars, toolbars, and so on. (Hint: Full-screen mode can be toggled in Acrobat or Adobe Reader by pressing Cmd+L/ Ctrl+L.) If your PDF is a kiosk presentation—a self-running set of slides meant to be left unattended—you can set the interval between the advancement of slides by enabling the Flip Pages Every *x* Seconds option.

Page Transitions   Sticking with the idea of a PDF as slide show or presentation or, even better, to liven up e-books, e-magazines, and e-catalogs, you can add page transitions that perform wipes, fades, and other effects as the reader, you, or the timer advances from one page or slide to the next. Choose From Document if you've used the Pages panel or Page Transitions panel to add transition effects, or select one from the list. Unfortunately, the Page Curl transition effect is not available for use in PDFs; it's Flash only.

Buttons and Media   If you didn't already know, PDFs can fully support rollover buttons and embedded movies and sounds. If your document contains any of these, and you choose Include All, these multimedia items will become part of the PDF just as they're part of the InDesign layout. If you *don't* want this live media—say, if you want to send a nonfunctional, flat proof of the interactive PDF to the client—choose Appearance Only. That option will effectively turn videos and buttons into pictures using their current appearances in the layout—or using the "poster" frame or image you may have embedded in videos like QuickTime movies.

Image Handling   We've already gone through all of these options in the other export formats above, so I'll spare the agonizing back and forth of "I've already read about these options; I don't need to read it again" and "but what if the author included a nugget of info in this latest description that wasn't in the others?" These options determine the format and quality of the layout's images as they will appear in the PDF.

PDF Security

Before we get into the settings accessible from the Security button at the bottom of the Export to Interactive PDF dialog, I need to provide a warning. PDFs are *not* entirely secure.

No matter how you may secure your PDF—if you restrict printing or making changes, even if you require a password just to open the document—I can break that security and print your PDF, change it to my heart's content, or peek into that PDF without knowing the password. True, I'm a PDF expert, but I'm not the only one who can crack open a secured PDF. *Anyone* can do it with a little knowledge, a freely available application, and even an application that comes *pre-installed* on one of the world's two largest operating systems. It would be irresponsible of me to explain how to break PDF security, but trust me; it's not difficult to do. That said, it does take a certain level of knowledge to do it, a level of knowledge that the vast majority of the people who might want to read your PDF do not possess. The following security options are for those people and will keep those people from doing whatever it is you don't want them doing with your PDF. Just keep in mind that a minority of potential readers will be able to do everything you don't want them to do, if they choose.

Bottom line: Don't bet the farm on PDF security.

COMPRESSION

To conserve space and reduce file size, images and other document contents are often resampled to lower resolution at export time. The Compression pane is where you control the quality of this output (see Figure 12.18).

FIGURE 12.18
The Compression pane

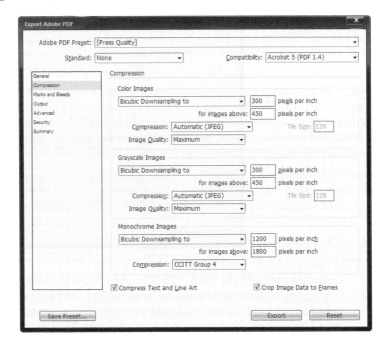

Each type of content has its own options. Color and grayscale images are self-explanatory, while the Monochrome Images section refers to one-color (black-and-white) bitmap images.

Downsample Method   The first dropdown field in all three sections is the Downsample Method list, which determines the algorithm used to recompose image data when the number of pixels in the image is reduced as a consequence of the settings to the right. Your choices for downsampling are as follows:

Do Not Downsample   Leaves images alone; does not change their resolution.

Average Downsampling To   Averages the colors of all pixels in the sample area to create a color that is the average of all of them. For instance, if you were downsampling a picture that was half red and half blue, the pixels along the border between the two colors would wind up purple.

Subsampling To   Subsampling picks up the color of a pixel in the center of an area and makes all the pixels in the area that color.

Bicubic Downsampling To   Bicubic downsampling uses an algorithm filled with weird math notations that go completely over my head. Suffice it to say that this method typically delivers the best quality of the three.

Downsample Resolution   The number field to the right of the Downsample Method field is the Downsample Resolution. Beneath that is the Resolution Threshold field. Combined, these three fields say, "For images whose resolution is equal to or greater than [Resolution Threshold] pixels per inch, knock them down to [Downsample Resolution] pixels per inch using the [Downsample Method]." Thus, in the upper number field, enter the maximum resolution you want to allow images to be in the PDF.

Compression   Images added to the PDF can be compressed in different ways (after downsampling), with advantages and drawbacks to each. Choose here the method you'd like to employ:

None   Doesn't compress the images; leaves them at full quality and full file size. This is not advisable unless your print provider requests it because of prior issues with compressed images.

JPEG   Compresses images by converting them to JPEG and converting using that format's native lossy compression method. In JPEG compression, quality is traded for file size; the lower the quality, the smaller the size. When choosing this method, set the Image Quality field as desired.

JPEG 2000   (Available only when Compatibility is set to Acrobat 6 (1.5) or higher.) JPEG 2000 is a newer (heh, 10 years old) JPEG image specification that more efficiently compresses images with less image degradation. Images in this format have progressive display, meaning that larger images begin at the lowest quality and progressively render in tiles, or blocks of pixels, until the full resolution of the image is displayed. The Tile Size field sets the dimensions, in pixels, of the tiles.

ZIP   ZIP compression is best suited for images with large areas of the same color, repeating patterns, or lots of sharp divisions between colors. For continuous tone images, where colors transition less dramatically, use JPEG or JPEG 2000.

CCITT Group 3   (Monochrome Images section) This method compresses black-and-white images one line at a time like a fax machine.

CCITT Group 4   (Monochrome Images section.) A better compression method than CCITT Group 3; use this method for general bitmap compression.

Run Length   (Monochrome Images section.) This compression method is ideally suited to images that contain large areas of black and/or white with few transitions between the two.

Compress Text and Line Art   Compresses text and line art in the document without loss of detail or quality.

Crop Image Data to Frames   Exports only the portions of images visible within their frames. Any portions cropped out by frames are discarded. Typically you want this enabled.

MARKS AND BLEEDS

PDFs can contain many types of marks integral to the printing process but that will be trimmed off in the final piece. Typically, such marks are added by press or prepress personnel as part of their document preparations, but some situations call for them to be added directly into the PDF at export time. Figure 12.19 shows the result of adding all of the marks available on the Marks and Bleeds pane to the PDF.

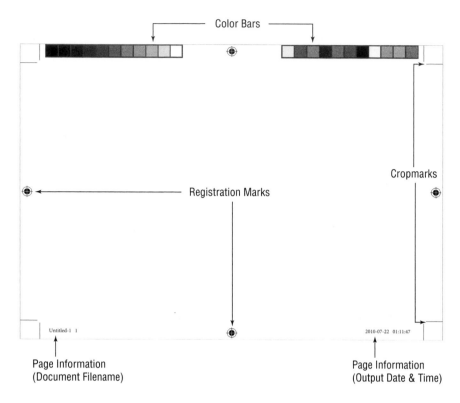

FIGURE 12.19
An exported PDF
containing all
printer's marks.

Color Bars

Cropmarks

Registration Marks

Untitled-1 1

2010-07-22 01:11:47

Page Information
(Document Filename)

Page Information
(Output Date & Time)

Under the Marks section, choose which marks you would like to add (see Figure 12.20). Selecting All Printer's Marks activates all the marks below it, or you can selectively switch them on or off.

FIGURE 12.20
The Marks and
Bleeds pane

Type   Although your only option here is likely Default, which means that the marks chosen to the left will be the default types and styles of printer's marks, the Type dropdown can contain other sets custom created for InDesign.

Weight   The thickness of the lines used to create crop marks and bleed lines.

Offset   The value here sets how far from the edge of the page to draw the printer's marks. This value must be larger than the bleed size.

In the Bleed and Slug area you can elect to Use Document Bleed Settings as specified in the New Document or Document Setup dialogs, or you can define a bleed area with the measurement fields. Check the Include Slug Area check box to incorporate into the PDF a slug area and its contents, if you created one.

ADVANCED

The OPI and Transparency Flattener sections are the same as those in the Print dialog's Advanced pane, so I refer you to that section in Chapter 11 if you need an explanation. The Fonts and Job Definition Format sections, however, are unique to PDFs.

Fonts are typically embedded within PDFs to nullify the need to send fonts with a document as external files. However, rather than include the entire character set of a font when not all the glyphs are used, you can save a significant amount on PDF file size by subsetting fonts or including only those characters that are actually in use. Set at 100% by default, this option tells InDesign to subset the font to in-use characters only when fewer than every single glyph is used. Reducing this value can force InDesign to embed the entire font if the number of glyphs used exceeds the percentage you set. Unless you have a compelling reason for doing so, I recommend leaving this field at 100%.

Job Definition Format (JDF) is a job-ticketing system, a set of instructions for prepress providers and automated systems that explain how to handle the file. Enabling this option adds a JDF ticket to the PDF and immediately opens the PDF in Acrobat Professional 7.0 or later to begin defining the instructions of the JDF.

Adobe PDF Presets

Once you have all your options set, you can simply click Export to generate a PDF. However, if you think you might use the same settings again in the future, save yourself some time and trouble by creating a preset.

The easiest way to create a preset is to set the desired options in the Export Adobe PDF dialog and then click the Save Preset button on the bottom left. InDesign will prompt you to name it, and you're finished. Then, next time you need those same settings, they're a mere two clicks away, on the Adobe PDF Preset menu at the top of the Export Adobe PDF dialog.

If you want to create a preset without going through the whole export process, you can do that too. Choose File ➤ Adobe PDF Presets ➤ Define to open the Adobe PDF Presets dialog (see Figure 12.21). There you'll see in the Presets list any existing presets (the bracketed ones are the defaults that ship with InDesign). Selecting one gives you the preset description, an expandable list of its settings, and any warnings about using the preset, such as when the preset states not to embed fonts.

FIGURE 12.21
The Adobe PDF
Presets dialog

1. Click the New button to open a startlingly familiar dialog box with a different title, the New PDF Export Preset dialog (see Figure 12.22).

2. Name your preset at the top.

3. Set your options exactly as you would when exporting a PDF for real.

FIGURE 12.22
The New PDF
Export Preset
dialog

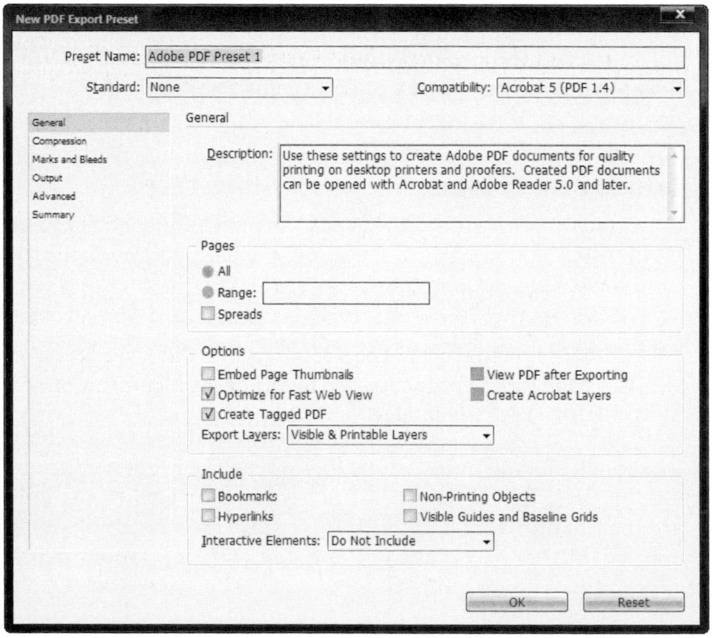

4. Click OK to save your preset to the Presets list.

You can edit your preset by highlighting it in the list and clicking the Edit button—or use the Delete button if you no longer want the preset.

5. Click Done in the Adobe PDF Presets dialog. Your preset will be ready for use next time you export a PDF (for print).

 Real World Scenario

EXPORT TO THE RESCUE

Carver Industrial Products (a pseudonym for a company that wishes to protect its identity) asked me to build a multichannel, multimedia publishing workflow for their extensive electrical supply catalog. The catalog is published quarterly in 12 languages and distributed to the world's power companies and their contractors. Print editions are produced in 9 of the 12 languages, and PDF catalogs are created in all languages. CIP, an American-based company, writes and creates new catalogs in-house in English and Spanish and then sends a digital edition of either the English or Spanish version to vendors in different countries for translation. Additionally, the cover of each new catalog is featured as an image on the CIP website corresponding to the catalog's language.

As you can imagine, the output portion of the workflow was easy, relying on InDesign's export abilities.

First, because not all of the translation service vendors had yet upgraded to InDesign CS5—in some countries CS5 was not even yet available for purchase—catalogs for translation were exported to CS4-compatible IDML. The vendors perform their translations directly in the IDML files sent to them and then return those files as IDML, which CIP's CS5-based production people can easily read, proof, and preflight.

The original English and Spanish versions, as well as the other-language versions of the catalogs, are exported to two sets of PDFs. The first set of PDFs is press ready and sent to CIP's print houses in the United States and other countries for final output. The second set of PDFs, which includes security settings to prevent changing the PDFs and low-quality-only printing, are generated and posted to CIP's websites for download and use by customers who don't receive, or prefer not to use, printed catalogs. Both sets of PDFs are quickly output from CIP's local English version of InDesign CS5 using two PDF Presets developed for the two types of output.

In order to get the cover of new catalogs onto CIP's websites, each language version is opened separately and its first page exported to JPG, ready for posting on the CIP website that corresponds with the language of the catalog.

Finally, more editorial-like portions of each catalog are exported to HTML, using the File ➤ Export for Dreamweaver command. The results of the export are cleaned up and massaged in a non-Adobe HTML editor and then integrated into the various CIP websites.

InDesign export handled all of Carver Industrial Products' content distribution needs—from print to PDF, Web image to HTML—even collaborating with other agencies still using InDesign CS4—painlessly and quickly.

The Bottom Line

Export Documents to IDML, XML, HTML/XHTML, and ePUB Formats   Not every document begins and ends in the same version of InDesign or even as an INDD document. Sometimes not every member of the team has upgraded to the latest version of InDesign. Even more frequently, content created and formatted in InDesign is destined for other uses besides print, besides within InDesign itself. The ability to export to IDML, XML, and HTML/XHTML means content isn't trapped within InDesign, that it can be repurposed for virtually any use you can think of, now or in the future.

Master It   Get your document to the Web. Open or create a document that contains a few pages of text mixed with images. Export that document to HTML, including CSS formatting and the best-quality JPEG format images. Proof your work in a Web browser.

Generate PDFs for Both Print and Onscreen Use   Exporting InDesign documents to PDF is, and will likely remain for a long time yet to come, the method by which most documents are sent to press. Designers prefer to send press-ready PDFs, and press and prepress shops prefer to receive press-ready PDFs. PDF is also growing as a final document format. With more and more content consumed directly on electronic devices and with long-awaited acceptance of e-books and interactive e-magazines, PDF has finally lived up to the potential its creator, John Warnock, foresaw in the early 1990s. InDesign is at the forefront of building consumable PDFs, now more than ever.

Master It   Export a PDF ready to send to your print provider for press output.

Export Pages as Images and Flash Content   Despite the strongest wishes of a certain fruity Cupertino-based computer and consumer product manufacturer, Adobe's Flash technology is, and will continue to be at least for the foreseeable future, an important part of the digital publishing landscape. Flash enables the delivery of rich, interactive, well-designed content to a variety of devices with a predictability and consistency not possible with HTML or other formats. And, as the world awakens to the new reality that "publishing" means more than ink on paper, Flash is becoming important even to InDesign-based designers.

Master It   In a new InDesign document, create a single-page document. On the page include bullet points summarizing what you learned in this chapter and how you can put that knowledge to work for you. Design the page well—make it an advertisement for you and your new knowledge—and then export it to Flash Player SWF as an SWF file wrapped in HTML, ready for upload to your website.

Chapter 13

Efficiency

Have you ever heard the term *prosumer*? Coined in 1980 by the futurist Alvin Toffler—in his book *The Third Wave*—as a blend of *producer* and *consumer*, the term was used to describe a possible future type of consumer who would become involved in the design and manufacture of products so they could be made to individual specification. These days, the term more often refers to amateurs or hobbyists who use professional-grade tools. A hobbyist's ideal page-layout application, used for birthday party invitations, band fliers, and custom Christmas cards, for instance, would be Serif PagePlus or Microsoft Publisher. A professional would choose a platform with more extensive features and finer control, something like InDesign or QuarkXPress. Prosumers are those who create invitations, fliers, and cards using gold standards such as InDesign or QuarkXPress.

For the prosumer, the key criteria in a page-layout application—and the most interesting parts of a book about the application—are those that unfetter creativity and offer design techniques and effects. Print professionals have the same requirements, but equally important is the ability of the application to effect—and of the book to teach—the fastest, most efficient means of *getting a job done*.

This chapter is *not* about the prosumer.

In this chapter, you will learn to

- ◆ Work efficiently with text
- ◆ Work efficiently with tables
- ◆ Work efficiently with objects

Working Efficiently with Text

Between InDesign's copious features and a little of the wisdom of experience, there are many ways to increase productivity when working with text and type objects, which is a good thing when you consider that setting and manipulating type is the biggest part of most professionals' work in InDesign.

Paragraph Styles

Paragraph styles are most definitely not a new concept. InDesign didn't invent them, and CS5 doesn't bring anything radically new to the concept. However, a remarkable number of professionals working under deadlines don't use them, thus wasting a tremendous amount of time and money. If you *do* use paragraph styles religiously *and* you're already adept at creating, modifying, and using them in InDesign, by all means feel free to skim or even skip this short

initial section—but do check out the following sections on style names, organization, nested styles, GREP styles, and more.

What are paragraph styles? Why should I use them? A paragraph style is a record of all paragraph-level attributes of text—formatting options that apply to all text between the start of the paragraph and the end. It's a record that can be reused to instantly style additional text with all the same attributes—typeface, font size, indents, paragraph spacing, rules, justification, bullets or numbering, underline, color, and more. Moreover, once a paragraph style has been applied to text, every attribute of that text can be altered throughout the entire document (or book) just by changing the paragraph style. You can literally reformat the text of a thousand pages in seconds. If you do nothing else to improve your productivity, nothing else to save yourself time and frustration, use paragraph styles.

Paragraph styles are, predictably, managed from the Paragraph Styles panel, which can be opened from Window ➤ Styles ➤ Paragraph Styles (see Figure 13.1).

FIGURE 13.1

The Paragraph Styles panel, with a few styles and groups already created

There are two ways to create a paragraph style:

◆ Define the style before formatting text.

◆ Create a style *from* formatted text.

The latter is the faster, more intuitive way because you set most, if not all, formatting on live text on the page and then simply create a style that records the formatting; you will work with familiar areas of InDesign such as the Paragraph and Character panels to *see* what the style will become.

1. So, set a line or paragraph of type on the page and format it however you like.

2. Highlight all or part of the paragraph, or simply leave the I-beam cursor within the paragraph.

3. On the Paragraph Styles panel, click the New button at the bottom. A new style will appear in the list with a default name, Paragraph Style 1; additional styles will be numbered sequentially.

4. Note that Paragraph Style 1 is *not* yet assigned to the text from which it was created. You'll still need to tag the text with the style by clicking Paragraph Style 1 once.

The style assignment will last until the end of the paragraph, a hard carriage return, as indicated by the presence of a pilcrow (¶), which you'll see if viewing hidden characters.

5. To apply the style to additional paragraphs, click within or highlight them (in whole or in part) and choose Paragraph Style 1 once more from the Paragraph Styles panel.

LOGICAL STYLE NAMES

Default style naming isn't very informative. *Was Paragraph Style 13 for figure captions or third-level numbered lists? Wait, wasn't it Paragraph Style 4 for figure captions and Paragraph Style 21 for third-level numbered lists?* You can see how confusing it can become quickly. Even if you know now exactly which default-named style is used for which text, will you remember six months from now? A year? If you need to bring in some help on the project or an update to, or derivation of, the project, will others know at a glance which style should be used for *this* text and which for *that*? In all cases, the correct answer is *very unlikely*. Give your styles descriptive names that make sense to you and to whomever else might have a reason to work with the document.

There are two ways to rename paragraph styles and two ways to access each way. The fastest way is to first highlight the style in the list and then Option+click/Alt+click the name itself. You'll be able to rename the style right on the panel. You can also double-click the style name in the list to do the same. If you double-click right on the characters, you'll be able to rename in place. If your double-clicking is a bit off, you'll open the Paragraph Style Options, which is the second way to rename styles (see Figure 13.2).

FIGURE 13.2
Paragraph Style
Options

On the top of the General pane of the Paragraph Style Options dialog is the Style Name field. Rename it there. And, while you're here, why not get even more organized?

CASCADING STYLES

The Based On field presents a list of all other paragraph styles defined in the document. InDesign's styles are *cascading styles*, meaning that Style B can be based on Style A, C on B, D on C, and so on. This is an important concept to grasp because it means that by carefully

basing styles on one another, you can effect broad changes across multiple styles by changing only one.

Let's say, for example, that you've chosen Adobe's Minion Pro type family for the majority of your document. Leaving out, for this example, styles not using Minion Pro, perhaps your paragraph styles would include the basic character formatting shown in Table 13.1.

TABLE 13.1: BASIC CHARACTER FORMATS IN THE DOCUMENT'S INITIAL PARAGRAPH STYLES

PARAGRAPH STYLE	FONT FAMILY	STYLE	SIZE	LEADING	FIRST-LINE INDENT
Body Copy	Minion Pro	Regular	10.5 pt	13.25 pt	0.25″
Body Copy First ¶	Minion Pro	Regular	10.5 pt	13.25 pt	0″
Kicker	Minion Pro	Bold Italic	12 pt	14 pt	1″
Caption	Minion Pro	Italic	8.5 pt	10 pt	0″
List - Num LVL 1	Minion Pro	Regular	10.5 pt	13 pt	0.5″
List - Num LVL 2	Minion Pro	Regular	10.5 pt	13 pt	1.0″
List - Unnum	Minion Pro	Regular	10.5 pt	13 pt	0.5″

Because more text will likely fall under the Body Copy paragraph style than any other, we'll designate that as the primary, or parent, style. Looking at the table, you should see many options among the other styles that are identical to those of Body Copy. Let's highlight them for clarity (see Table 13.2).

TABLE 13.2: COMMON CHARACTER FORMATS IN THE DOCUMENT'S INITIAL PARAGRAPH STYLES

PARAGRAPH STYLE	FONT FAMILY	STYLE	SIZE	LEADING	FIRST-LINE INDENT
Body Copy	Minion Pro	Regular	10.5 pt	13.25 pt	0.25″
Body Copy First ¶	Minion Pro	Regular	10.5 pt	13.25 pt	0″
Kicker	Minion Pro	Bold Italic	12 pt	14 pt	1″
Caption	Minion Pro	Italic	8.5 pt	10 pt	0″
List - Num LVL 1	Minion Pro	Regular	10.5 pt	13 pt	0.5″
List - Num LVL 2	Minion Pro	Regular	10.5 pt	13 pt	1.0″
List - Unnum	Minion Pro	Regular	10.5 pt	13 pt	0.5″

Each of the styles shares at least one common characteristic—the font family Minion Pro. Except for the Kicker and Caption styles, the rest have at least three options matching those of Body Copy. Whenever two or more styles share formatting options, you're presented with the opportunity to save yourself some work. You see, each paragraph style isn't *required* to store *all* the formatting options for a passage of text; it can contain as many or as few settings as you like. By setting styles to be based on one another, you leave all the *common options to a single style*, storing *only the differences* in the dependent styles.

Considering the styles in our tables and the commonalities we identified, Body Copy is our primary style based on nothing ([No Paragraph Style]) and holding all the core formatting options. Body Copy First ¶ will be based on Body Copy and therefore only contain the different first line indent; all other options it will inherit from its parent, Body Copy. The Kicker style will also be based on Body Copy, but it will use only its font family; the font style, size, leading, and first-line indents are all different, and those unique settings will be part of the Kicker style. Each of the other styles will also be based on Body Copy, cascading from the parent Body Copy style for shared attributes and holding onto only their unique values. The result would produce styles that look like Table 13.3. With all styles based on the Body Copy paragraph style, common values are left out of dependent styles (indicated by empty fields).

TABLE 13.3: REDUNDANT ATTRIBUTES ARE REMOVED IN STYLES BASED ON ONE ANOTHER.

PARAGRAPH STYLE	FONT FAMILY	STYLE	SIZE	LEADING	FIRST-LINE INDENT
Body Copy	Minion Pro	Regular	10.5 pt	13.25 pt	0.25″
Body Copy First ¶					0″
Kicker		Bold Italic	12 pt	14 pt	1″
Caption		Italic	8.5 pt	10 pt	0″
List - Num LVL 1				13 pt	0,5″
List - Num LVL 2				13 pt	1.0″
List - Unnum				13 pt	0.5″

Now that you have the concept down, you should be asking three questions:

◆ What are the point and value of cascading styles?

◆ How do I leave common traits out of a paragraph style definition?

◆ Other formatting attributes are shared between some of the other styles. Should they cascade off one another as well?

Let's start with the first question: *What are the point and value of cascading styles?* The point of cascading styles off one another is to eliminate redundancy in their definitions, and the value is that doing so increases efficiency. Looking once again at our cascading styles, you can see they

all share a font family, Minion Pro. What if you or the client decides that Officina Serif ITC Pro would be a better choice? Well, that's a single change—change the font family setting in the Body Copy style and the alteration will ripple down through all styles dependent on Body Copy. Suddenly, and with no further action on your part, Body Copy First ¶, Kicker, Caption, and your lists will also all use Officina Serif ITC Pro. Text assigned to the Kicker style will be Officina Serif ITC Pro Bold Italic, and text in the Caption style will be Officina Serif ITC Pro Italic. Not happy with Officina Serif ITC Pro? Change Body Copy's font family to Palatino Linotype or Times New Roman or Garamond Premiere Pro—whatever—and all dependent styles will inherit the change from their parent. Change the font size in Body Copy and all styles except those with unique values will change as well. Basing styles on one another eliminates redundant settings that become impediments when a common trait must change. The formatting of some or all the text in an entire document can be modified in seconds, with a single, facile task.

As for your second question—*How do I leave common traits out of a paragraph style definition?*—the answer is simple. In the Paragraph Style Options dialog, on the General pane, the Style Settings area lists the Based On style and only those additional settings that differ from it (see Figure 13.3). Before you base the style on another, the Style Settings area will display all formatting options defined in the style. As soon as you make a selection in the Based On field above it, all common attributes disappear from the Style Settings area. InDesign assumes you want the shared attributes inherited from—and changed along with—the parent style and so removes them from the child style itself.

FIGURE 13.3
Style settings for
the current para-
graph style

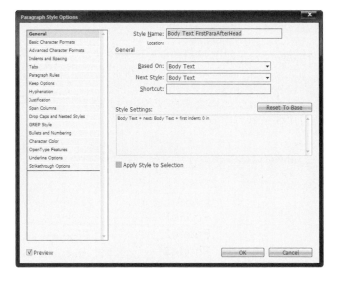

If any unique settings remain in the Style Settings area that you don't want to be unique, that you want to instead inherit from the parent style, delete them. Go to the appropriate pane in the Paragraph Style Options dialog, and clear the contents of the text field for the specific attribute. For example, if you want to remove a 0.25-inch right indent, go to the Indents and Spacing pane, highlight the value in the Right Indent field, and press Delete or Backspace on your keyboard. The 0.25-inch setting will immediately be replaced by the inherited value of the parent style, whatever is its right indent. Check boxes, radio buttons, and dropdown lists are similar—just clear their values.

Finally, you observed that the styles we've been working with in our tables shared other common attributes and asked, *Should they cascade off one another as well?* Yes, they should if you want true style efficiency. Styles may be cascaded numerous levels deep—Style B can be based on A, C on B, D on C. Inheritance will follow through all the levels. For example, if we based List - Num LVL 1 on Body Copy and List - Num LVL 2 on List - Num LVL 1, List - Num LVL 2 would inherit the options from *both* List - Num LVL 1 and Body Copy.

Carefully setting styles to be dependent on one another may sound complicated, but it really isn't—no more so than a child's game of matching like characteristics—*Which of these is like the others?* And, it yields tremendous productivity benefits.

AUTOMATIC SEQUENTIAL STYLES

Another area that helps greatly—and unlocks instant formatting of an entire, unstyled document (see the sidebar "Super Secret Revealed: Two-Click Formatting of an Entire Document")—is the Next Style field on the General pane of Paragraph Style Options. The Next Style field poses a simple question: *When you hit Return/Enter, what style do you want to use for the next paragraph?* Paragraph styles apply to an entire paragraph, from the character after a carriage return through, and including, the next carriage return. After that, in the following paragraph, you can keep the same paragraph style or automatically switch to another. For example, rarely does a subhead precede another subhead without intervening text. Therefore, I would open the Paragraph Style Options for the Subhead style and set its Next Style field to Body Copy; thereafter, every time I type a document subhead and hit return, I automatically begin typing the next paragraph in the Body Copy style.

Next Styles can be strung together as well, thus creating, under some circumstances, fully automatic, cascading paragraph styles with no need to even reach for the Paragraph Styles panel after the first line of the document. Consider a directory-style listing (see Figure 13.4). Each line is its own paragraph, each line has—or can easily have—its own paragraph style, and most important, the paragraph formatting is cyclical. Each listing or dataset begins and ends with the same styles that begin and end lines in other listings.

FIGURE 13.4
Typical directory listings with styles called out

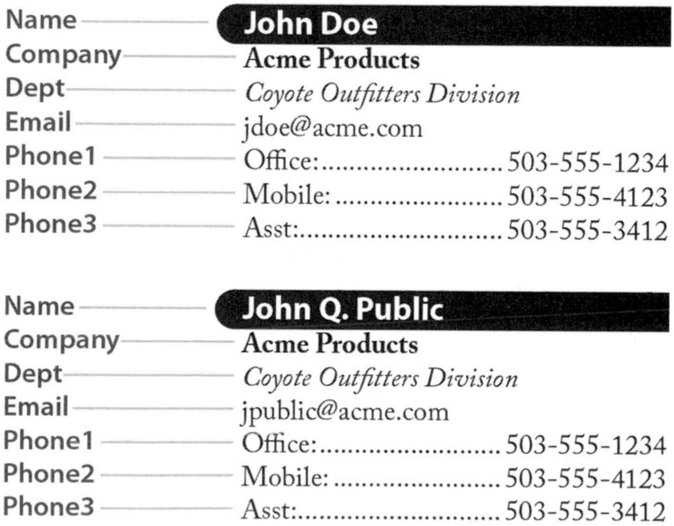

Name —————— **John Doe**
Company ——————— **Acme Products**
Dept ——————— *Coyote Outfitters Division*
Email ——————— jdoe@acme.com
Phone1 ——————— Office:......................... 503-555-1234
Phone2 ——————— Mobile: 503-555-4123
Phone3 ——————— Asst:............................503-555-3412

Name —————— **John Q. Public**
Company ——————— **Acme Products**
Dept ——————— *Coyote Outfitters Division*
Email ——————— jpublic@acme.com
Phone1 ——————— Office:......................... 503-555-1234
Phone2 ——————— Mobile: 503-555-4123
Phone3 ——————— Asst:............................503-555-3412

You can type a thousand of those listings, touching the Paragraph Styles panel only *once* thanks to Next Style:

1. In the options for the Name style, set the Next Style field to the Company style.

2. In Company, make Dept the next style.

3. In Dept, set Email as the next style and then Phone1 and Phone2 successively.

4. With the Phone3 style, set its Next Style field back to the beginning (i.e., back to Name).

5. Now, type the name, pick the correct paragraph style for the entry's name, and hit Return/Enter.

6. Type the company name, which will automatically be in the Company style, and hit Return/Enter.

7. Type the contact's department in the Dept style, and so on.

8. When you finish typing the assistant's phone number on the listing's last line, hit Return/Enter.

   The Next Style cascade will loop back to the beginning, setting the line after your carriage return in the Name style, ready for you to type the next contact's name.

Next Style saves a great many distracting trips to the Paragraph Styles and Character Styles panels in many, many types of documents. We'll get into the efficient use of character styles later in this chapter. For now, let's keep the focus on paragraph styles.

SUPER SECRET REVEALED: TWO-CLICK FORMATTING OF AN ENTIRE DOCUMENT

Criss Angel, David Copperfield, David Blaine, Siegfried & Roy, and all the world's other top magicians and illusionists belong to the International Magicians Society (IMS), an organization that, among other things, enforces among its members the policy that a magician never reveals the secret to his tricks. Thankfully, there is no similar body governing InDesign gurus, because what I'm about to reveal to you is, without exaggeration, one of the, if not *the*, best-kept secrets of the top InDesign gurus. It's often the big finale trick at conferences, and it's rarely shared in mass consumption media like a book or blog post because, well, knowing the trick is one of the reasons people call us InDesign gurus. You know me, I won't hold back any knowledge from you; the other gurus, though, might come gunning for me. If I suddenly have an "accident," you'll know the truth.

Here's the reveal, the result, of the trick: An entire document—from 1 to 1,000 pages—can be formatted with multiple paragraph styles in only two clicks of the mouse.

Like all great magic tricks, this one is achieved through preparation and misdirection. The preparation part is a matter of using cascading paragraph styles and the Next Style field. Going back to the directory example, every line of a directory listing carries a different paragraph style. By setting the Next Style field to every successive style required for the listing, and then looping the last paragraph style back to the first of a listing's styles, you can perpetually type directory listings that automatically style. But this trick isn't about automatic formatting as you type; this is about applying multiple styles instantly to a story *already* written. The preparation is the same, though: set up your Next Style fields.

Now that the trick has been prepared, you're ready to practice it in front of a mirror before moving on to a live audience.

1. Begin by setting the stage—pour your unformatted or improperly formatted text into InDesign. Although not absolutely necessary, for dramatic effect, simply because overset text can't be seen, you'll want to make sure that the entire story is placed on one or more pages, that there isn't any overset text.

2. Inform the audience of the extreme difficulty and danger involved in the following trick. Ask for total silence.

3. Place the text cursor somewhere within the story and press Cmd+A/Ctrl+A to select all.

4. Careful to use misdirection that prevents the audience from noticing the actions of your mouse cursor, go to the Paragraph Styles panel and right-click the first style in the chain of styles—the Name style in the directory listing example. Up will pop a context-sensitive menu you may think you know inside and out, top to bottom.

5. Around the middle of the pop-up menu will be a new command you've never seen before, one that is available nowhere and nowhen else in InDesign than when you have multiple paragraphs selected and have right-clicked a paragraph style that has a Next Style attribute set to something other than [Same Style].

6. There is the secret to the best trick of the greatest InDesign gurus: Apply [This Style] and Next. Click that command, and your entire document will format.

The command applies the first style—the one on which you right-clicked—to the first paragraph in the selected text. It then applies whatever style is defined in the first style's Next Style field to the second paragraph and then continues applying Next Style paragraph styles to every subsequent paragraph. Thus, you can format 1,000 pages of unformatted directory listings—or any type of document that uses successive paragraph styles—with two clicks.

Even a document like a newspaper or magazine article, one that isn't cyclic and doesn't loop the last style back to the first, can be formatted with this trick. Just make sure the last style—probably one for body copy—has [Same Style] set in the Next Style field. Then, after the kicker, headline, deck, byline, first paragraph, and first body copy paragraph are styled, every subsequent paragraph will also be assigned to the body copy style.

Now that you know the secret, don't tell anyone else. Sure, encourage them to buy their own copies of this book (my family has to eat), but until they do, let them think of *you* as the magician, as the guru, formatting multiple paragraphs, multiple pages, even whole documents, in only two clicks. Now *you* are one of the keepers of the secret. Welcome to the fraternity.

ORDERING STYLES

Paragraph (as well as character, object, table, and cell) styles are listed in the panel in the order of creation—a departure from earlier versions of InDesign that enforced an alphabetic arrangement. If you want alphabetic arrangement, choose Sort by Name from the Paragraph Styles flyout menu. You can also manually order styles and groups however you like—just drag them up or down within the panel list to create a custom sort order.

CS5
    If you were frustrated by InDesign's refusal to remember the sort order of styles in previous versions, rejoice: CS5 *does* now save the sort order inside documents. Thus, you can sort by name or create a custom order now, and the next time you open the document, the styles will have stayed that way rather than reverting to creation order.

STYLE GROUPS

Styles can be further organized into folder-like groups and nested groups much like Illustrator's or Photoshop's layers (see Figure 13.5).

FIGURE 13.5
Style groups make organization even easier.

By clicking the Create New Style Group button at the bottom of the panel, you can add expandable groups to the Paragraph Styles list (as well as to other styles panels' lists, which we'll discuss later in this chapter). Place styles in the groups by dragging them or by highlighting the styles and choosing from the panel flyout menu Copy to Group, which opens a destination group selection dialog, or New Group from Styles, which simultaneously creates a new group and moves the styles into it. You can even put one group inside another, nesting them.

Groups can be renamed like styles, by double-clicking their names, and can be opened or closed by clicking the arrow to the left of the group name. Helpful Open All and Close All Style Groups commands are on the flyout menu.

CLEANING UP STYLES

Paragraph styles are major productivity aids but only when in use. (So, uh, use 'em.) As you work, changing *this* passage of text, trying *this* visual effect or *that*, you'll undoubtedly end up with extraneous paragraph styles unused anywhere in the document. Leaving those alone makes for an unnecessarily bloated style list. Dump the styles you don't need. On the Paragraph Styles panel flyout menu is the Select All Unused command. Execute it to select (highlight) all the styles that aren't assigned to any text, anywhere, and then simply click the trashcan Delete icon at the bottom of the panel to delete those useless bits of clutter.

STYLE OVERRIDES

An *override* is any formatting that doesn't jibe with the style definition. For instance, if you set a paragraph in a roman (non-italic) typeface and then italicize a word or phrase within the paragraph, the italic text is overriding the paragraph style. Overrides are revealed as a plus sign (+) beside the style name on the Paragraph Style panel, but only when the overridden text is selected. If you select or place the cursor within the italic text in the example, a plus sign will appear next to the paragraph style's name in the panel. Move the cursor to another word that does adhere to the style definition, however, and the plus sign will disappear despite the

presence of overrides in the same paragraph. Selecting the entire paragraph also selects the overridden word and thus supplies the telltale plus sign. *Anything* done to a paragraph or a part of a paragraph that isn't specifically defined in the paragraph style is an override—text color, font, leading, paragraph indents, tabs, and so on.

In and of themselves, overrides are no big deal—they're just formatting options that aren't in the style definition. Heck, if all they are is an italic word or two, who cares, really? Many times, though, that plus sign signals something bigger than an emphasis here and there. For instance, an override in a collaborative layout could hint at a radical departure from the style guide by one of the layout artists. One accidental press of Option+Down arrow/Alt+Down arrow on the keyboard would increase the leading of a selected paragraph, potentially changing the text fitting for dozens of subsequent pages. Maybe someone inadvertently clicked the Registration color swatch instead of the Black swatch on the Swatches panel. Registration, as you know, is 100% of cyan, magenta, yellow, and black; a paragraph colored with Registration will look just as black as pure black onscreen, but it will print to all four CMYK plates and come off the press looking more like blurry scorched mud than crisp black. The plus sign is your only warning of these or other mishaps.

Restoring text formatting to the strict definition of the paragraph style is called clearing overrides. After selecting the word, words, paragraph, or story containing overrides, there are several ways to clear overrides:

◆ Choose the Clear Overrides command from the Paragraph Styles panel flyout menu.

◆ Force reapply the paragraph style by holding Option/Alt and clicking the style name on the panel.

◆ Use the Clear Overrides button at the bottom of the Paragraph Styles panel:

◆ Cmd+click/Ctrl+click to clear character-level overrides only (e.g., italics or kerning).

◆ Cmd+Shift-click/Ctrl+Shift-click to clear only overriding paragraph-level attributes such as indents, spacing, and drop caps.

USE CAUTION IN CLEARING OVERRIDES

Be careful clearing overrides by any method: The process is indiscriminate, and all overrides will be wiped out, wanted or not.

If you like the override and want to make the style incorporate it, thus updating all other text assigned to the same paragraph style to match the overridden text, highlight or place your cursor within only the differently styled word and choose Redefine Style on the Paragraph Styles panel flyout menu. Redefine Style incorporates the formatting options of the selected text into the style definition. For most people (your humble host included), Redefine Style is a lifesaver because it saves them from having to go into the Paragraph Style Options to make changes. Instead, formatting options can be changed on the page and then the style quickly updated to incorporate the new aesthetic.

In an ideal world, your document would never have a plus sign beside any style. Practically speaking, however, it's far too much darn work to never have overrides. I mean, changing a kerning pair in a headline is an override and produces that plus sign. What are you going to do,

create a character style for *every* little tweak and pluck? Certainly not. Just be careful, and, when it makes sense, use character styles. And, with that…

Character Styles

Paragraph styles are paragraph level and include in their definitions many character-level formatting options such as font family, font style, size, leading, scaling, color, OpenType options, and much more; paragraph styles apply to the entire paragraph, including the final paragraph mark (¶). If an entire paragraph will be formatted the same, a paragraph style will do the trick all by itself. However, if you expect words or phrases *within* paragraphs to differ in some respect from their surrounding text, regularly or occasionally, you'll want character styles defined to store, apply, and preserve those differences.

Predictably, character styles are managed on the Character Styles panel (Window ➤ Styles ➤ Character Styles). I won't dwell on the panel itself because it's almost identical to big brother Paragraph Styles. You have a list of styles, style groups, and many of the same commands on the flyout menu. Even their respective new style and style options dialogs are identical, but the Character version contains a subset of the panes found in the corresponding Paragraph Style New and Options dialogs (compare Figure 13.6 with Figure 13.2 that we looked at earlier). Character styles can also be based on one another, although, because they don't have anything to do with carriage returns, there is no Next Style field.

FIGURE 13.6
The Character
Style Options
dialog

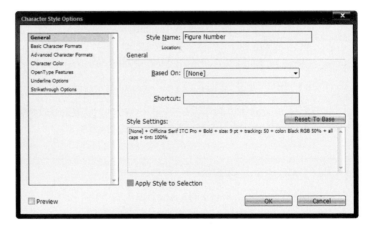

Think of character styles as sanctioned overrides. They change text formatting by the character or by the word, but they don't generate a plus sign and thus aren't wiped away by clearing overrides. Create character styles as you would paragraph styles—either by formatting text and then pressing the New button at the bottom of the Character Styles panel or by defining the style in the Character Style Options dialog ahead of placing text. To apply them, you must highlight text.

PARAGRAPH STYLES VS. CHARACTER STYLES

Paragraph styles may be applied when the cursor is simply within a paragraph, even if no text is selected, but character styles require specific text selection.

Character styles are ideal for a variety of uses. Here are just a few examples (see Figure 13.7 and the color version in the color insert section of this book):

◆ Using *run-in* heads.

◆ Underlining URLs in a document destined for distribution as a PDF (and in which those URLs will be live, clickable links; don't underline them otherwise).

◆ Adding other nondefault underlines and strikethroughs without having to go through the Underline Options or Strikethrough Options dialogs every time.

◆ Highlighting text (see the sidebar "Underline Styles for Hyperlinks" in Chapter 3, "Characters").

◆ Setting italic or bold type that will survive a deliberate or accidental clearing of overrides.

◆ Changing the color of bits of text.

◆ Styling the first line of a story larger or in all caps.

◆ Styling the numbers and bullets differently than subsequent text in numbered or bulleted lists.

◆ Differentiating the style of numbers or leaders in a directory- or TOC-style entry.

◆ Styling drop caps differently from the rest of the text in the paragraph. Note that drop caps themselves—whether to use them, how many lines tall they are, and how many characters wide they are—are paragraph-level attributes. Use character styles to alter typeface, color, and other options on drop caps already defined in paragraph styles.

FIGURE 13.7
Example uses for character styles

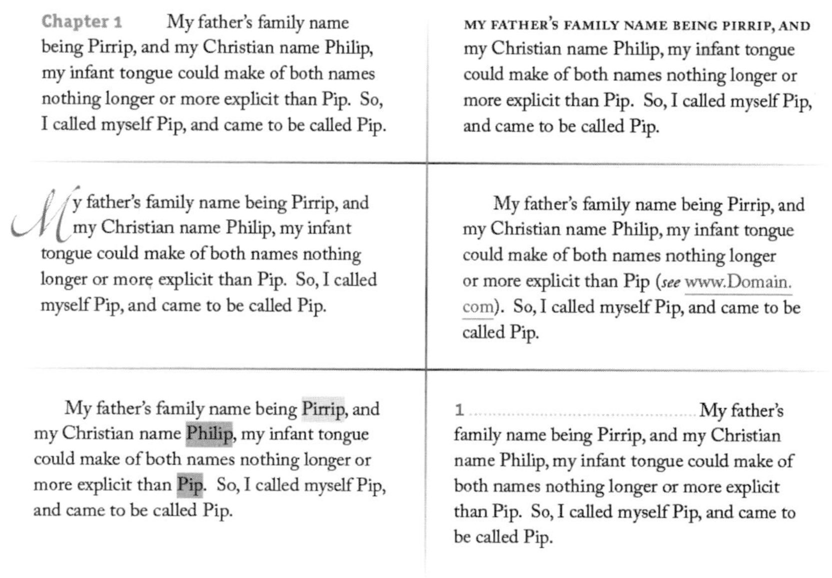

Chapter 1   My father's family name being Pirrip, and my Christian name Philip, my infant tongue could make of both names nothing longer or more explicit than Pip. So, I called myself Pip, and came to be called Pip.

MY FATHER'S FAMILY NAME BEING PIRRIP, AND my Christian name Philip, my infant tongue could make of both names nothing longer or more explicit than Pip. So, I called myself Pip, and came to be called Pip.

My father's family name being Pirrip, and my Christian name Philip, my infant tongue could make of both names nothing longer or more explicit than Pip. So, I called myself Pip, and came to be called Pip.

My father's family name being Pirrip, and my Christian name Philip, my infant tongue could make of both names nothing longer or more explicit than Pip (*see* www.Domain. com). So, I called myself Pip, and came to be called Pip.

My father's family name being Pirrip, and my Christian name Philip, my infant tongue could make of both names nothing longer or more explicit than Pip. So, I called myself Pip, and came to be called Pip.

1 .... My father's family name being Pirrip, and my Christian name Philip, my infant tongue could make of both names nothing longer or more explicit than Pip. So, I called myself Pip, and came to be called Pip.

Real World Scenario

FIND/CHANGE STYLES TO THE RESCUE

Mikayla L. worked as the final stop in a publication workflow that involved nine layout artists, each working on different portions of a 320-page quarterly. Her job was to collect and proof everyone's work, stitch it all together into a single publication managed by an InDesign book, and fix any mistakes before imposing the issue and sending it to press. Of course, the publication had a style guide, templates, and preconfigured paragraph and character styles; invariably, however, the articles and sections Mikayla received from the other creatives contained numerous style overrides in the form of local formatting—all of which Mikayla had to fix before the publication went to press. Making matters worse, the publication also ran per issue anywhere between 1 and 10 articles and pieces of articles from outside agencies and filler libraries. The outside contributions were formatted in ways that rarely bore any resemblance to Mikayla's templates.

Wrangling these wild styles should have been as easy as selecting paragraphs and applying or reapplying paragraph styles. Unfortunately, doing so cleared out *desired* overrides, most notably italic. Consequently, Mikayla found herself spending days staring at side-by-side comparisons of original pages and pages with correct paragraph styles, locating italicized words in the former, and manually italicizing the same words in the latter. The process took so long that she had to push up the issue closing date—which, of course, some members of the team understood to mean more time between submission and press for making last-minute rewrites, leading to more formatting cleanup and often on the same story more than once.

The real solution to Mikayla's problem lay with stricter enforcement of the publication's style guide, which was in the offing but still left her with a lot of extra work in the interim. Although style enforcement might improve the consistency of work from Mikayla's coworkers, policy changes for content from external agencies wasn't likely to improve as quickly as internal policy changes. By way of retaining Mikayla's direct control over fixing the publication, I enacted a two-step solution.

First, Mikayla and I identified all the formatting options that fell under the heading of "desired override"—in other words, any appropriately used character-level formatting such as italic, a couple of different underline and coloring styles used for assorted kinds of URLs listed in stories, and small caps for acronyms and occasional other uses. We created character styles to hold each of the settings—one for small caps, one each for the types of URLs, one each for italic and bold-italic. We also created a Regular character style that specifically disallowed all the formatting options of all the other character styles; using the Regular style would instantly strip off the effects of, say, the bold-italic style, reverting the selected text to non-bold, non-italic. We added these styles to the main template.

Step 2 was building and enacting a procedure to replace wanted style overrides with character styles and then remove all unwanted overrides. No sweat. Using Find/Change (Edit ➢ Find/Change), we searched for any italic glyph and assigned it to the Italic character style. You see those settings in the screenshot of the Find/Change dialog. Similar searches were run for each of the other format overrides that had matching character styles. Each replacement criteria set was saved as a reusable query.

To revert undesirable overrides back to their correct paragraph styles, additional searches were performed, one for each paragraph style. In that case, it was even simpler: both Find Format and Change Format were set to the same paragraph style and no other options. When InDesign performs a Find/Change with such criteria, it automatically strips off any overrides—but not those

properly assigned to character styles. So, to remove any unwanted overrides on the Body Copy style, Mikayla set Find Format to search for Paragraph Style: Body Copy; Change Format was also set to only Paragraph Style: Body Copy. InDesign rolled through all the stories in the document, finding every instance of text in the Body Copy style, and forced reapplying the paragraph style. Mikayla's problem was solved.

To make things even faster, and with the help of a JavaScript programmer in Mikayla's IT department, even all the Find/Change queries were automated. Now Mikayla just executes the Style Cleanup script from the Scripts panel. Formatting cleanup that used to take her days is finished within a couple of minutes.

BREAKING STYLE LINKS

When you change a style definition, all text assigned to the style will update accordingly anywhere in the current document. Sometimes, you'd rather freeze a particular passage of text, leaving it unchanged regardless of what happens to the style definition. To do that, disassociate the text from the style with the Break Link to Style command on either or both of the Paragraph Styles or Character Styles panels. The text will retain its formatting but will no longer update to reflect changes in the style.

Nested Styles

A *nested style* is a character style applied from Point A to Point B automatically. For example, you could specify that the first two words of any paragraph assigned to the First Graph paragraph style automatically adopt a different color, typeface, and an underline. If you're working on a product catalog, you could force every dollar sign ($) to one character style, the dollar amount to another character style, and the cents to a third style (perhaps one that makes the numerals superscript and underlined), all automatically.

Remember, when we discussed the Next Style choice on paragraph styles, how I said you can format an entire listing—and even multiple listings—by merely selecting the first paragraph style? Nested Styles is very similar but operates *within* paragraphs instead of being triggered by carriage returns. In other words, you can format an entire paragraph of many different character styles by merely selecting the first paragraph style.

1. Open the Paragraph Style Options for any style.
2. Go to the Drop Caps and Nested Styles pane (see Figure 13.8). In the upper portion, Drop Caps, is the introduction to nested styles.
3. Define the number of lines and characters to form the drop cap.
4. Choose a character style that applies only to the drop cap.

After the drop cap, the character style will stop applying to text, leaving the rest of the paragraph untouched. Thus, the beginning of the drop cap is Point A, the end Point B; it's a nested style.

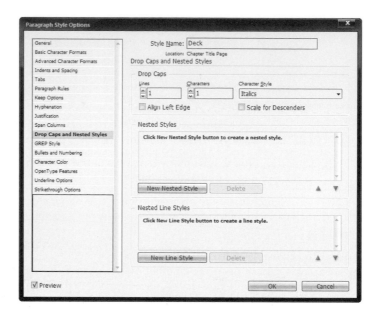

When you'd like to use something other than a drop cap as a nested style, move to the lower section and click the New Nested Style button, which will add a new row of four fields to the Nested Styles list. Before I describe the fields, though, I'd like to diagram the anatomy of a simple nested style so you can see what those fields do (see Figure 13.9). The character style (Heading 3 RunIn, it's called), begins with the paragraph and applies to text from the *run-in head* up until it reaches the nested style end marker, which, in this case, is a tab.

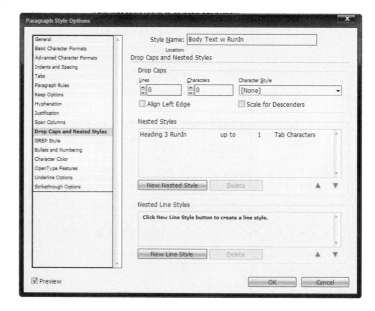

Back in the Nested Styles list, the row of fields is a statement—use *this* character style up to, or through, *X* instances of *that* stop character. Follow these steps to create a nested style:

1. In the first field, choose the character style to use.

2. Next, decide whether to style the stop character itself as well as the text before it.

   For example, if you set a colon as the stop character, choosing Through will apply the character style to the colon as well as to the text that precedes it; setting this field to Up To will apply the style to the text before the colon but leave the colon itself unstyled.

3. After that, choose how many instances of the stop character appear before it actually stops applying the character style.

   You can, for instance, continue applying the character style through the third tab from the beginning of the paragraph, or the fifth tab, or the ninth…

4. Finally, choose the stop character itself. You can use any single letter, number, punctuation, or symbol.

   The dropdown menu in this field presents several common options such as a tab character or forced line break, as well as sentences, words, and characters. Choosing Sentences, for example, you could style the entire first sentence of the paragraph whether that sentence is 2 or 40 words long. If the stop character you want isn't in the list, type it into the field, replacing whatever is there.

As you may surmise, you can add multiple nested styles that follow one another. In Figure 13.10 you can see a series of nested styles I might use for the prices in a catalog; on the right of the figure are the before and after of using the nested styles. (Note that the decimal point is still there but turned white by its character style.) The order of nested styles in the list is critical because each style picks up after the last has ended; instead of starting from the beginning of the paragraph, the second nested style would begin calculating from the end of the first nested style, from the Through or Up To character or break point. I couldn't, for example, put my Price Cents style directive ahead of the Price $. If I did, none of the styles that need to be applied before Price Cents would be applied. The arrows beneath the Nested Styles list enable the rows to be reordered as needed.

FIGURE 13.10

At left, the chained nested styles create the effect at the lower right. In the upper right is the text before applying nested styles.

Pay attention to the fact that there's a [None] item in the list of character styles. That's powerful and important. You must begin styling from the beginning of a paragraph, but if you want the first part of a paragraph—say, through the first tab—to match the paragraph style and not any particular character style, create a nested style that applies the [None] character style through or up to the first tab. *Then* add a new nested style that begins applying something special from that point onward. You can even reuse [None] or any character style in multiple nested styles in the same chain.

Your stop character can be just about any character you can type—and many invisible ones such as spaces, tabs, and returns. This is what makes nested styles so powerful. They apply automatically to text, adapting to the text itself. Still, this method assumes that an appropriate stop character can be found in the text where you want it. What if there isn't? What if you want to control where a nested style stops applying, but you don't have a consistent stop character in each of the paragraphs with nested styles? For situations like that, you can insert a special, invisible stop character marker in the text where you need it.

On the Type ➢ Insert Special Character ➢ Other menu is the End Nested Style Here marker, which corresponds to an option on the Stop Character field dropdown in the Paragraph Style Options's Drop Caps and Nested Styles pane. Placing the End Nested Style Here marker in text, and choosing that as the stop character, limits the effect of a nested style to precisely the point you decide.

What if you want to style only the first line of a paragraph regardless of how many words or characters that may be, regardless of whether the last word in the line is complete or hyphenated? Can you just set the nested style stop character to End of Line? Yes, but not in the Nested Styles list. Rather you have to use the Nested Line Styles list. They're similar, but Nested Line Styles applies only to full lines of text (not sentences). Click New Line Style and then select the character style and number of lines to which to apply it. You can set a different character style per line in a paragraph if you like. Note that nested styles trump nested line styles; if you apply a nested style to the first word in the paragraph and a nested line style to the first line, the first word will match the condition you set for it in Nested Styles while the rest of the line adheres to the style set in Nested Line Styles.

Nested styles added to the paragraph style apply anywhere that paragraph style is applied. If you want to use a nested style only once, in a spot instance, choose Drop Caps and Nested Styles from the flyout menu on the Paragraph panel or the Control Panel in Paragraph mode.

GREP Style

Now that you've mastered nested styles and nested line styles, you might be feeling pretty powerful—and you should; you can automatically format every paragraph you want, beginning to end, with penultimate control. When you're ready to graduate to ultimate control, move to the GREP Style pane of the Paragraph Style Options dialog (see Figure 13.11). *GREP* is the acronym for "global / regular expression / print," which is shortened to "g/re/p". Way back in 1973 when Ken Thompson created g/re/p to be an application for UNIX, the name mattered. Since then, Ken's creation has blossomed into its own language and method of querying and searching for all operating systems and many applications (like InDesign), and the long form of its name has been all but forgotten. These days, the name is just "grep," "Grep," or "GREP," depending on the capitalization preference of the software author. InDesign uses the all-caps version, GREP.

FIGURE 13.11
The GREP Style
pane with a GREP
style ready to
reformat ordinals

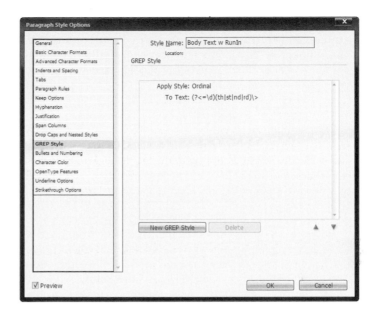

Whereas nested styles work sequentially, starting at the beginning of a paragraph and moving inward looking for stop characters, GREP styles apply character styles to text that matches a pattern, wherever that text may appear in a paragraph. For example, let's say you want to convert the textual part of ordinal numbers (e.g., 1st, 5th, etc.) to superscript. You don't necessarily know where in a paragraph the ordinal will appear, so you can't use nested styles to apply a superscript character style. A GREP style makes it easy.

1. Just click the New GREP Style button.

2. Choose the appropriate character style to apply.

3. In the To Text field in the GREP Style list, enter the following regular expression:
   `(?<=\d)(th|st|nd|rd)\>`.

That expression tells InDesign to find any number digit followed by "th," "st," "nd, " or "rd" at the end of the word and to apply the selected character style to matching text (but not to the number itself). And InDesign will do it, whether the matching text is the first word in a paragraph, the last, or somewhere in the middle, and whether there is a single occurrence of the ordinal text or one hundred. Any paragraph to which that paragraph style is applied will be searched for text matching the GREP expression.

Another example of GREP styles is how they can help book production personnel. Do you lay out technical books a la *Mastering InDesign*? I do, more and more lately as I write my own and lay out others' print and e-books. A handy expression you might find useful is one that applies a character style to figure and table references in text. Though it can be used for final output—maybe you want figure references in a certain different font or style—you can also use it to temporarily make figure references stand out—maybe change the text color to magenta or apply a highlight effect behind the reference—to aid you in finding the right locations to place figures themselves.

Whip up the character style you want for figure and/or table references, and then use this expression: `(?i)(Figure|Table)\s\d+` . If your figure references are different, perhaps "Illustration" or "See Fig" is how they're typically listed, replace "Figure" or "Table" or *add* a search term after "Table." Just separate each term with the pipette vertical line.

FREE GREP REFERENCE CHEAT SHEET

GREP is incredibly powerful, and like most powerful things, it has many secrets. That's why I've put together a cheat sheet of GREP regular expression symbols and codes. It'll help you with GREP Style and the GREP tab of Find/Change. Just visit `http://iampariah.com/projects/other-projects` to download the cheat sheet free as a printable PDF.

GREP is not unique to InDesign. It's actually from the UNIX world, but I won't bore you with all of that. Besides, we already covered the basics of GREP in terms of the Find/Change dialog, in Chapter 8, "Stories." It's a search language of regular expressions. If you can write an expression to search for it, you can apply a character style to it with GREP Style.

Master GREP styles, and you quite literally may never have to manually apply a character style again.

Text Variables

As of the release of InDesign CS5, Adobe owns three page-layout applications:

◆ PageMaker, which reached an official end of life in 2003 yet continues to enjoy a large and loyal following

◆ InDesign, which was conceived by PageMaker creator Aldus (acquired by Adobe in 1994) as the replacement for PageMaker

◆ FrameMaker, a robust technical-document-publishing application that is decidedly unfriendly to creative types

Although PageMaker and InDesign differ in their approaches, there is nothing the former does that the latter doesn't. The same can't be said of FrameMaker. That application has always led the pack in its ability to create an unlimited assortment of adaptive text variables and automatically numbered items and lists. Maintaining three separate page-layout applications is a strain for a company like Adobe because, to a large degree, its layout applications compete with one another. More important, PageMaker and FrameMaker are both (by computer standards) ancient code bases that cannot be readied for the publishing demands of today, much less tomorrow. In fact, FrameMaker for Mac hasn't even been updated to work with OS X; the Mac version was officially discontinued a few years ago because sluggish sales wouldn't justify the expense of rewriting the elderly code.

PageMaker's features were easily replaced by InDesign, but Adobe couldn't replace FrameMaker with InDesign without rendering InDesign as unintuitive and noncreative-friendly as the other. Slowly, however, Adobe is training InDesign users to expect more-advanced, more-powerful, more-complicated features. In expectation of the day when it can finally retire FrameMaker, InDesign acquired anchored objects, numbered lists, XML structuring, scripting, and *text variables*.

When you insert a page number marker on a master page, you are really inserting a text variable. It isn't static data; rather, it updates itself with every page. In its simplest form, a page number is a mere digit; activate section or chapter numbering and the page number will include the unique number of each section or chapter (and possibly text, too, if you've defined it to do so in the Document & Section Numbering Options) as well as a numeric, alphabetic, or mixed-numbering page number. That's a text variable: *text that changes automatically to meet current conditions.*

The obvious benefit to productivity of using a text variable is that certain bits of text that would otherwise have to be written and edited by hand are inserted and changed automatically. Place the text variable once and forget about it; it will alter its information to match changing conditions in the document, computer, or what have you. Used wisely, the result can be a significant time savings—particularly with repeating text such as a product name.

What would be a practical application of a custom text variable? Consider this scenario: You're the production manager at a direct-mail production house. As part of your company's services, you offer clients several predesigned, ready-to-fly templates. Your templates are built such that only the client's name, logo, and contact info (phone, fax, address, and URL) change; all other information and design are static from one client to the next. Instead of changing the client-specific information in its three or four locations manually—or even doing a Find/Change—insert text variables in the appropriate template locations. To change the client company name, simply change the single value in the text variable's definition, and all instances of that variable in the layout copy will update to match. Setting up all the requisite custom data—company name, phone, address line 1, address line 2, and so on—would involve each being one text variable. If you hooked InDesign into your client or job database via scripting or XML, you could even automate the entire process of changing text variables and sending the document to print or PDF.

VARIABLE TEXT TYPES

InDesign CS5 ships with eight predefined, ready-to-insert text variables:

Chapter Number	Last Page Number
Creation Date	Modification Date
File Name	Output Date
Image Name	Running Header

They can be inserted in a text frame by selecting Type ➤ Text Variables ➤ Insert Variable. Once inserted, a variable takes on the formatting of surrounding text and is thus ready to use instantly. You may not want to use the defaults for everything, however, so you can define your own variables from Type ➤ Text Variables ➤ Define. In the Text Variables list are the defaults and any you've created or imported from other documents via the Load button.

TEXT VARIABLE WRAPPING

Note that text variables *will not wrap* across multiple lines; instead they will squish horizontally and, if pushed too far, eventually overset. (This is incredibly frustrating, by the way.)

As implied above, you can have numerous text variables of different or all the same types. You can, for instance, have several different running header type text variables in use in the same document. Click the New button in the dialog to create a new text variable. In the New Text Variable dialog, 10 different types of variables are available, and each has its own unique options to set:

Chapter Number   This type of variable displays the current chapter number with optional text before and/or after and using the numbering style selected (see Figure 13.12). Flyout menus to the right of the Text Before and Text After fields enable easy input of special glyphs and markers. Although you may paste into the Before and After fields text that is copied from another field or the document text, special characters will not paste in correctly and must be inserted using the flyout menus.

FIGURE 13.12
Options for Chapter Number text variables

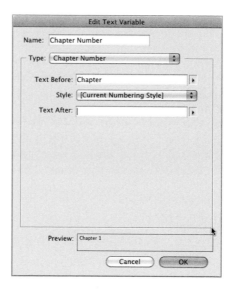

Creation Date   Useful for inserting into the slug area or a note the date and/or time at which a document was created, this variable offers a highly customizable array of date/time formats from the flyout menu to the right of the Date Format field (see Figure 13.13). Naturally, the field also accepts text input, so you can separate date/time components with standard punctuation and marks.

Custom Text   This variable type offers but one text entry field that can accept pasted or typed content and special glyphs and symbols from the menu to the right of the field. Use custom text variables for anything not accounted for by default. For instance, create text variables named "Company Name," "Phone," "Address Line 1," "Address Line 2," and so on to build the ready-to-fly templates in the scenario I mentioned previously. Then, changing the template for each customer is not a matter of replacing multiple instances of that common information manually but instead just a trip back into the text variable (via the Edit button in

the Text Variables dialog) to change the contents of the Text field for each of those variables. A few seconds' work, and the template is customized for each client and ready to print.

File Name Placing the name of the current document into the slug area is a common practice, one that this text variable makes a snap. Before and after text is complemented with two options, Include Entire Folder Path and Include File Extension, that, respectively, insert the complete path to the file on disk and the document file extension (see Figure 13.14).

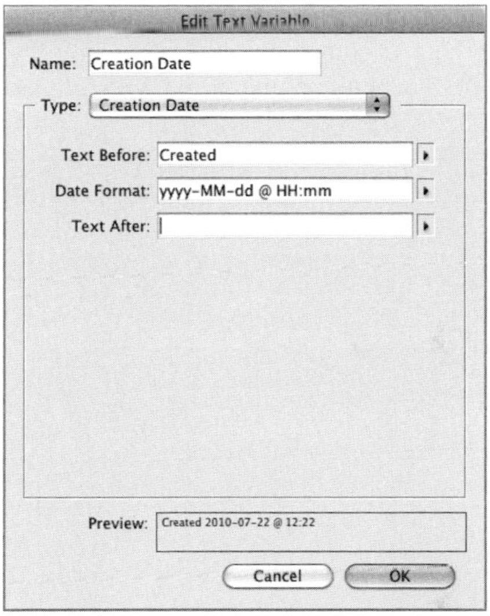

FIGURE 13.13
Options for Creation Date text variables

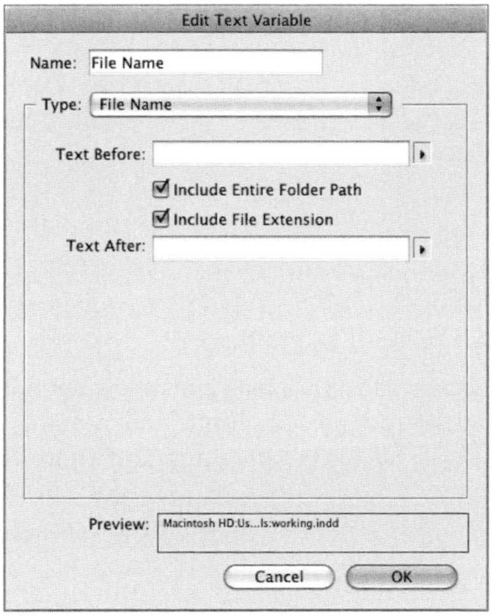

FIGURE 13.14
Options for File Name text variables

Last Page Number   Undoubtedly among the most commonly used, the Last Page Number text variable can be used to create a folio in the form of *Page X of Y* where *X* is the current page number inserted from the Type ➤ Insert Special Characters menu and *Y* is the number of the last page in the document, added via a text variable. Standard optional before and after text is accepted, as are a numbering style (e.g., Arabic, Roman, alphabetic, etc.) and a scope—whether to use the last page number of the section or document (see Figure 13.15).

FIGURE 13.15
Options for Last
Page Number text
variables

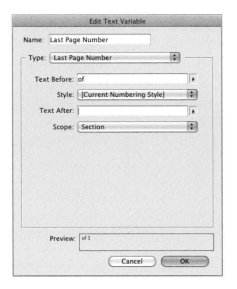

Metadata Caption   Remember back in Chapter 6, "Objects," when we discussed Live Captions? The Metadata Caption text variable is the same thing, but packaged as an insert-anywhere text variable rather than a Live Caption object. From the Metadata field you can choose any piece of file, document, or object metadata—from who it was lasted edited by to the aperture speed of the camera that took the image (if you're using it with an image)—as is available in Live Captions (see Figure 13.16). Before and After fields enable you to add any text you like around the variable itself.

Modification Date   With options identical to the Creation Date text variable type, Modification Date records the last, rather than the first, time the document was saved.

Output Date   Again, like Creation Date and Modification Date text variable types, Output Date offers number options for formatting the date/time when the document was output—printed, packaged, or exported to PDF. Output date variables are useful for document-tracking purposes, but with a little creativity they can prove valuable for other uses—say, to automatically insert the date of printing, which can itself be used in the slug area or even on the page, within a document, to display the date of a newsletter or newspaper edition.

The last two text variable types, Running Headers (Paragraph Style) and Running Headers (Character Style) require a little more space to explain.

FIGURE 13.16
Options for Meta-
data Caption text
variables

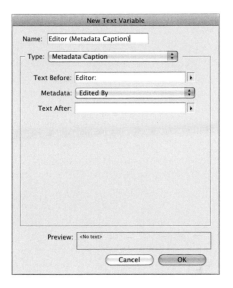

RUNNING HEADERS AND FOOTERS

When you insert text at the top or bottom of a page, you're creating headers or footers. Adding the Current Page Number marker into master page headers and footers adds a relatively simple text variable with the page number and possibly section and chapter numbers or identifiers. In the same or a different text frame, you can also add the Section marker to enhance a folio with something to the effect of *Chapter 11* or *Section IV*. The dynamics at work with automatic page numbers and section numbering are excellent and much needed, but they only go so far. Page numbers, for example, are cognizant of only the current section and page numbers and any prefixes or suffixes added. Section markers don't even consider the page level. Wouldn't it be great if page headers noted not only the section or chapter number but also the subsection? What if every instance of the Heading 1 paragraph style was reflected in the page header? In publications such as catalogs, directories, indexes, and glossaries, wouldn't it be cool to have the first product, person, entry, or definition on the left-read page noted at the top of that page and the last product, person, entry, or definition in the spread noted at the top of the right-read page for easy reference, as with a dictionary or telephone book?

All of that—and more—is possible (without resorting to FrameMaker) with the Running Header (and footer) text variable type. In Figure 13.17 you can see a single-page header from a fairly standard personnel or membership directory. The anatomy of this header, created entirely on the document master page, is very, very simple. First, on the left, is a standard Current Page Number marker. Beside it is the first running header text variable, with the second running header text variable anchored to the page's inside margin. Both variables look for appearances of a particular character style (the EntryName character style in this case). The left variable uses the first instance of that character style on the page, echoing text set in that style, while the right variable repeats whatever it hears in the *last* instance of the character style. I would use identical variables—perhaps even the exact same master page—in a dictionary to include the first and last definitions of words on the page in the page header.

FIGURE 13.17
Text variables
enable dynamic
headers in this
membership
directory.

There are two variations of the Running Header text variable type: one that echoes text assigned to a specific paragraph style and one that watches for the use of a character style. It's simple to choose: do you want to echo an entire line of text or merely part of it? In the case of the personnel directory (see Figure 13.17), personal names were not set on lines by themselves; rather, they were set as the first part of a line with additional data—birthdates—tabbed off to the right. I didn't want the birthdates included in the header, so I used a nested style to automatically give each entry's personal name the EntryName character style and told the text variables to listen for that particular style.

A running header (footer, too, mind you) is entirely style dependent. If you want to take advantage of this new feature, you *must* use paragraph and/or character styles, as discussed earlier in this chapter. Moreover, you must be careful to use a particular style only to format the specific text you want to appear in the header (or footer; last time, honest). Once you have a document and text containing the appropriate styles, create a new text variable, choosing Running Header (Paragraph Style) or Running Header (Character Style) as appropriate. In Figure 13.18, you can see the settings I used in the Edit Text Variable dialog to create the membership directory dynamic running header.

FIGURE 13.18
Options for the
directory running
header text variable

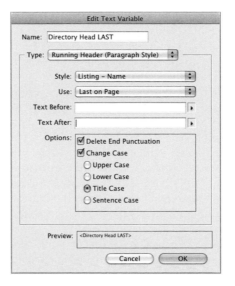

Style   Choose the paragraph or character style the variable should echo.

Use   Either the first or last instance of the selected style on the page.

Text Before/After   As with other text variable types, these fields allow you to enter static text, punctuation, and symbols around the variable text.

Delete End Punctuation   Use this option particularly when the variable is based on paragraph styles to strip off any punctuation appearing at the end of the echoed text.

Change Case   A very nice little feature, the four options in this section allow you to change the case of echoed text without altering the original. For instance, if the trigger text on the page is mixed case (e.g., *Burke, Samuel D.*) and you'd rather it be all caps in the header (e.g., *BURKE, SAMUEL D.*), choose the Upper Case radio button. To get fancy, setting just the last name in all caps and the rest in mixed case (e.g., *BURKE, Samuel D.*), use multiple variables and multiple character styles inserted via nested styles. You can also use multiple variables to create a LAST, First name setup when the page itself actually lists names First Last.

Once you've defined your text variables, simply insert them into text frames using the Type ➤ Text Variables ➤ Insert Variable menu. Any custom variables you've created will appear on that menu.

Note that text variables are document specific, like styles. Therefore, if you want to create a global text variable for use in several documents, or at least available for use in future documents, create the variable with no documents opened. Alternatively, if you've already created the variable in a document and want to make it globally available for future documents, close all documents and use the Load button in the (Define) Text Variables dialog.

Also in that dialog is the Convert to Text button, which, when clicked, will convert all instances of the highlighted variable throughout the document to static (nonvariable, nonupdating) text.

Conditional Text

Conditional text, added in CS4, enables you to hide and show any length of text, from a single character to pages' worth of copy, much like you hide and show layers, but with a couple of differences. There's even a very Layers-like Conditional Text panel (see Figure 13.19). Although there is some overlap between what you can accomplish with conditional text and text variables or layers, conditional text is, at best, a solution to unique needs and, at worst, another tool in your belt.

FIGURE 13.19
The Conditional
Text panel, with
a few conditions
already created

THE NEED FOR CONDITIONAL TEXT

Many of us produce documents that will be output to multiple versions or editions. For one example, you might be producing the same brochure with text in English, Spanish, and French. Another common example would be a textbook, in the teacher's edition of which appear the answers to exercises, while the student's edition contains only the exercises. I'm sure you can think of other examples of effectively the same document containing two or more different sets of text.

Layout artists typically employ two methods of producing such documents, both with significant limitations.

The Multiple Document Method   Closely related variations on the same document are often created as multiple, disconnected documents—for instance, an English version, a Spanish version, and a French version. All three contain the same layout and graphical elements, text is formatted with the same paragraph and character styles, and, with the exception of the language in which the copy is written, they are identical in every way. Usually one version is created first—the version in the native tongue of the layout artist—and the other language files are created via Save a Copy from the original, and then the text is translated. The major drawback to this method is that the layout artist has three separate documents to manage. If the client requests a font or leading change, a change that reflows the entire document and requires nipping and tucking of image placement, text frame options, and so on, all those changes must be performed thrice.

The Layers Method   The other time-honored technique of exchanging one set of copy for another in the same layout keeps everything in one document, thus eliminating the drawback of the multiple document method. Text frames containing English-language copy are placed on a layer separate from all other objects, while similar layers contain the Spanish and French text frames. Outputting one language is often as easy as simply turning its corresponding layer on and the others off. When the lengths of all variations of the copy are approximately the same, the layers method is perfect—all text is formatted using the same styles, so a change that affects one language layer affects all language layers. Images and other objects are placed on separate layers and can be changed for all versions with a single action, and the artist has but one document to track and manage.

But what happens when the copy variations aren't the same approximate length? Take the teacher's edition of a textbook, for example. Student editions of the books get problems to solve and exercises to complete, while the teacher's edition must have all of that *plus* the answers and results. One method is to put the teacher's edition material in a sidebar, which works when the layout has the space for a sidebar and the answers and results are short enough to fit into that space. Oftentimes the additional content required for a teacher's edition just won't work with the layers method because the copy is too large to fit within the empty areas of the student edition page.

Conditional text solves the problems inherent in both the multiple document and layers methods.

◆ First, it keeps all the copy in a single document, which eliminates the multiple document drawbacks.

◆ Second, conditional text appears (or hides) inline, actually within the same text frames as the text that will show in all editions. Thus, instead of relying on finding an empty place in, say, the student edition copy to insert the teacher's edition text, the student edition copy adjusts and reflows to accommodate the inclusion of the conditional teacher's text when present.

As you can see in Figure 13.20, which shows "The Bottom Line" exercises from Chapter 3 of this book, an instructor's version of the book could display the exercise solutions directly beneath the "Master It" exercise description itself, while the normal, student edition of the book

would omit the solutions (not that that's how we've laid out this book, but we *could* have). Both editions show the same description and exercise; only the inclusion of the solutions is edition specific. The always-visible copy reflows to accommodate the inclusion or omission of the conditional copy. The same reflow would happen if, instead of whole paragraphs, the conditional text were but a sentence or two or a few words inside otherwise always-visible paragraphs.

FIGURE 13.20
(Above) The normal or student edition of the book; (below) the same spread with the inclusion of copy only for the instructor's edition (highlighted)

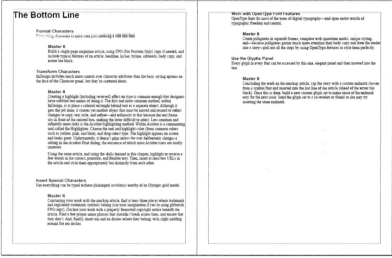

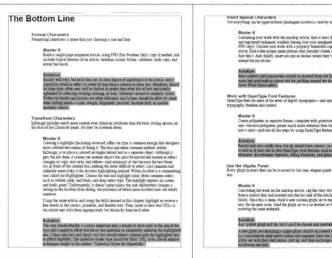

USING CONDITIONAL TEXT

Conditional text, in my humble opinion, is a misnomer. To me, the term sounds like it describes a feature wherein InDesign looks for certain conditions, and if conditions are met, it automatically inserts text; if those conditions aren't met, the text isn't inserted—basically an if-then-else

directive that runs automatically. Sadly, this is not the case. Rather, Conditional Text should more appropriately be called "Show/Hide Text," because that's how it works: Text is shown or hidden as the result of manually toggling the show/hide eyeball icon.

Let's run through an exercise to get a feel for working with conditional text:

1. Create a text frame and enter into it a few paragraphs, some of which you'll want visible in all editions, some you'll want shown only in a specific second edition. The paragraphs can be different languages, student/teacher editions, region-specific news or sales info, or whatever.

2. Leaving the always-visible paragraphs alone, select one of the edition-specific paragraphs—be sure you highlight the entire paragraph, including the invisible pilcrow (¶) that marks the end of the paragraph.

3. On the Conditional Text panel, click the New Condition button at the bottom, which will pop-up the New Conditional dialog box (see Figure 13.21). In it, name your condition, something like *Spanish* or *Teacher's Edition* or whatever.

FIGURE 13.21
The New Condition
dialog box

InDesign calls out conditional text to you in the layout with visual indicators as defined in the Indicator section of the New Condition dialog box. These indicators won't print, unless you specifically direct InDesign to do so by selecting Show and Print in the Indicators field at the bottom of the Conditional Text dialog; they're onscreen cues to enable you to quickly identify which content is conditional and to which condition it belongs.

A. From the Method menu, choose the method and appearance for your indicators, either Underline or Highlight. (I used Highlight in the previous figures.)

B. If you opted for Underline, then select either Wavy, Solid, or Dashed in the (Underline) Appearance dropdown list.

C. Finally pick a color for your underline or highlight. If your document contains multiple sets of conditional text—for example, two or more optional language sets—you'll want to set each condition's appearance to be different for easy identification of text assigned to each condition.

D. Click OK when finished.

4. Back in the Conditional Text panel, you now have your condition, but the text is not yet assigned to it. Note the checkmark in the second column of [Unconditional]. The checkmark indicates that the selected text is visible when that condition is visible.

[Unconditional] can't be hidden; it's the condition for your always-visible text. So, place a checkmark beside the condition you just created by clicking within that column; doing so should automatically remove the checkmark from beside [Unconditional].

You've now defined that highlighted paragraph of text to omit from the always-visible text and show only when your new condition is visible.

5. Toggle the visibility eyeball beside your new condition to see it show and hide, and the surrounding text to move down to accommodate its inclusion or move up to fill the hole left by your conditional text's absence.

6. Select another paragraph and assign it to your existing condition by adding a checkmark beside the appropriate condition, thus automatically removing the checkmark from beside [Unconditional].

Of course, if text reflowing is a problem for your layout, don't use conditional text. Instead, use layers, text variables, or multiple documents.

As I noted previously, conditional text is not limited to whole paragraphs—it can be one paragraph or one hundred, a single word in the middle of a paragraph or a single glyph. Think about that for a moment as you reflect on what types of objects you know InDesign considers to be, or treats like, text. Tables are text objects, so you could use conditional text to control the display of parts, or the entirety, of a table. Anchored and inline graphics and frames, too, are treated like text. The images and frames themselves aren't, of course, but their anchor markers *are* text. Thus, you could highlight an inline graphic or the marker for an anchored object and set it to display only on one or more conditions. When those conditions are not visible, the remaining text will reflow to fill in the space left by the hidden inline or anchored object.

USING CONDITIONAL SETS

A story may contain any number of conditions, visible in any combination—some on, some off. Also, each bit of text can belong to multiple conditions; you could, for example, have a list of upcoming county-wide events visible in both the regional and city-specific editions of your newsletter, while lists of events taking place only in certain cities are shown only within their respective cities' editions.

As another example, take technical instruction about dealing with plug-ins in Photoshop CS5. In an article that gives instructions for manually adding or removing Photoshop CS5 presets like actions, contours, or patterns, I would have to write the article to encompass the unique paths to Photoshop's presets present in all the operating systems currently used by large portions of Photoshop users. That would have to include Mac OS X and four different versions of Windows. Giving all those paths is somewhat tedious for me as the writer, but more significantly it's confusing for readers (thanks a lot, Microsoft). To get to the Patterns preset folder, I would have to list all of the following paths:

Mac OS X: `Applications/Adobe Photoshop CS5/Presets/Patterns`

Windows XP/2000: `C:\Program Files\Adobe\Adobe Photoshop CS5\Presets\Patterns`

Windows 7/Vista (32-bit): `C:\Program Files (x86)\Adobe\Adobe Photoshop CS5\Presets\Patterns`

Windows 7/Vista (64-bit): `C:\Program Files\Adobe\Adobe Photoshop CS5 (64 Bit)\Presets\Patterns`

Also, because Photoshop CS5 installs both a 32- and 64-bit edition on Windows 7 and Vista, I would have to tell readers to make changes in *both* the paths listed for Windows 7/Vista (32-bit) and Windows 7/Vista (64-bit), something users of Mac OS X or Windows XP and 2000 need not read. So, if I were publishing the same article in *Macworld Magazine*, *PC World Magazine*, and *XP-User Magazine* (the last one is made up), I would want different editions of the article for their respective readerships. *Macworld* readers won't care about the Windows paths, just like *XP-User* readers don't need to worry about the paths for OS X and Windows 7. But if I were also publishing the same article in *Layers Magazine*, which is platform agnostic, I would need all four paths listed. Table 13.4 shows which paths will be needed by which publication.

TABLE 13.4: PATHS REQUIRED BY DIFFERENT ARTICLE VERSIONS

PATH FOR:	MACWORLD	PC WORLD	XP-USER	LAYERS
Mac OS X	☑	☐	☐	☑
Windows XP/2000	☐	☑	☑	☑
Windows 7/Vista (32-bit)	☐	☑	☐	☑
Windows 7/Vista (64-bit)	☐	☑	☐	☑

The most efficient means of producing the same article layout for all four publications is to assign paths to one or more text conditions, which is where conditional sets come in handy.

A conditional set is simply a recording of which conditions are active and inactive at the same time—much like Layer Comps in Photoshop. Because my article on working with Photoshop CS5 presets will be published to four different magazines, each requiring a different set of paths to be listed, I would set them as conditional text. But because some paths must belong to multiple conditions, I'll expedite (and reduce the likelihood of error) showing and hiding each path by employing conditional sets. I would create conditional sets for each of the four magazines.

First, I would create text conditions per path line, a la Figure 13.22. Instead of turning this on and off manually as I output each version of the article, I'll create publication-specific sets to automatically show and hide the appropriate conditions.

FIGURE 13.22
Each path line is
assigned to one
text condition.

The Set field is hidden from the Conditional Text panel by default. To show it, choose Show Options from the panel flyout menu. Beneath the Indicators field you'll now see the Set field (see Figure 13.23). Using sets is easy: Toggle the visibility of conditions as needed for a specific situation. For instance, for the Macworld set I'm about to create, I'll hide all the paths except the one

for Mac OS X. Then, on the Set menu, choose Create New Set, and in the resulting dialog box, name the set. Repeat for any additional sets. For me that means turning on all four conditions for the Layers set, showing just the XP condition for XP-User, and hiding the OS X condition while showing all three Windows conditions for my PC World set. Effectively, I've created sets that match the table.

FIGURE 13.23

The Set dropdown menu on the Conditional Text panel

Now, every time I select one of those sets from the Set menu, it will automatically show only the text conditions visible at the time the set was created, hiding those that were hidden when the set was created. If I goofed up, hiding or showing one or more conditions that should be the opposite in the set, I can simply set the visibility as it should be and then choose the Redefine [Set] command from the Set menu.

If, after creating sets, you add a new condition, it won't be accounted for in the sets. You can add it to them by using the Update All Sets command from the Set dropdown.

If you find yourself using the same conditions and/or sets in multiple documents, go back to the Conditional Text panel's flyout menu. There you'll find commands to load conditions from other documents, which brings in just the conditions, and a command to load conditions and sets. When the sets come into your new document, they'll retain their definitions of which conditions are to be shown and hidden. Thus, you can quickly move through a new document assigning conditions to text, knowing that your sets will automatically make the appropriate conditional text visible or invisible when desired.

Data Merge

Digital printing is faster and, generally speaking, more efficient than traditional lithographic printing. There is little to no *run-up* or *run-down*, which saves paper, and even during the job, fewer raw materials are consumed. These, of course, are some of the major reasons digital printing is spreading so rapidly. Another significant reason is the fact that digital printing is *plateless*, meaning data flows directly from a computer to the ink impression system without film or plates. Consequently, it's not cost prohibitive to print in very small quantities as it is with offset printing. Each page printed on a digital press can be different without significantly increasing the production budget. That fact has caused the variable data printing (VDP) mini-revolution in which every-

thing from advertisements (Publix Supermarkets) to the cover of a 40,000-subscriber magazine can be customized to each individual receiving the piece (the June 2004 issue of *Reason*).

How is it accomplished on the design side? you may ask. In essence and execution, it's very simple. Designers and compositors lay out all the static elements within the original digital document; then, wherever customizable data must appear, they insert markers or tokens. The variable data is contained within a database. At one of two points during document production and output, the markers or tokens in the layout are replaced one at a time by the records in the database, creating unique *one-off* documents.

I say there are two points during which the database records may be inserted and unique pages generated. The more powerful and flexible of the two methods is to do it concurrently with output. Numerous high-end systems exist to host potentially very large databases of text and imagery and—just before or during RIP—to create the one-offs from a layout template. That's the production option. The other option, which works better for simple text and image replacement and in short runs of fewer than 500 versioned one-offs, is to perform the variable data, multiple one-off creation *before* sending the document to RIP. Using this latter option, the designer creates all the variations as a single, continuous document and sends it to press, asking that every page be printed only once.

VDP OF 300 ONE-OFFS

An example of creation-time variable data printing was a flyer distributed to attendees of the InDesign Conference Master Class in October 2006. The flyers advertised an InDesign plug-in I created (now obsolete due to improvements in InDesign CS5) while simultaneously giving away a free license to, and serial number for, another InDesign plug-in. Each of the 300 one-page flyers contained a unique software serial number. Everything else about the flyers was static—same imagery, same ad copy, and so on. With only one line of text to change per copy, using a full-blown VDP system at press time would have been overkill. Instead, I used InDesign's built-in VDP function—data merge—to suck in the list of serial numbers and generate the 300 pages for me. After exporting the 300-page InDesign document to PDF, I had a single copy (of all 300 pages) digitally printed for pennies per page.

Data merge can insert many different types of variable text into a layout. It can even insert images as variable data objects. In addition to serial numbers and sales flyers, data merge can be used on numerous other types of documents. Mailing labels and envelopes, of course, come immediately to mind. I've also used, or helped my consulting clients use, data merge for such things as the following:

◆ Rapidly producing new business cards for 200 employees, pulling personnel names, titles, departments, e-mail addresses, phone extensions, and EPS images of special, employee-specific certification logos from a list generated out of the human resources database

◆ Pulling in data from a database that matched customers' previous purchases with related, as-yet-unpurchased items to produce sales flyers specifically tailored to the buying habits of 8,500 customers

◆ On-demand printing of children's books in which each customer's child's name, age, gender, birth date, and description appear within the content of the book

◆ Producing regionalized versions of association newsletters wherein local chapter information, events, contacts, photos, and maps are inserted among global material sent to all members nationally

◆ Pulling requisite data from a FileMaker Pro database into visually interesting InDesign layouts for one-at-a-time estimates, invoices, contracts, and proposals

◆ Laying out one hundred 500-page membership directories, including name, title, company, profession, legal specialties, certifications, honors, phone number, and photograph from Excel spreadsheets

◆ Creating point-of-sale signage and shelf tags for the entire inventory of a national department-store chain by designing only a single layout (signage and shelf tags were printed on the same page and then separated in finishing) and then importing product name, price, SKU, and other information from the stock database the retailer maintains anyway

These are but a few of the variable data projects I've worked on within InDesign (and PageMaker before it). There are others, and there are many, many possible uses for which I've not had the chance to employ data merge. If you need content customization in three or more copies of the same layout, use data merge. It's very simple.

Let's get the basic terminology out of the way first. There are a few terms you need to know to work through a data merge in InDesign. It's a process of merging a list of data (*data source file*) into a layout document (*target document*) to produce a third, commingled set of data and layout, the *merged document*. The merged document is what you then send to press or a desktop printer.

THE DATA SOURCE FILE

The data source file is where all the unique data is stored. InDesign cannot *directly* use a database such as FileMaker, Bento, Microsoft Access, or MySQL as a data source file; Adobe left such direct integration to third-party plug-in makers and system integrators. What InDesign *does* link to are *flat-file databases*—in other words, comma- or tab-separated text files. Every database and spreadsheet application built since the 1980s has the ability to export its data to comma- and tab-separated text files. Don't be deterred by the fact that you can't hook straight into InDesign from Excel or FileMaker; all you have to do is find the data you want in the source application and export it to comma-separated text as a CSV file or to tab-delimited text as a TXT file. In most cases, the export process can be automated in the database or spreadsheet application. If you aren't the database person in your organization, talk to whomever is; she'll know exactly how to get the data out into CSV or TXT files.

Within the data source file, as in any database, data is separated into fields—one piece of data (e.g., a person's name is one field, his address another field, his phone number a third)—and records. All the fields that make up a single entry are one record; the next person's name, address, telephone, and so on are another record. Records are separated in the data source file by paragraph returns, creating rows of fields. Every record will generate a new InDesign page when the merge is effected.

The very first record in your data source file should be a header row or list of field names (e.g., Name, Address, Phone). This helps you and InDesign identify what goes where. It's very important that each record have the same number of fields—even if the field is blank. For instance, if you're working with addresses, some entries may have a country listed while others do not. *All* such records *must* have a country field. When the record has no data in the field, leave

it blank, ensuring that there is still a tab or comma position for that record's country field. The following lines, an example of an address-based, comma-delimited data source file, illustrate my point; note the second record:

```
CITY, STATE/PROVINCE, COUNTRY, ZIP/POSTAL

Beaverton, OR, USA, 97007
South Boston, MA, , 02127
Alberta Beach, AB, Canada, T0E 0A0
```

Because data source files may only be comma or tab separated, and because every instance of a comma or tab communicates to InDesign that a new field has begun, you cannot use commas or tabs as actual text. For example, *red, white, and blue* is construed as three separate fields instead of a single field value. If you want to use commas in your text, either use tab delimitation for the data source file or enclose the text containing the comma in quotation marks—*"red, white, and blue."* For tabs in text, leave them out of the data source file entirely; instead, insert two separate field placeholders in the InDesign target document with a tab between.

THE TARGET DOCUMENT

The target document is an InDesign layout that's unremarkable save for the fact that placeholders stand in for the actual data to be printed. You may design the merged document and insert placeholders on either (but not both) the document or the master pages. If your variable data layout is more than one page, design it on the document rather than on the master pages. If, however, it's a single page or several pages that are each assigned their own master pages, there is a distinct advantage to putting the placeholders on a master page: The merged document may be updated to reflect changes in the data source file, something not available when the placeholders are on the document pages. A master page containing placeholder fields should be applied to the first page in the document.

After creating a data source file with the header row, lay out the target document exactly as it will ultimately print. Add all imagery and static text, but leave blank the variable data markers; you'll insert those in short order. First, you have to connect the data source file to the target document via the Data Merge panel.

INITIATING DATA MERGE

Open the Data Merge panel from Window ➢ Utilities ➢ Data Merge, and do the following:

1. From the panel flyout menu, choose Select Data Source and navigate to the CSV or TXT data source file you created.

2. Before clicking Open, check Show Import Options at the bottom of the dialog. You'll then be presented with the Data Source Import Options dialog box (see Figure 13.24).

FIGURE 13.24
The Data Source Import Options dialog

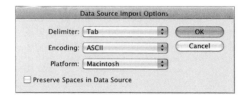

If InDesign does not correctly identify the delimiter in the file, you can change to Tab or Comma, adjust the file encoding and platform, and choose between keeping or stripping off leading and trailing spaces (spaces between words are preserved regardless).

3. Click OK in Data Source Import Options, and the Data Merge panel will populate with the fields in the header row of your data source file (see Figure 13.25).

FIGURE 13.25
After import, the Data Merge panel displays the header row fields in the first record.

4. Return to the places in your layout where variable data should be inserted.

5. Position the cursor in the text at the correct point, and click once on a field name in the Data Merge panel. Doing so will insert the placeholder for that field wrapped in double braces—for example, <<Address>>.

6. Insert the remaining placeholders the same way.

Figure 13.26 shows how a simple address label might look with field placeholders inserted. Beside each field name you'll see the page number on which you inserted that placeholder. If you insert the same placeholder on multiple pages, or multiple times on the same page, you'll see all of the page numbers listed.

FIGURE 13.26
Placeholders in place on a mail label

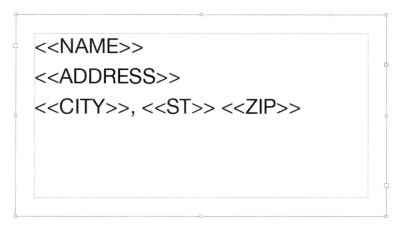

<<NAME>>
<<ADDRESS>>
<<CITY>>, <<ST>> <<ZIP>>

If you make changes to the data source file after import, choose Update Data Source from the Data Merge panel flyout menu. To replace one data source with another, choose Select Data Source again, or choose Remove Data Source, and then begin again.

Placeholders may be added anywhere text can go—alone in a text frame, amid lines of other text, in the middle of a paragraph, inside a table, within a text on a path object—and they are in all respects treated like normal, nondynamic text. Style placeholders using the same character, paragraph, and other formatting options; you can even use paragraph, character, table, and cell styles on them. In other words, variable data should be formatted to appear like any other text in your document, not like direct mail advertisements of old where one's name was inserted in the middle of a sentence in a different typeface with two inches of white space on either side. Take note that InDesign inserts only the variable text exactly as contained in the data source document. InDesign will neither add nor remove spaces, tabs, or anything else before or after the variable text. Therefore, be careful to insert any wanted spaces, tabs, and so on around the placeholder in the destination document. Similarly, make sure the data in the source is cleaned up and devoid of extraneous spaces, punctuation, tabs, and anything else you don't want in the final, merged document.

Merging Data

With your field placeholders in place, it's time to see what's going to happen in the merge:

1. Switch to the target document page containing the placeholders.

   If you inserted them on a master page, go to a document page based on that master; note that you may need to create a document page or two or reapply the master.

2. At the bottom of the Data Merge panel, check the Preview option, which will substitute one of the actual records of your data source file for the placeholders.

   It's always a good idea to preview the merge before actually merging data. Beside the Preview option, in the bottom right of the panel, navigation buttons enable you to proof how each record will look before finalizing the data merge operation.

3. If you notice blank lines in your merged data, go to the Data Merge panel flyout menu and choose Content Placement Options (see Figure 13.27).

FIGURE 13.27
Content Placement
Options

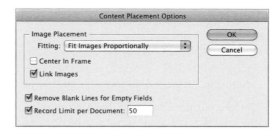

4. Check the option at the bottom, Remove Blank Lines for Empty Fields, to, well, remove blank lines created by empty fields.

   If a record contains a blank field, the space will be hidden. For example, when using two lines for addresses, those records wherein only one line is filled will leave the second address field blank, causing an ugly gap in the text. Remove Blank Lines for Empty Fields removes the line as if it was never there. To mitigate problems inherent in working with

longer documents, you may also limit how many records are merged into one document file. If when working with 100 records you set a limit of 50, InDesign will create two merged documents. The remaining options should be familiar to you from working with placed images. Shortly I'll explain how use images in a data merge.

5. Once you're satisfied with the preview, choose Create Merged Document from the panel flyout menu, or click the button at the bottom of the panel.

Up will pop the Create Merged Document dialog (see Figure 13.28) Here, you can specify exactly which records to merge. This is especially useful if a printer malfunction eats one or two pages; you don't have to run the entire merge again.

FIGURE 13.28
Create Merged
Document dialog

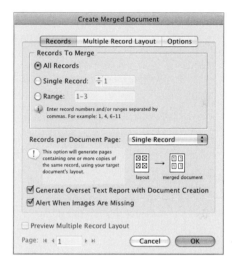

Records per Document Page determines how many copies of the merged data will appear on each page:

♦ For form letters, flyers, and other one-page-per-reader variable-data documents, use Single Record per page.

♦ Choose Multiple Records per page for mailing labels and other *ganged* layouts where multiple, variable-data content needs to appear on the same page.

If the Records per Document Page dropdown is grayed out, there's a reason—two, possibly. InDesign will allow only one record per page merging if either of the following conditions is in effect in the target document:

♦ If the field placeholders are used on document pages in a multiple-page document (instead of on a master page).

♦ If placeholders appear on more than one master page (both pages in a spread count as more than one master page).

For best results with placing multiple records per page, use nonfacing pages in the document.

6. Do check the Generate Overset Text Report with Document Creation and Alert When Images Are Missing options because they provide important feedback about two common problems:

 ◆ Merged text doesn't completely fit within the area assigned to it (or merged text causes static text to not fit).

 ◆ Images can't be found.

7. If you *are* setting multiple records per page, make sure to check out the Multiple Record Layout tab (see Figure 13.29).

FIGURE 13.29
Create Merged
Document dialog
Multiple Record
Layout tab

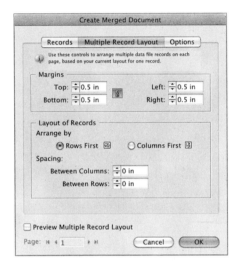

Here you can define the page margins, the gutters between columns and rows, and whether labels or business cards or name tags or what have you build left to right and then top to bottom (Rows First option) or top to bottom first (Columns First option).

The Options tab contains the same controls as the Content Placement Options dialog discussed a moment ago.

8. When you're ready, click OK to merge records into a new document.

If you've elected to use a single record per page, you'll have one InDesign document with a page count equal to the record count. The merged document is what you'll save and send to print.

If you put field placeholders on the master page, data can be updated later without regenerating the entire merged document. After making changes in the data source file or in the layout of fields on the master page, choose Update Data Fields on the Data Merge panel's (return to Figure 13.25 for this panel) flyout menu. If your changes are more extensive than adding records or rearranging elements on the page—for instance, if you added a new field to every record—you will need to re-create the merged document from the target document.

MERGED IMAGES

Variable data isn't always textual data. Sometimes, you want to exchange images. That's easy. First, in the data source file, differentiate the field containing image paths with an *at symbol* (@), and then reference images by path in the fields. For instance, the following examples from a comma-delimited data source file reference full image paths on Windows:

```
NAME, @PHOTO

John Doe, D:\headshots\johndoe.jpg
Bob Roberts, D:\headshots\bobroberts.tiff
```

And on Mac:
```
NAME, @PHOTO
John Doe, HD:headshots:johndoe.jpg
Bob Roberts, HD:headshots:bobroberts.tiff
```

SPECIAL USE OF THE @ SYMBOL

In Microsoft Excel the @ symbol is used for special functions. Therefore, it could be problematic to make the @ the first character of a cell when organizing data sources in Excel. If this becomes an issue for your work, precede the @ with a straight single quote or foot mark (') such as: '@PHOTO. Upon export from Excel to CSV, the straight quote will be omitted.

Insert the image field placeholders just as you would text field placeholders. Instead of putting them in text frames, however, drag the placeholder from the Data Merge panel (see Figure 13.25) into a graphic frame—if you want a stand-alone image, that is; if you want an image inline among text, add it to a text frame. You can also put the image field placeholder inside table cells, which hold either text or imagery. Regardless of where you put it, until the merge is actually effected, an image placeholder will display as only the textual field name.

Working Efficiently with Tables

Tables and tabular data are common in printed matter and are becoming more common as InDesign gradually replaces Adobe FrameMaker as the long- and technical-document publishing tool of choice. With each new version of InDesign, tables become easier to work with and more feature rich. Table-related features aren't as cool or widely publicized as, say, attribute-level transparency or multiple-asset placing, so fewer people realize how InDesign can raise productivity when working with tables.

Live Linking to Excel Spreadsheets

Although tables are used for more than simply laying out spreadsheets, the fact remains that a great deal of the tabular data laid out on the InDesign page comes directly from Microsoft Excel. InDesign will place an Excel spreadsheet via File ➢ Place, which you probably already knew. And that's where a common problem begins.

Spreadsheets and other tabular data change *often*, frequently more often than editorial copy. Typically, designers place the Excel data and style the table, its cells, and their data with the Table panel (Window ➢ Type & Tables ➢ Table) and all the various options on the Table menu. It seems that, no matter what the data you're styling, someone always needs to revise it at the last moment. You'll no sooner finish styling the table, getting it just right, when a new version of the Excel spreadsheet arrives by email. At that point, many InDesign users find themselves faced with a choice: replace the old data with the new and then manually style the table all over again, or try to find the differences between the two versions and manually update the table one cell at a time. Either way, updating tabular data from an external source is a pain in the neck—but it doesn't have to be.

Squirreled away at the bottom of the File Handling pane of InDesign's Preferences is an important check box for anyone who places Excel spreadsheets. It's the option to Create Links When Placing Text and Spreadsheet Files. That option is disabled by default, which means that, when you place textual documents and spreadsheets, they instantly become embedded in InDesign; there is no link to the original, and if the original document is changed, you have to place a whole new copy into InDesign. However, if you check Create Links When Placing Text and Spreadsheet Files, every time you place an Excel document into InDesign, it will be linked instead of embedded. If the original document is later changed or replaced, it can be updated in InDesign from the Links panel just like an image. Most of the formatting is retained, too!

What doesn't survive when a linked Excel document is updated are changes you've made to the data itself within the table on the InDesign layout page, the addition of running header or footer rows, and other structural attributes of or changes to the table. Styling *does* survive— particularly if you use table and/or cell styles (we're getting to those). Still, the time saved not having to reposition and restyle the entire table will usually outweigh the time required to rebuild the few elements that are lost when updating from the linked file. You'd have to rebuild and reconfigure them with or without linking the rest of the data anyway.

The downside to Create Links When Placing Text and Spreadsheet Files is that *all* textual assets placed into InDesign become linked. That includes Word, RTF, TXT, and other textual documents as well as Excel files. For some, that's a benefit; for others, it's a liability. After all, most of the time you'll want to place copy into the layout and then not have to ship the original Word or RTF document to press as part of the package. Working around this consequence is no problem really. With such documents—and with Excel documents, if you like, right before going to press—highlight the appropriate file link in the Links panel and select Embed Link from the panel flyout menu. The link to the original document will be broken, embedding the content in the InDesign layout. You can even select multiple assets in the Link panel list and embed them en masse.

Table Styles

Yes, Virginia, there is a Santa Claus. And, yes, InDesign has table styles.

A much-requested feature in any page layout application is table styles. InDesign has 'em. In fact, there are two parts—table styles and cell styles. Tables styles record and apply table level formatting attributes such as borders, row and column spacing, strokes, and fills—including alternating fills. No longer must you manually set the options for each table in the document!

Table styles and cell styles work just like paragraph and character styles. They have their own panels on the Window ➢ Styles menu, the Table Styles and Cell Styles panels (see Figure 13.30).

Styles are added the same way—with the New button at the bottom of the panel—and may be reordered or grouped into folders. To apply them, merely highlight the appropriate content—a table or some of its cells—and click the appropriate style in the Table Styles or Cell Styles panel. You can even load styles from other documents with the Load Table and Cell Styles commands on the flyout menu of either panel or the Load Table Styles or Load Cell Styles on the respective panel's flyout menu.

FIGURE 13.30

The Table Styles and Cell Styles panels

Editing a table style presents the Table Style Options dialog (see Figure 13.31), which looks very much like the Paragraph Style Options. On the General pane, one style can be based on another to take advantage of ultra-convenient cascading of styles. At the bottom, five dropdown fields enable choosing cell styles for different parts of a typical table: header and footer rows, left and right columns, and body rows (i.e., the rest of the table). Of course, the cell styles must be created on the Cell Styles panel before you can choose them in this dialog. The rest of Table Style Options is all the options you'll find in the Table Options dialog and Table panel.

FIGURE 13.31

Table Style Options dialog

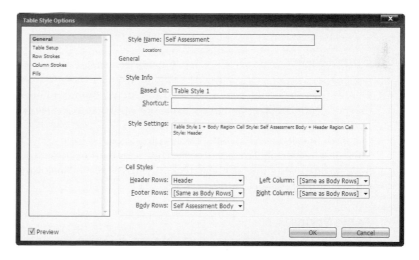

Cell styles are to table styles what character styles are to paragraph styles. In a cell style, you define individual cell attributes such as diagonal lines, strokes and fills, cell insets, vertical justification, baseline offset, clipping, and text rotation. Moreover, among the text-formatting options is the ability to choose a paragraph style to apply to type within table cells.

You can also choose a table style at the time you *create* a table. With the Type tool inside a text frame, choose Table ➤ Insert Table to open the familiar Insert Table dialog. At the bottom of the dialog is a list of all existing table styles; choose one and your new table will insert with full formatting. Similar options appear when you place an Excel document and select Show Options during the place operation. Figure 13.32 shows both dialogs side-by-side. Selecting the table style at the time of insertion or creation of multipage tables spares the minor chore of having to select across pages and then choose appropriate table and cell styles.

FIGURE 13.32
Insert Table dialog (left) and Microsoft Excel Import Options (right)

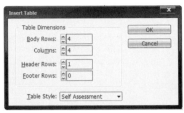
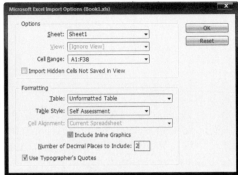

Working Efficiently with Objects

Working efficiently with objects also entails employing reusable styles but goes beyond to reusable *objects* as well.

Object Styles

Let's review: InDesign operates on a container-to-content model where everything in the document is either content—text, images, paths—or a container to hold content. Text, for instance, must be contained in either a text frame or a path text object. In addition to container and content, InDesign also cares about attributes. Thus, InDesign deals with containers and content and with the attributes of each. Paragraph and character styles govern text-content formatting attributes but not the attributes of the frame containing the text. Paragraph styles, for instance, have no bearing on the number of columns in the text frame or the transparency of text. That and much more are left to the dominion of object styles, which record and apply the attributes of containers.

If you open the Object Styles panel from the Window ➤ Styles menu, you'll find three preloaded entries—[None], [Basic Graphics Frame], and [Basic Text Frame] (see Figure 13.33). Each style is listed in brackets denoting that it is undeletable; you can edit these styles and change their definitions, but you can't get rid of them. The [None] style you want because it wipes out pretty much every attribute—fill, stroke, effects, everything. [Basic Graphics Frame] and [Basic Text Frame] reduce a selected object to default options; for a graphics frame, for example, that means 1 pt black stroke, no fill, nothing else.

FIGURE 13.33

Object Styles panel

One extremely useful option is the ability to set a user-created object style as the default for newly created graphics or text frames. Remember, a graphics frame is not only one into which you'll place imagery; it's also any unfilled decorative path such as a block of color, an ellipse, and so on. On the Object Styles panel flyout menu, choose any existing object style from the Default Graphic Frame Style submenu to format every new graphic frame *as you draw it*, which is an even faster and more efficient method of styling multiple objects than drawing and then applying the style. The Default Text Frame Style offers the same choice for text frames.

The rest of the panel is remarkably similar to the other four Styles panels, with a reorderable style list, the ability to group styles in nested folders, and buttons for New, Delete, Clear Overrides, and Clear Attributes Not Defined by Style. *What's the difference between the latter two?* Object styles can be defined to include every possible attribute but are rarely so defined. Instead, many attributes are simply not enabled. For instance, you may have an object style that doesn't include a drop shadow. Now, if you applied the style to an object and then selectively gave the object a drop shadow, that effect is an attribute not defined by the style. Clear Overrides, on the other hand, is relevant if the style *does* define a drop shadow but you later change the shadow angle on the individual object.

Double-clicking a style or choosing Style Options from the panel flyout menu will open the robust Object Style Options dialog (see Figure 13.34). *Every* attribute that may be given to a container—and many for content—is organized within this dialog. On the General pane, in the Style Settings area, is an expandable tree detailing the attributes defined in the style. The list of attributes on the left matches the summary of Style Settings and offers in one place access to just about every option you can set on the Swatches, Stroke, Effects, Story, Text Wrap, and other panels and in the Corner Options, Text Frame Options, Anchored Object Options, Effects Options, and other dialogs. Beneath the deceptively named Basic Attributes list is a replicated Effects Options section. Using the Effects For dropdown menu to select the element affected, you can apply the various Photoshop-esque transparency effects to containers and contents and individually to fills, strokes, text, and images.

Although most creatives prefer to design a live object on the page or pasteboard, applying needed attributes, *and then* produce an object style from the object, others know precisely what they want and can build the style in Object Style Options from scratch, by setting options without an object ready. Which way you choose depends on your particular work style. The Preview check box at the bottom of the dialog will show changes in a selected object as you make them either during initial style creation or later tweaking.

FIGURE 13.34
The Object Style
Options dialog

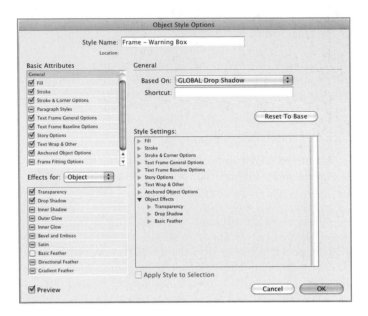

Libraries

The utility of proprietary application object libraries has been greatly diminished with modern innovations such as placing native format graphic files (e.g., PSD, AI, PDF) into the layout; the ability to place one InDesign file as an asset inside another; *snippets*; accessible visual digital asset managers (DAMs); and the ability to drag and drop pictures from a DAM, the file system (e.g., OS X Finder and Windows Explorer), and other applications. Once upon a time, a library palette was the pinnacle of convenience and productivity. Now, libraries are no longer essential, but they're still very handy for improving efficiency in many solo and group workflows. Besides, they're kind of fun.

Libraries are floating, mini DAMs inside InDesign (see Figure 13.35). They allow objects created or placed in InDesign to be duplicated and placed elsewhere in the same or other documents without copying and pasting. Objects added to a library may be linked images that are, in reality, scattered about one or more hard drives or network resources. Library assets can be text frames (with or without text), native InDesign paths, objects with effects, groups of objects, even an entire page. These objects can be arranged and sorted in various ways within the library and then added to a document simply by dragging them out of the library and dropping them on the page or pasteboard.

FIGURE 13.35
A library panel

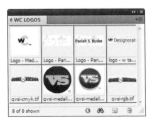

If you're a freelancer with no repeat clients or the print shop's in-house document fixer, you probably won't have much use for libraries these days. I recommend everyone *else* at least try using a library—or two, three, or more—because having at your fingertips all your frequently used objects can save massive amounts of time and effort over other methods of inserting objects. Consider some of the following uses:

◆ All your company's or client's logos can be stored—versions in RGB, CMYK process, CMYK plus spot colors, grayscale, black-and-white; logos with and without the tagline; full logos; iconic logos.

◆ Advertising-supported publications can store all their variously sized ad space placeholders and ready-for-content frames in a library ready for drag-and-drop placement (instead of keeping a list of ad sizes taped to the side of the monitor).

◆ Periodicals, catalogs, and other longer documents that use several layout templates for different types of pages can insert each page layout—inclusive of its text frames, graphic frames, and all other elements—as a single library entry and place all the pieces onto a blank page by dragging just one entry from the library.

◆ Photos and illustrations slated for potential use in a document can be collected from various sources and locations and organized together into a library for side-by-side evaluation.

◆ Any object or bit of text used from once in a while to in every project can be collected into a library, keeping them always available for the next new document for the client or in the project.

Now that you're beginning to see the value of libraries, let's make one:

1. Open or create a document with several objects on a given page. These can be any type of object—text, placed imagery, paths drawn in InDesign, and so on.

2. Choose File ➤ New ➤ Library. InDesign will prompt you to save the library, which creates an INDL file.

   After you save the library, a new panel will appear bearing as its title the filename you chose (e.g., *Acme Logos*). The library itself will be blank.

NAMING YOUR LIBRARY

InDesign suggests the default name of *Library.INDL*. Don't use the default. Give the library a *meaningful* name. If this will be a library of logos for your client Acme Corp., name the file *Acme Logos .INDL* and save it in the folder where you save Acme Corp. assets or documents. If you use libraries well, you'll probably find yourself creating them for several clients, projects, and other purposes. Naming them all *Library.INDL* and saving them to a default location like My Documents or your Home folder won't seem like a very smart decision when you need to archive all documents related to one client or project to DVD-ROM.

3. One at a time, select objects on the document page and drag them into your library panel. Notice how each becomes a new library entry with a thumbnail and *Untitled* as its legend. We'll set aside the legend for now.

Snippets

Snippets are reusable content similar to libraries but with two key differences:

◆ First, whereas libraries collect multiple objects into a single list, snippets are new external assets not gathered together into a panel.

◆ Second, library objects do not remember positioning data, but snippets do.

A snippet is an encapsulated segment of XML code, but don't let that put you off—after finishing this sentence, you need never again consider the words *snippet* and *XML* together. What is important, and the reason I mention it, is that XML can contain text, path data, imagery, attributes—all the structural data and everything InDesign needs to re-create a container, its content, and their attributes. Snippets even remember their relative location on the page and the layer(s) on which they originated. In the simplest terms, a snippet is a piece of an InDesign page externalized. Snippets may be passed around and traded like baseball cards.

Create a snippet by selecting one or more objects with the Selection tool, and then drag the object(s) out of InDesign to drop on your desktop. An INDS file will be created, which is like any other file and can be managed through the file system, Bridge, or what have you. If the idea of dragging something out of an application onto the desktop gives you the heebie-jeebies, use File ➤ Export; in the Export dialog, set Save As Type to InDesign Snippet.

Placing snippets in documents is just as easy—through File ➤ Place or by dragging from the desktop into InDesign. Upon dropping (or placing), the object(s) dragged to the desktop will instantly appear with all formatting and appearance intact and on the layer(s) from which they originated. By default in InDesign CS5, snippets will drop at the cursor location rather than at the position on the page from which they originated. Changing that behavior is a toggle. In Preferences, on the File Handling pane, change the Snippet Import option. Position at Original Location will place the snippet in exactly the same place on the page as the original set of objects from which the snippet was created. Position at Cursor Location will place the snippet content wherever a loaded place cursor is clicked or where a snippet dragged from the desktop is dropped.

Style Shortcuts

All styles—paragraph, character, table, cell, and object—may be assigned to keyboard shortcuts on the General pane of their options dialogs. To set a keyboard shortcut, click in the Shortcut field and press the keyboard keys that will serve the particular style—for instance, Cmd+5/Ctrl+5. Assigning keyboard shortcuts to styles is not a new feature; neither is the fact that it's so limited as to be almost useless.

The primary limitation to style shortcuts, you see, is that they *require* use of the numeric keypad—the set of number keys out to the right of full-sized keyboards. Every shortcut must be one or more modifier keys—Cmd, Opt, Ctrl, Shift on Mac or Ctrl, Alt, Shift on Windows—plus a numeric keypad number. Thus, the first limitation is that usually alphabetically named styles must be bound to arbitrary numbers. *(Did I put the RunIn Head paragraph style on Ctrl+Shift+Num 5, Ctrl+Num 5, or was it something plus the 6?)*

Next, you have to recognize that, on most keyboards, any of these options are two-handed keyboard shortcuts, which are only—and not always—slightly more convenient than reaching for the mouse and clicking an entry on a panel. The choice of shortcuts is also limited by the fact that many key combinations are reserved for use by the operating system. On Windows, for example, you cannot use Alt and a number without also choosing Shift or Ctrl because Alt plus

the numeric keypad numbers is reserved for system-wide insertion of special characters—for example, to insert a copyright symbol, press Alt+0169.

Finally, the biggest limitation to keyboard shortcuts for styles is again the numeric keypad. Laptops don't have them, nor do many slim desktop keyboards. Most laptop keyboards have a pseudo-numeric keypad created by depressing the Function key (often labeled as *Fn* and unique to laptops) and then pressing other keys (such as U, I, and O for 4, 5, and 6 or another mapping of numeric keypad functions to existing keys). So, in addition to pressing one, two, or three modifier keys and a number key, those using laptops or slim keyboards must press Function. Worse, pressing Function often changes the function of a modifier key. Option on a Mac PowerBook, for instance, becomes Alt when the Function key is depressed. Therefore, it is impossible to press Opt+Shift+Num 6 on a PowerBook's built-in keyboard.

Until Adobe adds styles to the customize Keyboard Shortcuts dialog and opens up the rest of the keyboard to style shortcuts, the feature is more of a hindrance than a help. The only exception I would proffer is default styles. Leave your custom styles unassigned to shortcuts, but binding the Basic Paragraph paragraph style, the None character style, and similar defaults for table, cell, and object styles to shortcuts can be very useful and universal because every document you create has these defaults (though you may not use them). For instance, some people find it very helpful to put Basic Paragraph on the numeric keypad's 1 key, the None character style on 2, and so on. For the rest of their styles they use something far more efficient: Quick Apply.

Quick Apply

Quick Apply was introduced way back in InDesign CS2, although most users still have no idea it's there or what it does. Even if you *do* know Quick Apply, don't skip over this section—CS5 is the Col. Steve Austin version of Quick Apply. Adobe sat down with InDesign, with Quick Apply, and Kevin Van Weil said, "Gentlemen, we can rebuild it. We have the technology. We have the capability to make the world's first bionic application menu. Quick Apply will be that application menu. Better than it was before. Better… stronger… faster."

Quick Apply's bionics make it an enhanced menu of paragraph, character, object, table and cell styles, and menu commands and scripts all together in a single, rapid-action list. In other words, you might be able to hide the Paragraph Styles, Character Styles, Object Styles, Table Styles, Cell Styles, and Scripts panels and reclaim the screen real estate they consume. You really have to see Quick Apply to understand it. Press Cmd+Return/Ctrl+Enter, and the Quick Apply menu will appear (see Figure 13.38).

The basic operation of Quick Apply is simple: In the search field above the list, begin typing the name of a style in the current document. As you type, the list of available options will shrink, filtered to those styles, commands, scripts, and variables that begin with what you typed. The first option matching your input will be highlighted. To choose it, applying the style or whatever to a selected object or text, simply press Return/Enter. If the highlighted item isn't what you want, type more of the name or use the up and down arrows on your keyboard to navigate the list. *Can I select something with the mouse?* Of course; it's a scrollable list, after all. But the main point of Quick Apply, with its simple Cmd+Return/Ctrl+Enter activation shortcut—the ability to type a part of a name and use Return/Enter to apply it—is to *spare* you the need to take your hands off the keyboard. Its secondary point, which does just as much for productivity, saves you from searching through various panels and menus hunting for something whose name—but not exact location—you already know. When you press Return/Enter to apply a selected style, Quick Apply retreats out of your way.

FIGURE 13.38
The Quick Apply
menu

At the top of Quick Apply are two buttons (see Figure 13.38). The lightning bolt hides the Quick Apply menu itself. You may recognize it as appearing on all the individual styles panels and the Control panel, where the same button will hide or show Quick Apply. Next, the down-facing arrow lets you choose what to show in the Quick Apply menu (see Figure 13.39). That's right, Quick Apply includes not only all the styles but also text variables, scripts, text conditions, and every menu command in InDesign: those on the menu bar at the top of the application, those on panel flyout menus, and even many that don't appear anywhere else in the user interface. You can quite literally *run InDesign exclusively from Quick Apply*. (Note that scripts are, by default, not included in Quick Apply. To include them, activate that option from the Show/Hide menu.) You can even include in Quick Apply menu commands hidden by customizing menus.

FIGURE 13.39
The Show/Hide
menu in Quick
Apply toggles the
inclusion of list
contents as well
as provides filter
codes.

Beside each type of entry in the Show/Hide menu is a parenthetic special code—for instance *(p:)* beside Include Paragraph Styles. With so much available on the Six Million Dollar Menu, typing just a few letters into the search field will undoubtedly return numerous commands, styles, and so on. The expansive focus of Quick Apply therefore becomes a hindrance to its own utility. Rather, it *would* but for the filter codes. If you want a table style, for example, preface your search with *t:*, which filters the Quick Apply list to show only table styles. Use *m:* for menu commands, *v:* for text variables, *p:* for paragraph styles, and so on. The Show/Hide menu is a complete key to filter codes.

Quick Apply even makes it easy to *edit* a style. Pressing Cmd+Return/Ctrl+Enter opens Quick Apply, but pressing the shortcut again while Quick Apply is open will open the editing options for the selected style, command, script, condition, or variable. With an object style selected, for instance, pressing Cmd+Return/Ctrl+Enter will open the Object Style Options dialog for that particular style. With a *text variable* selected, Cmd+Return/Ctrl+Enter opens the Text Variables dialog.

Scripting

To one degree or another, anything you can do manually in InDesign can be automated via a script. Such scripts can be written in Mac-only AppleScript, Windows-only Visual Basic Script, or cross-platform JavaScript. They can do something as simple as preload the Swatches panel with your corporate colors, and they can perform highly complex, multistaged operations such as turning a blank page into a press-ready layout. Using scripts, InDesign can also be connected to other applications—for example, data from a spreadsheet or database can be sucked into InDesign and laid out automatically (which is awesome for data merge). The possibilities are limited only by your imagination and coding skill.

Covering what can be done and how to do it is far beyond the space available in this tome. Entire books have been written on the subject, and Adobe wrote one of the best—the *InDesign CS5 Scripting Guide*. There are three variations of the *InDesign CS5 Scripting Guide*: one each for AppleScript, Visual Basic Script, and JavaScript. You'll find them as PDFs in the `Adobe InDesign Documentation\Scripting` folder on the InDesign or Creative Suite DVD. If you don't have your DVDs on hand, you can also grab copies free of charge from `www.adobe .com/products/indesign/scripting/`. You'll want to begin with the *Adobe Introduction to Scripting*, progress through *Adobe InDesign CS5 Scripting Tutorial*, and use the *Adobe Creative Suite JavaScript Tools Guide* and the three script-language-specific versions of the *InDesign CS5 Scripting Guide* for reference (under the heading of "InDesign CS5 In-Depth Scripting Guides" on that page).

Accompanying the scripting tutorial and reference documents are hundreds of sample scripts that do everything from creating printer presets to unlinking text frames, from placing text files to laying out events calendars. In addition to those, hundreds of other scripts are floating around the Internet, most created by other InDesign users to address specific workflow needs.

The Adobe Exchange (`www.adobe.com/cfusion/exchange/`) used to be a place to look for InDesign scripts and other resources, but it's hopelessly out of date. As of fall 2010, the InDesign Exchange contains five scripts uploaded between 2002 and 2006. The rest of Adobe Exchange tends to also be perpetually outdated due to, as I understand it, a lack of personnel still at Adobe

to run the place. Instead of the Exchange, here are a few vastly more current online locations to find InDesign scripts and many more resources and freebies for InDesign, other Creative Suite applications, and design in general:

- ◆ http://www.indiscripts.com
- ◆ http://jsid.blogspot.com/
- ◆ http://gurusunleashed.com/
- ◆ http://workflowprepress.com/
- ◆ http://workflowfreelance.com
- ◆ http://www.creativepro.com/search/node/indesign+script
- ◆ http://www.indesignmag.com/

Full disclosure: I have no association with InDiscripts.com and JavaScripting InDesign, beyond being friendly with both site owners, but I write for, often finding those great InDesign scripts featured in, all the rest of the sites. I also own GurusUnleashed.com, WorkflowPrePress .com, and WorkflowFreelance.com.

As you search for already written InDesign scripts, I would hope you'll find ones that function on your platform. If you don't know what I mean, see the sidebar "Making Scripts Peer Friendly."

Making Scripts Peer Friendly

At this point, I would like to emphatically request that, should you create scripts for InDesign or InCopy, you do so in *JavaScript*. Only Mac-based InDesign and InCopy users can use AppleScript, and only Windows-based users can use Visual Basic Script (aka VBScript). Both, however, can use JavaScript scripts in InDesign. Few things are more frustrating than scouring the Web for days on end in search of a script to solve a problem, finding the perfect script, and then realizing that you can't use it because it was written for the other platform.

While all three languages (JavaScript, AppleScript, and VBScript) offer unique advantages—and the latter two enable file-system integration that, because of security concerns at the level of the operating system, JavaScript can't—most platform-specific scripts written by InDesign users *don't* use those advantages or integrate with the file-system. In other words, they *could* have been written in cross-platform JavaScript but weren't. From what I've seen, many script writers have a tendency to write specifically for their own platform as a first choice, not even considering that their scripts might be of use to someone on the other platform. With the split between Mac- and Windows-based professional creatives hovering right around 50/50 (yes, I *am* certain of that), it's naïve to think that only Mac users will need or want to do *this* or *that* in InDesign. I'm not just talking about Mac-based script writers, either; there are plenty of highly useful VBScript InDesign scripts out there that confound Mac users with a need.

For the foreseeable future, Windows will never do AppleScript and Mac will never do VBScript. If you write a custom script, *please* write it in JavaScript if at all possible. Don't punish your fellow creatives and production people, a great many of whom have no say in which operating system they get to use at work.

When you've written or obtained scripts you'd like to use, you have to give them to InDesign. Do that by closing InDesign and copying the scripts to the correct location for your platform:

Mac OS X `Users/[username]/Library/Preferences/Adobe InDesign/Version 7.0/en_US/Scripts`

Windows XP/2000 `Documents and Settings\[username]\Application Data\Adobe\InDesign\Version 7.0\en_US\Scripts`

Windows 7/Vista `Users\[username]\AppData\Roaming\Adobe\InDesign\Version 7.0\en_US\Scripts`

When you relaunch InDesign, the scripts will be available in the User group on the Scripts panel, which can be opened by choosing Window ➢ Utilities ➢ Scripts. Under Application in the panel, you'll also see numerous sample scripts that are not in the locations noted (see Figure 13.40). If you want to crack these open to help you learn scripting or even to delete them, you'll find them in the InDesign application installation location:

Mac OS X `Applications/InDesign CS5/Scripts/Scripts Panel/Samples`

Windows 7/Vista/XP/2000 `Program Files\Adobe\Adobe InDesign CS5\Scripts\Scripts Panel\Samples`

Windows 7/Vista (64-bit) `Program Files (x86)\Adobe\Adobe InDesign CS5\Scripts\Scripts Panel\Samples`

FIGURE 13.40
The Scripts panel

To execute a script on the Scripts panel, double-click it.

Note that many scripts function only when a specific condition has been met—such as preselecting certain types of objects or highlighting text. Indeed, many scripts that manipulate or work from objects require that objects be *named*. This is where the Script Label panel comes into play. The Script Label panel (Window ➢ Utilities ➢ Scripts) has no buttons, no flyout menu, and, apparently, nothing else (see Figure 13.41). Actually, the entire panel is a single text field. Select

an object on the page or pasteboard, click once inside the Script Label panel, and begin typing a name or label for the object. That's it. That's all it does. But, once named with the label a script expects, the object can then be manipulated by the script.

FIGURE 13.41
The Script Label
panel

Script writers can attach scripts and scripted functions to InDesign documents and to menu commands.

A (FREE) BETTER SCRIPTS PANEL

Script Bay is a free Scripts panel replacement from In-Tools.com released July 2010. As of this writing, it can run within and execute scripts from InDesign, Illustrator, and Photoshop. The author plans to expand it to support Flash, Fireworks, and Bridge as well. Here is the author's list of features:

◆ Script Bay offers the ability to run scripts located anywhere on your hard drive.

◆ Scripts can be viewed in either a list-view or tree-view.

◆ The list of scripts can be dynamically filtered, and scripts can be launched via keyboard navigation.

◆ Scripts can be edited directly in the built-in Script Bay script editor.

◆ Multiple scripts or folders full of scripts can be run in a single command.

◆ Script files can be moved, duplicated, deleted, and renamed directly within the panel.

◆ Scripts run in the Script Bay panel can be undone in InDesign as a single undo.

◆ Scripts can be easily "installed" into the host application.

◆ Script Bay has a default "cross-application" folder, and scripts placed in this folder are automatically available to all CS applications.

◆ Script Bay supports drag and drop for moving around script files as well as loading scripts into the script editor.

◆ Scripts can be added to Script Bay from anywhere on your hard drive by simple drag and drop.

Check it out and download it free from `http://in-tools.com/wordpress/script-bay/script-panel-replacement-for-the-entire-creative-suite`.

The Bottom Line

Work Efficiently with Text   Text takes up the most space in the average InDesign document. Unfortunately, editing and *re*styling text occupies the majority of a creative's time in the document. Used wisely, paragraph and character styles, nested styles, text variables, and data merge eliminate repetitive actions and hours of work.

> **Master It**   Use Excel, a database, or Notepad/TextEdit to create a new flat-file database of information. The data may be anything you like—a mailing list, product listings for a catalog, directory listings, and so on—but should include at least three fields and three rows. Save the file as either comma or tab delimited; this will be your data source file.
>
> Beginning with a blank InDesign document, build a variable data target document to hold the records from the data source file. Include static information as well as field placeholders. Format all text—static and placeholders—and create paragraph and character styles to make the initial and follow-up formatting easier. If you have appropriate places to employ nested styling, do so.
>
> When the target document is ready, effect a data merge to generate a press-ready variable-data project.

Work Efficiently with Tables   Table and cell styles make it a one-click operation to format tabular data and to instantly update all tables to match future formatting changes.

> **Master It**   Begin with a table of data. If you have tables in preexisting InDesign documents, use those (save the document under a different name, just in case). If you don't have such documents already, create a new layout and add at least two tables; the sports or financial sections of today's newspaper are excellent places to find tabular data you can use for FPO. Style one table with alternating fills, custom strokes of your choosing, and appropriate text formatting using paragraph styles. When the first table is styled to your liking, build table and cell styles, and then use them to format the second table.

Work Efficiently with Objects   Working efficiently doesn't end with text and tables. Graphics, paths, and containers are part of any InDesign document, and creating and editing them productively are also important to the efficient InDesign-based workflow.

> **Master It**   Using either your own or a client's various media logos (RGB, CMYK, grayscale; with and without taglines; iconic and full logos; and so on), build a shareable, reusable logo library. Now create a second library of text frames and other objects you use at least occasionally. Make sure to give each an object style before adding it to the library so that other objects can quickly be styled to match and so that formatting changes don't take too much time. Don't forget to label objects in both libraries for rapid identification and filtering by you or your coworkers.

Chapter 14

Collaboration

Few InDesign users operate in a vacuum, creating documents from start to finish all on their own. The majority of modern workflows, even among freelancers, entail some form of collaborative content creation. Perhaps it's a group of designers cooperating on the packaging for a large product line; maybe it's designers and copywriters crafting the perfect advertising creative. In the past, much like print and Web, West Berlin and East Germany, the personnel, activities, and especially software tools employed by design and production have always been separate from, and often mutually unfriendly toward, copywriting and editorial. All of that is changing. More and more print workflows are embracing digital content delivery; Germany has been unified. Most importantly, the software, which has always been, at best, reluctantly compatible and, at worst, openly hostile toward one another is actually beginning to cooperate, coordinate, and collaborate. Creatives keep on designing while writers keep on writing, but the barriers that separated them from each other and their peers are being torn down as fast as the Berlin Wall.

However—and with whomever—you collaborate, InDesign can speed and improve the process. In this chapter, you will learn to

◆ Collaborate with other designers

◆ Collaborate with writers and editors

◆ Collaborate with anyone on any file

◆ Send documents for review

◆ Share reusable settings

Collaborating with Other Designers

No man is an island, entire of itself; every man is a piece of the continent,
a part of the main.

—*John Donne, Meditation XVII (1572–1631)*

Whether you need to collaborate with the person over the cube wall from you or across the planet, InDesign has several powerful ways to coordinate joint efforts among creatives.

Saving to Older Versions of InDesign

Not all of us upgrade as quickly or regularly as others. Many (many, many) people skipped InDesign CS4, for example, two-stepping from CS3 up to CS5. For some, InDesign CS3 is ideal, with all the features needed for their particular work; they don't need or want CS4 or CS5 and will not upgrade to it for a while, if ever. (I doubt *you* are included in this group; after all, you obviously bought a book titled *Mastering InDesign CS5 for Print Design and Production*.) Others may lust after a new version but simply can't justify its price tag. Whatever the reason, it becomes necessary on occasion to move documents between the latest and earlier versions of InDesign.

The fact that InDesign CS (CS1, version 3.0) did *not* save backward for compatibility with 2.0 (the first commercially successful edition of InDesign) brought forth a public outcry so vociferous that it echoed for years throughout the halls of Adobe and many press and prepress shops around the world. That outcry led to the creation of the InDesign Interchange file format with its .inx file extension. Interchange files could be created and opened by InDesign CS1, CS2, and CS3. Thus, files could be exchanged among any of those versions of InDesign with little to no loss of function. Of course, once InDesign users had that ability, they stopped screaming for it. This led Adobe to apparently think it was no longer necessary. When the clamor for broad backward file compatibility died down, Adobe got rid of it. Well, technically they just limited it.

Unfortunately, InDesign now takes the QuarkXPress route of saving only one version back. You can export from CS5 to the CS4-compatible InDesign Markup Language (IDML) format, but that same format cannot be opened in CS3 or earlier versions. Instead, you must export to CS4-compatible, open the file in CS4, and then save it back out from CS4 to InDesign Interchange in order to open the file in CS3.

This, of course, is a major problem for creative and production personnel alike due to several factors:

- ◆ Only a fraction of InDesign users upgraded from CS3 to CS4.

- ◆ Many shops won't immediately upgrade to CS5.

- ◆ Many users, once they have upgraded, throw away or sell their older versions.

- ◆ Once Adobe releases a new version of its software, it ceases sales of older versions.

CS5-to-CS3 collaboration requires that someone have a copy of CS4 installed in order to convert the IDML file to an INX file. Of course, only a minority of the market actually *has* InDesign CS4, and, since the release of CS5, it's not easy to buy a copy of CS4. Thus, Adobe has created a conundrum—you *can* save backward between the latest (CS5) and the most popular (CS3) versions of InDesign, but only if you have the version the fewest people bought (CS4). Naturally, the solution Adobe favors is that everyone upgrade to CS5. Real-world pragmatism renders that option unfeasible for many, though. If you count yourself among those who can't upgrade to CS5 or who work with others who can't upgrade to CS5, you'll have to do the double-version save-back two-step.

1. In InDesign CS5, choose File ➤ Export and, from the Save as Type dropdown list, select InDesign Markup (IDML).

2. In InDesign CS4—yours, your collaborator's, or one belonging to some kind soul offering save-back conversions—use File ➤ Open to open the IDML file you created.

3. Still in CS4, choose File ➢ Export. This time, set Save as Type to InDesign CS3 Interchange (INX).

4. Open the INX file via File ➢ Open in InDesign CS3.

5. After editing in CS3, you can keep the file as an INX or save it to a normal INDD file, both of which CS5 (and CS4) can open without any additional steps.

6. If, after editing in CS5, the document must be sent back for further work in CS3, repeat steps 1–5.

Yeah, I know; that workflow sucks. It gets worse if you need to save back for CS2. That version won't open the INX files created by CS4; instead, you'll need to save out again as an INX from CS3. I wish I had something better to offer you, but that's all Adobe built. None of the InDesign plug-in makers or scripters has risen to the challenge to provide a better way, either.

Maintaining a round-trip editing workflow between different versions of InDesign is tedious but doable. My best advice is to always keep at least the latest two versions of InDesign—or *any* mission-critical creative application—installed or at least installable for just such scenarios. Personally, I keep a minimum of three versions of each application installed on at least one Windows and at least one Mac workstation. I also keep several versions installed on my laptops in case I need to save backward while traveling or visiting a collaborator's office.

One Document, Many Designers

Dividing a multipage document into multiple documents of one or more pages each and then collecting the pieces under a Book file is a common collaboration workflow. So common is it that I've given it a name—the Book File Collaboration Workflow™. Under this method, members of the design team work on pieces of the whole, and each piece is at least one full page. If the team members work from a single network file repository, each piece of the publication stays in synch with all other pieces with regard to section and page numbering, style consistency, and other shared document attributes. If they *don't* work from the network, shared attributes are updated when their pages are delivered to the person in charge of assembling and managing the parts into a whole publication (the paginator).

SETTING UP THE BOOK FILE COLLABORATION WORKFLOW

To set up Book file collaboration, begin by analyzing the document to be created or edited. How many creatives will work on it? Does it have inherent break points for apportionment? For instance, if the publication is a magazine, could the "Letter from the Editor" column page be broken out into its own document for one designer to work on while the "News Bites" spread and subsequent department and features pages are given their own documents and handed to other designers? If logical content separators aren't as obvious, look for more subtle separations where the document could be divided.

Once you've identified where the publication can be separated, make the pieces:

1. Begin with the complete publication in a single document. Set on the master page(s) folios, page headers and footers, and any other common elements that will appear on all or at least the majority of the document's pages. Although you're unlikely to need the full publication document again, save it for safety anyway.

2. On the Pages panel (Window ➤ Pages), select all the pages that will *not* be in the first constituent part and delete them.

   You should then have a document containing only the page(s) that will be assigned to the first designer. The pages *must* be contiguous; if you want to give pages 2–5 and 10–15 to the same team member, make one document for pages 2–5 and another for 10–15.

   If the document contains the Current Page Number special character, the document pages will renumber after the other pages are deleted. Ignore the page numbers. They'll be fixed automatically in a few steps.

NUMBERING PAGES MANUALLY

If you manually insert page numbers, *stop doing that!* InDesign has robust section- and page-numbering options that can handle nearly any page enumeration scenario with far less work than the unnecessarily masochistic practice of manually inserting and changing page numbers. Read about *page numbers, section numbering,* and *text variables* in this book before you say, *Oh, InDesign won't do automatically what I need for page numbering and identification.*

---

3. Because you're still working in the one and only full publication document, and you've probably just deleted the majority of the publication, *don't save.* Instead, choose File ➤ Save a Copy. When prompted, name the document something both you and the designer who will work on it will understand. If the section you're creating is the first of 10 parts of the May issue, a name like May-p2-5.indd would be ideal.

   Click OK when ready. Save a Copy saves a copy of the document without saving or closing the original document.

4. Press Cmd+Z/Ctrl+Z to undo the deletion of pages and return to the full document.

5. Repeat steps 1 through 4 for each subsequent section of the document, saving a copy of each part, until all the pieces are saved out to their own documents.

6. Go to File ➤ New ➤ Book and create a new InDesign INDB Book file with the same name as your publication. After you save, a blank Book panel will appear; its name will be that of your publication.

7. On the Book panel's flyout menu, choose Add Documents (or click the plus sign button at the bottom of the panel).

8. In the Add Documents dialog, choose all the publication part files you just created.

9. Click the first file in the list to select it, and then, holding the Shift key (on both Mac and Windows), click the last file in the list. All intervening documents will also be selected.

   Click the Open button, and the documents will populate the Book panel.

10. If the documents are not in their correct order, drag them within the list until they are correct. Automatic page numbers will update across all the files, putting them back into place in the scheme of the overall document.

11. Send the section documents to the designers who will be responsible for them.

Using the Book panel, you, as the publication manager, will be in control of the overall publication cohesion. If your team is working from a network file server, place all the component documents, the INDB Book file, and documents' linked assets in a folder on the server, and have team members open from, and save to, the same documents and folder. Your view of the publication through the Book panel will then always be in synch with the most recently saved changes to any pages of the publication. If your team works remotely from one another or for another reason cannot open and save files in a central repository, ensure that, as each piece comes back to you, you overwrite originals with new versions, which will also keep your Book panel updated.

Rearranging the individual documents in the publication is as easy as dragging them within the Book panel. If section A, for instance, must now come after C instead of before section B, simply drag A down to the correct place in the Book panel. Pages throughout the rest of the publication will instantly renumber to reflect the change. You don't even need to involve the designer working on section A!

If you later need to make changes to the segments, to move pages between publication sections, for instance, that's easy:

1. Open both the source and destination documents by double-clicking each in the Book panel.

2. In the source document, the one from which pages will be moved, choose Layout ➤ Pages ➤ Move Pages, which will open the Move Pages dialog (see Figure 14.1).

FIGURE 14.1
The Move Pages
dialog

3. In the Move Pages dialog and the Move Pages field, enter the page number(s) of the page(s) to move from the source document to the target document.

   Use hyphen-separated numbers to specify a range (e.g., 1-3) and comma-separated numbers for nonsequential pages (e.g., 1,3).

4. Change the Move To field from Current Document to the name of the destination document, and then, using the two Destination fields, tell InDesign precisely where to drop the page(s).

5. Check Delete Pages After Moving so they will be removed from the source document.

6. Click OK, and the pages will immediately move from the source to the target document.

7. Save both, and you're finished; the Book panel will update itself.

If you only want to *copy* pages between documents, leaving the originals in the source document but also adding them to the target, don't check Delete Pages After Moving. This is a handy trick for those situations where someone comes along and says, "Hey! Wouldn't it be cool if every chapter suddenly began with a splash page?" Folks who work on magazines, telephone

directories, and other such advertising-supported periodicals love that particular trick because it makes it easy to insert newly sold full-page or full-spread ads into the middle of a feature article or other publication section that can't—or shouldn't—be broken into still more documents.

Speaking of periodicals…

WHEN BOOK FILE COLLABORATION WON'T WORK

The Book File Collaboration Workflow has one hard rule—in order for automatic page numbering and unified output to work, each component document must comprise strictly contiguous pages with no blank or extraneous pages. For magazines, newspapers, newsletters, magalogs, and other documents where stories jump, pausing on a particular page, skipping other content pages, and then picking up again farther into the publication, the one rule of Book file collaboration could be a problem. (If your publication doesn't jump stories, it's not a problem.) InDesign can't thread a single, continuous story across multiple documents; threaded frames may only be in the same document. Therefore, if a feature article jumps from page 19 to page 32, you're left with a dilemma. You have a choice among four possible solutions for that dilemma:

Single Document Workflow   Make pages 19–32 one document, inclusive of all content pages between, thus making it impossible for more than one designer to work at any given time on any page between 19 and 32.

Redundant Pages Workflow   Make pages 19–32 one document, but leave blank any pages not directly part of the single feature story. Any intervening pages and sections are still their own separate documents, enabling other designers to work independently and concurrently on their respective pieces. This method isn't new—it's what magazines and other periodicals typically employ. There are two downsides to this method: automatic page numbering goes haywire because of the extraneous pages, and it forces extra pagination work and a greater potential for mistakes immediately before going to press.

Many component documents using this method include numerous pages that serve no function other than as placeholders for content on which someone else is working. When the pages are locked down, just before the issue is put to bed, someone has to sit down and either combine all the components into a single document via drag and drop or go through each document, printing or exporting content pages manually while ignoring placeholder pages. When pages are exported to PDF, EPS, or another format, the numerous resulting files are then either combined into a single document (for instance, one large PDF), imposed in-house into a single document, or named after their page numbers and sent out for imposition (whereupon someone hopes very, very hard that the imposer doesn't make a mistake).

Book File Collaboration Workflow   Continue with the Book File Collaboration Workflow, making page 19 one file, page 32 another, and dividing the intervening pages as needed and independently of the jumped story. In that case, the story is manually broken on page 19, with its last line tweaked and a jumpline inserted, and then the overflow copy is added manually and independently to page 32, again with a manually inserted and maintained *Continued From* jumpline. Last-minute edits to the story or to the layout that affect story composition require editing two documents instead of one, often cutting a word or line from *this* one to paste into *that* one.

Assigned Content Workflows   Augment or replace the Book File Collaboration Workflow with a different methodology. See if your workflow can employ the InCopy LiveEdit Workflow

(Adobe's term, not mine) or the Placed Page Collaboration Workflow (I was the first to coin this one, so please send me a nickel every time you use it) or both. I'll discuss both of these methodologies shortly—the latter in the very next section, "One Page, Many Designers," and the former a few pages hence in the section "Collaborating with Writers and Editors."

Just to be clear: If your publication *doesn't* jump stories outside the pages assigned to each creative, you *can* use the Book File Collaboration Workflow without the aforementioned problem. *Do* still read the rest of this chapter, though, because none of these methodologies is necessarily exclusive of the others.

One Page, Many Designers

Yesterday there was a one-to-one, one-designer-to-one-page, relationship so inflexible it may as well have been cast in iron. Today, the paradigm has shifted. With InDesign a many-to-one relationship is possible. Many designers may work simultaneously on one page—or, more accurately, on *portions* of the same page. In Figure 14.2 you'll see a flowchart diagramming an example of what I've dubbed the Placed Page Collaboration Workflow.

FIGURE 14.2
Diagram of a Placed Page Collaboration Workflow in use on a single page (See the color insert section of this book for a full-color version of this figure.)

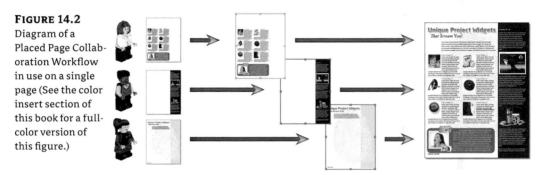

In the diagram, a single-page magalog layout is divided into three separate areas. Three separate designers will work concurrently, one on each area, all never leaving InDesign. Kim (at the bottom with the ponytail) is the lead designer on the page. She has created the page grid and will be adding background imagery, the headline, deck, page introductory paragraph, and static elements like the folio. She has also assigned portions of the page to other designers working in InDesign or perhaps even in InCopy's layout view. Rachael (the redhead), is responsible for copyfitting and setting the product listings in the middle of the page as well as the feature box at the bottom of the page, while Carlos (in the middle) takes care of designing the sidebar. Previously, trying to split the work on one page among three designers meant each would have to take a turn, each one waiting to begin work until the last has finished. All three designers under this scenario *are* working concurrently, on the same page, in InDesign.

The principle is simple, one with which you're already intimately familiar. Let's look at the basics of your current workflow.

If you work on advertising-supported publications, for instance, you almost certainly accept PDF or EPS press-ready ads from agencies, right? Someone far away designs an ad and FTPs it to you, and you drop it as is into the appropriate slot in your layout. If you don't accept outside creative into your layouts, you *do* create elements and sections of at least some pages in Photoshop

or Illustrator. That artwork (or agency art) is placed into InDesign as a linked asset. Should the asset need to be altered, it's edited in its native application and the link merely updated in InDesign. Thus, while you're working on the composed page in InDesign, someone else could be working at the same moment and independently in Illustrator on the pie chart for page 6. Neither of you will hinder the other's work because, as a linked asset, that AI or PDF pie chart is a wholly separate document from your INDD layout. You do this day in and day out with placed assets, so you know how it works.

Now, substitute another INDD file for the AI or PDF. Instead of a pie chart, page 6 contains a table or other elements better done in InDesign than outside it. InDesign accepts *other InDesign files as placed and linked assets*. That's what Rachael, Carlos, and Kim are doing. Each is working in InDesign on a separate INDD document. The final, composited page in the Figure 14.2 flow-chart is a fourth document (or not; maybe Kim is working in the master layout while Rachael's and Carlos's pieces will be placed into her document). For the sake of argument, let's assume a fourth document collects the three designers' separate documents. The compositor uses File ➤ Place or drag and drop from Bridge, Finder, or Explorer to import the designers' three separate INDD files exactly as he would a trio of TIFFs, PSDs, PDFs, or whatever. The placed assets are then arranged to form the composite page—just like pages you lay out every day with images and artwork created outside InDesign. That's the Placed Page Collaboration Workflow.

Another cool aspect of compositing a page by placing INDD files is that the compositor's tasks of manual asset positioning and transforming can be completely eliminated. Glance again at Figure 14.2, paying particular attention to the component pieces. Notice that they're all the same size and, except for Kim's background, contain copious white space. Each piece is the exact size of the final page. If your composited INDD document is 8.5×11 inches, make each page asset 8.5×11 inches. The bounding box of each placed page will then also be 8.5×11 inches. Not only does that enable each designer to work with a sense of how his work fits into the page as a whole, it also means the asset can be placed with minimal positioning work. Rachael's, Carlos's, and Kim's art can all be placed at the same time, aligned to each other's top and left edges with two quick clicks of buttons on the Control panel or Align panel, and then easily positioned to the 0,0 origin. No one has to zoom in and precisely position the pieces to one another because they are all the same size, ready to align perfectly with one another. Cropping is unnecessary, too, because empty space on the InDesign document page is transparent; each asset will show through the negative space in the one above it. They'll even blend with each other if transparency or blending modes are used. In my flowchart, the black background of Carlos's sidebar is set to a Multiply blending mode at 85%. When it overlays the fingerprint image in Kim's section of the page, the sidebar will enable the white fingerprint ridges to show through as 85% black ridges. The red feature box also blends with the other part of the fingerprint via another blending mode.

How do I know what everyone else is doing? I can't lay out a page in a vacuum. Again, InDesign can place other InDesign files as assets. So, to keep abreast of what everyone else is doing in his portion of the page, place each page component document on the pasteboard. Assuming everyone is working from files stored on a network server accessible by all, Rachael can place on her pasteboard Carlos's and Kim's INDD documents, Carlos can place Rachael's and Kim's, and so on. When any one of them saves the document, InDesign will notify the others that the linked asset has been changed and ask if the link should be updated. If you have a good group of people fastidious enough to clean up after themselves, they can even place the other designers' documents

on the page instead of the pasteboard. The effect then is that three people are all working simultaneously on the composite layout. (Fair warning: It can be a little creepy at first to watch parts of your page change as if by supernatural means.)

SOLVING THE PROBLEM WITH BOOK FILE COLLABORATION

C'mon. Do you really expect me to assign three designers to one page? No, of course not, at least not in most workflows. Don't take me too literally. The one-page example and diagram can be interpreted literally or as an allegory for a much larger document. Collaborating via placed pages works even better with multiple pages. Remember previously when I listed the types of documents and circumstances under which a Book File Collaboration Workflow won't work? Well, the Placed Page Collaboration Workflow *does* work on those documents and under those circumstances.

Periodicals often follow a common workflow based on division and duplication—Divide and Copy and Conquer, I call it. Initially, a template is created containing all the pages in the book. Department and regular features pages are laid out, ad pages are assigned, and FPOs are inserted for feature article spreads and other content. Then you, the creative director, sit down and plan the page parceling. You may divide it equally among your designers and production artists. You would then save one additional copy of the template for each designer. Alternatively, you might apportion the template by logical structure. In that case, regardless of the number of people working on the next issue, you would divide the document into its spaces. For instance, the three pages blocked out for the first feature article would be a single space and one complete copy of the template, the two pages for the "Letters to the Editor" department another copy, and so on until all sections of the publication have been accounted for in copies of the initial template.

Figure 14.3 diagrams the common Divide and Copy and Conquer method of designing and laying out periodicals. In this case, the publication has been apportioned to the three production artists plus pages for yourself (you're at the bottom of the flowchart; I wouldn't be so presumptuous as to make a LEGO person of you). Earlier we talked about jumping a story from page 19 to page 32, which is where the flowchart picks up. Pages 1 through 18 we'll assume have been assigned to other production artists. Rachael, Carlos, and Kim are your best people, anyway. They're busy folks, but then they're LEGO designers; they have no lives and don't need coffee breaks. The green pages are Rachael's to design, the blue belong to Carlos, the red to Kim, and the goldenrod are yours (you can see the full-color version in the color insert). Ad pages are blocked out entirely, awaiting PDF and EPS ads that will be dropped in during pagination.

Examine the flowchart. This type of collaboration is common because it offers the benefit of maintaining automatic page numbering. The feature story jumps from page 19 to page 32, and, by leaving all intervening pages in place, page 32 is numbered as such without the need to manually type 32 into a text frame and change it should pages be added, deleted, or reordered. Because all four copies of the template are complete copies, Rachael knows she's working on pages 21–23 while Carlos has pages 25, 26, and 28, Kim has pages 30–31, and you have the feature story on pages 19 and 32. Everyone knows where her or his work falls within the book, and the publication TOC can then be built by hand with reasonable assurance of its accuracy (automatic TOC generation is impossible at this stage because there are four copies of every page, so the various versions cannot be tied together via a Book file).

FIGURE 14.3
Flowchart of a common periodical publication workflow

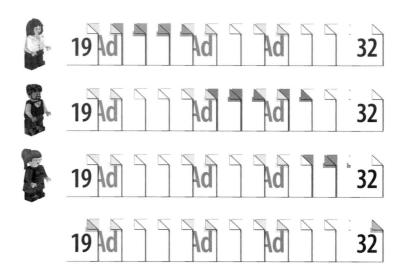

Regardless of its benefits, this type of collaboration has significant inherent problems. Can you spot them? I found several:

No Flow   Let's start with the fact that there are no arrows. Flowcharts are supposed to have arrows, right? I mean, that's the *flow* part of *flowchart*. There are no arrows because nothing moves; nothing and no one interact. Rachael does her thing, Carlos his, Kim hers, you yours. None of you has the slightest idea what the others are up to. That's a problem in itself, but it also leads to other problems. Such as…

Working Blind   You, the creative director, have no insight into, or oversight of, what your people are doing short of walking up behind them or asking them to stop productive work to print or email proofs. If you don't get proofs (or peer over shoulders), odds are good you'll be surprised by the pages at the eleventh hour and find yourself asking for changes. Even if you do get proofs, how often is it practical to check up on and coordinate with your designers? If Kim does something that doesn't work with Carlos's design, one of them has to change, but after how many work hours have been invested? How much does each change cost you?

Redundant Changes   Everyone is working from a separate and complete copy of the entire publication template. Magazine structures don't often change without rebuilding the entire template, but they do change from time to time. Pages in other types of multipage, team-effort publications are often shuffled around with pages added or removed here and there. In a workflow of the sort shown in the diagram, such a change is a nightmare. To add a page in the middle of the publication or shift one section behind another entails coordinating with each of the designers to make the identical change in every copy of the template. Done infrequently by very organized, detail-oriented creatives, such structural alterations can be accomplished smoothly. The difficulty and likelihood of mistakes increases in direct proportion to the frequency and number of such changes and with the level of stress on the creatives. One slipup and you could be spending quite a bit of time trying to puzzle your publication back together.

Pagination PIA   Pagination with this type of publication is a royal pain in the… neck. At the end of the publication cycle, someone must sit down with all the pieces of the publication

and pull out only the original pages from each version and then combine all those pieces into a single publication. Typically this is done by saving each page individually to EPS or PDF and then placing those one at a time into yet another template duplicate.

The workflow presented in Figure 14.3 is extremely common. It's also a huge waste of time and money because, for many such workflows, there's a better way.

Let's review the key production problem that forces a Divide and Copy and Conquer workflow. If you have a magazine, newspaper, newsletter, magalog, or other document with jumped stories, you can't divide the publication into multiple Book panel-managed files without severing the threading between frames of jumped stories. You also can't break out the pages in between the story jumps and expect automatic page numbering to work across the book. You *can*, however, use placed pages in addition to a Book file to give you everything—automatic page numbering, threaded jumped stories, and concurrent productivity—*without* risky structural alterations or grueling pagination work at the end.

The chart in Figure 14.4, which continues with the example of a story that jumps from page 19 to page 32, demonstrates placing pages in a multipage document. In this case, the creative director is using both a Book file and placed pages. To handle the jumped story, one booked document includes pages 19 through 32 inclusive. Intervening pages are assigned out to Rachael, Carlos, and Kim. The designers work in separate INDD documents that are placed as linked assets in the main document; there are no redundant, unused pages in the documents the designers receive. Each component document is either single pages or multiple pages, whichever is needed. Multipage INDD document assets can be placed just as easily as can multipage PDFs—one page at a time. Therefore, even though Carlos's three pages are nonconsecutive, broken by the full-page ad on page 27, he can still carry a threaded story through all three pages. When his pages are placed into the main publication document, they're placed as pages 25–26 and 28; he *works on* consecutive pages even though they won't be *printed as* consecutive pages. He doesn't have to break the text flow; he can work in a single three-page document, enjoying threading and all the other benefits of working in only one document, without causing problems for the main document. In fact, Carlos's pages can be moved around in the main document (and renumbered automatically) without the need to even involve Carlos.

I get it: The Placed Page Collaboration Workflow is alien—it might even sound insane. But do yourself the favor of thinking it through and of comparing it with how you're currently managing multiple designers working on the same multipage document. I have personally been a contributor to, and manager of, all the same workflows I described above, and more. Yes, they work, but they don't work *well*. Rather, the Divide and Copy and Conquer method on which so many publications rely is itself a workaround to the lack of genuine collaboration built into our software. It's an insane workflow that we made work year after year because we didn't have anything better. Now there's something better, something that will save you measurable time and money, if you'll give it a shot.

There is legitimate use for Placed Page Collaboration in the occasional one-page document. But it's with multipage documents that it really shines—particularly if, for one reason or another, you can't use Book File Collaboration or using it alone doesn't solve your workflow problems. By freeing creatives from the need to sit on their hands or perform busywork while waiting to get access to documents, your organization saves money and time. You'll also save time and money by eliminating the need for a paginator to impose in a scramble at the last minute, going through all the full-document templates, selecting and imposing all the needed pages sitting here and there among dozens of empty or FPO pages.

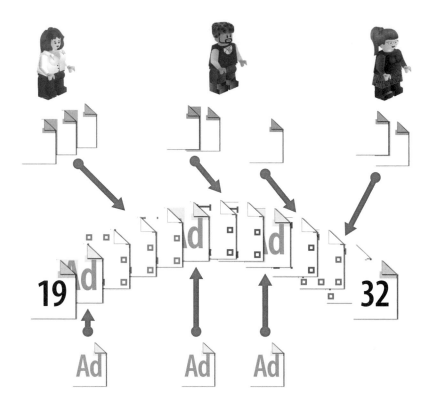

FIGURE 14.4
Diagram of a Placed Page Collaboration Workflow in a multipage document (See the color insert for a full-color version.)

GOING TO PRESS WITH PLACED PAGES

Point made, but there's no way it will print. Why not? Why is it that every time someone presents a new way of doing things in InDesign, the first response is always, *I bet it won't print.* QuarkXPress doesn't suffer this kind of cynicism. Placing INDD files inside other INDD files is *exactly* like placing Illustrator AI files or even EPS images. It's another linked asset, albeit one that can have its own linked assets, but it prints, packages, and exports to PDF just fine. Again, I can personally attest to it.

So, how *do I output*? Same as any InDesign document you did yesterday or last week—print it, package it, or export it to PDF. You can also do all of those through a Book panel the same way you did it before you placed pages.

One thing you'll be glad to know is that InDesign's Package feature is placed-page aware. When you place INDD pages into another INDD document, you've created a layer of nesting. The *placed* INDD can have its own fonts and linked assets—and even contain other placed INDD files. Potentially you could build from placed pages an infinite Russian matryoshka doll where every placed INDD has inside it another placed INDD, and inside that is another INDD, and so on. How far into that nest of linking will the Package command go? As far as I can tell, all the way. Just for kicks I tried six levels deep. Package found and collected unique images and fonts used at each level. So, if you have DocA.indd placed inside DocB.indd, File ➤ Package will find all the fonts and linked assets used by DocB.indd. One of those linked assets is DocA.indd, so InDesign will collect that and put it into the packaged project's Links folder, too. At the same

time, InDesign recognizes that DocA.indd itself has font and asset dependencies, so it grabs all those as well. And, it updates the links in *all* collected INDD files to point to images and other assets in the Links folder.

Placed Page Collaboration Workflow. It just works. Remember where you heard it first.

Collaborating with Writers and Editors

Design—graphic designers, production artists, compositors, and typesetters—and editorial—copywriters, journalists, editors, and authors—have, since time immemorial, often been pitted against one another by the secular and incompatible tools and technologies on which they each depend. Editorial passes its text to design for copyfitting and layout, taking the copy out of the sight and control of its creators. Editorial must then wait for proofs to be returned from design. Changes—and there are often changes—have to be passed incrementally to designers to effect; after the first handoff, editorial must rely completely on design to update and correct what is editorial's own work. That could be frustrating for anyone. Equally frustrating is the other side of the process where design personnel frequently must interrupt work on current pages to go back and edit text on previously completed pages. Frustration could lead to resentment and to conflict between the two departments. At the heart of all of it is the software.

The sky is blue, water is wet, editorial uses Microsoft Word. This undisputable fact of life is not because Microsoft Word is perfectly suited for copywriting and editing. Far from it. It has numerous flaws and quirks that increase the difficulty of day-in, day-out writing and editing. It's the only choice for editorial for one simple reason: Nothing better has come along. Or, maybe that should read, "nothing better has been presented to editorial." There *is* competition to Microsoft Word, but writers aren't using it for one of three reasons: They don't know what other options are out there; the other word processors don't integrate better than, or even as well as, Word with other applications in the workflow; or their employers, who suffer under one or both of the first two reasons, don't give editorial a choice.

When it comes to Word competitors like Corel WordPerfect, WordStar, OpenOffice.org Writer, the Mac-only Pages, and others, switching from Word offers no advantage to the design-editorial collaboration. None of these applications integrates into InDesign (or its competitors) any better (but frequently worse) than Word. Not one of them addresses the potential frustrations and slowdowns in the design-editorial collaboration.

Solving the Design-Editorial Collaboration Problems

In Chapter 8, "Stories," you were introduced to InDesign's editorial companion, InCopy, and given an explanation of the basics for using it as a stand-alone word processor. I won't rehash that introduction here. This section is about how the designer or production person handles the InDesign side of the InDesign-InCopy collaboration. It's not about *you* writing and editing stories in InDesign this time. It's about you enabling *editorial staff* to write and edit stories in your InDesign documents. Before we get into the mechanics of that, however, I want to briefly explain why your design and editorial collaboration workflow needs InCopy.

InCopy addresses the largest and most common problems on both sides of the design-editorial collaboration.

Editorial's Biggest Problem   Editorial must hand off its work to design and loses control of the copy at that point. Editors will not have direct interaction with the copy again before

to let the InCopy user choose his color first. Then he'll need to inform you of his color choice by phone, email, or carrier pigeon so that you may set the same color within the assignment—or not. The Color field is entirely optional and exists solely to give you, the InDesign user, a visual cue in the Assignments panel of who owns what content. Assignments in the panel will be tinted to the assignee's color, but that's where the utility of this field ends.

FIGURE 14.8
The New Assignment dialog

When you create an assignment file, an ICMA document will be written to disk. Each story added to the assignment will be exported as an ICML. The Location for Assignment File section tells you where on your computer (or the network) these files will be saved. Clicking the Change button enables you to browse your system for a new place to save the documents. If your editorial department collaborators are on the same network, set Location for Assignment File to a shared folder on the network, one to which you, your fellow designers, and the editors have both read and write access. If your editors work remotely from other locations, you'll need to make use of packaged assignments, which we'll discuss later in this chapter; for now, choose a convenient location on the network or your computer.

The Include section is extremely important. Here is where you determine how much of the layout InCopy users see when they open the assignment and work with it in InCopy's InDesign-like Layout view. Story and Galley view, which do not show the layout, are unaffected by the Include options. Your choices are as follows:

Placeholder Frames If chosen, this option makes solid gray boxes of all frames not directly a part of the assignment. Any content within those frames will be hidden from InCopy users' view. Any frames that *are* in the assignment—including graphic frames—*will* be visible and editable in InCopy's Layout view.

> *Recommendation*: Choosing Placeholder Frames is very much like setting InDesign's display performance to Fast Display, with the same benefits: less distraction, and pages draw to the screen very quickly. If editors find themselves distracted by page elements that are not theirs, or if they report that InCopy moves sluggishly while they edit, consider using the Placeholder Frames option.

Assigned Spreads   Assignments may consist of multipage threaded stories as well as multiple disconnected stories spread across several pages. Therefore, with the Assigned Spreads option, an InCopy user has the ability to see in InCopy's Layout view all the assigned *and* unassigned content from those pages (in spreads). Any pages or spreads that are *not* part of the assignment will be excluded. Of course, although visible, unassigned content will not be editable in InCopy. Like InDesign's Typical Display display performance mode, images included in the assignment to InCopy users are low-resolution proxies ideal for onscreen viewing and suitable for output on a desktop printer. The images and graphical elements are not, however, of a high enough quality that editors should rely on them for fine detail.

> *Recommendation:* Assigned Spreads is already the default option, and I recommend that you consider using it most often. One of the key benefits to the tight integration between InDesign and InCopy is the ability for editors to see and write in the real WYSIWYG layout page within InCopy. Sending full views of assigned spreads gives editorial a window on the layout that, in most cases, helps them better visualize the impact of, and limitations on, their copy. Usually it benefits the publication overall; however, in some cases it can be a hindrance. Some editorial staffers find that looking at an in-progress or unfinished page is confusing (even though they don't *have* to look at it; InCopy has two other views that hide the layout).

All Spreads   With this option, the entire document, not only the spreads containing assigned frames, will be sent and viewable in InCopy's Layout view. The InCopy user will be able to edit only the content assigned to him, however. Choosing this option generates larger files and may cause sluggish InCopy performance on computers with less RAM and hard drive space.

> *Recommendation*: I recommend using the All Spreads option only in assignments for those who absolutely must see the entire document—namely, top-of-the-chain editors. For most lower-level editors, it's overkill and can slow down InCopy running on low-spec computers.

Let's leave discussion of the Linked Image Files when Packaging check box option to the section "Collaborating with Remote Editors," coming up.

6. When you have all the options for your first assignment set, click the OK button.

7. Although you now have a new assignment in the Assignments panel, it's still empty, devoid of assigned content. On the document page, select one frame and go to Edit ➢ InCopy ➢ Add Selection to Assignment.

8. You'll see the assignment you just created on that list; choose it as the destination for the selected content.

   If you haven't recently saved the document, InDesign will kindly prompt you to do so, and then it will export the content to an ICML file, which is indexed by the ICMA assignment file. The ICML InCopy document will be created in a `Content` folder beneath the location you chose for the ICMA. For instance, if you chose to save the assignment to your desktop in a folder titled `MyDocument Assignments`, the ICML will be saved to `MyDocument Assignments\Content`.

9. In the Assignments panel, your assignment will now list the assigned frame. It will also show a yellow, out-of-date caution sign beside the assignment name. Regrettably, InDesign does not automatically update assignments as it does INDB Book files. Select the assignment in the panel's list and choose Update Selected Assignments from the panel flyout menu, which will write the change (the new ICML to index) to the ICMA file.

If you and your editors are on the same network, call up an editor and tell her where to find the assignment. When she opens the assignment file (the ICMA, not the ICML story file) in InCopy, she can edit the frame content all she wants. She can be editing in InCopy while you work on the layout in InDesign—even while you make changes to the frame size and positioning! When one of you saves your respective documents, the other will be notified and given the opportunity to update the view onto the other's content.

Congratulations! You've just assigned content to an editor. You were a good foster parent for the story, but it was time. You just returned the copy to the custody of its rightful parent. Now the *editor* will take care of raising the story to maturity while *you* focus on *your* baby, the layout.

 **Real World Scenario**

PUBLISH TO PRINT, PDF, AND WEB, WITH INCOPY AS THE PIVOT POINT

Pilsen Dynamics produces a bimonthly, magazine-style newsletter for its employees, shareholders, customers, and vendors. The newsletter, the *PD Report*, is a marketing tool featuring articles about the company's accomplishments, products, and research and development efforts, but it also takes a broader view of industry trends and concerns. The four-color and saddle-stitched printed edition is distributed to various points in North America via direct mail; it is sent to overseas customers and vendors as an RGB PDF. Although the print edition is the pride of the *PD Report*, various content from each issue—such as the feature articles, calendar of events, and letter from the CEO column—are simultaneously published to the Pilsen Dynamics's intranet, which is accessible by employees, contractors, and certain vendors. One of the chief benefits to the online version is the ability to spark discussion through bloglike comments appended to each article.

The workflow is the epitome of team-based collaboration.

Work on an issue begins with in-house writers submitting their ICML articles and accompanying photographs (often a selection of possible photos) directly to the production department. Production, working from an InDesign INDT template file, places the first-draft ICML files and photos and then generates InCopy assignments for the publication's editors. Because all work is done in-house, all files are written to a shared server, accessible by production and editorial personnel (and later by the intranet team).

Often a writer submits several possible photos for an article, or production itself offers stock photo or stock illustration candidates. All possible images are placed into a folder named to mirror the ICMA filename, and the final selection is left to the article editor. Adobe Bridge is now included with all of Adobe's stand-alone, CS3 version applications, so even the InCopy-based editors can visually browse the folder, rate and label images, and, if they aren't happy with any candidate image, use the Adobe Bridge interface to Adobe Stock Photos to select and license a new photograph or illustration. Once an image is selected, editors place it into an assigned image frame directly within InCopy.

Editors and writers go back and forth perfecting the copy while production personnel continue designing the rest of the publication.

When a story has reached its final form, the editor executes a JavaScript script from the InCopy Scripting panel. The script performs a number of small but important tasks:

◆ Accepts and commits to all revisions and changes in the document

◆ Inserts a nonprinting "FROZEN COPY" note at the top of the story to prevent other editors from later modifying the story

◆ Exports the document dictionary to be later merged with other editors' dictionaries by a server-side script, thus creating a central repository of all new words and spelling or hyphenation exceptions (the single dictionary will be imported into every editor's copy of InCopy to ensure that everyone on the team has the most current list of words)

◆ Exports the story to an XML file

◆ Checks in the assignment

When all editors have completed their work and checked in their assignments, the production department updates and reviews content and generates a single RGB PDF version of *PD Report*. The PDF is made available to the personnel who will send it to overseas recipients. It is also sent to the printer, who will convert from RGB to CMYK in preflight and print the hard copy edition. But, the collaboration doesn't end there.

If a story were only going to press and PDF, there would be no reason to mark the story "FROZEN COPY," accept all revisions, or export an XML version. Editors could simply tell production when editing had been completed; no special mark inside the story would be necessary. Similarly, changes made to the article with InCopy's change-tracking enabled wouldn't mar the finished output; notes and markups are nonprinting. And, InDesign has no use for the XML version when content is linked via the Assignments panel. All of these functions are required to output the story to the company intranet.

While the print edition is in production at the outsourced print shop, the internal intranet team goes to work on the exported XML stories. Using a custom script as a bridge, they suck the XML stories into an MSSQL database running on their .NET server. The script maps InCopy's XML structure to required database fields and converts formatting tags to HTML, including CLASS and ID attributes so that the content can be styled by the site's existing CSS style sheet. With the article now available via the intranet's content management system and, ostensibly, ready for publication, the intranet team turns to the story images. With the final publication PDF as a guide, they select the story images in Adobe Bridge and execute, from within Adobe Bridge, a Photoshop batch action to size and downsample images and to save Web-compatible PNG copies of the images in the same folder. Finally, they manually add references to the images to the online stories.

Using InCopy as the pivot point, all the departments can use the same content to publish to print, PDF, or the intranet with little wasted or duplicated effort. Each department maintains control over the content in its area of expertise while using technology to streamline the hand off of content to the next department. Ahh, creative efficiency.

of the interview subject's headshot, I might assign the photo frame to them as an InCopy story, too. The other editors—copyeditor Linda, production editor Dassi, and acquisitions editor Mariann—would also need a pass at the copy, but they'll need to see the same copy that goes to Sam or Tom. Therefore, I wouldn't create assignments for them. Instead, Sam and Tom would send *their* assignments on to the next person in the chain from within InCopy. As the InDesign layout artist, my concern with the copy ends with the assignment and delivery to the first step in the chain and doesn't pick up again until just before going to press, when I perform my final proof of all pages.

Once you have all your empty assignments created, they'll appear on the InCopy ➤ Add to Assignment menu available from the Edit menu and all those other places. You can add each story or graphic frame one at a time to the correct assignment. That's a lot of clicking, though. Why not just drag? You can drag any frame from the layout and drop it onto an assignment in the Assignments panel to add the content to that assignment. When all content that must be assigned has been added to the correct assignment, choose Update All Assignments from the panel flyout menu to write changes into the ICMA documents.

ASSIGNING PHOTOS

InCopy users can, if you let them, place and replace images in graphic frames. Reporters, for example, can supply their own story photos. Many designers use this ability to get the photo from the InCopy user but later tweak the cropping, scaling, and other attributes of images in InDesign. In other words, assigning a graphic frame to an InCopy user can lighten your workload a little bit more without sacrificing any control.

Graphic frames are assigned just like story frames—through the same menus and methods. Then, in InCopy, editors can use the File ➤ Place command and a Place dialog and options identical to InDesign's to insert imagery into the checked-out frame. Once the image is inserted, they can perform basic manipulation tasks like scaling and repositioning the image, but, again, they cannot edit the frame size, shape, position, or visual attributes.

REARRANGING ASSIGNED CONTENT

If you inadvertently add a story to the wrong assignment, or priorities change and you need to move content from one person's assignment to another's, just drag the content entry in the Assignment panel's list from one assignment to another and update all assignments. The ICML won't change or be overwritten. Only the ICMA assignment files will change, removing the reference to the ICML from one and adding it to another.

From the Edit ➤ InCopy menu, you can quickly add all story frames, all graphics, or all story and graphic frames on the current layer to a particular assignment in one step. This is a handy way to get all content onto the Assignments panel quickly. Once they are there, you can drag and drop individual frames to other assignments.

UNASSIGNING CONTENT

To pull content out of an assignment altogether, highlight its entry in the Assignments panel, click the trashcan icon at the bottom, and update the assignment. The content will then re-embed in the InDesign document. Note that this action does not delete the ICML file; it only breaks the link between the content in the layout and the external ICML document.

RENAMING ASSIGNED FILES

ICML files are named by combining the filename of the originating InDesign document with the first few words of the content in the ICML and exported frame. The ICML files *can* be renamed, but there's very little point in doing so because their names on the Assignments panel *cannot* be altered from the first name InDesign gives them. Yeah, I know: *Whose brilliant idea was that?* If you'd still like to change the name of the ICML file, follow this procedure:

1. Open the InDesign file containing the assigned ICML file in question.

2. Rename the ICML file on disk.

3. In the InDesign Links panel, the linked ICML file will suddenly go missing because it was renamed (indicated by the red circle beside its name). Select the missing link in the list and click the Relink button.

4. In the Relink dialog, choose the newly renamed ICML and click Open. The missing link status will disappear, and the Links panel entry will change to reflect the new filename.

5. Switch to the Assignments panel, where the assignment containing the ICML story will show the yellow caution sign to indicate that the assignment is out of date.

6. Select the assignment and choose Update Selected Assignments from the panel flyout menu.

OVERRIDING CHECKOUTS

In any team effort, someone must be in charge of the overall project. This is a matter of practicality, operational security, and workflow integrity. Indeed, if the LiveEdit Workflow afforded everyone equal power, if no one could override anyone else, one forgotten check-in the night before deadline could bring the entire project to a grinding halt. Fortunately, power is *not* shared equally between InDesign and InCopy. Although most publications are captained by someone who uses InCopy—a managing editor, editor in chief, or publisher—in the LiveEdit Workflow, it's the InDesign side of the collaboration that holds final technological authority (don't tell editorial!).

It happens. Someone goes home sick or leaves for the night forgetting to check in stories on which they'd been working. In the InDesign document, you'll see content checked out, and you can't fix that typo on line 7. Do you call the missing editor at home? Should you call IT to come hack into the editor's computer? Nah. Start editing the story in InDesign. It will prompt you to check out the story, which will then generate a warning that someone else already has it checked out. At that point you'll be offered the option to re-embed the story, overriding the checkout and any unsaved changes the editor may have made. Once embedded back into the InDesign document, it's native, editable text (or a picture) again. Exercise caution in overriding a checkout because what gets embedded is the version already on the InDesign page—the version from the last read of the assigned ICML. If the absent writer made any changes to the checked-out content, those will be lost.

To give the assignment to another InCopy user, add the frame to an assignment again just as you did the first time.

Recovering from Broken Assignment Files

When you create assignments and generate story files, ICML documents are added to the Links panel (Window ➤ Links) as linked assets. Thus, even though a story is part of an assignment managed via the Assignments panel, it is also a linked external asset and is therefore under the dominion of the Links panel. I would say that better than 99% of the time, you won't need to even think about the fact that assigned stories are also managed through the Links panel. The only time you will care is when something goes wrong with the assignment.

If the ICMA assignment file was lost, accidentally deleted, or somehow became corrupted, you could ostensibly be in a serious pickle. On a couple of occasions I've had clients call me in a panic because something happened to the ICMA and they could no longer update stories in InDesign or even work on them in InCopy. Of course, as is the order of the universe, such catastrophes never happen earlier than mere hours before a deadline. There's no need to panic, though, because the Links panel rides to the rescue.

Remember, an assignment ICMA is like a Book file INDB. The assignment file contains nothing more than its own name, the name and color of the assignee, and a list of ICML documents; the actual content of stories is within ICML files. As long as they survive, your assignment file can be re-created.

Collaborating with Remote Editors

Up until now we've been talking mostly about collaborating with network peers who have read/write access to the same shared folders as you. What about remote or mobile workers on either the InDesign or InCopy side of the assignment?

In my experience migrating *many* workflows, *many* writers and editors, to collaborative InCopy-InDesign workflows, those that include at least one remote or mobile worker outnumber those that have all design and editorial personnel in-house. Originally, Adobe's LiveEdit Workflow was built entirely around the belief that everyone would have read/write access to the same central file location. That, of course, handicapped any workflows that weren't all networked yet still wanted collaborative efficiency, control, and freedom with InCopy and InDesign. Worse, because InCopy shows all stories in the assignment in a continuous interface, many editorial department recipients of ICMA and ICML documents had difficulty with the idea that they needed to return multiple email attachments to the designer (see Figure 14.13). *It looks like one document, so why do I have to send several documents?* That confusion often led to only ICMA assignment files being sent back to layout artists; of course, ICMA files alone are useless to anyone. Additionally, using File ➤ Open in InCopy showed both the ICMA and ICML files to the InCopy user. Given the fact that Mac and Windows applications may hide many document filename extensions by default, the editors' confusion was further compounded by having several similarly named files and no clear indicator of which they needed to select in the File Open dialog.

Adobe's answer to these problems was assignment *packages*, single files that, like a ZIP or StuffIt archive, include multiple files compressed into one. In this case, the contents of the package are assignment files, ICML stories, and, optionally, linked image assets used by the layout in the assignment. As I alluded to previously, assignment packages are intended for remote workers, but they aren't *solely* for remote workers. They also address the very real, very large problem of too many files confusing users and paralyzing the InCopy side of the workflow. Both InCopy and InDesign can open and work with assignment packages and send them to each

other. InCopy users only have to deal with a single package file—InCopy will extract the ICMA and ICML on the fly as part of the file-opening process and will recompress the files again after closing the ICAP package. *And*, the act of sending a package to InDesign or InCopy users auto-matically checks out content to the recipient, preventing accidental double modification by the sender or anyone else.

FIGURE 14.13
Opening an assignment file in InCopy presents a Story Editor view of all assigned stories inline for easy editing.

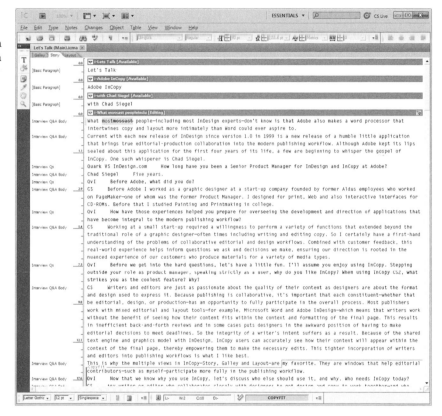

To create a package from within InDesign, begin by creating an assignment as usual and adding content. In the Assignment Options dialog, decide whether to check that option we skipped earlier, Include Linked Image Files When Packaging. Including them allows InCopy users to see high-resolution images but increases the size of the package. Excluding them causes InDesign to generate and include low-resolution proxies that are fine for onscreen viewing and printing to desktop laser and ink-jet printers. I recommend the latter, especially if you intend to email the package. With the assignment and content created, choose Package for InCopy from the Assignments panel flyout menu. You'll be prompted to name the new package. After you save the package, a cute gift box in InCopy purple will appear beside the assignment name in the Assignments panel (see Figure 14.14). At the same time, the content in the packaged assign-ment will be checked out.

FIGURE 14.14
Packaged assign-
ments are denoted
by special icons—
an InCopy pack-
age (left) and an
InDesign package
(right).

You can send the package to your editorial colleague by FTP, email, or even pocket flash drive. If your plan is to email the package, save yourself a couple of steps. Instead of choosing Package for InCopy from the Assignments panel flyout menu, choose Package for InCopy and Email. In one fell swoop InDesign will package up the assignment, pop open an email, and attach the package to the email. Fill in the recipient's email address and maybe a friendlier message than "Your assignment is attached," and click Send. Now get to work on the next project while editorial takes care of writing, editing, and polishing the copy without burdening you.

On the other side, your editorial counterpart will receive the package by email. She should then save it to disk and open it in InCopy—either by double-clicking the ICAP file or using the File ➢ Open command in InCopy. When she's finished editing and it's time to send the content back to the layout, she should choose File ➢ Package ➢ Return for InDesign and Email to generate and send an IDAP package back to you (see Figure 14.15). Her InCopy package will lock down the content as checked out to someone else (you).

FIGURE 14.15
InCopy's Package
menu

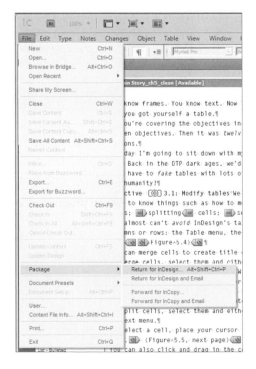

When it arrives, you can either double-click the IDAP or choose Open Package from the fly-out menu on the Assignments panel. The package will marry up with the INDD layout, updating and checking in the assigned frames in that publication.

Instead of sending the package back to you, the InCopy user can also send it to other InCopy users. That's what the Forward for InCopy and Forward for InCopy and Email commands in the Package menu do. Either will create a new ICAP InCopy package, lock and check out the content, and send it on to the next editor who needs to review the same content. That next editor will either send it back to you or on to the next editor in the chain for review and markup.

One crucial limitation of the Package For system is the fact it can be used only from InDesign to InCopy, InCopy to InDesign, and InCopy to InCopy. You can't package for another InDesign user. That's a problem when designers need to collaborate, or when, as in about one-third of the publishing workflows with whom I consult, editorial also works in InDesign rather than in InCopy.

Adobe hasn't given you a way to accommodate remote or mobile workers collaborating with InDesign, but I will; see "Collaborating with Anyone on Any File," later in this chapter.

Copy before Layout

Up to this point, the way we've been talking, it may seem that everything, including the copy, begins in InDesign. That's not necessarily true. Often that's the case exactly—you design a frame-first layout or template and then build InCopy assignments from empty frames or frames filled with placeholder text. Just as common, however, are workflows that begin with editorial personnel writing first drafts and then you laying out those first drafts to build a document. How does collaboration and the LiveEdit Workflow fit into a workflow wherein copy is written before layout begins? Not too dissimilarly, as it turns out.

Here's one common scenario:

1. A freelance writer writes his first draft in Microsoft Word and submits the DOC (or DOCX) file to his editor.

2. The editor imports the DOC file into InCopy for initial editing and saves the document as a native ICML InCopy document.

3. Even as the InCopy document is exported back to a Word-compatible RTF document and sent to the writer for revision, the editor passes the first-draft ICML to the design department so that page allocation, illustration, and layout may begin.

4. The designer places the ICML document and begins page composition.

From this point, the workflow can progress along two possible routes, as detailed in the following sections.

Placing the Document as a Linked Asset

You can place the ICML document as a linked asset and forgo assignments altogether. ICML documents are native InCopy documents. Functionally, they are identical to the ICML story files generated when content is added to an assignment—except they are not wrapped in assignments. There will be no check-in/checkout control via the Assignments panel in either application. Double modification is prevented by the fact that, in a network environment, only one

person at a time may open the file from the shared location. If all parties are not working from the same shared folder, there is no protection against double modification of the copy.

Additionally, unassigned ICML files do not include layout information or a layout preview. Switching to InCopy's Layout view while editing such a story presents a blank page rather than the copyfit page. More importantly, because unassigned ICML files do not include bidirectional communication with InDesign, editors will not know if copy over- or undersets. The ICML remains in the custody of editorial personnel. When they change and save the file to a shared network folder, it is updated within InDesign like any external asset managed by the Links panel.

I don't recommend this option because it is functionally no different than placing native Word DOCs. Editorial isn't allowed the insight into how text fits into and looks on the page, and it will be up to you to verify their work after every revision, ensuring that copy hasn't overset, cutting off the end, or underset, leaving empty lines. This negates several of the most important benefits of using InCopy in the publication workflow. You're back to babysitting the page copy, and editorial is back to requesting proofs after every revision.

BUILDING AN ASSIGNMENT AROUND AN INCOPY DOCUMENT

Instead of leaving the ICML document as a stand-alone linked asset, you place it the first time and then build an assignment around it. The assignment is then saved to a shared folder or sent as an assignment package back to the editor. The ICMA then enables check-in/checkout, prevents double modification, and gives the editor a window onto—and the ability to edit within—the laid-out page.

The downside to creating an assignment after beginning with an ICML is not a technological one but a habitual challenge. For everything to work, the editor must stop using his ICML file directly and switch to opening the ICMA assignment or ICAP assignment package. In fact, if the assigned version was saved to a different location than the original ICML, he must delete the original ICML. For some editors, these simple alterations to the familiar process of using the same story file from start to finish can be quite confusing, which leads to mistakes and frustration.

Keep in mind that the computer experience of some editorial people is limited solely to default, uncustomized installations of Web browsers, the corporate email client, and Microsoft Word. I'm not speaking derogatorily about writers and editors here (remember, I'm both as well as a designer). Rather, I'm pointing out the reality that editorial's work demands much less interaction with, and knowledge of, technology than does production's work. Technologically challenged personnel may save all their documents to a single location on their hard drives, leading to massively overcrowded Home (Mac) or My Documents (Windows) folders. They will therefore likely save the ICMA or ICAP to the same folder containing the original ICML, which, if they don't delete the original ICML, will probably result in the wrong file being edited at some point.

If you opt to generate assignments after receiving first-draft ICML documents for initial placement—and I heartily advise that you do—be prepared to assist members of the editorial team who are not comfortable with technology. I recommend you create a numbered list of steps to take after the assignment has been delivered to them. Include in the list how and where to save email attachments (if you email assignment packages); how to locate and delete the original ICML; how to open the ICMA or ICAP, paying special attention to the fact that some editorial computers will not show the .icma or .icap filename extension; and, if using assignment packages, how to send the package back to you or on to the next editor. Print out these instructions for each editor, and suggest that each affix it to the side of his monitor until he's gone through the new procedures a few times.

Collaborating with a Big Cheese

If the editor in chief, quality control, or other nondesign person needs access to edit the majority of stories in your publication, don't send just assignments. Send the InDesign document (or documents) itself, too. InCopy can directly open and save (but not create) INDD files. Then, the InCopy-using Big Cheese can check out and edit the contents of *any* frame in the document. The Big Cheese can also use the Track Changes feature in InCopy to record his or her changes, as well as to approve or reject copy changes made by other editors. Of course, the frames themselves cannot be altered. Note that you will still need to create one or more assignments, and add all stories to it or them. InCopy can open the INDD, but in order for it to checkout individual stories, those stories must be external ICML files managed by an ICMA assignment. The Big Cheese will just never have to directly deal with them; instead he will open and work with the INDD directly, while InCopy manages the assignment and individual story files in the background.

Tracking Changes

CS5

Like InCopy for several versions, InDesign CS5 can now finally track text changes, too. Changes tracked by either InCopy or InDesign automatically continue to be tracked in the other. Most tracked changes are visible only in Story Editor, but, with Track Changes enabled, InDesign will highlight all text insertions and preserve deletions and replacements as highlighted, struck-through text. Each change may then either be approved or rejected, or all changes may be approved or rejected wholesale.

Enable change tracking on one or all stories in the current document by selecting the appropriate command from the Type ➤ Track Changes menu. There you may also navigate between changes, as well as approve or reject individual changes or all changes in the current story in the document.

Or you can do all of that and more on the new Track Changes panel, which you'll find hiding on the Window menu's Editorial submenu (see Figure 14.16). The buttons along the top of the panel are, in order:

Enable/Disable Track Changes in the Current Story

View/Hide Changes

goto Preview Change

goto Next Change

Accept (the current) Change

Reject (the current) Change

Approve All Changes in the Story

Reject All Changes in the Story

FIGURE 14.16
The Track Changes
panel

Beneath the buttons the three fields tell you

◆ Who made the change (using whatever name was given to InDesign or InCopy in the User dialog)

◆ The date and time the change was made

◆ What type of change it was, whether inserted or deleted text

Track Changes is a much-needed improvement, even though it tracks only inserted, deleted, or replaced text, not object-level operations or even style changes to text. Still, it fills a hole that drove many editors back to Word just to have change tracking.

Collaborating with Anyone on Any File

Let's be brutally honest here: Adobe doesn't get the concept of collaboration. In spite of—no, in large part *because* of—the way in which InDesign and InCopy interrelate, because of the failed and now discontinued Adobe Version Cue file versioning "technology," it's obvious that Adobe either doesn't understand that the modern creative professional works within a team of creative professionals or they simply don't know how to build software to account for that fact.

They've long known that more than 90% of users of one Adobe creative pro product also use another and that nearly as many also use three or more Adobe products. Yet it's only in the last three versions of Creative Suite that Adobe has truly focused on making some of their products really look and work alike, making the experience of a single user moving from, say, InDesign to Illustrator to Photoshop familiar and consistent. Of course, Web Suite stars Flash, Fireworks, and Dreamweaver don't have the same user experience as InDesign, Illustrator, and Photoshop, so, clearly, Adobe is still trying to get the single-user workflow down. They haven't even begun to get the multiuser workflow.

InCopy and InDesign are in version 7, but neither the LiveEdit workflow nor the Package For features actually addresses the needs of a collaborative design and editorial workflow. For that matter, assignments are clunky and error prone, but we're stuck with that for now. As to the rest, well, there are inexpensive and usually free non-Adobe solutions to make everything work. Thanks to third-party file synchronization services like Dropbox, we're *not* bound to the idea that every collaborator must be on the network or to the requirement to use clunky, counterintuitive packages.

Dropbox Remote Collaboration

When you need greater collaborative control than offered by the built-in Package For features, turn to a third-party file-synchronization service. There are plenty of them out there, but I recommend Dropbox. Dropbox (`http://Dropbox.com`) is an on-demand or always-on (your choice) file-synchronization service. Once the minimal software is installed on both your computer and your collaborator's, and the files on which you wish to collaborate are added to your shared `Dropbox` folder, changes made to the files by one of you will instantly update the copy on the other's computer. In other words, you'll be working on the same files, without dealing with packaging. Dropbox is platform agnostic, meaning it can synchronize files from your Mac to your collaborator's Windows machine and vice versa—I even have Dropbox on my Android OS phone and my iPad.

Moreover, Dropbox has built-in version control (see Figure 14.17)! Want to compare the version of a layout as you last left it against the changes made overnight by the editor in New Delhi? Easy!

FIGURE 14.17
The Dropbox.com version-control interface managing versions of a file on which I'm collaborating

I'm not trying to sell you on Dropbox; there are several similar services out there. Before Dropbox I used Windows Live Sync (`http://sync.live.com`) which has great features but lacks Dropbox's versioning backup and comparison. I have personally brought the third-party file-synchronization collaboration model into over a dozen workflows, and every one of them *immediately* worked better, more efficiently, and more securely, recognizing the following benefits:

Automatic File Synchronization   No one has to package files or email them to one another. As long as every team member has Internet access, the files are automatically kept in synch across all team members' computers.

Notification of Changes   Dropbox (and, again, other third-party file-synchronization services) offer the option of alerting users via a desktop pop-up window when new files are added or new versions of files have been downloaded. This gives team members a heads-up about changes they may need to review.

Nonlocal Check-in/Checkout Control   Whether a story is checked in or checked out is a flag set in the file itself. Thus, when assignments and stories are managed via Dropbox, and someone checks out a story for editing, that story gets locked to all team members no matter where they are, just as if they were all working from a local network.

Version Tracking, Comparison, and Accountability   Because Dropbox creates a backup of a document as a new version every time someone makes a change, it provides clear accountability of who changed the document and when, enables comparison of versions, and allows the project manager to roll back the document to a prior version instantly.

Any Document Collaboration   InDesign assignments and packages can manage only InDesign's documents and assets—INDD, IDML, INCA, and ICML documents and their images. Because Dropbox (et al.) is not a part of InDesign, it can manage *any* files on which your team needs to collaborate, including all the InDesign-related files as well as PDFs, Microsoft Word and Excel documents (both of which may be made into linked assets for

placement into InDesign), Photoshop or Illustrator documents, HTML files, QuarkXPress documents—*anything*. Thus, it's not just an InDesign-InCopy solution but a full workflow collaboration solution.

Give Dropbox or another service a try, even among collaborators who share a network connection, and I guarantee you'll see immediate benefits. At the very least, the file versioning and version comparison alone are worth the (usually free) cost of the Dropbox service.

Sending Documents for Review

When a document needs to be sent to a client for review, most of us create and send a PDF. That PDF then comes back to us inclusive of comments and markups. If you're like me, you open the PDF in Acrobat over on one monitor, bring up the original document in InDesign on another monitor, and go page-by-page through both files making changes.

I'll spare you the long discussion of how to create and manage PDF-based reviews for two reasons:

◆ First, it's a complicated, inefficient process rendered moot by the inclusion of CS Review in InDesign CS5.

◆ Second, as I write this, Acrobat 9 is the current version, but by the time this book hits the shelves, Acrobat 10 will almost certainly be available, thus rendering many of the commands and screenshots I would provide useless.

Included in InDesign, Illustrator, and Photoshop CS5 is CS Review. Part in-application panel, part Web-based service, CS Review enables you to easily share snapshots of a document online and receive feedback directly in the application. It allows you to initiate and manage a review from directly within InDesign (or Illustrator or Photoshop, but that topic is for *Mastering Illustrator CS5* and *Mastering Photoshop CS5*) and then to review and accept, reject, and effect requested changes all directly in InDesign, in the document under review.

Connecting to CS Review

Before you can do anything with CS Review, you'll need an Adobe ID. An Adobe ID is your universal logon to all of Adobe's online services, including your product registrations, the user Forums, the (apparently abandoned) Adobe Marketplace, Acrobat.com, CS Live, and other services.

Chances are you already have an Adobe ID, if through no other action than simply registering an Adobe product (like InDesign CS5). If you've forgotten your Adobe ID or password, or you never obtained an Adobe ID, you can set one up for free. Just visit Adobe.com and click the Your Account link at the top. If there isn't one (the site changes from time to time like any other website), try going directly to the following URL: `https://www.adobe.com/cfusion/membership/`.

Once you have your Adobe ID, open the CS Review panel within InDesign from Window ➢ Extensions ➢ CS Review. The initial view on the panel will look like Figure 14.18. Click the Sign In button to enter your Adobe ID (email address) and password. When you do, the CS Review panel, which is really a portal with a direct link to Adobe's servers—and thus requires an active Internet connection in order to work—will log you into the CS Live system. Thereafter, the CS Review panel maintains an always-on connection to Acrobat.com/CS Live. Comments on any document currently under review will populate the panel.

FIGURE 14.18
The CS Review panel before logging in with an Adobe ID

Initiating a Review

You can send any InDesign document—in whole or in part—out for a Web-based review. And doing so is surprisingly easy. Let's walk through the steps:

1. Open or create an InDesign document you'd like to send for review, and make sure the CS Review panel is open as well.

2. From the bottom of the CS Review panel click the sticky-note-like Create a New Review button.

3. Up will pop the Create New Review dialog (see Figure 14.19). Enter the name of the review—something client friendly—and check Add Active Document to Review.

FIGURE 14.19
The Create New Review dialog

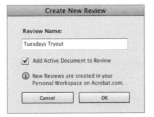

4. When you click OK in the Create New Review dialog, the Upload Settings dialog will appear (see Figure 14.20). Set the various options, which I'll discuss immediately below, and then press Upload. InDesign will then upload the document in its "parts" to CS Review on Acrobat.com.

FIGURE 14.20
Choosing the
Upload Settings for
the review docu-
ment

Before you click Upload, however, let's take a look at the various options available:

Page Range   In the Page Range section choose whether to send the entire document (All Pages) for review, just the current page, or a specific page range. Note that each page becomes what CS Review calls a "part." If you upload pages 1–3, each page will be termed a part in the CS Review panel, in the browser-based review window, and everywhere else. It's a tuh-mey-toh/tuh-mah-toh thing.

Quality   In a CS Review it isn't really the document pages that are shared, it's *snapshots* of the document pages, JPEG images. The Quality field effectively sets the resolution of the images created from the pages, either Low, Medium, or High.

Intent   Your Intent options are Print, Web, and Murderous. Choosing Print displays the snapshot(s) on the Web with overprint preview activated, and it sets the 100% zoom size to equal the paper size. Choosing Web deactivates overprint preview and sets the 100% zoom to match the pixel dimensions in the Document Setup dialog box. Choosing Murderous intent sends your document, IP address, and global positioning coordinates to local law enforcement for a PDF-based review.

View Online after Upload Complete   Check this option to, er, view it online after the upload completes. Just like viewing a PDF immediately after export, this option proofs your CS Review document to you but in a Web browser rather than in Acrobat. I recommend checking this not only so you can see how your newly initiated review looks, but because you *have* to go to the Web interface to invite clients to review it. Making it open automatically saves you a step.

5. After the document snapshot uploads, you'll have a new entry on the CS Review panel. The entry will carry the title you gave it along with a preview icon, the numbers of under-review pages, a count of the number of times the document has been viewed, and the count of comments left on the document (see Figure 14.21).

6. The next step is to invite clients to review the document. You can do this by clicking the Share button at the bottom of the CS Review panel, which is just a shortcut to launch the document's Acrobat.com CS Review page (see Figure 14.22). It's there that you must actually share the file. Click the Share File button in the lower-left corner of the window, and then click Share It with Individuals.

FIGURE 14.21
The parts of CS Review panel entries, showing documents under active review

Snapshot Thumbnail

Number of Active Reviewers and
Co-Authors Versus Number Invited

Number of Times the Review has Been Viewed

Number of Comments

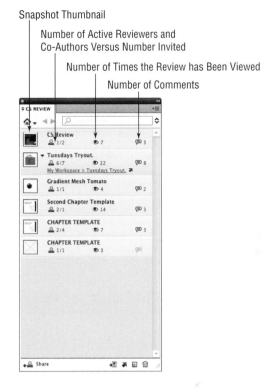

FIGURE 14.22
The CS Review page of a document

7. In the Share dialog, create a message to send to your client's personnel, inviting them to review the design online (see Figure 14.23). Enter comma- or semicolon-separated email addresses for recipients in the People to Share With field, set a subject, and enter a message. (There are also a few other options, and I'll discuss them shortly.)

8. Finally, click the Share button to send the email review invitations.

FIGURE 14.23
Inviting reviewers to the document

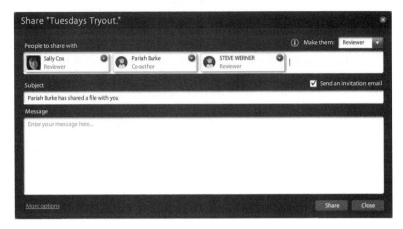

You have just initiated a review. Each of your invitees will receive an email similar to the one in Figure 14.24 inviting him to review your document. Note that each reviewer must have an Adobe ID, which he may obtain from Acrobat.com after clicking the review link in the email. Reviewing documents is entirely free to your invitees. For the first year at least after you install InDesign or any CS5 product, it's also free to you. As of this writing, Adobe has neither set a definitive time at which they will begin charging for CS Review nor the price(s) they'll charge. All they'll say to date is that it's "free for at least the first year."

FIGURE 14.24
A CS Review invitation email

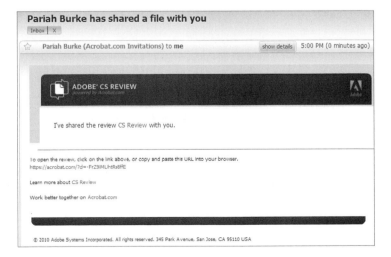

Review Sharing Options

Before getting into how the review will actually work, I want to explain those extra options we skipped in the Share dialog. Refer back to Figure 14.23 as we go through them.

In the top-right corner you may choose whether invited reviewers are actually reviewers or co-authors. Reviewers may add comments and delete their own comments but not others'. Additionally, after someone else replies to a reviewer's comment, the author of the original comment cannot delete the comment or the reply. Co-authors, by contrast, have all the same privileges you do. Namely, they can add parts (again, better known as "pages") to the review, add their own comments, and delete or flag comments and replies made by others.

Between the People to Share With and the Subject field is a check box labeled Send an Invitation Email. This may seem pedantic, but if you toggle it on and off you'll begin to understand the difference. With Send an Invitation Email checked, you will actually send emails to those listed in the People to Share With field. Uncheck the option, however, and Acrobat.com will not send emails, thus the Subject and Message fields disappear. You might not want to send emails if the people whom you're inviting to review the document *already* have Acrobat.com accounts. In that case, it won't email them, but it will add the document to their Acrobat.com personal workspaces (a list of documents active on the account). For example, let's say your client, Sarah, already uses Acrobat.com (maybe Sarah is a big Buzzword fan). Rather than clutter her inbox, you could disable the Send an Invitation Email option, enter Sarah's e-mail address in the People to Share With field, and click Share. Instead of an email, your new document will appear in Sarah's Acrobat.com workspace (think personal home page or dashboard). Sarah will notice it (hopefully) and open it for review.

At the bottom left of the Share dialog is a subtle hyperlink called More Options. Clicking it reveals the Re-Sharing options, which determine whether anyone with whom you or someone else has shared the document can herself share it with others, or whether only those designated as co-authors may share the document.

Not incidentally, you can also set each invitee's role—reviewer or co-author—individually without multiple trips to the Share dialog. Each recipient entry in the People to Share With field bears a black-and-white arrow in the corner. Clicking this arrow presents you with the option to remove the recipient and to indicate whether the recipient should be assigned the reviewer or co-author role.

After sharing the document, each of the review participants will be listed in the bottom row of the CS Review window. In each you will also find an arrow offering the same commands to change the participant's role or remove him entirely. Hovering over each participant's name will slide up a small tile informing you of the last time the person viewed or edited the document.

At any time you may invite more people to review the document—or see a list of those already been invited—from the Share File button in the bottom left of the CS Review window.

Reviewing Online

CS Review is not, by any stretch of the imagination, the most feature-packed document-collaboration or client-review service. The only markup possible is the addition of comments and replies to those comments. Reviewers can't draw lines or circles or cloud shapes, as they can with PDF-based reviews, nor can they highlight text—because there isn't any text; it's just a pixel image snapshot of your InDesign page. What it lacks in markup, though, it more than makes

up for in convenience because the review happens online, but the InDesign user can watch and interact with it entirely within InDesign itself.

Adding a comment to a page inside the Web-based CS Review session is a point-click-type operation. Your client clicks somewhere within the page snapshot, usually on the object or area about which she'd like to comment. Then the client types her comment. Where she clicked is now a marker for her comment, as indicated by a colored circle visible on the page snapshot when Comments Showing is enabled in the CS Review menu bar. The client may also click and drag to define a rectangular area for the marker rather than a small circle. The comment itself appears in the right sidebar (see Figure 14.25). Clicking, or just hovering the cursor over, either the comment or its marker will automatically highlight the other for easy identification. If a comment's marker isn't visible on the current page at the current zoom level, you can click the Jump To link at the bottom of the comment to alter the view to show the marker.

FIGURE 14.25
Comments and their markers in a document under review

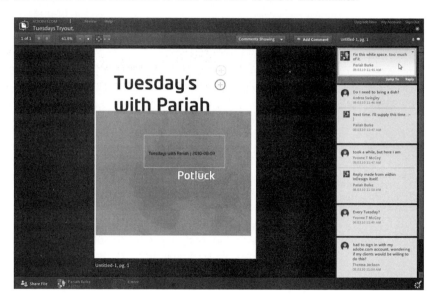

Each comment may also be replied to in order to create a threaded conversation. For instance, if Devon asks for a change, Aidan may reply to Devon's comment disagreeing with him. Kiley may then reply to Aidan in support of Devon's original comment. At some point you may want to jump in with a reply to the original comment or one of the rejoinders (or you might not; Devon, Kiley, and Aidan sound a little disorganized). Conversations can go quite deep.

You and anyone to whom you've given the role of co-author can delete comments by choosing that option from the little arrow menu that appears in the top-right corner of a comment when that comment is selected. You may also edit or copy the text of a comment or reply. Of course, as the InDesign user, you'll likely do all this from within InDesign.

Reviewing within InDesign

Getting back to InDesign, any comments added by any review participants on Acrobat.com will automatically also appear in the CS Review panel. Each part (page) in the review will be listed separately under the entry named after the full review title. Each page will list comments added

by reviewers, co-authors, and you, along with their replies and rejoinders (see Figure 14.26). The entire conversation is visible within the CS Review panel. Clicking a comment will show inline in the panel a thumbnail of its comment marker from the document snapshot; thus you can see the context for the comment!

FIGURE 14.26
Comments and their markers in a document under review

An even better way to understand the context of a comment is to see the comment markers *directly in the layout*. You can do that by clicking the button on the bottom of the CS Review panel marked Show Comments in Layout. With that on, the circles and/or rectangles created by your reviewers as comment markers become visible right on the pages of your InDesign document. The markers are not selectable objects on the page, though; they're merely overlay indicators—*magic markers*, if you will.

Right-clicking a comment on the CS Review panel pops up the familiar Reply, Copy Text, Edit, and Delete commands, as well as an option to View Online, which will launch the Web-based Acrobat.com CS Review window, and a submenu called Flag. As you work through the comments left in the document by your client and collaborators, flag each comment as To Do, Done, Approved, Rejected, Disregard, or Needs Review. Each flag creates a new reply to the comment (or reply), flagged as indicated, with or without annotation from the flagger.

A few other things to note about working with the CS Review panel:

◆ Beneath the title of each page in a review project is a space for a caption for that page. Double-click the word <*Caption*> to type in an optional description of that page.

◆ Clicking the Home button at the top of the panel returns you to the list of all active reviews.

◆ You need not have an under-review document opened in InDesign in order to see the number of times it's been viewed, how many comments it contains, and, indeed, even the comments themselves. All you need is InDesign opened with the CS Review panel visible.

- The CS Review panel doesn't manage just InDesign documents under review. The CS Review panel in any of the applications that use it—InDesign, Illustrator, and Photoshop—shows and enables you to manage all active reviews created from any of the programs—reviews of InDesign documents, Illustrator artwork, and Photoshop images, all from within InDesign or Illustrator or Photoshop.

- Right-clicking the entry for a page in an active under-review document offers you the option Open Source File, which will open the document in its creating application.

- When a review is finished, highlight it in the CS Review panel and click the Delete (trashcan) button.

- To initiate a second, separate review of the same document, choose Save As from the context-sensitive menu that appears when you right-click an active review.

- If you're managing many reviews at once, or a review has many comments, use the search field at the top of the panel to find what you're looking for.

Sharing Reusable Settings

Collaboration doesn't just mean sharing a page or a document. Often designers work together on separate documents within the project, on different projects of a larger campaign, or, especially within in-house creative and production departments, with a variety of different projects and campaigns that share common attributes. Whenever a designer re-creates something that would more easily be obtained another way, time and money are wasted. I don't know about you, but I *hate* blowing time or money on anything that doesn't bring a smile to somebody's face.

Although everything that follows has been covered, in depth, in other chapters, a review is warranted. Besides, here it's all in one place, in succinct how-tos. The following settings may be saved out of InDesign as reusable settings and then shared to other InDesign or InCopy users.

Dictionaries

User dictionaries, including added, removed, ignored, and excepted spellings and hyphenations, can be shared. (There's more on dictionaries in Chapter 8.)

Export   Go to Edit ➢ Spelling ➢ Dictionary and click the Export button. You'll be prompted to save a Word List.txt file. Change the filename to something unique and meaningful in case the recipient receives multiple exported dictionaries.

Import   Go to Edit ➢ Spelling ➢ Dictionary and click the Import button. When prompted, locate the TXT file you received from a collaborator. Importing a dictionary adds it to the current document's document-level dictionary. If you import a dictionary with all documents closed, the word list will become part of the default InDesign dictionary and thus applicable to all new documents you create.

Paragraph, Character, Table, Cell, and Object Styles

The various styles aren't saved to external files but rather become part of the INDD documents in which they're used. Thus, there is no export instruction. (More on all of these can be found in Chapter 13, "Efficiency"; paragraph and character styles are also discussed in Chapter 2, "Text," and object styles in Chapter 6, "Objects.")

On each of the Styles panels there is an Import command—for example, Import Character Styles on the Character Styles panel. Execute that command, and then, in the resulting Open dialog, navigate to and choose the INDD InDesign document or ICML InCopy document containing the styles you'd like to load into the current document. Loading styles with all documents closed makes those permanent parts of InDesign, and the styles will therefore be available in every new document you create.

Both the Character Styles and Paragraph Styles panels offer the Load All Text Styles command, which will load both character and paragraph styles in one step. Similarly, the Table Styles and Cell Styles panels have a command to load both of those in a single step as well.

Swatches

Like styles, color swatches are saved as part of the documents in which they're used. Unlike styles, however, they can also be saved to external files that can then be shared among other InDesign documents as well with Photoshop and Illustrator. (More on swatches can be found in Chapter 6.)

Export On the Swatches panel flyout menu, choose Save Swatches. This command is disabled until you select a nondefault swatch in the panel itself. When prompted, save the Adobe Swatch Exchange ASE file to disk.

Import Choose the Load Swatches command from the Swatches panel flyout menu in InDesign and load the ASE file. You'll find similar commands in Illustrator and Photoshop to import the same swatches.

Stroke Styles

You can share custom-designed striped, dotted, or dashed stroke styles. (You'll find more on stroke styles in Chapter 6.)

Export On the Strokes panel flyout menu, choose Custom Stroke Styles. If you have created any custom stroke styles, the Save button will be available. Click it and choose a destination for your stroke styles.

Import To import, return to the Custom Stroke Styles dialog and click the Load button.

Autocorrect Word Pairs

The moment you create or alter an autocorrect word pair via the Autocorrect pane in InDesign's preferences, a new file is created on disk to store it. There is no export. (Read more about Autocorrect in Chapter 8.)

Copy the language-specific XML file (e.g., `English USA.xml`) from the source system to the same location on the destination system. That location is as follows:

Mac `Applications/Adobe InDesign CS5/Presets/Autocorrrect/`

Windows XP/2000 `C:\Documents and Settings\[username]\Application Data\Adobe\InDesign\Version 7.0\en_US\Autocorrect\`

Windows 7/Vista `C:\Users\[username]\AppData\Roaming\Adobe\InDesign\Version 7.0\en_US\Autocorrect\`

Solution   If learners need help finding which menu commands are new or improved in InDesign CS5, remind them that the Window ➤ Workspace menu contains the New CS5 workspace, which, when active, will highlight such commands in blue. In the Edit ➤ Menus dialog box then, all the menu commands and submenus that must be disabled will note *Blue* in the right column. The directive to color additional menu commands green is another hint about how to accomplish the first part of the exercise. In the last part, disabling plug-ins, the results will vary. However, the only plug-ins disabled under Help ➤ Manage Extensions should be nonrequired APLN files with *Panel* in the name.

Change the Default Font, Colors, and More   Out of the box, InDesign CS5 uses Minion Pro 12/14.4 pt as the default text style and includes swatches for process magenta, cyan, and yellow and RGB red, green, and blue. These defaults are fine if your average document uses 12/14.4 Minion Pro and only solid process or RGB colors. But, if the average document you create requires another typeface, size, leading, other colors, or virtually any other option different from the defaults, change the defaults and save yourself some time.

Master It   Think about the documents you create most often. What is the type style—font family, font style, size, leading, and other formatting attributes—you use more than any other? Make those your new defaults. Do the same with your swatches, eliminating any colors you rarely use while adding those you use frequently.

Solution   All changes should be made with no documents opened. The result will vary widely from learner to learner, but at least something should be different about the Character and Swatches panels from the out-of-the-box configuration.

Carry Your Personalized InDesign Work Environment in Your Pocket or on Your iPod From freelancers brought into agency offices to assist with crunch time to students working in school labs, from round-the-clock production teams where different shifts use the same equipment to those dedicated enough to bring work home, seldom do creatives work solely on a single machine anymore. Creative and production personnel who switch computers waste a significant portion of their time customizing the InDesign environment of each computer on which they work even for a few minutes. To save time, nearly everything customizable about the InDesign CS5 working environment is portable. Customize one copy of InDesign, and carry your unique environment with you, making you instantly productive at any workstation.

Master It   After arranging your panels and customizing your keyboard shortcuts and menus, it's time to take your InDesign workspace with you. If you have a USB flash drive, an iPod, a smart phone, or even just a floppy disk handy, copy the files containing your customized environment to the storage device. Now, if a second computer is available with InDesign CS5 installed, install those files to that computer and set up InDesign CS5 your way.

Solution   The first step learners should undertake is to save a workspace as discussed in the section "Workspaces" in this chapter. While customizing keyboards and menu commands, they would have already created new sets of each but may need to save those sets again to reflect later changes. Once everything has been saved, they should follow the instruction in the section "InDesign in Your Pocket" to back up on the one system, and restore and activate on the second, their own workspaces, menus, and shortcuts.

Chapter 2: Text

Create and Fill Text Frames   Setting type is InDesign's primary function, and it performs that function better than any other application. The fundamental building block of type in InDesign is the text frame container and the text content.

> **Master It**   Create a new text frame, and then place the flawed text file, `bad-lorem.txt`, into it. Clean up the resulting text to make it readable. When finished with that, place the document `loremWord.doc` into the same text frame after the first imported document.

> **Solution**   As described in the how-to exercises under the "Getting Text into Text Frames" heading, students should import `bad-lorem.txt` and then the `loremWord.doc` document, making use of Show Import Options in both cases.

Span and Split Columns   The ability to set some paragraphs to span or split columns, reaching across multiple columns in the same text frame or further dividing areas of a frame to a greater number of columns, is a huge time and effort saver. Previously designers had to create multiple frames to answer these needs, resulting in significant time and effort spent creating all those frames, and even more when modifying them for every little change.

> **Master It**   Create an editorial-style page layout complete with headline, kicker, and byline, all spanning two-column body copy. Do it in one text frame.

> **Solution**   This exercise is exactly the one performed step-by-step in the "Spanning All Columns" section. Learners should follow those steps to achieve the results presented in the figures in that section.

Format Text Frames   Correctly formatting and configuring text frames will save effort and time not only now but also every time a frame or its content changes.

> **Master It**   Using the text frame created in the previous exercise, convert it from a single column into three, with a 0.25-inch gutter. At the same time, give the text some breathing room by setting top and bottom insets of 0.1667 inches and no inset on the sides.

> **Solution**   Using the Text Frame Options dialog, students should set the number of columns to three, change the gutter width, and uncheck Fixed Column Width. To effect the inset spacing, they will need to disable the Make All Settings the Same chain-link option and individually set the top and bottom insets.

Format Paragraphs   Paragraphs must be separated and styled to enable legibility and facilitate readability. That can be accomplished through alignment, indents, paragraph spacing, and drop caps.

> **Master It**   Continuing with the multicolumn frame of placed stories, let's make them readable. In the first full paragraph of each story, add a drop cap of two to three lines. Separate the same paragraphs from anything that may come before with a comfortably large paragraph space before. Give the rest of the paragraphs a correct first-line indent and, to control runts, a last-line right indent. Because we have three probably narrow columns, let's make clean, ragless paragraphs.

> **Solution**   The result should have two drop caps, first- and last-line indentation on all paragraphs except those with drop caps, and vertical spacing on the two lead paragraphs (those containing the drop caps). All should be set to force justify (no ragged edge).

4. In InDesign, configure Live Captions via the Caption Setup dialog to approximately match the settings in the following image. Note that the order of the caption rows, as well as the location for the caption, and any text before and after are all at the preference of the learner.

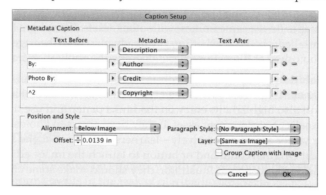

5. Choose File ➤ Place, and in the Place dialog navigate to and select the images previously modified in Bridge.

6. Still in the Place dialog, check the box beside the Generate Static Captions option, and then click OK.

7. Place the images. A Live Captions text frame whose content matches the assigned configuration should be automatically generated beneath each image.

Chapter 6: Objects

Use Attribute-Level Transparency and Object Effects   InDesign attribute-level transparency and transparency-based object effects allow more to be done inside InDesign with live object effects than ever before.

Master It   Place an image onto the page. Above that image, create a text frame and fill it with placeholder type. Fill and stroke the frame. Using the new attribute-level transparency and object effects…

◆ Give the frame an inner glow and blend it back with the photo such that the frame tints the photo.

◆ Make the type gradually disappear into its background as it moves from the top down.

◆ Give the stroke a drop shadow and blending mode that alter the background image just in the area of the stroke.

Solution   Results will vary widely with the images, colors, and blending modes chosen, but learners should all do each of the following:

◆ Select in the Effects dialog Settings for Fill, add an inner glow, and either alter overall transparency of the fill or change its blending mode.

◆ Select in the Effects dialog Settings for Text, and apply the default gradient feather with either a –90° angle or 90° and reversed.

◆ Select in the Effects dialog Settings for Stroke, change its blending mode, and apply a drop shadow.

Design Custom Stroke Styles   Although the stroke styles that come with InDesign are perfect for many occasions, they fall short of perfect for others. That's why InDesign lets you create your own.

Master It   Create a new Dash type stroke style that looks like the following graphic—dot-dot-dash-dot-dot—which is Morse code for *ID*, InDesign's identifier among the Creative Suite 3 icons.

Solution   Learners should create a new stroke style that looks like the one depicted here. Some variance in pattern length and individual dash length and spacing is to be expected.

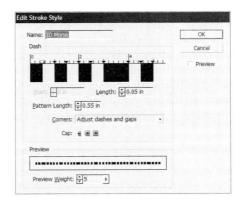

Create Mixed Ink Swatches and Share Swatches   Between creating mixed ink swatches and mixed ink swatch groups and sharing swatches across applications and documents, InDesign makes color fidelity and productivity easy.

Master It   Pick a new spot color and create shades of that spot by mixing black into a mixed ink group. Generate 10% tint swatches in the group. Save the document and exchange it with a partner. Both you and the partner should then add the mixed ink group swatches you both created into InDesign's default Swatches panel. If you're working alone, you can still do this portion of the exercise with the single document you created.

Solution   Following the instructions in the section "Mixed Inks" in this chapter, learners should first create a spot color swatch and then generate a mixed ink group with nine swatches, beginning with 10% black mixed with 100% spot color and progressing upward to 100% black. After saving and closing the document containing the mixed ink group, ensuring that no other document is opened in InDesign, learners should use the Load Swatches command on the Swatches panel to import swatches from that document into the panel to become part of InDesign's new default swatch list.

Chapter 9: Documents

Interact with Documents Visually and Change Zoom Level, View Modes, and Display Performance InDesign provides numerous means of changing the way you interact with documents, how fast they move, how you see them, and what you see.

Master It Open any InDesign document containing text and images on the same page. Open three different views of the same document, arranged simultaneously onscreen, zooming all to fit the page within the document window, and compare the views according to the following options:

- ◆ View 1: Preview mode with High-Quality Display display performance
- ◆ View 2: Layout mode with Fast Display display performance
- ◆ View 3: Bleed mode with Typical Display display performance

Solution Learners should open a document and then, using the Window ➢ Arrange ➢ New Window command, create two other views on the same document. They should then manually arrange the trio comfortably onscreen and by changing the View ➢ Display Performance setting and the different modes at the bottom of the Tools panel, establish the comparison described above.

Employ Page Transitions for PDF and SWF Output Page transitions add pizzazz to slideshow or Flash presentations.

Master It Open or create a set of slides in InDesign, one per page, and assign a different page transition to each page. At least some of the pages should use nondefault options for those transitions. Export your slideshow to interactive PDF or SWF and test it out.

Solution The results will vary depending on learners' preferred transitions and slides. What should be accomplished is that they have a playable PDF or SWF presentation that includes a selection of the 12 available page transition effects, and that some of those were customized from their default options via the Page Transitions panel.

Build and Manage Grids and Guides The foundation of any well-laid-out document is a well-thought-out grid.

Master It Create a new document and build a grid on the master page consisting of six equal columns and three equal rows within the page margins. Once that's done, apportion the top row into three equal sections.

Solution Learners should use the Layout ➢ Create Guides utility to create the initial grid with six and three, no gutters, and Fit Guides to Margins. Next, to divide the top row, they will have to manually drag down two horizontal ruler guides. After unlocking guides, they will precisely position the new manually created guides with the Transform or Control panel's Y field.

Work with Object-Oriented Layers The ability to see and interact with each object on the page via the Layers panel is a potentially large time and frustration saver, particularly when compared to other methods of selecting overlapping objects. Renaming object entries in the Layers panel helps you organize your work.

Master It Create a new document and place three similarly sized colored rectangles atop one another. The colors should be, in order from front to back, blue, red, and white. Use the Align panel (Window ➢ Object & Layout ➢ Align) to help line them

up if necessary. Then, in the Layers panel, reorder the objects such that, from front to back, they become red, white, and blue, and then rename the objects to **Foreground**, **Midground**, and **Background**.

Solution   Once the three rectangles have been created in the proper colors and sequence, learners should expand Layer 1 in the Layers panel by clicking its expansion arrow, which will reveal the entries for the rectangle objects. Learners should then drag and drop objects up or down as needed to reorder them into the prescribed color order. Each layer must then be renamed as instructed, by clicking, pausing, and clicking again the object entry to enter editing mode, and then its label must be typed in.

Create and Manage Book Files   Often one person finds it easier to work on longer documents by breaking them up into chapters or sections and connecting them via a book file. For workgroups wherein different people are responsible for different sections of the document, a book file is essential to productivity.

Master It   Working alone or in a group, create at least three InDesign documents of several pages of text each. Save each document, and then create a book file to connect the documents. Finally, create a single PDF from the entire book.

Solution   Learners should preferably team up to create InDesign documents and then designate one individual to create the book file. Once the book is set, the Export Book to PDF command should be chosen from the Book panel flyout menu.

Index Terms and Create an Index   An index helps readers find content. From simple keyword lists to complex, multilevel, topic-driven indices, InDesign handles them all, marrying index entries to referenced text through index markers.

Master It   Open or create an InDesign document containing a story of at least three pages in length. Working through the document, create index entries and cross-references for at least 10 words, one of which should be a word that repeats numerous times throughout the story (use a common word such as *the* if needed). Once the terms are indexed, generate and place the index story on a new page.

Solution   Learners may take several routes to accomplishing the indexing depending on the story and words chosen, although their methods should conform to those described in the sections "Creating Index Entries," "Cross-References," and "Power Indexing" under "Indexing" in this chapter. With all the options available to them in the Generate Index dialog, the final output will likely vary as well from learner to learner.

Create Tables of Contents   Tables of contents direct readers in logical or virtually any order to content, and InDesign's TOC options are varied and powerful for myriad uses.

Master It   Open or quickly create a rudimentary book-style document containing body text and several heading paragraphs utilizing at least two levels of headings. Create and assign paragraph styles for the body text and headings. Using what you've learned in this chapter, generate and place a hierarchal TOC.

Solution   Before beginning with the Layout ➤ Table of Contents command and the corresponding dialog, learners should create a document that has text and styles in the format of Heading 1, Heading 2, and Body Text, with several paragraphs of each style. Then, in the Table of Contents dialog, the Heading 1 and Heading 2 styles should be moved into the Include Paragraph Styles list, assigned Levels 1 and 2 respectively, and then the TOC placed into the document. The other options available for formatting the TOC will vary by learner.

Chapter 10: Preflight

Configure Color Management on Documents and Images Consistent color throughout the workflow is critical—even in grayscale jobs. With each version of Creative Suite, Adobe makes color management smarter, easier, and more consistent across the Creative Suite applications. However, the nature of color management is such that it works only if you configure it for the devices specific to your workflow.

Master It Configure Adobe Bridge to use the ICC profiles for your monitor and printer (or other output device) across all of Creative Suite. You can profile your devices yourself using Mac's Display Calibrator Assistant or Windows's Image Color Management. If you're configuring a high-end output device such as an imagesetter or proof printer, ask your print service provider for the most up-to-date ICC profile for the device. If you choose to configure color management for your desktop printer, either profile it yourself or visit the manufacturer's website; most OEMs include free, downloadable ICC profiles. These aren't specific to your printer's unique color-rendering characteristics, but they will get you close.

Solution Learners should profile their monitors using the basic method just described and obtain an ICC profile for an output device. Both should be installed through Adobe Bridge's Creative Suite Color Settings or even InDesign's individual Color Settings dialog.

Soft Proof Documents to Screen When software makers say *What You See Is What You Get (WYSIWYG)*, it's really not, not in the case of color, not from the typical working mode of applications. That's where soft proofing comes in. Its pixel-based preview still isn't a precise representation of what you can expect with ink on paper, but when configured correctly, InDesign gets it surprisingly close.

Master It Using one of your own documents or a sample from another chapter on this book's download page, proof the approximate expected output colors with your printer's ICC profile. Next, examine how the document will separate when sent to press and how transparency will flatten. Look for potential printing issues, and resolve them.

Solution Using the Customize Proof Conditions dialog and the Proof Colors command, learners will first observe their document colors shift into the chosen output device's gamut. Next, employing the Separations Preview and Flattener Preview panel, they'll look for problem areas.

Configure and Use Live Preflight and the Preflight Panel to Examine a Document for Problems Printing is about much more than just clicking the Print button. It requires planning and careful preparation. During design and certainly before output, you must make a number of design decisions critical to your artwork's printed quality. Then, when it is time to send away the job, you have options about how to do that.

Master It Create a new, comprehensive preflight profile. Name it **Check Everything**, give it a description to reflect that purpose, and set it to check for all the available conditions.

Solution Learners should follow the steps described in the "Creating a Preflight Profile" section to create the profile and then enable and set options for all the preflight conditions as described in the section titled "Preflight Conditions."

Chapter 11: Print

Manage the Inks Used in a Document   Ink Manager enables direct and granular control over the inks used in a document, including process and spot inks, ink type, neutral density, trapping sequence, and aliasing one ink to another.

> **Master It**   Aliasing one ink to another is an important task you may have to perform from time to time, particularly if you frequently place image assets created by different individuals or groups.

1. On the Swatches panel, create two spot color ink swatches—they can be any color, from any color library.

2. Create two large rectangles on a page, ensuring that they don't overlap. Color one rectangle using the first spot color and the other with the second.

3. Print separations of the file to your local laser or ink-jet printer. If you don't have one on hand, print separations to an Adobe PDF and then view the PDF file.

4. Back in InDesign, use Ink Manager to alias the second ink to the first.

5. Now print separations again, noting the difference in output this time from the previous separations print.

> **Solution**   At the end of the exercise learners should have three items: an InDesign document whose Swatches panel displays two spot colors; a first set of printed separations containing two plates, one for each colored rectangle; and a second, single-page separations output wherein both rectangles are printed as the same color, on the same plate.
>
> How to print separations is covered in the "InDesign Trapping vs. In-RIP Trapping" section under "Trapping," while aliasing one ink to the other is accomplished with understanding of the "Ink Manager" section on "Ink Alias."

Set an Object's Colors to Overprint   Overprinting is the process of setting an object's inks to print on top of any inks that may appear behind it. This results in mixing of the foreground and background colors. When the foreground color is black, the effect is minimal and may not be noticeable at all—particularly if all the black in the document always overprints ink beneath it. Overprinting cyan, magenta, or yellow, which are not as opaque as blank ink, on top of one another, however, will result in color mixing.

> **Master It**   Create two partially overlapping circles, each with a fill color and a heftily weighted stroke. Set the fill of the foreground circle to cyan and the fill of the background circle to magenta. Give both a 100% black stroke color. Now duplicate the pair of circles so that you have four circles—two sets—side-by-side. Configure the first set's foreground circle such that its fill overprints and the second set's foreground circle such that its fill is a knockout. Now activate Overprint Preview and examine the difference between the two sets of circles.

> **Solution**   After the learners create and assign fill and stroke colors to the circles, the foreground circle in the first set should be set to overprint by selecting the Overprint Fill option on the Attributes panel. Assigning a knockout option to the second set's

foreground circle is automatic; as long as Overprint Fill is *not* selected on the Attributes panel, the second circle will knock out ink behind it. Once the learner activates Overprint Preview, the result should be that the second set looks the same—a cyan circle partially obscuring the magenta circle behind it—while the first set shows cyan mixed with magenta in the area where the circles overlap.

Print Documents with Various Options   The Print dialog is the interface for printing documents to paper or even electronic files like PDFs or PostScript. Understanding the role of each of the panes is crucial to predictable printed output.

Master It   Open (or create) an 8.5×11-inch document and print a page or two to 8.5×11-inch paper, inclusive of all printer's marks. All marks must appear on the printed page.

Solution   Learners should print the document through the Print dialog available via the File ➤ Print command. In that dialog box All Printer's Marks should be enabled on the Marks and Bleed pane. In order to produce output wherein the artwork and those marks are printed, Scale to Fit must also be enabled on the Setup pane.

Produce Booklets and Output in Printer's Spreads   Imposing pages for output into printer's spreads or a bound document is a frequent need, one that many InDesign users look high and low to fill with a plug-in, all the while missing the fact that the function is already built into InDesign. Contrary to the terms most people look for within InDesign—*impose* or *imposition*, *paginate* or *printer's spreads*—Print Booklet is the tool for the job.

Master It   Create a new 32-page document. Now use Print Booklet to set up (but not necessarily print) a 2-Up Saddle Stitch booklet from the document. Be sure to account for the correct amount of creep, assuming you'd output to 28-lb bond stock.

Solution   The exercise should end with the Print Booklet dialog opened. The Booklet Type should be 2-Up Saddle Stitch. Following the creep calculation formula noted under "Creep" in the "Booklet Page Options" section, and after consulting Table 11.1, "Average thickness of common paper stocks," learners should have arrived at a Creep value of 0.0464 inches or 3.341 points. The Creep value is the number of signatures—four pages per signature, or 32 divided by 4, which yields 8 signatures—multiplied by the caliper of each sheet of paper, which, with 28-lb bond, is 0.0058 inches.

Package Documents, Images, and Fonts for Delivery or Archival   Packaging a document collects all the document image and font assets into folders along with a new copy of the InDesign document updated to point to those assets. Thus, packaging makes a document portable, reliant on no assets other than those in subfolders contained within the document's folder. A portable document can be easily transferred to service providers and collaborators or archived to CD or DVD.

Master It   Open any InDesign document that contains both images and text. Package the document such that it's ready for delivery or archival.

Solution   Learners should execute a package on the document via the File ➤ Package command and run through the Package dialog. Upon finishing the package, the learner should have a folder containing a copy of the InDesign document as well as two subfolders, `Images` and `Fonts`, containing all the assets required by the document.

Chapter 12: Export

Export Documents to IDML, XML, HTML/XHTML, and ePUB Formats   Not every document begins and ends in the same version of InDesign or even as an INDD document. Sometimes not every member of the team has upgraded to the latest version of InDesign. Even more frequently, content created and formatted in InDesign is destined for other uses besides print, besides within InDesign itself. The ability to export to IDML, XML, and HTML/XHTML means content isn't trapped within InDesign, that it can be repurposed for virtually any use you can think of, now or in the future.

Master It   Get your document to the Web. Open or create a document that contains a few pages of text mixed with images. Export that document to HTML, including CSS formatting and the best-quality JPEG format images. Proof your work in a Web browser.

Solution   Beginning with a document as described, the learner should choose File⯈ Export for ⯈ Dreamweaver, name the outgoing HTML file, and find himself or herself in the XHTML Export Options dialog box. The learner should choose settings on each of the dialog's panes that match the following images.

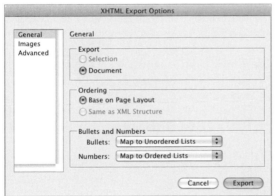 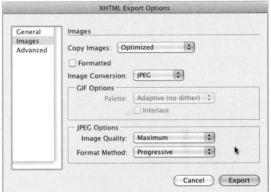

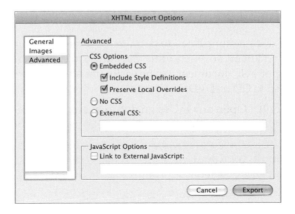

Generate PDFs for Both Print and Onscreen Use   Exporting InDesign documents to PDF is, and will likely remain for a long time yet to come, the method by which most documents are sent to press. Designers prefer to send press-ready PDFs, and press and prepress shops prefer to receive press-ready PDFs. PDF is also growing as a final document format. With more and more content consumed directly on electronic devices and with long-awaited acceptance of e-books and interactive e-magazines, PDF has finally lived up to the potential its creator, John Warnock, foresaw in the early 1990s. InDesign is at the forefront of building consumable PDFs, now more than ever.

Master It   Export a PDF ready to send to your print provider for press output.

Solution   Learners should choose File ➢ Export and make sure to change the Save as Type dropdown list to Adobe PDF (Print) rather than the default Adobe PDF (Interactive). In the resulting Export Adobe PDF dialog box, the [Press Quality] preset should be chosen from the Adobe PDF Preset menu and then the PDF exported without further changes to any options.

Export Pages as Images and Flash Content   Despite the strongest wishes of a certain fruity Cupertino-based computer and consumer product manufacturer, Adobe's Flash technology is, and will continue to be at least for the foreseeable future, an important part of the digital publishing landscape. Flash enables the delivery of rich, interactive, well-designed content to a variety of devices with a predictability and consistency not possible with HTML or other formats. And, as the world awakens to the new reality that "publishing" means more than ink on paper, Flash is becoming important even to InDesign-based designers.

Master It   In a new InDesign document, create a single-page document. On the page include bullet points summarizing what you learned in this chapter and how you can put that knowledge to work for you. Design the page well—make it an advertisement for you and your new knowledge—and then export it to Flash Player SWF as an SWF file wrapped in HTML, ready for upload to your website.

Solution   Of course, the content and appearance of the InDesign document and output files will vary with each learner, but the export process should be identical. Learners should choose File ➢ Export and set Save as Type to Flash Player (SWF). After they click Save, the Export SWF will appear. All options may be left at their defaults, or the learners may customize the options. The only requirements are that the All Pages and Generate HTML File options be selected. When finished, learners should have an SWF file embedded within an HTML file; opening the HTML file in a Web browser should properly display the SWF.

Chapter 13: Efficiency

Work Efficiently with Text   Text takes up the most space in the average InDesign document. Unfortunately, editing and *re*styling text occupies the majority of a creative's time in the document. Used wisely, paragraph and character styles, nested styles, text variables, and data merge eliminate repetitive actions and hours of work.

Master It   Use Excel, a database, or Notepad/TextEdit to create a new flat-file database of information. The data may be anything you like—a mailing list, product listings for a catalog, directory listings, and so on—but should include at least three fields and three rows. Save the file as either comma or tab delimited; this will be your data source file.

Beginning with a blank InDesign document, build a variable data target document to hold the records from the data source file. Include static information as well as field place-holders. Format all text—static and placeholders—and create paragraph and character styles to make the initial and follow-up formatting easier. If you have appropriate places to employ nested styling, do so.

When the target document is ready, effect a data merge to generate a press-ready variable-data project.

Solution   Owing to the multiple steps and complexity of this exercise, a great deal of variance in learners' results is to be expected. Upon completion, the learner should have a merge document with all data correctly imported. Additionally, all text in the document should be assigned to paragraph and/or character styles.

Work Efficiently with Tables   Table and cell styles make it a one-click operation to format tabular data and to instantly update all tables to match future formatting changes.

Master It   Begin with a table of data. If you have tables in preexisting InDesign docu-ments, use those (save the document under a different name, just in case). If you don't have such documents already, create a new layout and add at least two tables; the sports or financial sections of today's newspaper are excellent places to find tabular data you can use for FPO. Style one table with alternating fills, custom strokes of your choosing, and appropriate text formatting using paragraph styles. When the first table is styled to your liking, build table and cell styles, and then use them to format the second table.

Solution   Results will vary, but learners should end up with two (or more) identically formatted tables. Additionally, all text within the tables should be assigned to paragraph styles and cell styles.

Work Efficiently with Objects   Working efficiently doesn't end with text and tables. Graphics, paths, and containers are part of any InDesign document, and creating and editing them productively are also important to the efficient InDesign-based workflow.

Master It   Using either your own or a client's various media logos (RGB, CMYK, gray-scale; with and without taglines; iconic and full logos; and so on), build a shareable, reus-able logo library. Now create a second library of text frames and other objects you use at least occasionally. Make sure to give each an object style before adding it to the library so that other objects can quickly be styled to match and so that formatting changes don't take too much time. Don't forget to label objects in both libraries for rapid identification and filtering by you or your coworkers.

Solution   When finished, learners should have two INDL libraries. Every object in each library should be labeled. The majority of objects in the second library should have object styles assigned to them.

Chapter 14: Collaboration

Collaborate with Other Designers   Teamwork and workgroup-based creativity is common among larger publications. Collaborating efficiently is crucial but rare—until now.

Master It   Working alone or together with colleagues, create or convert a preexisting, multipage document into a candidate for the Placed Page Collaboration Workflow. Assign

content to coworkers, and have them design or alter the existing design of their portions of the publication and deliver their respective INDD documents back to you so that you may update and finalize the overall publication.

Solution   Learners should apportion a multipage document such that one or more separate pages are assigned to each member of the learner's workgroup. Content on those pages should be removed to separate InDesign documents and then placed back into the original locations as placed and linked INDD documents. The other members of the workgroup should edit their assignments and return the art to the team leader working with the core document. The leader will then update linked assets to bring the document current. Watch out for pages with duplicated content, which indicates that the learner forgot to delete the original objects from the core document subsequent to generating the assigned component documents.

Collaborate with Writers and Editors   It's a control thing, man. Laying out the page is the domain of the designer; editing the copy is the realm ruled by editors. Neither group wants governorship of either material forced upon (or even really given to) the other group. Thankfully, with InCopy, Adobe's best-kept secret, there's no longer a need for either editorial or design to give up its control, freedom, or field of view.

Master It   Open or create a layout containing at least two separate stories. Create assignments for two collaborators, assigning at least one story to each, and then generate and email an InCopy package for each assignment to its assignee.

If your collaborators have InCopy CS3 on hand, have them edit the stories and return them to you as InDesign packages. Finally, update the content in the layout from those packages.

Solution   If learners do not have access to InCopy or coworkers with InCopy, forgo the second part of the exercise. In the first part, the result should be an Assignments panel that lists two assignments with at least one content item each. Both assignments should display the purple gift box icon denoting that they've been successfully packaged. Also check File ➢ User to ensure that the learner correctly identified himself to InDesign, per the instructions in this chapter.

Collaborate with Anyone on Any File   The collaboration methodology built into InDesign and InCopy is really only usable by those on the same local network. If your team includes remote members, there's a much better method than resorting to the Package For features. Moreover, this better method isn't limited to InDesign and InCopy documents.

Master It   Partner with someone to collaborate on an InDesign document containing InCopy assignments and stories. One of you works in InDesign, creating layout and assigning frames, and then the other works in InCopy to fill the stories. Use the third-party remote file-synchronization solution I recommended to stay in synch with versions and check-in/checkout.

Solution   Both learners should establish Dropbox.com accounts and install the Dropbox software. The InDesign user should create a new assignment, add story frames to it, and then add the INDD and its ICMA and ICML files to her computer's Dropbox folder. The

InDesign user should then share the folder with the InCopy user via the Dropbox.com interface.

After receiving the documents, the InCopy user should open the ICMA assignment file, check out one or more stories, fill in content, and save and check in the stories. Within moments the updated content will produce yellow alerts on the Assignments panel in InDesign for the InDesign user.

Send Documents for Review   PDFs are great proofing and client-review tools, but nothing tops in-application review management via CS Review for speed, efficiency, and coordination of client project reviews.

Master It   Send a new or existing InDesign document off for review via CS Review. You may send it to a lab partner or friends or even send a live document to a client. If no one is available to help, send it to yourself using two different Adobe IDs. Have your partner(s) review the document, adding comments and replies. Then, within InDesign, examine requested changes, flag each comment or reply, and respond to them.

Solution   The learner should obtain an Adobe ID if he doesn't already have one and then start and invite others to a review from within InDesign using the CS Review panel according to the step-by-step directions listed in the "Initiating a Review" section. The learner's partner(s) or helper(s) should leave comments and requested changes within the Web-based review, and the learner should examine each requested change within InDesign. Each comment or reply should also be flagged as To Do, Done, Approved, Rejected, Disregard, or Needs Review, as discussed in the section titled "Reviewing within InDesign."

Share Reusable Settings   They say the definition of the word *insane* is doing something over and over while expecting different results. I agree with that definition, but I would like to propose my own addendum: Doing the same thing over and over when there's no reason to do it more than once is also insane. In this thing we do, there is more than enough insanity thrust upon us by deadlines, clients, limited budgets, malfunctioning software, temperamental RIPs, and so many other sources; we must do what we can to salvage our own peace of mind and maintain productivity. Save a brain cell; share a setting.

Master It   Examine your work: the typical documents you create and contribute to and the styles, swatches, and other reusable settings you use at least once a month. Save them all. Put them on a USB flash memory stick or email them home to yourself. Then, send them to your coworkers or lab partners, and ask for their reusable settings in return. Each of you should then load pieces you've exchanged into your respective versions of InDesign. It's time to collaborate efficiently.

Solution   Given that each learner will likely opt to save and share different types of reusable settings, there is no check against their progress other than that *something* was transferred between the InDesign users and successfully loaded into their copies of InDesign.

ASCII

(Acronym for American Standard Code for Information Interchange) This is the computer language that represents human-readable text. The English-based ASCII contains 95 characters, including the Latin alphabet and standard punctuation. TXT files are ASCII-encoded and thus are often referred to as ASCII files. More robust text-based file formats such as RTF and DOC are based on, but extend beyond, ASCII.

assignments

Within InDesign and its sister application InCopy, an assignment is a collection of one or more text or graphic frames separated from an InDesign publication and made available for work by an InCopy user or another InDesign user. Only one user may have any one InDesign INDD document opened for editing at a time. When assignments are used to apportion the document into linked and semi-autonomous sections of content, however, that single document may be edited by several people concurrently. A bidirectional check-in/checkout system further assists by maintaining version control and preventing double modification of assigned content.

B

baseline

The invisible line on which type stands. Glyphs such as *j, g,* and *y* have lower portions—called *descenders*—that descend below the baseline.

Bézier

In vector drawing, paths are created by placing *anchor points* on a virtual grid and then connecting those anchor points with *path segments*. In the Bézier drawing system of vector illustration, path segment angle and curvature are controlled by the anchor points rather than by the path segments. Bézier curves are parametric, meaning that the curvature in one end of a path segment affects and interacts with the curvature in the other end.

    The vector drawing tools in all of Adobe's applications—InDesign, Illustrator, Photoshop, and others—use Bézier curves.

blow out

When a device such as a printer or camera cannot render low percentages of color (in subtractive color models) or high percentages (in additive color models) and the result is a jump to 0% color, or pure white, the color is said to "blow out." For example, many offset presses cannot render less than 4% of a given ink; thus an area painted in 3% of a color will blow out and become no color at all. *Plugged* is the opposite of blow out; when very dark values become 100% color, or black.

Buzzword

An online, collaborative word processor from Adobe. Buzzword is part of the Acrobat.com and CS Live suite of Software as a Service offerings. (See also *Software as a Service, SaaS*.)

C

calibrate

To calibrate a device is to bring its color rendering or capturing ability as close as possible into alignment with the actual colors presented to the device.

caliper

The thickness of a sheet of paper expressed in thousands of an inch. For example, the caliper of 20 lb bond paper is 0.0038 inches.

CALS

CALS is a model for representing tables and tabular data in XML. (See *XML*.)

camel case

Originally termed "medial capitals," camel case refers to compound words or phrases where, instead of spaces, hyphens, or other separators, the words are joined together with each component word bearing a capital letter, often in the middle of the combined word. Common examples of camel case include "InDesign," "QuarkXPress," and "iPod."

cap height

The height of a given typeface's capital letter X.

carry-over

A notation to readers that the current point in a threaded story is not the beginning of the story, that it continues here from an earlier place. For example, "continued from page 10." Also known as carry-over line, continued line, or continue head. (See also *jumpline*.)

CJK

Shorthand for Chinese, Japanese, and Korean; most often used to describe a group of fonts containing glyphs for one or all three languages.

clipping path

A vector path embedded into, or attached to, an image or object that causes parts of the object to appear transparent. Unlike *alpha transparency*, clipping-path transparency does not offer levels of opacity; areas of color are either completely transparent (clipped) or fully opaque. Clipping paths may be added to images in Photoshop or Illustrator and are understood by InDesign and other page-layout applications. If an image does not contain a clipping path, one may be created inside InDesign to mask out (render transparent) parts of the image.

CMS

(Abbreviation for color management system; also for content management system and for the *Chicago Manual of Style*, which factored heavily into the editing of this book) A color management system connects calibrated color capture or render devices and their respective profiles, translating color data from one device to the next in an attempt to ensure consistently accurate portrayal of colors at each step.

CMYK

(Abbreviation for Cyan Magenta Yellow Black) CMYK is a subtractive color model wherein the more color added, the further the mix moves from white. CMYK, or process ink, is the standard for printing in North America and most of the world. Although CMYK has an extremely limited color *gamut*, it may be augmented through the use of spot color inks.

color profile

When a color rendering or capture device such as a computer monitor or scanner is profiled, its unique color interpretation characteristics are examined and recorded into a color profile and saved as an ICC or ICM file to be read by a color management system that translates and maintains consistent color between several devices' color profiles.

compound path

Two or more vector paths behaving as one.

compound shape

Two or more complete shapes (closed paths) behaving as one shape.

contextual orphan

An *orphan* is the first line of a paragraph left behind at the bottom of a column or page while the rest of the paragraph flows to the next column or page. A *contextual* orphan is what the author calls a short or single-line paragraph that, in context, should remain in the same column and on the same page as the paragraph it precedes but is instead left behind at the bottom of the previous column or page. For example, a single-line heading is its own paragraph but should always appear in the same column and page as the first paragraph it describes. (See also *orphan*.)

contextual widow

Similar to a *contextual orphan*, a contextual widow is a term coined by the author to describe a single-line or short paragraph pushed to the next column or page even though logic dictates that it should remain directly beneath the preceding paragraph. For example, a contextual widow would be the final, single-line paragraph of a bulleted or numbered list. (See also *widow*.)

counter

The holes or large open spaces within letter forms—for example, the holes in the letters *o* and *g*.

creep

Your neighbor with the telescope that always seems to be pointing in the direction of your bedroom window. A movie the comedian Eddie Izzard hoped to star in as a child. In the world of print, creep refers to the fact that the volume of sheets of paper displace other sheets of paper folded together. The edges of interior sheets stick out from the edges of enclosing sheets.

creep-in

Also called push-in, a creep-in is a negative inside or spine-side adjustment meant to push the page image inward toward the bound edge of a document to adjust for *creep*.

crossover

A crossover is bleeding ink into the spine of a bound document similar to the way the outer edges of ink are set to bleed off the page edges.

cross-reference

A directive advising the reader to reference a different section of, or item within, the current document. For example, directives to "See Figure X.Y" or, in an index, "See also: CMYK" are cross-references because at one point in the document they direct a reader to a different point in the same document. In InDesign cross-references are made of two parts: the *destination text* and the *source cross-reference*. Cross-reference is often referred to by the shorthand *xref*.

CSS

Cascading Style Sheets, the means by which styling is accomplished online. CSS style definitions and attributes such as font size, color, and much more are applied to HTML content tagged or named a particular way.

curve handles

In vector drawing, *anchor points* contain angle and curvature data to affect *path segments*. Curve handles are always present but only visible when the anchor point has more than 0° of curvature and/or more than a 0° angle. Dragging curve handles alters the angle and depth of curvature of path segments emanating from an anchor point.

D

data source file

When creating variable data printing (VDP) documents using InDesign's mail merge features, the set of comma- or tab-delimited variable data is stored in a data source file (a CSV or TXT file).

descender

The portion of a *glyph* that extends below the text baseline, such as with the lowercase letters *g*, *q*, and *j*.

destination text

The target of a *cross-reference* directive's *source cross-reference*.

direction lines

See *curve handles*.

drop rule

A vertical rule or line separating columns or rails.

duplexing

Printing on both sides of a piece of paper.

E

em

A relative measurement equal, in theory, to the width of a typeface's capital *M* and to the cap height of the typeface. For example, type set in 12 pt should theoretically have a 12 pt em measurement; 10 pt type should have a 10 pt em. In practice, with digital fonts, the capital *M* is rarely the width of a full em, although an em is still usually the same width as the cap height of the font.

em dash

A horizontal dash one *em* wide.

en

A relative measurement equal, in theory, to the width of a typeface's capital *N* and slightly more than half width of an *em*.

en dash

A horizontal dash one *en* wide.

endpoint

An anchor point at the beginning or end of an open path.

ePUB

The file extension and format of the XML-based e-books standardized on by digital book readers such as Apple's iBooks, Amazon's Kindle, Adobe Digital Editions, and other e-reading platforms.

F

flat-file database

A collection of data stored in an ASCII-based format such as a comma- or tab-delimited TXT file rather than in a traditional database.

flattening

The process of removing transparency and generating opaque objects from the areas of color created by overlapping one or more transparent objects with nontransparent objects.

flush

The clean edge of type. For example, this page is printed with type flush left, meaning that the type aligns along the left to create a clean edge.

flush left

Text aligned uniformly to the left margin.

flush left and right

See *force justified*.

flush right

Text aligned uniformly to the right margin.

folio

A page number. Also refers to the page itself and to large sheets of paper that are folded once and bound.

force justified

Text aligned to *flush*, clean edges on both the left and right sides of the column, is justified. In most justified paragraphs, last lines that are too short to fill the width of the column remain left, right, or center aligned. However, when even short last lines are made to justify, creating a uniform rectangle but with large gaps possibly introduced between words or letters, the paragraph is called force justified. Some newspapers, for example, force justify text.

format building blocks

Components of cross-reference formats, which may include static text, dynamic text such as the page number `<pageNum/>` building block, styling directives such as the `<cs name=" "></cs>` building block that assigns a character style to one or more building blocks, and other types. See *cross-reference*.

FPO

(Abbreviation for For Position Only) Temporary content—text or imagery—placed to estimate size, position, or usage of other content to be inserted later.

G

gamma

The frequency of radiation that turned Dr. Bruce Banner into the Incredible Hulk. Also the luminescence value of color as measured in tones of gray.

gamut

The range of color values possible in a particular color space, device, or color-production process.

gang

Printing multiple pages from one or more jobs on a single, large sheet of paper to save production time and costs.

ganged

See *gang*.

glyph

A single character, pictogram, mark, or entity within a font or language.

greeking

Content—usually text—that is used in place of final copy (aka FPO text). In InDesign, when text appears onscreen below a size limit set in the preferences, the text is replaced by black-and-white patterning, which is also greeking. The term derives from the expression "It's all Greek to me," indicating that something cannot be read or is gibberish.

GREP

GREP, originally a Unix command-line search application created in 1973 by Ken Thompson, is a regular expression query or search language used within InDesign and many other applications. GREP allows for not only verbose queries (e.g., finding all instances of the word "the") but also queries of regular expressions, or fuzzy searches, wherein the user looks to find patterns, such as any three letters beginning with "t," or any digit, any letter, and so on. GREP is used within InDesign in the Find/Change dialog box to enable searching for, and possibly replacing, virtually any text. It is also used in GREP Styles, which enables applying character styles to type that matches patterns or regular expressions. Although GREP has all but completely separated as its own word independent of its original longer form, GREP is indeed an acronym for "global/regular expression/print," which translates to "search globally among the text for a regular expression and return (or print, in old Unix) the result."

gutter

Traditionally either the space between pages in a *spread* or the space between columns or both. In InDesign, the gutter describes only the space between columns.

H

hanging punctuation

Punctuation and parts of *glyphs* allowed to shift in part or wholly beyond the *flush* edge of text to create a more optically balanced flush edge instead of a physically clean flush edge.

hard proof

Any printed version of a document short of the final output.

HSL

(Abbreviation for Hue, Saturation, and Luminosity [or Lightness]) A color model that describes a color in terms of its hue, saturation, and luminosity values; interchangeable with HSB (Hue, Saturation, and Brightness).

I

ICC profile

See *color profile.*

IDML

An abbreviation for InDesign Markup Language, an XML-based, tagged format version of a document. Also the file extension of such documents when exported to InDesign Markup Language. IDML files are often used when it becomes necessary for users on different versions of InDesign to collaborate because IDML files are version agnostic within InDesign CS4 and CS5.

imposed

See *imposition.*

imposition

Sometimes called "digital stripping" or pagination, imposition is the process of placing pages into the correct order for printing such that, when folded, a sheet containing multiple pages will make the pages readable in the correct order. (See *printer's spreads* and *reader's spreads.)*

in port

The place on a threaded text frame through which text flows into the frame. The in port is located near the upper-left corner of a text frame and on the left end of a type on a path object. Opposite the in port is the *out port.*

inset

A margin on the interior of a text frame that pushes type inward from one or more edges of the frame.

IPTC

Abbreviation for the International Press Telecommunications Council and the label for a set of metadata defined by that body as the most important for general and editorial usage Imagery and other content. (See *metadata*.)

J

jumpline

A directive to readers that a threaded story resumes at a later point. For example, "continues on page 83." Also known as continue line or jump head. (See also *carry-over*.)

K

kerning

The relative distance between a pair of letters. Kerning values are adjusted on the Character panel or the Control panel's Character mode to reduce or increase space between two characters whose shapes create awkward gapping or collision.

knockout

When two or more colors overlap, the foreground color can either *overprint*, which often causes mixing of colors from the background into the foreground color, or knockout such that the lower or background ink is removed, punching a hole through it in the shape of the foreground color area, thus preserving the appearance of the foreground color.

L

layer comp

In Photoshop, a layer comp is a recording of the state of an image's layers at a given moment in time. Layer comps register the visibility, opacity, blending mode, and position of individual layers and may be used to switch between design variations without the need for creating multiple documents. InDesign honors and employs layer comps stored in Photoshop PSD documents such that design variations created in Photoshop may be placed and changed on the InDesign page without a return trip to Photoshop.

leader

Marks, *glyphs*, or symbols representing or preceding a tab. For instance, in many tables of contents, entries are connected to their page numbers by a series of dots/periods or a continuous rule (really underscores). Those dots or underscores are the leader.

leaf

See *signature*.

left-read

In a bound publication or facing-pages document, the page to the left of the spine. In English- and other Latin-based-language publications, the left-read pages are even numbered. In Japanese, Hebrew, and sinistral publications reading from right to left, left-read pages are odd numbered. Although the term "left-read" is common, the proper name of the left-read or back side page in a bound document is the verso page.

ligatures

Two or more letters tied into a single character. Generally, when certain pairs, triplets, or quartets of individual letters or *glyphs* are combined, their shapes cause awkward collisions—for example, *f-i* and *f-t*. In old metal and block type as well as older TrueType and Type 1 fonts, ligatures were extra, single characters added to fonts that combined the shapes of individual colliding letters in a way that avoided collision. In modern OpenType fonts, ligatures are created by combining special variants of each individual character drawn to accommodate such combinations and avoid collision while maintaining the individuality of each letter.

Verso

See *left-read*.

W

widow

A paragraph's last line appearing as the first line in a new column or page. Bringhurst limits the definition of widow to only the paragraph's last line beginning a page, but the definition has expanded through common usage to also include the last line beginning a new column. (See also *contextual widow*.)

wireframe

A skeletal representation of the shape of a three-dimensional object.

workspaces

In InDesign and other Adobe applications, the workspace is the entire environment of the application interface, including menu configurations and panel arrangements. Most such applications enable the user to save, recall, and often even share environment settings as a "workspace" file. InDesign comes with several predefined workspaces on the Window ➤ Workspace menu.

WYSIWYG

(Acronym for What You See Is What You Get) Basically, what you see onscreen is what will print. InDesign is the first page-layout application to offer true WYSIWYG, particularly with regard to transparency, vector graphics, and object interactions on the page.

X

xref

Shorthand for cross-reference. (See *cross-reference*.)

XMP

(Abbreviation for Extensible Metadata Platform) A technology coauthored by Adobe that allows *metadata* to be embedded in file formats based on XML or containing an XML layer. Common XMP metadata includes author and copyright holder information, camera settings (for photographs), licensing restrictions, and archival data such as categories, description, and keywords. The extensible part of XMP is its ability to go beyond predefined metadata fields and include any information a file author sees fit to store in the XMP layer.

XSLT

An abbreviation for XML Stylesheet, a set of rules defining how XML data will be transformed into another data format such as HTML. (See *XML* and *HTML*.)

Z

Z-order

Three-dimensional (3D) space is plotted on three axes: X (the horizontal plane), Y (the vertical plane), and Z (the depth plane). Within two-dimensional or pseudo-three-dimensional applications such as InDesign, full understanding of, and support for, the Z-axis and 3D objects is not available. Out of necessity, however, objects can be stacked above or below, in front or behind, one another. This stacking is done along the Z-axis and is referred to as the Z-order of objects.

Index

Symbols

, (comma), 556
@ (at symbol), 561
+ (plus sign), 530

A

Above Line Alignment
  (Anchored Object Options
  dialog), 247–248
above-line anchored objects,
  247–248
Absolute Colorimetric (Intent
  Color Settings), 429
ACE. *See* Adobe Certified Expert;
  Adobe Color Engine
Acrobat (Adobe Acrobat)
    CMS, 430
    Document Properties dialog,
      460–461
    PostScript, 441–442
Actual PPI (Link Info section), 196
Actual Size, 506
Add (Pathfinder command),
  144–145
Add Anchor Point tool, 131, 140,
  159
Add Bullets dialog, 326
Add Items on Page, 568
Add Items on Page as Separate
  Objects, 568
Add Pages To (Smart Text Reflow),
  323
Add Publisher Entry, 502
Add/Remove Rows (Caption
  Setup dialog), 209–210
Adobe Acrobat. *See* Acrobat
Adobe Bridge. *See* Bridge
Adobe Buzzword. *See* Buzzword
Adobe Caflisch Script Pro, 104, 109
Adobe Caslon Pro, 103, 105, 106,
  107, 108, 112, 116, 118
Adobe Certified Expert (ACE), 429
Adobe Color Engine (ACE), 429
Adobe Exchange, 573
Adobe Extension Manager, 20

Adobe Flash. *See* Flash
Adobe Graphics Engine, 375
Adobe HOW Design Conference,
  373
Adobe Illustrator. *See* Illustrator
Adobe Illustrator Clip Board
  (AICB), 186
Adobe Illustrator documents. *See*
  AI documents
Adobe InDesign CS5. *See* InDesign
Adobe In-RIP Trapping, 460–462
Adobe Myriad Pro, 39, 98, 106, 110,
  116
Adobe PDF Presets dialog, 517–519,
  624
Adobe Photoshop. *See* Photoshop
Adobe PressReady, 424
Adobe RGB, 422, 423, 426, 427, 432.
  See also RGB
Adobe RSS newsfeeds, 12
Adobe Stock Photos, 12, 598
Adobe Swatch Exchange (ASE)
  files, 240, 241, 623
Advanced Mode (CMS), 425
Advanced pane
    Export Adobe PDF dialog, 517
    OPI Image Replacement, 442,
      470, 496
    Print dialog, 469–470
    XHTML Export Options
      dialog, 492–493
Advanced tab (Export EPS, Export
  SWF), 495–496, 499–500
After-Blending Intent, 431
AI documents (Adobe Illustrator
  documents), 165, 172–175, 216.
  See also PDFs
AICB (Adobe Illustrator Clip
  Board), 186
Align panel, 11, 270, 415, 586
Align Stroke, 228
Alignment field (Caption Setup
  dialog), 210
Alignment From Reference Point
  Proxy, 203
Alignment option (Bullets and
  Numbering dialog), 327

alignment options (paragraphs),
  52–54
All Affected Objects
  (Transparency Flattener), 438
all caps, 89
All Caps command, 91
All Pages Must Use Same Size and
  Orientation, 450
All Rasterized Regions
  (Transparency Flattener), 438
All Small Caps command, 109–110
All Spots to Process, 456
All Spreads, 597
Allow Graphics and Groups to
  Resize option, 290
Allow Master Item Overrides on
  Selection (Pages panel), 311
Allow Ruler Guides to Move, 290
Allow Split Footnotes, 345
alpha channels, 166, 167, 170
alpha transparency, 126, 165, 195
alphanumeric ordinals, 92
Americana, 82
Anchor Marker option, 250
anchor points
    Add Anchor Point tool, 131,
      140, 159
    adding/removing, 131
    Convert Anchor Point tool, 140
    Convert Point menu, 155, 156
    converting, 130–131, 155, 156
    Corner command, 156
    corners v., 122
    curves and, 127–130
    Delete Anchor Point tool, 131,
      136, 140
    editing (Direct Selection tool),
      150–154
    heart drawing, 150–154
    Illustrator and, 128
    path segments and, 122
    paths and, 122
    Plain command, 156
    Smooth command, 156
    Symmetrical command, 156
    term usage inconsistency, 128